EU Regulation and Transatlantic Trade

European Monographs

Editor-in-Chief Prof. Dr. K.J.M. Mortelmans

In this series European Monographs, this book EU Regulation and Tranatlantic Trade is the thirty-seventh title.

The titles published in this series are listed at the end of this volume.

EU Regulation and Transatlantic Trade

Sebastiaan Princen

KLUWER LAW INTERNATIONAL
THE HAGUE / LONDON / NEW YORK

Published by:
Kluwer Law International
P.O. Box 85889, 2508 CN The Hague, The Netherlands
sales@kli.wkap.nl
http://www.kluwerlaw.com

Sold and Distributed in North, Central and South America by:
Kluwer Law International
101 Philip Drive, Norwell, MA 02061, USA
kluwerlaw@wkap.com

Sold and Distributed in all other countries by:
Kluwer Law International
Distribution Centre, P.O. Box 322, 3300 AH Dordrecht, The Netherlands

Library of Congress Cataloging-in-Publication Data

Princen, Sebastiaan.
EU regulation and transatlantic trade / by Sebastiaan Princen.
p.cm.-- (European monograph series ; 37)
Includes bibliographical references and index.
ISBN 9041118713 (alk. paper)
1. Foreign trade regulation--European Union countries. 2. European Union--United States. 3. European Union countries--Commerce--United States. I. Title. II. European monographs ; 37.

CRC-prepared by: G.J. Wiarda Institute, Utrecht Institute for Legal Studies, Boothstraat 6, 3512 BW Utrecht.

Printed on acid-free paper.

ISBN 90-411-1871-3

Kluwer Law International incorporates the imprint of Martinus Nijhoff Publishers

Printed and bound by Antony Rowe Ltd, Eastbourne

TABLE OF CONTENTS

List of Abbreviations ix

1. Introduction and research problem

1.1 Internationalisation and domestic regulation 1
1.2 Overview of this study 4
1.3 The California effect 5
1.4 The research problem 10
1.4.1 The choice of policy areas 10
1.4.2 The type of standard 12
1.4.3 The countries involved in the process 13
1.4.4 Delimitation in time 17
1.4.5 The research problem 18
1.4.6 The selection of cases and the research questions 21
1.5 The research design and the use of theory 23
1.5.1 Causal inference from multiple case studies 23
1.5.2 The use of theory 26
1.5.3 Process-tracing 27
1.5.4 The use of sources 29
1.6 Outline of the book 32

2. A theoretical framework 35

2.1 Introduction 35
2.1.1 The California effect and the two-level game approach 35
2.1.2 Preferences and constraints 37
2.2 International bargaining 39
2.2.1 Regulatory trade measures and the terms of trade 40
2.2.2 Strategy and commitment in international bargaining 45
2.2.3 Argumentation and legitimacy in international bargaining 47
2.2.4 The role of international law 49
2.3 Domestic politics and international bargaining 54
2.3.1 Domestic politics and the national interest 54
2.3.2 Governmental actors 57
2.3.3 Formal ratification by parliaments 59
2.3.4 Informal ratification by interest groups 61
2.3.5 The initial situation 65

2.4 The interaction between international and domestic politics 65
- 2.4.1 Affecting the target country's win-set 66
- 2.4.2 Affecting the initiator country's win-set 72
- 2.4.3 Manipulation of the win-set in the domestic context 73
- 2.4.4 Transnational actors and coalitions in two-level games 74

2.5 Summary and hypotheses 76

3. The European leghold trap regulation 79

3.1 Introduction and background 79
3.2 The European ban 82
3.3 The potential impact of the European Regulation on the US and Canada 84
- 3.3.1 The regulation of traps and trapping in the US and Canada 84
- 3.3.2 Trappers and the fur industry in the US and Canada 88
- 3.3.3 The (potential) impact of the European Regulation 90

3.4 Compatibility with GATT/WTO law 95
- 3.4.1 The GATT/WTO's prohibitions 96
- 3.4.2 The general exceptions in GATT Article XX 98
- 3.4.3 The European leghold trap Regulation and GATT Article XX 107

3.5 Negotiating an agreement 109
- 3.5.1 The early initiatives 109
- 3.5.2 The ISO process 111
- 3.5.3 The negotiations between Canada, the US and the EC 113
- 3.5.4 The International Agreements on Humane Trapping Standards 124

3.6 The implementation of the agreements and further domestic developments 126
- 3.6.1 Developments and implementation in the US 127
- 3.6.2 Developments and implementation in Canada 130
- 3.6.3 Developments and implementation in the EC 131

3.7 Conclusions 132
- 3.7.1 A California effect or not? 132
- 3.7.2 Explaining the outcomes 136

4. The European ban on the use of growth-hormones in meat production 147

4.1 Introduction and background 147
4.2 The European ban on the use of growth-hormones 149
4.3 The initial situation in the US and Canada and early developments 151
- 4.3.1 The initial situation in the US and Canada 151
- 4.3.2 Early developments 155

4.4 International developments and the WTO cases 157
4.4.1 Standard-setting in the Codex Alimentarius Commission 157
4.4.2 The SPS Agreement and the cases before the WTO 159
4.5 The process after the WTO cases 166
4.5.1 Arbitration and retaliation 166
4.5.2 Developments in the EC 169
4.5.3 The talks on compensation and the exports of non-treated beef 178
4.5.4 Regulatory developments in the US and Canada 182
4.6 Conclusions 183
4.6.1 A California effect or not? 183
4.6.2 Explaining the outcomes 186

5. Genetically modified foods and food products 193

5.1 Introduction and background 193
5.1.1 What is genetic modification? 193
5.1.2 The promises and risks inherent in agricultural biotechnology 196
5.1.3 International work on GM food safety 199
5.2 The initial situation in the US and Canada 201
5.2.1 The initial situation in the United States 202
5.2.2 The initial situation in Canada 208
5.3 The European regulation of GM foods 210
5.3.1 Horizontal and vertical legislation 211
5.3.2 Developments in the late 1990s 216
5.3.3 The shifting political balance in the EC 222
5.4 International developments 227
5.4.1 Debates in international forums 228
5.4.2 Compatibility with GATT/WTO law 233
5.4.3 GATT/WTO law and the Cartagena Protocol 237
5.5 Reactions in the US and Canada 242
5.5.1 Impact on trade and bilateral initiatives 242
5.5.2 Domestic developments in the US 248
5.5.3 Domestic developments in Canada 252
5.6 Conclusions 256
5.6.1 A California effect or not? 256
5.6.2 Explaining the outcomes 260

6. The European data protection directive 269

6.1 Introduction and background 269
6.1.1 Data protection and international trade 269
6.1.2 International work on data protection and transborder data flows 271

6.2 The EC data protection Directive 274
- 6.2.1 History and background 274
- 6.2.2 Directive 95/46 and data transfers to third countries 278

6.3 The European Directive and international trade law 284

6.4 The European Directive and the US 288
- 6.4.1 The initial situation in the US 288
- 6.4.2 Domestic developments after the adoption of the European Directive 293
- 6.4.3 Setting the stage for an agreement 296
- 6.4.4 The Safe Harbour negotiations 299

6.5 The European Directive and Canada 307
- 6.5.1 The initial situation in Canada 307
- 6.5.2 Reactions to the European Directive and further developments 311

6.6 Conclusions 316
- 6.6.1 A California effect or not? 318
- 6.6.2 Explaining the outcomes 320

7. Summary and conclusions 329

7.1 The eight cases and their outcomes 329

7.2 Explaining the outcomes 334
- 7.2.1 Changing constraints 334
- 7.2.2 Changing preferences 348
- 7.2.3 Expanding participation 356
- 7.2.4 Providing an answer to the research problem 357

7.3 Generalising the conclusions to other cases 362
- 7.3.1 Generalising the conclusions to other issues 363
- 7.3.2 Generalising the conclusions to other issue areas 366
- 7.3.3 Generalising the conclusions to other countries 368

List of interviews 371

References 375

Index 417

LIST OF ABBREVIATIONS

AAFC	Agriculture and Agri-Food Canada
AB	Appellate Body (in WTO dispute settlement)
ABA	American Bankers Association (US)
ACB	Associated Credit Bureaus (US)
ACLU	American Civil Liberties Union (US)
ADI	Allowable Daily Intake
AFBF	American Farm Bureau Federation (US)
AIA	American Insurance Association (US)
AMI	American Meat Institute (US)
AMS	Agricultural Marketing Service (US; part of USDA)
APHIS	Animal and Plant Health Inspection Service (US; part of USDA)
ASA	American Soybean Association (US)
ASTA	American Seed Traders Association (US)
AWI	Animal Welfare Institute (US)
BEUC	European Bureau of Consumers Unions (EC)
BIC	Ballot Issues Coalition (US)
BIO	Biotechnology Industry Organization (US)
BMP	Best Management Practices (US)
BSE	Bovine Spongiform Encephalopathy (or: 'mad cow disease')
BST	Bovine Somatotropin (also: Bovine Growth Hormone)
CAC	Codex Alimentarius Commission (falls under FAO and WHO)
CAN$	Canadian Dollars
CAHT	Canadian Alliance for Humane Trapping
CAP	Common Agricultural Policy (EC)
CBA/Canada	Canadian Bankers Association
CBA/US	Consumer Bankers Association (US)
CBD	Convention on Biological Diversity
CDMA	Canadian Direct Marketing Association (later: CMA)
CDT	Center for Democracy and Technology (US)
CEC	Commission of the European Communities/European Commission (EC)
CFHS	Canadian Federation of Humane Societies
CFIA	Canadian Food Inspection Agency
CFR	Code of Federal Regulations (US)
CFS	Center for Food Safety (US)
CGSB	Canadian General Standards Board
CHC	Canadian Health Coalition
CIAA	Confederation of Agri-Food Industries (EC)

CICS	Canadian Intergovernmental Conference Secretariat
CITES	Convention on International Trade in Endangered Species
CMA/Marketing	Canadian Marketing Association (formerly: CDMA)
CMA/Medical	Canadian Medical Association
CoE	Council of Europe
COG	Chief of Government
COPA/COGECA	Committee of Agricultural Organisations in the European Union (EC)
CPhA	Canadian Pharmacists Association
CSA	Canadian Standards Association
CSI	Coalition of Service Industries (US)
DB	Society for the Protection of Animals ('Dierenbescherming'; Netherlands)
DES	Diethylstilbestrol
DFAIT	Department of Foreign Affairs and International Trade (Canada)
DG	Directorate General (EC; part of the European Commission)
DG Sanco	Directorate General for Health and Consumer Protection (EC)
DG I	Directorate General for External Affairs (later split into, among others, DG Trade)
DG III	Directorate General for Industry (later: DG Enterprise)
DG VI	Directorate General for Agriculture (later: DG Agriculture)
DG XI	Directorate General for the Environment (later: DG Environment)
DG XII	Directorate General for Science, Research and Development
DG XV	Directorate General for the Internal Market and Financial Services (later: DG Internal Market)
DG XXIV	Directorate General for Consumer Affairs (later merged into DG Sanco)
DMA	Direct Marketing Association (US)
DoC	Department of Commerce (US)
DSB	Dispute Settlement Body (under the WTO)
DSU	Dispute Settlement Understanding (part of WTO Agreements)
EC	European Community (until 1993: EEC)
EEC	European Economic Community (since 1993: EC)
ECJ	European Court of Justice/Court of Justice of the European Communities (EC)
EP	European Parliament (EC)
EPA	Environmental Protection Agency (US)
EPIC	Electronic Privacy Information Center (US)
ERS	Economic Research Service (US; part of USDA)
ETP	Eastern Tropical Pacific
EU	European Union

FAQ	Frequently Asked Question (part of the Safe Harbour agreement)
FACE	Federation of Fieldsports Associations of the European Union
FAO	Food and Agriculture Organization (part of the United Nations)
FCRA	Fair Credit Reporting Act (US)
FDA	Food and Drug Administration (US)
FEDMA	Federation of European Direct Marketing Associations (EC)
FIC	Fur Institute of Canada
FMI	Food Marketing Institute (US)
FoE	Friends of the Earth
FOIA	Freedom of Information Act (US)
FPCHT	Federal Provincial Committee for Humane Trapping (Canada)
FSIS	Food Safety Inspection Service (part of USDA)
FSR	Financial Services Roundtable (US)
FTC	Federal Trade Commission (US)
FTCA	Federal Trade Commission Act (US)
FVO	Food and Veterinary Office (EC; part of DG XXIV, later DG Sanco)
FWS	Fish and Wildlife Service (US; part of USDA)
GAO	General Accounting Office (US)
GATS	General Agreement on Trade in Services (part of WTO Agreements)
GATT	General Agreement on Tariffs and Trade (since 1995 part of WTO Agreements)
GDP	Gross Domestic Product
GMA	Grocery Manufacturers of America (US)
GM	Genetically Modified
GMO	Genetically Modified Organism
GRAS	Generally Recognized As Safe (US)
GSP	Generalised System of Preferences
HEW	(Department of) Health, Education and Welfare (US; later HHS)
HHS	(Department of) Health and Human Services (US; formerly HEW)
HFC	Hormone Free Cattle (Programme)
HIPAA	Health Insurance Portability and Accountability Act (US)
HNN	High North News
HSUS	Humane Society of the United States
IAFWA	International Association of Fish and Wildlife Agencies (US)
IFT	Institute of Food Technologists (US)
IFTF	International Fur Trade Federation
IHAC	Information Highway Advisory Council (Canada)

IIA	Information Industry Association (US)
IITF	Information Infrastructure Task Force (US)
ILO	International Labour Organization
IMF	International Monetary Fund
INAC	(Department of) Indian and Northern Affairs Canada
IP	Identity Preserved
ISB	Information Systems for Biotechnology (US)
ISO	International Organization for Standardization
ITI	Information Technology Industry Council (US)
ITO	International Trade Organization
JECFA	Joint FAO/WHO Expert Committee on Food Additives
JMC	Joint Management Committee
MAFF	Ministry of Agriculture, Fisheries and Food (UK)
MEP	Member of European Parliament (EC)
MGA	Melengestrol Acetate
MP	Member of Parliament (Canada)
MRCI	Ministry for the Relations with Citizens and Immigration (Part of the government of Quebec, Canada)
MRL	Maximum Residue Level
NAFTA	North American Free Trade Agreement
NFPA	National Food Processors Association (US)
NHTC	Non-Hormone Treated Cattle (Programme)
NIH	National Institutes of Health (US)
NOEL	No Observable Effect Level
NRF	National Retail Federation (US)
NTA	National Trappers Association (US)
OECD	Organisation for Economic Co-operation and Development
OJ	Official Journal (EC)
OMB	Office of Management and Budget (US)
OSTP	Office of Science and Technology Policy (US)
PIAC	Public Interest Advocacy Centre (Canada)
PIPEDA	Personal Information Protection and Electronic Documents Act (Canada)
PWG	Privacy Working Group (US; part of IITF)
SCF	Scientific Committee on Food (EC)
SCVPH	Scientific Committee on Veterinary Measures Relating to Public Health (EC)
SEA	Single European Act
SIA	Securities Industries Association (US)
SPS	(Agreement on) Sanitary and Phytosanitary Standards (part of WTO Agreements)
SSC	Scientific Steering Committee (EC)
TABD	Transatlantic Business Dialogue (US/EC)

TACD	Transatlantic Consumer Dialogue (US/EC)
TAED	Transatlantic Environmental Dialogue (US/EC)
TBT	(Agreement on) Technical Barriers to Trade (part of WTO Agreements)
TC 191	Technical Committee on Humane Trapping Standards (under ISO)
UECBV	European Meat Traders Association (EC)
UK	United Kingdom
UN	United Nations
US	United States
USC	United States Code
USCIB	United States Council for International Business
USCoC	United States Chamber of Commerce
USDA	United States Department of Agriculture
USTR	United States Trade Representative
WFRR	World Food Regulation Review
WHO	World Health Organization (part of the United Nations)
WTO	World Trade Organization (until 1995: GATT)

CHAPTER ONE

INTRODUCTION AND RESEARCH PROBLEM

1.1 INTERNATIONALISATION AND DOMESTIC REGULATION

Internationalisation has become one of the buzzwords in international politics. Although the concept of internationalisation has several dimensions, including at least economic, political and cultural globalisation (Tomlinson, 1999: 13-14; Waters, 1995: 7-9), much attention has focused on economic internationalisation and its consequences for policies in other areas. Economic internationalisation has occurred through the lowering of barriers to trade and investment, leading to the formation of international markets for various products. Many products no longer need to be produced in the same country they are consumed in. Partly, this is the result of technological and organisational changes, which have dramatically reduced the costs of international communication and transportation. Partly, countries have deliberately sought to reduce barriers to trade, such as tariffs, quotas and certain kinds of regulation, and to stimulate the free flow of goods and services across borders.

Economic internationalisation has aroused mixed feelings. On the one hand, it is often viewed as a way to improve welfare through international specialisation and competition. On the other hand, many critics of the process fear it will undermine the protection of other values, such as welfare state arrangements and regulatory standards in fields like environmental and consumer protection. Economic integration, so the critics argue, will lead to a 'race to the bottom' when it comes to the protection of those values. More stringent standards increase production costs, as a consequence of which firms will shift production to countries with less stringent standards. Therefore, countries may lower their standards in order to keep firms or even to attract them. The resulting process would be the subsequent lowering of standards to the 'lowest common denominator' or even below that: a 'race to the bottom.'

Cases of a race to the bottom have been reported by Genschel and Plümper (1997: 631-633) with regard to withholding taxes on interest income between member states of the European Community (EC)[1] and by Murphy with regard to shipping regulations at the global level (cited in Dietrich, 1996: 194, footnote

1 Since the Maastricht Treaty, which entered into force in November 1993, it has become customary to speak of the 'European Union' (EU). However, legally speaking, all issues in this study have taken place under the European Community part of the EU, and it was the EC that adopted measures and concluded agreements. I will therefore refer to the EC rather than the EU, except where the EU proper is meant.

105). According to an influential argument by Rehbinder and Stewart (1985: 9-12), harmonisation in the EC is likely to take place at the level of the member state with the least stringent regulatory standards when unanimity is required to reach a decision. Golub (1996: 328-330) reported a similar outcome in a study of the EC packaging waste Directive, which had been adopted by a qualified majority of EC member states. At the global level, Silverglade (2000) claimed that the formulation of international food standards has tended to reduce the stringency of those standards. Esty and Geradin (1998: 19-21) argued that even if formal regulatory standards are not lowered as a result of a race to the bottom, international competition will lead to a reduced willingness on the part of governments to raise environmental standards or to enforce existing ones, and they presented anecdotal evidence to support their claim.

The quintessential example of a race to the bottom has been state corporate law regimes in the United States (US). About half of the largest US corporations are registered in the state of Delaware (Charny, 1991: 428), arguably because it has the least stringent corporate law standards in the country in terms of shareholder protection against corporate management. Consequently, Vogel (1995: 5-6) dubbed the race to the bottom the 'Delaware effect.' Others, however, have challenged the idea that Delaware's corporate law system is the least stringent in the US (Charny, 1991: 430-434).

Yet, although the logic of the race-to-the-bottom argument has had wide appeal, both in popular and scholarly debate, a number of systematic empirical studies suggest that such a process has not occurred, at least not in the field of regulatory standards. Levinson (1996), reviewing the empirical evidence for environmental regulations, found little evidence for a race to the bottom. Similar results have been found for labour standards across states in the US (Krueger, 2000: 129-131). Others have challenged the theoretical argument behind the race-to-the-bottom thesis (Revesz, 1992; 1997; Trumbull, 2000).

More surprisingly, some authors have argued that internationalisation may lead to a strengthening rather than a weakening of standards. Such race-to-the-top processes were found by Vogel in the EC, the US and, to a lesser extent, the North American Free Trade Agreement (NAFTA) and bilateral relations under the General Agreement on Tariffs and Trade (GATT) or the World Trade Organization (WTO) (Vogel, 1995; 1997a; 1997b). He called this phenomenon the 'California effect' after the American state that has often played a frontrunner's role in raising regulatory standards in the United States.

A California effect takes place when a country (or a coalition of countries) exports its own (more stringent) standards to, or imposes them upon, one or more of its trading partners through the use of market access. For example, a country may ban or threaten to ban imports of products that do not conform to certain standards. If, in reaction, that country's trading partners raise their regulatory standards in order to remain able to export their products, a California effect has taken place.

In a quantitative analysis of the development of environmental standards in the US, Fredriksson and Millimet (2000) also found a 'race to the top' among US states, led by the state of California, but it is not clear whether this effect was related to trade. In studies of harmonisation processes, Eichener (1993; 1997) reported a California effect with regard to the harmonisation of environmental and occupational health and safety standards in the EC, and Genschel & Plümper (1997: 628-631) in international banking. Dietrich (1996) found that EC harmonisation of automobile emission standards led to a gradual strengthening of standards, although he did not expect such an effect to take place under the GATT/WTO.

The California-effect thesis focuses the attention on the way regulatory standards in one country may lead to a strengthening of those in another country through their trade effects. As a consequence, it highlights an unexpected and, to some, counter-intuitive result of economic internationalisation. However, as yet relatively little is known about the conditions under which trade will lead to a strengthening of regulatory standards. This study aims to narrow this gap by contributing to systematic theory about the conditions under which a California effect will occur.

In addition to contributing to systematic theory about the California effect, this study may also contribute to the public and political debate on economic integration. Economic integration has met with considerable resistance from public interest groups and politicians alike, who fear that it will undermine the accomplishments of modern (welfare) states. The creation of NAFTA is a vivid example of a debate that was dominated (at least in the US) by concerns over environmental, consumer and labour standards (cf. Hogenboom, 1998). Similar concerns in relation to the WTO and other international institutions have come to the fore by protests during recent summits, starting with the 1999 WTO Ministerial Conference in Seattle. An understanding of the effects which economic integration has on regulatory standards may contribute to this debate and can help to determine the conditions under which such integration should take place.

Two caveats should be made here, though. First, policy recommendations rest on normative judgements about the stringency of standards and the use of trade measures to promote them. It is not my aim to form or make such judgements in this study. All the study aims at is to provide some insight into the actual process of regulatory change as a result of trade. Second, this study does not attempt an assessment of the relative incidence of the California effect. Such a study would require a completely different design. It is hoped, however, that by developing a systematic account of the conditions underlying the California effect, more insight can also be gained into the probability that this process will actually occur.

1.2 Overview of this Study

In this study, I will examine four environmental and consumer protection issues in which the EC adopted more stringent process or production standards than the US and Canada, which potentially affected exports from those two countries. One issue concerns animal welfare, which is part of the broader field of environmental protection. The other three issues relate to consumer protection: two concern food safety, while the last issue deals with the protection of personal information. Because both the US and Canadian reactions to these differences in standards are examined, this makes for a total of eight cases. For each case I will examine whether the US or Canada actually strengthened its regulatory standards in order to maintain access to the EC market, and what factors contributed to that outcome.

The animal welfare issue, examined in chapter 3, concerns the EC ban on the use of leghold traps, and the concomitant ban on the import of furs from countries that had not either banned the use of leghold traps themselves or adhered to internationally agreed humane trapping standards. Since both the US and Canada allowed the use of leghold traps and international standards had not been formulated, this ban formed an important threat to their fur exports to the EC. In the end, the US and Canada avoided imposition of the ban by negotiating separate agreements with the EC on humane trapping standards. In both cases, trapping standards were strengthened as a result of the EC ban, although more so in Canada than in the US.

The first food safety issue, which will be discussed in chapter 4, is the EC ban on the use of growth-hormones in meat production, as well as on imports of meat that has been produced with their use. The US and Canada allowed the use of six growth-hormones, which were used mainly in beef production, which largely eliminated their beef exports to the EC. Yet, in contrast to the leghold trap issue, the 'beef-hormone' issue (as it has become widely known) did not lead to any strengthening of regulatory standards in the US or Canada.

The other food safety issue, examined in chapter 5, is the regulation of genetically modified foods and food products. Unlike the other three issues, it is more difficult to identify a clear EC measure that banned or threatened to ban imports from the US and Canada. Still, developments in the EC regulation of GM foods and food products during the second half of the 1990s, led to a considerable divergence with US and Canadian regulatory standards, which in turn restricted their export opportunities for certain agricultural products. Arguably, the European measures led to some limited degree of strengthening in US and Canadian standards, although only in an indirect sense and more so in the US than in Canada.

The fourth and final issue, which is analysed in chapter 6, is the EC data protection Directive. This Directive opened the possibility of blocking transfers of personal information to countries without an 'adequate' level of protection. In the mid-1990s, when the Directive was adopted, both the US and Canada had inadequate systems of data protection under the terms of the Directive, which potentially affected a wide range of exports to the EC that relied on the exchange of personal information. In response, the US negotiated a 'safe harbour' agreement with the EC, consisting of a set of data protection principles with which US firms could choose to comply when doing business with firms from the EC. Canada, by contrast, adopted general legislation to protect personal information in the private sector, partly in response to the EC Directive. As a consequence, both countries experienced a strengthening of data protection standards as a result of the European Directive, although in different ways.

These cases will be analysed on the basis of a theoretical framework that seeks to specify the conditions under which a California effect is likely to take place. The theoretical framework is based on Robert Putnam's 'two-level game' approach, which focuses on the interaction of international and domestic political processes that is central to the California effect. Putnam's original approach will be modified and specified in a number of ways, which will be discussed more extensively in chapter 2. In chapter 7, the conclusions of the case studies will be related to this theoretical framework to yield a number of general conclusions.

Most importantly, the outcomes of California-effect types of processes can be explained by looking both at the trade effects of differences in regulatory standards, at the costs of adopting more stringent regulatory standards for actors in the US and Canada, and at the way the arguments for the EC standards related to existing values and perceived problems in the US and Canadian domestic political debates over these issues. Moreover, not only did the EC standards have an impact on the political process in the US and Canada, but interest groups and government officials in the US and Canada also tried to undercut support for these standards within the EC, in which they succeeded in some cases but not in others. Apart from threatening to impose or actually imposing retaliatory measures and using arguments against the EC standards, they sometimes also invoked international (trade) law and sought to expand participation in the EC by involving trade officials in the process.

The case studies thus present a wide range of processes, both at the international and domestic levels, and both within the US, Canada and the EC. Before proceeding to the theoretical framework and the case studies, however, this introductory chapter will first discuss some of the existing literature on the California effect, the way I arrived at my research problem and the four issues, the choice for a case study approach, and the methods used in conducting the case studies.

1.3 The California effect

David Vogel has pointed to three factors he considers to be crucial in producing a California effect (Vogel, 1995: 260-268). First, the country imposing the more stringent standards needs to have a rich and large market in order to induce other countries to raise their regulatory standards to retain market access. In the exporting country, an important role is therefore played by export-oriented firms, which have an interest in retaining market access.

Second, the imposition of more stringent standards is more likely if they are supported by domestic producers that have an interest in imposing those standards on their foreign competitors. They may form coalitions with public interest groups, such as environmental groups, that are also interested in more stringent standards. Such coalitions are called 'Baptist-bootlegger coalitions,' after the two groups that supported the prohibition in the US, albeit for different reasons.

Third, agreements aimed at international integration may contribute to a strengthening of regulatory standards. Trade agreements, such as the GATT/WTO Agreements or the EC Treaty, may constrain the use of regulatory trade measures by the countries which are party to them, but they may also contain provisions aimed at the harmonisation of regulatory standards. If these international standards are more stringent than most countries' domestic standards, they may result in an overall strengthening of domestic standards. A California effect is more likely when a trade agreement offers more room for this kind of harmonisation.

In reviewing the cases of a California effect discussed in the literature, three main ways can be discerned in which such an effect may be produced:

- A country may require products to conform to certain standards;
- A country may require other countries to conform to certain standards, and;
- A country may have national standards harmonised in an international organisation.

Imposing standards on products

If a country requires products to conform to certain standards, foreign firms have to comply with the more stringent standards if they want to continue to export their products to the country that adopted those standards. If they do so, economies of scale may lead the firms to adjust their entire production to these more stringent standards because often it is less expensive to produce all products according to the most stringent standards than to maintain separate production lines for exports and domestic markets.

As a consequence, however, the export-oriented firms may face a competitive disadvantage on their home markets where they have to compete with firms that do not export their products and thus do not have to comply with the more stringent standards. It may therefore be an advantage for the export-oriented firms to have the more stringent standards accepted in their home countries as well. If they succeed, often in co-operation with public interest groups that support more stringent standards, the sequence is completed and the more stringent standards have been exported from one country to another.

A good example is the case of California's automobile emission standards. The state of California has been known for its relatively stringent environmental standards. According to the idea of a race to the bottom, this should have proved a severe handicap and downward pressures on California's standards should have resulted. Vogel, however, tells a different story (Vogel, 1995: 259):

> 'The California effect can be seen literally in the history of American automobile emission standards. The 1970 Clean Air Act Amendments specifically permitted California the option of enacting stricter emission standards than those required for the rest of the United States, an option which California chose. Consequently its standards remained stricter than those of any other state. In 1990, Congress brought national emission standards up to California's and once again permitted California to impose stricter standards. It also gave other states the option of choosing either national or California standards. In 1994 twelve eastern states requested that the federal government permit them to adopt California's new standards. These standards in turn are likely to become the basis for the next round of minimum federal requirements. California has now had America's strictest automotive pollution control standards for more than three decades. Thus, in stead of states with laxer standards undermining those with stricter ones, in the case of automobile emissions precisely the opposite has occurred: California has helped make American mobile emissions standards steadily stronger.' (Endnotes omitted).

California's automobile emission standards even travelled across the ocean to the European Community. In the negotiations on this issue in the EC, the US standards became a benchmark. They were supported by the 'green' member states of the EC and by car manufacturers that exported large numbers of cars to the US (mainly to California, as a matter of fact). After long debates and a number of compromises, the EC finally adopted standards that were similar to those in the US (Dietrich, 1996; Vogel, 1995: 63-77).

Imposing standards on countries

Sometimes, market access is not denied to individual products, but rather to products from countries that have less stringent standards than the importing country. In that case, the government of the exporting country is more directly involved. It will have to strengthen its standards, if its firms are to have market access to the country imposing the more stringent standards.

A good example of this type of measure is the US ban on tuna caught with dolphin-unfriendly methods (see Joseph, 1994; Vogel, 1995: 103-123). In 1972, the US enacted legislation to protect dolphins that were killed during the tuna catch in the Eastern Tropical Pacific (ETP). This legislation, and subsequent amendments, prohibited the use of certain fishing methods by tuna fishermen and required foreign governments to enact similar legislation, or their tuna could not be imported into the United States.

Although, by the late 1980s, the Mexican rate of dolphin kills had decreased under US pressure, it still remained above the American rate. Finally, in 1990, the US banned the import of Mexican tuna. Mexico, in turn, filed a complaint against the US with the GATT (the General Agreement on Tariffs and Trade, the predecessor of the World Trade Organization) and a dispute resolution panel was established.

In 1991, the panel reached its conclusion: the US was not allowed under GATT rules to ban a product because it did not conform to US process and production standards. Dolphin mortality did not affect the quality of the product (tuna) as such. The US legislation therefore sought to impose US standards on another country, which could not be allowed (for a more extensive legal analysis of this dispute, see section 3.4.2). This has since become the most famous example of the incompatibility between trade and the environment and it was strongly denounced by US environmental groups. The protection of dolphins had to yield to free trade, so it was argued.

Vogel shows, however, that this was not what actually happened. At the time of the Tuna-Dolphin case, Mexico and the United States were negotiating a free trade agreement that also included Canada; what was later to become NAFTA. In the process, the US government faced fierce opposition from labour unions and environmental groups which feared that many companies would leave the US in favour of Mexico with its low wages and lax standards. The Tuna-Dolphin case and the public outcry it provoked, were thus most unhelpful to the US and Mexican governments.

Despite the favourable outcome, the Mexican government did not bring the panel conclusion to the GATT Council for adoption, which would have given it an official status. Moreover, Mexico stepped up its dolphin protection programme and entered into an international agreement to protect dolphins in the ETP area. All in all, whereas the number of dolphins killed by US tuna fishermen alone had been 368,000 in 1972 (when the first item of US legislation concerning this issue was enacted), the total number of dolphin kills by fishermen from all countries was no more than 5,000 in 1993 (Vogel, 1995: 104 and 117, respectively). The mortality rate for each time a net was set by a fishing vessel decreased from more than 12 in 1986 to 1.5 in 1992 (Joseph, 1994: 13-14); for Mexican vessels alone, the decline was from 15 to 1.85 in that same period (Vogel, 1995: 107).

Harmonisation in international organisations

A process leading to a California effect can be strengthened if countries co-operate in international organisations with powers of harmonisation. Then, one member state can try to have its own (relatively stringent) standards accepted as international (minimum) standards. If these standards are binding on all member states, the general level of standards will be raised.

A good example of this type of California effect is the European Community's occupational health and safety standards. The EC is the best example worldwide of an international organisation committed to economic integration that has wide powers of harmonisation, i.e. the power to substitute European-wide standards for national ones. Vast areas of regulation have been brought under the competence of the EC, thus creating a powerful supranational organisation.

Most harmonisation measures have to be approved by the Council of Ministers, which consists of representatives of each member state's government. As was discussed above, scholars have tended to disagree about the likely outcomes of harmonisation processes. Some have argued that harmonised standards will most probably end up at the 'lowest common denominator.' Member states with less stringent standards have no interest in harmonisation at a more stringent level than their own, because it would undermine their existing advantage at that point. Especially when unanimity is required in the Council of Ministers, harmonisation would therefore normally end up at the level of the member state with the least stringent standards. If a qualified majority is required, the standards would be set at the level of the last member state needed to form a majority (Golub, 1996: 328-330; Rehbinder & Stewart, 1985: 9-12).

Yet, this was not what happened in the case of occupational health and safety standards. In the Single European Act, the EC Treaty revision of 1986, a specific legal base was created for this field of regulation. The Council of Ministers was given the power to enact Directives[2] in order to improve the 'working environment' (at that time Article 118^{A} EC Treaty, now Article 137; see EC, 1997j). The EC followed up immediately and developed a system of Directives to cover the field.

The content of those Directives was anything but the lowest common denominator. On the contrary, it formed a major innovation for almost all member states, with the exception maybe of Denmark and the Netherlands. Eichener (1993: 6 ff.) mentioned a number of innovative features of the Directives, the most fundamental of which is the broad concept of health underlying them: 'health' does not just mean physical health and the prevention of direct risks at work, but it also covers issues like stress, fatigue and the organisation of the workplace.

Eichener explained these outcomes by pointing at a number of institutional features of the European Community, such as the institutional interests of and the role played by actors at the EC level, most prominently the European Commission, and the advantages member states with relatively stringent standards had in the preparation of the Directives in terms of expertise and available manpower. In addition, he discussed several strategies which the European Commission could use to increase support for more stringent standards, including the use of elements from different member states' existing legislation, the mobilisation of non-governmental actors in the political process, and allowing room for weak implementation by the member states (see also Eichener, 1997: 597-606).

Although these three processes through which a California effect may occur can be distinguished analytically, they may coincide in specific cases. For instance, in the automobile emissions case discussed above, both the US requirements on European cars and harmonisation processes in the US and the EC played

2 The EC has a number of legal instruments at its disposal to enact standards. The most widely used instrument is called a 'Directive'; it specifies the goals to be attained, but leaves the form and instruments by which to achieve them to the member states (see Article 249 EC Treaty; EC, 1997j). See further below, in section 2.3.3.

a role. Another example, as we shall see in chapter 6, is the European data protection Directive, which opened up the possibility of blocking data transfers to countries without an adequate level of protection. In principle, this is an example of the second category: a measure imposed on a country. At the same time, international data protection standards had been formulated in the Organisation for Economic Co-operation and Development (OECD). Also, the EC Directive contained a number of exemptions for individual data transfers and foresaw adequacy findings for sectors of the economy, apart from the country as a whole. Thus, this issue combines all three types of processes.

1.4 The Research Problem

In section 1.1, the aim of this study was formulated as contributing to systematic theory about the conditions under which a California effect will occur. In order to arrive at the research problem to be examined in this study, this section will specify this general aim in a number of ways that relate to the policy areas to be covered, the type of standards in those fields, the countries involved in the process, and the time frame of the study.

1.4.1 The choice of policy areas

In this study, I will limit myself to regulatory policies. This excludes all distributive policy areas, such as taxation and social security. These areas are distinct in that they involve efforts to redistribute (large) sums of money from some groups in society to others. As such they are probably more vulnerable to a race to the bottom (see the interest taxation case in Genschel & Plümper, 1997; see also Scharpf, 1997: 525). However, the concept of the California effect was developed in the context of regulatory policies and it is probably most useful to develop it further in that context. At a later stage, the literature on regulatory policies may then be linked to the extensive literature on (changes in) the welfare state and to other distributive policy fields.

Within the area of regulatory policies, I will focus on two policy areas that have been at the centre of many debates over the impact of internationalisation on domestic policies: environmental and consumer protection. Environmental and consumer protection standards stand in contrast to 'economic' regulation such as corporate and contract law. Environmental and consumer protection standards are interventionist, in that they seek to redirect the outcomes of market processes; economic regulation is facilitative in that it provides the legal framework which parties in a market need to conclude transactions. As a consequence, all parties in a market have an interest in the good functioning of economic regulation and, to some extent, in its stringency. Economic regulation is what Ogus (1999: 410 ff.) has called a 'homogeneous legal product.'

Environmental and consumer protection standards, on the other hand, are 'heterogeneous legal products' on which the preferences of the parties affected may diverge because they often run counter to the interests of at least one of the parties. These standards impose costs on producers in order to protect other interests. Moreover, these other interests are often tied to important societal values. Consequently, the affected parties may differ greatly in their support for, or opposition against, more stringent standards or even the existence of those standards in the first place. These preferences will most likely also differ between countries, making 'spontaneous' convergence less likely (Ogus, 1999: 413-414).

This may be a highly stylised picture of the various policy areas, since some corporate standards can be argued to be primarily interventionist or 'heterogeneous' in nature (e.g. standards in corporate law protecting shareholders; cf. Ogus, 1999: 413) while some, say, consumer protection standards may well be facilitative or 'homogeneous.' Nevertheless, the distinction is likely to hold true for most standards in these areas.

Therefore, consumer and environmental standards are relatively unlikely candidates for a California effect. If it can be shown under which conditions they are actually subject to a California effect, this would also be a strong indication of the conditions under which this would be the case for standards in facilitative policy fields.

I will also exclude human rights. Trade measures in the form of economic sanctions have regularly been used in attempts to impose human rights on countries that have violated these rights. A quite extensive literature has emerged concerning the question whether and under what conditions these sanctions are effective (see e.g. Baldwin, 1985; Galtung, 1967; Glasius, 1999; Hawkins, 1997; Hufbauer, Schott, & Elliott, 1990; Klotz, 1996). Although important insights from this literature will be incorporated into my theoretical framework, I will not address the issue of human rights as such. This area is probably distinct in that it involves much more fundamental norms and affects more directly the power base of the targeted regimes than do environmental or consumer protection standards.

Moreover, violations of human rights are normally not related to competitiveness concerns, in that violations of human rights are thought to run counter to fundamental norms but not to enhance the competitiveness of firms. Consequently, human rights are not part of the debate on a race to the bottom as a result of economic internationalisation. Furthermore, in contrast to the measures I am studying here, human rights-related economic sanctions cannot be avoided by changing the way the affected products are themselves produced. Rather, they require changes in other (types of) standards that are unrelated to those products. The same applies to issues of criminal law.

Because human rights issues and economic sanctions adopted in response to them are distinct from most issues and measures in the fields of environmental and consumer protection, the underlying processes may also be different. They will therefore be excluded from this study, but in section 7.3.2 the potential relevance of this study for human rights-related sanctions and vice versa will be further discussed.

Labour standards fall in between environmental and consumer standards on the one hand, and human rights on the other. Some labour standards can be considered as human rights (as has been done in debates over child labour and other 'core' labour standards, see Langille, 1997: 32 and 34-37) and may involve important issues of power and authority (for instance, the rights of trade unions). In that sense, they are related to human rights issues. At the same time, other labour standards are less closely linked to issues of human rights and authority and are therefore more similar to environmental and consumer protection standards. Moreover, the debate over labour standards has had a strong economic element in that the stringency of labour standards may raise competitiveness concerns (Langille, 1997: 37-43; Lee, 1997: 177 and 179 ff.). As a result, the debate over labour standards and trade has partly run parallel to that over environmental standards and trade (see e.g. Charnovitz, 1992). However, as we will see below, labour standards have hardly been used by the EC to block imports from other countries, and they have not played a role in the relations between the EC and the US and Canada. Consequently, they will be excluded from the scope of this study, although in section 7.3.2 the relevance of my results for labour standards issues will be discussed as well.

I will not make any further distinctions between or within the two issue areas of environmental and consumer protection standards, since the issue area as such need not make much difference for the purposes of this study. Policy areas may differ in important factors, such as the influence and composition of interest groups, but these differences can be readily expressed in terms of those factors without referring to the policy area as such. This is a more fruitful approach because it yields more 'fundamental' explanations and because these factors may also vary across issues within issue areas, across countries, or over time.

1.4.2 The type of standard

Two types of regulatory standards can be discerned in the fields of environmental and consumer protection: product standards and process (or production) standards. Product standards refer to characteristics of products themselves, such as product safety standards, or maximum levels of certain substances in food. These standards can fairly easily be imposed on imported goods because product characteristics can, in principle, be tested for at the border. Process standards, on the other hand, refer to characteristics of the production process in which a product has been made. Examples include pollution emission standards for factories, or processing standards for food products. These standards have to be implemented and monitored at the site of production. They are therefore more difficult to enforce, and they are likely to be seen as greater and more direct intrusions in another country's own regulatory policies. Moreover, as will be discussed more extensively in the case study chapters, they are more likely to violate trade agreements. Finally, it is probably more difficult to command support among consumers or voters for restrictions on products based on the way they have been produced than based on their characteristics.

Consequently, Vogel (1997b: 563-565) and Scharpf (1997: 523-524) have argued that process standards are less likely to be strengthened in a California effect than product standards. Nevertheless, both the US and the EC have adopted several measures that have restricted imports of products based on the way they were produced, mainly in the environmental field. It is therefore particularly interesting to study cases involving process standards to see whether and, if so, how they have led to a California effect.

In between product and process standards lies the category of product-related process standards. These are process standards that are imposed in order to control certain characteristics of the resulting product. The best example is formed by food processing standards, which are imposed in order to guarantee certain minimum qualities of food products. These product-related process standards are employed because in some cases they may be more effective in preventing harm than direct product standards.

The difference between 'pure' process standards and product-related process standards is not always clear, as it depends on the objectives of a regulatory standard. Yet, the 'true' motives for adopting certain measures are often difficult to assess. In some cases, the protection of values in the country imposing the standards, the protection of values in other countries affected by those measures, and protectionism may all play a part in the process. Moreover, officially stated and 'real' motives may differ since the motivation lying behind a certain measure may be part of the political process. As a consequence, I will discuss both types of process standards.

1.4.3 The countries involved in the process

The choice for the EC's external relations

In terms of the 'source' of a California effect, this study will focus on the EC's external relations. Together with the US, the EC is the main potential source of a California effect at the global level, because the US and the EC are the two trade blocs that combine a large market and relatively stringent environmental and consumer protection standards. Focusing on one of the two has the advantage of increasing the comparability of the cases and reducing the influence of all kinds of contextual factors that are not of primary interest. The choice for the EC or the US is fairly arbitrary, but the EC is more interesting in that its role in producing a California effect has as yet received relatively little attention, as has the external dimension of EC regulatory policies more generally.

I will focus on the EC's external relations rather than relations between its member states because harmonisation within the EC has become the subject of an extensive literature. This issue has been discussed in or as part of general works on EC policy-making (such as Majone, 1996; Peterson & Bomberg, 1999; Wallace & Wallace, 1996; 2000) and in studies of specific issue areas (e.g. Eichener, 1993; Golub, 1996; Haverland, 1998). Therefore, a greater contribution can probably be made by focusing on the less widely researched area of the EC's external relations.

In principle, a California effect could take place between EC member states in the absence of harmonisation. However, the issue areas that are relevant to this study have largely been harmonised (see Howells & Wilhelmsson, 1997, and Jans, 2000, for overviews of EC consumer and environmental law, respectively). Within the EC, member states have only very few possibilities left to ban products from other member states because they do not conform to certain standards, especially when process standards are concerned. This is even more true when the regulatory standards have been harmonised at the European level (Sevenster, 1998).

For those same reasons, individual EC member states have also become less relevant in California-effect types of processes with non-EC members ('third countries'). Because of the internal market between the member states, a third country can easily circumvent one member country's more stringent (process) standards by importing through another member state and then relying on the relatively stringent rules for trade restrictions within the EC. In addition, as an increasing range of policy areas and issues have been harmonised on the European level, the authority to deal with third countries on these issues has, at least in principle, also shifted to the EC (Demaret, 1993: 357-367; Ziegler, 1996: 215-216). Therefore, the EC is a better candidate for studying the effect of regulatory standards on other countries than its member states.

At the same time, however, it can be argued that the EC, as a highly developed international organisation, is a distinct and unique actor in international politics. This would make it a most unlikely candidate for a study aimed at producing more general insights into the California effect. Still, it can be argued that the US is also a unique country, given its political institutions and interest group system that are quite distinct from what can be found in almost any other country in the world. The problem of generalisability is therefore not unique to the EC. Whichever cases or countries are selected, one always has to make clear to what extent one's results can be translated to other cases and countries. There is no reason to assume a priori that this problem is greater for the EC than for the US.

This is not meant to deny that the EC has certain specific characteristics, and they will be discussed where appropriate in chapter 2 and the case study chapters. In section 7.3.3, I will then come back to this issue and discuss to what extent the results of the case studies can be generalised to other countries.

The choice for the US and Canada

At the other end of the relation, this study focuses on the effects of EC measures on the US and Canada. This excludes, first of all, the adoption of more stringent standards by candidates for EC membership (mainly in Central and Eastern Europe) and the adoption of more stringent standards because of an association agreement with the EC (in the countries that are part of the European Economic Area and the countries around the Mediterranean). The exclusion of those countries is largely the result of a decision to focus on cases that involve the imposition of a single standard, which excludes processes in which the standard to be imposed is part of a broader package of standards a country has to conform to as a consequence of an agreement with the EC.

Excluding these countries focuses the debate more specifically on the link between trade and regulatory standards, for two reasons. First, when the adoption of standards is part of a broader package of regulatory reform, it is likely to be much less controversial than when it is imposed in isolation. To begin with, the political debate will then be focused less on any single standard, except maybe for some controversial ones. Furthermore, and more importantly, the adoption of standards is the outcome of earlier negotiations in which the whole package of standards to be adopted was negotiated against EC membership or free market access. The link between any single standard and the trade benefits to be held will therefore be relatively weak. When trade is affected by a single standard, the political struggle, both within and between the EC and the other country, will focus specifically on that standard and the specific measure at stake.

Second, a decision to apply for EC membership or to conclude an association agreement involves a much broader array of motives than purely trade-related ones. It may also involve political motives and, in general, is a 'strategic' choice about the orientation of a country vis-à-vis the EC. When the adoption of a single standard is at stake, this is much less so. Non-trade-related motives may play a role in these processes as well, but probably to a much lesser extent. This allows a more specific focus on the role of trade concerns in strengthening standards, to the exclusion of other mechanisms.

A second category of countries that is excluded are non-Western countries, including developing countries. There were three reasons for excluding these countries. To begin with, the number of EC process standards in the fields of environmental and consumer protection that (potentially) affect exports from developing countries has been fairly small. Even if labour standards are taken into account, too, only three measures can be found, all as part of the EC's Generalised System of Preferences (GSP). First, the GSP has included tariff preferences for countries that adhere to three 'core' conventions of the International Labour Organization (EC, 1994b: Article 7; EC, 1998e: Articles 10-15). Second, the GSP also includes tariff preferences for certain products from countries that manage their tropical forests in a sustainable way (EC, 1994b: Article 8; EC, 1998e: Articles 9-10 and 16-18). Finally, the GSP opens the possibility of excluding countries that use forced or prison labour, an option the EC exercised against Myanmar (EC, 1997d).

A second reason to exclude these measures is that they have affected different countries, rendering both empirical research and a comparison between potential cases very difficult. Thus, the measures relating to tropical forests affected mainly Malaysia, Indonesia and Brazil, the major exporters of tropical timber, while child labour is an important issue in countries like India and Pakistan.

Third, trade measures with regard to these issues have been adopted by both the EC and the US. It would therefore be difficult to distinguish between the effects of the EC and the US measures, which would in turn defeat the attempt to focus only on regulatory trade measures adopted by the EC.

These considerations do not apply to the Transatlantic relation (here meant to include both the EC-US and EC-Canadian trade relations). In general, the EC-US and EC-Canadian relations provide an interesting context for studying the California effect. First, a reasonable number of EC process standards have (potentially) affected exports from the EC and Canada.

Second, trade between the EC and the US and, to a lesser extent, Canada, forms an important part of total world trade. Not only is the EC-US trade relation one of the most important in the world, but these two countries have also formed the driving forces behind the GATT and the WTO, as well as other international forums dealing with environmental and consumer protection issues.

Third, the inclusion of both the US and Canada makes for interesting comparisons between two countries that are similar in some ways and different in others. Although the two countries' specific institutional frameworks differ, they are similar in a number of ways. These similarities occur mainly at a relatively high level of abstraction, in that they are both 'liberal democracies,' and 'market economies,' they are 'affluent,' have 'Western cultures,' and are 'North-American.' The effect of factors like this on California-effect types of processes is unclear and the explanatory variables in my theoretical framework will be formulated on a more concrete level. Still, it is likely that factors like 'culture,' 'democracy,' and being a 'market economy' have an impact on the way these processes develop and their outcomes. It is therefore useful to keep them more or less constant between the cases to be studied. The analysis will then focus on more concrete variables, on which the two countries may, and indeed often do, differ. Moreover, most EC process standards that have affected the US have also affected Canada and vice versa. As a result, the same issues can be studied in both relations.

At the same time, the two countries' trade relations with the EC differ. Canada is a very trade-dependent country: between 1996 and 2000, exports of goods and services made up between 38% and 45% of the Canadian gross domestic product or GDP (calculated from Statistics Canada, 2001b). However, the vast majority of Canadian trade has been with the US: between 1995 and 1998, around 80% of Canadian exports of goods went to and around 68% of Canadian imports of goods came from the US. In that same period, exports to the EC accounted for between 5.1 and 6.4% of Canadian exports, while imports from the EC formed around 10% of total Canadian imports (calculated from OECD, 1999: Vol. 1, p. 88).

The US is much less trade dependent, exports of goods and services forming only around 11% of its GDP between 1995 and 2000 (calculated from DoC, 2001). Canada and the EC were the most important trading partners for the US between 1995 and 1998, each accounting for around 18 to 19% of total US imports of goods, and around 20 to 22% of total US exports of goods (calculated from OECD, 1999: Vol. 4, p. 468).

The EC's external trade dependence is similar to that of the US, but it trades much more with the US than with Canada. Between 1995 and 1998, US imports formed between around 19 to 21% of total EC imports of goods, while Canadian imports were only 1.7 to 2.0%. Similarly, between around 17 and 21% of total EC exports of goods went to the US, and only 1.6 to 1.9% to Canada (all figures excluding trade among EC member states; calculated from OECD, 1999: Vol. 5, p. 316).

The EC-US and EC-Canadian relations therefore offer a combination of similarities and differences that allows for a meaningful comparison between them and useful variation on crucial explanatory variables at the same time. Again, in section 7.3.3, I will discuss the extent to which the results of this study can be applied to other countries and trade relations, including those with candidates for EC membership.

The drawback of examining only cases in the Transatlantic relation is that it becomes more difficult to generalise conclusions to other countries and relations. Arguably, that is the price that has to be paid for the benefits of comparability, and given the type of study I am doing it is probably unavoidable. It does mean, however, that generalisations to other cases can never be more than hypotheses, although careful reasoning may at least lead to well-argued hypotheses.

Moreover, in line with the discussion of the EC's characteristics above, most relations between the EC and third countries have some 'unique' characteristics. A number of countries in Eastern Europe are involved in the process of gaining EC membership, which means they have to adopt an extensive array of regulatory standards. Many other countries bordering the EC have specific association treaties with it. Many Third World countries have special relations with the EC member state they were once a colony of, and this special relation has often also been reflected in trade policies. Again, this need not preclude theoretical generalisation altogether, but it does make it more difficult.

1.4.4 Delimitation in time

The study will also be limited to processes that (predominantly) took place in the 1990s. This keeps the political context of the Transatlantic relation more or less constant, since the processes have taken place after the Cold War. Although the impact of this context is difficult to assess and probably ambiguous, it may affect the processes under study in a number of ways.

On the one hand, the predominance of security issues in the Cold War period may have dampened the importance of regulatory and trade issues in the Transatlantic relation. Although environmental and consumer issues are not likely to be linked to security issues directly, the security context of a (trade) relation may affect the way actors deal with an issue and, for instance, their propensity to burden their bilateral relation by elevating an issue to a trade dispute (cf. Rood, 2000: 182-183).

On the other hand, however, the US and the EC have sought to strengthen their co-operation in a number of ways during the 1990s. According to Krenzler and Wiegand (1999: 153), '[t]he revolutionary changes in Eastern Europe and Russia, and their far-reaching implications, led both sides to the conclusion that transatlantic bonds should be strengthened beyond the security arena (...) and that dialogue and cooperation between the EU and the USA needed to be improved.' Consequently, a number of bilateral initiatives have been taken to improve co-operation, mainly in the fields of trade and regulation, some of which will be highlighted in section 2.2.4.

These changes may have had an impact on regulatory issues between the EC and the US (and indirectly also Canada), but the precise form of that impact is difficult to ascertain. A further analysis of this impact would go beyond the scope of this study, however, and it is exactly to avoid this kind of issues that a delimitation of the study to the 1990s is useful. Even then, the EC-US relation experienced rapid developments during this period, but this is probably inherent in any choice of time frame and at least many of the most difficult contextual factors can be ignored.

At the same time, another important contextual factor, the international trade law regime, changed significantly during the 1990s. The change from GATT to WTO occurred in 1995 and meant an important development in international trade law in a number of respects, some of which will be discussed in section 2.2.4 and the case study chapters. This change is very useful, however, since it allows a closer analysis of the role of international trade law in California-effect types of processes. This role is part of the theoretical framework of chapter 2, and in chapter 7, a number of conclusions will be drawn concerning it.

1.4.5 The research problem

All in all the research problem of this study reads as follows:

> *Under what conditions will EC process standards in the fields of environmental and consumer protection that affect or have the potential to affect US and Canadian exports lead to a strengthening of standards in the US and Canada?*

The dependent variable is the occurrence of a California effect in the US and Canada, which is here defined as the strengthening of US or Canadian process standards as a result of the (potential) trade effects of the EC's (more stringent) process standards. The independent or explanatory variables are the conditions that lead to the occurrence of a California effect.

The concept of the California effect itself entails a causal link: between a strengthening of regulatory standards (the dependent variable) and the (potential) trade effects of another country's standards (the independent variable). I will call such standards 'regulatory trade measures' to reflect the fact that they are regulatory measures and that they (potentially) affect trade. This term distinguishes them from regulatory measures that do not affect trade and from 'traditional' trade measures that are specifically aimed at regulating imports, for instance through the imposition of quotas.

The EC is supposed to have adopted a regulatory trade measure if it has adopted a legal basis for denying market access to foreign products if they, or the country from which they are exported, do not conform to certain process standards. Whether or not the EC has adopted a regulatory trade measure does not therefore depend on whether or not it has actually used the legal basis in its dealings with other countries, that is, whether it has implemented the measure or actively threatened to do so.

It can be argued that a legal base that is not used does not affect trade and can therefore not be regarded as a regulatory trade measure in the proper sense. However, the possibility of trade being interrupted may have the same effects as the actual interruption of trade. Of course, this will depend on the likelihood of a regulatory trade measure being implemented, but this likelihood will often be difficult to assess. More importantly, the factors that determine this likelihood will partly be the same as those that determine the effects of a regulatory trade measure on other countries' regulatory standards. For instance, interest group pressure in the country imposing a regulatory trade measure may account for the use of a legal basis but, as will be argued in chapter 2, also for the credibility of the regulatory trade measure and thus for (part of) its effects on other countries. In order not to confound the argument it is better to distinguish the factors leading to a California effect from the factors leading to the adoption of a regulatory trade measure in the first place. What is important, then, is to distinguish between hollow, weak and strong regulatory trade measures, but this distinction may be part of the explanation of their effects.

The dependent variable in the concept of the California effect is the change in stringency of regulatory standards in the US and Canada. If those countries strengthen their regulatory standards in response to an EC regulatory trade measure, a California effect has taken place. This does not mean that the country completely has to accept the conditions attached to the regulatory trade measure. It is enough if some strengthening takes place, although the California effect is greater if the regulatory standards are strengthened to a greater degree.

The stringency of regulatory standards has two sides, because the regulatory standards themselves have two sides: on the one hand, they impose obligations on someone, on the other they protect someone or something. Thus, in defining the stringency of standards two approaches can be followed, depending on the point of view taken. First, a standard can be said to be more stringent if it imposes stronger obligations on someone. In abstract terms, 'imposing stronger obligations' can be read as 'imposing more costs.' Second, a standard can be said to be more stringent if it offers more protection to a third party.

These two approaches need not lead to the same result, since a standard may impose high costs without offering effective protection and vice versa. Since the main interest in the debate about trade and standards concerns the level of protection, that would seem to be an attractive approach. Yet, determining the effective protection offered by standards is a task that goes well beyond the scope of this study, as it requires both technical expertise and a set of (political) norms to judge what is 'effective' or 'useful.'

Hence, I will take a more objective approach by looking at the range of alternatives a standard allows or prohibits. The more a standard restricts the range of allowable actions, the more stringent it is. This definition still leaves open a number of other questions, especially: *who* do the standards protect, *in what respects*, and *how*? Sometimes it may not be possible to combine these dimensions into one measure of 'stringency.' Then, different directions and sizes of change will be found on these different dimensions. This may make a comparison between standards difficult or even impossible, in particular between issue areas. Hence, I will not attempt to formulate a general scale of stringency that can be used to assess all types of standards. Rather, I will discuss whether a strengthening has taken place for each case separately, taking into account the various dimensions of stringency relevant to that case.

The size and, possibly, direction of the causal link between a strengthening of US or Canadian regulatory standards and an EC regulatory trade measure are likely to be determined by a number of other factors that mediate the effects of the regulatory trade measure on the US and Canada; the regulatory trade measure is a necessary condition for a California effect to occur, but it is not a sufficient condition. In this study, I seek to formulate a set of conditions that are sufficient in producing a strengthening of US and Canadian regulatory standards as a result of an EC regulatory trade measure.

Schematically this can be demonstrated as follows:

Other factors
↓
EC regulatory trade measure ⟶ Strengthening of standards in the US or Canada

The 'other factors' are the real focus of this study and the identification of these factors is its main purpose.

1.4.6 The selection of cases and the research questions

In principle, the ideal design would select the cases to be studied based on variation in the explanatory variables. In case study research, where a small number of cases are studied, random selection may do more harm than good. In statistical studies, random selection serves several purposes. If the procedure is followed correctly, it may be assumed, among other things, that the influence of omitted variables (variables that have not been included in the research) is zero, because their influences even out across the sample. When studying a small number of cases, this cannot be assumed, leading to potentially serious biases (King, Keohane & Verba 1994: 124-126).

We are therefore better advised to make a theoretically informed selection of cases. Unfortunately, choosing on the explanatory variables requires a large number of potential cases. Even then, it will be impossible to find two cases that are similar and different exactly on the variables of choice, but at least the opportunities systematically to select cases are greater. Given the small number of potential cases in this study, such an approach is unfeasible.

Under the choices made in formulating the research problem, there are six potential EC regulatory trade measures that can be studied:

- The EC ban on meat produced with certain growth-hormones (EC, 1985; 1988a; 1996b);
- The (threatened) EC ban on furs from countries that allowed the use of leghold traps or did not adhere to internationally agreed humane trapping standards (EC, 1991);
- The EC eco-labelling scheme, which foresaw a voluntary label for products that were environmentally friendly, partly based on the production process (EC, 1992a)
- The (threatened) EC ban on cosmetics tested on animals (EC, 1993);
- The EC data protection Directive, which opened up the possibility of blocking transfers of personal information to countries without an adequate level of protection (EC, 1995);
- The EC regulation of GM foods and food products, which restricted their approval and required labelling partly based on the production process (EC, 1990b; 1997c; 1997f; 1998c; 2000a; 2000b; 2001a).

A maximum of four regulatory trade measures seemed reasonable given the scope of the study and the necessity to undertake an in-depth analysis of each issue and the reactions in the US and Canada. The eco-labelling scheme was not selected because it was a voluntary rather than a mandatory scheme. Consequently, it did not make market access conditional on complying with certain standards.

The cosmetics ban was not selected either, because the ban has not been implemented since the legal basis was created. Moreover, in 2000 the European Commission tabled a proposal to amend the Directive in order to restrict it to animal tests carried out within the EC (CEC, 2000c). In principle, whether or not the ban has been implemented is not relevant to its inclusion in this study. After all, the import ban on furs from animals caught with leghold traps was also implemented only after the US and Canada had reached an agreement with the EC (see chapter 3). Still, given the 'dormant' status of the cosmetics ban since the creation of its legal basis in 1993, this was the most logical issue not to include in the study. Nevertheless, in the chapter on the leghold trap ban, the issue of why the cosmetics ban was not implemented will be briefly discussed.

This leaves the four issues that were briefly reviewed in section 1.2. Technically speaking, this leads to eight cases: four regulatory trade measures times two countries that were affected by them. These eight cases need to be distinguished because they may differ, both on the explanatory variables and the outcomes. Thus, one country may and another may not have adopted more stringent regulatory standards in response to the same EC regulatory trade measure. Similarly, the variables that affected the outcome, such as the trade dependence of the country on the EC, may also have differed.

Studying these eight cases allows comparisons in two ways. First, cases can be compared for the same countries. Thus, the EC-Canadian cases can be compared amongst each other in order to arrive at conclusions, as can the EC-US cases. Second, the reactions of the US and Canada to the same EC regulatory trade measure can be compared. Because the substantive issues are often the same in the processes following one and the same EC regulatory trade measure, and because many developments in the EC are relevant to both the EC-US and EC-Canadian relations, the case study chapters will each discuss one regulatory trade measure and the reactions of both the US and Canada to that measure. I will refer to these four regulatory trade measures as the 'issues,' and to the eight reactions of the US and Canada as the 'cases.'

Methodologically, it is important to note that these eight cases are not completely independent, but linked in two ways: through the explanatory variables, and through their outcomes. The explanatory variables are linked in a number of ways. For instance, many of the same officials and interest groups have participated in the two food issues, the use of growth-hormones in meat production and genetic modification of foods. This results in a smaller variation between these issues. Also, a number of external developments have been the same for these two cases, such as the BSE crisis and the reform of the Common Agricultural Policy in the EC.

The cases are also linked through their outcomes. For instance, it is likely that developments in and their experience with the hormone issue have influenced the way US and Canadian officials and groups have dealt with the GM foods issue. These links are less strong with and between the other two issues, although in general these four issues are part of the same trade relations and have been linked in that way. For instance, as tensions were running high in the US-EC trade relation, partly because of the beef-hormone issue, governments on both sides were less likely to raise yet another trade dispute or start proceedings before the World Trade Organization.

The constraints in the choice of cases involve a risk of ending up with a set of cases that do not show sufficient variation or not on the right variables. As it is, however, the cases that will be examined in this study vary sufficiently, both in their outcomes and in most of the explanatory variables, to draw useful conclusions. In that sense, the selection of cases does not seem to have prejudiced the validity of the study to a great extent.

As to the links between the cases, they will be discussed in the case studies where they are relevant. As with the delimitation to cases in the Transatlantic relation, they may diminish the generalisability of the study's outcomes, but a careful analysis of these links may at least serve to make these limits clearer.

In order to arrive at an answer to the research problem, a number of research questions have to be answered. For each case, these questions read as follows:

1) Has a California effect taken place?
   - Has a strengthening of standards taken place in the US/Canada?
     - What regulatory standards were in place in the US/Canada before the adoption of the EC regulatory trade measure?
     - What regulatory standards were in place in the US/Canada after the adoption of the EC regulatory trade measure?
   - To what extent is this strengthening, if any, the result of the EC regulatory trade measure?
2) What factors may account for this outcome?
   - What was the value of the relevant explanatory variables in this case?
   - How did decision-making processes in the US/Canada and the EC develop after the adoption of the EC regulatory trade measure?

The explanation sought under the second question will be structured around a set of hypotheses that are derived from a theoretical framework. This framework is formulated in chapter 2, and the relevant hypotheses, which will be tested in the case studies, are presented in section 2.5.

1.5 The research design and the use of theory

1.5.1 Causal inference from multiple case studies

The research problem involves causal relations between a number of factors. The kind of answers I am looking for will take the following form: 'if factor A is present (or: has a high value), regulatory trade measures in the fields of environmental and consumer protection are more likely to lead to a strengthening in another country's regulatory standards.' Such a statement is meant to apply to all or most of the cases that conform to certain conditions.

In quantitative designs, generalisations are arrived at by randomly selecting a relatively large number of cases and measuring the values of certain variables in each of them. Then, the variables can be correlated by using statistical techniques, like multivariate analysis. If done properly, the probability that a correlation found in the research reflects a correlation in the population can be calculated statistically.

Together with the other requirements for causality, a causal relation can be inferred for the whole population, not just for the sample studied. Basically, two additional conditions have to be met to infer a causal relation (Cook & Campbell, 1979: 31): the explanatory variable has to precede the dependent variable in time, and the possibility of another variable influencing the dependent variable has to be ruled out. Then, it is justified to infer that the explanatory variable(s) indeed caused the phenomenon to be explained, that is, that the phenomenon would not have occurred if the explanatory variable(s) had been absent or had had different values (cf. the discussion and definition of causality in King, Keohane & Verba, 1994: 76-82). Causality is therefore always a matter of theoretical interpretation of a correlation.

In this study, such a design with large numbers of cases and statistical analysis is not feasible, or indeed desirable, for a number of reasons. First, the number of relevant cases is very small, even if the precise number depends on one's definition of 'regulatory trade measures.' For instance, as was noted above, the number of legal bases for process-related regulatory trade measures that have been created in the EC has been no more than about eight or nine. This number can be increased by treating every country that is affected by those measures as a separate case (which, in principle, is the correct thing to do) but even then the total number of cases will not be sufficiently large to use statistical techniques in a meaningful way.

Second, the adoption of standards in response to another country's regulatory trade measure is a very complex phenomenon. Many variables are involved that interact with each other and that are strongly embedded in their social contexts. Complexity as such is not a sufficient argument for not using quantitative designs, since it may be possible to simplify the phenomenon to make it manageable, or to quantify the interactions between factors themselves. The current state of theorising about the California effect, as well as the kind of variables that are likely to play an important role do not seem to allow such a simplification, however. We would run into severe risks of losing essential information if we wanted to put them into a quantitative mould. Since studying complex phenomena in their context is very time-consuming, this necessarily limits the number of cases that can be examined.

Third, case studies offer better opportunities for studying processes. Processes may be of interest in themselves; David Vogel's theory of the California effect, for instance, is not just a theory about outcomes, but also about the processes through which the outcomes are realised. Equally importantly, studying processes may also increase the plausibility of a causal inference. If we are able to find out which processes led to a certain outcome, we will be able to reach much firmer conclusions about causal links between variables. Case studies lend themselves relatively well to studying processes, especially the kind of political processes I am interested in, as it is often possible to trace the actors and their mutual behaviour, and the way they have brought about a certain outcome.

Although these are good reasons for carrying out case studies, generalisation from the cases studied to cases that have not been studied is problematic. Because only a small number of cases are studied, it may well be that the cases are not representative of the larger population of possible cases. Any causal inference may therefore be a product of the case selection, and may not apply to the wider class of cases. Some authors have argued that such a 'sampling logic' of generalisation cannot be applied to case studies (Yin, 1994: 36 and 47-49). Rather, case studies should be seen according to a 'replication logic,' just as multiple experiments. Then, multiple case studies serve as replications of each other (Yin, 1994: 45-47). As a consequence, multiple case studies are not well suited for generalisation to larger populations, but they can be used to generalise to theories.

This line of reasoning would support the kind of design followed in this study, because generalisation to theory is exactly what it aims at. Nevertheless, the distinction between theoretical and population generalisation is not that clear-cut (Swanborn, 1996: 68-69). Theories contain a number of propositions about causal relations between variables for some domain of units. Except at the highest level of generality, the domain of a theory is thus limited to a part of all possible units and an important task of research is to determine what the limits of a theory's application are. In that respect the problems of generalising to theories and generalising to populations are quite similar: in both cases it has to be shown how the cases studied relate to cases that a theoretical proposition seeks to cover.

The basic logic underlying causal inference from multiple case studies is often derived from Mill's methods of difference and agreement (Skocpol & Somers, 1980: 183-184). The method of difference can be used if cases have different outcomes. Then, if all cases have the same value on all potential explanatory variables, except one, the one explanatory variable whose value differs between the cases is the cause of the difference in outcomes. The method of agreement can be used if all cases have the same outcome. If all cases have different values on all potential explanatory variables, except one, then the one explanatory variable that has the same value in all cases is the cause of the similarity in outcomes.

Lieberson (1992) showed that causal inference based on these approaches is extremely vulnerable to the specific cases studied and the variables taken into account. When used in the context of case studies, he argues, some rather unlikely assumptions have to be made to arrive at generalisations to other cases. More specifically, he points at six crucial assumptions that have to be met:

- Causes are deterministic. That is, they have to produce the same effects in all cases. If the causal relations are probabilistic and vary between cases, then it becomes much more difficult to draw firm conclusions in any one case;

- There is only one cause. If an outcome can be explained in more than one way, it is not possible to decide which of the explanations is right. Consequently, no conclusion can be drawn, at least not when only two cases are studied. Since it is nearly impossible to find cases that differ or agree on all potential explanatory variables except one, as the methods of difference and agreement require, it will therefore often be impossible to reach a conclusion. In the methodological literature, this is often referred to as the problem of 'indeterminacy' (e.g. King, Keohane & Verba, 1994: 119-120);
- There are no interactions between variables. Sometimes, explanatory variables only operate in combination with other variables, but the methods of difference and agreement are not able to uncover these interactions;
- All possible causes have to be taken into account. If an explanatory variable that is important in reality is left out of the study, the conclusions can be severely misinterpreted;
- No errors have been made in the measurement of variables. If the value of the explanatory variables is not measured correctly, false conclusions will be drawn;
- The same pattern will occur in all other cases about which generalisations are made.

Lieberson's analysis has the merit of highlighting the assumptions underlying a strict application of the methods of difference and agreement. Still, his analysis is limited by its restriction to inductive studies that use the methods in a rather mechanistic way. Many of the six assumptions can be relaxed by using two strategies, thereby meeting much of the criticism implied in them and strengthening causal inferences drawn from case studies. These strategies are, first, the use of a theoretical framework and, second, careful process-tracing in the cases themselves (cf. Haverland & Princen, 1998: 30-33).

1.5.2 The use of theory

In chapter 2, a theoretical framework will be formulated and a number of hypotheses will be derived from it. It is these hypotheses that will in turn form the background to and will be tested in the case studies. Formulating and using a theoretical framework serves a number of interrelated purposes. To begin with, by working from a theoretical framework, the results of this study can be more readily compared with and integrated in the existing body of theory. As a result, the California effect is not studied as an isolated phenomenon, but as part of a wider range of social processes, and the conclusions can be related to these other processes. Furthermore, using a theory focuses attention in the case studies on potentially relevant factors. Since case studies offer a plethora of facts and developments, a theoretical framework serves to avoid being swamped by them.

Both arguments for using a theoretical framework also point to its drawback: by using a theoretical framework other potentially relevant factors may be excluded from a study, and by focusing the analysis in the case studies some developments or factors may be obscured. To some extent, this is a valid point of criticism. At the same time, however, it is also unavoidable in that undertaking case studies (or research more generally) always involves making choices among the multitude of facts that present themselves. If those choices are not made explicitly, a researcher will (have to) make them implicitly. Hence, a theoretical framework also serves to make explicit the assumptions and ideas that guide the case studies.

Moreover, by formulating an explicit theory, the assumptions and ideas that guide the study are structured by bringing them into one framework. In that way, they achieve a degree of coherence that moves them beyond a set of disparate notions. Finally, by explicitly formulating and structuring a theory, additional insights and implications can be yielded from the original set of assumptions and ideas, which may both serve to strengthen the theoretical framework itself and to enrich the empirical analysis in the case studies.

The use of a theoretical framework also meets some of Lieberson's points of criticism. First, the assumption that only one variable caused the phenomenon to be studied loses much of its relevance, since the case studies are no longer used inductively but to test certain hypothesised causal relations. Of course, the number of cases still limits the number of independent hypotheses that can be tested, but this can be met by process-tracing, as will be argued below.

Second, using a theoretical framework increases the likelihood that all or most relevant potential causes have been taken into account. Of course, it is always possible that some important variable is left out. In the case studies, I have sought to reduce this risk by confronting my conclusions and interpretations with the interpretations of the people I interviewed and of other studies of that case, where they exist. At some points, the case studies indeed yielded additional insights, which will be discussed in the case study chapters.

Third, the validity of generalisations to other cases can be increased by a correct specification of the conditions under which the conclusions will hold true. Of course, this entails an assumption in itself, in that these conditions cannot be tested in the case studies themselves. Therefore, it again has to be assumed that they have been correctly specified.

1.5.3 Process-tracing

An important instrument to make causal inferences more plausible and to avoid some of Lieberson's critique is the tracing of causal process between variables in a case study ('process-tracing;' George & McKeown, 1985: 35). This is particularly true of studies of political phenomena. If, for instance, it is stated that the combination of strong environmental groups and a big industry for pollution abatement equipment will increase the likelihood of a California effect, this statement can be made much stronger if we can show that the two sides formed a coalition, supported each other's proposals, and the like. Then, we will be much more confident that it was actually the combination of the two, rather than some other factor, that caused the California effect. Thus, process-tracing can be used to some extent as a substitute for statistical correlation in assessing a causal link.

Process-tracing meets a number of additional points of criticism raised by Lieberson. First, process-tracing can make causal inferences stronger for several variables in the same case study. Consequently, a larger number of causal relations can be demonstrated than would be possible if only the values of variables were taken into account.

Second, process-tracing is also well-suited to studying the interaction between variables. By showing how variables have (or have not) operated together in a case, their interaction can be studied, thus obviating much of Lieberson's criticism at this point.

Third, the risk that an observed causal relation is actually the result of another explanatory variable that was not taken into account can be reduced by showing the process underlying the causal relation. That way, the causal inference will be much stronger than when it is only based on a comparison of values of the explanatory and dependent variables, which meets much of Lieberson's point about all possible causes being taken into account.

Despite the improvements that can be made by using a theoretical framework and applying process-tracing, some of Lieberson's points remain valid. Thus, case studies are not well suited to examine probabilistic causal relations, at least not when they are meant to reach conclusions about frequencies or probabilities. Still, it seems possible to examine hypotheses in terms of more or less. Moreover, when drawing conclusions, the potential probabilistic character of those conclusions should be noted.

Likewise, measurement error remains an important potential problem. In case studies such as those carried out here, the term 'measurement' is used somewhat metaphorically, and some might prefer the term 'interpretation,' but the basic problem is the same. In the case studies, the validity of the measurement/interpretation has been increased by using different sources alongside each other and by confronting my conclusions with those of interviewees and existing studies. Moreover, differences of opinion or ambiguities in the measurement will be noted throughout the texts of the case studies to increase their reliability as much as possible.

Finally, it has to be assumed that other cases will reflect a similar pattern of causal relations if generalisations are made. This is not unique to case study research; it applies to the same extent to other designs that seek to generalise their conclusions. For instance, in statistical analyses, assumptions often have to be made about properties of the sample and the population if valid conclusions are to be drawn from certain techniques. As was argued in the previous subsection, this problem can be met at least partly by a correct specification of the conditions under which the theory will hold true, but in the end generalisations depend crucially on whether these conditions are correctly specified. Generalisations will therefore have the character of new hypotheses rather than established relations.

1.5.4 The use of sources

Several different (types of) sources have been used in conducting the case studies. Three types of sources were important:
- Official documents;
- Reports by other observers (secondary documents);
- Interviews.

Each type of source has its strong and weak points, and the value of these sources for specific purposes varies. Moreover, they have to be used in conjunction to produce better results; by systematically checking results from one source against another, a technique usually referred to as 'triangulation,' a firmer basis can be reached for one's conclusions.

The use of official documents

Official documents have two main uses. First, they give the authorised formulation of legal texts, be they laws or law-like legal instruments or concrete decisions and judgements. This use is fairly unproblematic as long as the proper legal interpretation methods are followed. Second, official documents give information about motives, behaviour and events. Government reports contain analyses of problems and perspectives, as well as overviews of events and motives for action. This aspect of official documents is more problematic, however, because they are always written with a (political) purpose in mind and for some audience other than the researcher (Yin, 1994: 82). A researcher can therefore not simply take this information from official documents as 'objective' information about the political process and the motives of actors in it.

As a consequence, some information in official documents may be more useful than others. As a rule, information about events can be treated with more confidence than information about motives or explanations of events. For instance, if an official document states that the government met with some interest group on a certain date, this can be used as a raw fact. Even here, caution is in place as events may be misconstrued or mentioned only selectively, but if one stays as close to the factual content of the message as possible, official documents may be useful (albeit limited) sources of information on these matters.

Moreover, apart from reporting on political processes, official documents are often important political facts in themselves. Thus, it may be politically highly significant if a government or interest group stated at some time that it would not support a measure. Even if this is not a 'true' picture of the government's or interest group's motives, the fact that they wanted to communicate this to someone else in the process is often a significant political fact.

In any case, the type of official document is important. Public statements and publications are most likely to have a strategic political purpose; they are what Moravcsik (1998: 81) called 'soft' primary sources. Confidential statements and minutes of meetings are more reliable as a source of information in this respect; they are 'hard' primary sources. When studying contemporary cases, it may often be difficult or impossible to obtain these confidential documents, however, in which case one has to resort to other, admittedly less reliable, sources.

The use of secondary documents

Most cases have already been reported or studied by others: journalists in newspapers and magazines, and other scientific researchers. Their reports give information about events and possible explanations for them. These reports can be and often are used as the basis or one of the bases for scientific case studies. The practice of using journalistic sources has been criticised on the ground that these sources are not primarily aimed at scientific reporting and may thus contain flaws and biases. Moreover, the interpretation given in journalistic sources cannot be used to support a researcher's explanation: this would simply amount to substituting that opinion for one's own. Scientific reports may be more reliable sources but here, too, one has to be cautious in using interpretations and explanations, especially when that report's sources are unclear, and when the study has a different aim and design.

In this study, secondary documents as well as soft primary sources will be used primarily as sources of factual information. Interpretations and explanations given in these documents will in principle not be used to support an explanation, unless no other and more reliable sources are available (cf. Moravcsik, 1998: 83).

The use of interviews and the selection of interviewees

Finally, interviews with key participants in the political process can give important information about that process (Yin, 1994: 85). Many (informal) contacts and events are not reported in official documents, although they may have been very important in the process leading up to a decision. By conducting interviews some of these events can be revealed and used in the analysis of a case. In addition, interviews provide the opportunity to test one's interpretation of events against that of people who participated in or have been close observers of those events. Moreover, they can shed more light on the interviewees' own actions and motives during the process. Nevertheless, it is important to treat this information with caution, too, since it can be biased in several ways:

- Interviewees may have forgotten events. This problem is greater the less recently events have taken place. Systematic bias also arises if interviewees have systematically forgotten certain types of events, for instance negative events (Deliens & Van Goor, 1984: 394-395);
- The interviewees' interpretation of questions may differ from what the interviewer had in mind;

– Finally, interviewees may try to rationalise their own actions and the processes they participated in (Deliens & Van Goor, 1984: 395). This type of bias is especially relevant to this study, since people often have an incentive to underestimate their own or others' power and successes in a policy process. On the one hand, successful participants may feel it is 'not done' to stress their own successes or they may fear it will affect their success in future negotiations (cf. Pfeffer, 1981: 49-50, who makes this point in the context of organisational processes). On the other hand, unsuccessful participants may want to present the outcomes of policy processes as the result of their own choices. As a result, the role of power processes or, for instance, the role of another country's actions, may be downplayed.

Some of these caveats can be overcome by a careful design and interpretation of results, but the main point here, too, is that the outcomes of interviews should as much as possible be checked against each other and against evidence from other sources.

Much of the value of interviews depends on the selection of interviewees, since their perspectives on and knowledge of events depend crucially on their backgrounds and the roles they played in the process. In a study like this, comprising four issues in the US, Canada, and the EC, the selection is even more important because the number of cases necessarily limits the number of interviews that can be conducted for any one case study.

In the selection of interviewees, I have followed some theoretical distinctions that will be elaborated in the next chapter. In that chapter, I distinguish between three types of government officials: 'policy officials,' who are responsible for a certain policy area; 'sponsoring officials,' who are responsible for a certain sector of the economy; and 'trade officials,' who are responsible for trade relations. I also distinguish between four types of interest groups: 'domestic firms,' which produce mainly for domestic markets, 'export-oriented firms,' which depend (to a relatively great extent) on exports, 'importing firms,' which rely (to a relatively great extent) on imports, and 'public interest groups,' such as consumer and environmental groups. As will be explained in chapter 2, each of these types of officials and interest groups is likely to have specific interests and ideas with regard to the stringency of regulatory standards and the use of regulatory trade measures.

Therefore, in selecting the interviewees, I have sought to include at least one interviewee from each type of official and interest group. Nevertheless, a number of adjustments had to be made to this general scheme. First, since firms were often not organised along the lines of 'domestic,' 'export-oriented' and 'importing,' these groups were merged. At the same time, it was often useful to include business groups from different stages of the production process. Second, sometimes the same person could cover more than one issue. For instance, the beef-hormone and GM foods issues were often dealt with by the same people in an organisation. Third, in some cases certain types of officials did not exist or had not been involved in the process. Finally, in a limited number of occasions it was not possible to contact a potential interviewee or the person concerned refused to be interviewed. In general, however, the general scheme of one interviewee for each type and issue in the US, Canada and the EC could be maintained.

Interviewees were selected in a number of ways. First, some persons were mentioned in official documents. Second, some persons were mentioned in organisational charts or on web sites. Third, and most importantly, the names of potential interviewees were obtained in earlier interviews. To that end, I started with a (small) number of interviews with US and Canadian embassy officials and some interest group representatives in the Netherlands. These interviews have not been used for the case studies themselves, but served as important sources of orientation and as starting points for the interviews in Brussels. Subsequently, a number of interviews were held in Brussels with officials from the European Commission and the US and Canadian Missions to the European Union, as well as interest group representatives that were based in Brussels. Finally, in January and February 2001, two trips were made, to Washington DC and Ottawa, respectively, to conduct interviews with US and Canadian officials and interest group representatives. These interviews all took place in person, and most of them were taped. Some interviews involved more than one person, either on the same issue or on related issues. Subsequently, two additional interviews were conducted by phone with interest group representatives in Canada. In total, 48 separate interviews were conducted for the case studies (excluding the preparatory interviews in the Netherlands), with a total of 67 persons.

In the 'list of interviews,' these interviews have been listed according to date, including the name of the organisation in which the interview took place and the issues that were discussed. If information from an interview was used in a case study, a reference is made to that interview. The references are not meant to indicate an official position of that government agency or interest group; they merely indicate that I used information from the interview to substantiate a particular claim I make in the case study, and they represent my understanding of the interviewee's statements.

In principle, reference is made to either an interest group, or a government agency at the level of (EC) Directorate General, (Canadian) department, or (US) department or agency. As one European Commission official in the GM foods issue did not allow reference to be made to the particular Directorate General, all European Commission interviews for that issue are referred to as 'European Commission.'

1.6 Outline of the book

In the next chapter, I will formulate a theoretical framework, based on a modified version of Robert Putnam's two-level game approach. From this framework, eight hypotheses will be derived that form the background to and will be tested in the case studies.

The next four chapters each deal with one issue, discussing the leghold trap, beef-hormone, GM foods and data protection issues, respectively. Each case study chapter is structured in a comparable way, discussing the following items:

- the background of the issue and a brief overview of the substantive debate underlying it;
- international standards in the field, if any, before the EC regulatory trade measure was adopted;
- the EC regulatory trade measure at issue;
- the initial situation in the US and Canada, in terms of their existing regulatory standards and the (potential) impact of the EC regulatory trade measure on their exports;
- further developments in international standard-setting on the issue;
- the compatibility of the EC regulatory trade measure with applicable international trade law;
- regulatory developments and the response to the EC regulatory trade measure in the US and Canada.

The precise sequence of these elements differs slightly between the four case study chapters to reflect differences in the way the issues developed. Still, each element is present, if relevant in a particular case. Finally, each chapter concludes by reviewing whether a California effect has taken place, and by explaining the outcomes of the cases on the basis of the hypotheses formulated in chapter 2.

In chapter 7, all cases will be discussed together to arrive at a general conclusion. First, a brief overview of the cases and their outcomes will be presented. Then, these outcomes will be explained by systematically comparing the cases. From this comparison, a number of general conclusions will be drawn that form the answer to the research problem in this study. Finally, the generalisability of these conclusions to a wider set of cases, issue areas, and countries will be discussed.

CHAPTER TWO

A THEORETICAL FRAMEWORK

2.1 INTRODUCTION

2.1.1 The California effect and the two-level game approach

According to the definition in the previous chapter, a California effect takes place if one country raises its regulatory standards because of a (threatened) withdrawal of market access by another country. I will refer to both threatened and implemented measures as 'regulatory trade measures.' The country that adopts a regulatory trade measure will be called the 'initiator country' or 'initiator.' The country that is affected by a regulatory trade measure is called the 'target country' or 'target.' A California effect takes place if the target country raises its standards (to a greater or lesser degree) as a result of an initiator country's regulatory trade measure.

This implies that the standard-setting process in the target country is affected by the initiator country's regulatory trade measure in such a way as to lead to more stringent standards. A theoretical framework therefore has to address two issues: how standards are set in the target country, and how regulatory trade measures affect this standard-setting process. Moreover, the use of regulatory trade measures is likely to be determined by domestic political processes in the initiator country. Hence in the California effect, domestic and international politics, as well as their interaction, come together.

A theoretical approach that captures this interaction well is the 'two-level game approach' that was founded by Putnam (1988; see also Evans, Jacobson & Putnam, 1993). This approach offers a useful framework for analysing the way in which domestic politics impacts international bargaining and vice versa.

The central insight of the two-level game framework is that international negotiations take place at two levels: at one level negotiators of different countries negotiate over the terms of an international agreement, at the other level each negotiator has to negotiate with his or her domestic constituents concerning the ratification of the international agreement. In the two-level game approach, 'ratification' refers not only to formal ratification processes, such as the formal procedures countries have for the adoption of international treaties. Rather, the term ratification is used 'generically to refer to any decision-process (...) that is required to endorse or implement a[n international] agreement, whether formally or informally.' This process may also involve 'bureaucratic agencies, interest groups, social classes, or even "public opinion"' (Putnam, 1988: 436).

The international and domestic levels are connected by the concept of a 'win-set.' A win-set is the set of international outcomes that can be ratified in a country.

Each country has its own win-set that is determined by domestic political processes. An international agreement can only be reached if there is an agreement that can be ratified in all countries involved or, in other words, if the win-sets of the countries involved overlap (Putnam, 1988: 437-438).

Apart from this domestic influence on international bargaining, events at the international level can also influence domestic politics and thus the win-sets of the countries involved. For instance, by expanding or restricting alternatives countries can make some international agreements more favourable for another country and others less so. Negotiators can even use international negotiations to change their own domestic win-set.

This approach is useful in analysing the California effect because the adoption of more stringent standards in response to a regulatory trade measure can be seen as a bargaining process in which two countries have to agree upon the conditions under which they conduct their trade. The initiator country may use a regulatory trade measure in a deliberate attempt to change the target country's standards, or such a change may be the side-effect of a regulatory trade measure that was adopted for other reasons. In both cases, the regulatory trade measure may result in a bargaining process between the initiator and the target with a view to reaching an agreement. Although the theoretical framework will be developed mainly with reference to regulatory trade measures as deliberate instruments, I will use the same hypotheses to explain the effects of both types of regulatory trade measures.

Moreover, although the two-level game framework has been formulated in the context of negotiations over (formal) agreements, it is also useful in the absence of an agreement or even of explicit negotiations. If the target country chooses to raise its standards as a reaction to the initiator country's regulatory trade measure, an 'agreement' can be said to exist between both countries in that they accept the same set of conditions under which to conduct their trade. This 'agreement' requires ratification in that the adoption of more stringent standards in the target country either takes place by a parliament (formal ratification) or has to be acceptable to a wider constituency (informal ratification). The two-level game approach is therefore useful for analysing both (formal) agreements and situations in which countries react to each other's actions without such a formal agreement and it has been applied to both types of cases before.

In this chapter, I will formulate a theory that explains how regulatory trade measures, either as instruments of international bargaining or as side-effects of domestic regulatory measures, affect the regulatory decision-making process and thereby the stringency of regulatory standards in other countries, and under what conditions they will lead to a California effect. This theory builds on the two-level game approach, but this approach will be modified and broadened in crucial ways.

As Moravcsik has pointed out, the two-level game framework, in its original formulation, is a metaphor rather than a fully-fledged theory:

> 'In order to generate empirical hypotheses about state behavior, Putnam's two-level-games metaphor requires more restrictive definition. It is essential to specify the prefer-

> ences of and constraints on the major actors. Three essential theoretical building blocks are needed: specification of domestic politics (the nature of the "win-sets"), of the international negotiating environment (the determinants of interstate bargaining outcomes), and of the statesman's preferences.' (Moravcsik, 1993: 23)

In the remainder of this chapter I will formulate these specifications, reversing the order of treatment in the quote somewhat. First, I will specify bargaining between unitary countries at the international level (Moravcsik's 'international negotiating environment'). Then, I will specify the domestic political process and the role of governments as linking pins between the two levels. In my theoretical framework, the role of governments substitutes for Moravcsik's 'statesman's preferences.' Finally, I will discuss the interaction between the international and domestic levels and derive a set of hypotheses from the theoretical framework, which will serve as the theoretical background to the case studies. Before that, however, I will discuss some concepts that form the basis for my theoretical specifications at each level.

2.1.2 Preferences and constraints

Although the California effect focuses on market access and regulatory *trade* measures, it would be a misconception to assume that regulatory trade measures can only affect another country's win-set through their trade effects. Rather, it is useful, as Baldwin (1985: 22-24) has argued in the context of economic sanctions, to distinguish between the instruments used to influence another country and the bases of that influence. The instruments refer to the tools used by countries in attempts to influence another country (here: regulatory trade measures); the bases refer to the causal conditions that determine a successful attempt. This distinction highlights the fact that success can be determined by a number of different power bases. Although regulatory trade measures are primarily economic instruments, their success need not rest (exclusively) on economic bases of power. For instance, success may also be achieved by the information about the initiator state's preferences that is conveyed in regulatory trade measures (cf. Baldwin, 1985: 24). Thus, the distinction between instruments and bases of power avoids the preconception that economic instruments can only have effect through economic causal conditions.

In specifying the theoretical framework at each of the levels, I will assume that actors make decisions by weighing the consequences of alternatives in the light of their preferences. Behaviour is then determined by two basic factors: preferences (or: goals) and constraints (cf. Siegers, 1992: 536). The preferences determine the values an actor attaches to alternatives or the trade-offs between those values, while the constraints determine which alternatives an actor can actually choose between. Actors' win-sets can thus be altered by changing either the constraints which those actors face or their preferences.

The distinction between preferences and constraints is central to my theoretical framework and, more generally, to any theoretical account that uses a rational choice approach. It is also relevant to many debates in current international relations theory that centre around the distinction between identities and constraints. For instance, the literature on the effects of international regimes is characterised by a debate between authors who emphasise the constraining effects of regimes and authors who stress the effects of international regimes for countries' identities or preferences (Checkel, 1997: 473). Scholars working in the economic theoretical tradition typically assume actors' preferences to be fixed, stable or given and seek to explain behaviour from changes in constraints facing those actors (e.g. Stigler & Becker, 1977). Constructivist (e.g. Klotz, 1996) and liberal (e.g. Moravcsik, 1997) scholars focus primarily on changes in preferences.

Preferences can be defined in terms of the values an actor attaches to different alternatives or, similarly, as an ordering of alternatives in terms of better or worse. Thus, the preferences of an actor define which alternatives are preferred to which other alternatives. For instance, a country or a firm within that country may prefer free trade over protectionism in agricultural products or vice versa. It becomes more complicated if more than two alternatives have to be rated, for example when actors have to rate combinations of free trade in agricultural and free trade in industrial products. Then, an actor's preferences could involve simultaneously a preference for protectionism in agricultural products and free trade in industrial products over free trade in both sectors, and a preference for the combination of free trade in both agricultural and industrial products over protectionism in both sectors.

The constraints facing an actor define the alternatives from among which the actor can choose. In the example given above, the constraints facing an actor (for instance, other countries' trade policies) may restrict its choice to either free trade or protectionism in both sectors. Then, the actor will choose free trade in both sectors, although it would have preferred free trade in one and protectionism in the other. However, given the constraints facing the actor, it did not have that alternative.

Although this distinction between preferences and constraints seems straightforward enough, it is still not conclusive because a change of preferences at one level can often be explained as a change in constraints at a higher level. For instance, if the actor in the example above (say, a firm) comes to favour free trade over protectionism in agricultural products, that can be seen as a change in preferences. It may well be, however, that the actor's preferences at a higher level (say, profit maximisation) have remained stable but that the firm's position in world markets has changed in such a way that free trade in agricultural products now yields more profits than protectionism, whereas the opposite was true before.

Similarly, if someone gives up smoking after reading a book on its negative health effects, that may be regarded as a change in preferences concerning smoking. Yet, at a higher level, that person may still hold the same preferences (e.g. regarding his health, or the balance between health and pleasure); only the perceived link between smoking and the more abstract value(s) has changed.

These two examples point at the more general insight that actors' preferences are ordered in a hierarchy of preferences, in which less abstract preferences can be subsumed under more abstract preferences. Behaviour could therefore in principle be explained by recognising some fundamental set of values (an actor's ultimate values). All less abstract preferences could then be deduced by systematically combining this ultimate value with some fundamental constraints, and so on until the level of concrete decisions is reached.

Although this approach allows one always to assume stable preferences, it is not very satisfactory in many situations. An actor's ultimate values are difficult to define. Moreover, ultimate values (e.g. 'happiness in life') tend to become virtually meaningless apart from the way they are operationalised. Furthermore, an actor's preferences at one level consist partly of values at a higher level and partly of causal beliefs about reality. Thus, if someone favours economic liberalisation in order to reduce unemployment, that implies not only a value judgement (less unemployment is beneficial), but also a causal belief about the link between liberalisation and unemployment (more liberalisation will lead to less unemployment). If the person's belief in that causal connection were to change, so would his preferences for liberalisation (cf. the concept of 'household production functions' in economic theory: Siegers, 1992: 538).

In defining preferences and constraints it is therefore important always to specify the level of abstractness at which they are defined. In this study I will define them at the level of governmental (regulatory) policies. Thus actors (be they individuals, firms, public interest groups, governments, countries, or whatever) have preferences for or against certain policies, given the consequences those policies have (in other words: given the constraints facing the actors). A change in an actor's behaviour can therefore be caused by:

- A change in constraints;
- A change in preferences, which in turn can be the result of:
  - A change in values at a higher level;
  - A change in causal beliefs concerning the effects of a policy.

Hence, an actor can also affect another actor's decisions in one of three ways: by changing the constraints facing the other actor, by changing the other actor's values at a higher level or by changing the other actor's causal beliefs. In the following sections I will formulate a theory that explains these changes in the context of the California effect.

2.2 International Bargaining

In this section I will analyse the effects of regulatory trade measures in the relations between unitary countries. Unitary countries are assumed to make decisions in the same way a rational individual does: by assessing the consequences of alternative courses of action and weighing them against a set of preferences. The assumption of unitary countries therefore ignores domestic political processes, by assuming that a country acts as if it were a unified actor (Milner, 1998: 767 ff.; Moravcsik, 1993: 6-7).

Under some circumstances this may be a useful assumption. In this section I will use it to study some general characteristics of (international) bargaining that can be analysed without direct reference to domestic political processes. In the next section I will then relax the assumption of unitary countries and incorporate domestic processes into the theory.

Following the discussion in the previous section, unitary countries can affect another country's decisions in one of two ways: by changing the constraints on that other country, or by changing its preferences. In this section I will first discuss the effects of regulatory trade measures on countries' constraints and then on their preferences.

2.2.1 Regulatory trade measures and the terms of trade

The bulk of the literature on regulatory trade measures (and economic sanctions) has focused exclusively on their economic effects. If an initiator country implements a regulatory trade measure, a target country incurs costs in the form of forgone trade profits and adjustment costs. If these costs are higher than the costs of complying with the initiator country's demands, then the target country will comply with the demands rather than suffer the regulatory trade measures. The effect of a regulatory trade measure should then be greater the more economic costs a target country has to incur (all other things being equal).

The basic argument underlying this analysis is that power derives from the dependence of one actor upon another: an actor has power over another actor if and to the extent that the latter actor is dependent upon the former (Emerson, 1962; Hirschman, 1980 (1945); Keohane & Nye, 1977). Dependence arises when an actor (say, B) has the ability to affect goals that another actor (A) values. For instance, B may have some commodity that A wants, or B may be able to secure A's safety. In these cases, A is dependent upon B. Now, if A and B have to reach agreement upon the sale of the commodity or the price at which B will secure A's safety, the outcome will reflect the asymmetry of the interdependence between the two: the more dependent A is upon B, the more concessions s/he will be willing to make in order to reach an agreement, and vice versa.

According to Emerson, 'the dependence of actor A upon actor B is: (1) directly proportional to A's *motivational investment* in goals mediated by A, and (2) inversely proportional to the availability of those goals to A outside the A-B relation' (Emerson, 1962: 32; emphasis in the original). The dependence of A upon B, and thus the power of B over A is therefore a function of two things: the value A attaches to the goals that B controls (in other words: A's preferences regarding the goals B controls), and the alternatives A has to attain these goals. Thus, if A can choose among a multitude of providers of some commodity, s/he will not be dependent upon any one of them, since s/he can always try to reach a better agreement with someone else. If, on the other hand, B has the monopoly over a commodity, A will have to reach an agreement with B or do without the commodity. This effect is independent from A's values regarding the commodity. Similarly, if two actors both rely on monopolist B for some commodity, the actor that wants the commodity most badly (values it most) will be more dependent and, as a consequence, willing to pay a higher price than the other.

This analysis is consistent with an analysis based on game-theoretic models of bargaining ('negotiation analysis,' see Sebenius, 1991). In these models, an actor will accept all agreements that are better than the alternative of no agreement. This alternative is not necessarily the situation at the moment of the negotiations (the 'status quo ante') but rather the situation that will arise as the result of unilateral action if an agreement is not reached. The value of an agreement at which an actor is indifferent between agreement and no agreement is called the actor's 'reservation value' (Raiffa, 1982: 37-38 and 45; Sebenius, 1991: 209). All agreements that are better than this reservation value are acceptable to the actor. Generally speaking, the outcome of a negotiation (and thus the relative power of the two actors) reflects the location of the actors' reservation values; the more agreements are acceptable to an actor, the weaker his or her bargaining position.

The location of the reservation values, in turn, reflects the relative 'need' to reach an agreement and is shaped by two factors:

- The shape of the actors' 'indifference curves,' that is, the preferences those actors have regarding the attainment of their various objectives (cf. Wagner, 1988: 467);
- The best alternatives the actors have.

This analysis therefore rests on the same conceptual foundations as the analysis based on dependence, because 'the shape of the actors' indifference curves' is equivalent to the actors' 'preferences' or 'values' and thereby Emerson's 'motivational investment.' The best alternative actors face is exactly the same as the second element in Emerson's definition of 'dependence.'

It is therefore justified to use insights and concepts from these two strands of analysis and theorising to complement and criticise each other. This allows us to use insights from the literature on dependence within a framework based on negotiation analysis (such as the two-level game framework).

These approaches are useful as a specification of the two-level framework, because they are also consistent with Putnam's basic concept of 'win-set.' The win-set is the set of international outcomes that can be ratified in a country or, in other words, all agreements that are considered to be better than no agreement (Putnam, 1988: 437). The size and shape of a country's win-set is therefore equivalent to the location of a country's reservation value, so one concept can always be substituted for the other.

As was stated above, B's power over A rests on A's dependence upon B. Conversely, B may well be dependent upon A for the attainment of some other goal, leading to a situation of mutual dependence or interdependence. It is therefore possible for two actors (such as unitary countries) to be dependent upon each other and, thus, to wield power *over each other*. This does not imply, however, that the relation is balanced in the sense that the mutual dependence or power is equal. On the contrary, interdependence is often asymmetrical with one actor having 'the edge' over the other actor in the relation.

Take, for instance, a baker and his customer. The customer is dependent (to some degree) upon the baker for obtaining his bread. The baker, on the other hand, is dependent (to some degree) upon the customer for selling his bread (i.e. for earning money). If the price of a loaf of bread is open to bargaining, and the two parties' bargaining skills are comparable, the outcome of the agreement will reflect the relative dependencies of the baker and the customer upon each other: if the baker needs the money more than the customer needs the loaf of bread, the price will go down and vice versa.

However, in general it is difficult, if not downright impossible, to compare the values of the agreement for the baker and the customer. This would require a comparison of utility between the two actors, something that is not possible unless some very restrictive assumptions are made. It is therefore also impossible to say which of the two gains most by an agreement (cf. Wagner, 1988: 407).

What we *can* do, however, is compare two actors and situations that differ in only one respect and see what differences this makes to the degree of dependence. For instance, the price of the loaf of bread should go down if the baker were to become engaged in fiercer competition with other bakers, while the price should rise if bread suddenly became much more popular than it was before (in both cases provided all other factors remain the same).

It is also possible to formulate hypotheses across units. Thus it could be expected that small, open countries are relatively more dependent upon their trading partners than big, closed countries (again, ceteris paribus), or that countries that trade a relatively large proportion of their GDP ('Gross Domestic Product') with one and the same trading partner are more dependent upon that trading partner than countries whose trade pattern is more dispersed. According to the power-dependence theory, it should therefore be easier to wield power over smaller countries and over countries that trade more heavily with one trading partner, all other things being equal.

In fact, this is exactly what Hirschman argued in his seminal study *National Power and the Structure of Foreign Trade* (1980 (1945)). In this book, first published in 1945, Hirschman analysed the use of trade relations to gain power over trading partners. This he called the 'influence effect' of trade. The influence effect derives from the dependence of a country upon trade with another country. More specifically, Hirschman stated that a country's dependence upon another country equals the costs it would incur by terminating the trade relationship with that other country. These costs are determined by three factors (Hirschman, 1980 (1945): 18):

- The direct losses resulting from the termination of the trade relation;
- The costs of the adjustment process the state has to go through as a result of the termination of the trade relation;
- The strength of the vested interests a state has in the trade relation.

Leaving aside the third factor (which will be discussed below, when the assumption of unitary actors is given up), the dependence of one country upon another with regard to their trade relation is therefore equal to the difference between the costs and benefits of maintaining the trade relationship and the costs and benefits in a situation without the trade relation. Even though two countries are party to one and the same trade relation, the costs of severing the relation may differ between them. The absolute size of the trade flow may be the same for both countries, but its relative size (as a percentage of GDP, for instance) will differ widely between big and rich, and small and poor countries. Moreover, the adjustment costs and/or the availability of alternatives may differ considerably between countries, both in absolute and in relative terms.

The country that has the highest stake in the relationship will be willing to make greater concessions to maintain it than the country that has a smaller stake. As a consequence, there will exist an asymmetrical interdependence between the two countries, which the less dependent country can use to extract more advantageous terms of trade (the relative prices at which goods are traded). This is the basis of the assertion that asymmetrical interdependence lies at the root of relative power in international economic relations and that bigger, richer countries can use trade (or, for that matter, investment or aid) relations to wield power over smaller, poorer countries, even in matters not directly related to the trade relation.

As Wagner (1988) has shown, however, it makes an essential difference whether one looks at the terms of trade as such or at the extraction of unrelated (political) concessions through trade relations. As was explained above, the terms of trade (such as one loaf of bread for some amount of money, or some quantity of commodity X for some quantity of commodity Y) in a relation are determined by the relative dependence of the parties involved (still leaving bargaining skills aside): the more dependent a party is, the worse its terms will become. Asymmetrical interdependence therefore offers an explanation for the outcomes of bargaining over terms of trade.

Yet, when one country wants to use its leverage in trade negotiations to extract concessions on other issues (like environmental standards) this is no longer evident. For even though the terms of trade reflect differences in relative power, the agreement still has to be agreed upon by both parties. Even though the more dependent country accepts a relatively bad agreement, the agreement is still better for that country than no agreement would be; if it were worse than no agreement, then the country would not have accepted the agreement.

Therefore, the stronger country cannot extract concessions on other issues if those concessions would make the agreement worse to the weaker country than no agreement would be. In terms of the negotiation analysis approach, the stronger country cannot extract concessions if the agreement is already at or close to the weaker country's reservation value. The concessions would make the agreement less valuable than the weaker country's best alternative (i.e. no agreement and hence no trade) and the weaker country would rather forgo the benefits of trade than to agree to the bad terms of trade plus the concessions on other issues.

Consequently, a country can only use trade relations to extract concessions on other issues if that country is willing to accept worse terms of trade. Within an existing trade relation, a country can only use the trade relation to extract concessions on other issues without changing the terms of trade if that country previously accepted worse terms of trade than it could have had; if, in other words, it did not exploit all its counterpart's dependence (Wagner, 1988: 473-474).

In principle, therefore, the capacity to link other issues to a trade relation does not depend on asymmetrical interdependence. The weaker country can just as well accept worse terms of trade in return for concessions on other issues as can the stronger country. The only thing that matters is that the country wanting to extract the concessions is able to offer a great enough improvement in terms of trade for the other country to be willing to make the concessions, no matter who makes the concessions and whose terms of trade become worse.

Still, although the capacity to link issues is not necessarily confined to the less dependent actor in a relation, it is generally easier for less dependent countries to use issue linkage in trade relations than for more dependent countries, for two reasons. First, the less dependent country is able to link issues at relatively lower cost than the more dependent country (Keohane & Nye, 1987: 734). The extraction of concessions on unrelated issues requires that the country demanding the concessions is willing to tolerate a deterioration in the terms of trade that is at least as great as the improvement in the terms of trade the other country demands in return for those concessions. Since the marginal utility of improving terms of trade for an actor can be assumed to decrease as the terms become better for that actor, the same absolute change in terms of trade is relatively less costly for an actor that has relatively good terms of trade; that is, the less dependent actor.

Second, when bilateral relations take place within a multilateral framework that serves to protect the most dependent countries, a less dependent country that is willing to break those rules can use the unexploited dependence on the part of the more dependent country to extract concessions on side-issues (Keohane & Nye, 1987). For example, the US and the EC have instituted systems of preferential trading that offer non-reciprocal market access to developing countries, terms that are probably more favourable than those that would have resulted from bilateral negotiations in which the asymmetrical dependence had been fully exploited. As a consequence, the US or the EC can use this unexploited dependence to extract concessions on other issues, an option which the more dependent developing countries do not have.

It is therefore still useful to view asymmetrical interdependence as a source of power in trade relations, as long as it is remembered that issue linkage has its price.

Being less dependent in a trade relation is neither a necessary nor a sufficient condition for being able to extract concessions on side-issues (Wagner, 1988: 473-474), but it does make it easier to pay that price.

Issue linkage can take several forms, but the form relevant to this study is the one in which a country links an issue on which it has no or little direct power (in this study: regulatory standards of another country) to another, unrelated issue on which it has more power (here: trade relations) in order to gain concessions on the former issue (see Sebenius, 1983: 289 ff., who also discusses other forms of issue linkage).

In the situation without linkage, the trade relation yields benefits for both countries. However, the size of the benefits depends on the terms of exchange between the two countries. If a strengthening of regulatory standards in some issue area provides no benefits to the target country, no agreement is possible when this issue is discussed by itself. By linking the two, previously unrelated issues, the cost-benefit balance changes for the target country. The combination of trade and more stringent standards may now yield positive net benefits, whereas previously the trade by itself yielded benefits but the more stringent standards did not. If the target country is a unitary actor seeking to maximise its net benefits it will therefore prefer the combination of trade and more stringent standards to the alternative of no agreement and it will adopt more stringent standards in order to maintain trade with the initiator country. Yet, the net benefits under the issue linkage are lower for the target country than the net benefits under the trade relation by itself. For the target country this puts limits on the extent to which it is willing to accept more stringent standards.

Unitary, rational countries can thus produce a California effect by linking more stringent standards in the target country and the terms of trade in their trade relation. This possibility hinges crucially on the capacity to actually forge this link, and to make credible commitments. To this I turn next.

2.2.2 Strategy and commitment in international bargaining

An analysis in terms of dependence (or reservation values) still leaves open several outcomes of a negotiation. Depending on the degree of overlap between ranges of outcomes the parties to a negotiation are willing to accept, the set of possible agreements (the 'bargaining set') may be smaller or bigger, but usually there is some room for manoeuvre within the bargaining set.

For instance, a country imposing a regulatory trade measure may be willing to accept a trade relation without more stringent standards, even though it would prefer the same trade relation with more stringent standards. If offered the choice between trade without more stringent standards or no trade at all, it may choose trade without more stringent standards. The target country, on the other hand, would be willing to accept a trade relation with more stringent standards, even though it would prefer a trade relation without more stringent standards. If offered the choice between trade with more stringent standards or no trade at all, it would thereby have to choose for trade with more stringent standards. Thus, although both countries would prefer to have it completely 'their way' they would also both be willing to accept an outcome that falls short of their highest preference, as long as it is better than their best alternative (in this case: no trade at all).

The eventual outcome therefore depends on the ability to make an irrevocable commitment to one's most preferred outcome, thereby leaving the other side the choice between that outcome or no agreement at all. If the commitment is successful, the other side will have to accept the other's preferred outcome. Each party to a negotiation therefore has an incentive to make an irrevocable commitment to its own preferred outcome before the other does, when it knows its own preferred outcome is still better than the other party's reservation value (i.e. when its own preferred outcome is part of the bargaining set) (Schelling, 1980 (1960): 22).

The result of an irrevocable commitment can be described in the terms used in the previous subsection. By making an irrevocable commitment, a country decreases its range of acceptable outcomes, and thus the bargaining set. The new, constrained bargaining set consists of better agreements for that country than the original bargaining set.

Hence, a country has to make an irrevocable (or at least credible) commitment to link the trade and standards issues. Moreover, this commitment has to be communicated convincingly to the target country. Similarly, the target country has to make a credible commitment rather to forgo trade than to accept the standards.

Now, the problem is that each party to a bargain has an incentive to pretend it is more committed than it actually is. Moreover, while each party has an incentive to use threats (or promises for that matter) during the negotiation, it also has an incentive not to fulfil them. If a threat is successful, it need not be carried out, but if it is unsuccessful, the threatening party has no incentive to carry it out afterwards.

The strategic problem a threatening country thus faces is how to make a credible commitment. This problem can be solved by deliberately incurring costs in case it would not fulfil its threat. The threatening country has to alter its structure of costs and benefits associated with carrying out the threat in such a way as to make it more costly to renege than to carry out the threat.

A unitary actor can do this by stressing the consequences of not fulfilling a threat for its reputation. If an actor is engaged in a series of negotiations with the same actor or a number of parallel negotiations, as most countries are, not fulfilling a threat will change other countries' estimate of that country's commitment in other negotiations. It will become increasingly difficult for a country not meeting its commitments to make credible commitments in other situations. By not fulfilling a threat a country therefore incurs costs to its reputation that may well outweigh any gains associated with non-fulfilment.

Apart from these costs in the international arena, a country may also incur domestic costs as a result of not meeting its commitments. These 'domestic audience costs' (Fearon, 1994: 577) may change a country's incentive structure decisively toward fulfilling its commitments after negotiations have failed.

In fact, incurring costs may be the best way for a country to show its resolve in the international arena. Whereas 'cheap talk' is not likely to make much of an impression on one's opponent, incurring costs shows that one is really committed to certain objectives (Baldwin, 1985: 107-108).

Not only does a country have to make a credible commitment, it also has to communicate it persuasively to the other country (Schelling, 1980 (1960): 28). Since each country knows that the other has an incentive to exaggerate its commitment, establishing a credible commitment is a process of learning by one's opponent (Fearon, 1994: 577). Countries have a number of strategies to communicate a commitment more persuasively to their opponents. Thus, a pledge of one's reputation is more credible if made in public than in private (Schelling, 1980 (1960): 29-30). A threat can also be communicated more credibly if it can be decomposed into smaller steps. By fulfilling a small part of the threat (e.g. blocking a small part of a trade flow) a country can increase the other country's estimate of its commitment (Schelling, 1980 (1960): 41). More specifically in the context of regulatory trade measures, a threat becomes more credible if it is more specific, naming the exact targets of the threat (Odell, 1993: 237). Finally, a commitment is more credible if it is more difficult for a country to rationalise its way out of it. If the threatening country's objectives are ambiguous, it is easier for that country to rationalise a failure to meet its commitments, which will influence others' estimates of its commitment (Schelling, 1980 (1960): 40).

The latter factor poses yet another dilemma for a country, however, because a threatening country also needs to leave some room for manoeuvre during the negotiations. If its objectives are so unambiguous as to leave no room for interpretation, this may enhance its credibility but it may also preclude any mutually acceptable agreement. This is, more generally, the dilemma of any commitment in a situation of uncertainty about the exact shape and size of the bargaining set: a firm commitment may improve one's gain from an agreement, but if it is pushed too far it may also preclude a mutually advantageous agreement altogether.

2.2.3 Argumentation and legitimacy in international bargaining

Compelling as the analysis of regulatory trade measures in terms of asymmetrical interdependence may be, the predictions it yields have often been contradicted by empirical evidence. For instance, one would expect smaller countries to yield more quickly to economic sanctions than larger countries, but this need not be the case (see e.g. Martin & Sikkink, 1993). Similarly, sanctions should be less effective if their economic effects could be reduced by smuggling or otherwise (Galtung, 1967), but this need not be the case either (Baldwin, 1985: 189-204; Klotz, 1996: 174-175). Also, asymmetrical interdependence often cannot account for differences among outcomes of different conflicts between the same countries (Odell, 1985;

Schoppa, 1999). Finally, this explanation cannot account for the effects of non-economic, or 'symbolic' sanctions, such as cultural and sports boycotts, which some authors argue to have been highly effective in some cases (Klotz, 1996: 189-190).

This can partly be explained by looking at domestic political processes, as will be done in the next section, but an explanation can also partly be found at the international level itself. As was argued in section 2.1.2, a distinction should be made between the instruments and the bases of power (Baldwin, 1985: 22-24). Regulatory trade measures are an instrument of power, but their effect may be contingent on bases of power other than only their economic effects. In terms of the conceptual framework laid out in the previous section, they will also depend on or even affect other countries' preferences. These preferences can be altered by either altering values at a more abstract level or by altering the causal beliefs in the other country.

Given the nature of the kind of processes we are studying here, a change in more abstract values is not very likely to occur. Such a process is quite fundamental and takes a long time to materialise. Regulatory trade measures are often too narrow and too much oriented toward the short term to effect such fundamental changes. Still, the legitimacy of a regulatory trade measure in the target country may differ according to its preferences and values. Moreover, they may affect causal beliefs, that is, the links actors perceive between their preferences regarding regulatory policies and more abstract values.

As some authors on economic sanctions have noted, sanctions signal a normative consensus in the initiator country or among the initiator countries. This normative signal may have important effects in the target country, especially if the target country shares core values with the initiator country. Following this line of reasoning, the economic effects of a sanction need not be primary. As a consequence, sports or cultural boycotts may be more effective than purely economic sanctions in producing a change in behaviour (Kaempfer & Lowenberg, 1999: 52-53).

Changes in causal beliefs take place through argumentation and persuasion. These arguments are more likely to be successful if the initiator and target countries share a set of common values. Then, the initiator country's arguments will relate more closely to the problems and possible solutions as they are perceived by the target country. Also, the initiator country will be perceived as being more trustworthy by the target country, if both share similar values and have a generally co-operative relationship. As a consequence the initiator country's arguments are more likely to be picked up by the target country and play a role in its decisions (Li, 1993: 353).

Changes of behaviour through constraints and through arguments are often seen as two distinct ways of exerting power. Many authors would even argue that argumentation is the opposite of power in that the target is still left with every alternative which it had before. Both processes have produced quite distinct strands of literature in international relations theory. There is a long tradition of analysis in terms of constraints and economic effects, while recently a new literature has emerged under the title 'constructivism,' which focuses almost exclusively on country identities and preferences.

Despite these distinct branches of literature, the two processes of constraining and arguing are often closely related. Many power processes do not only involve constraints or arguments. Rather, they involve combinations of the two, and it is often these combinations that are most effective in changing behaviour.

Pure arguments will only be effective to the extent that the two countries have identical or at least highly similar values. This would resemble purely co-operative situations that are very rare in reality. If the countries have mixed motives, the power of arguments will be limited because they do not change the available alternatives. Moreover, incurring costs by taking concrete regulatory trade measures shows the strength of one's preferences (Baldwin, 1985: 97-98).

Pure manipulation of constraints, on the other hand, may encounter fierce resistance from the target, as it will be perceived as coercion. Coercion without arguments is easily seen as illegitimate, which can be a reason in itself for the target country not to comply with the demands. Even if compliance is gained, the constraints need to remain in place in order to ensure future compliance. In that respect, the effects of argumentation may be more lasting and 'cheaper' for the initiator than the effects of coercion. Yet, coercion may be the only strategy if the countries' values are completely opposed.

Most conflicts, however, will display a combination of co-operation and opposition. They will therefore involve a combination of arguments and coercion. Manipulating constraints may make the argument more compelling to the target, whereas arguments may make the coercion more legitimate. In either case, the two processes reinforce each other to produce a change in behaviour, although the availability and precise effects of each strategy will vary across relations and issues according to their position on the scale between pure co-operation and pure conflict.

2.2.4 The role of international law

A focus on argumentation and legitimacy may also shed some light on the role of international law in California-effect types of processes. International law is a system of rules aimed at regulating the relations between countries. It consists roughly of two layers: first, general international law that applies to all countries in the world community, and, second, specific international law that derives from treaties and that only binds the countries that are party to these treaties. These international rules and norms also affect the issues at stake in the California effect.

Two types of international rules are relevant to the use and effects of regulatory trade measures. First, international trade law regulates the extent to which countries are allowed to use regulatory trade measures in the first place. The most important body of international trade law is formed by the agreements on the World Trade Organization (WTO), and before 1995 (when the WTO came into existence) by the General Agreement on Tariffs and Trade (GATT). Second, a number of international treaties and organisations play a role in the formulation of common, more or less harmonised standards in a number of areas, such as product quality, and environmental protection.

The GATT/WTO framework

The GATT/WTO framework of international trade law is among the most important bodies of international law in the Transatlantic relationship. Not only does it lay down the most stringent set of legal norms concerning trade between the EC and the US and Canada, but its development has also been largely driven by the interaction between the EC and the US, the two most important trading blocs in the world.

An extensive literature has emerged concerning GATT/WTO law in general, and its relation to regulatory trade measures in particular (for general overviews, see e.g. Jackson, 1998; Trebilcock & Howse, 1999; for specific issues, see the references in the case study chapters). A comprehensive review of this literature is beyond the scope of this study. Here, I will briefly sketch the main features of this framework, focusing on its design and institutional set-up. In the case study chapters, the substantive GATT/WTO rules relevant to those cases will be discussed.

The GATT was concluded in 1947. Originally it was meant as a preliminary treaty that would become part of a more comprehensive treaty for an International Trade Organization (ITO). This ITO was to become a fully-fledged international organisation to complement the International Monetary Fund (IMF) and World Bank organisations that had been created after the Second World War. However, in the American political climate of the time the idea of creating another powerful international organisation was not well received and the Treaty creating the ITO was not ratified by US Congress, effectively precluding its entry into force (Jackson, 1998: 38; Vernon, 1995: 330; Winham, 1998: 349).

The GATT remained in force as the legal framework regulating trade between a number of (then) developed, capitalist countries (Jackson, 1998: 39-41; Vernon, 1995: 330-331). In subsequent decades, the GATT was strengthened in a number of negotiating rounds in which tariff rates and quotas were gradually eliminated, and specific agreements on certain industries or issue areas were concluded (Jackson, 1998: 73-78).

Apart from agreements on reductions of tariffs and quantitative barriers to trade, the GATT also included a dispute settlement mechanism. Contracting parties could turn to the GATT for the establishment of a dispute settlement panel if they felt that another contracting party had engaged in discriminatory or protectionist practices. The panel would give an opinion about the matter which could then be adopted by the GATT General Council consisting of all contracting parties. Since unanimity was required in the General Council, each contracting party, including the country that had lost the panel case, could block the formal adoption of a panel report.

Nevertheless, the GATT dispute settlement mechanism developed a body of case law relating not only to tariffs and quotas, but also to regulatory standards, since they may form barriers to trade. By applying certain regulatory standards, foreign imports may be disadvantaged vis-à-vis domestic products. For instance, foreign producers may be less well equipped to meet those standards, because they lack the necessary technologies or because it would require additional investments. On the one hand, regulatory standards may be justified as a means to protect certain values or to offer a certain level of protection to consumers or the environment. On the other hand, domestic standards can also be used to protect domestic producers against cheaper or qualitatively superior foreign imports.

Because of their potential protectionist effects or abuses, domestic standards are directly relevant to international trade and the GATT/WTO has sought to reduce their use as protectionist tools. In GATT/WTO law a number of criteria have been developed to distinguish 'legitimate' domestic standards (those that are meant to protect other values) from 'illegitimate' (protectionist) ones.

As the level of tariffs and quotas was gradually reduced to virtually zero (at least in the field of industrial products), the importance of regulatory standards and other less tangible barriers to trade (such as technical standards, intellectual property rights and government procurement) increased. In the field of technical standards, a special agreement was concluded in 1979 as a result of the Tokyo Round of GATT negotiations. This was the Agreement on Technical Barriers to Trade or TBT Agreement (Jackson, 1998: 222-223). In this agreement, the contracting parties agreed to a somewhat stricter regime governing the application of this kind of standards to foreign imports. The TBT Agreement was aimed at increasing the role of scientific evidence in the justification of these barriers to trade, and in encouraging the adoption of international standards where possible. However, the dispute settlement system was as weak as it was for regular GATT disputes. Moreover, the GATT did not engage in setting international standards itself; this was left to other bodies, such as the International Organization for Standardization (ISO) in the field of industrial standards.

In the Uruguay Round of negotiations between the GATT contracting parties (between 1986 and 1994), the original idea of an international organisation in the field of trade was revived under the name of a World Trade Organization (WTO). The WTO was to become a 'real' international organisation on an equal footing with the World Bank or the IMF. The original GATT ('GATT 1947'; WTO 1994a) was included in the WTO Agreements (as 'GATT 1994'; WTO 1994b). Also, the multitude of separate agreements that had been concluded among (parts of) the contracting parties to the GATT were integrated into one legal package that all WTO members had to agree to (Winham, 1998: 351).

The construction of the WTO was part of an effort to strengthen the international trading regime, especially when it came to dispute settlement. As a result of the Uruguay Round, the dispute settlement procedure now consists of two tiers: a panel and an Appellate Body. Furthermore, the adoption of a panel or Appellate Body report can only be blocked by a unanimous vote among the WTO's members, reversing the logic of the GATT dispute settlement system.

Also, the TBT Agreement was strengthened in order to tie technical standards more closely to scientific evidence and to make it less easy for countries losing a dispute to evade the consequences (WTO 1994d). A separate Agreement on Sanitary and Phytosanitary Standards ('SPS Agreement;' WTO 1994c) was concluded to cover standards mainly relating to food safety. Like the TBT Agreement, the SPS Agreement requires regulatory standards that restrict trade to be based on a scientific risk assessment, and it lays great stress on the use of internationally formulated standards as a means of reducing trade restrictions.

International standards and agreements

The GATT and WTO have not themselves formulated international standards in fields like food safety or environmental protection. They have only regulated the use of domestic standards that affect international trade by the (GATT) contracting parties and (WTO) members. Other international organisations, however, are concerned with efforts to establish international standards in these fields. For instance, the Organization for Economic Co-operation and Development (OECD) has issued standards on biotechnology and data protection (see chapters 5 and 6). Similarly, the Codex Alimentarius Commission is a UN body that sets food safety standards (see chapters 4 and 5).

The standards of the OECD and the Codex Alimentarius are not binding upon their member countries; they are merely guidelines, which governments may or may not accept. Nevertheless, they may serve as important benchmarks because they reflect a consensus among governments and/or firms about the appropriate standards in a certain field. Moreover, some international standards may play a role in WTO dispute settlement under the TBT and SPS Agreements, as will be discussed in more detail for food standards in the context of the beef-hormone issue (see section 4.4).

Binding international standards may flow from international (multilateral) agreements. For instance, many environmental treaties contain standards that the contracting states have agreed to implement domestically. Some treaties contain trade provisions that regulate trade flows of certain products, sometimes even with countries that have not signed the treaty. In 1994, the GATT secretariat found that eighteen multilateral environmental treaties contained such trade provisions (Ahn, 1999: 820). Petersmann (1995: 2 and Annex VIII) listed 24 environmental treaties containing trade provisions. Some, such as the Montreal Protocol on Substances that Deplete the Ozone Layer, also contain trade restrictions against non-parties, both as a way to further the objectives of the agreements directly and as an incentive for non-parties to join the agreement (see e.g. Schlagenhof, 1995: 148ff.). The relation between trade provisions in environmental agreements (or multilateral agreements more generally) and GATT/WTO law will be discussed in more detail in the context of the GM foods issue, where it has potential relevance (see section 5.4.3).

Bilateral agreements in the Transatlantic relation

Apart from these multilateral agreements and organisations, the EC, the US and Canada have also concluded a number of agreements between them. The EC and the US in particular have built up quite an extensive body of trade-related agreements between them during the 1990s (Krenzler & Wiegand, 1999: 155-159; Rood, 2000: 185-187). Most of the agreements that are relevant to this study establish regular contacts and meetings between officials from both sides. Moreover, they provide institutionalised forums for business and public interest groups, the so-called 'Transatlantic dialogues.' These Transatlantic dialogues exist, among others, for the benefit of firms and business groups (the Transatlantic Business Dialogue, or TABD), environmental groups (the Transatlantic Environmental Dialogue, TAED) and consumer groups (the Transatlantic Consumers Dialogue, TACD). Consequently, the bilateral EC-US agreements provide an important institutional framework for dialogue between the EC and the US, which has played an important role in most of the issues examined in this study.

In comparison, the bilateral agreements between the EC and Canada have been more restricted in number and scope. Still, here too, a number of agreements set out a basic framework of regular talks and consultations, as well as joint work programmes (see in particular Canada & EU, 1996). In 1999, a formal forum was established for EC and Canadian firms and business groups, similar to the EC-US Transatlantic Business Dialogue. In general, however, the EC has tended to focus more on its relation with the US, and special institutional frameworks have played a more important role in the EC-US cases than in the EC-Canadian cases analysed in subsequent chapters. Where they have, they will be discussed in that case study.

The effects of international law

Regulatory trade measures therefore operate within an international legal context that may affect them in a number of ways. First, international trade rules may prohibit the use of certain regulatory trade measures. Second, international consensus on certain standards may affect the way target countries react to regulatory trade measures. In each case study chapter, I will discuss the specific rules of international law that are relevant to that case study.

Here, a preliminary issue is at stake: to what extent does international law affect the behaviour of countries in the international arena? Although this question is also relevant for domestic law, it is particularly pressing at the international level because of the absence of a centralised enforcement mechanism. Whereas most (but certainly not all) domestic legal systems are enforced by a central authority that, as the classic definition goes, 'has a monopoly over the legitimate use of force' (see Milner, 1991: 71), no such centralised authority exists at the international level.

The force of international law always rests on the consent of the countries subject to it. As a consequence, compliance with the rules of international law is always contingent upon those countries' willingness to respect the law. However, even if rules of international law are not obeyed, they may still play a role in that they weaken or reinforce the effect of a country's regulatory trade measure.

In my theoretical framework, international law will be assumed mainly to play a role in argumentative processes. International law forms a body of reference for the countries involved or, as the standard definition of international regimes states, a set of 'principles, norms, rules, and decision-making procedures around which actors' expectations converge in a given issue-area' (Krasner, 1983: 1). Reference to these expectations, which form a common set of values, can therefore confer legitimacy on a country's actions (cf. Hurd, 1999). A judgement that a country's actions do not conform to international law reduces that legitimacy.

The legitimacy of international rules depends on two factors. First, countries have to agree about the meaning or content of a rule of international law. To overcome differences regarding this meaning, international regimes may institute mechanisms to settle differences of opinion. Second, the countries have to agree about the values underlying the international rule. International rules that are highly contested, such as the non-intervention principle in humanitarian affairs, are not shared by all countries; a specific rule will therefore only command legitimacy in a specific case if a country accepts its general legitimacy.

Also, non-compliance may diminish the general legitimacy of the international rule. The transgressor can less legitimately invoke the rule in other cases or against another country. Transgression can therefore undermine the legitimacy of an international rule or the regime as a whole, as well as the image of a country in the international arena, which may damage its interests in future conflicts. A country may therefore choose to comply with an international rule because it has an interest in defending it or the associated international regime and/or its international image, even if transgressing the rule would be beneficial in a specific case. The long-term costs of transgression will be higher if the specific case has closer links to future cases under a regime and if the potential benefits of maintaining the international rule or regime in the longer term are greater.

As a consequence, the initiator country will usually try to diminish the costs of transgression by finding a way to justify its actions under international rules. The target country will usually challenge the legality of the initiator country's actions in an attempt to diminish its legitimacy.

2.3 Domestic politics and international bargaining

2.3.1 Domestic politics and the national interest

In the previous section I discussed international bargaining between unitary countries. This analysis proceeded from the assumption that a country has some 'national interest' which it seeks to promote in the international arena. This assumption can be justified in one of three ways (Milner, 1998: 768-769):

- By assuming that the national interest is defined by one actor in a country;
- By assuming that everyone in the country has identical preferences;
- By assuming that the domestic political process results in a single set of preferences that can be treated as if it resulted from a single actor.

None of these assumptions seems to be realistic in studying the California effect, although this may differ between issues and countries. In democratic countries, both the adoption of regulatory standards and of regulatory trade measures have been shown to be largely driven by domestic interest groups that, more often than not, have conflicting preferences (see Vogel, 1995). Even in non-democratic countries the ruling elite may consist of different factions that have conflicting preferences regarding regulatory and other policies (see e.g. Hawkins, 1997, for an analysis of conflicting interests within the ruling elite in authoritarian Chile). This effectively undermines the two first justifications of the unitary country assumption when it comes to the California effect, although it may still be a useful simplification in certain other cases.

The third justification is more promising, but it does not render the study of domestic politics obsolete. First, assuming a single set of national preferences is only useful if it is assumed that these preferences are stable. When changes in national preferences are allowed, these changes can again only be explained by domestic political processes. Second, even if the domestic political process results in a single, stable set of national preferences, an analysis of domestic political processes is needed to explain variations between countries. Such an analysis can only be avoided by assuming that the national preferences are determined by external factors, such as a country's position in the world system. This assumption is arguably not very realistic, however, in particular for 'low' political issues, like regulatory policies. A theory of domestic politics is therefore needed to explain national regulatory policies and the preferences which countries bring into the international arena.

Two steps can be discerned in the process through which regulatory trade measures may affect regulatory standards in the target country. In the first step, the initiator country decides to adopt a regulatory trade measure. The exact sequence may differ between cases: in some cases the initiator country may decide to restrict trade based on regulatory standards it adopted long before, while in other cases, the adoption of the more stringent standards and of the regulatory trade measures may go hand in hand.

In the target country, the initiator country's standards may add a completely new issue to the political agenda, or there may have been a domestic struggle about the stringency of the standards in the issue area before the initiator adopted the regulatory trade measure. In any of these cases the question should be answered why and how the initiator and target countries have come to adopt the standards and measures they have. This defines the initial situation of the process, which sets the stage for the subsequent developments and may affect the outcomes of that process.

In the second step, the regulatory trade measure may affect the initial situation in the target country. Conversely, the target may try to affect the political process in the initiator country with a view to diluting the regulatory trade measure. As a result, the target country decides whether or not to adopt more stringent standards in response to the regulatory trade measure. In general, the target country has four options:

- Not to adopt more stringent standards and to forgo trade with the initiator country;
- To (threaten to) start legal proceedings under an international dispute settlement mechanism;
- To retaliate against the initiator country. Normally, this will only take place after retaliation has been authorised under GATT/WTO law;
- To adopt the initiator country's standards straightaway.

Whatever the response, the target country may also enter into talks or negotiations with the initiator country with a view to finding a mutually acceptable agreement. After the target country has decided how to respond to the regulatory trade measure, the process may terminate or it may continue in mutual attempts to influence the other country.

In this section I will analyse the first step. This is the last building block required to formulate a theory of two-level games. It thereby offers the analytical tools that will be used in the next section to examine the process after the regulatory trade measures have been adopted (the second step in the process) and to formulate a number of hypotheses regarding the research problem in this study: under what conditions will a regulatory trade measure lead to a California effect?

In two-level games, two levels of domestic decision-making can be distinguished: governments, and actors that are involved in formal or informal ratification. The governmental level consists of actors that operate in international negotiations. The actors at this level ('officials') have a formal or informal veto over policies in that they can block or advance certain proposals (Putnam, 1988: 457). Yet, actors at the governmental level are dependent on domestic actors for the formal or informal ratification of their proposals and for the attainment of other goals.

Formal ratification is required when certain actors (for instance parliaments) formally have to accept a governmental proposal. Other societal actors often try to influence decision-making at the governmental and/or parliamentary level and may thus play a role in the informal ratification of a proposal. These interest groups can exert influence at both levels by giving or withholding valuable political resources, such as funds, co-operation in the implementation of policies or political support for policies and politicians. In practice some of these interest groups may even have an informal veto power in the decision-making process (Tsebelis, 1995: 306-308).

National policies are the outcome of political processes within and between both levels. Within the governmental level different officials have different preferences. These preferences are weighed in a political process between them. Within parliaments, political parties or individual parliamentarians usually have different ideas about the policies to be pursued. Finally, interest groups also have different preferences and compete for political resources such as public support, information and finances.

Public opinion is the most relevant if a proposal has to be approved by a referendum (Trumbore, 1998: 550). It is least relevant in issues that are decided entirely at the governmental level without much involvement on the part of interest groups, such as most security and military issues. The issues in this study fall somewhere in between these two extremes. Environmental and consumer protection issues are unlikely to be subjected directly to a referendum. On the other hand, in most countries, these issues are also likely to be subject to public debate and pressure by interest groups (although to varying degrees).

In the following analysis governments, parliaments and societal actors have to be taken into account as well as the links between them. Among the societal actors I will limit myself to the role of interest groups, since most regulatory standards will not be subject to a referendum.

Public opinion can also play an indirect role if certain issues play a decisive role in elections (Trumbore, 1998: 550). Although most types of issues at stake in this study are not likely to play an important role in elections, public preferences concerning them can be important for elected officials. In tense electoral systems salient issues may become important even if they are not of major concern to most voters. Moreover, environmental and consumer protection policies may affect a government's image among certain societal actors or the population at large, which may be an important asset for elected officials. Still, in any of these cases public opinion will most likely be formulated and mobilised by interest groups, so that it is probably justified to limit the analysis to the role of interest groups alone.

Thus, the formulation of national policies depends on processes at two levels. At one level, governmental actors struggle over national policy proposals and the definition of the 'national interest' therein. At the other level, parliaments or their equivalents have to approve the international agreement or national policy. Interest groups try to influence the outcomes of this struggle by effectively constraining or enabling certain courses of action. Links between actors at these levels may exist at various points in the political system.

The outcome of the political processes within and between the levels depends on the preferences of the actors, their incentives to become active in the political process, their resources, and the institutions that structure the political process. In the remainder of this section I will analyse these four factors at both levels, as well as the links between the two.

2.3.2 Governmental actors

Governmental actors play a crucial role in the formulation and implementation of national policies. They usually conduct international negotiations, formulate proposals and enforce existing standards. In that respect the government plays the role of the 'Chief of Government' (COG) in Putnam's formulation of the two-level game framework (Putnam, 1988: 456 ff.). In his analysis, and most studies that have followed it, the COG is the central figure between the international and domestic political processes. On the one hand, the COG negotiates international agreements with his or her counterparts in other countries. On the other hand, the COG has to negotiate with his/her domestic constituents concerning the ratification of the international agreements. Because of this central position, the COG and his/her international and domestic strategies are often the main object of analysis in two-level game studies.

However, rather than assuming one 'Chief of Government' it is more useful to view a government as composed of different actors with different preferences (cf. Evans, 1993: 401, 427-428). Moreover, in many existing studies the COG is the central actor, taking all the initiatives. Yet, as Knopf (1993: 628) has argued, societal actors are 'active players in their own right who can shape the agenda for interstate bargaining.' Although this is probably true in any issue area (Knopf's argument concerns bargaining over nuclear weapons), it is likely to be even more so for the issues that are the subject of this study: policy-making in environmental and consumer protection issues is probably more often decentralised and initiated by interest groups than decision-making in, say, security issues.

In the US and Canada, the US Government and the Government of Canada play the role of the government in this theoretical framework. In the EC, this is the European Commission, which has the exclusive authority to submit proposals and represents the EC internationally. Like its US and Canadian counterparts, the European Commission consists of various organisational units ('Directorate Generals' or DGs), which are concerned with different issues or policy areas.

In regulatory policy-making processes, three types of officials are most relevant: trade officials, 'sponsoring' officials (that are responsible for some part of the economy) and policy officials (that are responsible for issue areas such as environmental and consumer protection policies). In general these officials can be assumed to have contrasting *preferences*, in that they will have the greatest interest in their own policy field. Thus, trade officials will generally favour free trade over environmental and consumer protection, while the policy officials responsible for these issue areas will generally favour their own policy areas over free trade. Sponsoring officials will usually look after the interests of firms in 'their' branch of the economy. This may mean that they will favour less stringent standards when the standards decrease the competitiveness of firms in their branch. However, they may also defend regulation that protects existing firms in the market and support the imposition of more stringent standards on foreign competitors when this gives a competitive advantage to 'their' firms. This will depend on the composition of firms in their branch of the economy, however. The preferences of officials can therefore be assumed to be dependent on their institutional roles.

Officials will have an *incentive* to become active in the political process if their issue area is affected by a decision. The more important a decision is for their issue area, the more time and resources they will be willing to invest in the policy process. These *resources* consist of knowledge and expertise and sometimes funds, but typically governmental actors have formal powers and relations with other actors that they can use to influence the political process. Apart from preferences, incentives and resources, the outcome of the political process at the governmental level therefore also depends on the *institutional context* of this process. Most political systems have formal or informal rules governing the participation of officials in policy processes, which will mediate the representation of their interests in these processes.

2.3.3 Formal ratification by parliaments

The adoption of regulatory standards and regulatory trade measures is often subject to a formal decision-making procedure that involves a parliament or an equivalent body. In the US, this is US Congress, consisting of the Senate and the House of Representatives. In Canada, Parliament assumes this role. Yet, as we will see in the case studies, this need not always be the case: the US and Canadian governments have wide powers in a range of issue areas to adopt regulatory standards within existing legal frameworks. Moreover, governments can also choose to work on voluntary standards, which need not require any formal approval by a parliament.

In the EC, the formal ratification procedures are a bit more complicated than in the US and Canada. The EC has its own parliament, the European Parliament (EP), but its formal powers are relatively limited. The main decision-making body in the EC is the Council of Ministers, which consists of Ministers from the fifteen (before 1995: twelve) EC member states. 'The' Council of Ministers is a legal fiction: in reality, there are several councils comprising member state ministers in a certain area. Thus, the Environmental Council consists of environmental ministers, and the Agricultural Council of agriculture ministers. The General Affairs Council consists of the member states' foreign affairs ministers.

Depending on the issue area, decisions in the Council of Ministers are taken either by unanimity or by a qualified majority in which each member state has been assigned a number of votes, loosely related to its size. After the 1995 enlargement to fifteen member states, this means that under qualified majority voting a decision can be blocked by three large member states or by two large plus two small member states (see Peterson & Bomberg, 1999: 50).

The Council of Ministers is not to be confused with the European Council. The European Council is a meeting of EC member states' heads of governments that does not take official decisions itself but discusses broad issues and issues general guidelines. The actual decisions are then taken by the Council of Ministers (Kapteyn & VerLoren van Themaat, 1998: 182-186).

The role of the European Parliament in the decision-making process varies between issue areas. In some issue areas, like agriculture, the consultation procedure is used. Under this procedure, the EP gives its opinion on a proposal, but the Council of Ministers need not take that opinion into account. In other areas, for instance harmonisation measures for the internal market or measures to protect consumers, the co-decision procedure is used. Under this procedure, both the Council of Ministers and the EP have to approve a decision and otherwise they have to arrive at a compromise between them (Article 251 EC Treaty, EC 1997j; for a detailed legal analysis of the procedure, see Kapteyn & VerLoren van Themaat, 1998: 430-439). In between is the co-operation procedure, which has recently become less important however (Article 252 EC Treaty, EC 1997j; Kapteyn & VerLoren van Themaat, 1998: 427-428, footnote 506).

The formal powers of the EP have been strengthened in subsequent revisions of the EC Treaty. Until the Single European Act (SEA) of 1986, the consultation procedure was the only one in use, but the SEA added two new procedures that gave the EP a larger role. With the Maastricht Treaty of 1992, the co-decision procedure was introduced (Crombez, 1996: 200). Moreover, the applicable procedure for certain issue areas has been amended over the past decades, giving a greater role to the EP. Still, some areas remain largely outside the EP's remit. For this study, these areas include most notably agriculture (see Article 37.2 EC Treaty, EC 1997j) and external trade policies (Article 133 EC Treaty, EC 1997j).

All in all, the EC system of decision-making combines actors at the European level and the member state level. At the European level, the European Commission, the European Parliament, as well as the Court of Justice play a role in policy-making processes. Member states have an important role to play through the Council of Ministers. They are also involved through an elaborate system of committees consisting of member state representatives, which scrutinise many of the European Commission's implementing decisions (the so-called 'comitology system;' see Kapteyn & VerLoren van Themaat, 1998: 395-399).

Moreover, the implementation of EC measures usually takes place by the member states. The bulk of EC measures are taken in the form of so-called 'Directives,' which are binding 'as to the result to be achieved,' but 'leave open to the national authorities the choice of form and methods.' Regulations, by contrast, are EC measures that are 'binding in [their] entirety and directly applicable in all Member States' (phrases from Article 249 EC Treaty, EC 1997j). As a consequence, Directives need to be transposed into member state law to become effective (except for some limited conditions under which Directives are deemed to have 'direct effect;' see Kapteyn & VerLoren van Themaat, 1998: 535 ff.). Regulations do not have to be transposed, but in both cases the enforcement of measures largely takes place at the member state level.

The EC thus combines elements from 'traditional' states, which have centralised decision-making procedures, and international organisations, which have entirely intergovernmental decision-making procedures. The balance between these two elements has not been stable over the last decades, and we will see some examples of shifts in the case studies themselves. In general, it is often argued that the EP has become more important in most decision-making processes, for a number of reasons. First, as was noted above, the EP has obtained wider formal powers in subsequent revisions of the EC Treaty. Second, the EP has succeeded in using its political clout to influence decisions that formally lay outside its remit (Earnshaw & Judge, 1996: 124-125). Consequently, the EP has also played an important role in informal ratification processes.

In terms of my theoretical framework, this means that the (formal) ratification of regulatory standards and regulatory trade measures in the EC often has to take place by two bodies: the Council of Ministers and the EP. Formal ratification will the refore only take place if these two bodies can reach agreement among themselves.

The position of EC member states in the Council of Ministers is itself the outcome of domestic political processes. As a consequence, it has been argued that the EC's intergovernmental character requires an extension of the two-level game framework to three levels (see e.g. Collinson, 1999: 217; Patterson, 1997: 141). Apart from the international and EC levels, the member state level would constitute a third level. Although such an extension may yield additional insights into the political processes within the EC, it will not be pursued here, at least not systematically, for three reasons.

First, it would enormously complicate the analysis, since it would require an examination of member states' domestic decision-making processes, as well as their interaction with European and international processes. Second, it is difficult to separate the different levels within the EC, since these two levels have become increasingly intertwined. For instance, interest groups are often active at both the European and member state levels. Expanding the theoretical framework to three levels would unduly stress the intergovernmental aspects of EC decision-making at the expense of these European-level processes. Although the artificiality of a distinction in separate 'levels' is a point of criticism that can be levelled against the two-level game approach in general (see Collinson, 1999: 217), it can be argued that this is more problematic within the EC than in the international arena, where states are still the predominant actors. Third, adding a third level would not fundamentally change the theoretical hypotheses, since the same hypotheses would apply to the interactions between each of the three levels. I will therefore treat the EC as one single level in this theoretical framework. In the case studies, member state positions and their interaction with the EC and international levels will be discussed where they are relevant for the specific case.

2.3.4 Informal ratification by interest groups

The role of interest groups in political processes has been accorded quite an important place in contemporary studies on politics, sometimes even to the exclusion of other political actors (see mainly the literature on the economic theory of regulation: Becker, 1983; 1985; Peltzman, 1976; for a critique, see Farber & Frickey, 1991: 12 ff.). Although this may be too extreme a position, the role of interest groups in California-effect types of processes is probably an important one.

Four types of interest groups are typically concerned with regulatory standards and regulatory trade measures:

- 'Domestic firms,' which operate mainly or exclusively on the domestic market;
- 'Importing firms,' which use imported goods, either as an input into their own production processes or to sell them on their domestic markets;
- 'Export-oriented firms,' which rely partly or substantially on exports to foreign countries;
- 'Public interest groups' (such as environmental groups, consumer groups, human rights activists and labour unions), which pursue what they see as the public interest in a specific issue area (e.g. less pollution or the protection of consumers).

These four types of interest groups have distinct *preferences* for different outcomes of the process. Domestic firms have no stake in free trade, since they do not export their products. They may even oppose free trade if they have to compete with foreign imports, especially when they are less competitive than their foreign competitors (Vogel, 1995: 21). As a consequence, domestic firms in the initiator country will generally support the adoption of regulatory trade measures that impose more stringent standards upon foreign competitors. However, domestic firms in the (later to become) target country will oppose the adoption of more stringent standards in their country.

The interests of importing firms partly run parallel to those of exporting firms in the other country, in that they have an interest in free trade (or at least free imports) and that they have an interest in relatively competitive imports. Importing firms in the initiator country will therefore generally oppose the adoption of regulatory trade measures, since they will negatively affect their competitive position and because they may interrupt free imports of goods.

Export-oriented firms have to compete with domestic firms and with export-oriented firms from other countries on foreign markets. They will generally support the adoption of more stringent standards by other countries, because that will improve their competitive position relative to domestic firms in those countries. They will oppose the adoption of more stringent standards by their own country, because that will undermine their competitive position. In general, however, they have an interest in reducing the divergence of regulatory standards between countries, because such divergence leads to higher production costs if economies of scale can be gained by producing at one single standard (Vogel, 1995: 250).

The stance of export-oriented firms in the initiator country toward using regulatory trade measures will be ambivalent. On the one hand, these firms have an interest in having the target country adopt more stringent standards, but on the other they also have an interest in maintaining free trade or at least free export opportunities (Busch & Milner, 1994: 268-269; Hathaway, 1998: 580). When the use of regulatory trade measures leads to retaliation, trade flows are interrupted and free trade may be jeopardised. The position of export-oriented firms on the use of regulatory trade measures will therefore depend on the likelihood of quick success, but they will normally oppose the adoption of regulatory trade measures as protectionist devices (cf. the more extensive discussion in Milner, 1988: 21-22).

If no regulatory trade measures are taken, export-oriented firms in the (later to become) target country will oppose the adoption of more stringent standards, because that would harm their competitive position. This may change after the regulatory trade measures are imposed, but this will be analysed in the next section.

Finally, although a conception of the public interest could also involve fewer or less stringent standards, public interest groups typically favour more stringent regulatory standards. They will therefore support the adoption of more stringent standards in their issue area, as well as the use of regulatory trade measures if that promotes the adoption of more stringent standards in another country (Vogel, 1995: 21).

Interest groups that share the same preferences regarding policies can form coalitions. For instance, in the initiator country, public interest groups and domestic producers can form a coalition to support the use of regulatory trade measures since their interests run parallel at this point. David Vogel called this kind of coalition 'Baptist-bootlegger coalitions', after the two groups that both favoured the prohibition in the United States: Baptists out of religious convictions; bootleggers because they could make large profits from selling illegal alcoholic beverages (Vogel, 1995: 20-22).

Not only do these groups have different preferences, they will also have different *incentives* to become active in the policy process. In the economic theory of regulation it is generally assumed that interest groups have a greater incentive to become active if the stakes involved in the issue are higher and are more concentrated on certain groups (Evans, 1993: 412-414; Majone, 1996: 31 ff.; Ogus, 1996: 69 ff.). Thus, if the benefits of protection fall on a small group of producers, while the costs are spread over a large number of consumers, the producers have a stronger incentive to become active in the policy process than the consumers. Not only is it easier for the (small number of) producers to organise than it is for the (large number of) consumers, but the gains to be had are also much greater for any single producer than they are for any single consumer. Hence, both the costs are lower and the potential gains are greater for the producers than for the consumers, which gives the producers a much bigger incentive to organise political pressure than the consumers. This assumption has been shown to hold true in many cases, so much so that it has even been described as 'a standard proposition in political science' (Pierson, 1996: 18).

Nevertheless, this assumption seems to account less well for the influence of public interest groups. The benefits they pursue are almost by definition diffused among a large number of people that are difficult to organise. Although this may partly account for the relatively weak position of public interest groups in many issue areas, this line of reasoning would predict that public interest groups have hardly any influence at all in most policy processes, since the costs of more stringent regulatory standards are fairly easy to quantify and fall almost completely on a relatively small and easy-to-organise group of firms, whereas the benefits are diffuse and often intangible.

Public interest groups can therefore most usefully be seen as disseminators of information and organisers of public support. By gathering information and disseminating it to the public and policy makers, public interest groups can mobilise support for their objectives among both policy makers and the public at large. In this way they can help to overcome the collective action problems inherent in the issue areas they are active in.

Public interest groups are more likely to be able to do this when they have a large amount of organisational resources, such as members and finances. Moreover, they are more likely to raise support for issues that are highly salient among the population at large. These may include long-standing concerns, such as food safety in Europe and the US, or concerns that have a high symbolic value, for instance the protection of certain animals.

Interest groups have several *resources* by which they can try to influence the outcomes of political processes. These resources can roughly be divided into resources that relate to the issue at hand, and resources that are external to that issue. Relating to the issue, interest groups (both private and public) can participate in the formulation of policy, because of their expertise in that issue-area or because they are indispensable in the implementation of the policy. Firms, in particular, are often crucial in the implementation of policies and therefore have de facto veto power over important policy proposals. Public interest groups are less likely to have such power, but their knowledge and expertise can be very valuable in the formulation of proposals.

Resources that are external to the issue at hand include political support for elected officials and campaign contributions. For many public interest groups this is the most important source of political power. Highly reputed public interest groups can use their standing with the public at large to affect the public image of elected officials. As was stated above, this image can be very important in tense democratic political systems.

As was already explained above, the use of these resources in the policy process is mediated by *institutions*. Most important for the purpose of this study are the links between interest groups and state actors. These links can be more or less close, depending on the political and institutional dependence of state actors on interest groups. The institutional structure of a political system can give greater or lesser access to the policy-making process to (some) interest groups. In some systems, certain interest groups have an institutionalised role in the policy process, for example through a right to be heard or even formal veto powers. In general, interest groups will be more successful in a policy process the more (privileged) formal and informal access points to governmental actors they have in that process.

2.3.5 *The initial situation*

In both the initiator and the target country, the situation upon the adoption of a regulatory trade measure is determined by a political balance between domestic actors. This balance is defined by these actors' preferences and constraints, and their participation, which is determined by their incentives to become active and by the institutional rules governing participation in the decision-making process. By definition, however, in the initial situation the outcomes will be such that the initiator country decides to adopt a regulatory trade measure, and that the target country has adopted less stringent standards than the standards required by the regulatory trade measure.

The initial situation in both the initiator and the target country is important because it determines the further course of the process. The political support for and opposition against a regulatory trade measure in the initiator country determine the credibility of these measures and a threat to implement them. The political support for and opposition against more stringent standards in the target country determine the effort that is required to change the outcome of the target country's policy process, and the way actors in the target country will respond to the regulatory trade measure.

In the next section I will analyse the second step in the sequence: shifts in the target country's political balance as a result of the regulatory trade measure, and shifts in the initiator country's political balance as a result of activities by (actors in) the target country.

2.4 THE INTERACTION BETWEEN INTERNATIONAL AND DOMESTIC POLITICS

With the previous two sections I have filled in the three theoretical building blocks that are needed to formulate a *theory* of two-level games: theories about international bargaining, domestic politics, and the governmental actors connecting the domestic and international bargaining processes. Although these processes can be analysed in a sequential way, the most interesting part of the two-level game approach lies in its effort to model the interaction between them. As was outlined in the introduction to this chapter, domestic and international politics influence each other and developments at one level have ramifications at the other. In this section I will analyse the interaction between the two levels in order to account for changes in (domestic) regulatory standards as a result of (international) regulatory trade measures. From this analysis, I will derive a number of hypotheses about the conditions under which a California effect will take place.

Above it was argued that national win-sets (and thus policies) are the outcome of a political process involving domestic actors. These national policies are the result of a domestic political balance, involving domestic actors' preferences, the constraints facing them, and the institutional balance between them. In theory, it is therefore possible to discern three ways in which a country's win-set can be changed:

- By changing the constraints facing domestic actors in that country;
- By changing the preferences of domestic actors;
- By changing the (institutional) balance between domestic actors in the political process.

These processes work both ways. On the one hand, regulatory trade measures may affect the domestic political balance in the target country in one or more of these ways. On the other hand, the target country may try to affect the domestic political balance in the initiator country also in one or more of these three ways.

Hence, the conditions should be specified under which each of these three ways is likely to affect another country's domestic political balance in order to arrive at a theory of the California effect. In the next subsection I will first discuss the conditions under which a regulatory trade measure may affect the political balance in a target country. Then, I will discuss the conditions under which the target country, by engaging in talks, starting legal proceedings and retaliating, may affect the domestic political balance in the initiator country. These two sections are only concerned with the effects of strategies on actors in the other country, regardless of the type of actor that uses them. In subsection 2.4.3, I will discuss the use of these strategies between actors at different levels within the same country. Finally, transnational actors and transnational coalitions of actors will be discussed.

2.4.1 Affecting the target country's win-set

The initiator country's regulatory trade measures may affect regulatory standards in the target country. Since these standards are the outcome of domestic political processes, the effects of regulatory trade measures on those processes has to be assessed. Using the general scheme outlined above, three ways can be discerned in which regulatory trade measures may affect the outcomes of domestic political processes in the target country.

Changing constraints

First, regulatory trade measures can change the constraints facing domestic actors by linking more stringent standards to trade. Before the linkage the political costs of more stringent standards outweighed the political benefits (otherwise the more stringent standards would have been enacted anyway). By linking this issue to trade, however, the costs of not enacting more stringent standards are raised and, consequently, the benefits of enacting those standards are raised relative to the costs. Overall, this may alter the balance between the costs and benefits of enacting more stringent standards in such a way that it becomes politically more favourable to enact the more stringent standards.

So far, this analysis conforms to the unitary actor analysis provided in section 2.2. The two-level game framework, however, points at an important condition for effective linkage: the linkage will only produce change if the trade effects are *targeted* at powerful groups in the target country that oppose the adoption of more stringent standards (Kaempfer & Lowenberg, 1999: 47-48; Putnam, 1988: 450-451).

Hence, issue linkage will have little effect in two cases. First, when the trade effects are targeted at powerless groups, because these groups will not be able to make a change in national policies even if their incentives are changed toward supporting more stringent standards. Second, when the trade effects are targeted at groups that are already highly in favour of more stringent standards. These groups' support can be reinforced by changing their incentives, but if they are already heavily in favour of more stringent standards this will not make much of a difference in national policies.

Regulatory trade measures will therefore have a greater effect if they are targeted at groups that can make the difference between the adoption and non-adoption of more stringent standards, so-called 'pivotal groups.' By changing their incentives in such a way as to diminish their opposition against the more stringent standards or to increase their support for adopting them, the domestic political balance can be tilted toward the adoption of more stringent standards.

This analysis also suggests that general, across the board, or random linkage strategies are not very likely to be successful. These linkages may affect some marginal groups, but they are also likely to affect groups that already greatly favour more stringent standards or groups that are not influential in the policy process.

Changes in constraints can take place at either the governmental or the constituency level or both. At the governmental level, the constraints facing governmental actors may be changed in such a way as to tilt the balance of power toward support for more stringent standards. Without regulatory trade measures, governmental actors can be assumed to have the greatest interest in their own policy field. For instance, environmental officials will support more stringent standards, while trade officials will oppose them.

By imposing regulatory trade measures, the constraints on these officials change. For environmental officials, nothing will change: they already favoured more stringent standards over less stringent standards, no matter what the effects on trade. For the trade officials, however, the constraints may induce an important shift, because now they no longer have to choose between more stringent standards plus exports, and less stringent standards plus exports, but between more stringent standards plus exports and less stringent standards without exports. As a third alternative, the target country can choose not to comply with the demands and resort to the GATT/WTO.

As a consequence, trade officials will have mixed feelings about giving in to the demands. On the one hand, they will want to ensure exports; on the other, more stringent standards will reduce the competitiveness of their firms on world markets. Moreover, giving in to regulatory trade measures may create an important precedent in international trade relations by defining what countries are allowed to do in these trade relations, and by affecting other countries' estimates of the target country's resolve. Trade officials will have to weigh these different consequences against each other.

The alternative of not adopting more stringent standards without resorting to the GATT/WTO or retaliating is particularly unattractive for trade officials, because then the target country has neither exports nor a chance of lifting the regulatory trade measures. The choice will therefore primarily be between complying and going to the WTO. Several factors can be hypothesised to affect this trade-off.

Complying with the initiator country's regulatory standards will be more attractive when the consequences of the regulatory trade measures for the target country's exports are more serious. This is the case when the direct loss of exports is greater, when there are no or few alternatives, and when the adjustment costs in the target country are higher. Complying will also be more attractive if the costs of adopting the more stringent standards are lower. Then, complying will only harm the competitiveness of the target country's exports to a low degree.

Trade officials will only support going to the GATT/WTO or retaliating if it helps their objectives, i.e. to secure more exports in the future. This is the case if retaliation is likely to be successful and if the future negative consequences of giving in to the regulatory trade measure are likely to be more serious. I will not test these hypotheses on resorting to the GATT/WTO or retaliation separately, however.

The latter factor is a strategic assessment that involves weighing the consequences of giving in to the initiator country's demands. These consequences can be twofold. First, giving in will reduce other countries' estimate of the target country's resolve in trade conflicts. As a consequence other countries will be more likely to use regulatory trade measures in the future. Second, giving in without too much struggle may change the rules of the international game in favour of countries that want to use regulatory trade measures (in general, in certain fields, or in certain issues). This may lead to even more regulatory trade measures in the future.

Among the interest groups in the target country, without the regulatory trade measure, domestic and export-oriented firms were hypothesised to oppose more stringent standards, while importing firms and public interest groups were hypothesised to support them. Regulatory trade measures will not affect the position of importing firms and public interest groups as regards more stringent standards. Both groups will not support resorting to the GATT/WTO or retaliating either: public interest groups because they feel that the regulatory trade measures are justified, and importing firms because it would damage imports. As a consequence, importing firms may actively oppose retaliation in order to avoid disruption to their business.

Domestic firms will not change their position on more stringent standards either, since they are not affected by a regulatory trade measure. Export-oriented firms, however, may change their position as a result of the regulatory trade measure. Their trade-offs will run parallel to those of the trade officials outlined above, except that they will be more concerned with specific export opportunities than with the international trading system as a whole. They will therefore only support retaliation if it is likely to lead to quick success and if the future negative consequences of giving in to the initiator country's demands for their branch of industry are likely to be grave.

Thus, three hypotheses can be formulated concerning the effects of regulatory trade measures on regulatory standards in the target country:

- A regulatory trade measure will have a greater effect on a target country's political balance, the greater that measure's effect on the target country's exports;
- A regulatory trade measure will have a greater effect on a target country's political balance, the more that measure's effects are targeted at pivotal actors in the other country;
- A regulatory trade measure will have a greater effect on regulatory standards in the target country, the lesser are the costs of complying with that measure for actors in the target country.

Changing preferences

The second set of factors that affect the occurrence of a California effect relates to the preferences of actors in the target country. Above I defined preferences in terms of values and causal beliefs about the world. Preferences can therefore be changed by changing either those values or the causal beliefs, without changing domestic actors' constraints or (institutional) balance. This can only be done through persuasion and argumentation. By providing the necessary arguments, domestic actors in the target country may be persuaded to change their preferences and become more favourably disposed toward the initiator country's demands.

This is what Putnam (1988) called 'reverberation.' Schoppa (1993) discovered a special variety of this mechanism in his study of US-Japanese economic negotiations, which he called 'alternative specification.' The US deliberately supported policy alternatives that had not previously been considered in the policy process. In terms of my analysis: these alternatives had not been part of the order of alternatives that defined Japan's preferences. The US intervention led these new alternatives to be considered too, thus leading to a new preference ordering that included those new alternatives. In the end, this contributed to the attainment of US objectives in the negotiations.

A change in underlying values is generally not likely to take place in the kind of processes that are central to this study. A change in underlying values is a highly complex process that usually takes a long time to materialise, whereas I concentrate on relatively short-term regulatory trade measures related to specific regulatory standards. Nevertheless, regulatory trade measures will probably be more legitimate among actors in the target country if they tie in with their underlying values. Moreover, changes in preferences may occur through changes in causal beliefs.

Persuasion of this kind is most likely to be successful if the relations between the initiator and the target country are generally friendly and co-operative, because persuasion depends heavily on the credibility of the initiator (cf. Li, 1993; Schoppa, 1999). If the initiator is perceived to be co-operative and friendly toward the target country, its arguments will more readily be considered and accepted in the target country. This hypothesis cannot be examined in this study, however, since the EC-US and EC-Canadian relations do not differ fundamentally in their degree of co-operation.

Furthermore, arguments are more likely to be accepted if they respond to existing values and perceived problems in the target country. Then, the arguments will more quickly be taken up by governmental actors or interest groups in the policy process (Schoppa, 1993). Similarly, regulatory trade measure will probably be received more favourably if actors in the target country consider them to be motivated mainly be 'genuine' concerns (like environmental or consumer protection) rather than protectionism.

If, however, the initiator is seen as hostile or untrustworthy, its arguments may not be accepted or they will even be used against domestic supporters of the target country's position. One instance of this mechanism is the so-called 'rally round the flag' process, in which domestic actors unite in their opposition against foreign intervention (see e.g. Galtung, 1967). This mechanism also works in less extreme ways when policy change in the target country is interpreted as 'yielding to foreign pressure,' in particular when the regulatory trade measure is mainly seen as a protectionist measure. Foreign intervention then gives the defenders of the status quo in the target country a new argument against policy change, which may well lead to a contraction of the domestic win-set (Paarlberg, 1997: 423-425). As a consequence, support for resorting to the GATT/WTO or retaliation is also likely to grow under these circumstances.

Of course, all actors in a country will not hold the same values or perceive the same problems. In fact, much of the political debate in a country evolves around the definition of problems and values. Similarly, different actors in a target country may have different ideas about the motives behind an initiator country's regulatory trade measure. The hypotheses outlined above do not require that all actors share the same values or perceptions. They do require, however, that at least some powerful groups and officials within the target country share the values and perceived problems addressed in the regulatory trade measure. As Kaempfer and Lowenberg (1999: 51) have noted in the context of economic sanctions, these sanctions will only produce change in the target country

> 'if there exists within that country a reasonably well organized opposition group whose political effectiveness potentially could be enhanced as a consequence of sanctions. In

the absence of such a group, the sanctions might only strengthen the regime's pursuit of its (...) policy by helping to rally public opinion around the government.'

The same is probably true for regulatory trade measures: they will have a greater impact on the political balance if some groups or officials can use them to reinforce and legitimise their own calls for more stringent regulatory standards. The more groups and officials support the regulatory standards required by the regulatory trade measure, the greater the effect will be. Based on the analysis in section 2.3, it can be hypothesised that it is in particular policy officials and public interest groups that will be susceptible to the arguments behind a regulatory trade measure, since they can be assumed to support more stringent regulatory standards within the target country, but support may be broader and encompass other groups and officials as well. I will not test this as a separate hypothesis, however.

All in all, the following two hypotheses can be formulated:

- A regulatory trade measure will have a greater effect on regulatory standards in the target country, the more it ties in with deeply held values and perceived problems in the target country;
- A regulatory trade measure will have a greater effect on regulatory standards in the target country, the more actors in the target country perceive it to be motivated by genuine concerns rather than protectionism;

Changing the (institutional) balance

The final set of factors that affect the occurrence of a California effect relates to the (institutional) balance between actors in the target country, or the access various actors have to the decision-making process. A regulatory trade measure may affect this balance and an initiator country may even use this as a strategy.

Schoppa (1993) has called this strategy 'participation expansion': by linking an issue to another, previously unrelated issue, a whole new set of state officials and interest groups can be brought into the decision-making process relating to that other issue. If these new officials and groups are more likely to support the initiator country's point of view, the target country's policies may shift toward the initiator country's demands. His example concerns economic negotiations between the US and Japan: by linking domestic Japanese economic policy issues to the relation between the US and Japan, those domestic economic policy issues suddenly gained relevance for the bilateral relation. As a result, foreign policy officials became involved in the decision-making process on the economic issues, which had previously been dominated by a set of officials and interest groups not interested in policy change. The foreign policy officials, though, had a greater interest in good bilateral relations with the US than in maintaining the status quo in economic policy issues, which exerted pressure towards change in the economic policy issues.

Partly, this may be explained as a change in constraints facing the foreign policy officials, but linking the two issues also achieved something else: the narrow group of decision-makers about domestic economic policy was expanded to include actors that had distinctly different preferences as regards these issues. It is probably useful to distinguish between these two effects, because one may occur without the other: constraints may be altered without altering the institutional balance between actors, while the balance may be altered without altering the constraints facing the actors.

Although Schoppa found participation expansion to trade officials to have been an important factor in his Japanese case, its consequences for a California effect are ambiguous. On the one hand, trade officials may not oppose more stringent standards out of principle when they can enhance trade. On the other hand, however, they are also concerned about the country's credibility in future conflicts over other countries' regulatory trade measures, which may lead them to be less willing to give in. As a result, no single hypothesis can be formulated on the effects of participation expansion to trade officials in the target country.

2.4.2 Affecting the initiator country's win-set

The effects of regulatory trade measures do not only depend upon their (potential) impact on the target country, but also on the resolve of the initiator country. If the initiator country's threats are not credible because domestic support for them is lacking, the target country will be less likely to give in to the initiator country's demands (Odell, 1993). In line with Vogel's analysis, this suggests that regulatory trade measures will be most credible, and thereby effective, if they are supported by Baptist-bootlegger coalitions of public interest groups and domestic producers.

The target country can try to reduce the initiator country's resolve by changing the initiator country's domestic political balance. The ways in which it can do that are similar to the ways in which a regulatory trade measure can affect the target country's domestic political balance: by changing constraints facing actors in the initiator country, by changing their preferences, and by affecting participation and the institutional balance in the initiator country's decision-making process.

The *constraints* facing powerful actors in the initiator country can be affected by retaliating (normally, but not necessarily following a GATT/WTO dispute): the target country can impose trade (or other) measures against the initiator country in response to the latter's initial regulatory trade measures. Here, the same holds true as for the effectiveness of the initiator country's regulatory trade measures: the retaliatory measures are most likely to affect the initiator country's political balance if they affect more trade flows and if they are targeted at pivotal groups in the initiator country.

The target country may also try to affect the *preferences* of actors in the initiator country by persuading them of its reasons not to adopt more stringent standards. Here, too, the same conditions seem to apply as in the reverse case: the target has to be perceived as trustworthy and friendly in order for its arguments to be taken seriously. In addition, however, actors in the target country may point to the incompatibility of a regulatory trade measure with international law, both GATT/WTO law and substantive international standards in the field concerned. Opponents of the regulatory trade measure in the initiator country may then take up this argument to support their position in the domestic political debate (cf. Cortell & Davis, 1996: 453).

Finally, raising trade concerns may affect the *institutional balance* between actors in the initiator country's policy process by expanding participation. By linking more stringent standards and trade, decision-making about the more stringent standards will come to involve trade officials, who are more likely to favour sound trade relations over more stringent standards than are, for instance, environmental policy officials. This can be stimulated by the target country if it is able to raise the salience of the issue in its trade relations with the initiator country or if it is able to mobilise actors in the initiator country that are favourably disposed toward the target country's position.

Hence, three additional hypotheses can be formulated, one relating to constraints, one to preferences, and one to participation:

- A regulatory trade measure will have a greater effect on regulatory standards in the target country, if it is supported by both public interest groups and domestic producers in the initiator country;
- A regulatory trade measure will have a greater effect on regulatory standards in the target country, if it conforms to international law and international standards;
- A regulatory trade measure will have a smaller effect on regulatory standards in the target country, if the target country succeeds in expanding participation in the initiator country to trade officials.

2.4.3 Manipulation of the win-set in the domestic context

In principle, these ways of affecting a political balance can occur among actors at each level within the target and initiator countries. In the previous two subsections, the analysis was limited to manipulation of a win-set by actors in the other country. In some cases, however, interest groups and government officials may also try to manipulate their own country's win-set. This is especially likely if the governmental actors are more willing to reach an agreement with the other party than are other domestic actors.

The basic mechanisms underlying such changes in the win-set are the same as those described above. Yet, governmental actors often have more ways to influence their own domestic policy processes than foreign actors. For instance, they often have additional opportunities for changing their interest groups' incentives by linking other (domestic) issues or giving direct side-payments (see Mayer, 1992). Most of these possibilities are not available to foreign actors.

Domestic state actors also have more opportunities directly to influence the participation of interest groups and the institutional context. Ratification and other decision-making procedures can therefore not always be treated as given: they can sometimes be changed in order to facilitate or hamper policy change.

Finally, most (if not all) state actors will be seen by other domestic actors in the same country as being more trustworthy than foreign actors. As a consequence, they stand a better opportunity of changing those domestic actors' preferences than their foreign counterparts. This depends, however, on the standing of state actors with actors in their political system; a weak official will not be able to use this strategy. Officials in the initiator country therefore have an interest in the good standing of their counterparts in the target country if the target country's officials are more willing to agree to the initiator country's demands than other domestic actors. They may even actively try to raise their counterpart's domestic standing through highly publicised international meetings (Evans, 1993: 406-407; Moravcsik, 1993: 26; Putnam, 1988: 451-452).

Another way for state actors to change other domestic actors' preferences is through 'issue redefinition' (Friman, 1993). Issue redefinition refers to 'policy-makers' recasting a given issue – trying to persuade others that more inclusive policy concerns affecting core national values are at stake – in an effort to encourage concessions' (Friman, 1993: 389). Friman specifically discusses the redefinition of economic agreements as security issues. This kind of redefinition is not very likely to take place in the type of issues we are dealing with in this study. Nevertheless, an issue can be redefined in other terms, for instance in terms of human rights. Of course, a policy maker less willing to reach an agreement with the initiator country can also use this technique to contract the domestic win-set.

As was discussed above, policy officials and public interest groups are particularly likely to use another country's regulatory trade measure to advance their own position, although other actors can do so as well. There, it was decided not to formulate a separate hypothesis on policy officials and public interest groups, but to treat the matter as part of the hypothesis on deeply held values and perceived problems. In general, the role of regulatory trade measures in political processes between actors in the same country is already covered by the hypotheses outlined above. Thus, I will not formulate any new hypotheses here.

2.4.4 Transnational actors and coalitions in two-level games

Apart from trying to influence actors in the other country, actors may also form coalitions or alliances with actors in the other country in order to improve their chances of success. By forming a coalition actions in the two political processes can be co-ordinated and joint pressure can be exerted. These coalitions can be made between officials on both sides, between interest groups on both sides, and between governmental actors on one side and interest groups on the other (cf. Knopf, 1993).

A special group in two-level games is formed by transnational actors, such as multinational corporations and transnational interest groups (e.g. Amnesty International or Greenpeace). Because of their transnational character these actors have special opportunities to influence two-level games. Furthermore, their transnational character may lead to a distinct set of preferences regarding the stringency of standards and free trade.

The role of transnational actors has recently regained attention, with most studies concentrating on inter- or transnational public interest groups and coalitions (see Arts, 1998; Hogenboom, 1998; Risse, 1998). The assessment of these groups' power varies, but appears to be determined by a number of factors at the international and domestic level. Transnational interest groups are most effective when they operate in a highly institutionalised international environment, and when they can gain access to domestic policy-making processes (Risse, 1998).

Most international public interest groups have relatively few resources to influence policy makers. Their most important asset seems to be their expertise and knowledge in a field, which they can try to share with policy makers; they are much less seen as representatives of some groups of society or society at large (Arts, 1998).

Although transnational coalitions of public interest groups and international public interest groups may play a role in the political processes surrounding regulatory trade measures, the conditions under which they can affect these processes do not seem to differ from those discerned above for the processes among domestic actors. Consequently, they do not require any separate hypotheses.

The study of multinational firms is older than that of international public interest groups. They generally have more resources at their disposal, in the form of investments and other funds. At the same time, their activities are more strongly territorially based, which makes them more dependent on their host countries' governments (Risse, 1998).

As Milner has argued, multinational firms' preferences with regard to protectionism depend on their character. Multinationals may support protectionist trade barriers if they 'enter a market to circumvent such barriers and thus come to see them as a way to keep out other foreign competitors' (Milner, 1988: 20). If the multinational firm's activities in various countries are closely integrated, however, they will normally oppose protectionism since it may invite retaliation and disturb the intra-firm trade between its subsidiaries in different countries (Milner, 1988: 23; see also 24-26).

If a multinational's international operations are not integrated, it conforms to a domestic firm in my typology of interest groups, and it will behave accordingly. If its operations are closely integrated, it is an importing firm and an export-oriented firm at the same time. This means that its preferences with regard to the stringency of standards are ambiguous. As an export-oriented firm, it may support the adoption of more stringent regulatory standards in the target country if that helps to maintain trade flows. As an importing firm in the initiator country, it may oppose the adoption or implementation of regulatory trade measures since that will worsen its competitive position on the initiator country's market and may disrupt trade flows. As a consequence, multinationals may take different positions in the process: opposing the regulatory trade measure while it is being adopted, but supporting it when it becomes clear that it will be implemented. Moreover, multinational firms will probably be less interested in the stringency of standard than in uninterrupted trade flows. As a consequence, no single hypothesis can be formulated concerning the position of multinationals in these processes.

2.5 Summary and Hypotheses

Shifts in a country's regulatory standards can be explained by shifts in that country's domestic political process in which these standards are set. In this domestic political process, several actors play a role, each with their own preferences and faced by certain constraints as well as institutional opportunities to participate in the political process. The same is true of the decision to adopt a regulatory trade measure.

In this chapter, I have formulated a theoretical framework for explaining the effects of regulatory trade measures on other countries' regulatory standards. This framework has sought to specify the interaction between international and domestic political processes that is central to California-effect types of processes. In this final section, I will bring together the hypotheses derived from this framework that will form the basis for the case studies to be conducted in the following chapters.

In general, decisions on regulatory standards and regulatory trade measures were argued to depend on three factors: the constraints facing domestic actors, their preferences, and the institutional access opportunities to the decision-making process. The effects of a regulatory trade measure were assumed to depend on these three factors in the other country's domestic political system, as well as on the way the regulatory trade measure succeeds in changing them. Attempts by a target country to affect the political balance in the initiator country were assumed to depend on the same factors.

The hypotheses can therefore be grouped into three categories, relating to these three factors. First, a number of hypotheses can be formulated with regard to constraints. The effects of a regulatory trade measure on another country's domestic regulatory standards were hypothesised to be greater the greater are the effects of the regulatory trade measure on that country's exports. Moreover, the effects on the other country's regulatory standards will be greater, the more the trade effects are targeted towards pivotal actors. The same will be true for the effects of retaliatory measures adopted by the target country against the initiator country.

These hypotheses specify the benefits some actors in the target country will obtain from complying with the regulatory trade measure. However, they will weigh these benefits against the costs of adopting the required standards. Thus, a regulatory trade measure will have a greater effect on the target country's regulatory standards the lesser are the compliance costs of adopting the more stringent regulatory standards for actors in the target country.

Moreover, actors in the target country will only respond to a (threatened) regulatory trade measure if this measure or the threat to impose it is credible. In line with the 'Baptist-bootlegger' hypothesis, the credibility of a regulatory trade measure was hypothesised to be the greatest if that regulatory trade measure is supported by both domestic producers and public interest groups.

All in all, four hypotheses were formulated with regard to actors' constraints:

- A regulatory trade measure or a retaliatory measure will have a greater effect on another country's political balance, the greater that measure's effect on the other country's exports;
- A regulatory trade measure or a retaliatory measure will have a greater effect on another country's political balance, the more that measure's effects are targeted at pivotal actors in the other country;
- A regulatory trade measure will have a greater effect on regulatory standards in the target country, the lesser the costs of complying with that measure for actors in the target country;
- A regulatory trade measure will have a greater effect on regulatory standards in the target country, if it is supported by both public interest groups and domestic producers in the initiator country.

The second category of hypotheses relates to preferences. According to one hypothesis, a regulatory trade measure will have a greater effect on another country's political balance the more it ties in with deeply-held values and perceived problems in that other country. Moreover, it was hypothesised that a regulatory trade measure will have a greater effect if it is perceived to be motivated by genuine concerns rather than protectionism. Finally, the effect of a regulatory trade measure on the target country's regulatory standards will be smaller if it violates international law and standards. This last hypothesis was argued to affect both the perception of the regulatory trade measure in the target country, and the perception of a GATT/WTO complaint or retaliation in the initiator country.

Thus, three hypotheses can be formulated with regard to preferences:

- A regulatory trade measure will have a greater effect on regulatory standards in the target country, the more it ties in with deeply-held values and perceived problems in the target country;
- A regulatory trade measure will have a greater effect on regulatory standards in the target country, the more actors in the target country perceive it to be motivated by genuine concerns rather than protectionism;
- A regulatory trade measure will have a greater effect on regulatory standards in the target country if it conforms to international law and international standards.

The third and final category of hypotheses relates to the participation of officials in the decision-making process. It was argued that in the target and initiator countries, the institutional roles of policy officials, sponsoring officials and trade officials affect the effects of a regulatory trade measure. Regulatory trade measures can also alter these roles by involving trade officials in issues that were previously outside their remit. One hypothesis was derived from this:

- A regulatory trade measure will have a lesser effect on regulatory standards in the target country, if the target country succeeds in expanding participation in the initiator country to trade officials.

In the next four chapters, these hypotheses will be tested against the effects of four EC regulatory trade measures that affected the United States and Canada. In the final chapter, I will then draw a number of general conclusions concerning these hypotheses.

CHAPTER THREE

THE EUROPEAN LEGHOLD TRAP REGULATION

3.1 INTRODUCTION AND BACKGROUND

Trapping is one of the most controversial and emotionally-charged policy issues in many Western countries, as are animal welfare issues in general. On the one hand, opponents view trapping as a cruel and inhumane practice that violates basic entitlements which animals have. On the other hand, trappers see trapping as a legitimate activity, which is part of a valued lifestyle, and provides a useful tool for wildlife management. In this section I will highlight some of the general debates, as well as some more specific issues relating to trapping, that form the background to the European ban on furs from animals caught in leghold traps.

Opponents of trapping argue that animals have an intrinsic value, apart from the value they provide to humans, and therefore they have a right to life or at least a right to 'humane' treatment (cf. Vingerling, 1997: 7-8). Opponents also allege that trapping results in particularly cruel treatment of animals, as well as animal suffering. Moreover, fur, the product sought by most commercial trappers, has become a symbol for animal welfare activists in many Western countries, as it is considered to be a luxury for which good alternatives exist (Vingerling, 1997: 8) and fur-bearing animals generally have a wide appeal among the public at large.

Within the opposition to trapping, a distinction can be made between groups and people who oppose trapping and the use of furs out of principle because they believe there is no justification for killing animals for fur, and groups and people who focus on the way animals are trapped and fur is obtained. This is usually indicated by distinguishing between 'animal rights' and 'animal welfare' groups (e.g. Todd & Boggess, 1987: 72). The latter groups are concerned about improving trapping techniques and traps in order to reduce suffering by animals, rather than abolishing the practice of trapping as a principle. In practice, however, both positions are closely related, with the principled argument underlying much of the efforts to improve trapping, and suffering caused by trapping used to buttress the more principled position. Throughout this study I will refer to both groups as 'animal protection groups' (cf. Muth et al., 1998: 605).

Trappers and their supporters, on the other hand, start from the notion that, in principle, it is perfectly legitimate to use animals, as long as their existence is not threatened. Thus, they feel that there is nothing wrong in catching 'surplus' fur-bearers, and many trappers, in particular the politically more active ones, view it as an important part of their lifestyle. They even argue that trapping certain animals, as well as hunting them, is necessary to maintain healthy populations of animals and is therefore an important tool for wildlife management (see e.g. NTA, 1994: 32 ff.).

Moreover, many trappers resent the moralistic overtones of much of the opponents' arguments. Most trappers are completely comfortable with the idea of using animals, as well as the idea that man dominates animals, which stands in marked contrast with the moral objections to trapping held by the opponents. At the same time, they are among the most knowledgeable and affectionate people when it comes to wildlife and conservation issues (study results cited in Todd & Boggess, 1987: 70, and Fleishman-Hillard Research, 1999: 62-63).

Consequently, they feel they are unjustly stereotyped as cruel and insensitive by an animal protection community that is largely based in urban areas. Trappers pride themselves in being at the forefront of wildlife issues and consider themselves to be concerned with animal welfare as well (Interview 15-1-2001, NTA). Opponents of trapping, by contrast, are often dismissed as 'animal rights' activists, who place animals' rights on a par with human rights, a position that is definitely not that of the trappers (see e.g. NTA, 1994: 12-15).

Within the more general and fundamental debate about trapping, a number of more specific issues have arisen. First, it makes a great difference to many people *for what purpose* animals are killed. Trapping for fur generally meets with more opposition than trapping for pest and predator control, as fur is thought to be a luxury item that does not warrant killing animals, whereas pest and predator control are more likely to be seen as rational justifications for trapping. As a result, many people, as well as some governments, differentiate between the various purposes in their position on trapping issues.

Second, much of the debate has focused on *specific traps and trapping techniques* rather than the activity of trapping as such (for an overview of different types of traps and their development, see Novak, 1987b). One type of trap has attracted the most attention and has become the subject of intense dispute in itself: leghold traps. Leghold traps operate through jaws that grab an animal's limb and/or its body. They hold the animal until the trapper finds it and can choose to release or kill it. The leghold trap is therefore a so-called 'restraining trap,' a category that also includes other traps that are not intended to kill the animal, such as box traps, which hold animals by containing them in a cage or box.

Restraining traps can be distinguished from traps that are intended to kill animals, so-called 'killing traps,' for instance by hitting it with a weight or a spring-powered jaw. Snares, which are made from ropes or wires, can be used both as killing and as restraining traps, depending on the part of the animal's body on which they operate (legs, necks or bodies; see Liss, 1990: 164).

Restraining traps can also be used underwater. Then, their purpose is to keep animals under water until they drown or run out of oxygen, which makes them a killing trap. These types of killing traps are known as 'drowning' or 'submersion' traps.

Leghold traps have been the subject of controversy because opponents claim they are particularly cruel and non-selective (see e.g. Animal Alliance, CAHT & HSUS, 1999b; AWI, 1990b; 1994a; EP, 1990a: 16). According to animal protection activists, leghold traps may severely wound an animal. Leghold traps are said to cut deeply into the flesh of animals, crushing their bones. Out of pain, animals have been recorded to chew off the limb that has been caught in the leghold trap. Moreover, animals may suffer from severe stress while being restrained, in particular when they have to wait a long time for the trapper to check the trap. In addition, so the opponents of leghold traps claim, animals that were not intended to be caught ('non-target animals') may run into the trap, making it a non-selective means of capturing animals.

Trappers who use leghold traps, on the other hand, argue that the images used by the opponents are outdated (FIC, undated: 18-20). There are many different kinds of leghold traps and modern leghold traps are infinitely more humane than their predecessors. Although the injuries recorded by opponents may have occurred with older types, modern traps have been redesigned so as to avoid these injuries, so they argue. Furthermore, trappers tend to stress the importance of training and expertise in using traps, which they argue can prevent most catches of non-target animals. In the end, they claim, it is in the trapper's best interest to avoid injuries to furs and unwanted catches.

Much of the debate surrounding leghold traps has concentrated on steel leghold traps with teeth. Other types of leghold traps, however, use flat jaws to restrain an animal, or so-called 'webbed' jaws that are supposed to prevent the animal from chewing off its limb (Novak, 1987b: 947). Still other leghold traps use jaws that have been coated with rubber or plastic to reduce the impact of the jaws ('padded leghold traps'). In attempts to arrive at more humane traps, new types of killing traps have also been developed, the most popular of which is the Conibear trap, which was developed by the Canadian Frank Conibear in 1929 and has been produced since 1957 (Novak, 1987b: 948).

To the opponents of leghold traps these arguments are not convincing. They argue that even if injuries and suffering can be reduced by using newer traps, leghold traps are cruel as a class and can never live up to a decent standard of humaneness. Thus, they believe that leghold traps should be banned altogether. The level of controversy over this particular type of trap is also reflected in the opinions of North American wildlife professionals, who, a recent survey showed, are deeply divided on whether the use of leghold traps should be prohibited (Muth et al., 1998: 620-621).

A possible way out of this controversy would be to formulate standards to which traps would have to conform. In this vein, research since the late 1800s has sought to find more humane traps and trapping techniques. Although this approach would be acceptable to trappers and animal protection activists who focus on the welfare of animals, it is not acceptable to groups that view trapping as morally wrong in itself. They fear that trapping standards would primarily serve to legitimise a practice they detest even if it incrementally reduced animal suffering. Trappers, on the other hand, are often reluctant concerning processes to formulate trapping standards as they fear they will lose traps they deem valuable and replacing traps is expensive.

If the concept of trapping standards as a way of improving animal welfare is accepted, several issues arise in relation to these standards themselves. For killing traps, the main issue is the time that is required for a trap to kill an animal or at least to render it unconscious. For restraining traps, the main issues revolve around the indicators to measure animal suffering. In a restrictive interpretation, these would only relate to readily observable physical injuries, while many animal protection activists also demand the inclusion of behavioural indicators that signal stress and pain in animals.

The debate over leghold traps and trapping standards is often confounded by the fact that arguments concerning the humaneness of traps are mixed with arguments about the morality of trapping and arguments with regard to the conservation of (endangered) species. To both sides in the debate, the discussion over particular traps tends to mean much more than just that: it stands as a symbol of deeply-held beliefs about the way people should deal with animals and the role of trapping in such a lifestyle. It was against this background of polemic and ongoing controversy, both in Europe and in North America, that the EC decided to ban furs from animals caught by leghold traps.

3.2 The European ban

In the early 1980s, animal protection groups in a number of European countries started extensive campaigns against fur. Animal protection activism was strongest in Northwest Europe, in countries such as the United Kingdom, the Netherlands and Germany. By the late 1980s, leghold traps had been banned in five member states of the (then) EEC: the United Kingdom, Ireland, West Germany, Denmark and Greece (AWI, 1990d: 309-310; EP, 1990a: 17).

Europeans hardly trapped for fur, but trapping for pest control was important in a number of countries, in particular the Netherlands, Germany and Belgium, which trapped hundreds of thousands of muskrats a year (FACE, 1999: V.6-7 & Annex IV, at pages 30-34). The wild fur that was used in garments was imported, mainly from Canada, the US and Russia. In addition, a number of European countries, such as Denmark and the Netherlands, had large fur farming industries. The European fur manufacturing and retail industries were concentrated in Southern Europe, with Italy as one of the main fashion centres and Greece as a major centre for fur processing.

In the second half of the 1980s, animal protection groups in the UK pushed for a label on imported wild fur that would state if the animals had been caught by leghold traps (Hamilton et al., 1998: 576; Interview 17-1-2001, HSUS/AWI). After lobbying by mainly the Canadian government, this proposal was rejected by the UK government. Not long afterwards, however, the proposal resurfaced as a resolution in the European Parliament (EP).

In June 1988, two Members of the European Parliament (MEPs) tabled a written declaration calling for 'a Community-wide ban on the manufacture, sale and use of steel-jawed leghold traps' and 'the labelling of fur products imported into the EEC to indicate whether they derive from animals caught in these traps.' In September 1988, the declaration had been signed by a majority of MEPs and was sent to the European Commission (EP, 1988c).

Around that same time, the European Commission proposed a ban on the manufacture, sale and use of leghold traps as part of a Directive on the protection of habitats, plants and animals. This proposal related only to the use of leghold traps in the Community and not to their use in other countries (CEC, 1988: Article 15(b) & Annex IX(b)).

In February 1989, the EP's written declaration was followed by a resolution that restated the demand for a labelling regime for imported furs, except that it related to leghold traps in general, not just 'steel-jawed' leghold traps (EP, 1989). In calling for a labelling regime, as well as a Community-wide ban on leghold traps, the EP referred both to the alleged cruelty of these traps and to their indiscriminate nature, which could pose a threat to non-target animals, including endangered species.

In April 1989, the European Commission, through DG XI (Environment), submitted a separate proposal that would prohibit the importation of furs and fur products from countries that either had not banned the use of leghold traps or did not adhere to 'internationally agreed humane trapping standards.' The Commission proposal thus went further than the EP Resolution, which had merely called for a labelling regime. The ban would apply to furs from eight species, which were listed in an annex to the proposal. It would enter into force on 1 January 1996, unless the Commission chose to suspend its entry into force by two years if it found that a country had made sufficient progress toward developing humane trapping standards (CEC, 1989).

In its position on the Commission proposal, the EP proposed to include both the ban on leghold traps in the Community and the ban on the importation of furs in one Regulation. Its entry into force was proposed to take place on 1 January 1995, with a possible extension of one year. In the meantime, an interim labelling regime would have to be applied. Moreover, six species were added to the list of species that would be covered by the Regulation. Most controversially for North American trappers, the EP also included an amendment that would require countries to ban leghold traps *and* adhere to humane trapping standards (EP, 1990b).

On 25 March 1991, the Commission adopted a number of amendments that had been proposed by the EP (CEC, 1991). The import ban and the ban on leghold traps within the EC were combined in one proposal. The number of species covered by the Regulation was expanded to thirteen, only excluding the red squirrel, which had been included in the EP proposal but was caught by body snares rather than leghold traps. Also, the Commission endorsed the EP proposal for the date of its entry into force. It did not accept the proposal for an interim labelling regime, nor did it endorse the amendment requiring a ban on leghold traps together with adherence to humane trapping standards.

On 4 November 1991, the Environmental Council finally adopted Regulation 3254/91 (henceforth 'the Regulation') 'prohibiting the use of leghold traps in the Community and the introduction into the Community of pelts and manufactured goods of certain wild animal species originating in countries which catch them by means of leghold traps or trapping methods which do not meet international humane trapping standards' (EC, 1991). The Regulation combined bans on the use of leghold traps (but not their manufacture and sale; Article 2 Regulation) and the importation of furs and fur products from thirteen species if they came from a country that had not banned the use of leghold traps or did not adhere to 'internationally agreed humane trapping standards' (Article 3.1 Regulation). Twelve of these thirteen species were caught mainly in the US and Canada, one (sable) in Russia. The ban would enter into force on 1 January 1995 (Article 2 Regulation), but the Commission could suspend its entry into force by one year if it found that 'sufficient progress [had been] made in developing humane methods of trapping' in a particular country (Article 3.2 Regulation).

The proposed Regulation had attracted international attention even before it was adopted. During the whole legislative process, and to some extent even before, North American animal protection groups and the Canadian government had been heavily involved, lobbying, giving information and negotiating specifics of the proposal. I will defer the discussion of these efforts and the main issues in these debates to section 3.5, however, after I have outlined the regulatory and political context in which the (proposed) Regulation was received in the US and Canada (in section 3.3) and the GATT/WTO compatibility of the European Regulation (in section 3.4).

3.3 The potential impact of the European Regulation on the US and Canada

3.3.1 The regulation of traps and trapping in the US and Canada

In both Canada and the US, the regulation of trapping falls under the jurisdiction of sub-federal governments, that is, the provinces and states, respectively. In addition, work on trapping standards has been done at the national level, mainly in Canada. In this subsection I will discuss the regulation of traps (in particular leghold traps) and trapping in both countries.

In Canada, the provinces had the main responsibility for regulating trapping and setting trapping standards. The situation in the (at that time two, since 1999 three) territories was somewhat different in that these areas formally fell under federal jurisdiction. Still, many aspects of wildlife management, including trapping, were regulated by the territorial governments themselves (Slough et al., 1987: 1064). Federal jurisdiction could only be asserted through the constitutional provisions on interprovincial trade and commerce, which had been used in order to require permits for game to be traded across provincial borders (see e.g. Anderson, 1987: 1041). It had not been used for requiring certain trapping standards to be met, though. The federal government also had the power to regulate wildlife and trapping on federal lands, but by and large almost all trapping activities fell under provincial and territorial authority.

Taking the mid-1980s as the baseline, the situation in the field of trapping standards varied considerably between the various provinces and territories. The province of Ontario had relatively extensive trapping regulations. The province was the home ground of several animal protection groups, which had resulted in restrictions on the use of leghold traps and the requirement to check traps daily (Novak, 1987c: 1058). British Columbia had restricted the use of leghold traps in 1982 (Slough et al., 1987: 1072). Other provinces and territories did not have similar restrictions (Anderson, 1987: 1046; Slough et al., 1987: 1071-1072).

At the federal level, no formal trapping standards had been established. Nevertheless, the federal government had been involved in efforts to develop humane trapping standards at the national level, together with the provinces and private groups. Several trap research programmes had already been carried out in the 1950s and 1960s when, in 1973, the Federal Provincial Committee for Humane Trapping (FPCHT) was established (Novak, 1987b: 957 & 962). The FPCHT examined standards for humane traps and carried out research on existing traps. In some cases, improvements were suggested in order to bring traps into conformity with the Committee's standards (Novak, 1987b: 963-964).

After the FPCHT had finalised its work in 1981, the provincial and federal governments decided to create a more formal institution to continue the work on trap research and standards. This became the Fur Institute of Canada (FIC), which was created in 1983. Work by the FIC has been financed by both the provincial and federal governments. After its establishment, the FIC built a research facility in Alberta and started work on (voluntary) national standards for traps under the Canadian General Standards Board (CGSB). The first national standard for killing traps was passed around 1990 (Interview 15-2-2001, FIC).

Thus, by the time the European Regulation was adopted, Canada had gained considerable experience in trap research and had been working on national trapping standards for some time. In addition, the Canadian government had taken the initiative to form a working group on international humane trapping standards in the International Organization for Standardization (which will be discussed below).

The underlying rationale for both the national and international processes was mainly to allay concerns about the cruelty of certain traps and trapping methods among animal protection groups and the public at large. As a contemporary observer of and participant in these standard-setting processes argued, the 'development and implementation of efficient and humane trapping systems is an absolute requirement if trapping is to survive. Trapping shows little in the way of modern equipment, and the fur fashion industry has been negligent in its support of trap research. It was public pressure that moved reluctant governments to conduct trap research' (Novak, 1987a: 93; references deleted).

In the decades before the European Regulation, the US had experienced a great deal of activism from animal protection groups, in particular aimed at banning leghold traps. Even before that, in the 1920s and 1930s, leghold traps had come under attack, but at that time not so much by animal protection groups as by hunters, who feared their hounds would be caught in leghold traps during the hunt (Novak, 1987a: 89; DiStefano, 1987: 1087). Although the locus of activism against leghold traps had shifted to animal protection groups in the 1970s, injury to hunters' hounds was still cited as the main reason for Tennessee's 1985 requirement that leghold traps be padded (Linscombe, 1987: 1096).

In the late 1980s and early 1990s, when the European Regulation was being discussed and adopted, the pattern of regulation in US states was very uneven. Some states had banned the use of leghold traps, while others had restricted their use to certain areas or species. In 1991, states that had banned most uses of leghold traps included Rhode Island, New Jersey and Florida. States that had restricted their use included Delaware, Connecticut, Massachussetts and, to a lesser extent, North Carolina (DiStefano, 1987: 1087; Linscombe, 1987: 1096; Liss, 1990: 159). The state of New Jersey had the most comprehensive restrictions, banning both the use, sale, manufacture and possession of leghold traps (Liss, 1990: 159). All states that had banned or severely restricted the use of leghold traps in the early 1990s were located on the East coast. Bans or restrictions were largely absent in the South-eastern, Mid-western and Western states, although the states on the West coast had very active animal protection groups (Hamilton & Fox, 1987: 1111; Linscombe, 1987: 1096; Melchior, Johnson & Phelps, 1987: 1120). Between the mid-1980s, when New Jersey adopted its ban, and 1994, when Arizona passed a ballot initiative prohibiting the use of leghold traps on public lands, this situation would remain stable.

In addition to states that had banned or restricted the use of leghold traps, most states that allowed them did impose certain standards on these traps. In a survey of state trapping regulations published in 1990, a US animal protection activist found that 29 states had imposed limits on the allowable size of steel leghold traps, although these limits varied considerably between states, while sixteen states prohibited and ten others restricted the use of teeth. In addition, ten states had banned killing traps either altogether or on land, and sixteen states had banned all snares. Varying numbers of states had imposed standards relating to the use of bait, the placement of traps, accidental trapping of non-target animals, the way trapped fur-bearers were to be killed, trap identification, the intervals at which traps were to be checked, and fur catch reports. Finally, states had sometimes prohibited the catch of certain fur-bearers, in addition to federally protected endangered species (for the overview, see Liss, 1990: 161-181). All in all, there was an enormous variation among US states in the types of requirements and the precise standards they imposed, probably reflecting both differences in natural conditions and in animal protection activism.

The amount of activism in the US was also reflected in the number of legislative initiatives taken to restrict trapping. One source mentions a number of 361 anti-trapping bills introduced between 1968 and 1986. Of these, 30% were introduced at the federal level (cited in Fleishman-Hillard Research, 1999: 33). Yet, although US animal protection activism had resulted on bans in some states, much less work had been done on trap research and national trapping standards than in Canada.

Federal initiatives to regulate trapping could take one of two routes. First, the federal government could use its powers under the interstate commerce clause to regulate trade in furs between states. On this basis, standards could have been attached to the way these furs had been produced, but this would not have affected intra-state activities. Second, the federal government had the power to regulate trapping on federal lands, such as national parks.

Although bills to ban leghold traps had been introduced in almost every session of Congress since the 1960s, these initiatives never went very far. One source stated that of all the bills to ban leghold traps that were introduced between 1957 and 1990 only two received public hearings and none reached the floor of Congress (Liss, 1990: 159). Likewise, there had not been any national initiatives to formulate voluntary trapping standards, as had been done by the FPCHT and the FIC in Canada, a situation that would not change until 1996.

Leghold traps were widely used in both countries. In a study carried out in Ontario in the first half of the 1970s, trappers reported each to possess 73 leghold traps and 17 Conibear traps (a kind of killing trap) on average. A similar pattern was found in Alberta (Novak, 1987a: 67). A 1987 overview of trapping in the Southeastern US states estimated that 'the leghold trap is still the single most important tool for harvesting fur-bearers in the Southeast, and approximately 70% of the harvest of land fur-bearers and 86% of aquatic fur-bearers are taken by it' (Linscombe, 1987: 1092). Referring to New Jersey's ban on leghold traps, the NTA stated that '[t]his primary tool for the capture of canines, such as fox and coyote, is used also for most other fur bearers such as raccoon, mink, muskrat, opossum and skunk' (NTA, 1994: 36).

The use of leghold traps has probably been more widespread in the US than in Canada. In urban or at least settled areas, which are more prominent in the US than in Canada, killing-type traps are often used less extensively than in remote areas. In settled areas, leghold traps are used exactly because they do not kill and allow pets or other animals that may adventitiously run into the trap to be released (Interview 19-1-2001, IAFWA; Hamilton et al., 1998: 580). A Canadian official claimed that restraining traps (including leghold traps) were used only for 5 to 10% of all animals caught in traps in Canada (Stone, 1997: 24).

All in all, however, Novak's (1987a: 68) general conclusion from the mid-1980s probably still held true by the time the European Regulation was adopted: 'although

Conibear traps appear to be receiving substantial and increasing use, especially in aquatic sets, holding traps continue to predominate among land sets, especially in settled areas. However, snares receive substantial use among northern trappers.'

3.3.2 Trappers and the fur industry in the US and Canada

Together with Russia (formerly the Soviet Union), the US and Canada are the largest producers and exporters of wild fur in the world. In order to sketch the background against which the European Regulation was adopted and the US and Canada reacted to it, it is therefore necessary to examine how important trapping was and how the fur industry was organised in the two countries. In the next subsection I will then discuss the potential impact which the European Regulation had on the US and Canada.

Reliable data on trapping in the US and Canada are difficult to obtain, since trapping is a relatively unorganised activity in both countries. It is done largely by individual, mostly part-time trappers and not by organised firms. The pelts are sold at fur auctions or to local fur buyers and from there to manufacturers and retailers, for which better data are available.

The highly cyclical nature of fur markets is another problem in assessing the importance of trapping and furs. As fur prices and general economic conditions fluctuate, so does the number of trappers. The number and value of pelts in any one year may therefore be a poor indicator of the importance of the industry five years later or over the longer term.

In 1983/1984, the number of trappers in Canada was estimated to be around 100,000. This figure is likely to underestimate the actual number of trappers since 'sporadic' trappers may not be represented in the figures. According to Todd and Boggess (1987: 59-60), the actual number of trappers may be twice as high in some parts of Canada, and they cite a 1979 poll in Alberta that even showed trapping participation rates to be almost eight times as high as the official number.

In the US, the number of licensed trappers was around 450,000 in the late 1970s and early 1980s, but here too the actual number was probably much higher (Todd and Boggess, 1987: 60). The total number of trappers is likely to have decreased since the early 1980s as fur prices have declined (Interview 15-1-2001, NTA). In a 1996 report, the European Parliament cited that there were 100,000 trappers in the US and 80,000 in Canada (EP, 1996a: 25).

The fluctuations in the numbers of trappers are partly the result of the type of people that engage in trapping. For most trappers in the US and Canada, trapping is only a part-time activity and income from trapping is typically small. The number of full-time trappers is relatively small. Still, fur prices are important in that they allow trappers to recover (some of) the costs of trapping. As a result, many part-time trappers will only trap when prices are relatively high. Apart from a core of committed trappers, trappers thus come and go with fur prices. The most important motives for most trappers are related to the recreational aspects of the activity, rather than the added income (Todd and Boggess, 1987: 63; Fleishman-Hillard Research, 1999: 59-61).

This general picture does not equally apply to all parts of Canada and the US, however, and the motives for trapping may differ between the two. To begin with, trapping plays a much more important role in remote areas, where some (mainly aboriginal)[1] people trap, hunt and fish not only for pelts, but also for meat. They sell some of their furs as a means to gain cash income, but theirs is largely subsistence trapping as opposed to the recreational trapping practised by most part-time trappers.

As subsistence trapping is mainly carried out by aboriginal trappers in remote areas, it is much more prevalent in Canada than in the US, with the exception of Alaska. In general, trapping seems to be a more important source of income to Canadian than to US trappers. In a study of trappers in the states of Georgia, New Jersey and West Virginia, almost all trappers (84 to 94%) trapped part-time, whereas a number of Canadian studies showed a much larger proportion of trappers who relied on trapping for their income, at least in the winter (Todd and Boggess, 1987: 61). Within Canada, reliance on trapping is greatest in the Northern parts of the country, which includes not only the Northern territories, but also the Northern parts of most provinces. Yet, even here full-time trappers are rare (Todd and Boggess, 1987: 68-70).

Another difference between the US and Canada is that trapping in the US is more often related to pest and predator control. In the US, this is the main motive for trapping in many rural and urban areas, while it is an insignificant part of all trapping activity in Canada. Although the pelts of animals trapped as pests or predators are often sold, this activity is therefore likely to continue even in the absence of trade in furs.

Furs are sold at auctions, either directly by trappers or through local buyers. The two largest North American fur auctions are both in Ontario, Canada (Shieff & Baker, 1987: 863-864; Interview 15-1-2001, NTA). Consequently, the US and Canadian fur markets are practically one.

Moreover, there is no clear distinction between trapping for export and trapping for domestic use, since a trapper does not know where his (almost all trappers are male) furs will go next. The distinction between export and domestic use is further blurred by the highly international character of the fur industry. Thus, furs may go from the US to Canada to be sold at an auction, then to Europe or Asia to be processed and made into garments, and subsequently return to the US to be sold

1 Throughout this case study I will refer to 'aboriginal' trappers to denote a category of people that are also called 'indigenous,' 'native' or 'first nation.' All of these terms have slightly different meanings and connotations and have been used in different contexts, both by Europeans and North Americans. I will therefore stick to the term 'aboriginal,' which is used in the Canadian Constitution, to refer to Indian people in the US, and Indian, Inuit and Metis people in Canada.

(for an overview of the production process in the fur industry, see Shieff & Baker, 1987: 864 ff.).

The international fur trade therefore demonstrates an intricate web of fur and garment flows between North America, Europe and Asia. Consequently, the US and Canada both export and import furs and fur products in significant quantities at the same time (Shieff & Baker, 1987: 871, table 8 for Canada, and page 875, table 10 for the US).

At the production level, trapped wild furs are joined by fur from fur farms, where certain fur-bearing animals are bred for fur. The main species bred on fur farms is mink. In the US and Canada, the relative importance of farmed and wild fur has fluctuated over time. Between 1976 and 1984, the US produced between three and four million farmed mink furs per year, compared to between fifteen and eighteen million wild furs (Compare Shieff & Baker, 1987: figure 3 at page 865 and figure 4 at page 866).

In Canada, both the numbers and the value of farmed furs relative to wild furs have fluctuated over the last decades. In terms of the number of furs, trapped furs outnumbered farmed furs 2:1 from 1983 to 1988, but since then these numbers have evened out. However, the value of farmed furs has consistently been greater than that of wild furs, with the exception of some years during the mid-1980s and the early 1990s (Statistics Canada, 2001a).

At the production and retail levels, the fur industry is much more organised than at the level of individual trappers. It is also at these stages that the greatest part of added value is reached, particularly through the mark-up by manufacturers and retailers. Shieff and Baker (1987: 867) estimate that 54% of the retail price of a beaver coat is accounted for by mark-ups by manufacturers and retailers (at 13% and 41% of retail prices, respectively). The fur industry thus shows a remarkable combination of a traditional, economically fairly marginal and unorganised part (at the trapping stage) and conversely a highly international and profitable part (at the manufacturing and retail stages).

3.3.3 The (potential) impact of the European Regulation

Because of the nature of the fur industry and the issue of leghold traps, the potential impact of the European Regulation on the Canadian and US fur industries was and is difficult to assess and has been the subject of debate. These difficulties stem from three factors. First, legally speaking, only exports of furs from the thirteen species listed in Annex I of the Regulation would have been affected by a European import ban. Wild furs from other species would not have been covered and, as mink was not listed, most farmed fur could have been exported to the EC as well. In practice, however, the ban had the potential to affect a much wider range of furs, as it would probably have undercut the market for furs and fur products in general, just as the earlier European ban on certain types of seal skins, which will be discussed somewhat more closely below, had done for all seal skin products (Interview 9-2-2001, Canadian Mission/INAC).

Second, given the intricate nature of the international fur trade, it is difficult to pin down the proportion of furs that were destined for the EC or to distinguish this from the fur trade to other countries. In a narrow sense, one could look at furs that ended up as products in the EC. However, much of the fur trade consists of exports, re-exports and (re-)imports during the production process, in which European countries play an important role. European fashion designers also play a leading role in the use of wild furs. If the European market for wild furs had been lost and European designers had consequently switched to farmed furs, this would have affected fur markets outside the EC as well (Interview 29-9-2000, Canadian Mission). The strategic importance of the European market was therefore much greater than its size as a market for fur products alone.

Third, estimates of the impact of the European Regulation were heavily contested as these estimates themselves were politically highly relevant to the issue. Thus, trappers and industry in the US and Canada sought to present high figures in order to convince US and Canadian policy makers of the importance of their industry for the total economy, while animal protection groups have tended to play down the significance of trapping for the economy and for individual trappers. The absence of reliable information and established definitions on many aspects of trapping allowed each of these groups to inflate or deflate figures almost at will.

As a result, estimates of the importance of the US and Canadian fur trade with the EC, as well as the importance of the fur industry in the two countries, varied considerably. In this subsection I will try to highlight some of the data available on this issue. First, I will estimate the importance of the EC as an export market to US and Canadian fur producers. Then, I will discuss the importance of the fur industry within Canada and the US. Finally, I will discuss a number of non-economic differences between trapping in Canada and the US that made an important difference in the perceived impact of the European Regulation in the two countries.

The importance of fur exports to the EC

As to the importance of the EC as an export market for North American fur, differences in definition led to significant differences in estimates. Nollkaemper (1996: 241, notes 28 and 29) has cited figures from the Eurogroup on Animal Welfare which state that exports to the EC of the thirteen species covered by the Regulation formed 10% of total US fur exports in 1994; Canadian fur exports to the EC were estimated at 42% of total Canadian wild fur production. Others have estimated that 75% of North American wild fur exports went to Europe (Hamilton et al., 1998: 573). These differences are probably mainly the result of differences in definitions: the 10% figure relates exports in the thirteen species to total fur exports, which include other species as well as a large amount of farmed fur. Farmed fur is mainly mink, which is not covered by the Regulation. The 42% and 75% figures only look at exports of wild furs, excluding farmed furs. It is not clear whether these figures include only the thirteen species covered by the Regulation or fur from all species. In addition, the 75% figure includes furs that are traded through Europe, whereas it is unclear whether these are included in the 10% or 42% figures.

Other figures, from the first half of the 1980s, indicate that Europe (as a whole, not just the EC) was the main or one of the main destinations for US raw (i.e. both wild and farmed) furs and fur products, although during this period these figures decreased from 71% to 56% of total exports for raw furs and from more than 60% to around 40% of total exports for fur products, respectively (Shieff & Baker, 1987: 874). In that same period, Europe was Canada's main export market for raw furs, at slightly less than 60% of total raw fur exports, while the European share in Canada's exports of fur products dropped from more than 60% to less than 20% and it was gradually replaced by the US as the main export market for fur products (Shieff & Baker, 1987: 869 & 871, figure 10).

Given the cyclical nature of fur markets and the system of re-exports, these figures are very difficult to interpret or to apply to later years. However, whatever the precise figures, the European market can at least be said to have been the main or one of the main export markets for US and Canadian fur exporters, both as a destination for furs and fur products and as a centre of fur processing and fashion.

In turn, exports have made up the majority of US and Canadian wild fur production as a whole. In the period between 1977 and 1984, exports of US wild furs varied between 72% and 99% of total wild fur production; a similar pattern applies to Canada (Shieff & Baker, 1987: 865, 869 & 873). The economic importance of the European market to North American fur producers was therefore enormous and a ban on the export of furs to the EC would have had a great impact on these producers.

The importance of trapping for the US and Canadian economies as a whole

Estimates of the importance of trapping for the Canadian and US economies as a whole are beset with similar difficulties as those discussed above. Apart from the value of the furs and fur products, some estimates include the value of pest and predator control resulting from trapping in the total economic value of trapping. The NTA, for example, including a wide range of items at the trapper, trade, manufacture, farm and retail levels, arrived at the total economic benefits of trapping of US$ 4.35 billion in 1987 and US$ 2.95 billion in 1990. Moreover, it estimated the annual losses caused by wildlife at US$ 12.8 billion. Taking a more limited measure, the total value of fur exports (both wild and farmed, and both raw pelts and products) was said to be US$ 461.9 million in 1987 and US$ 261.6 million in 1990 (all figures cited in NTA, 1994: 24, 25 & 51). The Animal Welfare Institute, on the other hand, estimated the value of exports affected by the European Regulation at a mere US$ 23.3 million (AWI, 1995: 5).

In Canada, government officials claimed that the fur industry as a whole contributed some CAN$ 800 million to the economy (JMC, 2000). According to Statistics

Canada, the total value of pelts produced in Canada (both wild and farmed, but excluding fur products) varied between CAN$ 34 million and CAN$ 154 million in the period between 1985 and 1995 (Statistics Canada, 2001a).

Although these figures are relatively small in comparison to the total economies involved, they are still significant and at least higher than the exports involved in the beef-hormone issue, which will be discussed in the next chapter. In absolute figures, the size of the fur industry was smaller in Canada than in the US. In relative terms, it may have been somewhat larger in Canada than in the US, but given the difficulties with the available data this is difficult to substantiate.

Non-economic factors that determined the impact of an import ban

More important than the economic or monetary value of the fur trade and industry, the two countries differed significantly in other respects that had an important impact on the potential political costs of the European Regulation and the way the two governments looked at it. These differences related, first, to the role of aboriginal trappers in the two countries and, second, to past experiences with similar bans.

As the number of trappers greatly exceeded the number of employees in fur manufacturing and retail in both the US and Canada, and the dispute evolved around the activity of trapping, most of the focus and debate extended to trappers rather than other parts of the fur industry. In Canada, an important part of the background to this debate was formed by the position of aboriginal trappers in remote areas.

As was indicated above, trapping in the US is carried out mainly by part-time trappers. To them, income is not the main motive for trapping, although with low incomes the additional revenues from trapping may be important (Todd & Boggess, 1987: 62). Trapping plays a much more important role in remote areas, though, where (mainly) aboriginal trappers use trapping as part of a subsistence lifestyle. In Canada, the potential impact of the Regulation on aboriginal trappers played a much more important role than in the US, for two reasons.

First, the relative number of aboriginal trappers in Canada was higher than in the US. The percentage of aboriginal trappers in Canada was estimated to be around 29% of all trappers in 1984. However, this figure is probably an underestimate and other authors have mentioned figures of 50% or 60%. In the US, a 1980 survey found that 95% of all US trappers were white, although 25% reported some aboriginal ancestry (Todd & Boggess, 1987: 59-60).

Of course, all aboriginal trappers were not subsistence trappers. As was discussed above, the importance of trapping as part of a subsistence lifestyle was greatest in remote areas, and it mainly played a role in Northern Canadian communities. In these communities, trapping was done not only for the fur trade, but also for meat and other products. Moreover, as the Canadian government repeatedly argued, it would have been very difficult for many aboriginal trappers to switch to other lifestyles (Interview 9-2-2001, Canadian Mission/INAC). In the US, the issue of aboriginal trappers was important in Alaska, but in most US states it hardly played a role (Interview 19-1-2001, IAFWA).

Second, the political significance of aboriginal issues was much greater in Canada than in the US. According to Brock (2000: 341), several factors account for this difference. Aboriginals make up a greater proportion of the Canadian than of the US population (about 2.7% versus less than 1% of the total population; see Brock, 2000: 340); Canadian aboriginal people have been able to exert electoral influence in several parts of the country; their plight has not been overshadowed by that of other disadvantaged groups, like blacks and latinos in the US; and Canadian aboriginal organisations have much stronger links with the government than do similar organisations in the US. In addition, the issues of aboriginal rights and self-government have played an important role in Canada's constitutional debates over the past two decades, which may also have resulted in an increased importance of and sensitivity to aboriginal issues on the political agenda (Brock, 2000: 346 ff.; Jackson & Jackson, 2001: 178-179).

Apart from, although closely related to, the role of aboriginal issues, Canada had also had experience with an earlier European ban, which the US lacked. In 1983, the (then) EEC had adopted a ban on the importation of puppy seal skins and products made of those skins (EC, 1983). As a result of this ban, the exports of Canadian seal skins to Europe, which had been the most important market, were lost. Allegedly, this had a devastating effect on Inuit communities on Canada's Atlantic coast, which had relied heavily on the seal hunt during winter months (see e.g. EP, 1990a: 22; Hamilton et al., 1998: 575; Lynge, 1997: 39). The US had not been affected by the European ban. In fact, the US had imposed its own ban on seal skins under the 1972 Marine Mammal Protection Act.

The experience with the European seal skin ban conditioned the response of the Canadian government in a number of ways (Interviews 29-9-2000, Canadian Mission; 9-2-2001, Canadian Mission/INAC; see also Hamilton et al., 1998: 579). First, the Canadian government had become more aware of the potentially damaging effects which a European ban on furs could have for communities that relied heavily on those furs. Second, the European ban on seal skins had taught the Canadian government that markets for all furs could be affected by the European ban. The seal skin ban had only applied to certain types of seals, but in the end it had affected the whole market for seal skins, including skins from other types of seals that had been important to Canada. Third, the European seal skin ban included an exemption for products from aboriginal hunters (EC, 1983: Article 3), but this had not prevented their markets from collapsing. This was to condition the Canadian government's reaction to future proposals to exempt aboriginal fur products from an import ban. Fourth, and finally, the seal skin ban had led the Canadian government to reconsider its approach to this kind of issue. After the seal skin ban had been implemented, Canadian officials started looking for a way to counter the emotionally powerful arguments of (European) animal protection groups and they concluded that they needed an equally powerful symbolic issue to counter public opinion. This they found in the issue of aboriginals, and in the next European ban to arise, the leghold trap Regulation, it was decided actively to use this argument as a means of gaining credibility among the European public and European decision-makers (Interview 9-2-2001, Canadian Mission/INAC).

3.4 Compatibility with GATT/WTO law

When the European Regulation was adopted, no case involving a regulatory trade measure aimed at protecting animals in other countries had been brought before the GATT. Discussions of the GATT compatibility of the proposed measure are conspicuously absent from the legislative documents prepared by the European Parliament and the European Commission. In the early 1990s, however, the issue would gain much more attention with the widely-publicised panel reports in the (two) Tuna-Dolphin cases (GATT, 1991; 1994; see also section 1.3 of this study), and in subsequent years a small body of case law built up around this type of measure.

The Tuna-Dolphin cases were relevant to the leghold trap Regulation in three ways. First, the import ban in the European Regulation was very similar to the US ban on tuna caught by dolphin-unfriendly methods. In both cases, production standards were used to ban imports of products from other countries and in both cases the production standards related to the protection of animals in other countries. Although the two Tuna-Dolphin panel reports were never adopted and therefore never became part of GATT law, these reports (in particular the second panel report), probably provide a good representation of the state of legal thinking in the first half of the 1990s. Consequently, the conclusions in the Tuna-Dolphin cases were relevant for a legal assessment of the European Regulation, in particular at the time the import ban was planned to enter into force.

The relevance of the Tuna-Dolphin cases extended well beyond their legal significance, however. The timing of the Tuna-Dolphin cases was also important, in that they were decided exactly in between the adoption of the European Regulation and the date at which the import ban was planned to enter into force. As a result, awareness of the GATT aspects of the Regulation, on both sides of the Atlantic, was greatly increased in this period.

Finally, and maybe most interestingly, the European Regulation pitted some of the same countries against each other, but in reverse roles. In the second Tuna-Dolphin case, it had been the European Community that had claimed that the US ban on the import of tuna violated GATT law, and the US had defended its measures as being GATT compatible. In the issue of leghold traps, both countries again faced each other, but this time the US had reason to doubt the GATT compatibility of a European measure and the EC had to defend it.

Although in the end, the European Regulation never led to a GATT or (after 1995) WTO case, GATT/WTO law played an important role in the background and, for the reasons outlined above, it had an important effect on both US and EC strategies. In this section I will therefore discuss the GATT/WTO compatibility of the European Regulation, had the import ban been implemented. In doing so, I will focus not only on the Tuna-Dolphin cases, but also on subsequent developments in legal thinking on this issue that took place in the second half of the 1990s.

In order to assess whether a regulatory trade measure is GATT/WTO (in)compatible, a number of steps have to be taken. First, it has to be assessed whether the regulatory trade measure is covered by one of the GATT/WTO's prohibitions. If this is the case, then it has to be assessed whether the regulatory trade measure can be justified under one of the justifications in GATT Article XX. In this section, I will discuss both questions in general and as applied to the European leghold trap Regulation. First, I will discuss the GATT/WTO's prohibitions, and the extent to which an import ban under the leghold trap Regulation would have violated them. Then, I will examine the GATT/WTO's general exceptions in GATT Article XX. Finally, I will discuss these exceptions in relation to an import ban under the European leghold trap Regulation.

3.4.1 The GATT/WTO's prohibitions

The GATT/WTO framework (WTO, 1994a; henceforth 'GATT') is built around a number of key principles that reflect prohibitions of certain types of trade barriers and discrimination between trading partners. GATT Article I:1 contains the 'Most Favoured Nation' principle, which states that:

> 'any advantage, favour, privilege or immunity granted by any contracting party to any product originating in or destined for any other country shall be accorded immediately and unconditionally to the like product originating in or destined for the territories of all other contracting parties.'

Thus, every trading partner (that was a party to GATT or is a member of the WTO) has a right to the same treatment as the 'most favoured' trading partner.

GATT Article III lays down the 'National Treatment' principle: once a product has been imported it should be treated the same as an equivalent domestic product (a 'like' product in GATT terms) with regard to internal taxes and regulations. Internal taxes and regulations should therefore not serve to discriminate between domestic and imported products. More specifically, Article III:4 reads:

> 'The products of the territory of any contracting party imported into the territory of any other contracting party shall be accorded treatment no less favourable than that accorded to like products of national origin in respect of all laws, regulations and requirements affecting their internal sale, offering for sale, purchase, transportation, distribution or use.'

While Article I:1 prohibits discrimination between imported products from different countries, Article III:4 prohibits discrimination between imported and domestic products. With regard to regulatory standards, Articles I and III have the same scope, since Article I explicitly equates its scope with 'all matters referred to in [paragraph] (...) 4 of Article III.' A note to Article III extends the scope of this provision to 'any law, regulation or requirement (...) which applies to an imported product and to the like domestic product and is collected or enforced in the case of the imported product at the time or point of importation.'

This scope stands in contrast to that of GATT Article XI:1, which states that:

> 'no prohibitions or restrictions other than duties, taxes or other charges, whether made effective through quotas, import or export licenses or other measures, shall be instituted or maintained by any contracting party on the importation of any product of the territory of any other contracting party.'

In GATT case law, Articles XI and III have been treated as being mutually exclusive (Schoenbaum, 1997: 273). In a 1984 case, a GATT panel argued that:

> 'the General Agreement distinguishes between measures affecting the "importation" of products, which are regulated in Article XI:1, and those affecting "imported products", which are dealt with in Article III. If Article XI:1 were interpreted broadly to cover also internal requirements, Article III would be partly superfluous.' (GATT, 1984: paragraph 5.14)

A regulatory measure will therefore be covered by either Article III or Article XI, but not both. In the Tuna-Dolphin panel reports, it was concluded that the ban on tuna caught with dolphin-unfriendly methods could not be considered an internal regulation in the sense of GATT Article III. As the second Tuna-Dolphin panel report put it:

> 'Article III calls for a comparison between the treatment accorded to domestic and imported like *products*, not for a comparison of the policies or practices of the country of origin with those of the country of importation.' (GATT, 1994: paragraph 5.8; emphasis in the original)

Consequently, the tuna ban fell under Article XI and not Article III (likewise in GATT, 1991: paragraph 5.8-5.16; cf. Geradin, 1997: 44-45). Since the scope of Articles I and III is identical when it comes to regulatory measures, this conclusion would seem to extend to the relation between Article XI and Article I, as well, but a later WTO panel dealing with a regulatory trade measure based on process standards did not deem it necessary to go into that issue if a ban already violated Article XI (WTO, 1998b: paragraph 7.22-7.23).

The issue of the applicable GATT obligation was important because the US had argued that if its tuna ban were covered by Article III, it would not violate that provision since Mexican tuna was treated no less favourably than US tuna and was therefore not discriminated against (GATT, 1991: paragraph 3.20). Even apart from the factual claim that the tuna ban was no less favourable for Mexican tuna than for US tuna, it is doubtful whether it would have survived scrutiny under Article III. Discrimination occurs when 'like' (i.e. equivalent) products are treated differently. The crucial question with regard to this provision (and Article I) is therefore: when are products 'like' and when are they 'unlike'? For if it could be maintained that products that have been produced differently are unlike, then the differential treatment of those products would not violate these provisions.

Yet, in GATT/WTO case law, this question has been answered differently: the 'likeness' of products refers to characteristics of the product itself. Any differentiation between products should therefore be based on differences between characteristics of the products (e.g. danger to the health of consumers, or pollution during their use) and not on the processes by which they were produced. Thus, in an early GATT case relating to charges rather than regulatory standards, it was concluded that a Belgian measure imposing a levy on products from countries 'whose system of family allowances did not meet specific requirements,' had violated GATT Article I (GATT, 1952: paragraphs 1 and 3). A similar argument would seem to apply to process standards that fall under GATT Article I or III (cf. Jackson, 1998: 236-237).

As a consequence, an import ban or differential treatment of imported products on the basis of differences in process or production methods will usually violate one or more of these three GATT provisions. An import ban on the basis of the European leghold trap Regulation would have violated GATT Article XI, since it would have been based on differences in process standards. Only by relying on an exception clause could such a ban have been justified and be considered consistent with GATT/WTO law after all.

3.4.2 The general exceptions in GATT Article XX

In Article XX, the GATT provides a number of general exceptions to the prohibitions discussed above. GATT Article XX starts with an introductory statement (the 'chapeau') that states:

> 'Subject to the requirement that such measures are not applied in a manner which would constitute a means of arbitrary or unjustifiable discrimination between countries where the same conditions prevail, or a disguised restriction on international trade, nothing in this Agreement shall be construed to prevent the adoption or enforcement by any contracting party of measures:'

Then a number of purposes for which measures can be adopted, is mentioned. For the leghold trap Regulation, the relevant purposes include measures:

> '(a) necessary to protect public morals;
> (b) necessary to protect human, animal or plant life or health;

(...)
(g) relating to the conservation of exhaustible natural resources if such measures are made effective in conjunction with restrictions on domestic production or consumption.'

The interpretation and scope of these exceptions has been elaborated upon in a series of cases before GATT/WTO panels. The crucial question, then, is whether these exceptions can be used to justify regulatory trade measures that impose production standards upon other countries if they are meant to protect values in the exporting country.

This question is sometimes referred to as the problem of 'extraterritorial application of law.' Technically, however, this is not the case here. Extraterritorial application of law means that actions outside a country's jurisdiction are covered directly by that country's legal provisions. An example would be if one country required the application of certain environmental standards by firms in other countries and even threatened to punish foreign firms that do not comply. This type of legal norm is generally forbidden in international law, although even this is not always the case (e.g. in some cases of severe human rights related crimes).

Regulatory trade measures that are meant to impose process standards on other countries do not impose those standards directly. They do not seek to regulate the conduct of people in other jurisdictions. Rather they regulate imports coming into a country, which are traditionally considered to fall under that country's jurisdiction. Although these standards are based on actions in another country and they seek to change those actions, they do not constitute extraterritorial application of law as such. Thus it is better to speak of extraterritorial *protection* of values through regulatory trade measures. The general prohibition of extraterritorial application does not apply (Nollkaemper, 1998: 187-189).

The Tuna-Dolphin cases

The issue of extraterritorial protection of values has been widely debated within the GATT/WTO and outside. It came to the legal fore in the (in)famous Tuna-Dolphin cases between the US and Mexico, then still under the GATT. The central question in the Tuna-Dolphin cases was whether the US could prohibit the import of Mexican tuna if the tuna had not been caught with methods to reduce accidental dolphin kills. In the first panel established around this issue, Mexico challenged the US embargo of tuna from Mexico (the 'primary embargo'), as well as the 'intermediary nation embargo' on tuna from countries that still allowed the import of Mexican tuna, and the American labelling requirements. In the second panel, the (then) EEC and the Netherlands challenged the primary and the intermediary nation embargoes.

In both cases the panel concluded that the US measures were incompatible with GATT law, but the reasoning differed somewhat. The first panel examined the question of whether GATT Article XX (b) and (g) could be used to justify extraterritorial protection of values. From 'the drafting history (...), the purpose of this provision, and the consequence that the interpretation proposed by the parties [with regard to the question whether or not Article XX(b) can justify extraterritorial protection of values, S.P.] would have for the operation of the General Agreement as a whole' (GATT, 1991: paragraph 5.25), it concluded that those provisions did not allow such use; they could only be used to protect values in the importing country itself. With respect to Article XX(b), the main argument for this interpretation ran as follows:

> 'The Panel considered that if the broad interpretation of Article XX(b) suggested by the United States were accepted, each contracting party could unilaterally determine the life or health protection from which other contracting parties could not deviate without jeopardizing their rights under the General Agreement. The General Agreement would then no longer constitute a multilateral framework for trade among all contracting parties but would provide legal security only in respect of trade between a limited number of contracting parties with identical internal regulations.' (GATT, 1991: paragraph 5.27)

A similar argument and even wording was used in relation to Article XX(g) (GATT, 1991: paragraph 5.32)

This conclusion has been heavily criticised on a number of grounds (see e.g. Howse, 1998: 74-75; Joseph, 1994: 10; Mayer & Hoch, 1993; Trachtman, 1992: 150-151). For the present discussion, most relevant is the legal criticism that the panel had not used the proper rules of interpretation of international law as set out in the Vienna Convention on the Law of Treaties (UN, 1969). These rules of interpretation require that recourse be had, first, to the provision's 'ordinary meaning in the light of its object and purpose' (Article 31.1). A number of criteria that may count in determining this meaning are spelled out in Article 31.2. Only secondarily can supplementary means of interpretation, such as preparatory work, play a role in the interpretation and even then only to confirm the meaning resulting from the primary means of interpretation or when these primary means lead to a 'manifestly absurd or unreasonable' interpretation (Article 32). The first Tuna-Dolphin panel had not applied these rules properly by relying too much on GATT Article XX(b)'s drafting history and the Agreement's general purposes.

The second panel did use the criteria from the Vienna Convention and came to the conclusion that the scope of the provisions was not restricted to the protection of values in the importing country only (GATT, 1994: paragraphs 5.15-5.17 for Article XX(g); paragraphs 5.31-5.32 for Article XX(b)). In principle, they could therefore also be used to justify regulatory trade measures aimed at protecting values in other countries (GATT, 1994: paragraph 5.20).

The panel also concluded that the conservation of dolphins fell under the 'conservation of an exhaustible natural resource' as required by GATT Article XX(g) (GATT, 1994: paragraph 5.13). Similarly, the parties to the dispute, as well as the panel, agreed that 'the protection of dolphin life or health was a policy that could come within Article XX(b)' (GATT, 1994: paragraph 5.30).

Yet, Article XX(g) also requires a measure to 'relate to' conservation. According to earlier GATT case law the phrase 'relating to' had to be interpreted as meaning 'primarily aimed at' the conservation of exhaustible natural resources

(GATT, 1988: paragraph 4.6). This proved to be the stumbling block for the US ban on Mexican tuna, since the second panel argued that Article XX(g) could only justify measures if those measures themselves contributed directly to the protection of those values. If the success of the regulatory trade measures was contingent on changes in the target country's policies, it could not be justified under Article XX(g). This conclusion was reached in a few steps. First, the panel stated that:

> 'both the primary and the intermediary nation embargoes on tuna implemented by the United States were taken so as to force other countries to change their policies with respect to persons and things within their own jurisdiction, since the embargoes required such changes in order to have any effect on the conservation of dolphins.' (GATT, 1994: paragraph 5.24)

Since the text of GATT Article XX does not say whether this is allowed, the panel looked at 'the object and purpose of the General Agreement' (GATT, 1994: paragraph 5.25). From this, it followed that:

> 'measures taken so as to force other countries to change their policies, and that were effective only if such changes occurred, could not be primarily aimed either at the conservation of an exhaustible natural resource, or at rendering effective restrictions on domestic production or consumption, in the meaning of Article XX(g).' (GATT, 1994: paragraph 5.27)

Similarly, the panel considered that:

> 'measures taken so as to force other countries to change their policies, and that were effective only if such changes occurred, could not be considered "necessary" for the protection of animal life or health in the sense of Article XX(b).' (GATT, 1994: paragraph 5.39)

Hence, Article XX could not be relied upon to justify the US embargoes on tuna from Mexico and intermediary countries, and these embargoes were inconsistent with GATT law.

Both Tuna-Dolphin panel reports have never been adopted by the GATT General Council. Consequently, they have no formal legal force. Nevertheless, these two reports have served as benchmarks in the debate over the use of regulatory trade measures for extraterritorial protection of values. They have also been referred to in subsequent case law (see e.g. WTO, 1998b: paragraph 7.46). Moreover, they (especially the second panel report) seem to reflect a legal consensus among the GATT's contracting parties and, later, WTO members, which has only become stronger since. Generally, the use of unilateral trade measures to protect values in other countries is not regarded as appropriate, as has been restated most importantly in Principle 12 of the Rio Declaration (UN, 1992).

The Shrimp-Turtle cases

Under the WTO, another case has been brought before the dispute settlement mechanism that involves issues of extraterritorial protection of values, the so-called 'Shrimp-Turtle' case. The background of this case was similar to that in the Tuna-Dolphin cases, as it involved a US ban on the importation of shrimp from countries that had not adopted sufficient measures to avoid accidental killings of sea turtles during the shrimp catch. The US government would grant an exemption from the ban if a country could show that it had adopted measures similar to the requirements for US fishermen, if its rate of accidental sea turtle kills was equivalent to that in the US, or if there was no threat of sea turtles being taken during the shrimp catch, conditions roughly similar to the ones imposed in the Tuna-Dolphin cases (for details, see Howse, 1998: 76-77).

The panel examining the Shrimp-Turtle case took a somewhat different approach than the Tuna-Dolphin panels by first examining the chapeau of GATT Article XX, since it applies to all specific exceptions in Article XX. Its requirements should therefore, according to the panel, be fulfilled before the specific exceptions could come into play (WTO, 1998b: paragraph 7.28).

The panel's conclusions hinged on the interpretation of the prohibition of 'unjustifiable discrimination' in the chapeau, which it examined in the light of 'the object and purpose of the WTO Agreement' of which GATT had become a part by that time (WTO, 1998b: paragraph 7.42). According to the panel, the GATT and WTO Agreements provided for a multilateral trading system whose rules 'create the predictability needed to plan future trade' (paragraph 7.44). Then, the panel argued:

> 'if an interpretation of the chapeau of Article XX were to be followed which would allow a Member to adopt measures conditioning access to its market for a given product upon the adoption by the exporting Members of certain policies, including conservation policies, GATT 1994 and the WTO Agreement could no longer serve as a multilateral framework for trade among Members as security and predictability of trade relations under those agreements would be threatened.' (WTO, 1998b: paragraph 7.45)

Although based on an interpretation of the phrase 'unjustifiable discrimination' in Article XX's chapeau, this conclusion was almost the same as that reached in the Tuna-Dolphin cases, even in its specific wording (cf. GATT, 1991: paragraph 5.27; GATT, 1994: paragraph 5.26). The panel did not explicitly address the issue of extraterritorial protection of values and it did not proceed to examine the specific exceptions in Article XX(b) and (g). Instead, it declared the unilateral US measures to be inconsistent with GATT/WTO law and called for multilateral agreements to protect sea turtles (WTO, 1998b: paragraph 7.55).

Under the new WTO dispute settlement mechanism, a panel ruling could be appealed against, an option the US exercised. The Appellate Body unequivocally denounced the methods of legal interpretation used by the panel, because the latter had disregarded the 'ordinary meaning of the words of Article XX' (WTO, 1998d: paragraph 6.115), had not taken into account that the chapeau is concerned with the *application* of measures and not their 'general design' (paragraphs 6.115-6.116), and because the panel had described the 'object and purpose' of the GATT 1994 and the WTO Agreement in 'an overly broad manner' (paragraph 6.116). Also, the Appellate Body held, the interpretation of the chapeau could differ according to the specific exception at issue (paragraph 6.120). As a consequence, the panel's interpretation 'renders most, if not all, of the specific exceptions of Article XX inutile ['useless,' S.P.], a result abhorrent to the principles of interpretation we are bound to apply' (paragraph 6.121).

Having thus demolished the panel's line of argument, the Appellate Body proceeded to examine, first, the specific exceptions in Article XX(b) and (g) and, then, the chapeau, only to arrive at a strikingly similar conclusion, although for different reasons.

Having determined that sea turtles fell under 'exhaustible natural resources' (WTO, 1998d: paragraphs 6.127 ff.), the Appellate Body refused to 'pass upon the question of whether there is an implied jurisdictional limitation in Article XX(g)' (paragraph 6.133). Instead, it was noted 'in the specific circumstances of the case before us, there is a sufficient nexus between the migratory and endangered marine populations involved and the United States for the purposes of Article XX(g)' (paragraph 6.133). Here, the fact that sea turtles migrate into and from US territory provided such a 'nexus.' In that respect, this case was less extreme than the Tuna-Dolphin case, in which the value to be protected lay completely on another territory. Still, the Appellate Body thought the nexus to be sufficient to justify the goals of the US measure, even if a large part of the values to be protected were still outside US territory. How exactly this new demarcation between a sufficient and an insufficient nexus is to be interpreted in other cases remains unclear, however.

The Appellate Body then had to decide on the question whether the US measure 'related to' the conservation of sea turtles. In doing so it did not refer to the 'primarily aimed at' formula that had informed the second Tuna-Dolphin panel. The Appellate Body recognised that the US measure 'is designed to influence countries to adopt national regulatory programs requiring the use of TEDs ['turtle excluder devices', S.P.] by their shrimp fishermen' (WTO, 1998d: paragraph 6.138). Unlike the second Tuna-Dolphin panel, it did not consider this to be incompatible with the 'relating to' requirement. Rather, the conclusion was that 'the means are, in principle, reasonably related to the ends. The means and ends relationship (...) is observably a close and real one (...)' (paragraph 6.141).

After having established that the trade measures were also 'made effective in conjunction with restrictions on domestic production or consumption' (the final requirement of Article XX(g)), the Appellate Body ended up at the chapeau, as the panel had. Here, the question was whether the US measures were 'applied in a manner which would constitute a means of arbitrary or unjustifiable discrimination between countries where the same conditions prevail.' The Appellate Body concluded that the measure actually did constitute a means of arbitrary and unjustified discrimination, because of :

> 'its intended and actual coercive effect on the specific policy decisions made by foreign governments, Members of the WTO. Section 609 [the contested US measure, S.P.], in its application, is, in effect, an economic embargo which requires *all other exporting Members*, if they wish to exercise their GATT rights, to adopt *essentially the same* policy (together with an approved enforcement program) as that applied to, and enforced on, United States domestic shrimp trawlers.' (WTO, 1998d: paragraph 6.161; emphasis in the original)

Interestingly enough, the Appellate Body did not attack the US statutory provision as such, but rather the way in which it was implemented by the US administration, which was much less flexible than the original provision as enacted by US Congress. It is unclear, however, whether the statutory provision as such would have been sufficiently flexible for the Appellate Body's standards. The main problem seems to be that the US measures require 'other WTO members to adopt a regulatory program that is not merely *comparable*, but rather *essentially the same*, as that applied to the United States shrimp trawl vessels' (WTO, 1998d: paragraph 6.163; emphasis in the original). Although this is not explicitly stated, this would seem to imply that a measure requiring only a comparable programme, would have passed the test.

Even in that case, however, the measure would have failed on a number of other points of criticism levelled by the Appellate Body. First, shrimps from countries without a sufficient regulatory programme that had nevertheless been caught with turtle-friendly methods, were not allowed into the US, which constituted another means of unjustifiable and arbitrary discrimination (WTO, 1998d: paragraph 6.165). Second, the US was deemed to have failed to pursue multilateral negotiations for the protection of sea turtles (paragraph 6.166 ff.). Finally, the US had discriminated against countries by using different phase-in periods (paragraph 6.173-6.174), by making different efforts to transfer the required technology to the countries involved (paragraph 6.175), and in the way the certification process was operated (paragraph 6.178 ff.).

Regulatory trade measures based on process standards and GATT Article XX

All in all, these four reports do not offer a clear and principled answer to the question whether regulatory trade measures can be used to protect values in other countries (except for the first Tuna-Dolphin report, which was clearly overruled by subsequent case law, however). The general consensus seems to be that the text of Article XX(b) and (g) does not preclude the protection of extraterritorial values *in principle*. On the other hand, however, all the reports have emphasised the detrimental effect of unilateral measures on the world trading system. All have, sometimes in differing but often in strikingly similar words, stated that unilateral measures to protect values in other countries may unevenly impair the rights of other exporting countries and could undermine the open and multilateral character of the GATT/WTO.

In their specific grounds for declaring a regulatory trade measure to be GATT/WTO incompatible, the reports differ. Actually, the grounds seem to have 'moved up' from a clear rejection of the possibility of the extraterritorial protection of Articles XX(b) and (g) (first Tuna-Dolphin report), via the denial of a sufficient 'relation' or 'necessity' (second Tuna-Dolphin report), to the claim of 'arbitrary or unjustifiable discrimination' as set out in the chapeau (the two Shrimp-Turtle reports).

Extraterritorial protection of values seems to be allowed if it is connected to the protection of values on the territory of the country imposing the measures (such as in the case of the migratory sea turtles). How strong this link should be remains unclear. If the value is located entirely outside a country's territory, the existence of such a connection may be more difficult to maintain, although the fact that a measure is aimed at changing another country's regulatory policies may not, in itself, be enough to lead to GATT/WTO incompatibility (as was argued in the second Tuna-Dolphin case; the Appellate Body's Shrimp-Turtle report, however, does not seem to support this position, but then the facts of the case were also somewhat different).

In the legal literature, it has been argued that these measures might be justified under GATT Article XX(a): the protection of public morals (cf. Harrop, 1997: 82; Van Calster, 2000: 13-15). The argument would then be that the values to be protected abroad give rise to such intense sentiments in the country imposing the regulatory trade measures, that the measures are necessary to protect the public morals in that country. Then, the eventual value to be protected would again be in the country using the regulatory trade measures.

This argument has never been used in an actual case before the GATT or WTO, but it is likely to fail. This interpretation of 'public morals' would stretch the meaning of the expression very widely. In practice it would mean that a country could protect any value it or its 'public opinion' deemed to be worthy of protection. It could then justify regulatory trade measures simply by referring to that public opinion. This interpretation is probably a little too far-fetched for a GATT/WTO panel.

Apart from the fundamental issue of the extraterritorial protection of values, GATT/WTO panels have increasingly strictly scrutinised the application of regulatory trade measures under the chapeau of GATT Article XX. The chapeau requires that 'measures are not applied in a manner which would constitute a means of arbitrary or unjustifiable discrimination between countries where the same conditions prevail, or a disguised restriction on international trade.' As the Appellate Body argued in the Shrimp-Turtle case:

> 'The task of interpreting and applying the chapeau is, hence, essentially the delicate one of locating and marking out a line of equilibrium between the right of a Member to invoke an exception under Article XX and the rights of the other Members under varying substantive provisions (e.g. Article XI) of the GATT 1994, so that neither of the competing rights will cancel out the other and thereby distort and nullify or impair the balance

> of rights and obligations constructed by the Members themselves in that Agreement.' (WTO, 1998d: paragraph 159)

A measure fails this test if it is applied indiscriminately to countries where different conditions prevail or if it is applied differently to countries where the same conditions prevail. This results in a number of requirements of 'due process' and 'reasonability' in the application of a measure. The blunt application of a measure, regardless of differences in environmental or economic conditions will therefore violate the chapeau, as will differential treatment of producers that face essentially the same conditions.

This line of reasoning also became clear in another case, which related to product standards. The US had formulated a legislative programme to reduce air pollution by limiting the content of petrol sold within the US. To determine the allowable concentrations of certain pollutants in petrol, the composition of petrol sold in 1990 was taken as a baseline. Domestic refiners were allowed to use individual baselines based on the petrol they themselves had sold in 1990. Foreign refiners, by contrast, had to use a uniform statutory baseline set by the Environmental Protection Agency (WTO, 1996b, under I B ff.).

The US justified this difference in application by two arguments. First, the use of individual baselines by foreign refiners would run into administrative problems, since it would be unfeasible to verify and enforce these individual baselines outside the US. Second, according to the US government, the mandatory use of the statutory baselines by US refiners would have been 'physically and financially impossible because of the magnitude of the changes required in almost all US refineries' (WTO, 1996a: paragraph 3.52).

Both arguments were dismissed by the Appellate Body. It argued that adequate techniques existed for the verification and enforcement of individual baselines abroad. To make these techniques work, the US government would (and, according to the AB, should) have had to enter into co-operative agreements with the governments of the foreign refiners. The failure to pursue such co-operative arrangements was now held against the US government.

The cost argument for not imposing the statutory baselines on US refiners was not accepted either:

> 'This may very well have constituted sound domestic policy from the viewpoint of the EPA [the Environmental Protection Agency, the governmental body that administered the contested regulatory programme, S.P.] and US refiners. At the same time we are bound to note that, while the United States counted the costs for its domestic refiners of statutory baselines, there is nothing in the record to indicate that it did other than disregard that kind of consideration when it came to foreign refiners.' (WTO, 1996b, under IV)

In this case, like in the recent cases discussed above, the purpose of the contested measure was not at issue: clean air was considered to be an exhaustible resource, which the regulatory programme was meant to protect. It was the implementation and administration of this programme, however, that led to unjustifiable discrimination between US and foreign firms, as well as the lack of co-operative endeavours on the part of the government imposing its standards. In applying the chapeau of GATT Article XX, the Appellate Body sought to balance the rights and obligations of the different parties to the dispute by scrutinising whether the contested measures led to unreasonable or unnecessary discrimination between exporting countries or between exporting countries and the importing country.

All in all, when it comes to imposing process standards to protect values in other countries, such measures will probably always run into severe legal problems if the regulatory trade measure requires one uniform set of standards to be applied in all target countries, or if the opportunities for multilateral action have not been exhausted. For both points of criticism it is not clear what exactly a country should do in order to avoid them. As to the latter point (multilateral action) it has been argued that unilateral action is often a prerequisite for reaching multilateral agreement, and GATT/WTO law is thus depriving countries of an important means to achieve this.

Whatever may be made of this argument, it has not been accepted in GATT/WTO case law. Although an analysis of this case law does not lead to an unqualified 'no' to the question whether regulatory trade measures aimed at protecting values in other countries are compatible with GATT/WTO law, to date no such measure has been found to be completely GATT/WTO consistent. Hence, when the import ban under the European leghold trap Regulation had entered into force, its chances of surviving scrutiny under GATT/WTO law would have been slim. How specifically an import ban would have run into problems will be discussed in the next subsection.

3.4.3 The European leghold trap Regulation and GATT Article XX

Above it was already concluded that an import ban under the European Regulation would have violated the GATT Article XI obligation. Two more questions were important for determining whether an import ban would have violated GATT/WTO law: whether an import ban fell under one of the purposes discerned in GATT Article XX and, if so, whether the application of the ban conformed to the provisions of GATT Article XX.

Starting with the first question, the applicable exception of GATT Article XX had to be determined. In its preamble, the European Regulation did not refer to animal welfare or the humaneness of leghold traps. The stated purpose of the Regulation was rather 'the conservation status of threatened or endangered species of wild fauna both within and outside the Community' (Recital 6 Regulation). Recital 5 referred to the Berne Convention on the Conservation of European Wildlife and Natural Habitats, but since this was a European agreement it could not be binding upon the US or Canada. The Regulation also referred to the adequate protection of wild species (Recital 7 Regulation), but it is not clear whether this related to protection in the sense of conservation or protection from suffering.

Consequently, the exception of GATT Article XX(g), which relates to 'the conservation of exhaustible natural resources' has to be considered first. The European Regulation would probably have failed to be covered by this exception as most of the species listed in the Annex, and thus to be covered by the import ban, were not endangered. Another argument could be that leghold traps could inadvertently catch threatened species, but in that case it is not clear why only the thirteen species in the Annex were covered by an import ban. Moreover, the EC would have had a difficult time in substantiating that endangered species were actually being caught in leghold traps and that this contributed significantly to their extinction, something Canadian conservation groups denied (EP, 1990a: 21-22).

Failing GATT Article XX(g), the EC could have tried to defend the Regulation under GATT Article XX(b), which makes an exception for measures 'necessary to protect (...) animal (...) life or health.' As the Regulation was aimed at reducing suffering by animals, it would probably have been covered by the 'animal life or health' formula.

As we saw above, however, this exception can only be used to protect animals in other jurisdictions under very limited circumstances. The possibilities seem to be somewhat wider under the Shrimp-Turtle criteria than under the Tuna-Dolphin cases, since the Shrimp-Turtle AB Report requires only a 'sufficient nexus' between the value to be protected by a measure and the territory of the country imposing the measure in order for that measure to come under Article XX(g).

It is unclear, but doubtful, whether this line of argument would also apply to Article XX(b). It is also unclear what exactly is meant by a 'sufficient nexus,' even in the Shrimp-Turtle case itself. However, even if a sufficient nexus were enough to qualify for Article XX(b), or the European Regulation were considered to fall under Article XX(g), there would probably not have been such a sufficient nexus as there was no animal migration of any sort between North America and Europe (which apparently was the determining criterion in the Shrimp-Turtle case).

The whole issue of extraterritorial protection could have been avoided if the Regulation had been covered by GATT Article XX(a), granting an exception for measures 'necessary to protect public morals.' In that case, the import ban would not have been defended as a tool to protect animals in other countries, but as a tool to protect European consumers from buying furs from animals caught by traps they disapprove of. As was argued above, however, this defence would rather stretch the meaning of GATT Article XX(a) and would probably have failed.

Even if a GATT/WTO panel had in principle accepted a defence under one of the exceptions of GATT Article XX, the measure would have had to conform to a number of fairly stringent requirements regarding its implementation. These criteria were mostly developed under case law in the late 1990s, although some criteria were also used in the Tuna-Dolphin cases. An import ban under the European Regulation would have failed these tests in a number of ways. First, an import ban would have violated these requirements if the E(E)C had not pursued multilateral negotiations on the protection of fur-bearing animals before introducing the ban.

Second, the European Regulation required an outright ban on leghold traps or the adoption of international standards. This amounted to requiring regulations that were 'not merely comparable, but rather essentially the same,' to cite a phrase from the Shrimp-Turtle AB Report, which would have violated an important criterion outlined in that report.

Third, the Regulation did not allow for differences in trapping standards between sub-national governments. As the regulation of trapping was a state/provincial responsibility in the US and Canada, this was a relevant issue. Likewise, the European Regulation did not foresee an exemption for furs that had been caught without leghold traps, but applied to all furs from countries that allowed leghold traps, regardless of whether the fur-bearing animal had actually been caught by leghold traps or not. Possibly, it could have been argued that this was justifiable for enforcement reasons, since it would have been very difficult to differentiate between furs caught in different types of traps, but that would have given rise to a complicated legal argument.

Finally, the European Regulation did not make any provision for alleviating the effects of the ban on trappers in Canada and the US and it did not make any distinction between trappers in different situations, even though the EP had repeatedly stressed the importance of taking the effects on aboriginal trappers into account. As a result, an import ban would possibly have been regarded as disproportionate to the ends it was meant to achieve.

Thus, an import ban based on the European Regulation would most probably have violated GATT/WTO law. This was true in the early 1990s, when the Regulation was adopted, but also in the second half of the 1990s, when much of the negotiations between the EC, the US and Canada took place.

3.5 Negotiating an agreement

3.5.1 The early initiatives

North American groups and governments had been involved in the European debate even before the Regulation was adopted. US animal protection groups had been involved in the UK labelling proposal and the EP calls for labelling, giving advice and helping to draft the proposals (Interview 17-1-2001, HSUS/AWI).

On the other side, the Canadian government actively opposed the UK labelling proposal, lobbying the UK government to withdraw it (Interview 15-2-2001, FIC). At this stage US groups and the US government were less involved. This is probably due to the Canadian government's increased awareness of this type of issue after the European seal ban, as well as the greater potential political costs of the proposals in the Canadian context. This pattern seems to have remained the same after the EP passed its Resolution, but when the European Commission proposed its import ban, US groups became active as well.

In 1990 and 1991, the (US) National Trappers Association (NTA) sent two delegations to Europe to lobby against the proposal. The main issue at that point was the EP proposal to require both a ban on leghold traps and adherence to international humane trapping standards for a country to be exempted from the import ban (NTA, 2000: 12; for the proposal, see EP, 1990b: Amendment 14). In the end, this proposal was not adopted by the European Commission and did not end up in the Regulation.

The Canadian government continued its lobbying efforts. It used a number of arguments, including the effects the ban would have on aboriginal trappers in Canada. Unlike the more technical arguments about traps and trapping, this argument caught on with politicians and groups in Europe alike. In its resolution (EP, 1989), the EP had already devoted attention to the position of aboriginal trappers and this had become one of the main issues in the legislative debate, as many felt that the traditional lifestyles of aboriginals should be preserved.

As a result, a prolonged debate arose over the role of trapping and leghold traps in aboriginal lifestyles. Opponents of the Regulation argued that the fur trade was essential for aboriginal communities and that the European Regulation aimed to kill that trade (Lynge, 1997). In addition to the economic importance of the fur trade, trapping was also argued to be an important part of aboriginals' cultural and spiritual worlds (Interview 9-2-2001, Canadian Mission/INAC).

Supporters of the European Regulation, by contrast, claimed that using leghold traps was not a part of aboriginal trappers' traditional lifestyles, but was 'imposed upon them' (AWI, 1990a). In addition, the 1989 EP Resolution stated that 'in Greenland the use of the leghold trap has been banned since 1938 and this has had no adverse effects on the traditional hunting practices of the indigenous peoples of Greenland' (EP, 1989: recital H).

Although most of the debate referred to aboriginals in general, the issue was further complicated by the different positions taken by various aboriginal groups and individuals. Aboriginals were represented in some of the Canadian delegations that travelled to Europe in order to lobby against an import ban, but Canadian animal protection groups were also joined by an aboriginal from the Native Animal Brotherhood who argued for the opposite. In the spirit of the debate, each side accused the other of using and even 'buying' aboriginals to defend its own case (Interview 22-2-2001, Animal Alliance).

In February 1990, before publishing its report on the Commission proposals, members of the European Parliament travelled to Canada at the invitation of the Canadian government, a decision that was heavily criticised by animal protection groups (EP, 1990a: 20). After the visit, the MEPs expressed concern about the effects of a European ban on aboriginal Canadian trappers, but also stated that they were convinced of aboriginal trappers' 'genuine desire to eliminate the leghold trap from native trapping and move to humane trapping methods that are in line with the indigenous peoples' traditional respect for animals' (EP, 1990a: 25).

In the end, the effect of aboriginal issues on European decision-makers is unclear. It probably contributed to the decision to plan the entry into force of the ban for 1 January 1995 rather than at an earlier date, in order to give aboriginal trappers more time to adjust (see EP, 1990a: 18). At the same time, both the EP, the Commission and the Council of Ministers agreed to the import ban as proposed.

3.5.2 The ISO process

When the proposed ban on leghold traps became an issue within the EP and the European Commission, the issue of trapping standards had already been discussed in the International Organization for Standardization (ISO) for a few years. Following a suggestion to that effect during the CITES Ministerial Conference of 1983, the Canadian government had taken the initiative to commence a standard-setting process at the international level (AWI, 1990c: 6; NTA, 1994: 16).

At that moment, the Canadian government had already worked on domestic trapping standards for just over a decade (see subsection 3.3.1 above). In 1987, ISO Technical Committee 191 ('TC 191') was established to formulate 'humane trapping standards.' Initially, it was mainly trappers and wildlife agencies from the major fur-producing countries that participated in this committee (NTA & Trappers' Alliance, 1995: 5).

Chaired by Canada, TC 191 had been working on trapping standards for about four years when the European Regulation was adopted. Because of the Regulation, the ISO process gained new significance. Apart from banning leghold traps straightaway, countries could also be exempted from the import ban if they conformed to 'internationally agreed humane trapping standards.' In recital 6 of the Regulation, explicit reference was made to the work being done in ISO, which the EC would 'take into account.'

Consequently, in the years after the adoption of the Regulation, Canada and the US devoted most of their efforts to achieving consensus within ISO. In those same years, animal protection groups became increasingly aware of the standards being developed, which some argued would result in overly lax standards (Interview 29-1-2001, DB). Around 1993, animal protection groups began to become active in the process as well.

They did so in two ways. First, some groups tried to gain representation in existing national delegations to TC 191. They were not greeted with great enthusiasm by the groups that had previously made up those delegations, but because of the representational rules which standard-setting organisations operate under they could often achieve representation anyway (Interview 17-1-2001, HSUS/AWI). Second, groups in countries that had not been active in TC 191 started to form national delegations in order to broaden participation in the standards process (this occurred for instance in the Netherlands; interview 29-1-2001, DB).

As a result, TC 191 experienced a considerable increase in interest from national delegations which took different positions from the countries that had previously been active in the committee. In response to the influx of countries with large input from animal protection groups, the older participants tried to involve countries that were likely to be more supportive of their position, such as the former Eastern European countries (Interview 29-1-2001, DB), but the balance of power had shifted fundamentally in the course of a few years.

Within the animal protection movement, groups were split as to the goal to be achieved in the process (Interview 29-1-2001, DB). Some groups wanted to participate in order to prevent the adoption of any trapping standards, which they felt would legitimise cruelty. Other groups were interested in achieving trapping standards, albeit more stringent ones than those that had been discussed, in order to achieve at least some improvement in animal welfare.

In terms of concrete trapping standards, animal protection groups and the new European delegations demanded the inclusion of pain and stress in the standards as criteria of humaneness, which North American trappers argued were not objectively identifiable. Moreover, animal protection groups argued for 'instant kill' as a standard for killing traps, which met with the same objections on the part of trapping groups (Interviews 15-1-2001, NTA; 29-1-2001, DB).

The sudden participation of new groups and countries in TC 191 brought the process to a grinding halt. When the new groups and delegations appeared, the older participants had come close to an agreement on the standards (AWI, 1993; NTA, 1994: 16; 2000: 12). This consensus among the older participants was disturbed by groups that brought an entirely new set of views and demands to the table.

In addition, animal protection groups started a more fundamental debate about the name of the standard. They argued that calling trapping standards 'humane' was an oxymoron and it would therefore be better to delete this word from the title of the standard (Interviews 17-1-2001, HSUS/AWI; 29-1-2001, DB). In the February 1994 meeting of TC 191, a majority of national delegations voted to delete the word 'humane' from the title of the standard and to continue to work simply on 'trapping standards' (AWI, 1994b; NTA, 2000: 12).

These events had two important effects on the process. First, positions became more polarised and mutual distrust permeated the discussions. The older participants saw the new efforts by animal protection groups as mere attempts to frustrate the process (NTA, 2000: 12; NTA & Trappers' Alliance, 1995: 5), while animal protection groups felt that the process was being actively manipulated against their views and interests (see e.g. AWI, 1992a; 1992b). Second, by deleting the word 'humane' from the title, it became doubtful whether adhering to the standard, once it was there, would qualify for an exemption under the European Regulation, which required adherence to 'internationally agreed *humane* trapping standards' (emphasis added). According to North American participants, in early 1995, the European Commission, which had an observer status at TC 191, conveyed the message that the ISO standards would no longer be sufficient.

Although the ISO process was to continue, agreement had become very unlikely, as a result of mutual distrust and an almost even balance between sides in TC 191. In September 1995, a final attempt was made to achieve consensus. Although an agreement may have been achieved between the heads of delegations (Interview 29-1-2001, DB), the attempt ultimately failed. As a result, the process of formulating trapping standards was terminated in September 1995 and it was decided to concentrate on a (less controversial) trap testing methodology instead (CEC, 1995h; NTA, 2000: 15). Since early 1994, Canada and the US had already shifted their attention to direct talks with the EC, however, and the debates on the European Regulation had taken a different route.

3.5.3 The negotiations between Canada, the US and the EC

Starting direct talks

As soon as North American trappers and officials became aware that the ISO process was not going to yield any results, they moved toward resuming direct contacts with the EC. In Canada, the government had been active from the beginning, but in the US the main activities had come from trappers and animal protection groups. In order to involve the US government in the process, the NTA started to put pressure on the United States Trade Representative (USTR) through various channels (Interview 15-1-2001, NTA).

It mobilised state wildlife agencies and governors to push for action at the federal level. Moreover, it organised a meeting for the Congressional Sportsmen's Caucus, a group of Members of US Congress who are interested in hunting, trapping and fishing issues. Together with the US Department of Agriculture (which was responsible for animal damage control), state wildlife agencies and their representative, the International Association of Fish and Wildlife Agencies (IAFWA), the NTA prepared a document to outline its position (for the process, see NTA, 2000: 12; the document is NTA, 1994). After the meeting, the NTA formed an industry coalition together with IAFWA, the Fur Information Council of America, and Louisiana's wildlife agency. Later they were joined by the association of US fur traders (NTA, 2000: 13 & 14).

As it was, the Sportsmen's Caucus was one of the largest caucuses in US Congress and the issue was taken up by a number of Congressmen from the states of Louisiana and Alaska, which were among the most important trapping states in the US. After a letter (Brewster et al., 1994) from and a meeting with the Congressmen, the USTR promised to start talks with the EC in order to achieve an agreement based on the work done in ISO, or else to start proceedings under the WTO, which would come into existence about six months later (recalled in another letter from Members of Congress, Stevens et al., 1994).

These initiatives were countered by letters from other Congressmen, who requested the USTR not to challenge a European ban before the GATT/WTO (Kerry et al., 1994; Lowey et al., 1994). They were vastly outnumbered by those who supported action against the EC Regulation, however, and their position did not influence the USTR.

A few months before these activities in the US, in April 1994, the Canadian government had requested consultations with the EC under the GATT, the first step toward a GATT dispute resolution panel, but these consultations did not yield any agreement between the two parties. Given the clear incompatibility of the European Regulation with GATT/WTO law, the US and Canada could at this point have waited for the ban to be implemented in order then to move to a GATT/WTO dispute.

For several reasons, however, a GATT/WTO dispute was an unattractive option for both the US and Canadian governments, as well as the EC (cf. Dale, 1996: 449-450). The US did not want to resort to the GATT/WTO because it did not want to be branded as 'anti-animal' (Interview 19-1-2001, USTR). It had just lost the Tuna-Dolphin cases, which had provoked an outcry from animal protection activists within and outside the US. Being on the other side of a similar dispute was probably not an attractive prospect.

Apart from this consideration of image, the Canadian government was also greatly concerned about the effects of even a temporary import ban on (aboriginal) Canadian trappers who relied heavily on trapping. As a GATT/WTO dispute was likely to take some time, the European market would have been shut off for at least some five years. After that period, much of the potential harm could already have been done, and it would have been difficult to regain the market once the ban had been lifted. Moreover, it would have been more difficult to overturn a ban once implemented than to delay its implementation. Finally, if the EC had refused to lift its ban, Canada would only have gained some retaliation rights. All in all, the Canadian government was primarily concerned about retaining market access for Canadian furs, something that could have been damaged by commencing a GATT/WTO dispute (Interview 29-9-2000, Canadian Mission).

At the same time, moreover, both the Canadian and US governments thought they could work out an agreement with the EC and the threat of a GATT/WTO dispute would be a useful tool in the negotiations (Interviews 19-1-2001, USTR; 29-9-2000, Canadian Mission). The EC was therefore requested to suspend the import ban for one year, as the Regulation allowed, which was done in July 1994 (EC, 1994a).

Because of the activities by the USTR and the Canadian government, DG I – the European Commission's Directorate General responsible for external relations, including trade – became actively involved in the issue. To DG I, the prospect of a GATT/WTO challenge was at least as equally unattractive as to the US and Canadian governments. It was clear that the EC would have lost the case, which would have been all the more embarrassing given the EC's own position in the Tuna-Dolphin case. As a result, DG I preferred negotiations to the unilateral imposition of the import ban.

The move toward a separate agreement

In the course of 1995, several meetings took place between Canadian, US and European officials. The issue was raised at several high-level meetings and the US and Canadian governments exerted considerable pressure on the European Commission, both DG I and XI, to modify the Regulation (NTA, 2000: 14). When, in February 1995, European officials stated that the ISO process would no longer be sufficient for an exemption under the Regulation, pressures also mounted to work on a separate negotiated solution (see e.g. Breaux et al., 1995a). At the same time, aboriginal delegations continued to visit Europe, and Denmark was reported to have requested a change in the Regulation in order to accommodate the concerns of aboriginal trappers (HNN, 1995).

By spring 1995, the EC (through DG I), Canada and the US agreed to negotiate a separate agreement on trapping standards, which would qualify for an exemption under the Regulation's import ban. In the following months, a working party was formed, which mainly consisted of technical experts who had also been involved in the ISO process. After a first meeting between experts from Canada, the US and the EC in September 1995, they were joined by a Russian delegation and they became known as the quadrilateral working party.

Since the import ban was to come into effect on 1 January 1996, time was running out for the countries involved. In May 1995, the Commission reported to the EP that 'certain fur countries' had requested a suspension of the import ban and that it was considering the 'consequences of the situation' (CEC, 1995a). Nevertheless, in response to a series of questions from the EP in June, July and October 1995, the Commission stated that the implementation of the ban would proceed as planned and that the talks with Canada, the US and Russia would not prevent it from coming into force (CEC, 1995b; 1995d; 1995e).

In December 1995, however, less than a month before the planned entry into force of the import ban, the Commission presented a proposal to modify the Regulation and postponed the import ban by one year. In a letter to the member states, sent on 8 December, DGs I (external affairs) and XXI (customs) informed them that the Commission considered the implementation of the ban to be 'for the time being unfeasible.' National customs authorities were therefore requested to 'refrain from taking any action at frontiers from the beginning of next year' (CEC, 1995g).

The proposal to modify the Regulation was presented together with this decision (CEC, 1995h). In the explanatory memorandum to the proposal, the Commission stated that it had 'carefully considered the effects import restrictions as of 1 January 1996 would have on the development of international humane trapping standards and on the Community's obligations under international trade rules.' As a result, the Commission proposed to postpone the import ban and to amend the Regulation 'so as to facilitate its implementation and to make such implementation more proportionate to its objectives.'

The proposed amendments consisted of replacing Articles 3 and 4 of the Regulation with new provisions that stipulated that the Commission would 'enter into or pursue negotiations with third countries in order to achieve a framework agreement on humane animal trapping standards' (proposed Article 3). By the end of 1996, the Commission would review the progress that had been made and assess whether a country had banned the use of leghold traps or 'made sufficient individual progress in the development of humane trapping methods' (proposed Article 4.1). Either would qualify a country for an exemption from the import ban. Moreover, exemptions were foreseen for furs and fur products 'resulting from trapping activities carried out by indigenous people' (proposed Article 4.4) and for furs and fur products from those sub-national jurisdictions (such as US states and Canadian provinces) which complied with the Regulation's requirements (proposed Article 4.5). All in all, these amendments would have given the Commission some leeway in negotiating an agreement with Canada and the US and in postponing the implementation of the import ban during those negotiations.

The European Parliament vehemently opposed the proposals. On 14 December, it adopted a resolution in which it stated that the Regulation could not be amended without consulting the European Parliament, it deplored the fact that the ban would not be implemented by 1 January 1996, and instructed its President to look into the possibilities of taking the Commission to the European Court of Justice for failing to implement the Regulation (EP, 1995b).

The report on the proposal, drawn up by the EP Committee on the Environment, was equally critical. The Report argued there was 'no need to discuss the Commission proposal at length: the present Regulation is appropriate and is in force but lacks implementation provisions' (EP, 1996a: 18). Subsequently, the Report completely revised the proposal, adding implementation provisions and deleting most of the Commission's proposed amendments, although taking into consideration some concerns about sub-national regulations and aboriginal trappers. On 19 June 1996, the EP adopted a number of amendments to the Commission proposal, to the effect that the import ban would enter into effect immediately. Exemptions could also be granted for regulations at the sub-national level or those adopted by aboriginal communities (EP, 1996b). As this was clearly unacceptable to the Commission, the Regulation remained as it was.

In the meantime, however, the status of the import ban had become subject to another internal EC dispute. In its December 1995 letter, the Commission had stated that it did not want to implement the import ban on 1 January 1996. Formally speaking, however, this was not a decision the Commission could take, since the Regulation did not allow for further suspensions of the import ban.

Taking this view, the Dutch government decided to implement the import ban unilaterally as of 1 January 1996 (Netherlands, 1995; 1996a). In an attempt to dilute the effects of this unilateral ban on the negotiations with Canada and the US, the European Commission reacted swiftly, arguing before the Dutch government that member states did not have an independent authority to implement the ban (CEC, 1996a). The Dutch government reacted, however, by stating that it considered the ban to have automatically come into effect now that the Commission had failed to determine which countries were exempted from the ban (Netherlands, 1996b). In a case before the District Court of The Hague, Canadian aboriginal trappers also challenged the unilateral ban, but their claim was rejected (Netherlands, 1996c).

Despite these frictions between the European Commission and the EP and the Netherlands, the talks with Canada, the US and Russia continued. On 20 June 1996, after the fourth meeting of the quadrilateral working party, the experts presented their results. Not much progress had been made, as each side had basically restated its position within the ISO process (NTA, 2000: 15 & 17). After the experts had finished their work, the Council of Ministers authorised the Commission to negotiate a framework agreement on humane trapping standards and formal negotiations began (CEC, 1997a: 2). In these formal quadrilateral negotiations, the initiative moved to the trade representatives, who had been there as observers during the previous meetings.

Negotiating an agreement

During a number of formal and informal negotiating sessions, negotiators from the four countries worked on a framework agreement with a technical Annex that would be elaborated by technical experts (Interview 29-9-2000, Canadian Mission). The EC delegation consisted of officials from DG I and DG XI, which shared the lead on this issue. The Canadian delegation was led from the Canadian Mission in Brussels and included officials from the Fur Institute of Canada, the Department of Foreign Affairs and International Trade, the Department of Indian and Northern Affairs Canada, as well as provincial governments. In the US, the USTR had the lead, while the technical input came from the USDA and experts from state wildlife agencies and IAFWA.

In all three of the above, the constitutional authority for setting trapping standards lay at a lower level, be it with member states, states or provinces. In Canada, this problem was overcome by involving provincial governments in the process and discussing proposed agreements with them (Interview 29-9-2000, Canadian Mission). In the US, IAFWA set up a group of representatives from wildlife agencies in various regions in the US, which discussed the process with state regulators (Interview 19-1-2001, IAFWA). In the EC, any agreement had to be approved by the Council of Ministers, after consulting the EP.

Although they were not official members of the delegations, trappers were involved in drafting the national positions in the US and Canada. Trappers remained active outside the formal negotiations, too, sending their own delegations to the EC and hiring a European consultancy firm to keep them informed of developments in the EC (Interview 15-1-2001, NTA). The NTA kept Congress involved through another briefing in July 1996 (NTA, 1996).

In the EC, business groups were not very actively involved in the process. Some trappers and fur importers did assist Canadian and US negotiators by providing them with information, but in general they were much less involved than European animal protection groups or North American trapper groups (Interviews 29-9-2000, Canadian Mission; 15-1-2001, NTA; 9-2-2001, Canadian Mission/INAC).

Animal protection groups were effectively excluded from the quadrilateral negotiations. Still, they tried to influence the process from the outside. North American and European animal protection groups informally contacted European officials, both in the European Commission and the member states (Interviews 29-1-2001, DB; 17-1-2001, HSUS/AWI). In addition, they sought to involve the general public in the issue, by running advertisements in European and US newspapers (AWI, 1996; HSUS, 1997).

Between June and December 1996, the quadrilateral negotiations made quick progress. Agreement was reached on a set of definitions and technical trapping standards. In addition, both sides wanted to include some other elements in the agreement. To Canada and the US, it was important that the standards would not just apply to them, but to the EC as well. This meant including some European species alongside the thirteen (mainly North American) species in the Annex to the Regulation. Canada wanted to ensure that Canadian fur would not again be banned on animal welfare grounds. As a consequence, a provision to that effect was included, overseeing the implementation of the agreement was put in the hands of a Joint Management Committee, and the agreement included a dispute settlement procedure (Interviews 29-9-2000, Canadian Mission; 9-2-2001, Canadian Mission/INAC). Moreover, Canada and the US did not want the agreement to prejudice their rights under the WTO Agreements.

To the US, a binding agreement was more difficult to accept than it was for Canada. Although the authority for trapping standards lay with sub-national governments in both countries, it would probably have been more difficult to have US states accept international standards than Canadian provinces. Several factors accounted for this. First, there were far more states in the US than provinces in Canada, making co-ordination much more difficult and rejection by one or a few states much more likely. Second, as was explained in subsection 3.3.3, a European import ban would have affected Canadian trappers more severely than US trappers, placing Canada in a worse bargaining position. Consequently, the US refused to sign a binding agreement, and went on to negotiate a separate, non-binding agreement with the EC.

The shifting position of the EC

Within the EC, there were clear conflicts of interest between DGs and member states. DG XI had always supported an import ban, but DG I was more concerned about the possibility of a trade dispute over a trade measure that clearly violated WTO rules as well as general principles which the EC had publicly professed. The European Commission was clearly confronted with a dilemma. On the one hand, it had legislation that required an import ban. A refusal to implement it would have led to a serious conflict with the EP, which had increasingly become a force to reckon with in the EC, as well as animal protection groups and a number of member states.

On the other hand, implementing the ban risked a trade dispute with the US and Canada. It is doubtful whether officials in DG I even wanted the EC to be successful in a WTO case over the Regulation. An extensive use of unilateral trade measures could undermine trade relations with the US and the development of a multilateral free trade regime. Traditionally, the EC had always opposed the US tendency to resort to unilateral trade measures and this had been an important issue in both the Tuna-Dolphin case and the Uruguay Round of negotiations over the WTO (Vogel, 1995: 114; Winham, 1998: 364). Thus, in a 1996 Communication to the Council and the EP on trade and the environment, the Commission had stated that 'the most effective way of dealing with international environmental problems is through international and multilateral agreements, not by unilateral trade measures' (CEC, 1996b: 22). The use of process and production method-related measures, such as the leghold trap Regulation, was explicitly rejected as well (CEC, 1996b: 14).

Within the EC, the strongest support for the Regulation came from the European Parliament, which had played an important role in initiating the Regulation and remained committed to its original intent. This support came primarily from the EP Committee on the Environment, Public Health and Consumer Protection, and a group of MEPs that was interested in animal welfare issues and was known as the Intergroup (comparable to a caucus in US Congress) on Animal Welfare.

Even within the EP, however, a remarkable shift can be seen in the way GATT/WTO law was looked upon. Although the Committee on the Environment had the lead on this issue, the Committee on External Economic Relations was always asked to give an opinion on proposals as well. In its earlier opinions, the Committee on External Economic Relations supported the proposed import ban and commented that 'measures aimed at prohibiting import of goods made from the fur of species trapped by this method [leghold traps, S.P.] and originating in countries that still use it are an effective means of creating pressure to speed up action to ban the leghold trap' (EP, 1990a: 30).

This position had reversed by 1996, when the Committee was asked to comment on the Commission's proposals to amend the Regulation. Even though the Committee still 'agree[d] to ban cruel and inhumane methods of capturing and killing animals' it now 'consider[ed] [it] necessary to establish internationally agreed humane trapping standards in cooperation with third countries' and 'insist[ed] on the necessity of the European Union to respect its international trade obligations, especially in the framework of the WTO' (EP, 1996a: 26). Therefore, the Committee on External Economic Relations supported the Commission proposal, while the Committee on the Environment and the EP as a whole rejected it.

Although this point of view never prevailed in the EP, it is further witness to the change in thinking about unilateral trade measures, and the leghold trap Regulation, within the EC's external trade community, if not among a majority of MEPs. In the end, however, the EP would not have to approve an agreement on trapping standards with the US and Canada, although it could use its political clout to affect the Commission's position and the outcome of the vote in the Council of Ministers, as it had done before.

Besides the shift in the general policy orientation of the EC, the locus of decision-making also shifted during the process. The Regulation had originated in DG XI and the EC's environmental community, but gradually DG I and the external trade community took over. DG I became involved in the issue when Canada and the US turned the Regulation into a trade issue. Then it became clear that the Regulation could have ramifications beyond the realm of animal welfare and could influence Transatlantic trade relations.

From this time, DG I became firmly involved in the issue and its resolution. Allegedly, the idea of negotiations between the EC, Canada, the US and (later) Russia came up in discussions with DG I (NTA, 2000: 14). Up to 1995, questions from the EP about the import ban had been answered by the Commissioner for Environmental Affairs, but from that time they were increasingly answered by the Commissioner for External Affairs (see for instance CEC, 1995a; 1995b; 1995d; 1995e). When the Commission decided to postpone the import ban in December 1995, the letter to the member states was signed by the Directors General for External Affairs and Customs, not the Environment (CEC, 1995g). Similarly, the letter to the Dutch government concerning its unilateral implementation of the import ban came from DG I (CEC, 1996a). Thus, the locus of activity on the Regulation within the European Commission had shifted considerably during the course of 1995.

Within the Council of Ministers, however, decisions on the Regulation were still being made in the Environmental Council. Among the member states, support for the Regulation varied. The strongest supporters were the UK, Austria (which had joined the EU in 1995) and the Netherlands. The UK and Austria were probably the staunchest supporters of all and the North American lobbying efforts were largely lost on them (Interview 9-2-2001, Canadian Mission/INAC).

The Netherlands represented many of the contradictions Canadian and US trappers resented. On the one hand, the Netherlands had one of the most active animal protection communities in Europe. Fur had been an issue since the early 1980s and hardly any fur products were sold in the country. The Netherlands was also the only EC member state to impose the import ban on 1 January 1996 (as was discussed above). At the same time, it was one of Europe's biggest trapping countries, albeit not for fur but for damage control. Using drowning traps, the Dutch government trapped over 300,000 muskrats a year in order to prevent them from undermining dykes (Crasson, 1996: 'The Netherlands,' at pages 3-4; FACE, 1999: V.6-7). The Netherlands was also one of the biggest fur farming countries in Europe, together with Denmark, although almost all fur was destined for exports. This combination of factors made the Netherlands particularly vulnerable to allegations of hypocrisy and the trapping of muskrats was a recurring theme in the debates (Interview 29-1-2001, DB). Nevertheless, the Dutch government supported the Regulation, as well as a stringent agreement with Canada and the US.

Other countries were also supportive of the Regulation, but less strongly so. These were the pivotal member states in that they could make the difference between the acceptance and rejection of an agreement, and they included most notably Germany and to a lesser extent Belgium. Together with the UK and Austria, Germany and one other small member state (be it the Netherlands or Belgium) could form a blocking minority in the Council of Ministers.

The southern member states were less supportive of the Regulation. Animal protection groups were much smaller there than in the north-western countries and some, like Italy and Greece, had important stakes in the wild fur trade. France was the EC member state with most trappers (together with the UK; see FACE, 1999: Annex IV, at page 36; different figures are reported in Crasson, 1996: 'France,' at page 2). It was also the only member state to have a special trappers' association (FACE, 1999: V.11). The Scandinavian countries did not feel very strongly about the issue either. In Denmark, this was compounded by the relationship it had with aboriginal trappers in its former colony of Greenland, which exerted considerable pressure on the Danish government (HNN, 1995).

All in all, the European Commission had to come up with an agreement that would satisfy a qualified majority of member states, at least include some of the original intentions of the Regulation and avoid a trade dispute with the US and Canada. The US and Canada both had a clear interest in avoiding a WTO dispute and an import ban, Canada more so than the US. At the same time, they wanted to use the EC's weaknesses to arrive at an agreement that would conform more closely to their own interests and that would cover the EC as well.

Finalising and ratifying the agreements

In December 1996, the EC, Canada and Russia initialled an agreement on humane trapping standards. The US was not willing to sign a binding agreement and separate negotiations continued between it and the EC. Nevertheless, a way out of the dispute with Canada seemed near and the Commission presented the proposed agreement to the Environmental Council (CEC, 1997a).

At this point, it became clear, however, that the proposed agreement would not be supported by a qualified majority of member states in the Environmental Council. In its meeting of December 1996, the Environmental Council demanded a better agreement and the implementation of the import ban by March 1997 if no improvements had been achieved (Council, 1996). More specifically, it demanded action on the standards for drowning traps, the implementation date and the inclusion of some terms relating to leghold traps (Interview 29-9-2000, Canadian Mission).

In an attempt to force a decision, the proposal was presented to the General Affairs Council, consisting of ministers for foreign affairs, in February 1997. Although an agreement could be adopted by either council, the General Affairs Council did not yet want to take a decision. Rather, it stated that the agreement left 'room for improvement on certain points' and asked the Commission to re-open the negotiations (Council, 1997a), although maintaining that the final decision would be made by the Environmental Council (Council, 1997b).

The EP, which would have to be consulted on an agreement, voiced its opposition to the proposed agreement, as well as the decision to schedule the agreement for the General Affairs Council (EP, 1997b). In a preliminary Report on the agreement, the EP Committee on the Environment argued that 'the Agreement fail[ed] both in terms of its animal welfare and trade objectives' (EP, 1997c).

The European Commission, probably concerned that the fragile consensus with the Canadian government would be lost, decided not to re-open negotiations over the standards in the agreement themselves. At the same time, however, the Canadian government was requested to make some additional concession that could guarantee acceptance of the agreement in the Council. In the end, this demand was met by a separate Canadian declaration that the country would prohibit the use of 'all jaw-type leghold restraining traps' for seven species at the entry into force of the agreement, and the use of 'conventional steel-jawed leghold restraining traps' for another five species at a later time (EC, 1998a: Annex IV; Interview 9-2-2001, Canadian Mission/INAC).

In June 1997, the proposed agreement, with the Canadian declaration, was brought back into the Environmental Council and the Commissioner for External Affairs, Sir Leon Brittan, called upon the environmental ministers to approve it (CEC, 1997f; 1997h). Bilateral contacts by the presidency of the EC (at that time the Netherlands), revealed that the agreement would still be rejected and that 'the matter would have to be considered further' (Council, 1997c).

A month later, the agreement was reintroduced in the General Affairs Council, thus completing the shift from the environmental to the trade arena within the EC. On 22 July 1997, a qualified majority of member states in the General Affairs Council finally adopted the proposed agreement (Council, 1997d). The formal signature was suspended until an agreement between the EC and the US would have been reached.

In the end, only the UK, Austria and Belgium opposed the proposed agreement. For the other two pivotal member states, Germany and the Netherlands, the proposed agreement probably represented the most that could be obtained from Canada without provoking a trade dispute. The Netherlands was in a more delicate position in that it was the EC's president in the first half of 1997 and therefore responsible for transferring the file to the General Affairs Council.

In the first half of 1997, as agreement with Canada and the US seemed imminent, the European Commission also took steps to implement the import ban. In January 1997, a certification regime was adopted (EC, 1997a). A proposed list of species and countries that were exempted from the import ban (CEC, 1997g) was adopted on 22 July 1997, together with the agreement with Canada and Russia (EC, 1997g). The list already featured Canada and Russia, but not the US, which was still negotiating a separate agreement with the EC.

The US had not been willing to agree to a binding agreement, like the agreement between the EC, Canada and Russia. The agreement between the US and the EC would therefore take the form of an 'agreed minute' that would not be binding on the parties. Apart from that, many of the issues between the EC and the US were the same as those in the EC-Canadian negotiations, as were some of the last-minute moves in the negotiations.

In November 1997, the General Affairs Council stated that 'the latest United States proposals in these negotiations were unlikely to be approved by the Community as they stood' and that 'if certain improvements were not made to the United States' proposals by 1 December 1997, the ban on imports of furs provided for in Regulation No. 3254/91 would apply to the United States from that date' (Council, 1997e).

In order to secure acceptance of the EC-US Agreement, the EC again required some reference to leghold traps. In the end, this was included in a side letter to the agreed minute, which stated that the use of 'all jaw-type leghold restraining traps' would be phased out for two species within four years of the agreement's entry into force; for all other species, the use of 'conventional steel-jawed leghold traps' would be phased out within six years (EC, 1998d, at page 35). The NTA claims that the latter pledge was agreed upon only in the final stages of the negotiations, when the agreement between the EC, Canada and Russia had already been accepted (NTA, 2000: 17-18).

Given the non-binding character of the EC-US Agreement, acceptance by the same EC member states that had supported the Agreement with Canada was not self-evident. The position of Germany was particularly crucial, as it could form a blocking minority together with the three member states that had opposed the agreement with Canada. On 10 December 1997, just days before the General Affairs Council meeting, the USTR wrote a letter to the German minister for foreign affairs, insisting that the US would implement the agreement even though it was not binding, expressing its concern that German opposition to the agreement would mean its defeat and pointing toward the likeliness of 'a serious EC-US trade dispute' if that were to happen (USTR, 1997).

In the end, Germany voted in favour of the EC-US agreement. It was approved by the General Affairs Council on 12 December 1997 (Council, 1997f) and signed on 18 December 1997 (CEC, 1997m). The day before, Canada and the EC had already signed their agreement (CEC, 1997l). The agreements still had to go to the European Parliament for an opinion. The EP's final legislative resolutions were straightforward: it rejected both agreements (EP, 1997e; 1997f; 1998). At this point, however, adoption of the agreements by the Council had become a formality. The agreement between the EC, Canada and Russia was formally adopted by the Council in January 1998 (EC, 1998a); the agreement between the EC and the US in July 1998 (EC, 1998d). The list of exempted countries was amended to include the US on 2 March 1998 (EC, 1998b).

The agreements evoked mixed reactions. US and Canadian officials felt they had obtained an important victory by avoiding a European import ban and by tying the EC to an agreement on trapping standards that had not been foreseen by the Regulation and which tied in with the existing work on trapping standards, at least in Canada (e.g. Interview 9-1-2001, Canadian Mission/INAC). North American trappers were more reluctant about the idea of having trapping standards imposed on them, but were generally happy that they had been able to avoid a European import ban (see e.g. Noseworthy, 1997; NTA, 2000: 18). Animal protection groups on both sides of the Atlantic were very disappointed with the outcome of the negotiations, either because they thought the standards were too weak or because they had hoped for an import ban in order to effect a complete ban on leghold traps (Interviews 17-1-2001, HSUS/AWI; 29-1-2001, DB; 22-2-2001, Animal Alliance).

3.5.4 The International Agreements on Humane Trapping Standards

The agreements between the EC, Canada and the US were similar in a number of respects, but different in others. In this subsection I will outline both agreements. Using language that is commonly used in the US, the EC-US agreement will be referred to as 'the Understanding on Humane Trapping Standards' or 'the Understanding.' The EC-Canadian agreement will be referred to simply as 'the Agreement.'

The Agreement between the EC and Canada (see EC, 1998a) consists of several parts. The basis is a framework agreement that sets out a number of obligations for both parties. The substantive trapping standards are elaborated in Annex I to the Agreement; Annexes II to IV deal with some additional specific issues.

The core of the framework agreement is Article 7, which stipulates the commitments of the parties to the Agreement. Article 7 requires these parties to establish certification procedures for traps (Article 7(a)), to prohibit the use of traps that do not meet the standards in Annex I (Article 7(c)) and to ensure that trapping methods on their territory conform to the standards (Article 7(b)). Article 10 lists a number of derogations from these commitments, which can be granted on a case-by-case basis. They include most notably 'protection of public and private property' (Article 10(b)), which would relate to certain forms of animal damage control, and 'traditional wooden traps essential for preserving cultural heritage of indigenous communities' (Article 10(d)).

Other provisions complement these core provisions. Article 8 deals with the implementation of the trapping standards, while Article 9 provides for ongoing trap research, and an evaluation of the standards three years after the Agreement's entry into force. Several provisions are included that stress the importance of co-operation between the parties and the exchange of information (most specifically Articles 6 and 11), while Article 12 foresees the mutual recognition of approved traps.

Article 13 provides that 'no Party may impose trade restrictive measures on fur and fur products originating from any other Party,' except for endangered species under CITES. Article 4 emphasises that the Agreement does not affect the rights and obligations of the parties under the WTO Agreements. In order to ensure the implementation of these provisions, the Agreement also establishes an overseeing mechanism, consisting of a Joint Management Committee ('JMC;' Article 14) and a dispute settlement procedure (Article 15; further elaborated in Annex III).

Annex I to the Agreement defines standards for both restraining and killing traps. For restraining traps, sixteen indicators are discerned (Article 2.3 Annex I). Two relate to an animal's behaviour in a trap (self-mutilation and excessive immobility); the other fourteen relate to injuries and range from fractures to amputations and death. At least 80% of animals on which a trap is tested should not show any of these indicators for a trap to be approved (Article 2.4 Annex I).

For killing traps, time-limits are set to loss of consciousness and sensibility. These limits range from 45 seconds for ermines to 120 seconds for marten, sable and pine marten and 300 seconds for all other species. At least 80% of tested animals should be unconscious and insensible within these limits (Articles 3.2 to 3.4 Annex I).

Part II of Annex I specifies the 19 species that are covered by the Agreement. Besides the 13 species covered by the European Regulation's import ban, these include six European species that were not covered by the European ban. Part III elaborates the methodology to be used in testing traps, while Part IV provides for a research programme. Apart from a general commitment to carrying out research, this part includes specific commitments for Canada to carry out studies on raccoon, Russia on sable and the EC on muskrats (Article 6.2 Annex I).

Annex IV to the Agreement contains declarations by Canada and the EC. The EC promises not to implement its import ban during the ratification of the agreement. Canada declares that it will prohibit 'the use of all jaw-type leghold restraining traps' for seven species at the date of entry into force of the Agreement, and the use of 'conventional steel-jawed leghold restraining traps' for another five species at a later date.

The main difference between the EC-Canadian Agreement and the EC-US Understanding (see EC, 1998d) is that the latter is non-binding. Rather than by a framework agreement, the Understanding's core is formed by an Agreed Minute, which reflects the non-binding nature of the agreed standards. The standards are said to constitute a 'common framework' (Points 1 and 2 Agreed Minute). The EC and the US 'intend to encourage and support research, development, monitoring and training programs by their respective authorities that promote the use and application of traps and trapping methods for the humane treatment' of the species covered by the Understanding (Point 4 Agreed Minute). However, the US 'does not by its endorsement intend to alter the distribution of authority within the United States for regulation of traps and trapping methods' (Point 3 Agreed Minute).

Like the EC-Canadian Agreement, the Understanding is not supposed to affect the parties' rights and obligations under the WTO Agreements (Point 6 Agreed Minute). Although the Understanding encourages the EC and the US to 'monitor and report on progress' (Point 5 Agreed Minute) and to 'consult with each other' (Point 7 Agreed Minute), it does not contain any other provisions on implementation or oversight, such as the EC-Canadian Agreement's provisions on a JMC, dispute settlement and domestic implementation.

The Annex to the Agreed Minute contains mostly the same standards as those in the Agreement's Annex I, both for restraining traps and killing traps (Articles 2.3, 2.4, 3.3 and 3.4 Annex). The Understanding will also apply to the same species (Article 4.1 Annex). The only difference between the two annexes is the absence of a section on trap research in the Understanding and, therefore, of specific research commitments as well.

In a Side Letter to the Understanding (EC, 1998d, at page 35), the US points out it will apply the standards to an additional ten species. This wider application was in line with the development of 'best management practices,' which had started some years earlier (see subsection 3.6.1 below). In addition, the US pledged to phase out the use of 'all jaw-type leghold restraining traps' for ermine and muskrats within four years, and the use of 'conventional steel-jawed leghold restraining traps' for all other species under the Understanding within six years after the entry into force of the Agreement between the EC, Canada and Russia.

These were the standards the US, Canada and the EC had agreed to. In the years following the adoption of the Agreement and the Understanding, the implementation of these standards began. In addition, a number of domestic developments took place in the area of fur-bearing animals. In the next section, both the implementation and these subsequent developments will be reviewed in order to examine the impact of the Agreement and the Understanding on domestic standards.

3.6 The Implementation of the Agreements and Further Domestic Developments

After the Agreement between the EC, Canada and Russia was signed, it was ratified by the EC on 26 January 1998 and by Canada on 1 June 1999. Technically, the Agreement would only enter into force after all three parties had ratified it, but in an agreed minute that had been attached to the Agreement, Canada and the EC had agreed to apply the Agreement between themselves pending the Russian ratification (EC, 1998a, at page 42). Likewise, the entry into force of the Understanding between the US and the EC had been made contingent upon the ratification of the Agreement by all three parties, but the US agreed to apply the Understanding together with the EC-Canadian application of their Agreement (Interview 8-12-2000, DG Trade).

Overseeing the implementation of the Agreement is in the hands of a Joint Management Committee (JMC), consisting of representatives from the EC, Canada and Russia. The US is also represented on the JMC as an observer. The JMC meets annually to discuss progress in the implementation of the Agreement (and the Understanding).

Research efforts in the US, which were started in a domestic standard-setting process in 1996, have been co-ordinated with Canada's trap testing programme and, to a lesser extent, Russia's. The US has concentrated on restraining traps, while Canada has focused on killing traps, and the two countries will use each other's results. Co-ordination of the research efforts takes place through semi-annual meetings of technical experts from both countries and Russia. In terms of research methodology, an agreement on a trap test methodology was reached in ISO TC 191 and these standards were released in November 1999 (ISO, 1999a; 1999b).

In addition to activities related to the Agreement and the Understanding, both the US, Canada and the EC experienced a number of domestic developments in the area of trapping and fur. In this section I will discuss both these domestic developments and the activities each country has undertaken to implement their international commitments in order to discover to what extent the international agreements have affected domestic regulatory standards.

3.6.1 Developments and implementation in the US

During and after the negotiation of the agreement with the EC, the US experienced a great deal of domestic activity in the area of trapping standards. During the 1980s, much of this activism had focused on the national level and there had been several attempts to have US Congress pass legislation to restrict trapping or ban the use of leghold traps. During the 1990s, bills aimed at banning the use of leghold traps were routinely introduced and reintroduced in every session of Congress. These initiatives never went beyond the committee stage, however. Animal protection activists estimate the number of members of Congress that support their cause at around 100 (Interview 17-1-2001, HSUS/AWI), while, according to the NTA, Congress' Sportsmen's Caucus includes 50 Senators and more than 230 Representatives (Interview 15-1-2001, NTA).

Anti-trapping activists came close to a partial victory when, in 1999, the House of Representatives passed an amendment to the Department of the Interior's appropriations bill that would have banned trapping in national parks. The concurrent amendment in the Senate was defeated, however (NTA, 2000: 29 and 31; Interview 17-1-2001, HSUS/AWI). All in all, anti-trapping activists were therefore not able to make much headway on the federal level. Similarly, it proved very difficult to have state legislatures pass legislation to ban trapping or leghold traps. In the 1980s, this had only happened in New Jersey (Fleishman-Hillard Research, 1999: 33).

As a consequence, US animal protection groups shifted their focus to states that allowed ballot initiatives. Such initiatives are allowed in 22 out of the 50 states, and during the 1990s, initiatives were put to the ballot in several states. This strategy proved much more successful. In 1994, an initiative was approved in the state of Arizona that banned most traps on public lands, around 83% of the state's total land area. In 1996, a ballot initiative to ban most traps was passed in Massachusetts (which had already banned most leghold traps in 1975), while voters in Colorado adopted a ban on leghold traps and snares. In 1998, California followed suit by passing an initiative to ban steel-jaw leghold traps, and in 2000, another ballot initiative was passed, this time in the state of Washington (Fleishman-Hillard Research, 1999: 35; Interview 17-1-2001, HSUS/AWI).

Trappers reacted by actively opposing initiatives that would restrict trapping. In February 1998, the NTA, together with a number of other associations, formed the Ballot Issues Coalition (BIC) to that end (NTA, 2000: 37). They were successful in the state of Oregon, where a ballot initiative to ban leghold traps was defeated in 2000 (Interview 17-1-2001, HSUS/AWI).

Apart from opposing initiatives aimed at restricting trapping, trappers also supported a number of initiatives to enshrine trapping in state constitutions or to make it more difficult for ballot initiatives on wildlife issues to be passed. In 1998, the Minnesota state constitution was amended by a ballot initiative stating that 'taking game [is] a valued part of our heritage that shall be forever preserved for the people,' while in Utah an initiative was adopted that required a two thirds majority at ballot initiatives relating to wildlife protection (Fleishman-Hillard Research, 1999: 36). In 2000, similar initiatives were planned for Arizona and Virginia (NTA, 2000: 37).

Through these initiatives and their success, the legislative battleground over traps and trapping shifted to the state level. By using the instrument of popular initiatives, anti-trapping groups were able to bypass wildlife agencies and legislatures and appeal directly to voters, a majority of whom were known to oppose leghold traps. This strategy was limited, however, by the fact that ballot initiatives were only available in a minority of states.

In response to increasing animal protection activism in the early 1990s, the US also started its own process of setting (voluntary) trapping standards, which became known as 'best management practices' (BMPs). Up until the 1990s, the US had lagged behind Canada in both trap research and the development of trapping standards (see subsection 3.3.1 above). As activism against trapping, and the use of leghold traps in particular, kept mounting, this position became increasingly untenable.

By the mid-1990s, wildlife agencies and their association, IAFWA, started to think about the development of trapping standards that could be used as guidelines by state regulators and that would improve the acceptance of trapping among the public at large. This process was mainly a reaction to domestic activism, as it was feared that traps and trapping would come under fire or even be outlawed in an increasing number of states (see IAFWA, 1997: 1-6). As a consequence, the standards have been developed with a close eye on public opinion as regards traps and trapping (see e.g. Fleishman-Hillard Research, 1999). The European Regulation formed an important catalyst for the process in that it alerted state regulators to the growing opposition to trapping and the necessity to act upon it (Interview 19-1-2001, IAFWA).

The BMP process started in 1996, at the time when the US and the EC were working on an agreement. Although the BMP process had partly been provoked by the European Regulation, it in turn made an important difference to the US position in those negotiations. Because wildlife agencies and IAFWA were now working on domestic standards, and they thought that those standards would be necessary even in the absence of trade restrictions, it was easier for the US government to agree to international trapping standards. In the end, the US even promised to apply the standards in the Understanding to an additional ten species, because the BMP process already included those species.

The BMP process was started and has been carried out by IAFWA together with state wildlife agencies. Responsibility for the implementation of the EC-US Understanding lies with the Fish and Wildlife Service (FWS), part of the US Department of Agriculture. The FWS provides the funds for the development of the BMPs, but the actual research has been carried out by IAFWA.

Trappers have been closely involved in the BMP process through the NTA. They have actively participated in discussions about the design of the BMP research and its results (Interview, 15-1-2001, NTA; NTA, 2000: 26-28). Animal protection groups have been largely excluded from participation, as IAFWA feels they would use the process to prevent BMPs from coming into existence (Interview 19-1-2001, IAFWA). As a result, animal protection groups have only had access to limited information from parts of the research that were funded by the federal government (Interview 17-1-2001, HSUS/AWI).

At the same time, however, co-operation between the NTA and the wildlife agencies represented by IAFWA has been marked by slightly different agendas as well. Although trappers have traditionally been the primary constituency for wildlife agencies, the agencies see the BMP process as essential for dealing with the sentiments of a wider public, including animal protection groups, which are increasingly viewed as part of the agencies' constituency as well. Trappers, on the other hand, have often been more reluctant to support a process that threatens to discourage the use of traps they find useful and legitimate.

As a consequence, part of the BMP process' results have been treated confidentially by IAFWA to prevent outcries not only from animal protection groups, but from trappers as well (Interview 19-1-2001, IAFWA). On the part of the trappers, this has given rise to increased distrust and frustration with the process (NTA, 2000: 27-28). Still, the participation of the NTA in the BMP process continues to date and the first BMPs are scheduled to be released in the coming years (see also IAFWA, 2000).

3.6.2 Developments and implementation in Canada

Canada's trap research under the Agreement with the EC (and Russia) was in line with its domestic trap research programme, which continued in the second half of the 1990s. The programme was carried out by the Fur Institute of Canada. The federal government is involved by funding 50% of the costs of the research programme through Environment Canada's Canadian Wildlife Service.

The standards in the Agreement and the results of the trap research will be implemented through the adoption or revision of national standards on killing, restraining and submersion traps. In 1996, the Canadian General Standards Board (CGSB) published a national standard for killing traps, which itself was a revised version of an earlier standard (CGSB, 1996). As of early 2001, the standards for restraining and submersion traps were still being debated, but much of the Canadian trap research had already been carried out. The bans on certain types of leghold traps for certain species that Canada had agreed to in the final phase of the negotiations with the EC was due to be implemented for the 2001/2002 trapping season (Interview 15-2-2001, FIC). Similarly, provinces may have to change their regulations to conform to the national standards once they are published, but as for now it is unclear whether this will require significant changes.

Apart from participating in the CGSB's national standards process, animal protection groups were also active on the legislative front. Like in the US, it proved very difficult to achieve changes through legislatures, both at the federal and provincial levels. In contrast to US groups, Canadian groups did not have the option of introducing ballot initiatives in order to impose bans at the provincial level.

The strategies of Canadian animal protection groups have therefore focused on two other points. First, they have campaigned for or against candidates in specific ridings (voting districts for the Canadian parliament). Support for animal protection groups is typically too small to have an impact on election results across the board in an electoral system that uses districts, like Canada's. Animal protection groups (as well as some environmental groups more generally) have therefore targeted a smaller number of candidates who are important as regards the issues which these groups advocate (Interview 22-2-2001, Animal Alliance; Environment Voters, 2001).

Second, efforts have been directed towards cities. Some provinces generally allow municipalities to regulate trapping, while in others, municipalities can request specific authorisations to do so. This possibility has given rise to a campaign to ban 'urban trapping,' which was initiated by Canadian animal protection groups (Animal Alliance, CAHT & HSUS, 1999a). Like in some US campaigns, these efforts focus mainly on highly urbanised areas as a stepping-stone toward more comprehensive bans.

Despite these changes in strategy, the domestic political process seems to have developed differently from that in the US. The emphasis has been more on the standards process, which is older than the US BMP process and, being a formal standards process, involves a wider variety of groups. Legislative initiatives have been more difficult to achieve and have therefore played a smaller role.

3.6.3 Developments and implementation in the EC

As was shown above, the institutional balance within the European Commission had shifted from DG XI/Environment to DG I/Trade during the negotiations on the leghold trap Regulation with Canada and the US. Having started as an environmental measure drafted by DG XI, DG I had gradually moved in. By the time the Agreement and the Understanding had been adopted, the issue had thus largely been transformed into a trade issue.

In addition, the emphasis had shifted from banning leghold traps to conducting trap research and setting standards for all traps – not just in Canada, the US and Russia, but also in the EC itself. The EC and its member states had much less experience in conducting trap research than Canada and the US, so the fulfilment of the EC's commitments would require a number of new initiatives rather than the continuation of existing processes.

Within the European Commission, no DG was the one logical locus for these responsibilities (Interview 8-12-2000, DG Trade). In principle, DG XI/Environment would be the most logical DG to be responsible for this issue, since the Regulation was initiated there and the process had now moved back to substantive issues of animal welfare. The main tasks of DG XI in the field of animals related more to conservation than to animal welfare, however, and by the end of the negotiations DG XI had probably lost most of its interest in the issue of trapping altogether.

Another possibility was DG VI/Agriculture, which was responsible for animal welfare in the farm sector. This responsibility was clearly connected to agriculture, however. Moreover, in 1999 responsibility for the Scientific Committee for Animal Welfare was shifted to the newly formed DG Sanco (health and consumer protection), tying it even more closely to issues of human health and food safety. Finally, if the emphasis were to be laid on traps as products, DG Enterprise could also have been considered, responsible as it is for the internal market in many products.

As it was, no DG really felt responsible for the file and it therefore remained where it was: with DG I, later DG Trade. DG XI/Environment commissioned a study on trapping practices in the EC (FACE, 1999), but did not engage in the other responsibilities under the Agreement. DG Trade represented the EC on the Agreement's JMC and issued a tender for the muskrat study which the EC was required to do under the Agreement's terms. No eligible candidate could be found, however (Interview 8-12-2000, DG Trade).

As a result, the EC has not yet taken any steps toward implementing the Agreement and the Understanding, other than the study commissioned by DG Environment (JMC, 2000). As to the research commitments, Canada has offered to conduct the muskrat study for the EC (Interview 15-2-2001, FIC). This still leaves the issue of implementing the trapping standards that are to come out of the Agreement's standard-setting process, which would probably require the adoption of a Regulation or Directive through the EC's legislative process.

The second half of the 1990s also saw a great deal of activity in the related area of fur farming. After campaigns by animal protection activists, fur farming had already been reduced in the UK. In the Netherlands, which had a sizeable fur farming industry almost exclusively for export purposes, the industry had gradually become subject to more stringent regulations. Finally, fur farming was prohibited in the UK in November 2000 (MAFF, 2000; UK, 2000). In January 2001, the Dutch government announced that it would also ban fur farming within ten years (Dutch Government, 2001). Both initiatives were explicitly based on ethical rather than animal welfare considerations. The issue of fur thus continued to arouse strong feelings in some of the EC member states, as the focus of animal protection activists had moved from trapping to fur farming. Other EC member states voiced their opposition to the UK and Dutch proposals, so the issue is likely to return to the EC's agenda as well (cf. Staatscourant, 2001).

3.7 Conclusions

In the previous sections I have outlined the European leghold trap Regulation and its impact on trapping standards in the US and Canada. An overview of the main events in this process is provided in table 3.1.

In this concluding section I will bring together various elements from the analysis in order to answer two questions: has a California effect occurred, and what factors have contributed to this outcome?

3.7.1 A California effect or not?

For a California effect to occur, two conditions have to be met. First, a strengthening of standards needs to have taken place, which requires a comparison between domestic standards before and after the process. Second, if a strengthening of standards has occurred, it needs to be the result (at least in part) of the European Regulation, which requires a distinction to be made between the domestic and international sources of regulatory change.

In both Canada and the US, the authority to set trapping standards lay at the subnational level, with provinces/territories and states respectively. At that level, the regulatory situations in Canada and the US varied when the European Regulation was adopted (see subsection 3.3.1 above). In Canada, the provinces of Ontario and British Columbia had more stringent regulations than the other provinces or the territories. No province had adopted a ban on the use of leghold traps and some provinces hardly had any standards relating to the humaneness of traps at all. In the

	In the EC	In Canada	In the US	At the international level
1983	EC ban on imports of puppy seal skins			
1983		Creation of the Fur Institute of Canada		
1987				Creation of ISO TC 191
1988	EP adopts written declaration			
1990		The first national standard for killing traps is passed		
1991	Adoption of Regulation 3254/91			
1991-1994				Tuna-Dolphin cases under the GATT
February 1994				The term 'humane' is voted out of the ISO standard's title
April 1994		Request for consultations under GATT		
Middle of 1994			USTR approaches the European Commission	
Late 1994			Successful ballot initiative to ban leghold traps in Arizona	
1995	US, Canada, EC (and Russia) start talks on a separate agreement			
1996			Start of the BMP process; successful ballot initiatives in Massachusetts and Colorado	
July 1997	EC-Canadian agreement is approved by the EC's General Affairs Council			
December 1997	EC-US Understanding is approved by the EC's General Affairs Council			
1998				Shrimp-Turtle panel and AB reports under the WTO
2000-2001	The UK bans fur farming; the Dutch government announces a ban			

Table 3.1: Main events in the leghold trap process

US, a few states had banned leghold traps or restricted their use. In the vast majority of states, however, the use of leghold traps was still allowed. Most states had adopted at least some trapping standards, but these varied considerably.

At the federal level, no formal standards had been adopted in either country. In Canada, however, a national standard-setting process had been started in the mid-1980s, and Canadian efforts in trap research dated back at least to the early 1970s. In the US, much less work had been done in the way of either trap research or formulating trapping standards.

The baselines for comparison therefore differ between the two countries. For each country, I will now summarise the situation by the end of the process (at least, until early 2001) and assess whether a strengthening of standards has taken place, as well as the extent to which such a strengthening has been the result of the European Regulation.

Canada agreed to a binding agreement with the EC that contains technical standards for traps. All traps that are used for the nineteen species covered by the Agreement will have to conform to those standards. At the moment, these standards have not yet been implemented, but when they are they will be somewhat more stringent than existing national standards in Canada (Interview 22-2-2001, Animal Alliance). As a result, the Agreement between Canada and the EC will result in a strengthening of trapping standards in Canada. Since the Agreement is a direct consequence of the European Regulation and its potential trade effects, it is a clear example of a California effect.

In addition, Canada agreed to a prohibition on the use of leghold traps for certain species. Formally speaking, this is a strengthening of standards, too. It is likely, however, that leghold traps were hardly used for these species anyway and that the Canadian declaration was more of a symbolic gesture at the end of the negotiations than a substantive concession (Interview 9-2-2001, Canadian Mission/INAC).

Apart from the changes as a result of the agreement with the EC, some initiatives have been taken at the local level. So far, these initiatives have been few and far between. They reflect changes in Canada's domestic political debate and the strategies followed by Canadian animal protection groups. There is no indication that these changes are related to the European Regulation, neither in a direct nor in an indirect manner, so they cannot count as examples of a California effect.

The US agreed to a non-binding Understanding with the EC. The substantive standards in the Understanding are identical to those in the EC-Canadian Agreement. When implemented, these standards will probably mean a strengthening of trapping standards in most US states, although to a lesser extent for the few states that have already banned or severely restricted the use of leghold (or other) traps than for others.

The Understanding was adopted after the US had started its process to formulate best management practices (BMPs). The Understanding therefore hardly means a strengthening of standards in comparison to the standards that would have come out of the BMP process. The BMP process itself, however, is also partly a consequence of the European Regulation and the threat of an import ban. Although the BMP process was primarily developed to address domestic concerns among US animal protection groups and citizens, the Regulation operated as a 'wake-up call' for many US wildlife agencies and IAFWA. In that sense, the BMP process is also partly the result of the European regulatory trade measure.

By early 2001, no BMP had yet been released. The eventual effects of the BMP process were still uncertain and would much depend on both the standards resulting from the studies and the extent to which states choose to adopt these standards. Animal protection groups are generally sceptical about the likely changes the BMP process will make (Interview 17-1-2001, HSUS/AWI). Others think that the BMP process will make a significant change (Interview 19-1-2001, IAFWA), although in some states the BMP standards may result in the return of traps that had previously been banned (Interview 15-1-2001, NTA).

All in all, the final outcomes of the BMP process are still uncertain. Still, to the extent that these outcomes will strengthen trapping standards at the state level, they are related to the European Regulation and import ban, both directly (through the Understanding) and indirectly (as a catalyst for the BMP process).

Apart from the BMP process, the US witnessed a great deal of activism at the state level through the use of ballot initiatives. In the 1990s, ballot initiatives to ban leghold traps, completely or on public lands, were adopted in four states, and one state adopted a ballot initiative that severely restricted trapping in general. These changes form a clear strengthening of standards, but they do not seem to be related to the European Regulation. They reflect changing strategies and possibly increased political sophistication on the part of animal protection groups, who have sought to tap into the public opposition to leghold traps in certain states. These changes in strategy do not seem to be related, directly or indirectly, to the European Regulation or the threat of an import ban, so these developments cannot count as examples of a California effect.

Overall, a California effect seems to have taken place in both Canada and the US. The effect is different in the two countries, however. In Canada, the threat of an import ban has led to a binding agreement that was largely in line with existing domestic regulations. The substantive standards seem to have been strengthened, however, as a result of the Agreement. The US agreed to a much weaker agreement, in that it is non-binding and depends on voluntary compliance by states. Changes in substantive standards are still unclear and will probably be smaller across all states than across all Canadian provinces. On the other hand, the European import ban did give an impetus to the development of national standards and a national trap research programme, something which had been absent in the US until the mid-1990s.

In addition to the impact on the US and Canada, the agreements resulting from the European Regulation may also mean a strengthening of trapping standards in the EC. The Regulation prohibits the use of leghold traps, which is both wider and narrower than the standards in the Agreement. It is wider in that it bans all leghold traps, not just those that do not meet certain standards; it is also narrower in that it does not restrict the use of other types of traps, which the standards in the Agreement cover as well.

When those standards are implemented in EC law, this will probably mean a considerable strengthening of trapping standards in most EC member states. As of the beginning of 2001, however, the implementation of these standards still seemed remote. The European Commission has not yet established an effective organisational framework for the implementation of the Agreement. Once this is done, an EC Directive or Regulation will have to be drafted to adopt the standards EC-wide and the draft will have to go through the EC's legislative procedures. Despite these caveats, this issue shows an interesting phenomenon, and one that is absent from the other three issues: not only did the EC's regulatory trade measures result in a strengthening of standards in the US and Canada, they may also lead to a strengthening of the EC's own trapping standards as a result of the negotiations with Canada and the US.

3.7.2 Explaining the outcomes

How can the outcomes of these two cases, as discussed in the previous subsection, be explained? Such an explanation would have to account not only for differences between the Agreement and the Understanding, but also for their similarities. Both countries accepted the negotiation of trapping standards as a solution to the dispute and in the end both countries accepted identical standards. Moreover, both countries promised to phase out certain types of leghold traps for certain animals in an attempt to assuage European opposition to the proposed agreement. The main difference between the Agreement and the Understanding is the binding character of the former and the non-binding character of the latter. Although an important difference in terms of the California effect, it was by no means self-evident that the US and Canada should both arrive at an agreement on trapping standards with the EC in the first place.

In this subsection I will seek to explain these outcomes using the hypotheses drawn up in chapter 2. In that chapter, it was argued that the political balance in another country can be affected in three ways: through constraints, through preferences, and through participation expansion. A number of hypotheses were formulated about the conditions under which each was likely to take place.

Changing constraints

Four hypotheses were formulated in relation to constraints. First, it was hypothesised that *a regulatory trade measure or a retaliatory measure will have a greater effect on another country's political balance, the greater that measure's effect on the other country's exports*. Both the US and Canadian wild fur industries relied to a great extent on the European market, either directly (through sales of products in Europe) or indirectly (through the European fur processing and fur fashion industries). The threat of a European import ban therefore had significant potential economic consequences for trappers and fur producers in the two countries.

This seems to explain why the US and Canadian governments were compelled to reach an agreement with the EC that would guarantee continued access to the European market. Because of the enormous potential impact of a European ban, this was an issue neither government could easily ignore. Thus, the size of the trade effects seems to have conditioned the necessity to react to the threatened import ban and the willingness to reach an agreement on the part of the US and Canadian governments.

At the same time, this case shows the difficulties in assessing the size of trade effects when an industry shows an intricate web of exports and imports in various stages of the production process. Then, it becomes increasingly difficult to distinguish exports to, for instance, the EC from exports in general. Moreover, whether an export market is seen as 'important' becomes as much a strategic decision as a matter of arithmetic.

Although the size of the trade effects may explain the willingness to reach an agreement, it does not explain the specific reaction of the two countries and the agreement that was eventually reached. More specifically, it does not explain why the two countries chose to negotiate an agreement on trapping standards rather than to ban leghold traps, which would also have guaranteed access to the European market.

Neither the US nor Canada retaliated or threatened to do so directly. They did use the threat of resorting to the WTO, however, which could have resulted in retaliation once the case had been won. Indirectly the US and Canadian threat to resort to the WTO can also been seen as an attempt to change constraints on European actors. This would explain much of the difference in the outcomes between the Canadian and US cases, since the US had much more credible means of retaliation in its relationship with the EC.

The threat to resort to the WTO may have changed the constraints on some players, especially by the end of the negotiations, when the Netherlands and Germany were persuaded to support the Agreement and the Understanding in the General Affairs Council. Still, the size of any retaliation would have been limited and it did not feature in any of the debates within the EC. Moreover, as will be explained below, the effect of the threat to resort to the WTO was as much an example of participation expansion and of the role of WTO law in argumentative processes as of a change in constraints.

The second hypothesis relating to constraints stated that *a regulatory trade measure or a retaliatory measure will have a greater effect on another country's political balance, the more that measure's effects are targeted at pivotal actors in the other country*. This may explain much of the differences between the Agreement and the Understanding. In Canada, the potential impact of a European import ban was targeted more closely on a politically significant group than in the US, which increased the potential political costs of an import ban for the Canadian government. Relatively more Canadian than US trappers relied on trapping for their incomes or livelihood. In addition, these trappers were mainly to be found among aboriginals, who generally played a more important role in Canadian than in US politics. As a result, the consequences for aboriginal trappers tended to play an important role in determining Canada's position. This was reinforced by the previous experience Canada had had with the European ban on seal skins, an experience the US had not had. As a result, the costs of not reaching an agreement (and the EC implementing an import ban) were higher for Canada than for the US, which weakened Canada's bargaining position vis-à-vis the EC.

According to the third hypothesis relating to constraints, *a regulatory trade measure will have a greater effect on regulatory standards in the target country, the lesser the costs of complying with that measure for actors in the target country.* In both Canada and the US, the costs of banning leghold traps were much higher than the costs of adopting trapping standards. In Canada, an agreement on trapping standards tied in with existing work and would potentially only require incremental changes to existing regulations. In the US, once it was decided to start work on BMPs, this was also the case.

This may explain why both countries chose to negotiate trapping standards rather than banning leghold traps. Yet, as will be discussed below, this probably also had a lot to do with deeply-held values and perceived problems among government officials and trappers in the two countries.

The fourth hypothesis relating to constraints stated that *a regulatory trade measure will have a greater effect on regulatory standards in the target country, if it is supported by both public interest groups and domestic producers in the initiator country.* This hypothesis points to the role of Baptist-bootlegger coalitions in increasing the credibility of a regulatory trade measure. In the leghold trap issue, Baptist-bootlegger coalitions do not seem to have played an important role. In general, there is no evidence of strong involvement by the European fur industry and the interviews on both sides of the Atlantic confirm this assessment.

The role of European fur farmers is an interesting one in this issue. From the perspective of my theoretical framework, European fur farmers were 'domestic producers' and consequently they could have supported the import ban as a way to keep out foreign wild furs. Some North American officials certainly suspected a protectionist interest on the part of the fur farming industry (Interview 29-9-2000, Canadian Mission).

Whatever tacit support fur farmers may have given to the import ban, they certainly do not seem to have been actively involved in the adoption of the European Regulation and they did not openly speak out in favour of the import ban. Fur farmers were involved in, for instance, the Dutch working group for ISO TC 191, but their participation seems to have been informed more by a desire to improve the image of fur than by outright protectionism (Interview 29-1-2001, DB).

In the early 1990s, fur farmers therefore seem to have been fairly uninvolved in the issue, although they have been reported to have advised US trappers to get rid of leghold traps in order to safeguard the industry's image in the late 1980s. This changed in the second half of the 1990s, however, as fur farming itself began to be attacked more seriously in a number of countries, and the International Fur Trade Federation (IFTF) stepped in in support of the trappers. During that same period, US hunters, who had lobbied for bans on leghold traps in the 1920s and 1930s and had not been very involved in the debate in the early 1990s, also became more supportive of trappers (Interview 15-1-2001, NTA).

The reason why both groups abandoned opposition to certain traps and even came out in support of trappers, was that the issue of trapping had a strong symbolic significance and had become part of much wider campaigns against fur and the harvesting of (fur-bearing) animals. Both fur farmers and hunters feared, probably quite correctly, that their activities would be next to come under siege. As a result, the debate on trapping and leghold traps became part of a much wider debate on the use of fur-bearers, in which fur farmers and hunters could no longer afford to ignore or even attack trapping as they had done previously, even if such attacks had been in their short-term interests.

Changing preferences

The second set of hypotheses was related to preferences. The first hypothesis under this heading stated that *a regulatory trade measure will have a greater effect on regulatory standards in the target country, the more it ties in with deeply-held values and perceived problems in the target country.* This probably played a very important role in this issue. In both Canada and the US, a ban on leghold traps was considered to be an unacceptable outcome. However, as was discussed above, trapping standards fitted in well with existing processes in Canada, and later also in the US. Whereas the impact of a European import ban conditioned the *willingness* to find a solution, the existence of a tradition of trap research and trapping standards seems to have conditioned much of the *substance* of the eventual outcomes in this case.

This is probably so for a number of reasons. First, it was more convenient for officials in Canada and the US to work with trapping standards, since they had already used the approach before. Second, using trapping standards as a solution made the outcomes look less like something that had been imposed by the EC, which also contributed to their acceptability. Third, finding a solution in line with existing work required a much smaller realignment in domestic coalitions than a different course of action would have required. Because work on trapping standards had been done, most interested groups already supported the concept and efforts only had to go into convincing them to accept changes within that approach. In the US, this was less so before the BMP process was started, but once US wildlife agencies and, to a lesser extent, trappers had decided to go ahead with this approach, the same dynamics may have been at play as well.

As was argued above, this may partly have had to do with the costs of complying with trapping standards as compared to the costs of complying with a ban on leghold traps. This is probably only part of the explanation, however. A ban on leghold traps also ran counter to the ideas which US and Canadian trappers and many wildlife officials had about trapping and animal welfare. In both countries, the use of leghold traps had been the subject of debate between trappers and animal protection groups. The debate over this issue was characterised by intense controversy and polemic, in which a ban on leghold traps had become tied to an animal rights position, at least in the eyes of trappers and many officials.

Since the European Regulation had been supported by animal protection groups in Europe and the US, it became part of this controversy and quickly became associated with an animal rights position. This made the European Regulation and a ban on leghold traps based on it much more difficult to accept for US and Canadian trappers and officials. Therefore, the nature of and positions in the domestic political debates in the US and Canada conditioned the way in which the European Regulation was interpreted and reduced its acceptability among important actors in both countries.

By contrast, trapping standards were not associated with an animal rights position. The idea of formulating international trapping standards was essentially Canadian, and had been supported by Canadian officials and (some of the) trappers. Canada had had quite some experience in trap research and setting trapping standards domestically, which it had already tried to bring to the international level in the ISO process. When the ISO process failed, the negotiation of trapping standards with the EC was therefore a logical step for Canada to take. Besides the concept of trapping standards, Canada could also take the results of its domestic process and TC 191 to the table, which further increased the acceptability of an agreement.

In the US, much less experience had been gained in setting trapping standards at the national level. The US had played an active role in the ISO process, but domestically little work had been done. Mounting activism in the US, combined with the European Regulation, made wildlife agencies aware of the value of trapping standards in gaining public acceptance of trapping and avoiding further successes by animal protection groups. Given these considerations, a Canadian-style programme of trap research and standard-setting was an attractive alternative to US wildlife agencies. Once the US had embarked on this course of action, an agreement on trapping standards with the EC became more feasible as well. This also explains why the US and Canada agreed to the same set of standards, although in different forms.

Although the hypothesis was formulated with regard to the target country (here, the US and Canada), deeply-held values and perceived problems also played an important role in the way the EC reacted to the US and Canadian initiatives and its acceptance of trapping standards that would cover European species, as well. Two arguments by the US and Canadian governments have been mentioned as being important in their approach to this issue.

First, the US and Canadian governments argued that trapping standards would mean a larger increase in animal welfare than a ban on leghold traps, and that the

Regulation as it stood could only be meant to block fur trade and eliminate trapping. To some animal protection groups (as well as, possibly, some MEPs and officials of DG XI/Environment), the European Regulation was indeed a welcome instrument in their fight against trapping and the fur trade in general, and they were probably more interested in an import ban that would further these objectives than in a solution that would allow trapping to continue, even in a modified form. At the same time, a number of other groups and officials were indeed mainly motivated by animal welfare considerations. To them, it was difficult to reject the idea of formulating humane trapping standards, and even for the groups that wanted to undermine the fur trade it was more difficult openly to support that objective rather than the (more acceptable) objective of improving animal welfare. Given this position, the rejection of an agreement on humane trapping standards became increasingly untenable.

As was discussed above and will be discussed below, European trade officials had a clear interest in avoiding the implementation of an import ban. To them the proposal to negotiate an agreement on humane trapping standards offered a satisfactory way out: one that would avoid the import ban from coming into force, while at the same time being defendable as the best solution for improving the welfare of trapped animals. Opponents of the Agreement and the Understanding subsequently focused on the substantive trapping standards contained in them, but the concept of an agreement on trapping standards became difficult to contest.

Second, many interviewees mention the role of the aboriginal trapper argument in the debates. According to people on both sides of the Atlantic, this was the argument that really caught on with European politicians, even involving all kinds of societal groups that sought to protect aboriginals' traditional lifestyles. These references show that the perceived consequences of an import ban on (mainly Canadian) aboriginals played an important role in the debates.

In terms of concrete changes in position, however, aboriginal issues seem to have had a much smaller impact. The EP was as strongly in favour of an import ban and opposed to an agreement in 1997 and 1998, as it had been in 1990. The consequences for aboriginal trappers were mentioned as an issue which an import ban had to take into account, but this was no less the case in the early resolutions passed in 1988 and 1989. Moreover, in its reports, the EP Commitee on the Environment demonstrated a considerable amount of scepticism concerning the Canadian government's claims about the effects on aboriginals and the importance of leghold traps in their traditional lifestyles. All in all, aboriginal issues do not seem to have made much of a difference in the EP's position on the issue.

Similarly, animal protection groups were not too impressed by the Canadian government's arguments. They were concerned about the effects on some groups of aboriginal trappers, but they did not accept the argument as a reason not to impose an import ban. During the process, they only showed support for a labelling regime for furs coming from aboriginal trappers, but this was a proposal that had already been part of the EP's earliest proposals.

DG I/Trade's concerns related mainly to the trade consequences of the import ban and its efforts were mainly focused on avoiding a trade dispute. The argument of aboriginal trappers was not used in supporting the decision to suspend the ban and start negotiations in 1995, although it might have been a useful argument in addition to the trade consequences. It is less clear whether the aboriginal trapper argument had an impact on DG XI/Environment, but its position does not seem to have changed much during the process.

Among the EC's member states, finally, the positions remained fairly stable during the process. The UK and Austria were strong supporters and the aboriginal trappers argument did not change that. In the end, Belgium also opposed the agreements. Denmark was reported to have brought up the issue of aboriginal trappers, but that seems to have had more to do with Denmark's historical links to Greenland than with Canadian aboriginal trappers. The Netherlands was in a difficult position because of its reliance on trapping muskrats for damage control, an argument that was also frequently used by North American trappers and officials.

Some officials claim the aboriginal trappers argument made the greatest difference in Germany, which in the end was a pivotal member state in the Council of Ministers (Interview 9-2-2001, Canadian Mission/INAC). It appears, however, that eventually the difference was made primarily by transferring the issue from the Environmental to the General Affairs Council. The absence of a qualified majority in support of the Agreement in the Environmental Council suggests Germany opposed the agreement there, too. As to the Understanding with the US, trade concerns probably played an even larger role, as is also witnessed by the US letter to the German minister for foreign affairs on 10 December 1997, which emphasised the potential trade dispute that would arise out of German opposition to the Understanding.

Thus, the issue of aboriginal trappers seems to have been more important in the debates than in determining the positions of the main players on the European side. This is probably true for both the decision not to implement the import ban in 1995 and for the adoption of the Agreement in 1997. In both cases, the most important shift was between arenas: from DG XI to DG I in 1995 and from the Environmental to the General Affairs Council in 1997. This ties in with the hypothesis on participation expansion, which will be discussed below.

According to the second hypothesis relating to preferences, *a regulatory trade measure will have a greater effect on regulatory standards in the target country, the more actors in the target country perceive it to be motivated by genuine concerns rather than protectionism.* There is little evidence that the European Regulation was seen as a protectionist device by most actors in the US and Canada. To some extent, the lack of participation by European fur farmers may have contributed to this assessment. Most actors seem to have acknowledged that the Regulation was mainly supported by animal protection activists.

As was discussed above, although their intentions were seen as genuine in the sense of not being protectionist, most US and Canadian trappers and officials did not find them acceptable. Moreover, they argued that the proponents of an import ban were not interested in animal welfare but in eliminating trapping, and in that sense the motives behind the Regulation were not considered to be 'genuine.' As was argued above, this probably contributed significantly to the resistance against the European Regulation and a ban on leghold traps in the US and Canada.

The third hypothesis relating to preferences stated that *a regulatory trade measure will have a greater effect on regulatory standards in the target country if it conforms to international law and international standards*. The US and Canadian claims of the GATT/WTO incompatibility of an import ban played an important role in shifting the EC's position during the process. As was discussed in considerable detail in section 3.5.3, the GATT/WTO argument was being taken increasingly seriously by European officials. Partly this can be seen as the result of a change in constraints, but the argument was also effective because of a change in policy orientation within the EC and the fact that the European Regulation ran counter to many principles which the EC had itself defended in the international trade arena. Because of this, the US and Canada could effectively use the GATT/WTO incompatibility as an argument against the European Regulation.

In general, the role of GATT/WTO law in this case is interesting. On the one hand, the US and Canada did not resort to the GATT or later the WTO, and an agreement was reached despite the apparent GATT/WTO incompatibility of a European import ban. This would seem to point to a weak role of GATT/WTO law in this case. On the other hand, however, the EC's position seems to have been affected primarily by the GATT/WTO incompatibility of its own measure, and the threat of a GATT/WTO case was used with great skill by the US and Canada, even though they themselves preferred to avoid a case. At the same time, the EC was protected by the GATT/WTO regime. Because even a temporary ban would have caused tremendous damage to trappers in Canada and the US (but more so in Canada), and a GATT/WTO case would probably have taken some five years, commencing a case was not very attractive to the US and Canada. Without such a case, however, the EC was largely shielded from retaliation by the US and Canada. All in all, GATT/WTO law therefore seems to have played a crucial role in this case, although not always explicitly so and not always in ways which one would expect.

The change from GATT to WTO in 1995 seems to have increased the importance of international trade law considerations within the EC. Under GATT dispute settlement procedures, a country that was party to a dispute could block further proceedings and the adoption of a panel report. Under WTO rules, this was no longer possible, which strengthened the dispute resolution mechanism. Consequently, DG I/Trade gained more interest in the leghold trap Regulation around the time when the WTO was created.

This conclusion is supported by similar developments surrounding the European cosmetics Directive. In 1993, the EC adopted an amendment to its cosmetics Directive that foresaw a ban on cosmetics tested on animals by 1 January 1998 (EC, 1993). This ban would also apply to imported cosmetics and it was therefore comparable to the leghold trap Regulation in that it would ban imports based on differences in animal welfare standards during the production process. For that reason, it most likely also violated GATT law.

Around 1996, immediately after the WTO had been created and the leghold trap issue had gained more attention, the trade aspects of the cosmetics Directive also started to come to the fore. Within the European Commission, DG I/Trade lobbied against implementing the marketing ban because it would be inconsistent with GATT/WTO law (Interview 9-11-2000, DG Enterprise). The Directive allowed the European Commission to postpone the implementation of the ban, and this was done several times in the second half of the 1990s. In 2000, the European Commission published a proposal for an amendment that would replace the marketing ban on cosmetics tested on animals with a ban on animal tests for cosmetics within the EC (CEC, 2000c). This ban would no longer cover imported cosmetics and be GATT/WTO consistent, which was cited as the main reason for the proposal. Hence, here too the European Commission's position shifted under the influence of international trade law considerations, and this shift coincided with the creation of the WTO.

Expanding participation

The final hypothesis related to participation expansion. According to this hypothesis, *a regulatory trade measure will have a lesser effect on regulatory standards in the target country, if the target country succeeds in expanding participation in the initiator country to trade officials*. The leghold trap issue is a clear example of this mechanism at work, since the US and Canada succeeded in involving EC trade officials in the matter, which arguably led to the most important shifts in the EC's position during the course of the issue. Participation expansion therefore seems to be one of the keys in explaining the EC's position during the process.

This issue also shows a good example of a *restriction of participation*, something that is not covered by my hypotheses. When the three countries decided to work on an agreement on trapping standards, animal protection groups were effectively excluded from the process. This removed many of the controversies that had precluded an agreement in ISO. In contrast to the rules governing standard-setting bodies, which allow public interest groups to participate, the direct negotiations between the US, Canada and the EC could be conducted on those terms which the governments themselves chose. Although animal protection groups had some input through DG XI/Environment, most of the negotiations were confined to trade and wildlife officials as well as trappers, which greatly increased the likelihood of an agreement, albeit one which animal protection groups were not happy with.

General conclusion

The leghold trap process shows important shifts in both the US, Canadian and EC win-sets, which in the end made it possible to reach an agreement. The threat of an import ban led to an expansion of the Canadian win-set since it posed a threat to the incomes of trappers. In the US, this was the same, but the shift in the Canadian win-set was greater because of the higher degree of targeting of a European ban on aboriginal trappers. This led the Canadian and, to a lesser extent, US governments to act in order to avoid the import ban from coming into force and increased their willingness to reach an agreement.

At the same time, banning leghold traps remained unacceptable to either country, both because of the compliance costs associated with a ban on leghold traps and because a ban was considered to be not at all legitimate among US and Canadian trappers and officials. However, formulating (more stringent) trapping standards tied in with the existing Canadian approach. In the US, a similar approach was adopted in the mid-1990s, as animal protection activism led to bans on leghold traps in an increasing number of states. Therefore, an agreement based on trapping standards was acceptable to both countries.

The EC win-set was expanded, too, by the GATT/WTO incompatibility of an import ban and the US and Canadian threat to file a complaint with the WTO. International trade law considerations had gained in importance within the European Commission with the creation of the WTO. Once DG I/Trade became involved in the issue and took over the initiative, the EC's willingness to reach an agreement increased significantly. Moreover, since the main argument for an import ban was the improvement of animal welfare, an agreement on trapping standards could be defended as a better way to further this objective than an import ban itself. In the end, the involvement of the EC's trade community proved decisive, both in starting talks with the US and Canada over an agreement, and in the acceptance of the final agreements, which were adopted in the General Affairs rather than the Environmental Council.

CHAPTER FOUR

THE EUROPEAN BAN ON THE USE OF GROWTH-HORMONES IN MEAT PRODUCTION

4.1 INTRODUCTION AND BACKGROUND

One of the most widely publicised trade disputes between the EC and the US and Canada has been the battle over the use of growth-hormones in meat production. This dispute led to a series of WTO cases and has remained highly contentious to date. In this chapter I will analyse this dispute and the developments behind it.

Hormones play important roles in regulating physiological processes in animals (as well as humans). They are important in the areas of reproduction, growth and development, and the maintenance of the internal environment, and for the production, utilisation and storage of energy. One hormone may perform various functions at the same time, while combinations of hormones may perform one particular function (see e.g. WTO, 1997a: paragraph 2.7). Because of the roles which hormones play, they have important effects on the growth and development of animals.

Although all animals produce their own hormones, the effects can sometimes be increased by adding hormones to the naturally produced ones. One group of hormones used for this purpose are the so-called anabolic steroids. These growth-hormones can broadly be divided into oestrogens, which are female sex hormones, androgens, or male sex hormones, and progestogens, which play a role in maintaining pregnancy. When these hormones are used for growth-promotion purposes, this is normally done in combinations (or compounds) of an oestrogen and another type of anabolic steroid in order to enhance the effects on growth (Preston, 1999: 125).

Apart from anabolic steroids, other types of hormones and other non-hormonal substances can also be used for growth-promotion purposes in animals, for instance antibiotics and beta-agonists (CEC, 1995f: 14-16). Although the European ban covered (some of) these substances as well, they were not the focus of the dispute with the US and Canada, and I will not discuss them further.

Anabolic steroids can be either natural or synthetic. Natural (or 'endogenous') hormones are the ones that animals already produce themselves. These hormones can be added in order to heighten their effect. Natural growth-hormones include estradiol 17ß (an oestrogen), progesterone (a progestogen), and testosterone (an androgen). Synthetic (or 'xenobiotic') hormones are artificially produced substances that mimic the operation of natural hormones. They include zeranol and DES (two oestrogens), trenbolone acetate (an androgen), and melengestrol acetate (MGA, a progestogen) (Hancock, Wagner & Anderson, 1991: 256; WFRR, 1999).

Most growth-hormones are released through a pallet that is inserted behind the animal's ear. This method ensures that the hormones are released gradually. Moreover, the ear itself is not used for human consumption. Other hormones are added to animal feed. Among the hormones mentioned above, this is the case for MGA, but it was also so for DES when it first appeared on the market.

The use of hormones for growth-promotion purposes primarily takes place in cattle, and to a lesser extent in sheep (Preston, 1999: 124). Administering growth-hormones has several effects: animals will need less time to reach their full weight, they require less feed to do so, and the meat will be leaner. Studies have found that the use of growth-hormones increased growth rates in cattle by some 10 to 30%, feed efficiency by 5 to 15%, and the leanness of the meat by 5 to 8% (see the slightly different figures in Beermann, 1995: 48 and Preston, 1999: 123; for overviews of the results of studies using different hormones in different types of cattle, see Renaville et al., 1995: 86 and Sejrsen et al., 1995: 88-91).

In terms of human health effects, much debate has concentrated on the carcinogenic effects of hormones. In the 1970s, the hormone DES was found to cause cancer, and its use was subsequently banned in Europe and North America. There has been little indication, however, that this is true for all hormones. For the other growth-hormones mentioned above, scientific risk assessments have shown no or negligible adverse health effects (see e.g. CEC, 1995f: 20-21; Preston, 1999: 130), although some, like estradiol, are more controversial than others (see e.g. Doyle, 2000: 5-7).

Much of the debate on the carcinogenic nature of growth-hormones has revolved around the level of acceptable risk. Some groups and regulators have taken the position that the absence of any risk is the only acceptable level when it comes to carcinogens, a so-called zero-risk approach. This is the rationale underlying the Delaney clause in the US Food and Drugs Act (21 USC 348(c)(3)(A)), which prohibits the approval of any carcinogen, and it would also become the justification for the EC's ban on growth-hormones. Others, however, have claimed that zero-risk does not exist and that the best we can do is to determine a level below which no observable adverse effects occur.

For the natural growth-hormones, both the risk assessment and the detection of their use are made more difficult because they are already present in meat. The use of natural growth-hormones only adds incrementally to the natural levels of these hormones in meat, and is often undetectable since natural hormone levels vary. Moreover, they also occur in other food products and they are also produced by humans themselves. Hence, producers of growth-hormones have claimed that 'estrogen concentrations in beef are infinitesimal, barely distinguishable between implanted and endogenous concentrations, and of little significance when compared with daily production by the body or compared to other food products' (Hancock, Wagner & Anderson, 1991: 280). Of course, this is not the case for synthetic hormones, but here the proponents of their use would argue that it is not necessary to ban them altogether if a level of these hormones in meat can be determined below which they do not affect human health.

Apart from the debate over the acceptable levels of risk, several other issues also make it difficult to assess the health effects of growth-hormones (cf. CEC, 1995f: 5). First, most studies have focused on the effects of using single hormones, while the implants of hormones that are actually used contain more than one hormone. Fewer studies exist on the combined effects of these hormone compounds. Second, most tests of hormones assume the use to be in conformity with good veterinary practice, i.e. the right doses, implanted in the right way. It is rather difficult, however, to assess to what extent actual use conforms to these good practices. For instance, if hormones are injected, rather than released through pallets behind the animal's ear, the concentrations of hormone residues in the animal's meat will be much higher, while the use of the hormones is more difficult to reveal in farm inspections. Although it is often argued that such use of hormones is not beneficial to the farmer, the possible or, to some, likely difference between 'ideal' practices and 'actual' practices has still caused considerable debate.

Moreover, and most important for this case study, consumer perceptions and socio-economic considerations may also play important roles in regulatory decisions on growth-promoters. Arguably, it was these two factors that combined in the early 1980s to produce a European ban on the use of growth-hormones in meat production.

4.2 THE EUROPEAN BAN ON THE USE OF GROWTH-HORMONES

In Europe, the fear of growth-hormones was heightened in the late 1970s by allegations that they caused disorders in the sexual development of children (for an analysis of one such case, see Fara et al., 1979). In the early 1980s, a number of Italian children were reported to have grown oversized genitals as a result of hormone-treated veal. These reports triggered a ban on hormone-treated meat by the Italian government and calls for a consumer boycott by European consumer organisations (WTO, 1997a: paragraph 2.26). Since these events affected the European Community's internal market for beef and veal, the EC (at that time still the EEC) stepped in to regulate the use of hormones in meat production.

In November 1980, the European Commission proposed a complete ban on the use of natural and synthetic hormones in meat production, except for therapeutic purposes. In addition, maximum residue limits would be established for meat imported into the EC (CEC, 1980, in particular Articles 3-5).

In the Agricultural Council of Ministers, however, the member states were divided over the course to take. While some countries wanted to ban all hormones, the UK, Ireland and Belgium argued for retaining the availability of the three natural growth-hormones estradiol 17ß, testosterone and progesterone, while the UK and Ireland also opposed a ban on the two synthetic growth-hormones zeranol and trenbolone (WTO, 1997a: paragraph 2.27; see also Meng, 1990: 820). The proposal was based not only on Article 43 (at that time) of the EEC Treaty (now

Article 37 EC Treaty; EC, 1997j), which formed the basis for agricultural policies, but also on Article 100 (then) EEC Treaty (now Article 94 EC Treaty; EC, 1997j), which covered the harmonisation of national laws. Unlike Article 43, which required a qualified majority in the Council of Ministers, Article 100 EC Treaty required unanimity, which meant that one member state could block the adoption of the proposal.

In July 1981, the Council therefore adopted a compromise. Directive 81/602/EEC banned two types of growth-promoting substances, stilbenes and thyrostats, immediately – a decision that was uncontroversial – but suspended a decision on the five other hormones until more research had been carried out. This further decision was to be taken by unanimity as well. The proposal to establish residue limits for imported meat had been deleted from the final Directive. Instead, it was prohibited to market any meat, including imported meat, from animals that had been treated with the substances covered by the Directive (EC, 1981: in particular Articles 2-5).

In the years following the adoption of the Directive, a scientific working group chaired by the UK scientist Lamming studied the health effects of the five hormones. In an interim report, released in 1982, the working group concluded that the three natural hormones presented no risks to human health, while the effects of the two synthetic hormones were still unclear. These conclusions were supported by three EC Scientific Committees (CEC, 1985a; Lamming et al., 1987: 389).

In line with the consensus among the scientific working group and the scientific committees, the Commission proposed to allow the use of the three natural hormones while provisionally banning the use of the two synthetic hormones (CEC, 1984). This proposal met with strong resistance from the European Parliament (EP) and European consumer groups, as well as some member states. The Commission sought to avoid a deadlock in the Council by basing its proposal exclusively on Article 43 EEC Treaty, which required only a qualified majority, even though Directive 81/602 had foreseen a unanimity decision on the five remaining hormones (cf. Meng, 1990: 821).

In September 1985, the scientific working group was ready to publish its final report, which would basically restate its interim conclusions on the natural hormones and declare the two synthetic hormones safe as well. A few weeks later, however, the EP adopted a resolution calling for a complete ban on all hormones for growth-promotion purposes (EP, 1985). Caught between the cliff and the sea, the Commission decided to block the release of the scientific working group's report and propose a complete ban on the use of any natural or synthetic hormones (CEC, 1985b; McNiel, 1998: 104). In 1987, the working group published its conclusions after all, as 'a group of scientists working together as individuals' (Lamming et al., 1987).

In the Council, a complete ban was opposed by the UK and Denmark, while France and Ireland had specific objections (Meng, 1990: 821). After some textual amendments had been made by the Commission (CEC, 1985c), the Council adopted Directive 85/649/EEC on 31 December 1985, extending the ban to the five other growth-hormones (EC, 1985). The UK and Denmark voted against the proposal; Ireland abstained (Meng, 1990: 821). The UK continued its battle against the ban in the Court of Justice of the EC, where it claimed certain procedural requirements had been violated in the adoption of the Directive. In February 1988, the Court ruled that the Directive was indeed void on procedural grounds (ECJ, 1988), but on 7 March of that year it was readopted as Directive 88/146/EEC, which was substantially the same as the 1985 Directive (EC, 1988a).

The 1985 and 1988 Directives extended the prohibition contained in the 1981 Directive to the use of all hormones for growth-promotion purposes. Only limited exceptions were foreseen for therapeutic purposes (Article 2 of either Directive). Moreover, imports of hormone-treated meat from third countries were prohibited. The decision to implement this import ban would have to be taken before 1 January 1988 (Article 6.1 and 6.2 of either Directive).

As a consequence, the European ban on the use of growth-hormones had direct effects on trade with the US and Canada, which both allowed the use of the five growth hormones. In the late 1980s, the EC and the US therefore started talks on the trade implications of the hormone ban.

4.3 The Initial Situation in the US and Canada and Early Developments

4.3.1 The initial situation in the US and Canada

In both the US and Canada, the use of growth-hormones in meat production was widespread. In the US, several growth-hormones and compounds of growth-hormones had been approved since the 1950s. These approvals were given by the Food and Drug Administration (FDA), an independent federal agency that, among other things, has the authority to approve new veterinary drugs. The first hormone to be approved for growth-promotion purposes was DES, in 1954, but it was again banned in 1979 when it turned out to be a carcinogen. Yet, in the previous decades, several other hormone implants had been approved for use in cattle, too, and they included all five hormones banned by the EC (for overviews, see Beermann, 1995: 60 and Preston, 1999: 124).

In addition, the FDA had set maximum residue levels for the five hormones in meat. For the synthetic hormones, these were the levels that were maximally allowed in meat, while for the natural hormones they defined the maximum allowable increases over the normal levels of these hormones in meat. As long as the actual residue levels did not exceed these maximums, the meat could be marketed (Doyle, 2000: 2).

Although the FDA also has a general authority over food safety inspections, fresh meat, poultry and processed eggs are excluded from the FDA's remit (21 USC 392(a)). Instead, meat inspections fall under the authority of the US Department of

Agriculture (USDA). They were carried out by the USDA's Food Safety Inspection Service (FSIS).

In Canada, approvals were given by Health Canada, the federal department of health. It had banned the use of DES in 1973 (MacNeil, 1995), but it had approved compounds containing all five hormones that were banned by the EC in 1985 (WTO, 1997b: paragraph 2.10). Monitoring of food safety was done by several departments. For meat this was Agriculture and Agri-Food Canada's (AAFC) Food Inspection Directorate. In 1997, the Food Inspection Directorate was merged with divisions from other departments to form the Canadian Food Inspection Agency (CFIA), which is responsible, among other things, for monitoring the safety of food products, including fresh meat and meat products.

In addition to the five hormones banned by the EC in 1985/1988, the US and Canada had also approved the use of MGA. MGA was also covered by the European ban, which brought the total number of growth-hormones under dispute to six. Since these hormones were mainly used in the production of beef, the issue became widely known as the 'beef-hormone' issue.

The use of growth-hormones was widespread in both countries and some had been used since the late 1950s. According to US producers, some 90% of cattle in feedlots were treated with these hormones (cited in WFRR, 1999). The US government claimed that about 70% of all US beef was hormone-treated (WTO, 1997a: footnote 25 at paragraph 4.9). The Canadian government estimated the percentage for Canadian beef to be a little over 75% (WTO, 1997b: paragraph 8.208).

One of the reasons why the use of growth-hormones was more widespread in North America than in Europe, was that in Europe beef production was closely linked to milk production (Grant, 1997: 122; Revell, 1988: 1-2). About two thirds of all European beef came from cows that had been used for milk production. In such a system of meat production growth-hormones are not very useful. In Canada and the US, however, almost all beef came from specialised cattle herds that were raised in feedlots. It is in these animals that the use of growth-hormones yields the greatest returns (Interview 11-1-2001, AMI).

Estimates of the added return on animals as a result of using growth-hormones range between US$ 44 to US$ 80 dollars per animal (figures cited in McNiel, 1998: 100 and WFRR, 1999, respectively; see also Beermann, 1995: 49, who cites a reduction in feed costs of US$ 50 and increased retail values between US$ 50 and US$ 75, and Preston, 1999: 125, who mentions an economic benefit between US$ 20 and US$ 75 per animal).

Exports of North American beef to the EC consisted of two parts. First, Canada and the US exported prime beef, which was subject to a quota of 11,500 tonnes per year shared by the two countries. This quota was meant for 'high quality beef,' also known as 'Hilton beef.' Any exports above the quota were subject to prohibitively high tariffs, but the quota was never completely filled even before the European ban on hormone-treated beef imports was implemented (WTO, 1999b: paragraph 54).

Second, the EC imported beef offal, mainly from the US. Offal imports into the EC were not subject to a quota. Between 1986 and 1989, the US annually exported some 65,500 tonnes of beef offal to the EC. Although the average prices were lower for offal than for high quality beef, total US offal exports had a higher value than US high quality beef exports (WTO, 1999b: Annex I). Canada also exported beef offal to the EC but much less than the US, and comparable to its exports of high quality beef (WTO, 1999c: Annex I).

In terms of direct losses, the economic impact of the European ban was limited. Given the restrictive European import regime for prime beef, exports to the EC formed only a negligible part of the total beef production in both countries and the loss of the European export market had relatively limited effects for US and Canadian producers. Vogel (1995: 159) reported that Canadian beef exports to the EC formed only some 0.02% of its total beef production in 1987. In the late 1980s, US beef exports to the EC amounted to about US$ 120 million a year, making up less than 5% of its total beef exports and about 0.6% of the total US beef production estimated at US$ 20 billion (figures taken or calculated from Vogel, 1995: 167-169).

For both countries, however, and in particular for the US, the whole issue was closely linked to the ongoing debate over the liberalisation of world trade in agricultural products and the alleged protectionism of the EC's Common Agricultural Policy (CAP). Agriculture had always been one of the most developed policy areas in the EC. The original EEC Treaty foresaw the establishment of a 'Common Agricultural Policy,' which would serve a number of purposes. On the one hand, the CAP was meant to create a common market for agricultural products, and on the other it was meant to assure both the availability of food supplies at reasonable prices and a decent income for farmers (McMahon, 2000: 23-24).

These objectives were pursued by establishing common minimum prices for agricultural products above world prices. In order to protect EC agricultural products from cheaper foreign imports, variable import levies were established on foreign imports (Grant, 1997: 67; McMahon, 2000: 98 ff.). The CAP's minimum prices soon led to surpluses in several agricultural products, including beef (Grant, 1997: 122; McMahon, 2000: 42-43; for figures on beef surpluses, see Revell, 1988: 9-11). In order to remedy this situation, the EC started to buy the surplus supplies itself and subsidised the difference between EC and world prices in order to stimulate exports.

From the perspective of the EC, the restrictive import regime and the subsidisation of agricultural products were logical corollaries to the CAP's internal measures and necessary to achieve its objectives. In EC parlance, they were an expression of the principle of 'Community preference,' which stated that European producers should be subject to more favourable conditions than their foreign competitors (Grant, 1997: 68; McMahon, 2000: 96-97). To most third countries, however, they were an example of blatant protectionism leading to a distortion of international trade in agricultural products.

As a result, agricultural trade and the CAP had become a contentious issue in trade relations between the EC and the US. Canada essentially took a similar position on these issues as the US, as both countries were important agricultural exporters. During the Uruguay Round of negotiations over the GATT, which started in 1986 and would eventually lead to the conclusion of the Agreements on a World Trade Organization (WTO) in 1994, agriculture was again one of the most important issues.

To the US and Canada, the EC ban on hormone-treated beef was therefore just another example of a European regulatory measure with protectionist effects if not protectionist intentions. The debate leading up to the ban had given them some reason to be suspicious. Although the official purposes of the Directives, as they had been adopted by the Council, had always stressed the health risks and the confidence of European consumers in meat markets, the EP had used other arguments as well.

In its October 1985 Resolution, the EP had pointed not only to the possible health risks of hormones, but it had also cited the 'overproduction of meat and meat products in the European Community which adds considerably to the cost of the CAP' as one of the reasons for supporting a ban on all growth hormones (EP, 1985: recital I). In another Resolution, adopted in 1988, the EP again stressed both safety concerns and 'surplus meat stocks' as well as 'the survival of traditional farming' as reasons strictly to enforce the ban on the use of growth-hormones in the EC and the ban on imports of hormone-treated beef. Moreover, it recommended a world-wide ban on growth-hormones as part of the Uruguay Round of GATT negotiations (EP, 1988b).

It was exactly this perspective on agricultural policies and trade that the US and Canada were opposing in international trade negotiations. Consequently, the European hormone ban was probably also significant as part of the wider debate on agricultural trade and as a matter of principle. If the two countries had accepted the EC ban on growth-hormones, this could have set a precedent for the use of similar measures in the future, something both countries wanted to avoid.

In relation to other concrete issues, debates within the EC also gave rise to concerns on the part of the US and Canada. In another 1988 Resolution, the EP had explicitly linked the issue of hormones in beef to the issue of BST, a hormone that is used to increase milk production in dairy cows (EP, 1988a). In the Resolution, the EP voiced concerns over the effects of the use of hormones on the socio-economic structure of European farming and called for the application of the hormones ban on imports from third countries at the same time. Moreover, BST was produced by methods of biotechnology and in the preamble to the Resolution the EP made an explicit reference to an earlier Resolution on the effects of biotechnology on European farming (EP, 1988a: recital A). As we will see in the next chapter, biotechnology was just in the process of becoming an important new technology in agriculture at that time (see also Peterson, 1989).

Thus, the hormones issue was linked to a much wider set of (potential) agricultural (trade) issues. Developments in the hormones issue could have important implications for these other issues. As a consequence, the European hormone ban had much wider economic implications than the limited size of Transatlantic trade in beef and beef products would suggest.

4.3.2 Early developments

The US and Canadian governments had already lobbied against a European hormone ban in the early 1980s (WTO, 1997a: paragraph 2.27; Meng, 1990: 820). When the complete ban was finally adopted in 1985, it became an important bone of contention in the Transatlantic relationship.

After bilateral consultations had not yielded any results, the US requested the formation of a group of technical experts under the TBT Agreement in March 1987. The TBT Agreement was an agreement under GATT that dealt specifically with regulatory standards. Under the GATT system, however, both parties had to agree to commence proceedings, and the EC blocked the US request arguing that process standards, such as the hormone ban, were not covered by the TBT Agreement (WTO, 1997a: paragraph 2.34; see also Hammonds, 1990: 841; Meng, 1990: 825; Vogel, 1995: 165).

According to the 1985 Directive, the ban on the use of hormones, as well as on imports of hormone-treated beef, was scheduled to come into effect on 1 January 1988 (EC, 1985: Article 10). In mid-1987, the US beef industry, through the US Meat Trade Policy Council, filed a request for retaliation with the United States Trade Representative (USTR). In the course of that year, the US threatened to retaliate against the EC if the latter would ban the imports of US beef. The European Commission, in turn, threatened to impose counter-retaliatory measures against the US (CEC, 1987).

In November 1987, the EC decided to suspend the entry into force of the hormone and import ban by one year (EC, 1987), which was followed by a US suspension of its retaliatory measures by one year as well (McNiel, 1998: 110). Officially, the EC suspension was meant to facilitate the transition for European farmers to a prohibition on the growth-hormones, but it was probably mainly aimed at winning some time for talks with the US (Meng, 1990: 824-825).

During 1988, the European Commission and US officials sat down to discuss a way out of a trade dispute. Initially, the European Commission was quite flexible in its search for a solution. In the course of 1988, however, anxieties concerning the risks of growth-hormones were stirred up once more in the EC, as it was discovered that a large black market existed for these hormones. As a result, political pressure strictly to apply existing standards increased and the Commission's room for manoeuvre evaporated, making it more difficult to reach an agreement (Interview 11-1-2001, AMI). The only change made was that the EC exempted animal feed from the import ban, which affected (a relatively small amount of) beef imports for pet food (Meng, 1990: 826; Vogel, 1995: 161).

On 1 January 1989, the European import ban took effect, and the US implemented its retaliatory measures. In response, the EC requested a GATT dispute settlement panel to examine the legality of the US retaliation, but that request was turned down by the US (WTO, 1997a: paragraph 2.35; see also Hammonds, 1990: 842; Meng, 1990: 826).

In the course of 1989, the EC and the US reached an 'Interim Agreement' on exports of non-treated beef. Under this agreement US producers could continue to export beef to the EC if it had been certified not to be treated with growth-hormones. This beef would be monitored under the so-called Hormone Free Cattle (HFC) Programme. The hormone-free beef could be exported under the regular US/Canadian quota for beef imports into the EC, and the US retaliation would be reduced by the amount exported under the HFC Programme. The EC and Canada did not come to any agreement at this time, nor did Canada adopt separate retaliatory measures.

Within the EC, support for the hormone ban had become quite widespread by this time. European farmers and meat producers were worried about the image of meat in European markets, in particular after the illegal hormone scandals of 1988. European importers did not have great stakes in imports from the US and Canada. Only British tongue canners were active in supporting the US position, since they relied to some extent on processing US tongue (Interview 11-1-2001, AMI).

In the US and Canada, little support could be found for changing the standards regarding hormone-treated beef. As was indicated above, the use of hormones was widespread and was considered to be an important part of the US and Canadian competitive advantage in beef production. Moreover, some of these hormones had been used for several decades and they were considered to be safe for consumption, even by most US and Canadian consumer groups.

In 1989, the Texas Secretary of Agriculture, Jim Hightower, offered to provide non-hormone treated beef for the European market (Meng, 1990: 827; Vogel, 1995: 168). In the end, however, this initiative did not materialise, and the exports of non-treated beef remained fairly low.

In 1993, the European Commission introduced a proposal that had three purposes (CEC, 1993a). First, it would codify the various provisions of the earlier Directives by bringing them together. Second, it would strengthen the enforcement of the hormone ban within the EC and introduce stronger penalties for violations. Third, the proposal would introduce a ban on beta-agonists, non-hormonal growth-promoting substances (including most notably clenbuterol) that had become popular in the EC after the use of growth-hormones had been banned (see e.g. for Germany: Meyer, 1991: 300).

At the same time, the European Commission made new attempts to strengthen the scientific basis underlying the hormone ban. In 1985, the Commission had blocked the publication of the report by the Lamming group but it organised a scientific conference to discuss the health risks of the use of hormones in meat production in late 1995. The general conclusion of the conference was that the use of these hormones did not pose health risks to consumers. More specifically, it was concluded that 'there [wa]s no evidence for possible health risks to the consumer due to the use of natural sex hormones for growth promotion;' for the synthetic hormones, it was concluded that '[a]t the doses needed for growth promotion, residue levels are well below the levels regarded as safe' (CEC, 1995f: 20-21). It was also pointed out, however, that little was known about the effects of administering growth-hormones in combinations, which was the common practice, and that all risk assessments crucially depended on the hormones being administered in accordance with good veterinary practice (CEC, 1995f: 5).

Despite the conference's general conclusion that the use of the five growth-hormones was safe, the process of adopting a codified ban on hormones, thyrostats and beta-agonists continued. On 29 April 1996, Directive 96/22/EC was adopted (EC, 1996b). The Directive replaced the earlier Directives from the 1980s and contained a complete ban on the use of hormones, thyrostats and beta-agonists in meat production. Substantively, this did not make a difference to the dispute with the US and Canada, since that dispute focused on the six growth-hormones mentioned above. In legal terms, however, it was now Directive 96/22/EC that became the focus of the dispute.

4.4 International developments and the WTO cases

4.4.1 Standard-setting in the Codex Alimentarius Commission

Since the mid-1980s, debates on setting international standards for growth-hormones in meat had been ongoing in the Codex Alimentarius Commission. The Codex Alimentarius Commission is a United Nations body that is administered jointly by the Food and Agriculture Organization (FAO) and the World Health Organization (WHO). It sets voluntary international food standards that serve as guidelines for its member countries. The EC has never been a member of the Codex Alimentarius Commission, but its member states are and the European Commission has observer status.

For substances such as growth-hormones, Codex may formulate two types of standards (see the description in WTO, 1997a: paragraphs 2.17-2.18; see also CEC, 1995f: 4). First, it may determine the Acceptable Daily Intake (ADI) of the substance. The ADI expresses the maximum amount of that substance which a person can safely ingest every day during his or her complete lifetime without experiencing adverse health effects. ADIs are calculated on the basis of animals tests. In these tests, the maximum daily intake of the substance is determined for which it has no negative effects on the animal, the so-called 'no observable effect level' (NOEL). The NOEL is then multiplied by the body weight of humans relative to that of the test animals, and divided by a safety factor (normally 100) to arrive at an ADI for humans.

Based on these ADIs, Maximum Residue Levels (MRLs) can then be determined. These express the maximum level of residue in food products that is recommended in order to keep daily intake below the ADI. In regulatory practice, the MRL is the most significant standard, since this is the standard imposed on producers of food products.

In Codex, the US (and Canada) sought to establish MRLs for growth-hormones in meat. The establishment of any MRL greater than zero ran counter to a complete ban on hormones, like the one the EC had just introduced, since it would allow the use of hormones as long as the residues remained below the level specified in the MRL.

These Codex standards were elaborated in a number of steps. Since the standards concerned residues of hormones in meat, one of the first steps involved the Joint FAO/WHO Expert Committee on Food Additives (JECFA), an advisory committee in the field of food additives. JECFA adopted recommendations for the three natural hormones and zeranol in 1987 and for trenbolone in 1989 (WTO, 1997a: paragraph 2.20). It did not consider MGA, which was less of an issue at that time.

For the two synthetic hormones, zeranol and trenbolone, JECFA recommended the establishment of MRLs in beef and beef products. For the three natural hormones, however, the establishment of MRLs was not deemed to be necessary. These natural hormones were always present in meat anyway and the natural residue levels varied within certain limits. The increase as a result of treating animals with natural hormones would remain well within these natural limits, as long as the hormones were administered 'in accordance with good animal husbandry practice' (cited in WTO, 1997a: paragraph 2.21).

The JECFA recommendations became the subject of intense dispute in the Codex Alimentarius Commission, pitting the EC and its member states against the US, Canada and other beef exporters. The JECFA recommendations were adopted as draft standards in 1989 (for the three natural hormones and zeranol) and 1991 (for trenbolone). However, no consensus could be reached on an actual Codex standard.

In 1994, the Codex standard-setting process gained new significance with the conclusion of the Uruguay Round of negotiations under the GATT, which created the World Trade Organization. One of the WTO Agreements was the Agreement on Sanitary and Phytosanitary Standards (SPS Agreement), which would come into force on 1 January 1995, together with the creation of the WTO. The SPS Agreement sought to discipline the use of standards aimed at protecting the health of humans, animals and plants that formed barriers to trade. The SPS Agreement will be discussed in more detail below, but important in the context of the Codex process was that under the SPS Agreement Codex standards obtained a special status as benchmarks against which national standards could be evaluated.

As a result, the standard-setting process itself became the subject of debate in the Codex Alimentarius Commission. In early 1995, the EC was reported to have called for a special meeting to discuss how Codex standards were set (EU Food Law, 1995a). Moreover, the EC argued for the inclusion of other than purely scientific criteria in the risk assessment. These other criteria could include, for instance, environmental considerations or consumer concerns (EU Food Law, 1995b: 12).

Finally, in June 1995, the Codex Alimentarius Commission adopted standards for the five hormones in a vote (WTO, 1997a: paragraph 2.20). These standards conformed to the JECFA recommendations given some years earlier. The vote was fairly narrow, with 33 countries voting in favour, 29 against, and seven abstaining. It was denounced by the European Commissioner for Agriculture (CEC, 1995c). Together with the standards for the hormones, the Codex Alimentarius Commission also decided not to allow other than purely scientific criteria in the standard-setting process (EU Food Law, 1995c).

Given the new role of Codex standards under the SPS Agreement, the establishment of MRLs was an important victory for Canada and the US. As a result of the establishment of these standards and the new WTO Agreements, they could now renew their legal challenge to the European import ban.

4.4.2 The SPS Agreement and the cases before the WTO

In March 1996, the US and Canada, together with Australia and New Zealand, held consultations with the EC under the WTO's dispute settlement procedure. As was to be expected, these consultations did not yield any results. Consequently, in April 1996, the US requested the establishment of a WTO panel (WTO, 1997a: paragraph 1.1-1.4). Before going to the WTO, the US had already removed its retaliatory measures against the EC, since retaliation without having first resorted to WTO dispute settlement was incompatible with WTO law.

In September, Canada requested the establishment of a panel as well (WTO, 1997b: paragraph 1.3). By requesting its own panel, rather than joining the US complaint as a third party, the Canadian government wanted to ensure that it could impose its own retaliatory measures after it had won the case (Interview 15-2-2001, DFAIT).

Under the new WTO rules, the EC could no longer block the request for a panel, which makes this the only case discussed in this study that has led to a GATT or WTO panel (and later also a case before the WTO's Appellate Body). Moreover, these were the first cases to be decided under the SPS Agreement (WTO, 1994c; henceforth 'the SPS Agreement' or 'SPS'). Because the two cases were formally separate, the US and Canada sometimes used slightly different arguments in their submissions, and they resulted in two separate panel reports. Still, the panels consisted of the same three persons and some of the hearings were held together.

The establishment of the WTO panels moved the process away from bilateral discussions and consultations. From now on, the process would take place in the context of the formal WTO procedure and attempts to reach a solution outside this forum stopped. It was only after the cases had been decided by the WTO that bilateral contacts were again to be resumed (Interviews 15-2-2001, DFAIT; 20-2-2001-II, DFAIT).

To start with the conclusions of the Panel and the Appellate Body (AB) report, both found that the European import ban violated the SPS Agreement and was therefore inconsistent with WTO law. The reasoning behind these conclusions, and the grounds upon which they were reached, differed however. Since these differences played a role in the reactions to the reports and the further development of the issue, I will discuss them in somewhat more detail.

The SPS Agreement and the Panel reports

The Panel reports were published on 18 August 1997 (WTO, 1997a; 1997b). Although the US and Canadian reports differed on some details, they were almost identical in their reasoning and conclusions, which was not surprising given the fact that the issues at hand were identical and the same panel had examined both cases. In the remainder of this section I will therefore always refer to the US report (WTO, 1997a; henceforth 'Panel Report').

The WTO Panel concluded that the EC import ban violated the SPS Agreement on three points (Paragraph 9.1 Panel Report):

- For all hormones except MGA, the European import ban violated Article 3.1 SPS since it had not been based on relevant international standards and it had not been justified under Article 3.3;
- For all hormones, the ban violated Article 5.1 SPS since it had not been based on a risk assessment;
- For all hormones, the ban violated Article 5.5 SPS since the EC had adopted 'arbitrary or unjustifiable distinctions in the levels of sanitary protection' resulting in 'discrimination or a disguised restriction on international trade.'

These conclusions were reached in a series of interpretative steps, most of which subsequently became the subject of appeal by one of the parties to the dispute. The Panel made a distinction between MGA, for which no international standards had been set by the Codex Alimentarius Commission, and the other five hormones, for which such standards did exist. According to Article 3.1 SPS, domestic standards should be 'base[d] (...) on international standards, guidelines or recommendations, where they exist.' In Annex A:3(a) to the SPS Agreement, the guidelines established by the Codex Alimentarius Commission were designated as 'international standards, guidelines or recommendations' for the purpose of the SPS Agreement.

The provision on international standards is made effective in dispute settlement proceedings by reversing the burden of proof if a country complies with them. Article 3.2 SPS states that 'sanitary or phytosanitary measures which conform to international standards, guidelines or recommendations shall be (...) presumed to be consistent with the relevant provisions of this Agreement and of GATT 1994.' Nevertheless, in Article 3.3 the SPS Agreement allows WTO members to adopt more stringent standards 'if there is a scientific justification, or as a consequence of the level of sanitary or phytosanitary protection a Member determines to be appropriate.'

From the provisions of Articles 3.1 and 3.2, the Panel inferred that the term 'based on' in Article 3.1 SPS should be read to the effect that domestic standards should 'conform to' international standards. Since Article 3.3 SPS equated not being based on international standards with adopting a higher level of protection, the Panel went on to argue that a domestic standard was not 'based on' an international standard if it offered a different level of protection (Paragraph 8.72 Panel Report).

Since ADIs and MRLs had been established for five of the hormones under dispute, the European standards, which required zero residues of the growth-hormones, offered a higher level of protection than the level reflected in the international standards. As a consequence, the European standards were not 'based on' international standards (Paragraph 8.75-8.77 Panel Report).

In a further interpretative move, the Panel treated Article 3.3 SPS as an exception to Article 3.1, similar to the relation between Articles XX and, for example, III GATT. Thus, it argued that WTO members had to base their domestic standards on international standards, unless they could justify their standards under Article 3.3 SPS (Paragraph 8.86 Panel Report). Article 3.3 SPS explicitly states that higher standards have to conform to the criteria laid down in Article 5 SPS, dealing with 'assessments of risk and determination of the appropriate level of sanitary or phytosanitary protection,' so the Panel continued to examine those provisions (Paragraph 8.83 Panel Report).

No international standards had been established for MGA. As a consequence, Article 3.1 and 3.3 SPS were irrelevant to the European ban on that hormone, but it was still subject to scrutiny under Articles 2 (on 'basic rights and obligations') and 5 SPS. Here, too, the Panel examined whether the European ban conformed with Article 5 (Paragraph 8.251 Panel Report).

The Panel's examination under Article 5 focused on two provisions: Article 5.1, which required that a measure be based on a risk assessment, and Article 5.5 SPS, which required a degree of consistency in the level of protection offered in different situations. As to Article 5.1, the Panel concluded that risk assessments, in the sense of scientific evaluations of risks, existed for all hormones except MGA (Paragraph 8.111 Panel Report). As a result, the ban on MGA was considered to violate Article 5.1 immediately (Paragraphs 8.255-8.258 Panel Report). For the other five hormones, the Panel examined whether the European ban was 'based on' the risk assessments.

To answer this question, the Panel inferred a procedural and a substantive requirement from Article 5.1. First, procedurally, risk assessments had to be 'taken into account' in the establishment of the standard, which the Panel concluded had not been the case in the EC's decision-making processes concerning the ban (Paragraphs 8.113-8.116 Panel Report).

Second, substantively, the Panel stated that the 'scientific conclusion reflected in the EC measures' should conform to 'any of those reached in the studies' (Paragraph 8.117 Panel Report). The EC had submitted a number of studies as risk assessments. After an examination of these studies and the information given by scientific experts during the proceedings, the Panel found that the evidence overwhelmingly concluded that the hormones were safe if used appropriately (Paragraphs 8.118-8.124 Panel Report). A number of studies submitted by the EC were deemed insufficient since they addressed the risks of categories of hormones in general, while the Panel required risk assessments to focus on the risks of residues in food of specific hormones used as growth promoters. Moreover, these categorical studies had been taken into account in other, specific risk assessments (such as the JECFA reports), which had concluded that the hormones did not pose a health risk (Paragraphs 8.127-8.128 Panel Report).

The European ban, on the other hand, reflected the conclusion that meat was only safe to eat if it did not contain any residues. Consequently, the European ban had not been 'based on' a risk assessment in the sense of Article 5.1 SPS (Paragraphs 8.136-8.137 Panel Report).

Finally, the Panel examined Article 5.5 SPS to see whether the EC had adopted unjustifiable distinctions in the level of protection offered in different situations, leading to restrictions on trade. To that end, it compared several standards, which can be grouped under two headings. First, it compared the level of protection offered with regard to natural and synthetic hormones used for growth-promotion purposes (for which no residues were allowed) and the level of protection offered with regard to naturally occurring hormones produced by the animal itself (which were not regulated). Second, it compared the level of protection offered with regard to the six hormones and the level of protection offered with regard to carbadox, an anti-microbial agent used in pig feed for growth-promotion purposes.

In order for a standard to violate Article 5.5 SPS, three elements had to be proven: different levels of protection had to be adopted in different situations; these differences had to be unjustifiable; and the differences had to lead to 'discrimination or a disguised restriction on international trade' (Paragraph 8.174 Panel Report). The Panel concluded that all three elements were present in the comparisons outlined above.

Since the EC allowed residues of naturally occurring hormones, while not allowing residues of similar added hormones, it had adopted different levels of protection that were not justifiable by health concerns (Paragraphs 8.191 & 8.197, and 8.212 & 8.214 Panel Report). The Panel also found that these differences led to discrimination or a disguised restriction on international trade, for a number of reasons. First, the measures restricted trade (Paragraphs 8.203 and 8.216 Panel Report). Second, in several EC documents they had been supported by concerns other than those based on health (Paragraphs 8.203 and 8.217 Panel Report). Third, the ban tended to affect US and Canadian beef more than European beef, because the use of growth hormones had been more widespread in the US and Canada than in the EC before the ban entered into force (Paragraphs 8.205 and 8.217 Panel Report). Thus, the European measures also violated the third element of Article 5.5 SPS and thereby the provision as a whole.

The comparison with carbadox was somewhat more complicated. Carbadox is an anti-microbial agent used in feed given to pigs, which was allowed in the EC. Although carbadox is not a hormone, it is also used as a growth promoter and the risks associated with it are of the same nature as those associated with hormones (i.e. they are potentially carcinogenic; Paragraph 8.220 Panel Report). Although the EC argued that the risks of carbadox were fundamentally different from those of growth hormones, as it was used differently, the Panel concluded that this difference in the level of protection was not justified either (Paragraph 8.238 Panel Report). The Panel also concluded that the difference led to discrimination or a disguised restriction on trade. It did so for the same reasons outlined above in the comparison with naturally occurring hormones (Paragraphs 8.241-8.242 Panel Report). In addition, the Panel pointed out that the hormone ban applied to the beef sector, in which the EC had surpluses and was less concerned with international competitiveness. By contrast, carbadox was used in the pork sector, which did not exhibit these surpluses and in which international competitiveness was a much greater concern. Consequently, the difference in the level of protection seemed to be driven by economic or protectionist motives, as well (Paragraph 8.243 Panel Report).

Having concluded that the European ban violated Articles 3.1, 5.1 and 5.5 SPS, the Panel did not consider other claims put forward by the US and Canada, and concluded that the ban violated WTO law. All the parties appealed against this conclusion; the EC since it contested the Panel's conclusions, the US and Canada since they thought that the Panel should have gone further on some issues.

The AB report

The Appellate Body (AB) discussed all the appeals together and published its conclusions on 16 January 1998 (WTO, 1998a; henceforth 'AB Report'). Although it upheld the Panel's final conclusion that the European ban violated the SPS Agreement, it reversed many of the Panel's specific findings and arguments. Several of the AB's conclusions were of a procedural nature, but others related to the Panel's substantive findings as well.

First, the AB argued that the term 'based on' international standards, in Article 3.1 SPS, did not mean that domestic standards should 'conform to' such standards. According to the AB, the ordinary meaning of the two terms was quite distinct, and the link the Panel had made between Article 3.1 and 3.2 SPS had been unwarranted. Furthermore, according to the AB, Article 3.1 SPS lay down a harmonisation objective to be attained rather than a legal obligation:

> '(...) harmonization of SPS measures of Members on the basis of international standards is projected in the Agreement, as a *goal*, yet to be realized *in the future*. To read Article 3.1 as requiring Members to harmonize their SPS measures *by conforming those mea-*

> *sures with international standards*, guidelines and recommendations, *in the here and now*, is, in effect, to vest such international standards, guidelines and recommendations (...) with *obligatory* force and effect. (...) the *SPS Agreement* itself sets out no indication of any intent on the part of the Members to do so.' (Beef-hormone case, AB Report, paragraph 165; emphasis in the original)

Likewise:

> 'Under Article 3.1 of the *SPS Agreement*, a Member may choose to establish an SPS measure that is based on the existing relevant international standard, guideline or recommendation. Such a measure may adopt some, not necessarily all, of the elements of the international standards.' (Beef-hormone case, AB Report, paragraph 171; emphasis in the original)

As a result, the AB considerably weakened the obligation inferred from Article 3.1 SPS by the Panel. This was reinforced by the AB's conclusion that Article 3.3 SPS was 'an autonomous right and *not* an "exception" from a "general obligation" under Article 3.1' (Paragraph 172 AB Report; emphasis in original).

Second, the AB upheld the Panel's conclusion that the European measures had not been based on a risk assessment and thus violated Article 5.1. In doing so, however, it made a number of important qualifications. Thus, the risks did not have to be quantifiable (Paragraph 184-186 AB Report). The AB also acknowledged that the EC was not required to rely on laboratory experiments alone; the risk assessment could also include factors that were not amenable to laboratory research, such as the extent to which a measure could be enforced. In the words of the AB:

> 'It is essential to bear in mind that the risk that is to be evaluated in a risk assessment under Article 5.1 is not only risk ascertainable in a science laboratory operation under strictly controlled conditions, but also risk in human societies as they actually exist, in other words, the actual potential for adverse effects on human health in the real world where people live and work and die.' (Paragraph 187 AB Report)

Later in the report, the AB argued that this included:

> 'the taking into account of risks arising from failure to comply with the requirements of good veterinary practice in the administration of hormones for growth promotion purposes, as well as risks arising from difficulties of control, inspection and enforcement of the requirements of good veterinary practice' (Paragraph 205 AB Report)

Moreover, a risk assessment did not only have to be based on the majority or mainstream of scientific opinions:

> 'Article 5.1 does not require that the risk assessment must necessarily embody only the view of a majority of the relevant scientific community. (...) In most cases, responsible and representative governments tend to base their legislative and administrative measures on "mainstream" scientific opinion. In other cases, equally responsible and representative

> governments may act in good faith on the basis of what, at a given time, may be a divergent opinion coming from qualified and respected sources.' (Paragraph 194 AB Report)

Finally, the Panel's procedural requirement for a measure to be 'based on' a risk assessment was deemed irrelevant (Paragraph 189 AB Report). Nevertheless, the AB maintained that:

> 'Article 5.1 (...) requires that the results of the risk assessment must sufficiently warrant – that is to say, reasonably support – the SPS measure at stake. The requirement that an SPS measure be "based on" a risk assessment is a substantive requirement that there be a rational relationship between the measure and the risk assessment.' (Paragraph 193 AB Report; see also a later conclusion in the context of Article 2.2. SPS: WTO, 1999a: paragraph 84)

The European measures failed this test (Paragraphs 197 and 201 AB Report). Although the AB had opened the door to the consideration of administrative and enforcement concerns, it concluded that the EC had failed to demonstrate what risks were involved with regard to those concerns in this case (Paragraph 207-208 AB Report).

In an important other issue related to the risk assessment criteria, the EC had argued that the 'precautionary principle' should be taken into account. The precise meaning of this principle is the subject of considerable debate, but generally speaking it says that if there is reason to believe that some food product carries certain risks, but it is not yet known exactly which risks and how high they are, countries should be allowed to take measures anyway.

In the SPS Agreement, precautionary measures can only be provisional, though, and the risk assessment has to be carried out within a reasonable period of time (Article 5.7 SPS). Although the AB acknowledged that this does not mean the role of the precautionary principle is necessarily limited to that single provision of the SPS Agreement (Paragraph 124 AB Report), it also made it clear that 'the precautionary principle does not override the provisions of Articles 5.1 and 5.2 of the *SPS Agreement*' (Paragraph 125 AB Report; emphasis in the original). This was confirmed in a later case, where Article 5.7 SPS was described as 'a *qualified* exemption from the obligation under Article 2.2 not to maintain SPS measures without sufficient scientific evidence' (WTO, 1999a: paragraph 80).

As a third conclusion related to the Panel report, the AB reversed the Panel's finding that the European measures violated Article 5.5 SPS. As to the comparison between added and natural hormones, the AB argued that 'there is a fundamental distinction between added hormones (natural or synthetic) and naturally-occurring hormones in meat and other foods.' If the EC were required to apply the same level of protection to naturally occurring hormones, this would entail 'such a comprehensive and massive governmental intervention in nature and in the ordinary lives of people as to reduce the comparison itself to an absurdity' (Paragraph 221 AB Report).

Nor did the AB consider the distinction between added hormones for growth-promotion purposes and those for therapeutic reasons to be unjustifiable, since the latter were used on a much smaller scale and under the responsibility of a vet (Paragraphs 223-225 AB Report).

Finally, the AB did find that the distinction between the hormones and carbadox was unjustifiable. Still, it argued that this distinction was not a restriction on trade since it was:

> 'unable to share the inference that the Panel apparently draws that the import ban on treated meat and the Community-wide prohibition of the use of the hormones here in dispute for growth promotion purposes in the beef sector were not really designed to protect its population from the risk of cancer, but rather to keep out US and Canadian hormone-treated beef and thereby to protect the domestic beef producers in the European Communities.' (Paragraph 245 AB Report)

There was something in the AB Report for everyone and all parties hailed the AB's conclusions (CEC, 1998a; USTR, 1998). The US and Canada could claim that the AB had upheld the Panel's conclusion that the European measures violated WTO law. At the same time, the EC could claim victory in a number of interpretative issues, which appeared to open the window to retaining the ban. Since the AB had reversed the conclusions relating to Articles 3.1 and 5.5 SPS, its conclusions now only rested on the EC's violation of Article 5.1 SPS. As we will see below, this left some room for debate about how the report's conclusions would have to be implemented, which the EC used to avoid lifting the ban.

With the AB Report, the illegality of the import ban on hormone-treated beef under WTO law had been established. However, a further issue was what consequences this should have for the European measures. It was around this question that the process evolved after the AB Report. Although the US, Canada and the EC resumed talks on the issue, the process had now moved firmly onto legal grounds and the WTO was to be revisited several times more in the years to come.

4.5 The process after the WTO cases

4.5.1 Arbitration and retaliation

On 13 February 1998, the Panel Report, as modified by the AB Report, was adopted by the WTO's Dispute Settlement Body (DSB). Although they could have done so under the WTO's dispute settlement procedures, the Panel and the AB had not provided any suggestions about the measures the EC had to take in order to correct the situation. Both had merely recommended that the EC bring its measures 'into conformity with its obligations' under the SPS Agreement (Paragraph 9.2 Panel Report; Paragraph 255 AB Report).

The way in which this was to be done became the subject of subsequent debate. According to the US and Canada, the illegality of the European ban meant it had to be lifted as soon as possible. The EC, on the other hand, argued that the real problem was not the ban, but the lack of sufficiently specific risk assessments to support it. As a consequence, it proposed to conduct additional risk assessments and only to lift the ban if these assessments failed to provide support for the ban.

As the three parties could not agree upon an implementation period, the issue was returned to the WTO for arbitration. According to WTO procedures, the standard implementation period for a WTO conclusion was 15 months, which could be reduced or extended, according to the 'particular circumstances' of the case (WTO, 1998c: Paragraph 23). The US and Canada argued that 10 months was sufficient to withdraw the EC measures, while the EC asked for 39 months: two years to complete the risk assessments and another fifteen months to take appropriate legislative action, if necessary (WTO, 1998c: Paragraphs 5, 15 and 19). While not deciding on the appropriateness of conducting additional risk assessments per se, the arbitrator did reject the EC's argument that such assessments had to be taken into account in determining the implementation period:

> 'Withdrawal is the *preferred* means of implementation under Article 3.7 of the DSU ['Dispute Settlement Understanding,' S.P.], and *prompt compliance* with the recommendations and rulings of the DSB is essential under Article 21.1. It would not be in keeping with the requirement of *prompt* compliance to include in the reasonable period of time, time to conduct studies or to consult experts to demonstrate the *consistency* of a measure already judged to be *inconsistent*.' (WTO, 1998c: Paragraph 39; emphasis in the original)

Since the arbitrator did not find any arguments for a shorter implementation period either, he decided the reports' conclusions had to be implemented by 13 May 1999, 15 months after the reports had been adopted (WTO, 1998c: Paragraph 48).

This did not stop the European Commission from setting up additional risk assessments and asking for further scientific advice from some of its scientific committees. At the same time, thought was being given to the steps to be taken when the deadline would pass. On 16 February 1999, the Commission informed the Council and the European Parliament that it was considering (a combination of) three options (CEC, 1999a):

- Compensating the US for lost exports by giving certain trade concessions;
- Retaining the ban as a temporary precautionary measure under Article 5.7 SPS;
- Allowing US meat into the European market under a labelling requirement.

Also, the Commission indicated that the additional risk assessments would not be completed by 13 May and the implementation of the WTO ruling might therefore not take place by that date. These options were also presented to the US (CEC, 1999b). After meetings between US and EC officials, the USTR expressed 'deepening concern' with the EC stance in this case (USTR, 1999a).

At that same time, the US and Canadian governments were preparing possible retaliatory measures, which they could take under WTO law if the EC did not comply. A few days after the deadline for compliance had passed without the EC withdrawing its measures, the US and Canada requested the DSB to authorise the use of retaliatory measures covering European products whose value equalled that of their lost trade in beef to the EC. The US estimated its loss at US$ 202 million per year, and Canada at CAN$ 75 million per year. The EC did not agree and the matter was referred to arbitration under the WTO, which was carried out by the original panel that had examined the European import ban (WTO, 1999b; 1999c).

The issue of retaliation revolved around the correct methodology for assessing the value of foregone US and Canadian exports in beef under the High Quality Beef quota as well as lost exports of edible beef offal. After consideration of all parties' arguments, the arbitrators established the amount of retaliation at US$ 116.8 million for the US, and CAN$ 11.3 million for Canada (WTO, 1999b: Paragraph 83; WTO, 1999c: Paragraph 72).

Together with the retaliation claim, the USTR had published a list of products, among which it would select the products to be covered by the retaliatory measures (consisting of additional 100% duties). The main item on that list was pork and pork products, whose total average annual exports from the EC to the US totalled some US$ 210 million in the period from 1996 to 1998. This caused considerable concern among European pork exporters, particularly from Denmark, who started to lobby the European Commission to reach an agreement on compensation in order to avoid the retaliatory measures (Interviews 26-9-2000, COPA/COGECA; 30-11-2000, UECBV).

In the US, retailers protested against the retaliatory measures, arguing that 'duties on consumer products will inevitably result in higher prices and fewer choices for consumers' and called for a settlement of the dispute. In case that would prove to be impossible, the retailers requested the USTR to remove certain items that were difficult to replace from the list of targets for retaliation (FMI, 1999).

Yet, at that point in the process, the USTR had little choice but to proceed with retaliation if no agreement could be reached on compensation by the EC. After the arbitrators had decided the amount, the USTR published a final list of products to be subjected to additional 100% duties on 19 July 1999. The UK was exempted from retaliation because of its long-standing opposition to the hormone ban (USTR, 1999b).

Likewise, Canada imposed its retaliatory measures on 1 August 1999 (DFAIT, 1999). Coming up with a list of products that was acceptable to Canadian importers had also proved to be quite difficult. Eventually, the products on the final list were those on which the Canadian government had received the fewest negative comments (Interview 20-2-2001-II, DFAIT). Again, the UK was specifically exempted from the retaliation, a decision that was applauded by the UK government (MAFF, 1999b).

4.5.2 Developments in the EC

During the process starting with the complaints filed with the WTO, the issue had turned almost exclusively into an international trade issue. The domestic debates did not show many developments and insofar as they did, they tended to reinforce the existing positions.

In the EC, the domestic ban on growth-hormones was not subject to any challenges and for the interest groups most closely involved the issue became more or less latent, except for the trade aspects (Interviews 14-8-2000, BEUC; 26-9-2000, COPA/COGECA; 30-11-2000, UECBV). As long as the European Commission did not propose any changes to the ban on the use of growth-hormones, they did not feel compelled to change their position or take any action, but most interviewees were convinced that the ban would attract extensive support if it were to be challenged (also Interview 7-8-2000, US Mission).

In the 1990s, these positions were reinforced by a series of food scares that raised public awareness of food safety risks in the EC. Even though some changes were made in the structure of the CAP, which reduced the level of import protection offered to European farmers, other developments contributed to a strengthening of support for the hormone ban in the context of the CAP. Both developments therefore merit some more detailed attention.

Food scares and consumer concerns

The most important food scare to occur in the EC during the 1990s was the BSE scare. BSE (Bovine Spongiform Encephalopathy), or 'mad cow disease' as it has become commonly known, is a disease that makes a cow's brain look like a sponge by causing small holes to appear in it (BSE Inquiry, 2000: 10). The disease was first discovered in the UK in the second half of the 1980s. Although at the time a number of measures were taken to avoid a spread to other cows and humans, the risk of transmission to humans was thought to be small (BSE Inquiry, 2000: 13-14).

Supported by scientific advice, UK government officials reassured the public that appropriate measures had been taken and that beef was safe to eat. Even when the media reported cases in which BSE had been transmitted to cats and pigs, the risk of transmission to humans was considered to be low and no new measures were thought to be necessary. In the first half of the 1990s, the disease seemed under control and only minor adjustments were made to reinforce the existing measures (BSE Inquiry, 2000: 15-17).

During 1995, however, several cases of the (fatal) Creutzfeldt-Jakob disease were reported in the UK. This disease did the same to people as BSE did to cows, but despite concerns on the part of the public and some scientists, the UK government maintained its position that beef was safe to eat. In March 1996, a scientific advisory committee reported that the cases of Creutzfeldt-Jakob represented a new variant of this disease and that they were probably linked to BSE in cows (BSE Inquiry, 2000: 19).

On 20 March 1996, the UK government therefore announced that new precautionary measures were needed since BSE could probably be transmitted to humans. Despite the attempts to reassure the public by adopting rigorous measures, the announcement was met with a public outcry in the UK and the rest of Europe. Not only were people concerned about the safety of beef, but many also felt that government officials had deliberately underplayed the risks of BSE and misled the public into thinking that eating beef was safe, even though they knew it was not (BSE Inquiry, 2000: 22).

Up to mid-2000, 170,000 British BSE cases were reported and 4.7 million British cattle had been slaughtered to prevent its further spread. During that same period, about 80 persons had contracted Creutzfeldt-Jakob disease as a result of exposure to BSE (BSE Inquiry, 2000: 1-2). Initially, almost all cases had occurred in the UK (CEC, 1997j: 82), but in late 2000, an outbreak of BSE was also reported in France and in the Netherlands.

The BSE scare had a number of consequences that also impacted other areas of food safety, such as the hormone ban. First, it raised doubts about the safety of food in general. Food safety, which had always been a contentious issue, suddenly received a new impetus and was pushed higher on the public and political agendas. These concerns were reinforced by a number of other food scares in the second half of the 1990s relating to, among others, salmonella and e-coli (Chambers, 1999: 97).

Second, the BSE scare raised suspicion about the validity of scientific evidence, or at least the way it was used by public authorities. Until the March 1996 announcement, scientists had generally considered the risks of transmission of BSE to humans to be low and UK government officials had gone to great pains to avoid an unwarranted scare. To many people, this proved, at best, the fallibility of science or, at worst, the way in which science was being abused by government officials to serve commercial interests.

Third, the episode showed a number of weaknesses in the way food scares were handled in the EC. In the early 1990s, the EC had taken several measures to restrict the exports of British beef to other countries in the EC. After the 1996 announcement, they were replaced by a complete ban on British beef exports (McMahon, 2000: 53). The whole process led to a serious crisis in the relations between the UK, the other EC member states and the European Commission, in which at one point the UK government even decided to block decision-making processes within the EC in order to expedite the lifting of the export ban on UK beef. Moreover, the European Commission's handling of the issue was arguably poor, partly because of the low priority food safety issues had within the Commission (for a more extensive analysis of these episodes, see Grant, 1997: 126-129). All in all, it was felt that the EC did not have the ability to act swiftly and efficiently in dealing with this kind of crisis and that national, possibly protectionist, sentiments were allowed to play too large a role in the process.

The BSE crisis also attracted considerable attention from the European Parliament (EP). Despite the extension of EP involvement in many policy areas (see section 2.3.3 above), the role of the EP in agricultural policies was limited to mere consultation; all decisions in this area were still taken exclusively by the Council after proposals from the European Commission. The 1997 Treaty of Amsterdam foresaw a co-operation procedure, and thus closer EP involvement, in the adoption of 'measures in the veterinary and phytosanitary fields which have as their direct objective the protection of public health' (EC, 1997j: Article 152.4(b)). Nevertheless, this was a limited authority and the Treaty of Amsterdam would only enter into force on 1 May 1999, after it had been ratified by all the member states.

Despite the limits on its formal authority in this field, the EP decided to set up a Committee of Enquiry into BSE in July 1996 (EP, 1996c). After the Committee had released its recommendations in February 1997, the Parliament adopted a Resolution threatening to use its power to force the Commission to resign if the recommendations had not been carried out before November 1997 (EP, 1997a). Such a 'conditional motion of censure' probably ran counter to the spirit, if not the letter, of the EC Treaty (then Article 144, now Article 201 EC Treaty, see EC, 1997j), but it followed in the 'European Parliament tradition of exploiting new methods to gain influence,' as one observer put it (Chambers, 1999: 96).

As it was, the conditional motion of censure forced the European Commission to co-operate with the EP and in October 1997 it submitted a report containing a whole range of measures relating to BSE and food safety in general (CEC, 1997j). Already before that, the Commission had produced several documents dealing with food safety issues (CEC, 1997d; 1997e). The system of scientific committees in the field of consumer health and food safety had also been reorganised by redefining their tasks and creating a Scientific Steering Committee (EC, 1997e; 1997h).

In the late 1990s, the Commission was reorganised and all units dealing with food safety were brought together in a new Directorate General for Health and Consumer Protection ('DG Sanco,' after its French acronym). All scientific committees were brought under the new DG Sanco's remit. Moreover, the Commission developed plans to set up an independent European food safety agency (CEC, 2000a).

In general, food safety and consumer concerns seem to have gained a more prominent role in the European Commission's work. As several interviewees, both within and outside the Commission, pointed out, consumer concerns were given more emphasis in the Commission's proposals during the second half of the 1990s, and consumer groups gained better access to the decision-making process, often at the expense of business and agricultural groups. This tendency was reinforced throughout this period by recurring food scares and new cases of BSE.

The BSE scare therefore formed an important background to the hormone ban in the second half of the 1990s. Even though it had not led to the ban, it served as a strong reinforcement. It had made it politically even less attractive to propose a lifting of the ban. In addition, it had discredited the use of scientific evidence to disprove risks to human health, which had been the most important element in the US and Canadian arguments against the hormone ban. As a result, it reinforced the position of the European consumers' association, BEUC, which had already consistently supported the hormone ban (BEUC, 1999b). It may even have strengthened the ban in that the labelling of US and Canadian beef, which had been an option before, was no longer seen as a viable solution to the trade issue (Interview 26-9-2000, COPA/COGECA).

Reforming the CAP

Another set of developments within the EC related to the CAP. The original CAP functioned for a number of decades after its inception in the early 1960s, but during the 1990s several developments contributed to a gradual liberalisation of European agricultural markets. The first set of developments was mainly of an internal nature. The CAP had been designed at a time when the EC was still a net importer of agricultural products. However, as was already noted above, the policy's minimum prices and protection at the borders soon led to surpluses in several agricultural products.

Because the EC started to buy surplus supplies itself and to subsidise the difference between EC and world prices in order to stimulate exports, the budgetary burden on the EC increased enormously during the 1980s. In 1985, the CAP accounted for 75% of the EC's budget and although this figure dropped in subsequent years, it remained well above 50% (Grant, 1997: 76). It became clear that some form of agricultural market liberalisation was needed to address these consequences of the CAP.

At the same time, a number of third countries became increasingly dissatisfied with the CAP's protectionist effects, which had steadily reduced import opportunities into the EC. These concerns were reinforced by the EC's subsidisation of agricultural exports, which distorted international trade even further (Mahler, 1991: 35). Within the GATT of 1947, agriculture had obtained a protected position at the insistence of the US, which later even obtained a special waiver for its own agricultural policies (Hoekman & Kostecki, 1995: 200 and 166-167; Trebilcock & Howse, 1999: 247). As agricultural exports became more important to the US, however, the US government's position shifted toward support for agricultural trade liberalisation. The US certainly also had a long tradition of government intervention in agriculture, but in the course of the 1980s and 1990s US agricultural policies were transformed to reflect a more market-oriented approach (Skogstad, 1998: 473-475).

During the Uruguay Round of GATT negotiations, the issue of agricultural trade and the CAP became one of the most important issues once again – so much so that an agreement was highly unlikely without some form of agricultural trade liberalisation. During the negotiations, the US was joined in its demands for agricultural trade liberalisation by a group of fourteen other relatively efficient and export-oriented agricultural producers, which also included Canada. In the negotiations on agriculture, these countries operated together and became known as the Cairns Group (Hoekman & Kostecki, 1995: 202 ff.; Mahler, 1991: 38-39).

In 1992, the US and the EC reached an agreement on the issue, which would become the basis for a separate Agreement on Agriculture under the WTO Agreements (Trebilcock & Howse, 1999: 261-263). In it, countries committed themselves to replacing all quantitative restrictions on agricultural imports by tariffs (so-called 'tariffication') and to reduce these tariffs over time. For the EC, this meant an additional impetus to reform the CAP in order to meet international competition (for opposing views on the relationship between the GATT negotiations and CAP reform, see Paarlberg, 1997, and Patterson, 1997).

As a result of these internal and international pressures, the CAP has gradually been liberalised since the early 1990s. The most significant decisions were taken in the MacSharry reforms of 1992, named after the then European commissioner for agriculture (see Swinbank, 1993: 360). Although these reforms were mainly targeted at the cereals sector (i.e. wheat, maize and barley), they also affected beef policies. As part of the reform package, the intervention price for beef was reduced by 15%, to be effected in three steps until 1995 (EC, 1992b).

These reforms did little to alleviate budgetary pressures, since product subsidies were replaced by direct income support based, in the case of beef production, on heads of cattle (Swinbank, 1993: 363; for some budget figures, see CEC, 1997b: 21-22). The reforms arguably did not have much effect on the production of beef in the EC, although some observers have argued that they presented an important shift away from product subsidies, which could form the basis for further reforms at a later stage (e.g. Grant, 1997: 123 & 78).

Between 1992 and 1994, EC beef production fell by 16%, while exports to the former Soviet Union increased (Grant, 1997: 123). As a result, the EC did not have to buy any beef surpluses between the end of 1993 and early 1996 (CEC, 1997b: 15). In 1996, however, the BSE crisis led to a 7% drop in beef consumption within the EC, which came on top of a steady decline by some 200,000 tonnes per year between 1993 and 1995 (CEC, 1997b: 8-9 & 23). Starting in 1996, the EC therefore had to buy surpluses once again, which was compounded by purchases of meat from animals that were slaughtered as part of the measures against BSE. Because of commitments undertaken as part of the Uruguay Round Agreement on Agriculture, these could not be exported with a subsidy (Grant, 1997: 128; Skogstad, 1998: 472).

The BSE crisis thus had important consequences for the CAP as well, and it is difficult to assess how the CAP reforms will work out in the long run. On the one hand, the direct effects of the CAP reform seem to have been limited and they arguably do not present a fundamental shift in EC agricultural policies (Skogstad, 1998: 471-473). In terms of beef prices, the European Commission estimated that European beef prices would still be 20 to 25% higher than US beef prices after 2000 (CEC, 1997b: 27).

On the other hand, they were the most significant reforms of the CAP to date, and they may have larger effects in the long run. In March 1999, the Council of Ministers agreed to reduce beef prices by a further 20% as part of Agenda 2000, the package of Commission proposals designed to prepare the EC for the enlargement towards Central and Eastern European countries (McMahon, 2000: 176-177). The CAP reforms would therefore seem to have weakened the protectionist motives for maintaining the hormone ban somewhat.

At the same time, however, the structure of the CAP was reinforced by another development, which is often referred to as 'multifunctionality.' The concept of multifunctionality refers to the notion that agricultural production serves or should serve more functions than the production of food alone. Most importantly, agriculture is seen as an important element in the conservation of the natural landscape in Europe. A more 'industrial' approach to agriculture is argued to jeopardise this function. Moreover, European agriculture has been confronted with increasing concerns in other fields, such as animal welfare and environmental protection (Grant, 1997: 208).

The idea of multifunctionality has, in a way, provided a new underpinning of interventionist agricultural policies in the EC, as well as protection at the EC's borders to protect European agricultural producers from products that have not been produced according to the same standards. According to Grant (1997: 203), '[f]arm interests are increasingly seeing environmental policy as a means of retaining subsidies for agriculture. If farmers are not to be paid for producing surplus products, then perhaps they can be paid for looking after the countryside.'

Multifunctionality also has an external dimension, as it creates pressures to protect European agricultural products that have been produced according to relatively stringent standards, against cheaper foreign imports that have not. Thus, in its Agenda 2000 proposal, the European Commission pointed to the 'need to introduce environmental and social standards at international level and to take into account consumer concerns' (CEC, 1997i: Part 1, chapter III.2).

All in all, the CAP has experienced important changes over the last decade. On the one hand, the use of direct protectionist and interventionist measures, such as subsidies, duties and import quotas has gradually been reduced. On the other hand, the EC continues to view agriculture as a 'special' industry and has imposed various new requirements on its producers. Since these new requirements are linked to issues like animal welfare and food safety, they are mainly of a regulatory nature. As can be seen in the beef-hormone and the GM foods issues, these regulations may also affect foreign imports.

The positions of European interest groups

To many outside observers, new regulatory requirements on foreign imports are merely an example of new protectionism and the outcome of a search for alternative protectionist measures now that the traditional measures have become less suitable. To European farmers, however, the regulatory restrictions on foreign imports are only a logical extension of standards imposed within the EC and are needed to ensure fair competition between EC and foreign producers (Interview 26-9-2000, COPA/COGECA).

This view has consistently been reflected in the positions taken by COPA and COGECA, the two most important European farmers' associations, which operate a joint secretariat in Brussels. In the beginning, farmers' organisations from Denmark and the UK opposed the hormone ban or argued for the labelling of US beef (Interview 26-9-2000, COPA/COGECA). In the end farmers' associations reached a joint position, however, and since then COPA/COGECA have always supported the European ban on growth hormones as a way of ensuring consumer confidence in beef products.

Concomitantly, they have argued for similar restrictions on foreign imports. In the beef-hormone issue these restrictions could be based on the ban's justification on health grounds: if the hormones were banned because they posed a risk to consumers, it was only logical that imported beef had to conform to the same standards. At the same time, COPA/COGECA also called upon the EC to 'place agricultural trading and market liberalisation in a setting which brings international recognition of the constraints imposed on European farmers and agricultural products and does not call into question the principle of Community preference' (COPA/COGECA, 1999a).

This argument is even more clearly pronounced in COPA/COGECA's position on the EC's ban on BST, a hormone that promotes milk production in cows. Initially, the EC considered banning BST for a number of reasons, including animal welfare, human health and the socio-economic consequences which BST would have for agricultural production (cf. Vogel, 1995: 172). In the end, however, the EC (as well as, for instance, Canada) banned the use of BST on animal welfare grounds alone, since the risks to human health were unclear. In order to avoid a clear violation of GATT/WTO rules, this prohibition applied only to the use of BST in the EC and not to imported milk that was produced with BST, for instance in the US (EC, 1999e).

Although COPA/COGECA supported the ban on BST, they called for new studies on the human health effects of BST with a view to basing the ban on that ground, which would open the possibility of banning imports of milk produced with BST. Moreover, they requested from the Commission that 'the decisions taken at the Community level, which reflect the wishes of European society but which also put European agriculture in a less favourable situation in terms of competitiveness in relation to the third countries, be taken duly into account in the WTO agricultural negotiations' (COPA/COGECA, 1999b).

A different position on the hormone ban could be expected from the importers of US and Canadian beef, who lost their imports as a result of the import ban, or from exporters who suffered from the retaliatory measures. It seems, however, that both the imports and exports of meat were too small to effect a change in meat traders' positions. In the early 1980s, UECBV, the European meat traders association, called for measures to restore consumer confidence in meat and it supported the hormone ban as a way to achieve that (Interview 30-11-2000, UECBV). Although some of UECBV's members were importers and/or exporters of meat, this was only a small part of the association's total membership. The meat trade industry did not therefore primarily consist of 'importing' or 'export-oriented' firms, but of 'domestic' meat trading firms, which operated mainly in the European market. As a consequence, UECBV's position was somewhat mixed, calling attention to the consequences which the ban had for international trade in meat, but at the same time supporting the hormone ban as a European measure, as well as COPA/COGECA's conception of 'fair trade.'

Although some importers may have been affected by the loss of beef imports from the US and Canada, the overall impact was too small to make much of a difference, especially since, at that time, there was no shortage of beef in the EC. The only imports that had more than a marginal significance for meat importers was tongue from the US, which was of a higher quality than other tongue. Nevertheless, the volume of these imports was relatively small (Interview 30-11-2000, UECBV).

When the US installed its retaliatory measures against the EC, the main meat sector affected by those measures was the Danish pork industry. They had already had concerns about retaliation before the hormone ban was established, and continued to argue for solutions that would alleviate the retaliatory measures. They were joined by some other agricultural producers that had been hit by the retaliation. UECBV requested the European Commission to consider the labelling of US beef as a way to avoid retaliatory measures, but it did not formally endorse that option. COPA/COGECA continued to oppose labelling altogether, as long as European farmers were not allowed to use the hormones (Interviews 26-9-2000, COPA/COGECA; 30-11-2000, UECBV).

Thus, even if the European hormone ban was not adopted for protectionist reasons, the structure of the CAP resulted in broad support for the import ban among agricultural groups. European farmers had an interest in banning US and Canadian beef, even if the actual amounts of beef coming into Europe had always been limited. Meat traders had only limited interests in the trade effects of the ban and the interests of importers became even smaller as the industry adjusted to the reduction in beef imports. In that sense, the CAP and the trade effects of the hormone ban have reinforced the support for the ban within Europe.

Other business groups have been much less involved in this issue. The pharmaceutical industry, which produces the hormones, has opposed the ban (Interview 30-11-2000, UECBV), but this does not seem to have made much of a difference to the EC's position. Retailers, which have been very active in the GM foods issue (see the next chapter), have been much less involved in the hormone issue (Interview 29-9-2000, EuroCommerce).

In 2000, US Congress adopted a bill that would require the USTR to rotate retaliatory measures between products, the so-called carousel approach. On 18 May 2000, this bill was signed into law by the President. Under the carousel approach, retaliatory measures would shift every six months from one set of products to another (US, 2000: Section 407). This had the potential considerably to broaden the range of producers and EC member states affected by the US measures and to increase the uncertainty surrounding exports to the US. It raised considerable concerns on the part of (meat) exporters from EC member states that had so far been unaffected by the retaliatory measures (Interview 30-11-2000, UECBV).

On 26 May 2000, the USTR invited comments on a revised list of products for retaliation, which would still affect all EC member states except the UK (USTR, 2000). After more than 400 comments had been received, the USTR indicated that it needed more time to implement a new retaliation list (US Mission, 2000). As it was, the USTR had not supported the adoption of the carousel approach to begin with. Partly this was the result of doubts as to the WTO compatibility of the approach (Interview 19-1-2001, USTR), which led to an EC request for consultations on 5 June 2000. Until now, however, the US has not implemented the carousel approach, which has laid the issue to rest for the time being.

All in all, consumer groups supported the ban for human health concerns, while domestic producers supported it to protect themselves against foreign imports. This coalition was even formally established when COPA/COGECA and BEUC issued a joint statement in support of the ban. In response to the European Commission communication on the WTO decisions, they stated that 'the current ban on imports of hormone treated beef must be maintained on the basis of the precautionary principle' (COPA/COGECA & BEUC, 1999).

Developments within EC institutions

This pattern of support was also reflected in the positions of the European Commission, the European Parliament and the EC member states, which showed broad support for the ban. Decisions on the hormone ban were taken by the Agricultural Council. Although some member states (some interviewees mentioned the UK and Denmark) may have been more willing to consider alternatives to the import ban, they do not seem to have fought it actively in the Council of Ministers. The EP has also vigorously supported the hormone ban and resisted the labelling of US and Canadian beef.

In response to the AB Report, the European Commission started a series of seventeen studies to provide for additional risk assessments, which it argued was what the AB Report mandated. On 30 April 1999, the Commission's Scientific Committee on Veterinary Measures Relating to Public Health (SCVPH) issued its review of existing risk assessments of growth-hormones in meat, one of the studies commissioned by the European Commission. The SCVPH argued that the assumptions underlying previous risk assessments 'disregard[ed] a number of important factors,' such as differences in the effects on humans from different age groups, the increase of hormone-related diseases in some countries, abuse of hormones in actual practice, and the effects of combinations of different growth-hormone compounds (SCVPH, 1999: 69-70). On the basis of the materials reviewed, the Committee argued that 17ß estradiol was a complete carcinogen, while the risks of the other five hormones could not be estimated quantitatively with present knowledge (SCVPH, 1999: 73).

The European Commission welcomed the report as support for the hormone ban and stated that lifting the ban was no longer an option (CEC, 1999d; 1999e; 1999f). The UK government, however, commissioned a review from a sub-group of its own Veterinary Products Committee. In October 1999, the sub-group published its report, which concluded that the evidence in the SCVPH's report did not support a complete ban (MAFF, 1999c).

A few months earlier, JECFA had released a report in which it reconsidered its earlier recommendation not to establish ADIs or MRLs for the three natural hormones. In the new report ADI's were recommended, but MRLs were still deemed unnecessary because 'the available data on the identity and concentrations of residues of the approved veterinary drugs in animal tissues indicate a wide margin of safety for consumption of residues in food' (JECFA, 1999: 13). Although the recommendation to establish ADIs meant a partial change in the previous recommendation, the main issue in the beef-hormone issue was residues in meat and on that issue JECFA's position remained unchanged.

In a reaction to the British and JECFA reports, the SCVPH restated its opinion, claiming that the two reports 'did not provide convincing data and arguments demanding revision of the conclusions drawn in the opinion of (…) April, 30th, 1999' (SCVPH, 2000: paragraph 2.3). Subsequently, the European Commission introduced a proposal to make the ban on 17ß estradiol permanent and to maintain the ban on the other five hormones on a provisional basis (CEC, 2000d). This, so the Commission argued, would bring the EC closer to compliance with its obligations under the WTO Agreements. Significantly, the proposal was based on the EC Treaty provision for veterinary measures relating to the protection of public health, and no longer on the provision for agricultural policies like all previous Directives on the hormone ban. As a result of this shift and the amendments made by the Treaty of Amsterdam, the proposal will therefore have to go through a consultation procedure with the EP. This is likely to strengthen the support for the hormone ban within the EC even further.

The Canadian and US governments argued that the SCVPH opinions did not contain any new evidence and that the Commission proposal was therefore based on the same evidence that had been found insufficient in the WTO cases (DFAIT, 2000). Thus, the scientific debate has not progressed much since the early stages of the dispute: the US and Canadian governments maintain there is no evidence that the six hormones present health risks, while the EC argues there is no conclusive evidence that they do *not* present any risks.

4.5.3 The talks on compensation and the exports of non-treated beef

While the US and Canada were preparing their retaliatory measures, talks about compensation were held with the EC. These talks were held separately between the EC and the US, and the EC and Canada. In the talks, an attempt was made to come up with a compensatory package that would satisfy US and Canadian producers and thereby prevent retaliatory measures from coming into effect.

Although talks were held with both the US and Canada, the EC focused most of its attention on the US (Interview 20-2-2001-II, DFAIT). Probably, it wanted to achieve an agreement with the US first and then to offer a similar package to Canada. The other strategy, to elaborate an agreement with Canada first, was not viable in this case since any agreement would be useless if it were not accepted by the US.

Several possible solutions were discussed during the compensation talks. One option might have been the labelling of imported hormone-treated beef. This was unacceptable to European farmers if they were not allowed to use growth-hormones themselves. Moreover, it would have required a change in the Directive, which would have been difficult to achieve given the uncompromising position of the EP on this issue.

Labelling was therefore never an official option, although it was considered on both sides of the Atlantic. It proved impossible, though, to reach agreement on the form of the label. To the US government and producers, a label of origin (that stated something along the lines of 'meat imported from the US' or a US flag) would have been acceptable, but any reference to adverse health effects or carcinogenity was not. To the European Commission this was crucial, however, and a mere label of origin was insufficient. Consequently, the option was quickly dropped (Interviews 26-9-2000, European Commission; 11-1-2001, USDA; 11-1-2001, AMI; 19-1-2001, USTR).

Labelling was not discussed in the talks between the EC and Canada, although the Canadian industry was receptive to the idea. However, the labelling of Canadian beef could have run into additional problems since Canadian producers were also engaged in a dispute with some US producers who demanded a country of origin label for Canadian beef on the US market. Accepting a labelling solution in the dispute with the EC could have set a precedent in that dispute (Interviews 9-2-2001, AAFC; 20-2-2001-II, DFAIT).

Another form of compensation that was discussed related to the Hormone Free Cattle (HFC) Programme which the US and the EC had established in 1989. In 1995, Canada and the EC had also agreed upon a protocol for the export of non-treated beef. The first batch of beef produced under this programme was exported from Canada to the EC in 1998 (FVO, 1998a: point 5.7).

In the late 1990s, both programmes became the subject of dispute between the EC and the US and Canada in their own right, although more so between the EC and the US. These disputes were the result of inspection trips made by the European Commission's Food and Veterinary Office (FVO; part of the Commission's DG for consumer protection, first DG XXIV, later DG Sanco) in order to monitor the implementation and enforcement of the programmes.

The first inspection trip to the US was made in November 1997. According to the European officials on that mission, the HFC Programme demonstrated several deficiencies in terms of controls on the use of growth-hormones. Follow-up trips were made in July 1998, June/July 1999, November 1999, and January/February 2000 (FVO, 1998b; 1999a; 1999b; 2000a). The reports of these missions were all highly critical of the way the programme was being implemented. The July 1998 report recommended the immediate suspension of beef (and other meat) imports from the US as well as of the Interim Agreement that formed the basis of the beef imports (FVO, 1998b: paragraph 5.1). After the USDA promised to take action on the deficiencies identified in the report, this was not done (FVO, 1999a: 5).

In early 1999, European scientists who were carrying out one of the seventeen studies commissioned after the AB Report discovered that 12% of US beef and beef products that were exported under the HFC Programme contained residues of synthetic hormonal substances. To European officials this demonstrated the 'deficiencies of the US Hormone Free Cattle Program and the ineffectiveness of the residue controls' (FVO, 1999a: 6). In April 1999, a '100% test and hold' requirement was introduced, under which all batches of imported beef from the US would be tested for hormonal residues before they could enter the EC (EC, 1999b). Initially, the US was to come up with a satisfactory solution before 15 June or all imports would be blocked; later, the deadline was extended to 15 December (EC, 1999a; 1999c).

In response to the criticism in the two reports and the discovery of the hormonal residues, the US Food Safety Inspection Service (FSIS), which was responsible for monitoring residues in fresh meat, decided to create a new programme in co-operation with the Agricultural Marketing Service (AMS), another division of USDA (Interview 11-1-2001, USDA). After another highly critical EC report in July 1999 (FVO, 1999a), the FSIS suspended all exports of US beef to the EC until the new programme would be ready. In August 1999, a new programme was established under the name 'Non-Hormone Treated Cattle' (NHTC) Programme. AMS would certify producers of non-treated beef, while FSIS would monitor the beef and certify it for export (FVO, 2000a: 6). One month later the export of beef to the EC was resumed (FVO, 1999b: 3 & 5).

During a visit in November of that year, FVO officials concluded that the NHTC Programme showed several flaws and again recommended that all imports of fresh meat from the US should immediately be blocked (FVO, 1999b: 10). This recommendation was not adopted by the Commission's Standing Veterinary Committee, however, and the deadline for implementing a complete ban was first extended to 15 February and then to 15 March 2000 (EC, 1999f; 2000c; FVO, 2000a: 5). In a final trip to the US, FVO officials made several recommendations for improving the NHTC Programme (FVO, 2000a: 19-21), but they did not recommend the immediate suspension of imports from the US. After the FSIS had announced some changes in the NHTC Programme and the Standing Veterinary Committee had given a positive opinion, the European Commission lifted the deadline for blocking the imports of non-treated beef from the US (EC, 2000d; FVO, 2000a: 23).

In its visits to Canada, FVO found some deficiencies in Canada's Hormone Free Cattle Programme, as well. Still, its recommendations were less drastic than in the case of the US. In May 1998, a visit was made to assess Canada's residue control programmes. By that time, no beef had been exported under Canada's HFC Programme, but exports would start shortly. Although some deficiencies in Canada's HFC Programme were noted, no suspension of imports were recommended. FVO officials did recommend the suspension of imports of Canadian prime veal and offal, but Canada had not exported any prime veal or offal to the EC for human consumption in the previous year anyway (FVO, 1998a: paragraphs 5.7 & 7).

The Canadian Food Inspection Agency (CFIA) and Health Canada proposed some changes in the HFC programme in February 1999, and in September 2000 FVO officials made another visit to Canada (FVO, 2000b: 6). The report concluded that the 'HFC programme as currently operating does not give sufficient guarantees that beef is free from HGPs [Hormonal Growth Promotors, S.P.]' (FVO, 2000b: 26). The European Commission was advised to 'take appropriate steps to ensure that only food commodities of animal origin, which comply with EU food safety requirements, are imported from Canada' but no immediate suspension was recommended (FVO, 2000b: 28).

In December 2000, Health Canada and the CFIA proposed an action plan to remedy some of the deficiencies which the FVO officials had discerned (Health Canada & CFIA, 2000). During this process, exports under Canada's HFC Programme continued.

Exports under both the US and Canadian HFC Programmes remained small, however. Between 1996 and 1998, US exports of beef offal and high quality beef accounted for a little more than US$ 34 million (WTO, 1999b: Annex I). Canadian exports were a mere CAN$ 4.5 million (WTO, 1999c: Annex I). Following the decision to install a 100% test and hold requirement for US beef after the detection of hormonal residues in 1999, exports under the US HFC Programme declined dramatically: the US government claimed that exports of high quality beef declined by about 75% in May and June 1999, while exports of beef offal declined by some 98% (WTO, 1999b: paragraph 45).

It was against this backdrop that the EC and the US worked on a compensation package. The EC offered compensation in the form of increased quotas and reduced tariffs for exports of non-treated beef products to the European market. The US and Canadian governments (as well as the beef producers) had a somewhat ambiguous position on those proposals. On the one hand, they were careful not to set a precedent for future issues and to stress that compensation could only be a temporary solution pending the withdrawal of the import ban. On the other hand, they wanted some assurance from the EC that a compensation package in the form of non-treated beef exports would remain in place for at least some five to ten years, since producers needed at least two years to raise non-treated cattle and then some more to make such a programme profitable. In the end, no agreement was reached because US and Canadian producers feared that the compensation would be withdrawn once the EC had completed its additional risk assessments. This fear was fuelled by remarks from European officials to this effect, as well as the Commission proposals for reinforcing the ban in May 2000 (Interviews 11-1-2001, AMI; 11-1-2001, USDA; 18-1-2001, AFBF; 19-1-2001, USTR; 9-2-2001, AAFC; 20-2-2001-II, DFAIT).

By the end of 2000, the talks on compensation between the US and the EC failed. At that moment, US retaliatory sanctions had been in place for a year and a half. Talks between the EC and Canada started when it became clear that the EC would not come into compliance by the WTO's deadline of 13 May 1999. Most of the time, these talks were relatively informal since the EC gave priority to reaching an agreement with the US first. The talks between the EC and Canada ended when Canada installed its retaliatory measures. Although there was some periodical resurgence of activity between the EC and Canada afterwards, this did not yield any results (Interviews 9-2-2001, AAFC; 20-2-2001-II, DFAIT).

4.5.4 Regulatory developments in the US and Canada

In the US and Canada, the hormone issue did not gain much prominence on the public or political agenda. US and Canadian producers continued to support the use of hormones. Some were willing to allow labelling or to produce hormone-free meat for the European market, but they did not support any changes in domestic standards, arguing that the European ban was unjustified.

Nor did most consumer groups oppose the use of hormones in beef production. Some smaller groups did raise the issue of the health risks associated with hormone-treated beef. In Canada, for instance, the issue was raised by the Canadian Health Coalition (CHC), in response to the 2000 inspection report by the EC's Food and Veterinary Office (CHC, 2000a; 2000b). Subsequently, the issue was picked up by a major Canadian newspaper (Globe and Mail, 2000). In the US, the Organic Consumers Association (OCA) drew attention to publications on the issue of growth-hormones in beef production (Canadian Press, 1999; LA Times, 1999). Even for these groups, however, the potential health risks of, for instance, BST featured far more prominently in their campaigns than those of hormones in beef.

Moreover, among the larger consumer groups, there was little support for a ban on growth-hormones in meat production (Interviews 14-8-2000, BEUC; 22-1-2001, Consumers Union; 16-1-2001, FDA; 19-7-2001, Consumers Association of Canada). They argued that the evidence against the hormones was not compelling and that hormone-treated beef had been consumed safely for several decades. Likewise, US and Canadian consumers did not seem to be very concerned about the use of growth-hormones and the market for non-treated beef, which had always existed in both countries, remained very small.

Opposition against the use of growth-hormones in beef production has therefore remained limited in both countries. By contrast, the campaigns against genetically modified foods were supported by a much broader spectrum of consumer and environmental groups, as we shall see in the next chapter.

These positions were also reflected in the position taken by the Transatlantic Consumer Dialogue (TACD), which was formed in 1998 to provide a platform for consumer groups from the US and the EC. In its statement on the hormone issue, it supported the EC's right to maintain its ban, but it did not go as far as to call for a ban in the US (TACD, 1999c). This stands in marked contrast to the positions taken in the GM foods and data protection issues (which will be discussed in the next two chapters), in which the TACD explicitly called upon the US government to adopt more stringent domestic standards. It therefore reflected the position of most US (and Canadian) consumer groups on the hormones issue: they did not want to undermine the EC ban, but they did not call for a similar ban in their own country either.

During the whole process, US and Canadian beef producers opposed any changes to the approval of the six hormones that were banned by the EC, arguing that the European measures were driven by trade rather than health concerns. They supported the US and Canadian decisions to resort to the WTO and to adopt retaliatory measures (Interview 11-1-2001, AMI). As was noted above, some importers opposed the inclusion of specific items in the retaliation packages, but they did not support a change in the domestic regulations regarding the use of growth-hormones.

4.6 Conclusions

An overview of the main events in the beef-hormone issue is provided in table 4.1. In this section I will discuss the outcomes of this process in terms of a California effect, and the factors that led to those outcomes.

4.6.1 A California effect or not?

This case represents a clear example of a continuing stalemate between, on the one hand, the EC and, on the other, the US and Canada. Neither the US nor Canada has changed its domestic standards for the use of growth-hormones in meat production. Such a change could have taken several forms. First, the US or Canada could have banned growth-hormones that were previously allowed. Second, regulatory authorities in the two countries could have adjusted their approval criteria or procedures in response to the European ban. Third, these authorities could have set additional limitations on the use of certain growth-hormones or meat produced by growth-hormones, for instance by requiring labelling. None of these three potential changes have taken place.

	In the EC	In the US	In Canada	At the international level
1950s		First approvals of growth-hormones		
Early 1980s	Hormone-related scare in Italy			
1981	First EEC Directive on growth-hormones			
September 1985	Completion of the Lamming report			
December 1985	The EEC bans all growth-hormones			
1987	The US request the formation of an expert group under the TBT Agreement. The request is blocked by the EEC			
1987 and 1989				JECFA recommendations on five hormones
1988-1989	Talks leading to the interim agreement on exports of hormone-free beef			
1 January 1989	Import ban enters into force	US imposes retaliatory measures		
1 January 1995				SPS Agreement enters into force
June 1995				Adoption of Codex standards on hormones
March 1996	Start of BSE scare			
April 1996	Adoption of Directive 96/22			
April and September 1996		US government files complaint with WTO and lifts retaliation	Canadian government files complaint with WTO	
August 1997	WTO panel reports			
January 1998	WTO AB report			
Middle 1998			First Canadian exports of hormone-free beef to the EC	
April 1999	'100% test and hold' requirement on US hormone-free beef exports			
April 1999	SCVPH report			
July and August 1999		US imposes retaliatory measures	Canada imposes retaliatory measures	
May 2000	The Commission proposes to give the hormones ban a new basis			
End of 2000	Talks on compensation eventually fail			

Table 4.1: Main events in the beef-hormone process

As to the production of non-hormone treated beef in Canada and the US, there is no indication that this has increased over the last ten years, at least not as a result of the European import ban. Both countries have established programmes for hormone-free beef exports to the EC, but the quantities exported under these programmes have remained limited. In principle, these programmes could form the basis for an increase in domestic non-treated beef production by providing an infrastructure of certified producers and facilities, but there is no indication that this has happened either.

Finally, the international standards on growth-hormones in beef have not been strengthened in response to the European ban. In 1999, JECFA recommended the adoption of ADIs for the three natural growth-hormones, which it had not deemed necessary in the late 1980s. Yet, it did not recommend MRLs, which were the most significant type of standard in the hormone issue. Moreover, Codex standards have not yet been changed as a result of the JECFA recommendations.

At the same time, the EC has not relaxed its own standards. It has rather strengthened them by applying stricter enforcement mechanisms and by banning additional growth-promoting substances. Since the WTO cases, the EC has been working on obtaining new scientific evidence to support the hormone ban and it does not seem to be willing to lift or relax it in the near future.

In terms of the trade aspects of the issue, there were two possible ways out of the dispute. First, the EC, the US and Canada could have agreed on a set of MRLs for imported meat, possibly ones which were more stringent than the Codex MRLs. It is doubtful whether more stringent MRLs would have been acceptable to the US and Canada, but at least it would have moved the debate to more acceptable grounds for these two countries. To the EC, however, allowing residues of growth-hormones in imported meat has been unacceptable. As a result, this option was not feasible.

A second potential solution might have been the labelling of imported hormone-treated beef. This option has been briefly considered by all the parties to the dispute. In the end, however, no agreement could be reached. Within the EC, a labelling solution would have encountered strong resistance from the European Parliament, and European farmers and consumer groups. Apart from the principle of labelling, no agreement could be reached on the form of a label either: the European Commission insisted on a reference to the potential health effects of hormone-treated beef, while the US and Canada were not willing to go beyond a label of origin. Consequently, the labelling option was not pursued any further.

Hence, in terms of my theoretical framework, the win-set of the EC did not overlap with the win-sets of the US and Canada. It looks as if the US and Canadian win-sets have remained fairly stable during the whole process and have not changed as a result of the European ban. The EC's win-set may even have become smaller during the process, as some options that seemed (remotely) acceptable in earlier stages became (absolutely) unacceptable at later stages. In the next subsection I will examine why this is so and how the outcomes of this case can be explained.

4.6.2 Explaining the outcomes

In explaining the outcomes I will follow the hypotheses as formulated in chapter 2. In these hypotheses, three ways were discerned in which regulatory trade measures and retaliatory measures may affect other countries' political balances and win-sets: by changing constraints, by changing preferences, and by expanding participation. I will discuss each of these three ways and the hypotheses related to them.

Changing constraints

To begin with the constraints, my first hypothesis stated that *a regulatory trade measure or a retaliatory measure will have a greater effect on another country's political balance, the greater that measure's effect on the other country's exports*. In this case, exports of beef to the EC were relatively insignificant to the US and Canada. Both countries exported less than 1% of their annual beef production to the EC in the years before the European ban. This was partly the result of the EC's restrictive import regime for beef, which already made it difficult for foreign producers to compete on the European market. Similarly, the US and Canadian retaliatory measures affected only a small part of European exports.

According to my second hypothesis, *a regulatory trade measure or a retaliatory measure will have a greater effect on another country's political balance, the more that measure's effects are targeted at pivotal actors in the other country*. The European import ban was not particularly targeted towards specific groups in the US and Canada. Some producers may have been affected more than others, but then their number was very small and they could easily switch to the domestic market or other export markets. The number of producers under the non-treated meat programmes has remained too small to form a important voice in the US and Canadian debates. Therefore, targeting played no role in the US and Canada.

The US and Canadian retaliatory measures were targeted somewhat. First, they excluded the UK, which had been an opponent of the European ban. This did not wield much leverage, however, since the retaliation still affected fourteen out of fifteen member states. In actual practice, the US retaliation mainly affected Danish pork exporters. There are indications that these producers started a lobby for an agreement between the EC and the US, but pork producers, and Denmark as a member state, were not particularly pivotal. As a result, they were not able to make the difference between the adoption or rejection of an agreement with the US (or Canada).

The application of the carousel approach by the US would have increased the range of actors potentially affected by the retaliatory measures, mainly by increasing uncertainty on the part of European exporters, but this approach was never applied. Even then, it is doubtful whether the extent of the retaliatory measures would have been sufficient to effect a change in the EC's position on the import ban.

Taking the extent and the targeting of the EC ban into account, it is clear that it hardly had any impact on US and Canadian producers. As a result, there was not much need for the US and Canadian governments to change their domestic standards in order to avoid the European ban from affecting their products. Likewise, the US and Canadian retaliatory measures were too limited to induce the EC to give in to the two countries' demands. This case study therefore seems to confirm the conclusion drawn in the leghold trap case that the extent and targeting of trade measures seem to determine a government's necessity to react to them and their willingness to reach an agreement.

In the third hypothesis it was stated that *a regulatory trade measure will have a greater effect on regulatory standards in the target country, the lesser the costs of complying with that measure for actors in the target country*. In this case, the costs of complying were enormous for the US and Canada, and this seems to a large extent to have determined their positions. Changing the domestic standards for the use of growth-hormones (in this case: banning the use of these hormones) would have been expensive in two ways.

First, the direct costs would have been high. As was explained in section 4.3.1, the use of growth-hormones had significant effects on the costs of producing meat. If the US and Canadian governments had banned the use of growth-hormones, these benefits would have been foregone, and the position of North American beef producers on world markets would have deteriorated. These costs were so high because the hormones had been used for decades. As a result, their use had become widespread and attempts to reverse this situation would have encountered strong opposition.

Second, conforming to the European measures would have had significant consequences for disputes on related issues and the ongoing debates over agricultural trade liberalisation. Giving in to the European import ban would have set an important precedent, since the EC could have resorted to similar regulatory measures in a wider range of issues. Consequently, the hormone ban had the potential to affect almost all agricultural trade between North America and the EC, which considerably increased the costs of conforming to the European standards.

The fourth hypothesis stated that *a regulatory trade measure will have a greater effect on regulatory standards in the target country, if it is supported by both public interest groups and domestic producers in the initiator country*. The occurrence of this kind of *Baptist-bootlegger coalitions* in the country imposing a regulatory trade measure was hypothesised to increase the credibility of that measure.

This case shows a textbook example of a Baptist-bootlegger coalition in the EC. On the one hand, the hormone and import bans have been supported by European consumer groups, represented by BEUC, which were concerned about the potential health risks of hormone-treated beef. On the other hand, the bans were supported by European farmers and their representative COPA/COGECA, which demanded protection from cheap foreign beef imports.

The import ban was initially opposed by a limited number of producers that were highly dependent on US offal imports. After some years, however, these producers had either adjusted to the new market conditions or gone out of business, which further reduced any opposition to the ban from business groups.

This dual support base has been reinforced by recurring food scares. In the early 1980s, one such scare led to the ban in the first place. In 1988, the discovery of a large black market for illegal growth-hormones reduced the room for manoeuvre which the Commission had in negotiating an agreement with the US. In the second half of the 1990s, several food scares, but most notably the BSE crisis, reinforced consumer concerns and affected European beef markets. Changes in the CAP may have reduced the need for direct protection against foreign imports somewhat, but the concomitant rise of regulatory burdens on European farmers has led them to renew calls for protection.

As would be expected on the basis of the hypothesis, this has led to very strong support for the hormone ban as well as the ban on imported hormone-treated beef. It has therefore served to constrain the EC's win-set considerably, reducing it even further in the course of the process. As result, the European ban has been very credible and the chances of it being lifted have been small.

Although this effect is perfectly in line with the hypothesis outlined above, the support by European farmers seems to have had another effect as well. Apart from constraining the EC's win-set, as was expected by the hypothesis, the open support by European farmers and the apparent significance of protectionist motives behind the ban may also have reduced the US and Canadian win-sets. In both countries, the European ban has mainly been seen as a protectionist measure, which has made it more difficult to comply with the European standards for a number of reasons.

First, it would have been more difficult to 'sell' a change in domestic standards if it was a reaction to foreign protectionist measures. Second, the perception of the ban as a protectionist measure reduced the trustworthiness of the EC as a partner for an agreement, since US and Canadian producers and officials feared the EC would withdraw from an agreement once it had found another basis for the hormone ban. These two reasons will be discussed more closely below in the context of the hypotheses on preferences. Third and finally, as was explained above, because of the protectionist aspects of the ban, it became linked to a wider set of disputes between the EC and the US and Canada about agricultural trade liberalisation.

The existence of an open Baptist-bootlegger coalition probably reinforced these concerns on the part of the US and Canada. As a result, Baptist-bootlegger coalitions may affect not only the win-set of the country imposing a regulatory trade measure, but also the win-set of the country affected by that measure. In that sense, they may actually reduce the likelihood of a California effect, as this case study seems to suggest.

Changing preferences

The second way relates to groups' and officials' preferences. Under this category, I formulated a number of hypotheses. First, it was hypothesised that *a regulatory trade measure will have a greater effect on regulatory standards in the target coun-*

try, the more it ties in with deeply-held values and perceived problems in the target country. In this case, the European ban did not tie in with any perceived problem in the US or Canada. Most hormones had been approved for use as growth-promoters decades before the European ban, and their safety had not been questioned since.

Consequently, the potential health risks of these hormones did not figure on the agenda of food regulators (FDA and Health Canada) or mainstream consumer groups. Apart from a small number of consumer groups, these health risks were considered to be remote and their use for such a long time was seen as proof of their safety. Apparently, the reversal of the approval of DES in the 1970s had not changed this perception.

Hence, to most consumer groups, the safety of growth-hormones was not an issue and they preferred to focus on other issues. For the FDA and Health Canada, reversing the approval of the hormones without new and conclusive scientific evidence would have undermined their trustworthiness as competent and independent regulatory authorities.

Conversely, the same was true for the US and Canadian arguments against the hormone ban. The European Commission seems to have been susceptible to the scientific arguments brought forward by the US and Canada in the 1980s. After all, the Commission had also proposed to allow the use of the hormones after the Lamming working group's interim report had concluded they were safe. European consumer groups, the European Parliament, and most EC member states were not impressed, however. They had far less confidence in scientific studies that claimed to disprove human health risks and were therefore less willing to accept the US and Canadian arguments. This stance was strengthened by the BSE crisis, which showed one clear example of scientific studies that had underestimated human health effects (in this case of an animal disease).

Second, *a regulatory trade measure will have a greater effect on regulatory standards in the target country, the more actors in the target country perceive it to be motivated by genuine concerns rather than protectionism.* In this case, the US and Canadian governments as well as producers overwhelmingly considered the European hormone ban to be a protectionist measure. They did not consider it to be driven by genuine concerns about human health. This perception made a change of domestic regulations less acceptable and made it more acceptable to file a complaint with the WTO.

Furthermore, the perceived protectionist intent of the European measures made it more difficult to arrive at an agreement on increased imports of non-treated beef. US and Canadian producers feared the EC would withdraw its concessions once it had formulated a new scientific basis for the hormone ban, which would have undermined any gains from producing the non-treated beef. Consequently, they were not willing to accept the EC's offers for improved access as a means of compensation.

The third hypothesis relating to preferences stated that *a regulatory trade measure will have a greater effect on regulatory standards in the target country if it conforms to international law and international standards*. In this case, both international trade law and international standards were important. As to international trade law, the cases before the WTO have shown that the European import ban violates GATT/WTO law. This has probably reinforced the US and Canadian positions on this issue.

It does not, however, seem to have led to a change in the EC's position. Most probably, this is because the European ban was imposed in the 1980s and had been in force for more than seven years when the US and Canada filed their complaints with the WTO. In that period, the European Commission had always maintained in public that the ban was necessary to protect human health. As a result, it was much more difficult for the EC to reverse the ban than it would have been if it had come into force more recently.

This ties in with the conclusion in the case study on leghold traps (in the previous chapter), in that a GATT/WTO case seems to be more effective as a threat than as a means to address an existing regulatory trade measure. This conclusion is also supported by the EC's decisions on BST. Although the scientific evidence concerning BST appears to be rather similar to that for the growth-hormones in beef, the European ban on BST does not extend to imported milk produced with BST (the equivalent of imported hormone-treated beef). Adopting the ban on the basis of human health effects would most likely have led to another dispute with the US and a case under the SPS Agreement. These considerations probably played an important role in the decision to ban BST on the basis of animal welfare, even if this meant imports could not be blocked. In that sense, the beef-hormone cases before the WTO may have had an impact on EC policies, but not in the beef-hormone issue itself.

Besides international trade law, the standards formulated by the Codex Alimentarius Commission have been relevant. This is so because of the role they play under the SPS Agreement, but also as a body of international guidelines that countries can look to in formulating their own standards. In this case, the European hormone ban contradicted the Codex standards and these standards did not have any influence on the European ban. Here, too, the fact that the European ban had been in place before the Codex standards were adopted has probably reduced their effects on European standards. Moreover, the Codex standards were adopted after a narrow vote in which the EC member states opposed their adoption, as well as the underlying criteria on which the decision was based. As a result, the Codex standards have not enjoyed much support within the EC, which has translated into the EC ignoring them in the development of its own standards.

Changing participation

The third and final way in which measures can affect another country's political balance (and thereby its win-set) is by expanding participation. The hypothesis stated that *a regulatory trade measure will have a lesser effect on regulatory standards in the target country, if the target country succeeds in expanding participation in the initiator country to trade officials*. In this case, participation has been expanded by the cases before the WTO and the negotiations preceding and following these cases. As a result, trade officials have been heavily involved in the issue, but they have tended not to undermine the positions taken by other officials.

All in all, differences between types of officials do not seem to have made much of a difference in this case. In the US and Canada, agricultural (sponsoring) officials, food regulators (policy officials) and trade officials have all defended the existing domestic standards and rejected changes to these standards. In the EC, the DGs for agriculture, which can be considered the 'sponsoring official' and had the lead in most of the process, and consumer protection (the 'policy official') both supported the hormone ban. DG Trade has also supported this position in talks with the US and Canada.

This is not to say that there were no differences in opinion between these officials. Most likely, they did differ on specific aspects such as the acceptability of certain types of labels or their willingness to accept certain types of compensation. Yet, these differences did not lead to changes in the more fundamental positions taken by the governments and the outcomes of this issue. In that sense, participation expansion did not lead to a change in win-sets, probably for the reasons discussed above under the hypothesis on GATT/WTO law.

General conclusion

To wrap up these arguments, the US and Canada could largely afford to ignore the European import ban because of its limited effects on US and Canadian producers. A change in domestic US and Canadian standards was unlikely since the hormones had already been used for decades. This resulted in widespread support for their use among both producers, who relied heavily on growth-hormones, and consumer groups, who did not see much reason for concern about their safety. Moreover, the whole issue was closely related to wider debates on agricultural trade liberalisation that pitted the EC against the US and Canada on a much wider range of issues. These positions were reinforced by the perception that the European ban was mainly informed by protectionist motives.

Within the EC, support for the hormone and import ban was widespread among agricultural groups, which wanted to protect their members against cheaper imports, and consumer groups, which were concerned about possible health risks. Both positions were strengthened in the course of the process, and the US and Canadian retaliation was too limited to make much of a difference. Because the hormone ban preceded the SPS Agreement and the Codex standards, it became more difficult for the EC to reverse its policies in response to the WTO cases and the decisions in Codex.

CHAPTER FIVE

GENETICALLY MODIFIED FOODS AND FOOD PRODUCTS

5.1 INTRODUCTION AND BACKGROUND

5.1.1 What is genetic modification?

Depending on one's perspective, the story of genetic modification starts in the second half of the 20th century, in the late 19th century, or around 1800 BC. In fact, this seemingly innocent question already reveals many of the controversies underlying the debate over this technology.

Genetic modification (or 'genetic engineering' as it is often called)[1] takes place if genes from one organism are inserted into the cells of another organism by molecular techniques. Through genetic modification certain desired traits can be conferred on living organisms. Genetic modification is used for a number of purposes, such as the production of medicines by bacteria and the modification of plants (and, possibly, animals) for food production. In this chapter I will limit myself to the regulation of the latter kind of genetic modification, which is known as 'agricultural biotechnology.'

According to its proponents and most biotechnologists, genetic modification is basically an extension of traditional breeding techniques. Farmers and plant breeders have been trying to improve their crops by selectively crossing and back-crossing varieties in order to obtain certain desired traits. Since this also comes down to an exchange of genes from one variety to another, genetic modification is merely the continuation of these traditional techniques with other means. In this view, the story of genetic modification therefore started with the discovery and rediscovery of Mendel's genetic laws. Some even stress a longer continuity, which stretches back to 1800 BC when humans started to use yeast and to ferment wine (IFT, 2000: 42).

Opponents of biotechnology, on the other hand, see genetic modification as fundamentally different from traditional breeding techniques, since it allows more fundamental changes in an organism's genetic structure. As a result, genetic modification allows a degree of human intervention in nature that is unprecedented by any other technique, which raises all kinds of scientific and moral questions. Consequently, opponents see no continuity with earlier techniques and date the

---

1 The terminology is not entirely clear in this field. I will use 'genetic modification,' which is the term used by the EC Directives covering these techniques. The US government, however, uses the term 'genetic engineering' for these techniques and uses 'genetic modification' to cover both the modern (recombinant DNA) techniques and the traditional breeding techniques (FDA 1999a).

beginning of genetic modification to 1953, when Watson and Crick discovered the structure of DNA, or in the early 1970s, when the recombinant DNA techniques were developed (for an overview of this development, see Wright, 1994: 71-78).

After these techniques had been developed, a heated debate arose over the desirability and consequences of genetic modification. In this period, research in biotechnology and the debate surrounding it focused on medical applications, for instance the production of medicines by bacteria. A regulatory framework was put in place to regulate the foreseen risks, but by the early 1980s the technology had become less controversial and regulatory safeguards were again relaxed. At the beginning of the 1980s, the first genetically modified medicines were marketed. These applications of genetic modification were relatively uncontroversial and did not arouse much public debate (for a detailed analysis of the political debate and regulation in the 1970s and early 1980s, see Wright, 1994).

During the 1980s, a number of scientists and firms also started to investigate the possibilities of agricultural biotechnology, which related both to genetically modified (or: GM) foods and food products, and to non-food plants (like tobacco and cotton). Initially, this did not stir much controversy, but when GM foods came out of the test fields and onto the food markets, the issue reoccupied centre stage yet again.

The first GM plants were planted for commercial purposes in the mid-1990s. Since then, the estimated acreage for the growth of GM plants (both food and non-food plants) has gradually increased from 1.7 million hectares in 1996 to 27.8 million hectares in 1998 (James, 1998: 3) and more than 44 million hectares in 2000 (James, 2000b). The three leading countries in agricultural biotechnology have been the US, Argentina and Canada, which in 1999 accounted for some 72%, 17% and 10% of global GM crop area, respectively (James, 2000a; the figures for 2000 show an increase in Argentina's share, see James, 2000b). The main GM crop has been soya, which in 1999 accounted for 54% of the global area of GM crops, followed by maize (28%), cotton (9%) and canola, a kind of oilseed rape (also 9%) (James, 2000a; the 2000 figures are almost identical, see James, 2000b).

In this case study, I will limit myself to genetically modified foods and food products. Although most of the environmental issues related to GM food crops are also relevant to non-food crops, GM food crops have raised specific concerns on the part of consumer and environmental groups since they and the products derived from them are meant for human consumption.

To understand the alleged promises and risks inherent in these crops and food products, some basic insight into the techniques and uses of genetic modification is necessary. Genetic modification takes place if a gene that carries a desired trait is inserted into another organism. The desired trait can take several forms, which can be broadly divided into production and consumption benefits. At the production stage, genetic modification can produce various effects, two of which are most common.

First, if a plant is vulnerable to certain pests, a gene can be inserted that makes it produce its own insecticide. For instance, Bt maize produces the toxin normally produced by the Bacillus thuringiensis, which kills European corn borers, the most important pest to threaten maize (Levidow, 1999: 12). New Leaf Potatoes also produce Bt toxin to protect them against the Colorado potato beetle (Doyle, 1999).

Second, plants can be made resistant to some herbicide. One popular group of plants in this category are the so-called 'Roundup Ready' plants (mainly soya and oilseed rape). Roundup, or glyphosate, is a very powerful, 'total' herbicide that kills all weeds. Indeed, it is so powerful that it would also kill the crops themselves if used on traditional varieties. Yet, by inserting a gene that confers tolerance against Roundup, the herbicide can be used without damaging the crops themselves.

In 2000, 74% of GM crops (food and non-food combined) were of the herbicide-tolerant type. Insect resistant crops accounted for 19% of GM crops. Crops that exhibited both traits at the same time occupied some 7% of the 1999 acreage (James, 2000b).

Various other genes have been inserted at the production stage, too. The first genetically modified crop to be approved in the US was the 'Flavr Savr' tomato, in which a gene was inserted that delayed the rotting process. Strawberries have been developed that can be frozen. These GM crops have not yet become very important, though, accounting for less than 1% of the global acreage of GM crops in 1999 (James, 2000a). Until now, the commercial use of agricultural biotechnology has been confined to plants, but there have been several tests with GM animals, like a salmon that produces its own growth hormones (ISB, 2000).

The first wave of GM products mainly provided these kinds of producer benefits, although proponents also point at the environmental benefits of these products. Benefits to consumers were indirect at best. Genetic modification can also be used to change the products themselves, however, and thus provide consumption benefits by changing their nutritional composition. This type of GM product is expected to become more important in the future, but some already exist. For instance, a GM rice has been developed that offers additional vitamin A and iron (IFT, 2000: 43).

Together with the gene conferring the desired trait, usually two other genes are inserted (Doyle, 1999). First, a 'promoter' gene, which ensures that the gene expresses itself, i.e. will become active in the crop. A gene has to be 'turned on' in order to be effective. In traditional breeding this takes place through the natural gene structure of the organisms. If a gene is transferred to a different species, however, this natural system no longer works, because the host species does not recognise or understand the expression mechanism of the inserted gene. Therefore, another gene has to be inserted to ensure that the gene expresses itself: the promoter gene.

Second, producers need a way to assess whether genetic modification has succeeded. There are several techniques for inserting a gene, but it is not certain that the transfer will take place in all cells. In order to sort out the genes in which the transfer has taken place from those in which it has not, a 'marker' gene is included in the package. This marker gene confers resistance against some antibiotic. As a result, a cell will become resistant against the antibiotic if, but only if, the transfer has succeeded. Now, by spraying the antibiotic on the treated cells, only the modified cells will survive and can be used for further processing. Although the antibiotic resistance marker gene is only used in the production phase of the crop, it is normally not removed from the modified cells afterwards.

5.1.2 The promises and risks inherent in agricultural biotechnology

According to its proponents, agricultural biotechnology holds great promise for the quality and efficiency of food production. The arguments generally presented in favour of this technology point at several kinds of benefits that can be expected from it.

First, GM crops are said to be environmentally friendly, since they reduce the amount of pesticides and herbicides sprayed on the plants, thus conserving soil, water and energy (IFT, 2000: 43). Data have been reported indicating a decrease in the use of pesticides by 26% of farmers growing Bt maize (AFBF, 2000a; Doyle, 1999). A United States Department of Agriculture (USDA) study found reduced use of pesticides and herbicides in most cases of Bt maize and Roundup Ready soya beans, although in some cases the effect was small or insignificant (USDA, undated).

Second, future GM crops should be able to conform more closely to consumer wishes. By genetic modification, crops can be produced that taste differently, have a lower fat content, or are more healthy in other ways (IFT, 2000: 43).

Third, GM crops may produce higher yields, leading to higher production of food for lower prices. The profitability of GM crops is difficult to determine because it depends on a number of other factors, such as weather conditions and the intensity of pest and weed problems in any one year. As a result, the profitability may differ between years and sometimes the extra costs of planting GM seeds (which are more expensive than traditional seeds) are not off-set by decreased spraying costs or increased yields. Nevertheless, research in Illinois has indicated that planting Bt maize should be profitable in 7 out of 10 years; Roundup Ready soya beans have about the same yield as conventional soya beans, but farmers can save some US$27 per acre on overall growing costs, due to savings on pesticides; pesticide costs for New Leaf Plus Potatoes, which produces toxins against Colorado potato beetles and aphids, would be some US$60 to US$90 less per acre, depending on specific conditions; Roundup Ready Canola also produces greater yields and greater profits per acre (all cited in Doyle, 1999).

It is also often pointed out that agricultural biotechnology has the potential to increase agricultural production in developing countries, for example by creating crops that are resistant against certain pests or that can survive in dry or cold climates. According to many proponents, agricultural biotechnology is therefore a sheer necessity to feed the growing world population in the coming decades.

Opponents are more sceptical about the effects on food production in developing countries. They argue that the current food problems are not the result of insufficient production techniques, but of the way food production is organised in developing countries (Greenpeace, undated: paragraph 2)

In addition to their scepticism about the alleged benefits, the opponents of agricultural biotechnology warn against a number of risks they feel GM crops and foods pose. Generally, two types of concerns can be discerned: concerns about food safety and concerns about the environment.

The concerns about food safety focus on two aspects: possible allergenicity and the transfer of antibiotic resistance marker genes. Opponents of GM foods fear these foods may contain new allergens or that allergens will be transferred together with the desired trait. The prime example of allergenicity as a result of genetic modification is the case of the Brazil nut gene that was inserted into soya plants. It turned out that people who were allergic to Brazil nuts were also allergic to the soya from the genetically modified plants. Although this was discovered during the development of the plant and the soya was never placed on the market, the example is still referred to by opponents (see e.g. Consumers International, 1999; Consumers Union, 1999a; 1999b; Greenpeace, undated: paragraph 5; TACD, 2000a). Proponents point out, however, that no approved GM crop has ever been proven to contain new allergens.

Another food safety concern relates to the antibiotic resistance marker genes. It is feared that these genes may be transferred to viruses, which would then acquire the antibiotic resistance themselves, rendering many antibiotics useless. For instance, a common antibiotic resistance marker gene codes for resistance against ampicillin, an antibiotic that is often prescribed against certain viruses. If microorganisms in the human body would take over the marker gene from the GM food, they would also become resistant against ampicillin (Consumers International, 1996; 1999; Greenpeace, undated: paragraphs 4 & 6; TACD, 2000a). Again, there is no evidence that this kind of transfer has actually taken place, but opponents warn that if it does, it is already too late.

Environmental concerns relate to the plants themselves and to the effects on insects in their environment. Some fear that GM plants may become weeds or may confer their genetically modified traits on weedy relatives that live nearby. This would have dire consequences, since the genetic modification would make it much more difficult to extinguish the GM plants, for example if they had become resistant against herbicides (Greenpeace, undated: section 3). Closely related is the concern that GM plants and their next generations may crowd out other varieties of the same species, reducing the number of different varieties available (the biodiversity). Apart from the intrinsic value of having many different types of plants and animals, biodiversity is also valuable as a source of genes (Doyle, 1999). As natural circumstances change, it is easier for a species to adapt if there is a pool of possible genes that may contain useful traits. By reducing biodiversity this pool is depleted, and so are the opportunities for future adaptations.

The concerns about both the generation of weeds and biodiversity relate to the degree of cross-pollination among plants. Several studies have been conducted to examine the circumstances under which this takes place and the rate by which the GM trait is dispersed among non-treated plants. So far, this has yielded no clear evidence of far-reaching dispersion of the GM traits (AFBF, 2000a; Doyle, 1999).

Genetically modified plants that produce their own toxin (such as Bt crops) may affect insects in their environment. Some have raised concerns about the effects on non-target insects that are exposed to the toxin. A much-debated study in this field concerns the effect of the Bt toxin on monarch butterflies, a benevolent species. In an article published in Nature, some researchers reported that in laboratory experiments the larvae of this species suffered from exposure to the Bt toxin. Others have pointed out, however, that these results are specific to the circumstances of the experiments, which are not likely to be replicated in natural situations (AFBF, 2000a; BIO, 1999a; 1999b; 2000e). Field studies reportedly showed minimal impacts on monarch butterfly populations (Doyle, 1999). According to some, Bt crops could indirectly even stimulate non-target species by reducing pesticide use (Doyle, 1999; IFT, 2000: 45).

Others have warned against the possibility that the insects the toxin is meant to control build up resistance against that toxin. In each group of insects, some may be (partially) resistant against a toxin. By natural selection these insects will survive and after a while the whole or a large part of the population may have become resistant against the toxin.

This process of building up resistance among the target insects is essentially unavoidable, but producers have sought to delay it by a combination of techniques (Doyle, 1999; Levidow, 1999: 14). By giving high doses of the toxin, most insects are killed, leaving only a few insects to multiply. Another technique consists of planting non-modified crops alongside modified crops. The insects that live off the non-modified crops will not build up resistance to the toxin. When they cross with resistant insects that have lived off the modified crops, the resistance trait will be diluted. These so-called 'refuge' areas normally consist of some 20% of total plantings, sometimes up to 50%.

For all these concerns, the pattern of argument is the same: proponents argue that there is no scientific evidence that any of these problems will occur on a larger scale than under traditional breeding methods (e.g. IFT, 2000: 43), while opponents argue that too little is yet known about the effects of genetic modification, especially outside experimental settings and when it comes to long-term effects.

Underlying these different views of the risks of genetic modification are the different views of genetic modification indicated at the beginning of this chapter. According to its proponents, genetic modification is essentially an extension of traditional breeding techniques. In a way, the traditional techniques might even be more dangerous since, together with the desired traits, all kinds of other traits are transferred as well. By inserting only some specific genes, modern genetic modification can avoid such unwanted transfers and reduce the associated risks. They also point out that many of the potential problems associated with genetic modification (such as the introduction of allergens and the acquisition of resistance to toxins by target insects) are no different from what could occur under traditional techniques. Thus, there is no a priori reason to suspect that modern techniques pose greater or different risks than the traditional ones. Since almost twenty years of studying and experimenting with genetically modified crops have not revealed any special risks there is no reason to treat them any differently than traditional crops, so the proponents argue.

Opponents, on the other hand, see genetic modification as fundamentally different from traditional breeding techniques. Genetic modification allows the insertion of traits from completely different species into a crop, something which is not possible with traditional breeding techniques (see e.g. Consumers Union, 2000a). This kind of gene transfer between species is likely to lead to unexpected consequences, since the way the genes will behave in the host cell cannot be predicted from our knowledge of traditional crossing. Even if the opponents acknowledge there is no specific scientific evidence for these risks, they argue that it is better to be cautious because the potential risks are enormous and once a problem occurs it may be too late. By analogy, some opponents point to the unforeseen effects of transfers of certain species to other habitats or the unforeseen characteristics of synthetic chemicals in their early days. Consequently, they argue that there is reason to expect adverse consequences and one should apply the precautionary principle that it is best to be too careful when potentially high risks are unknown but likely.

These different perceptions of the risks of GM crops and foods are reinforced by the moral or religious concerns some people have over genetic modification. Some opponents feel that the technology allows unjustified human intervention in nature, a view that is evidently not held by people who see genetic modification as an extension of traditional breeding.

All sets of concerns (moral, environmental, and food safety related) have played a role in the debate over GM foods and food products. The different arguments are often voiced together or are bound together. In this case study, I will limit myself to the food safety aspects of genetic modification, though. The environmental and moral concerns and regulatory developments in these fields will only be taken into account insofar as they have influenced the debate over and regulation of food safety aspects.

5.1.3 International work on GM food safety

International work on the safety of GM food products has taken place in several forums. In this field, it was the Organisation for Economic Co-operation and Development (OECD) that played a pioneering role. As early as 1982, the OECD published a report on biotechnology (OECD, 1982). In 1983, the OECD formed an Ad Hoc Group of National Experts to study the safety assessment of biotechnology.

This group published reports on safety considerations in 1986 and 1992 (OECD, 1986; 1992).

The OECD's most important contribution to the development of GM food safety regulation concerns the 'substantial equivalence' approach, which was developed in a 1993 report (OECD, 1993). This approach uses existing, 'traditional' food products as a benchmark against which to assess the safety of new, genetically modified food products. If a GM (or any other new) food product is compositionally similar to an already existing food product with a history of safe use, there is no reason to treat it any differently than the existing food product. What counts is therefore not the *production method* as such, but the characteristics of the food *product*. As the report explains:

> 'The concept of substantial equivalence embodies the idea that existing organisms used as food or as a source of food, can be used as the basis for comparison when assessing the safety of human consumption of a food or food component that has been modified or is new.' (OECD, 1993: 11)

A safety assessment should therefore focus on similarities and differences between the new food product and its traditional counterpart, if it exists, for instance a GM soya bean and a traditional soya bean that has been consumed safely for many years. The two products can be compared with each other in terms of their composition, the levels of possible toxicants and allergens and the like, under the intended conditions of use. Then:

> 'knowledge that a new food or food component(s) was derived from organism(s) whose newly introduced traits have been well-characterised, together with a conclusion that there is reasonable certainty of no harm as compared with its conventional or traditional counterpart, means that a new food or food component(s) can be considered substantially equivalent.' (OECD, 1993: 11)

If that is not the case, 'the identified differences should be the focus of further evaluations' (OECD, 1993: 12).

The concept of substantial equivalence is consistent with the view of biotechnology as an extension of traditional breeding techniques. Genetic modification is not seen as risky in itself, and consequently there is no need for specific regulations (an argument already voiced in OECD, 1986: 42). Only insofar as a GM food product is different from other food products, in terms of *product* characteristics, should it be subjected to further safety assessments. The process of genetic modification is likely to change some product characteristics, which will necessitate an assessment of these differences, but this is not unlike other modifications made to food products and not related to the technique of genetic modification in itself.

The OECD's work in this area is important because, as we will see, it has served as an important baseline in international debates over the regulation of GM foods. The US and Canadian governments explicitly base their policies on the OECD's concept of substantial equivalence (which, of course, they have themselves helped to develop in the OECD working groups) and, more generally, it has set the terms for the debate over this issue for proponents and opponents alike.

5.2 The initial situation in the US and Canada

The GM food issue differs from the other issues in that it is very difficult to mark a clear starting point in the process to be studied. Of course, in all cases the definition of a starting point or initial situation is a little arbitrary. Most issues do not come 'out of the blue' or move from one static equilibrium to another; they have been around for a long time, and the trade measure may only be the start of a new phase in that longer process. Still, in the other three issues one can reasonably point at some process that was started by a European trade measure and, correspondingly, some initial situation that was affected by the trade measure.

In the GM food issue, however, the processes in the EC, US and Canada have run largely parallel. In the early 1980s, all three gained some experience with medicines that were produced through GM techniques. The use of genetic modification for food did not start until 1990, when the first GM food additive was approved in the US, and the mid-1990s, when the first GM food products started to appear on North-American and European shelves.

GM foods therefore were, and still are, a relatively new phenomenon. The EC, the US and Canada all had to find their way in this new issue area, in which all kinds of new concerns were raised by public interest groups. Even if the basic regulatory approach was laid down relatively early (as in the US government's 1986 Coordinated Framework), the particular standards have been subject to change and challenges since then, especially as public concern as regards the issue started to increase during the second half of the 1990s.

At some point in this process, the EC adopted certain trade measures that became part of an already dynamic political debate in the US and Canada. Because of the dynamism and flux of this new issue area, it is much more difficult to disentangle cause and effect in these cases and to determine the exact contribution of the EC's trade measures to their outcomes.

Nevertheless, it is possible to discern some sort of 'basic approach' which the three governments have taken and then to examine changes of, but more often within, this basic approach. In this section I will sketch the basic approaches of the US and Canadian governments. The next section describes the development of the EC regulation of GM foods.

5.2.1 The initial situation in the United States

The 1986 Coordinated Framework and the FDA

The US government was very quick to establish a regulatory framework for GM crops and foods. Already in 1986 a 'Coordinated Framework' was published. In 1992, the Food and Drug Administration published its 'Statement of Policy on Genetically Modified Food.' The basic approach taken in these two documents was highly similar and has also remained unchanged until now.

In June 1986, the Office of Science and Technology Policy (OSTP), part of the Executive Office of the President, published a 'Coordinated Framework for Regulation of Biotechnology' (OSTP, 1986), after drafts had been published in 1984 and 1985 (OSTP, 1984; 1985). The Coordinated Framework sought to address the multifaceted character of the new technology by bringing together the various agencies that were responsible for regulating different aspects of biotechnology. In doing so, the Coordinated Framework relied on existing legislation. This legislation already contained procedures and standards for the assessment and monitoring of new food products derived from traditional techniques, which were carried over to GM foods. The introduction of new legislation to cope specifically with genetically modified products was not deemed necessary.

The Coordinated Framework consisted of two parts. In the first part, the OSTP outlined the authorities of the agencies involved. For each product, one agency was made responsible; if more than one agency had authority, a lead agency was established. Moreover, a co-ordination mechanism was put in place that would facilitate the exchange of information and that would provide common definitions to be used by all agencies with the stated goal that 'the reviews conducted by each of the regulatory agencies are (...) of comparable rigor' (OSTP, 1986: 23303).

Under the Coordinated Framework, the responsibility for the safety of GM crops and food products is shared by three agencies. The US Department of Agriculture, through its Animal and Plant Health Inspection Service (APHIS), is responsible for the safety of the growing of crops. Its main concern is whether a GM crop has the potential to become a plant pest that could harm other plants in its environment. The Environmental Protection Agency (EPA) is responsible for the environmental effects, including the use of pesticides and the allowable residues of pesticides on food products. The Food and Drug Administration (FDA) is responsible for assessing and monitoring food safety, including the implementation of the pesticide residue levels set by the EPA.

In the second part of the Coordinated Framework, each agency separately indicated how it would deal with GM products under its authority. To complete the administrative overview, the Occupation Safety and Health Administration published safety standards for workers in the biotechnology industry, and the National Institutes of Health (NIH) discussed their guidelines for research conducted with NIH grants. Here, I will further focus on FDA as the main regulator of food safety aspects.

The Food and Drug Administration is a federal agency with powers over the safety of medicines and foods, excluding poultry and meat products. Since 1979, it has been part of the Department of Health and Human Services. In the FDA statement that was part of the Coordinated Framework, the agency did not introduce any new requirements or procedures. 'Rather,' it stated, 'the administrative review of products using biotechnology is based on the intended use of each product on a case-by-case basis' (OSTP, 1986: 23310). Also, since 'no particular statutory provision or regulation deals expressly with food produced by new biotechnology (...) when confronted by an issue concerning the regulation of food produced by new biotechnology, the Agency will apply the relevant statutory or regulatory provisions' (OSTP, 1986: 23312).

FDA's powers in the context of GM foods are based on the Federal Food, Drug and Cosmetic Act (21 USC Chapter 9). First, FDA can block the sale of any food product that it deems unsafe. This authority can be used once a product is already on sale and is based on Section 402 (21 USC 342), which deals with 'adulterated foods.' It defines an adulterated food, among other things, as a food which 'bears or contains any poisonous or added deleterious substance which may render it injurious to health' (21 USC 342 (a)(1)). According to FDA's statement in the Coordinated Framework, 'courts have agreed with the agency's interpretation of this section that any substance that is not an inherent constituent of food may be regulated as an "added substance"'. The same holds true if 'the quantity of the constituent exceeds the amount that would normally be present because of some technological adjustment to the product' (OSTP, 1986: 23312). FDA has wide powers to block the marketing of adulterated foods and to prosecute those who have put them on the market.

Second, under Section 409 of the act (21 USC 348), FDA has to authorise food additives before they are marketed. This provision was introduced in 1958, in response to the increase in chemical food additives, but it is also applicable to changes in the composition of foods due to genetic modification. As a consequence, whole foods whose composition has been changed by genetic modification may also fall under Section 409 (cf. FDA, 1992: 22990 and 21 CFR 170.30(f)(2)).

A food additive needs to be approved by FDA before it can be marketed, except when it is 'Generally Recognised as Safe' or 'GRAS.' Food additives can be GRAS because they have a long history of safe use before 1958 (e.g. sugar or salt) or because they have been recognised as GRAS by FDA (see 21 USC 321(s) and 21 CFR 170.30). If not, the food additive has to go through a regulatory procedure to assess its safety on a number of aspects (like allergenicity). Companies have the obligation to determine themselves whether a new food additive needs clearance under this procedure. If FDA is convinced that the food additive is safe, it will issue a 'food additive regulation' and the additive can be used in food products and marketed.

Foods that have been changed through genetic modification are not automatically subject to the food additives procedure. In some cases, genetic modification only produces a substance in the food product that has already been present in similar food products before or that has had a history of safe use in other products. In such cases, the substance that is produced by genetic modification may be GRAS and does not need to go through the food additive procedure. However, FDA warned that 'a substance (...) that is GRAS could lose its GRAS status solely because it was produced or modified by new biotechnology (...) if the substance (...) has been altered in such a way that it can no longer be generally recognized by qualified experts to be safe' (OSTP, 1986: 23313). In addition, FDA issued some guidelines it would use in determining the safety of GM food (OSTP, 1986: 23313).

The first approvals and the 1992 Statement of Policy

In March 1990, FDA took its first decision concerning a food additive that had been produced by genetic modification. It concerned chymosin or rennet, an enzyme that is used in the production of cheese. Previously, the enzyme could only be obtained from animals which produced it naturally, but now it could also be produced by a genetically modified micro-organism. Since natural chymosin had already been used in the production of cheese, FDA affirmed that the GM chymosin was also GRAS and therefore needed no pre-market approval as a food additive. Important considerations included that the GM and natural chymosin had the same structure, and that the micro-organisms that produced the enzyme, as well as the antibiotic resistance marker genes, were destroyed during the process (FDA, 1995).

In the early 1990s, the first whole GM food was also introduced. Calgene's Flavr Savr tomato (which had been modified to delay the rotting process) went through an extended assessment in order to assess its safety. The tomato had been expressly picked by Calgene to serve as an example for other GM foods (ISB, 1994a). Although, technically, it did not have to request authorisation, Calgene went through the complete food additive procedure in order to receive an authorisation for this product (FDA, 1994b; 1995; ISB, 1994b). First, in November 1990, the antibiotic resistance marker gene was submitted for an advisory opinion. Subsequently, the whole tomato was submitted for an advisory opinion in August 1991. In January 1993, the request for the marker gene was transformed into a fully-fledged food additive petition. After the tomato and the marker gene had gone through an extensive evaluation process, FDA finally gave its approval in 1994 and issued a formal food additive petition for the enzyme that was coded by the marker gene, the only new substance in the Flavr Savr tomato (FDA, 1994b; 1998: Appendix 1).

In the meantime, in May 1992, FDA had published its 'Statement of Policy: Foods Derived from New Plant Varieties,' which contained more specific guidelines about this type of GM food (although, technically, it concerned new crops derived from both traditional and GM techniques). The basic principles underlying the Statement of Policy were the same as those in the Coordinated Framework: GM foods would not be treated as a separate class as such, but only insofar as genetic modification had led to differences in the food products (FDA, 1992: 22984-22985).

After a restatement of these general principles, the Statement of Policy discussed the statutory bases and the procedures to be followed in more detail. It also discussed the risks associated with the new techniques, but concluded for most risks that 'the likelihood of a safety hazard is typically very low' (FDA, 1992: 22986). As to the agency's powers and practices under the Federal Food, Drug and Cosmetic Act, it stated that 'FDA considers the existing statutory authority under Sections 402(a)(1) and 409 of the act, and the practical regulatory regime that flows from it, to be fully adequate to ensure the safety of new food ingredients and foods derived from new varieties of plants, regardless of the process by which such foods and ingredients are produced' (FDA, 1992: 22939).

In its assessment of GM foods, FDA used the concept of 'substantial equivalence,' which at that time was being developed and discussed by the OECD's Group of National Experts (FDA, 1992: 22992). In most cases, FDA argued, the characteristics of a GM food product are no different from those of existing products. If, for instance, a gene is inserted that produces a certain protein that has already been present in existing food products and has been proven to be safe, there is no reason to assume that it will pose any other or greater risks merely because it is produced through a different technique (i.e. genetic modification).

The assessment of a GM food product (like any other new food product) thus focused on any differences with existing food products. If such differences existed, the new trait would fall under the procedure for new food additives and become the subject of further scrutiny and tests. Rather than carrying out tests itself, FDA would monitor tests done by companies themselves. If FDA concluded that these tests had been conducted properly and revealed no unacceptable risks, the food product would be authorised for sale.

Although in general FDA did not expect most GM crops to fall under the premarket review of Section 409, it did encourage firms 'to work cooperatively with the agency to ensure that the new products are safe and comply with applicable legal requirements' (FDA, 1992: 22991), 'even though such consultation is not legally required' (FDA, 1992: 22930). In order to determine the proper action to be taken, the Statement of Policy included a guidance section, in which a 'decision-tree approach' was taken. By answering a number of yes/no questions in five flow charts, firms would arrive at one of three conclusions: 'new variety not acceptable,' 'no concerns,' or 'consult FDA.'

Besides the use of Sections 402 and 409, the Statement of Policy also addressed the issue of labelling of GM foods. FDA's authority to regulate the labelling of food products derived from Section 403(a)(1) of the Federal Food, Drug and Cosmetics Act (21 USC 352(a)), which prohibits 'false or misleading' labels. A label was deemed to be false or misleading if, among other things, it did not reveal 'material facts' (21 USC 321(n)). According to FDA, 'material' meant that labelling was only required if the product 'pose[d] special health or environmental risks,' if the label could 'mislead the consumer in the light of other statements made on the label,' or if a food's common name suggested a characteristic that it no longer had because of the changes made (FDA, 2001b).

In keeping with this general approach, FDA stated that labelling was only necessary if 'a new plant variety differ[ed] from its traditional counterpart such that the common or usual name no longer applie[d] to the new food, or if a safety or usage issue exist[ed] to which consumers must be alerted' (FDA, 1992: 22991). The method by which the product had been obtained (in this case genetic modification) was not considered to be relevant ('material,' in the law's terminology) and did not have to be labelled.

After the Flavr Savr tomato had gone through the extensive food additive procedure, FDA concluded that subsequent food products did not have to meet the same stringent risk assessment criteria and installed the informal consultation procedure that had already been advocated in the Statement of Policy. This procedure was supported by the biotechnology industry, which wanted to safeguard public confidence in its products without having to go through all kinds of mandatory procedures, and by FDA's Food Advisory and Veterinary Medicine Advisory Committees, which agreed that notification and consultation were sufficient (FDA, 1998, Appendix 2; 1999a).

Refinement of the approach

FDA elaborated on its consultation procedure in a guidance that was first published in 1996 and updated in 1997 to reflect some organisational changes within FDA. In it, FDA emphasised that it:

> 'does not conduct a comprehensive scientific review of data generated by the developer. Instead, the FDA considers, based on agency scientists' evaluation of the available information, whether any unresolved issues exist regarding the food derived from the new plant variety that would necessitate legal action by the agency if the product were introduced into commerce.' (FDA, 1997a)

Each consultation procedure would be overseen by a Biotechnology Evaluation Team, consisting of experts from different divisions of FDA. The guidance document further specified the steps to be taken both in the initial and in the final consultations. The outcome would be formally notified to the firm and filed.

In addition, a number of specific issues were discussed in the years after the publication of the Statement of Policy. In 1994, FDA organised a conference on the allergenicity of GM food crops. During this conference, the likelihood and detection of allergens in GM foods was discussed (FDA, 1994a).

Another issue of interest was the presence of antibiotic resistance marker genes in GM foods. In the Statement of Policy, the potential risks associated with these genes had already been pointed out. In 1998, after consultations with experts, FDA published a guidance on the use of antibiotic resistance marker genes and requested comments on it (FDA, 1998).

In it, FDA acknowledged that 'the likelihood of transfer of an antibiotic resistance marker from plants to microorganisms in the gut or in the environment [was] remote' and that it 'would likely be insignificant when compared to transfer between microorganisms, and in most cases, would not add to existing levels of resistance in bacterial populations in any meaningful way.' Despite these reassuring words, the agency called for an evaluation of antibiotic resistance marker genes on a case-by-case basis and it noted that a gene should not be used if it coded for resistance against the only antibiotic available for some form of treatment. After consultations with experts, FDA concluded that the approach taken in the authorisation of the Flavr Savr tomato and its antibiotic resistance marker gene had been scientifically sound and sufficient (FDA, 1998).

As a result, the policies of the Coordinated Framework and the Statement of Policy remain valid today. From 1994 up to and including 1999, FDA completed consultation procedures for 46 varieties on the basis of this policy (even though some may still have awaited approval from USDA and EPA; FDA, 2000a). The food additive procedure was not used for any GM food product in that period. FDA claimed that all marketed GM food products had been reviewed in these consultations even if, legally speaking, they were not mandatory (FDA, 1999a). Officials of the biotechnology industry supported the procedure as a flexible way to ensure consumer confidence and one claimed that the consultation procedure was 'de facto mandatory' and that the industry regarded it as such (BIO, 1999d).

Formally speaking, FDA's regulatory approach to GM foods did not differ from its approach to new foods derived from traditional breeding methods or chemical innovations. No new legislation or regulations were formulated, but GM foods were accommodated within the existing framework. The core of FDA's approach is that it looks solely at the characteristics of the product, not at the method by which it has been produced.

Still, in practice, FDA has been more careful in its dealings with GM foods than with other foods. Partly this may have been a reaction to the novelty of the techniques involved and the possibility that they had unanticipated consequences. Partly, this may also have had to do with the sensitivity of the issue among the public at large. Although the American public has generally had a positive attitude towards GM foods, the biotechnology industry has always been concerned to assure public trust in its products. As a consequence, it has always supported FDA's policy of informal consultations in order to ensure that federal oversight over GM foods is visible to the public.

Although FDA's policy received broad support among the biotechnology industry and scientists, environmental and consumer groups were more critical of the new technology. Criticism focused on FDA's reliance on industry data for its evaluation of food safety risks, and on the absence of mandatory labelling. In the second half of the 1990s, as GM foods began to be marketed in the US, the opposition increased, as did public concerns over GM foods.

5.2.2 The initial situation in Canada

With the US and Argentina, Canada is one of the leading countries in agricultural biotechnology. Canada's main GM food crop is GM canola, a kind of oilseed rape. More than half of Canada's canola acreage is planted with genetically modified crops. Other GM crops are less widely spread. The strategic importance of biotechnology for the Canadian economy was discussed in the National Biotechnology Strategy, which was first established in 1983 and renewed in 1998 (CFIA, 2000).

Canada's regulatory regime for GM foods is broadly comparable to the US framework, although the division of authority differs, as do some specific procedures. The general framework for the regulation of biotechnology was laid down in the Federal Regulatory Framework for Biotechnology, which was published in 1993 (CFIA, 2000). In this Framework, the division of tasks between federal agencies was established. Moreover, it was decided to use existing legislation and institutions to regulate biotechnology products, including GM foods.

The authority over GM food crops has been divided between two agencies. Health Canada, the federal department of health, is responsible for food safety standards and conducts safety assessments of new food products. Initially, the Food Inspection Directorate of Agriculture and Agri-Food Canada (AAFC), the federal department of agriculture, was responsible for the environmental aspects of GM crops, for GM animal feeds, and for field trials. In 1997, the Food Inspection Directorate was merged with a number of other governmental agencies to form the Canadian Food Inspection Agency (CFIA), which officially falls under Agriculture and Agri-Food Canada, but operates independently (Interview 21-2-2001, CFIA).

The regulation of food safety by Health Canada takes place under the Food and Drugs Act and its associated regulations. Like the American framework, the Canadian Food and Drugs Act distinguishes between post-market and pre-market controls. According to Article 4, it is forbidden to sell a food product if, among other things, it 'has in or on it any poisonous or harmful substance,' or if it 'is adulterated.' Adulterated food is defined more narrowly in Article B.01.046 and Division B.15 of the associated Regulations, which contain lists of ingredients and their allowed concentrations. If a food contains a higher concentration of those ingredients, it is considered to be adulterated.

Food additives need pre-market approval before they can be marketed, unless they are 'used, recognized, or commonly sold as an article or ingredient of food' (Article B.01.001 Food and Drugs Regulations). Division B.16 of the Regulations, which deals with food additives, includes tables of additives that have been approved, with their approved use and their maximum allowable levels in food products. A food additive can be added to these tables by submitting it for approval to the Minister of Health (Article B.16.002 Food and Drug Regulations).

Other types of ingredients and whole foods, such as pesticides and infant foods, are also subject to pre-market approval. However, whole GM foods as such do not fall under the food additive provisions or one of the other pre-market procedures. In reaction to the appearance of GM foods, Health Canada therefore developed its 'Guidelines for the Safety Assessment of Novel Foods' (Health Canada, 1994), which were published in September 1994 after some years of drafting and consultation.

'Novel foods' are food products that are new on the Canadian market. The concept includes 'foods that result from genetic modification and exhibit new or modified characteristics that have previously not been identified in those foods, or that result from production by organisms exhibiting such new or modified characteristics' (Health Canada, 1994: 4), although it is not limited to GM foods alone. Separate guidelines were formulated for novel fibres.

The approach taken in the Guidelines was broadly similar to that in FDA's 1992 Statement of Policy. It acknowledged that 'food produced by novel processes may require notification prior to sale,' but that 'd[id] not mean that a safety assessment of a novel food (...) w[ould] be required in all cases' (Health Canada, 1994: Vol. I: 3). The concept of substantial equivalence was explicitly used as the basis for the policy, which meant that 'notification may not be required if the modification to the product or process is not significant' (Health Canada, 1994: Vol. I: 4). However, it also stated that 'developers are encouraged to consult the Food Directorate in the early stages of product development in order to reach agreement on whether notification is required' (Health Canada, 1994: Vol. I: 5). In an annex to Volume I of the Guidelines, a number of charts were used to assess the necessity of notification. By answering a number of questions, a producer could discover whether a new product called for consultations with the Food Directorate or an assessment under the food additive provisions, or whether notification was not in fact required.

Volume II of the Guidelines dealt with genetically modified micro-organisms and plants. Here it was explicitly stated that 'the application of genetic modification does not inherently increase or decrease the risk associated with an organism' and that 'the emphasis of the safety assessment will be on the product and not on the process used to develop it' (Health Canada, 1994: Vol. II: 3). The approach built on the substantial equivalence approach in that 'once substantial equivalence to an existing food product can be established, no additional safety testing would be required. Where similarity or degree of equivalence cannot be established, a more extensive safety assessment may be necessary' (Health Canada, 1994: Vol. II: 4). The next two chapters in Volume II of the Guidelines described the information that was needed to assess GM micro-organisms and plants, and their products.

Labelling is a joint responsibility of the CFIA (prior to 1997: AAFC's Food Inspection Directorate) and Health Canada, Health Canada being responsible for any health and safety aspects of labelling (CFIA, 1998a). In 1993 and 1994, several public consultations were held on the issue of labelling, resulting in proposed guidelines that were published in December 1995 (AAFC, 1995).

In these proposed guidelines, an approach similar to that used by FDA was proposed: GM food products would have to be labelled if they presented 'potential health and/or safety risks for individuals or population segments,' or if 'significant compositional or nutritional changes from the traditional food source' had occurred; a general labelling requirement for GM food products was rejected (AAFC, 1995: 5-6). These proposals were supported by business groups, whereas some public interest groups argued for the mandatory labelling of all GM food products (CFIA, 1997: 8).

In the end, the Canadian government did not require the mandatory labelling of GM food products as a class. Rather, labelling was required if there were significant concerns or changes related to the food product itself, for instance possible allergenicity. Labelling of the process of genetic modification (either that it has been used or, conversely, that it has not been used) could only take place on a voluntary basis (CFIA, 1998a).

Although the exact procedures may differ somewhat from the US regulatory framework, if only because the internal distribution of authority differs, the general approaches of the two countries have been highly similar when it comes to the food safety aspects of GM foods. Both FDA and Health Canada have focused on characteristics of GM foods, rather than on the process by which they are produced. In assessing the safety of a GM food product, a comparison is made with traditional food products that are considered to be safe. If the GM food product shows no significant differences with such a traditional food product, it is considered to be safe as well (the idea behind substantial equivalence). Likewise, the mandatory labelling of the process of genetic modification is not in place.

The similarity between the two countries' regulatory frameworks can also be seen in the number of approved GM crops. Between 1994 and 1999, inclusive, Health Canada issued 43 novel food decisions (Health Canada, 2000), compared to 46 completed FDA consultations in the US. Many GM varieties have been approved in both countries.

Given these broad similarities, Canada and the US have sought to harmonise their review processes. Thus, in July 1998, officials from Health Canada, the CFIA and APHIS met to discuss the molecular genetic characterisation that is part of both countries' review processes (CFIA, 1998b), which led to an agreement on this issue (Interview 21-2-2001, CFIA).

5.3 The European regulation of GM foods

The EC policies on GM foods have generally been more restrictive than those of the US or Canada. Still, the situation is not black and white. The EC has been mixed over the issue, with both proponents and opponents of GM foods seeking to affect the regulatory process. However, the balance between the two sides has shifted over the last decade or so, leading to a more restrictive regulatory framework than the US and Canada have in place. Partly, this shift is the result of changing concerns over GM foods, but it has also had a lot to do with the EC's distinct decision-making structures and procedures when compared to the US and Canada.

5.3.1 Horizontal and vertical legislation

The EC regulatory framework consists of 'horizontal' and 'vertical' legislation. The horizontal legislation concerns a number of Directives which regulate genetically modified organisms (GMOs) in general, not limited to certain product categories. The vertical legislation is made up of several Directives and Regulations that regulate specific categories of GMOs and GM products, such as GM foods or GM seeds.

The horizontal Directives

Work on the EC-level regulation of biotechnology started in the late 1980s. In a 1987 Resolution, the Council identified biotechnology as a key area for regulatory action (Council, 1987), which resulted in two (horizontal) Directives: 90/219 on the contained use of genetically modified micro-organisms (EC, 1990a), and 90/220 on the deliberate release into the environment of genetically modified organisms (EC, 1990b; henceforth 'Directive 90/220').

Unlike the US and Canada, the EC thus chose to adopt separate legal instruments for the regulation of GMOs. This was the outcome of a fierce political battle between the DGs involved in biotechnology policy, in which DG XI (Environment) supported horizontal legislation based on a precautionary approach and was able to take the initiative during the formulation of the Directives (for a detailed analysis of the political process leading to the Directives, and in particular the conflicts within the European Commission, see Patterson, 2000: 324-333).

For the purpose of this study, Directive 90/220 was the most relevant piece of horizontal legislation. Initially it covered all deliberate releases of GMOs, including the marketing of GM food products. With the adoption of the Novel Foods Regulation in 1997 that role changed somewhat, but that will be discussed below. Directive 90/220 sought to harmonise the member states' approval procedures for GM products and to provide for one single application and approval procedure for their marketing in all EC member states.

To that end it established a two-tiered approval procedure. First, the producer or importer of a GM product had to submit a notification to the competent authority for the approval of GM products in the member state where the product was to be marketed (Article 11.1 Directive 90/220). Under Article 4.2, each member state had to designate such a competent authority for the purposes of the Directive. The contents of the dossier to be submitted were stipulated in Annexes II and III of the Directive. Upon examination of the notification (and, if necessary, after additional information had been submitted), the competent authority had the choice of either withholding approval, which would end the procedure, or giving a favourable opinion. In the latter case, the dossier was forwarded to the European Commission, together with the favourable opinion (Article 12.2).

The European Commission in turn forwarded this package to the competent authorities of all the other member states, which could raise objections to the favourable opinion (Article 13.1). If no objections were raised, the competent authority that had examined the notification would give written consent to the applicant (Article 13.2). If objections were raised, however, the procedure continued. The competent authorities were supposed to reach an agreement among themselves first, for instance if additional information was requested. If the competent authorities were not able to reach a consensus, the decision moved to the Community level (Article 13.3).

The European Commission then decided on the approval, subject to a regulatory committee consisting of member state representatives. This committee had to approve the draft Commission decision with qualified majority or it could reject it with unanimity. If the Committee rejected the draft decision or if it failed to take a decision, the European Commission had to submit the draft decision to the Council of Ministers, which could approve the product by qualified majority. Also if the Council failed to take a decision, the Commission would again take over, and adopt its draft decision (Article 21).

After a GM product had been approved, the competent authority to which the notification was originally submitted, would give written consent to the producer or importer and the product could be marketed in all EC member states.

This procedure reflected many of the peculiarities of EC decision-making. It involved decision-making at both national and European levels. Moreover, it allowed for the major involvement of the member states, through the competent authorities, a regulatory committee and eventually even through the Council of Ministers if no consensus could be reached among the competent authorities. This stood in marked contrast to the procedures in the US and Canada, where independent governmental agencies oversaw GM food products and where the authorisation procedure took place exclusively at the federal level.

The choice for a separate legal framework to regulate GM food products seemed to point to a different conception of GM foods. Rather than viewing them as varieties of traditional foodstuffs that need no special consideration merely because they have been produced differently, the enactment of separate standards seemed to imply that GM foods pose specific risks, different from traditional foods. Otherwise, no specific standards would be necessary. The difference between the European and North American frameworks has therefore often been characterised as the difference between a process-based and a product-based approach (Patterson, 1999: 10-11).

Still, the actual difference in standards was not as clear-cut as this difference in approach might indicate. In the US and Canada, although the regulation of GM foods was formally no different from 'traditional' new foods, the oversight did turn out to be more stringent. For instance, in the US, the voluntary consultation of FDA by producers amounted to a more stringent procedure than the one used for traditional foods. Similarly, the stringency of a regulatory approach does not only depend on the principled choice of whether or not to adopt a separate legal framework, but also on the criteria that are used in the risk assessment. If those are substantively similar, the difference in standards will be smaller than suggested by the principled choice for product or process-oriented regulation.

Although the Directive gave a list of information that was required in the notification, it remained silent on the methods of risk assessment to be used in evaluating this information. The requested information, however, showed striking similarity to that requested in the US and Canada in that it focused on scientifically ascertainable risks related to the product itself; moral and consumer concerns related to the technique of genetic modification did not seem to play a role, nor did economic concerns about the effects on the agricultural sector. Moreover, the risk assessment as foreseen by the Directive seemed to be based on the concept of substantial equivalence, as much as the US and Canadian approaches. Also, Directive 90/220 initially did not require any labelling of GM foods on the basis of their production method. In fact, no separate provision was made for labelling GM foods as opposed to other foods.

In practice, the differences between the European, US and Canadian approaches were therefore not so great at the beginning of the 1990s. The main difference seems to have been the degree of formalisation of the approach: whereas FDA and Health Canada relied on voluntary consultation under their regulations, the EC installed a separate legal framework. And whereas the US and Canada did not require a formal pre-market approval of GM foods, the EC did.

The Novel Foods Regulation

In 1997, Regulation 258/97 concerning novel foods and novel food ingredients was adopted (EC, 1997c; henceforth the 'Novel Foods Regulation'). This was a piece of vertical (product-specific) legislation which specifically regulated foods and food ingredients produced by, among other things, GM techniques. According to Article 1 of the Regulation, novel foods included foods and food ingredients containing GMOs or produced from GMOs. However, food additives and flavourings did not fall under the Regulation since they were regulated in separate Directives.

The procedure foreseen in the Novel Foods Regulation was essentially the same as the procedure in Directive 90/220. If a producer or importer wanted to market a novel food, it had to submit a request to the member state in which the product was first to be marketed. That member state would carry out an initial assessment to determine whether an additional assessment was necessary (Article 4.1 and 4.2 Novel Foods Regulation). It would then send its conclusions to the European Commission, which would forward it to all the other member states for their comments. The member states and the Commission could then make comments or raise objections to the approval of the product (Article 6). If objections were raised or the initial assessment had led to the conclusion that an additional assessment was necessary, an authorisation at the EC level would become necessary (Article 7). This European authorisation process would take place through the same procedure described above for Directive 90/220, including the regulatory committee procedure and, if necessary, a decision by the Council of Ministers by qualified majority (Article 13).

On 29 July 1997, the European Commission published a recommendation 'concerning the scientific aspects and the presentation of information necessary to support applications for the placing on the market of novel foods and novel food ingredients and the preparation of initial assessment reports' (EC, 1997i). This recommendation, which had been prepared by the Commission's Scientific Committee for Food, contained guidelines for the initial assessment of applications under the Novel Foods Regulation. It was based on the concept of substantial equivalence, although it acknowledged that the 'establishment of substantial equivalence is not a safety or nutritional assessment in itself, but an approach to compare a potential new food with its conventional counterpart' (Point 3.3 Recommendation). The recommendation specified a number of issues that had to be taken into account in the assessment of food safety, such as toxicological requirements, allergenicity and the assessment of marker genes. In Section 4, six categories of novel foods were discerned that differed in the degree of complexity and thus in the exact criteria to be used. In the subsequent section and the tables annexed to the recommendation, a number of 'structured schemes,' comparable to FDA's decision trees, were used to address the specific questions to be asked in the risk assessment for each of these categories.

The Novel Foods Regulation contained a simplified procedure for novel foods which, among other things, had been produced from but did not contain GMOs (for example, oil pressed from GM soya beans). If these products '[we]re substantially equivalent to existing foods or food ingredients' (Article 3.4 Novel Foods Regulation), they only had to be notified to the European Commission (Article 5 Novel Foods Regulation).

Directive 90/220 provided that its safety assessment procedure did not 'apply to any products covered by Community legislation which provides for a specific environmental risk assessment similar to that laid down in this Directive' (Article 10.2 Directive 90/220). The Novel Foods Regulation provided for such a similar procedure with regard to the food safety aspects of GM foods. Hence, products that fell under the definition of novel foods did not have to go through the procedure under Directive 90/220, but this only concerned products insofar as they were marketed as foodstuffs. GM crops still needed authorisation under Directive 90/220 to be planted. Thus, GM soya or maize needed authorisation under Directive 90/220 to be marketed as a crop, but products derived from them needed authorisation under the Novel Foods Regulation. Broadly speaking, Directive 90/220 could therefore be described as covering the environmental aspects of GM crops, while the Novel Foods Regulation covered the food safety aspects.

The Novel Foods Regulation also imposed labelling requirements which, at the time of its adoption, were more stringent than those under Directive 90/220. Article 8 of the Novel Foods Regulation provided that novel foods had to be labelled to inform consumers of the presence of a GMO or of any characteristic 'which render[ed] the novel food or food ingredient no longer equivalent to an existing food or food ingredient.' In the latter case, the label also had to indicate the method by which the different characteristic had been obtained, i.e. genetic modification. These labelling requirements also applied to products that had gone through the simplified procedure of Article 5 Novel Foods Regulation.

Extending the labelling requirements

The difference between the labelling provisions of the Novel Foods Regulation and Directive 90/220 did not last for long. In June 1997, the European Commission used its power to adapt to technical progress Annex III of the Directive to establish mandatory labelling for GMOs approved under Directive 90/220 (EC, 1997f). In this amendment, the Commission envisaged two types of labelling: a label that indicated that a product contains or consists of GMOs, and a label that indicated that GMOs may be present. The latter label was to be used when non-GM foods were mixed with GM foods and there was no certainty about the presence of GMOs in the final product.

For the two GM food products which had been approved under Directive 90/220 prior to the Novel Foods Regulation (a herbicide-tolerant soya bean, and a herbicide-tolerant Bt-maize), Council Regulation 1139/98 was adopted to provide for mandatory labelling in May 1998 (EC, 1998c). This Regulation did not contain the 'may contain' formula which the Commission had used in its amendment to Directive 90/220, since the Council (as well as the EP, and business and consumer groups) felt that this would be confusing and unclear: either GMOs were present or not and products had to be labelled accordingly.

Both the amendment to Directive 90/220 and Regulation 1139/98 required the labelling of products that contained proteins or DNA from GMOs. This meant, for instance, that GM soya had to be labelled, as well as other food products containing GM soya. If the product did not contain DNA or protein from GMOs, like oil from GM soya that is chemically identical to oil from non-GM soya, it did not have to be labelled, however.

After the adoption of the Novel Foods Regulation and the amendments to Directive 90/220, the EC's regulation of GM foods thus experienced a considerable strengthening when it came to labelling. In marked contrast to the US and Canada, the EC now required the mandatory labelling of all food products containing GMOs, even if the products themselves were substantially equivalent to their traditional counterparts. Thus, the Flavr Savr tomato, had it been approved in the EC, would have had to be labelled as a GM product, while it did not have to be in the US and Canada. The same was true for food products containing GM ingredients (for instance pizzas containing GM maize).

The European labelling requirements did not extend to food products produced from GMOs which were substantially equivalent to traditional food products, but if they were not substantially equivalent, the method by which the change had been made (in this case: genetic modification) had to be indicated on the label. This, too, meant a departure from the American and Canadian standards, because although they required the labelling of changes in GM food products, they did not consider the method by which these changes had been effected to be relevant and thus worthy of labelling. The European labelling regime was to be strengthened even further in 2000, which will be discussed below.

In terms of the assessment of food safety, at least on paper the European approach differed less from the US and Canadian approaches than the labelling regimes. Like under Directive 90/220, GM food products had to undergo a mandatory authorisation procedure under the Novel Foods Regulation, whereas formally they did not have to do so in the US and Canada. In practice, this difference may not have been so important, however.

As was discussed above, the approaches did not differ greatly, since the same methodology and risk assessment criteria were foreseen by the European, US and Canadian frameworks. Also, the data for the risk assessment came from the producers of the products themselves in both the EC and the US and Canada. Neither the competent authorities in the EC member states and the European Commission, nor FDA and Health Canada, conducted their own tests to determine the safety of GM food products. Rather, they set standards for the tests to be conducted by the producers and reviewed these tests accordingly.

Although the 'black letter' risk assessment criteria did not differ so much between the two sides of the Atlantic, the actual use of these criteria by the authorities did. Moreover, a number of developments led to a gradual strengthening of the European regulation of GM foods during the late 1990s.

5.3.2 Developments in the late 1990s

At least four such developments are relevant to our story. First, a number of member states took unilateral measures to restrict or ban the sale of GM foods. Second, the approval process came to a halt when a number of member states gathered a blocking minority in the Council of Ministers. Third, in early 2000, two labelling regulations were adopted that refined the existing labelling requirements and extended them to food additives and colourings. Finally, the revision of Directive 90/220 led to a new Directive that significantly strengthened the formal approval criteria for GM products. In this subsection I will discuss these developments. In the next subsection I will analyse why they occurred.

Unilateral measures by the member states

On 3 April 1996, the European Commission approved the marketing of Monsanto's GM soya beans in the EC (EC, 1996a). On 23 January 1997, approval was given to European company Ciba-Geigy's GM maize that was both herbicide-resistant and produced the Bt-toxin (EC, 1997b). With the approval of these first two GM food crops, the debate started to heat up considerably in Europe.

It was in particular the approval of the Bt-maize that spurred controversy. Its approval process highlighted many of the tensions in the EC's regulatory framework (see EP, 1999: 42). After the French competent authority had proposed to approve Ciba-Geigy's Bt maize, seven other competent authorities registered their objections, while the European Commission supported the approval. In the regulatory committee the European Commission had to submit its proposal to, no qualified majority could be mustered for approval, so that the decision had to be referred to the Council of Environmental Ministers. In the Council, thirteen out of the fifteen member states opposed the Commission proposal to approve the Bt maize, but since unanimity was required in order to reject a Commission proposal, no decision could be taken. As a consequence, the Commission had to take a decision and, after having obtained advice from three scientific committees, the approval was granted.

Immediately after the French competent authority had given its written consent, Austria and Luxembourg unilaterally banned the sale (and, in the case of Luxembourg also the use) of the Bt-maize (CEC, 1998c: 2; 1998d: 2). Under Article 15 of Directive 90/220, member states were allowed to do so if they had 'justifiable reasons to consider' the product 'a risk to human health or the environment,' but only on a provisional basis. After three European Commission scientific committees had indicated that Austria and Luxembourg had not produced any new evidence regarding the Bt-maize, the Commission considered these bans to be unjustified and proposed to revoke them.

At first, the European Commission tried to force Austria and Luxembourg to withdraw their bans (see CEC, 1998c; 1998d), but this effort was blocked in the Council of Ministers. As anxieties over GM foods started to rise, the European Commission became more reluctant to use legal means and the Commission's actions were temporarily stalled.

Other unilateral initiatives by member states included restrictions on the planting of GM crops in Denmark in late 1998 (Danish EPA, 1998) and a Greek ban on field trials with GM crops in early 1999 (EuropaBio, 1999c; IFT, 1999). In August 2000, the Italian government suspended the marketing of four products derived from but not containing GM maize that had gone through the simplified procedure of Article 5 Novel Foods Regulation, arguing that these products were not substantially equivalent to existing foods or food ingredients as was required for the simplified procedure to apply (SCF, 2000: 2).

The de facto moratorium

During the late 1990s, the political balance in the Council started to shift. Already in April 1997, the European Commission had indicated that the number of countries in the Council opposed to GM foods had increased so as to make a qualified majority in the Council for the approval of pending applications under Directive

90/220 unlikely (CEC, 1997c). Nevertheless, several more crops were approved in the following year, four of which were approved by the regulatory committee.

With the growing number of member states that had serious second thoughts about GM crops, however, this became increasingly difficult. During the June 1999 Council of Environmental Ministers, France, Denmark, Greece, Italy and Luxembourg demanded more stringent standards. In a statement, these member states pointed to 'the importance of the Commission submitting without delay full draft rules ensuring labelling and traceability of GMOs and GMO-derived products' and stated that 'pending the adoption of such rules (...) they will take steps to have any new authorisations for growing and placing on the market suspended' (Council, 1999: Annex). In response, Austria, Belgium, Finland, Germany, the Netherlands, Spain and Sweden stated the intention 'not to authorise the placing on the market of any GMOs until it is demonstrated that there is no adverse effect on the environment and human health' (Council, 1999: Annex). Although the European Commission could have continued to approve GMOs as long as not all member states opposed approval (as it had done in the case of the Bt maize), it argued that it would not be wise to stir up anxieties even more by using these formal powers (Interview 9-11-2000, European Commission).

This amounted to a 'de facto moratorium' on the approval of new GM crops under Directive 90/220, starting in October 1998 when the last GMO had been approved in the EC. At that time, eighteen GMOs had been approved, while fourteen applications were pending (CEC, 2000e: 3). The moratorium was not formalised, since there was no legal basis for a formal moratorium on GM crops in either Directive 90/220 or any other piece of EC legislation.

Although this 'de facto moratorium' related only to Directive 90/220 and not to the Novel Foods Regulation, it had an impact on the whole GM food approval process. In fact, a parallel situation occurred in which a number of GM foodstuffs were pending under the Novel Foods Regulation's approval process. The notification of substantially equivalent food products derived from GM crops, but not containing added DNA or proteins themselves, continued as it had done before (CEC, 2000e: 4-5; Interviews 31-8-2000 and 9-11-2000, European Commission).

Strengthening the labelling requirements

Besides the developments discusses above, the EC's labelling requirements were strengthened as well. In January 2000, the EC strengthened its labelling requirements in two ways. Commission Regulation 49/2000 (EC, 2000a) amended Regulation 1139/98 and dealt with the labelling of products that are not supposed to contain GMOs, but that have adventitiously been mixed with some GMOs. For instance, a producer that has tried to separate non-GM from GM soya beans, may still be confronted with a small amount of GM soya beans in his or her final product. According to Regulation 49/2000, this product need not be labelled as containing GMOs, when the adventitious presence of GM food ingredients does not exceed 1% per ingredient. Thus, if a product contains soya, no more than 1% of the soya should be GM. If the presence exceeds this threshold, the product has to be labelled like any other GM food product.

Commission Regulation 50/2000 (EC, 2000b) extended the existing labelling regime to food additives and flavourings, which had previously been exempted because they fell under different legal frameworks. As a result, food additives and flavourings that contained GMOs or that were no longer equivalent to existing additives and flavourings also had to be labelled.

The revision of Directive 90/220

The de facto moratorium and the strengthening of the labelling requirements took place during the revision of Directive 90/220, and were partly installed in anticipation of that revision. At first, the impetus for the revision had come from the European Commission's wish to improve the competitiveness of the European biotechnology industry. In its White Paper on Competitiveness, Growth and Employment (CEC, 1993b) and the Communication on Biotechnology and the White Paper (CEC, 1994a), the Commission had considered biotechnology to be one of the key innovative sectors for the future (see also the next subsection). The follow-up to the Communication was the Report on the Review of Directive 90/220/EEC in the Context of the Commission's Communication on Biotechnology and the White Paper (CEC, 1996c), which appeared in December 1996. This report examined the need for proposals relating to four objectives outlined in the Communication on Biotechnology and the White Paper:

- To increase the flexibility of Directive 90/220;
- To increase the uniformity of the approval process between Member States;
- To give notifiers more opportunities to benefit from the uniform EC approval system;
- To facilitate the link between Directive 90/220 and product legislation (such as the Novel Foods Regulation, which was also discussed at the time).

The report then discussed a number of proposals relating to Part C of the Directive, which dealt with the placing on the market of products containing GMOs, in order to expedite the approval process and formulate more uniform risk assessment criteria. Also, the report announced proposals for specific labelling requirements without yet specifying their content.

Thus, the proposed revision of Directive 90/220 was supposed to 'streamline' the approval process in order to speed it up and to strengthen the regulatory environment for biotechnology firms. Most concerns of the critics of biotechnology were not addressed. The report did not discuss what risks would have to be taken into account in the risk assessment, nor did it call for strengthened labelling rules. In line with the Communication's statement that deliberate releases 'have not given cause for concern, and evidence is accumulating to the effect that genetically modified plants do not differ from non-modified plants other than in the specific character conferred by the introduced gene' (CEC, 1994a: 3), the report sought to address administrative inefficiencies and obstacles to innovation, rather than the concerns voiced by environmental and consumer groups.

In its reaction to the Report, the European Parliament called for the inclusion of an 'ethical, economic and social dimension' in the approval process, mandatory labelling of all products containing GMOs, and the introduction of limited approval periods after which the effects of the GMO would have to be evaluated (EP, 1997d).

In February 1998, the European Commission published its proposed amendments to Directive 90/220 (CEC, 1998b). By this time, the emphasis had shifted to the risks of GMOs and the need to strengthen the standards of Directive 90/220. After a series of Commission proposals, and positions by the EP and the Council of Ministers, an agreement between the Council and the EP was finally reached in December 2000, and Directive 2001/18, which replaced Directive 90/220, was adopted in March 2001 (EC, 2001a; henceforth 'Directive 2001/18'). In the Council of Ministers, France and Italy abstained (Council, 2001). The new Directive will have to be transposed in member state law before 17 October 2002.

In limited ways, the Commission's original idea of streamlining the approval process has been retained in Directive 2001/18. First, in order to centralise the approval process and to provide for an independent source of information in case of conflicting opinions, consultation with a Scientific Committee has become mandatory when approval is opposed by the European Commission or the competent authority of a member state (Article 28 Directive 2001/18).

Second, the procedure involving the regulatory committee of member state representatives has been changed. Originally, the Commission proposed to use a procedure that would require a simple majority in the Council of Ministers, which would eliminate the possibility of a deadlock as in the case of Ciba-Geigy's Bt maize (CEC, 1998b: 5). Eventually, however, Directive 2001/18 used the general framework for regulatory committees adopted in 1999 (EC, 1999d; see Article 30.2 Directive 2001/18). Under this procedure, the regulatory committee and the Council of Ministers can adopt or reject the Commission's proposal with a qualified majority. Since unanimity is no longer required to reject a proposal, the Council's role in the approval process is somewhat strengthened by this change. Moreover, the EP can become involved in the procedure, even though it cannot block an approval (see EC, 1999d: Articles 5.5 and 8).

More importantly, however, the new Directive strengthens the EC's approval criteria in a number of ways. First, the factors to be taken into account in the Directive's risk assessment have been broadened. They now explicitly include 'potential adverse effects (...) either direct and indirect, immediate and delayed, on human health and the environment' (Annex II, point A Directive 2001/18). Also, the Directive invokes the precautionary principle as the leading principle in the risk assessment, leaving its precise meaning open (Recital 8, Articles 1 and 4.1, and Annex II, point A). Moreover, in a recital to the Directive, it is stated that member states 'may take into consideration ethical aspects' (Recital 8).

Second, the new Directive requires the labelling of GMOs 'at all stages of the placing on the market' (Article 21.1 Directive 2001/18). In its June 1999 Common Position, the Environmental Council also decided to complement the labelling requirements by 'provisions on the traceability of GMOs enabling competent authorities to keep track of GMOs through the various stages of their market life' (Council, 1999). These provisions were not yet incorporated in Directive 2001/18, but the European Commission submitted a separate proposal on this issue in July 2001 (CEC, 2001b).

Third, authorisation will be granted for a limited period of ten years. After that period, the GMO has to be re-evaluated and the authorisation renewed for subsequent periods of ten years (Article 15.4 Directive 2001/18). The approvals that have been given under Directive 90/220 have to renewed, although under a lighter procedure (Article 17.1(b)).

Fourth, the use of antibiotic resistance marker genes will be phased out. They will be prohibited for GMOs that are placed on the market by 2004 (Article 4.2 Directive 2001/18).

Finally, the European Commission has promised to submit a proposal on the liability of producers for environmental damage before the end of 2001 (Recital 16 Directive 2001/18). In its first reading, the EP had called for the strict liability of GMO producers for any health or environmental damage resulting from their products, which would impose liability for damage regardless of fault on the part of the producer. Although this amendment was not taken up by the Commission and the Council and the EP eventually voted not to include an amendment to this effect, this issue will resurface again when the Commission presents its proposal.

Like Directive 90/220, Directive 2001/18 contains a provision that exempts a GM product from its scope if it has been authorised under another piece of EC legislation that is 'at least equivalent' to Directive 2001/18 (Article 12.1 Directive 2001/18). A procedure for determining equivalency will be stipulated in a separate Regulation, however, and until then GMOs have to go through the procedure of Directive 2001/18 (Article 12.3 Directive).

As a result, the revisions made in Directive 2001/18 also affected the Novel Foods Regulation. In July 2001, the European Commission proposed a new Regulation to replace the Novel Foods Regulation's provisions on GM foods (CEC, 2001c). The proposed Regulation covered all food products containing or produced from GMOs, and it harmonised approval and other criteria with those of Directive 2001/18. It also proposed to delete the Novel Foods Regulation's simplified notification procedure for substantially equivalent GM food products. Moreover, it included a further strengthening of labelling requirements in that all food products that were covered by the new Regulation would have to be labelled as containing or being produced from GMOs.

The move toward more stringent standards

All in all, the EC standards regarding GM foods have been strengthened considerably over the last few years and are likely not to be relaxed again in the foreseeable future. The approval process under Directive 90/220 has come to a complete halt, which has also affected the approval of new food products under the Novel Foods Regulation. Directive 2001/18 has strengthened the EC's approval criteria in several ways.

Therefore, although some 60% of European foods are estimated to contain GM soya or products derived from it, the acreage planted with GM crops in Europe has been negligible. In France and the UK, several test fields and silos containing GM maize were destroyed by activists (ISB, 1998a; Margaronis, 1999). In the summer of 2000, some fields that had been planted with seeds adventitiously mixed with GM varieties were discovered in France and Sweden. The competent authorities ordered the complete removal of all seeds. The anxieties are therefore not likely to cool down in the short run and even if the approval process is soon resumed, it will remain under close scrutiny by sceptical member state governments and public interest groups.

The labelling requirements have also been strengthened considerably since 1997. Food products containing GM ingredients have to be labelled, as well as food products in which adventitious GMOs are present above the 1% threshold. If food products produced from but not containing GMOs differ from their traditional counterparts, the process by which they have been produced has to be put on the label, too. These labelling requirements have also been extended to food additives and flavourings. These requirements are not likely to be relaxed soon. Rather, the July 2001 proposals on traceability and the Novel Foods Regulation may even lead to a further strengthening of labelling requirements, in that the whole production process will have to be reviewed and not only the product. This would mean a clear choice for the kind of technology labelling that has been eschewed by FDA and Health Canada alike.

5.3.3 The shifting political balance in the EC

The developments in the European regulation of GM foods can be linked to a number of changes in the political process underlying it. These changes have taken place on different levels: among the public at large, in the activities of public interest groups, among the EC member state governments, among European business groups, and also to some extent in the European Commission. In this subsection I will examine the different positions of the actors in the process and trace how and why they have changed over the years.

The situation in the first half of the 1990s

In the early 1990s the EC's position on GM foods was already mixed. On the one hand, the public at large was less positive about GM foods than the public in the US and Canada, but without concrete examples of GM foods on the shelves or in the fields, it did not become a real issue. Public interest groups (environmental and consumer groups) did raise the issue intermittently, but they did not pursue the kind of systematic campaigns that were to mark the debate in the late 1990s.

The positive elements in the attitude toward GM foods (or biotechnology more generally) can be found in a number of Commission documents released throughout the 1990s. In them, the Commission stressed the potential of biotechnology and its importance in relation to European competitiveness in the world market. In its White Paper on Growth, Competitiveness and Employment, the Commission presented biotechnology as one of the key areas for future development, together with information technology and the audiovisual sector. The Commission claimed that 'biotechnology has emerged as one of the most promising and crucial technologies for sustainable development in the next century' because it 'enables the creation of new products and highly competitive processes in a large number of industrial and agricultural activities' (CEC, 1993b: 15).

The White Paper's recommendation that the regulatory framework should be adapted so as to facilitate the development of the biotechnology industry was further elaborated in a 1994 Communication on 'Biotechnology and the White Paper,' which analysed the existing regulatory framework. In the Communication, it was claimed that there was 'increased confidence among scientists in the safety of genetic engineering' (CEC, 1994a: 2) and that 'evidence is accumulating to the effect that genetically modified plants do not differ from non-modified plants other than in the specific character conferred by the introduced gene' (CEC, 1994a: 3). Moreover, the Commission acknowledged 'that the biotechnology regulatory framework is a factor impacting on industrial competitiveness, which confirms the need for balanced and proportionate regulatory requirements' (CEC, 1994a: 3). As a result, the Commission proposed to modify the existing framework both through adaptation to technical process and by amendments to existing legislation. In the remainder of the Communication, a number of changes were proposed to make the framework more flexible and less restrictive if no adverse effects had been shown. At the same time, the Commission was aware of the public scepticism regarding biotechnology and sought to change this attitude by giving more information (CEC, 1994a: 11).

As in the formulation of Directive 90/220, these Commission positions were the outcome of a fierce battle between the DGs involved, in particular between, on the one hand, DG XI (Environment) and on the other DGs III (Industry) and XII (Science, Research and Development) (Patterson, 2000: 335-337). Nevertheless, the DGs that sought to promote biotechnology in the EC (DGs III and XII) were able to have their position accepted as that of the European Commission's.

Member state governments were split over the issue, with Denmark and Germany being the most serious critics of the technology. Other member states were more positive however. These differences were reflected in the transposition of Directive 90/220 into national laws: within the room for manoeuvre given by the

Directive, France was reported to have adopted the most biotechnology-friendly legislation, while Germany and Denmark enacted much less favourable laws (Schenkelaars, 1996: 161). In any case, only a minority of the member states in the Council of Ministers seem to have had serious concerns about biotechnology and GM foods.

From the mid-1990s onwards this situation started to change, due to both the fact that GM foods were actually beginning to be approved and marketed, and a number of developments outside the area of GM food policy as such, which nevertheless had a strong impact on its development.

The rise in public concerns and public interest group activism

Among the public at large, the latent fears of GM foods became more open as the first GM foods were approved and marketed in 1996 and 1997 (for a comparison between public opinion in the US and the EC in these years, see Gaskell et al., 1999). These fears were reinforced by a number of events that shook public confidence in the food regulatory system and in science more generally, such as the BSE crisis, which was discussed more extensively above in section 4.5.2.

Public concerns about GM crops and foods differed greatly between EC member states. They were most strongly felt in the UK, where the BSE crisis had originated and which now developed a strong sentiment against GM foods. Public opinion in the Southern European countries seems to have been least concerned about the issue.

Public interest groups were quick to capitalise on this change in mood and may also have contributed to it by starting campaigns to warn the public of the risks of GM crops, and to demand clear labelling of GM foods. Two types of public interest groups were active in this process. Environmental groups, led by Greenpeace and Friends of the Earth, were the most vocal opponents of GM foods. They emphasised both the possible effects on the environment (like cross-pollination with non-GM varieties and ethical concerns about 'tampering with nature') and possible food safety risks. They called for a strengthening of the approval system or, more often, a ban on GM crops and foods (see e.g. Greenpeace, undated).

Consumer groups were less radical in their opposition, although the national groups differed in their exact positions. Nevertheless, their consensus position as advocated by BEUC, the European Consumers Organisation, did not reject the use of biotechnology in food as such, since the negative effects were not proven and most consumer groups recognised that the technology could also have positive consequences for consumers. Rather, they focused on the issue of consumer choice and demanded the mandatory labelling of GM foods and food ingredients derived from GM products. In addition, BEUC argued for more stringent approval criteria, strict liability and time-limited approvals (BEUC, 1998; 1999a). A campaign for consumer choice was started by BEUC in 1997 (Interview 14-8-2000, BEUC).

These campaigns and the consumer concerns underlying them were fuelled by occasional research that showed possible health or environmental risks of GM foods and crops. One of the most widely debated and most controversial claims was made by scientist Arpad Pusztai in a BBC documentary in August 1998. He reported to have found signs of intestinal changes in rats eating GM potatoes. The scientific validity of his results was heavily disputed from the outset, which resulted in his retirement from the research institute where he was working and a number of prominent journals refusing to publish his results (ISB, 1998b; Lancet, 1999a; 1999b). Nevertheless, his claims became a renewed source of concern for public interest groups and part of the public alike.

Shifts among the member states

At the same time as public concerns rose, the number of member state governments having serious doubts about GM foods increased as well. After the 1995 EC enlargement Sweden and Austria joined the ranks of Denmark and Germany in the Council of Ministers. Moreover, a number of other member state governments became less positive than they had been previously.

As was noted above, the opposition by some member state governments led to a number of unilateral bans and restrictions on GM crops and foods, even if they had been approved on the European level. The British position was remarkable in this respect. On the one hand, the British public and some British environmental groups had been the strongest opponents of GM foods, which was reflected in calls for more stringent standards by the UK Ministry of Agriculture and Food (MAFF, 1998; 1999a). On the other hand, however, the British government remained one of the defenders of GM foods in the Council of Ministers and did not support the de facto moratorium.

Nevertheless, the relative balance in the Council of Ministers shifted toward a minority in favour of more stringent regulations that was able to block any decisions under qualified majority voting. A number of interviewees indicated that it was in particular the change in the French government in the summer of 1997 that was significant in this respect. Before the change, France had been rather positive about GM foods, as was witnessed by its relatively favourable legislation transposing Directive 90/220 and by its position in the Council of Ministers. With the change to a Socialist-Green government, this changed. As a result, not only did the French position in the Council change, but the French competent authority also refused to give written consent to two GM food products which had been notified to it before the change in government and had subsequently been approved in the European procedure, even though it had given a favourable opinion at the beginning of the procedure.

Shifts among business groups

The shifts among the public at large, public interest groups and member state governments did not leave the industries involved in GM foods untouched. Under pressure from consumers and public interest groups, retailers were the first to shift their position. During the late 1990s, several supermarkets, in particular in the UK, worked toward the removal of GM foods from their house brands or even from all the products which they sold (IFT, 1999). EuroCommerce, the European organisation of retailers, declared its support for the mandatory labelling of GM food products and requested an extension to additives and aromas (EuroCommerce, 1998; 1999).

The retailers were followed by a number of food processors, which decided no longer to use GM ingredients in their products. CIAA, the Confederation of the Food and Drink Industries in the EC, remained more reluctant, however. It accepted labelling on the basis of added DNA and proteins but unlike EuroCommerce it did not support any further expansion of the labelling rules and stressed that labelling should focus on product characteristics rather than production techniques (CIAA, 1997; 1999). Still, in the first week of May 1999, seven European supermarket chains and three multinational food processing companies decided to ban GM foods altogether, as a reaction to the increased consumer concerns (Lancet, 1999b).

The farmers' position was less clear on this issue and they kept relatively silent in the debate. They had a particularly strong interest in consumer concerns since planting decisions have to be made around a year before the products are to be sold. Given the increasing uncertainty about the market for GM crops in Europe, hardly any farmer chose to grow GM crops. Within the European farmers organisation, COPA/COGECA, farm groups from different member states took different positions on the regulation of GM foods and crops, leading to a number of abstentions in the formulation of COPA/COGECA's official position (Interview 26-9-2000, COPA/COGECA; see also the endnotes to its position in COPA/COGECA, 2000). Still, COPA/COGECA publicly supported the de facto moratorium during the revision of Directive 90/220, as well as labelling, traceability, and a ban on antibiotic resistance marker genes. COPA/COGECA also stressed that '[i]t is essential that the regulatory approach taken by the EU also covers imported products, especially processed foods derived from GMOs' and called for the assessment of 'the economic (...) impact of this technology on the structure of EU agriculture and the future of rural areas' (COPA/COGECA, 2000), thus linking the regulation of GM foods and crops to the Common Agricultural Policy, which was discussed above in the context of the beef-hormone issue (in sections 4.3.1 and 4.5.2).

The European biotech industry was, not surprisingly, the staunchest defender of GM foods. To them, the breakdown of the approval system meant a direct threat to business. They disputed many amendments to the approval procedure, such as the ban on antibiotic resistance marker genes (EuropaBio, 2000b) and time-limited approvals (EuropaBio, 1999a), as well as the imposition of strict liability for damage to the environment or human health (EuropaBio, 2000c). Moreover, they opposed the introduction of mandatory labelling as it was thought to scare consumers and become a negative label in public perception. As an alternative, they advocated positive, 'GMO-free' labelling. They were unable, however, to change the general climate surrounding GM foods in the late 1990s, although they may have contributed to the EP's rejection of the proposal to include strict liability (i.e.

liability independent of any fault on the part of the producer) for environmental damage by GM crops in the revision of Directive 90/220 (Interview 7-8-2000, US Mission).

The position of the European Commission

All along the debate, the Commission remained relatively positive toward the technology, although it was also concerned about regaining consumer confidence in food safety. Within the Commission, a number of changes took place to ensure this. The role of the scientific committees was strengthened and responsibility for those committees was transferred to DG Sanco, the new DG for health and consumer protection (the successor of DG XXIV). In 2000, the Unit responsible for the Novel Foods Regulation was transferred from DG Enterprise (formerly DG III) to DG Sanco. The approach also became more consumer-oriented, although this preceded the shift between DGs and probably had more to do with the food scares of the 1990s than with the institutional changes (Interview 31-8-2000, European Commission). Within the European Commission, the initiative for legislation relating to GM products has therefore again shifted to DGs Sanco and Environment, with the other DGs (such as DG Enterprise) being involved only when a proposal has already reached an advanced stage (Interview 9-11-2000, European Commission). Support for more stringent standards was also reinforced when, in May 1999, the Commission's Scientific Steering Committee recommended banning the use of all antibiotic marker genes from GM foods (SSC, 1999: 9).

Thus, the balance of interests in the EC shifted considerably between the early and late 1990s. In the early 1990s, the Commission, the biotechnology industry and most member states in the Council of Ministers supported the development of GM foods, while the opposition remained mostly silent. By the end of the 1990s, however, the Council of Ministers had blocked all further approvals under Directive 90/220 and supported more stringent standards, while public interest groups were engaged in massive campaigns to warn about possible risks. As a result, retailers had sided with those demanding mandatory labelling and traceability, while food processors and farmers had also been forced to forgo the use of GM crops. This left only the Commission, the biotechnology industry and some member state governments (mainly the UK) on the side of the active proponents of GM foods, with the Commission being significantly more open to consumer concerns than it had been in the first half of the 1990s.

5.4 International developments

The European measures regarding GM foods have had a significant impact on debates in international forums. Conversely, these debates have had an impact on the political processes in the US, Canada and the EC. In this section, I will discuss the debates that have taken place in a number of international forums, the negotiation of the Cartagena Protocol on Biosafety being the most important. I will also analyse the legal status of the EC's regulations under the GATT/WTO framework and the Cartagena Protocol.

5.4.1 Debates in international forums

Since the early 1990s, international debates over GM foods have taken place in several forums. Work within the OECD has continued to build on the groundwork which had been laid in the early 1990s (e.g. in OECD, 1993). The Ad Hoc Group of National Experts was replaced by a Working Group on the Harmonisation of Regulatory Oversight in Biotechnology and a Task Force for the Safety of Novel Foods and Novel Feeds, which were established in 1995 and 1998 respectively. The OECD's efforts have focused mainly on the harmonisation of the information used in risk assessments (CAC, 2000b: 5), but it has also been called upon by the G8 Heads of Government to study 'the implications of biotechnology and other aspects of food safety' (G8, 1999: point 43).

Debates in the Codex Alimentarius Commission

Despite the ongoing work in the OECD, the focus of governments seems to have shifted to the Codex Alimentarius Commission (Interview 16-1-2001, FDA). This is probably due to three factors. First, the Codex Alimentarius Commission formulates food safety standards that serve as benchmarks in trade disputes under the World Trade Organization's Agreement on Sanitary and Phytosanitary Standards (SPS). Consequently, Codex standards have stronger legal effects than OECD guidelines. Second, the Codex Alimentarius Commission has more specific expertise when it comes to formulating food standards. Third, the range of actors involved is much wider in the Codex Alimentarius Commission than in the OECD. The Codex Alimentarius Commission, working under the United Nations' Food and Agriculture Organization (FAO) and World Health Organization (WHO), has a wider membership of countries. Moreover, it offers more room for participation by (domestic) interest groups, making it a more open forum than the OECD, something which came to be valued by governments as the public debate over GM foods became more intense.

The FAO and the WHO, which are jointly responsible for the Codex Alimentarius Commission, began work on GM foods in the early 1990s. In a number of reports on the basis of expert consultations, it was concluded that GM foods did not pose fundamentally different risks than traditional foods and the concept of substantial equivalence was endorsed as the best basis for the assessment of GM foods (FAO & WHO, 1991; 1996).

Likewise, the Codex Alimentarius Commission did not find it necessary to create specific committees to deal with GM foods. In 1991, it endorsed the conclusions and recommendations of the FAO and WHO's 1990 joint consultation (as laid down in FAO & WHO, 1991) and decided that the Codex General Subject Committees would deal with GM foods within their respective fields of competence. This decision was reinforced in 1995 (CAC, 2000a: 6).

In 1999, however, the Codex Alimentarius Commission decided to establish a specific working group after all. Under its terms of reference this Ad Hoc Intergovernmental Task Force on Foods Derived from Biotechnology should:

> 'develop standards, guidelines or recommendations, as appropriate, for foods derived from biotechnology or traits introduced into foods by biotechnology, on the basis of scientific evidence, risk analysis and having regard, where appropriate, to other legitimate factors relevant to the health of consumers and the promotion of fair trade practices.' (CAC, 2000a: annex 2)

The Ad Hoc Task Force met for the first time in March 2000 to discuss its areas of work, work priorities and some principles underlying the risk assessment of GM foods. In the participants' reactions to these issues, the familiar disagreements resurfaced. Canada stressed the importance of the concept of substantial equivalence and the work that had been done by the OECD (CAC, 2000c, Part I: 2-4). The US agreed and added that 'the Task Force should limit its initial discussions to food safety and nutritional assessment of foods derived from biotechnology' (CAC, 2000c, Part I: 13).

The EC, by contrast, called upon the Task Force to focus on 'questions related to food derived from modern biotechnology, on the protection of consumer health and fair trade and, where appropriate, include the consideration of other legitimate factors and the Code of ethics as established by the Codex Committee on General Principles' (CAC, 2000c, Part I-Add.1: 3). As the key concepts in relation to these issues, the EC identified the precautionary principle, 'traceability and monitoring,' and 'the consideration of other legitimate factors.' Unlike Canada and the US, it did not refer to the OECD's work on substantial equivalence.

During the first meeting, a compromise was reached on the areas of work that included most of the concerns and issues raised by the US, Canada, and the EC. Two ad hoc working groups were established to elaborate texts (CAC, 2000d), but at the second meeting of the Task Force, the debates were still preliminary (CAC, 2001b). Still, at the 2001 meeting of the Codex Alimentarius Commission, all countries agreed in principle that the safety, and in particular the allergenicity, of foods produced through genetic modification should be tested before these foods enter the market (FAO & WHO, 2001). This was a very general statement, however, which included elements that were uncontroversial in the EC, the US and Canada alike. The more contentious issues were still left to be decided later.

The issue of GM food labelling has been discussed in the Codex Committee on Food Labelling. It has been discussed at several meetings since 1994. A proposal to add a labelling requirement if an allergen has been transferred, was approved during a meeting in May 2000 (CAC, 2000e: iv & Appendix III).

Other labelling issues have proceeded much less quickly. In the field of mandatory labelling, different proposals have been tabled. For the May 2000 meeting,

Canada, which chairs this Committee, presented two options: one in which labelling would only be required if the product had been significantly changed (the US and Canadian approach), and one in which the label would have to state that a food had been derived from genetic modification if the food product contained DNA or proteins resulting from the genetic modification or if it differed significantly (the EC approach). During the meeting, India and Norway, supported by some other delegations and observers, such as Consumers International, proposed a labelling requirement for all GM foods and food ingredients, regardless of any differences in the products themselves. This issue was not resolved and consequently it was returned to the third step of the Codex procedure, in which a proposed draft standard is sent to member states and observers for their comments (CAC, 2000e).

For the Committee's 2001 meeting, a new draft was prepared by a drafting group, consisting of the most vocal countries in the process. The new draft sought to combine the two options presented by Canada and also included a provision relating to the comprehensive, process-based approach advocated by India and Norway (CAC, 2001a). Consequently, the draft effectively offered a choice of three different approaches and concentrated on the standards that should apply when using each approach.

Even in the drafting group, it had not proved possible to reach consensus on this draft, however. For instance, Canada preferred the draft to specify that its standards relating to process-based labelling were only meant to apply to voluntary labelling schemes (CAC, 2001a: Annex II, p. 14). India, on the other hand, rejected the sections on exemptions and thresholds as being contrary to its preferred comprehensive labelling approach (CAC, 2001a: Annex II, p. 15). As a result, the draft remained at step 3 of the Codex procedure after the Committee's 2001 meeting (CAC, 2001c).

The Cartagena Protocol

In the end, the negotiations concerning the Biosafety Protocol (which later became known as the Cartagena Protocol) became the most important forum for this issue. These negotiations took place in the context of the United Nations' Convention on Biological Diversity (CBD), which had been concluded in 1992. In the CBD, the contracting parties had agreed to a set of principles regarding biodiversity. Both the EC and Canada are parties to the CBD, but US Congress failed to ratify it. In Article 19.3 CBD, the intention was stated to develop a protocol that would address trade in GMOs. Even though this protocol was to deal mainly with environmental issues and not food safety per se, it has had great relevance for the debate over food safety issues as well.

In 1995, negotiations started on the Biosafety Protocol. Although, technically, the US could not become a party to this agreement, not being a party to the CBD itself, it was invited to participate anyway, since it was (and is) the most important producer and exporter of GMOs. Initially, the deadline for presenting an agreement was set for 1998, but due to diverging views in the working group preparing the draft, this deadline could not be met.

The participants to the negotiations formed five groups (Cosbey & Burgiel, 2000). The Miami Group was formed by the US, Canada, Argentina, Australia, Chile and Uruguay, the main GM producers and exporters, which had an interest in keeping trade in GMOs as free as possible. Its main opponent was the so-called 'Like-Minded Group' of developing nations, which wanted to protect their biodiversity against imports of GMOs. They demanded more opportunities to block GMO imports if necessary. In between these camps were three groups of countries: the EC, the countries from Central and Eastern Europe, and the Compromise Group (consisting of Japan, Mexico, Norway, Singapore, South Korea, Switzerland and, in the final negotiating session, New Zealand).

Having started as negotiations between the developed and developing states, the negotiations eventually also became a forum for the controversy between the US and the EC (Falkner, 2000: 301). In February 1999, the parties to the negotiations met in Cartagena, Colombia, but were unable to reach a consensus. One of the most controversial issues was whether the Protocol should cover only living GMOs that were meant to be introduced into the environment, such as seeds, or also GM 'commodities,' products intended to be used as food, feed or for processing, such as GM soya, GM maize and GM canola. The Miami Group argued for a narrow scope, since the Protocol was supposed to address environmental issues and commodities would pose no risk in that respect. The Like-Minded Group demanded a wider scope, arguing that the environmental effects of commodities was unclear. Some also argued for the inclusion of commodities on human health grounds (Cosbey & Burgiel, 2000).

Another important point of disagreement concerned the balance between environmental and trade concerns and the relation to the WTO. The Miami Group wanted the Protocol to be subordinated to the WTO Agreements, whereas the EC and the Like-Minded Group wanted it to be an exemption to the WTO. This issue was particularly important, since the EC, the US and Canada were simultaneously working on this issue within the framework of the WTO. Falkner (2000: 35) argues that the proposals to establish working groups on biotechnology under the WTO were meant to effect 'a shift in the institutional context within which biosafety issues would be debated, away from the CBD's emphasis on biodiversity protection and towards the WTO's objective of trade liberalization.'

Finally, the EC wanted to include the precautionary principle in the Protocol. This was not acceptable to the Miami Group, which feared that it could be used as an excuse for protectionism (Cosbey & Burgiel, 2000).

In February 2000, the parties at last reached an agreement in Montreal, Canada (UN, 2000; henceforth 'Cartagena Protocol'). An Advance Informed Agreement procedure was established for the transboundary movement of living GMOs, except those that are 'intended for direct use as food or feed, or for processing' (Article 7.2 Cartagena Protocol). Importing countries can refuse living GMOs if a risk assessment has established risks for the environment or human health (Articles 10 & 15). Moreover, the Protocol allows socio-economic factors to be taken into account (Article 26).

Products intended for use as food or for processing are subject to a (lighter) notification procedure. Importing countries retain the right to refuse them, again based on a risk assessment (Article 11). Annex II specifies the information required for the notification, which should include a risk assessment (Annex II, point (j)). The requirements of the risk assessment are set out in Annex III. They include information about the recipient and donor organisms, characteristics of the genetic modification and the GMO, information on the intended use, and information on the receiving environment (Annex III.9). In the risk assessment itself, novel characteristics that may have adverse effects on biodiversity have to be identified, 'taking also into account risks to human health' (Annex III.8(a)).

The precautionary principle was finally included as a general objective and in two specific provisions. The preamble refers to the 'precautionary approach contained in Principle 15 of the Rio Declaration,' which is reiterated in Article 1 on the Protocol's objective. Without using the phrase 'precautionary principle' or 'approach,' Articles 10.6 and 11.8 state that 'lack of scientific certainty due to insufficient relevant scientific information and knowledge (...) shall not prevent [a] Party from taking a decision, as appropriate, with regard to the import of the living modified organism.'

The Protocol also provides for the labelling of GMOs intended to be used as food, feed or for processing (Article 18.2). The formulation of precise requirements for labelling have been postponed to later negotiations, to be conducted within two years after the entry into force of the Protocol.

Its relation to other international agreements, most notably the WTO Agreements, remains unclear. In the end, the Protocol only deals with this issue in its preamble where it simultaneously states that 'this Protocol shall not be interpreted as implying a change in the rights and obligations of a Party under any existing international agreement' but that this recital 'is not intended to subordinate this Protocol to other international agreements.' In the end, so it reads, 'trade and environment agreements should be mutually supportive.'

During the negotiations, some business groups warned against the trade effects which a Protocol could have (GMA, 1998), and business groups from both North America and Europe formed the Global Industry Coalition to present a single position to the negotiators of the Protocol (Interview 15-2-2001, BioteCanada). In the end, however, the Protocol was looked upon fairly favourably by most groups in the EC, US and Canada. Environmental groups were happy to see the precautionary principle incorporated into the Protocol text. Business groups hoped that the Protocol would provide a basis for harmonised risk assessment procedures, which in the end would facilitate trade in GMOs (see e.g. EuropaBio, 2000a), but others feared protectionist uses of the precautionary approach endorsed in the Protocol (ASA, 2000b).

Canada did not sign the Cartagena Protocol straightaway. Only after internal government debates and consultations with domestic groups did the Government of Canada decide to sign the Protocol. To the signature it attached a declaration, clarifying its interpretation of some provisions and specifying a number of issues that would have to be settled during the implementation of the Protocol (Government of Canada, 2001b). First, the Government of Canada wanted to make sure that the Cartagena Protocol would not prejudice its rights under the WTO. Second, it explicitly excluded food safety considerations from the Protocol's scope, interpreting the phrase 'impact on human health' narrowly, to include only impact 'resulting from adverse impacts on biodiversity.' Third, it required clarification of the rules on labelling before it would ratify the Protocol. Finally, a number of more minor issues were identified that needed to be specified. This way, the Government of Canada sought to reduce the potential impact of the Cartagena Protocol on international food safety standards, as well as on its domestic regulation of GM foods and food products. It also clarified its position on a number of contentious issues that had to be decided in the talks on implementation following the conclusion of the Protocol itself.

5.4.2 Compatibility with GATT/WTO law

The European regulation of GM foods thus operates within a complicated international legal framework. On the one hand, it is subject to the WTO's standards. On the other hand, this policy area has been debated in many international forums, in which some measure of harmonisation has been sought. In this subsection, I will discuss the compatibility of the EC's approval process and labelling requirements with the WTO Agreements and the other international standards, insofar as they have been put in place.

The EC approval process

The most relevant WTO agreement to this issue is the SPS Agreement (WTO, 1994c; henceforth 'the SPS Agreement' or 'SPS'), which lays down standards for the assessment of national regulatory standards dealing with, among other things, food safety if and when they impede trade. As was discussed in section 4.4.2 in the context of the beef-hormone dispute, the SPS Agreement provides that national regulatory standards have to be based on a risk assessment. In that dispute, the WTO panel and Appellate Body both concluded that the EC's measures had not been based on a risk assessment, in that there was no 'rational relationship' between the prohibition on hormone-treated beef and the underlying risk assessments.

The GMO case is different in a number of respects, however. First, the European framework does not ban the sale of foods derived from GMOs altogether. Directives 2001/18 and 90/220 and the Novel Foods Regulation lay down standards for the risk assessment to be conducted before the approval of GM products. Such an approval system as such does not violate the SPS Agreement, as long as the approvals are based on a risk assessment.

Second, while in the beef-hormone issue all available evidence (except for some minor exceptions) indicated that the banned growth hormones did not pose a threat to human health, there is significant debate about the risks of GMOs, even within the scientific community. Even if most scientists agree that there is no reason to treat GMOs as an entirely different class of organisms, it is generally acknowledged that GMOs might pose certain risks under certain conditions. Moreover, there is significant debate about the precise nature and extent of those risks, with some scientists taking a more sceptical approach than others.

An additional complicating factor is that the GMO issue has different aspects. These aspects conform to a variety of possible risks, such as ecological risks, the risk of the spread of antibiotic resistance, the risk of inserting allergens into GM foods, etcetera. Disagreements among scientists about the risks of GMOs partly run along the lines of these respective areas, with ecologists generally being more sceptical than microbiologists.

As a consequence, it does not seem excessive to impose an approval procedure on GM products, as long as the approval process focuses on scientifically ascertainable risks. The European risk assessment procedure seems to do that, at least on paper. It takes into account risks for human health and the environment and evaluates them according to scientific principles. It is unclear how the same level of protection could be attained by less trade-restrictive means.

The SPS Agreement also requires risk assessments to be based as much as possible on internationally formulated standards. The standards developed by the Codex Alimentarius Commission count as such. Since the Codex has not approved specific GMOs, such approvals cannot be used in the assessment of the EC's approval system. When it comes to the procedures used to evaluate GMOs, however, the EC seems to follow generally agreed upon international standards, such as the 'substantial equivalence' approach, that have been developed within several international forums. The EC has also played an active part in these international processes.

The role of other factors, such as consumer and socio-economic concerns, is much more contentious within the framework of the SPS agreement, but officially they do not play a role in the EC's risk assessments, although Directive 2001/18 seems to offer some room for 'ethical aspects.' Accordingly, no specific GM food product has ever been rejected in the EC because of these 'non-scientific' factors.

Under the SPS Agreement, precautionary measures are only allowed as provisional measures pending further risk assessments. As was discussed in the context of the beef-hormone issue, the precautionary principle cannot override the SPS Agreement's provisions on risk assessments. Since Directive 2001/18 explicitly takes the 'precautionary principle' as the basis for risk assessments, the revised Directive has the potential to come into conflict with the SPS Agreement. This depends entirely on the way this principle will be used in practice, however.

Besides, in the period discussed in this case study, Directive 90/220 was still in force, and that Directive did not officially endorse the precautionary principle.

Most of the US and Canadian criticism has not focused on the EC's formal risk assessment criteria, however, but on the way the framework has operated in practice. It is said to be politicised, intransparent and unnecessarily slow. If this were to be the basis for a claim before the WTO, it would have to concern the rejection of a specific GM product, rather than the process as a whole. Politicisation of the process is not a violation of the SPS Agreement in itself; it would only violate the Agreement if non-scientific factors were to determine a decision not to approve a product. Since many products have been approved and the debate on approvals has often concerned scientific issues, a rejection would have to be found that could be argued not to be 'based on' a risk assessment. Then, this decision, rather than the system as a whole, could be brought before the WTO.

The transparency requirements of the SPS Agreement concern the prompt publication of SPS measures and the existence of a single enquiry point (Article 7 and Annex B SPS). The fact that the European approval process is complicated and the deliberations are not always open to public scrutiny does not seem to violate these provisions.

Finally, the speed of the approval system is subject to the provisions in Article 8 SPS and Annex C on 'control, inspection and approval procedures.' Point 1(a) of Annex C states that these procedures 'are undertaken and completed without undue delay and in no less favourable manner for imported products than for like domestic products.' Before the de facto moratorium under Directive 90/220, European approval procedures were quite lengthy, but it is not certain whether they were 'unduly' lengthy. Even FDA took four years to evaluate the Flavr Savr tomato, and approval procedures for some non-GM products have taken several years in the US and Canada, too. Moreover, the EC's approval procedures do not appear to have been less favourable for US or Canadian than for European GM crops and foods.

This could be different under the de facto moratorium, which can be interpreted as a deliberate slowdown of the process. Still, here too, it is not clear whether the resulting delay has been 'undue' in terms of the SPS Agreement. The de facto moratorium could also be interpreted as a (de facto) ban on GM products that is not based on a risk assessment but on non-scientific factors. The Council of Ministers took care, however, not to frame the moratorium as a formal ban, but as a temporary measure while more stringent regulatory standards were being developed. Since this implies a precautionary approach, this would bring the de facto moratorium under the scope of Article 5.7 SPS.

According to Article 5.7 SPS, states can take precautionary measures as long as they are temporary and the risk assessment is carried out within a reasonable period of time. It can be argued that this is the case here: the EC has put a temporary ban in place while awaiting further developments. Given the complexity and the rapid scientific developments underlying this issue, this could be argued to be justified. This might change, however, if the European ban were to become a semi-permanent feature of the European regulation of GMOs, but during the period over which I am examining this issue, the de facto moratorium would seem to be allowable under both Article 5.7 and Annex C of the SPS Agreement.

All in all the European approval process seems to fall within the latitude allowed by the SPS Agreement. With the de facto moratorium the EC has come closer to a ban based on non-scientific factors or to 'undue delays' in its approval process, which would violate the SPS Agreement. As long as the approval process has not been completely blocked (as it is under the de facto moratorium), some further strengthening of the risk assessment criteria would not seem to violate the SPS Agreement's provisions, given the Agreement's scope for countries to determine their own level of protection and the debate on the risks of GMOs.

The EC labelling requirements

In principle, the labelling of products falls under the Agreement on Technical Barriers to Trade (WTO 1994d; henceforth the 'TBT Agreement' or 'TBT'), except when 'labelling requirements [are] directly related to food safety' (Annex A, paragraph 1 SPS Agreement). The applicable agreement if the EC labelling system were to come before a WTO panel would therefore depend on the basis of that system, but since I have limited myself to the food safety aspects of GM foods, I will focus on the SPS Agreement.

Under the SPS Agreement, the same rules apply to labelling requirements as to other SPS measures. Since the EC and the US have not been able to agree on labelling standards in the Codex Alimentarius Commission, there are no relevant 'international standards, guidelines or recommendations' to be taken into account. Still, the labelling requirements have to be based on a risk assessment and to conform to the more detailed rules laid down in Article 5 SPS. For instance, in the beef-hormone issue, a mandatory labelling scheme for hormone-treated beef would probably have violated the SPS Agreement as well, since it would have been based on the same (insufficient) evidence as the complete ban (Pardo Quintillán 1999: 171).

On the one hand, the EC's labelling system would seem to be more vulnerable to a WTO challenge than the approval procedures, since the labelling scheme is mandatory, whereas the approval procedures have merely been slow and restrictive. Moreover, the EC's labelling regime is more clearly related to consumer concerns, apart from scientifically ascertainable health risks. Consumer concerns have not played that role in the approval procedures, at least not officially.

As a result, the labelling requirements offer a clearer target for a WTO challenge than the approval procedures. Above, I have already argued that the EC's approval system would probably survive scrutiny under the SPS Agreement, although some caveats had to be made. Some of the same arguments of scientific uncertainty would apply to the EC's labelling requirements, as well, but even then the EC could probably offer little scientific evidence for health risks specifically related to GM foods as a class. It would also be more difficult for the EC to justify the labelling requirements as provisional measures under Article 5.7 SPS, since they have become more or less permanent features of the EC's regulation of GM foods.

On the other hand, once they are deemed to be based on a risk assessment, the labelling requirements would seem to be less vulnerable to a WTO challenge than the approval procedures. Article 5.6 SPS Agreement requires that a measure is 'not more trade-restrictive than required to achieve [the] appropriate level of sanitary and phytosanitary protection, taking into account technical and economic feasibility.' Labelling requirements are more likely to pass this test than are approval procedures, since in most circumstances labelling is the least trade-restrictive measure available, short of allowing a product on the market without any restrictions.

In the final analysis, however, much would depend on the basis for and the form of the label. As to the basis, in the EC legislation so far, labelling is required if either added DNA or proteins can be shown to be present or if the product is no longer substantially equivalent due to genetic modification. In the latter case, the process by which the product has been produced has to be mentioned as well. This is probably a more acceptable solution than a labelling requirement that would be based on an examination of the production process per se, without any link to the final product, but mentioning the process could be argued to serve no purpose in terms of the protection of health, while it could discriminate against (imported) GM foods.

Given the acceptability of the labelling requirements themselves, another important consideration for a WTO panel would be the actual form and implementation of these requirements. If the label were to be negative to the effect that it would discriminate against GM products when compared to non-GM products, it would not be acceptable. Also, the implementing procedures would have to be proportional and not unnecessarily burdensome for the imported products. In general, the EC's regulations can be said to conform to these requirements, but then the crucial question remains whether they are based on a risk assessment in the sense of the SPS Agreement.

The labelling requirement would therefore seem more likely to violate the SPS Agreement than the approval procedure, although it would be a more difficult case to make than the hormone issue. The EC could also try to use a different basis for the labelling requirement. In that case, the TBT Agreement would apply, and the legal considerations might be different, but that analysis is beyond the scope of this study. The approval procedures would seem to fall within the scope of allowable action under the SPS Agreement, at least for now.

5.4.3 GATT/WTO law and the Cartagena Protocol

How could the Cartagena Protocol affect the legal status of the EC's measures? During the course of the process under study here, the Cartagena Protocol was not yet in force. It was only signed in January 2000 and opened for signature later that year. Before the fifty states required for its entry into force have ratified it, some time will have passed.

Nevertheless, the Cartagena Protocol gives an important insight into the development of international law in this area. And even though the US is not a party to the CBD, of which the Protocol is an extension, it actively participated in the negotiations. It may therefore feel bound by the Protocol's provisions, at least in practice, even if it does not ratify it. As a result, the Protocol is a significant instrument to gain some understanding of the 'state of the art' in international law regarding trade in GMOs.

The Cartagena Protocol seems to offer more opportunities for importing countries to block GM products than the SPS Agreement. It contains the precautionary principle, which under the SPS Agreement can only be used to support temporary measures. Some have taken this to imply that the precautionary principle has become a principle of international (environmental) law (Cosbey & Burgiel, 2000). In any case, the Cartagena Protocol allows its parties more leeway in restricting or blocking imports of GMOs than the SPS Agreement, even if the Protocol's criteria are mainly limited to biosafety considerations. Still, this may also include 'risks to human health' (Annex III.1 Cartagena Protocol) and socio-economic considerations (Article 26 Cartagena Protocol). The interpretation of the clause 'risks to human health' is the subject of debate, however, as was witnessed by the Canadian government's remark that it should only relate to risks resulting from 'adverse impacts on biodiversity.'

The relationship between the Cartagena Protocol and the WTO Agreements

Given the possible incompatibility of the Cartagena Protocol and the SPS Agreement, a crucial question is what is the relationship between the Cartagena Protocol and the WTO Agreements. This is a specific case of the relationship between multilateral agreements in general, an issue of some notoriety among international legal scholars (Sinclair, 1984: 93; Czaplinski & Danilenko, 1990: 12-13). Until now, no country has ever disputed a trade measure taken pursuant to a multilateral treaty, but it is not very clear what role such a treaty would play in the GATT/WTO dispute settlement proceedings (see also Nollkaemper, 1998: 195 ff.).

The safest assumption seems to be that trade provisions from another multilateral agreement cannot be invoked against a country that is a member of the WTO but not a party to the other multilateral agreement. In that case, Article 30.4(d) of the Vienna Convention on the Law of Treaties (UN, 1969; henceforth 'the Vienna Convention') stipulates that the agreement to which both countries are a party will prevail (cf. Geradin, 1997: 49-50). Thus, the EC cannot invoke the Cartagena Protocol against the US, since the US is not a party to the Protocol.

If the countries are both members of the WTO and parties to the other multilateral agreement, the situation becomes more complicated. Assuming that both Canada and the EC will ratify the Cartagena Protocol, this would be the situation between them. In the absence of a legal hierarchy between the GATT/WTO Agreements and the Cartagena Protocol, some rules are needed to solve this type of conflict. The provisions of the Vienna Convention do not cover all situations in which conflicts between international agreements occur. Still, the Vienna Convention and customary international law provide some tools for solving this issue.

First, as foreseen in Article 30.2 of the Vienna Convention, an agreement itself can stipulate that it is subordinate to another agreement, which is the clearest way of establishing a priority between agreements. The GATT/WTO Agreements do not contain such a provision, despite proposals to that effect in the literature (see e.g. Petersmann, 1995: 42-43; Schlagenhof, 1995: 151-153; Geradin, 1997: 49-50).

The Cartagena Protocol does contain language on its relation to other international agreements, but it does little to clarify the issue. As was noted above, the Protocol uses vague and somewhat contradictory language in its preamble and has avoided the issue in the treaty text altogether. Although Cosbey and Burgiel (2000) point at the Protocol's significance in that its 'not (...) subordinate' phrase uses the strongest language in any multilateral environmental treaty and that 'it would be very difficult (some suggest politically impossible) for the dispute panel to ignore the Protocol's wording,' it is unlikely that it will be of much use in determining its relation to the WTO Agreements.

Second, if the agreements at hand do not contain a provision on their relation to each other, Article 30.3 of the Vienna Convention, dealing with successive treaties relating to the same subject-matter, may be relevant. That provision states that if two treaties have been concluded which relate to the same subject-matter, the later treaty prevails (see also Article 30.4). Using that rule, the Cartagena Protocol would take precedence over the WTO Agreements.

However, it is not clear whether the GATT/WTO Agreements and the Cartagena Protocol 'relate to the same subject matter.' This question is clear when it comes to a treaty that is specifically meant to succeed another treaty, such as GATT 1994 and GATT 1947. It is much less obvious when it concerns, for instance, trade restrictions in a multilateral environmental agreement and the GATT/WTO Agreements. Although the relevant provisions of both treaties concern trade restrictions, the treaties as such do not relate to the same subject-matter. Moreover, as Sinclair (1984: 98) has argued, the requirement that agreements relate to the same subject-matter should be 'construed strictly. It will not cover cases where a general treaty impinges indirectly on the content of a particular provision of an earlier treaty.' Arguably, this is the case in the relation between the Cartagena Protocol and the WTO Agreements, so the rules on successive treaties do not seem to apply here.

Still, even if it were accepted that the GATT/WTO Agreements and the Cartagena Protocol relate to the same subject-matter, Article 30 of the Vienna Convention would yield some unsatisfactory results (cf. Schlagenhof, 1995: 150). For instance, until 1994 probably all trade provisions in environmental treaties would have taken precedence over the GATT, since they were mostly concluded after the 1960s. However, with the conclusion of the WTO Agreements in 1994, the situation would have been reversed, even though this was never specifically meant to be the outcome by the countries concluding the WTO Agreements. Moreover, trade provisions in multilateral treaties concluded since 1994, such as the Cartagena Protocol, would take precedence over GATT 1994, while those in older treaties would not.

Third, if the rules on successive treaties do not apply, the relation between international agreements becomes a matter of interpretation. To begin with, the provisions of the Cartagena Protocol and the WTO Agreements could be interpreted so as to eliminate a conflict between them (cf. Czaplinski and Danilenko, 1990: 13). This approach would also be supported by the phrase in the Cartagena Protocol's preamble that states that 'trade and environment agreements should be mutually supportive.'

This approach could go a long way in preventing conflicting interpretations between the Cartagena Protocol and the WTO Agreements in concrete disputes. Still, conflicting interpretations could possibly arise on a number of points (cf. Phillips and Kerr, 2000: 69-74). For instance, as was pointed out above, the role of the precautionary principle differs between the Protocol and the SPS Agreement: the Cartagena Protocol specifically states that 'lack of scientific evidence (...) shall not prevent' a country from blocking the imports of certain GM products 'in order to avoid or minimize (...) potential adverse effects,' whereas the SPS Agreement only allows such measures on a provisional basis. Also, the Cartagena Protocol allows the inclusion of socio-economic factors in the risk assessment, something the SPS and TBT Agreements do not.

If it is not possible to reconcile the interpretation of the Cartagena Protocol and the WTO Agreements, the principle that more specific provisions and agreements prevail over those that are more general would apply. Although this principle is not stated in the Vienna Convention, it is widely recognised as a rule of customary international law (Sinclair, 1984: 96; Czaplinski & Danilenko, 1990: 20-21). The Cartagena Protocol is arguably a more specific agreement than the GATT 1994 or the SPS and TBT Agreements, since the Protocol covers trade in GMOs while these WTO Agreements cover trade (or trade in plants and animals) in general. This conclusion is contingent, however, on the interpretation of (provisions in) the Cartagena Protocol and the WTO Agreements.

This interpretation is complicated by the declarations made by the Government of Canada upon signing the Protocol. These declarations concerned the relation to the WTO Agreements both directly, in that the Government of Canada considered the Protocol not to prejudice any of its rights under other international agreements, and indirectly, in that it excluded human health effects not resulting from impacts on biodiversity from the Protocol's scope, thus qualifying the relation between the Protocol and the SPS Agreement.

These kinds of 'interpretative declarations' are a hotly contested issue among international legal scholars. Some consider them to be reservations as defined in Article 2.1(d) of the Vienna Convention, at least when the declarations are meant to specify conditions for ratification (for this debate, see e.g. Horn, 1988: 229-235; Sinclair, 1984: 52-54). If the Canadian declarations were considered to be reservations in this sense, that would be problematic because the Cartagena Protocol explicitly prohibits parties from making reservations (Article 38 Cartagena Protocol).

However, the Government of Canada's declarations are not formulated as specific conditions for ratification but as principles that should guide the implementation of the Protocol, and given the Protocol's prohibition on reservations probably quite intentionally so. For some of the reservations this makes sense, as they concern issues that still have to be settled in further talks. For others, most notably the relation to other international agreements and the interpretation of the term 'risks to human health,' this is less evident since they could be seen as attempts to modify the legal effects of the Protocol. Even here, however, they could also be seen as attempts to clarify the meaning of ambiguous terms and provisions, the purport of which is not directly clear from the Protocol itself.

The role of other multilateral agreements in GATT/WTO case law

Whatever the rules of international law on the relationship between the Cartagena Protocol and the WTO Agreements, in the end it will be a WTO panel or the Appellate Body that will decide on this issue when a trade dispute arises (cf. Palmeter & Mavroidis, 1998: 412). The relation between the GATT/WTO Agreements and other bilateral and multilateral agreements also played a role in the Tuna-Dolphin and Shrimp-Turtle cases, which were discussed in section 3.4.2 of this study. In the second Tuna-Dolphin case, a number of other multilateral agreements related to the protection of dolphins. Referring to the rules of interpretation of Articles 31 and 32 of the Vienna Convention, the panel dismissed the relevance of these agreements, claiming that:

> 'the agreements cited by the parties to the dispute were bilateral or plurilateral agreements that were not concluded among the contracting parties to the General Agreement, and that (...) did not apply to the interpretation of the General Agreement or the application of its provisions.' (GATT, 1994: paragraph 5.19)

Apparently, the panel required an agreement to be concluded among *all* the parties to the GATT in order to have relevance for the interpretation of GATT. It is not clear how the Vienna Convention's rules could be construed to support this claim, and according to Palmeter and Mavroidis (1998: 411), the panel's reasoning was 'illustrative of the tendency of GATT panels to disregard public international law when it came to interpreting the General Agreement' (cf. in general Kuyper, 1994: 229-232).

In the Shrimp-Turtle case, the issue emerged again when the US invoked the Convention on International Trade in Endangered Species (CITES), to which all the countries involved in the dispute were parties and which included sea turtles as an endangered species. This argument was dismissed by the panel, however, arguing that CITES related to trade in sea turtles, while the US had restricted trade in shrimps. Moreover, CITES did not mandate the specific protection measures required by the US (WTO, 1998b: paragraph 58).

This outcome was logical given the facts of the case. Given the nature of the obligations under CITES, the panel did not have to consider further issues concerning the relation between the WTO Agreements and other multilateral agreements, although the fact that it discussed the provisions in CITES could be seen as an acknowledgement of their potential relevance to the dispute. In that sense, the Shrimp-Turtle panel would fit into a more general tendency of GATT/WTO panels and the Appellate Body not to interpret GATT/WTO law in isolation from other sources of international law (Palmeter & Mavroidis, 1998: 413).

Still, under the current status of GATT/WTO case law, it is unclear to what extent a WTO panel would allow its interpretation of the SPS and TBT Agreements to be influenced by the wording of another agreement that is, in principle, unrelated to it, in particular when there is uncertainty about its meaning in relation to concrete measures. If it were to use the applicable rules of international law, an analysis such as the one presented above would suggest itself, even though this analysis did not yield unambiguous results.

A further legal analysis of these issues would be more of an attempt to contribute to the legal debate over the Cartagena Protocol than to analyse it. For the purposes of my analysis, the presence of these issues in themselves is important, however, since they point both at the high degree of ambiguity surrounding the Cartagena Protocol and its legal status, and at the fact that the Protocol is still in the stage of development. The Government of Canada's declarations should therefore primarily be seen as attempts to set an agenda for these subsequent developments, which will no doubt be countered by other countries and groups that hold opposing views. In the end, much will depend on how the general provisions of the Protocol are going to be elaborated and interpreted when it comes to the EC's practical approval procedure and labelling requirements, and both are not yet entirely clear.

5.5 Reactions in the US and Canada

5.5.1 Impact on trade and bilateral initiatives

The impact of the EC measures on US and Canadian exports

The European measures (both the de facto moratorium and the strengthened labelling requirements) have affected exports of GM crops and foods from the US and Canada, although to differing degrees. These exports have been affected both directly and indirectly. Directly, some US and Canadian producers experienced decreasing exports to the EC as a result of the European standards. Indirectly, the European measures affected exports to other countries. Moreover, they threatened the future prospects of US and Canadian exports to the EC.

The main GM crops exported by the US are soya beans and maize. The vast majority of both products is produced, distributed, processed and marketed in bulk. In this process, the maize and soya beans from different sources are not separated but handled without distinction. As a result, the distinction between GM and non-GM varieties is lost and containers of maize or soya beans typically contain both varieties. This system allows for considerable economies of scale in handling the maize and soya beans but makes it impossible to trace soya beans and maize to their source of production.

A very small part of the harvest is so-called 'identity preserved' or IP. IP corn or soya beans consist of non-GM varieties that are kept apart from other varieties during the whole process of growing, harvesting, distribution, processing and marketing. Even then, some commingling with GM varieties may occur, as the machines and containers used to process the IP varieties are often also used for GM varieties and may contain traces of GM maize or soya beans.

Since the economies of scale inherent in the bulk system are lost, IP varieties are more expensive and have to be sold at a premium in order to be profitable. The only way to overcome these inefficiencies within the bulk system would be to ban the use of GM varieties altogether, which would imply higher production costs in growing the crops themselves, however.

Both maize and soya beans were among the first flow of GM crops. GM varieties of both crops were first planted in 1996 and their relative acreage has increased steadily each year since then. It was estimated that in 1999, some 50% of soya bean and 36% of maize acreage in the US was planted with GM varieties (cf. CEC, 2000b: 11; BIO, 2000c).

The stories of their exports to the EC differ a great deal, however. European self-sufficiency in maize was around 100% between 1996 and 1999 (CEC, 2000b: 36). Nevertheless, there were some imports and exports, as well as imports of maize gluten feed. Some 75 to 80% of maize in the EC is used for animal feed and only 7% for direct human consumption (CEC, 2000b: 35). The US exports about 20% of its maize, but only a few percent of US maize exports find their way to the EC (cf. CEC, 2000b: 40; USDA, 1999: 48).

The US share in European maize imports dropped from 86% in 1995 to 12% in 1999 (CEC, 2000b: 36). The decline of US maize exports to the EC is largely due to the differences in approved varieties. Whereas the US has approved eleven GM maize varieties, the EC has approved only four (EuropaBio, 1999b; CEC, 2000b: 40). When US maize growers started to grow varieties that had not been approved for the EC market, this effectively ended their export opportunities to the EC (Interview 25-1-2001, NCGA). Because of the bulk system, it was prohibitively expensive to separate the approved and unapproved maize, leading to the presence of unapproved maize in every container and every product made from US maize. In 1998, USDA estimated the losses due to the blocked export opportunities for maize to be around US$ 200 million (USDA, 1998: 34); in 2001, the US General

Accounting Office reported a decline of US maize exports to the EC from US$ 300 million in the mid-1990s to US$10 million around the year 2000 (GAO, 2001: 10).

Such a decline has not occurred in the case of soya beans. The EC hardly has any soya bean production itself; between 1995 and 1999, the EC produced between 6% and 12% of its domestic need for soya beans. It has therefore depended almost completely on imports from other countries, including the US. US exports of soya beans to the EC account for about 15% of American production, or 30% of American soya bean exports (CEC, 2000b: 34-35).

Warned by the example of the US maize exports, the American Soybean Association (ASA) made efforts to block the marketing of GM soya bean varieties that had not been approved in the EC (Interview 31-8-2000, ASA). Thus, in 1999, the ASA convinced AgrEvo not to market or plant its LibertyLink soya bean, which had only been approved in the US (ASA, 1999a). As a result, almost all GM soya beans used in the US are Roundup Ready varieties, the only variety which has also been approved in the EC.

Despite these efforts, the amount of soya beans exported to the EC declined quite considerably between 1997 and 1998, but USDA has attributed this to price competition with Argentinian soya beans, rather than to the European controversy over GM foods (Interview 31-8-2000, ASA; CEC, 2000b: 39). This is not surprising as about 80% of US soya bean exports to the EC is used for animal feed (ASA, 2000a: 63). Moreover, Argentina is itself one of the leading countries in GM crops.

Although about 60% of all processed foods contain soya beans or soya bean products (e.g. soy oil), only one or two percent of soya bean exports are used for human foods (Interview 31-8-2000, ASA). The use of US soya beans for human foods has suffered more from voluntary reformulation of house brands by supermarkets and labelling requirements. For US soya bean exports as a whole, this has not made much of a difference, however.

Thus, US maize exports suffered a significant decline in a small volume, while US soya bean exports experienced a negligible decline in a large volume, at least when it comes to the trade effects of the divergence between European and US regulations. As a consequence, the direct trade effects of the European regulations on US exports have been relatively minor.

Canada's main GM crop is canola, a kind of oilseed rape that has been specifically developed in Canada. By 1999, about half of Canada's canola acreage was planted with GM varieties. Canadian canola growers are highly dependent on exports as more than 80% is exported, either as seed, as oil or as meal (Western Producer, 2000b). Exports to the EC are not very important, however. They reached a peak in 1994, when Canada exported CAN$ 425 million worth of canola to the EC, having followed a rather erratic pattern before this (Interview 7-8-2000, Canadian Mission; cf. the export statistics for canola meal, oil and seed in Canola Council, 1999; 2000). Since 1994, canola exports to the EC have dropped to virtually zero, mainly because Canada's GM canola varieties have not been approved in the EC. This export share has been taken over by other countries, mainly

China. As a result, the Canadian canola industry has not suffered from the lost export opportunities to the EC, even though production reached a peak in the late 1990s. Moreover, since Europe and Australia reportedly have surpluses of non-GM canola, there is little use for Canadian producers to engage in identity-preserved or non-GM canola exports. Consequently, the EC has lost priority as an export market for Canadian canola producers in the short term (Western Producer, 2000b).

Ironically, Canadian soya bean exports to the EC increased somewhat, because Canadian soya bean growers were much smaller than their US counterparts and already segregated various soya bean varieties for niche markets in Japan and Korea. Segregation of GM and non-GM soya beans fitted into this system well and, as a result, Canadian farmers were able to capture part of the European market for IP soya beans, although it remained a minor export crop compared to canola (Interviews 7-8-2000, Canadian Mission; 20-2-2001-I, DFAIT).

Apart from the loss of direct exports to the EC, exports to other countries were also indirectly affected by the European measures. First, some countries adopted similar standards as the EC or became more reluctant to import GM products because of the EC's stance. Second, countries that exported to the EC themselves were reluctant to import GM products from the US and Canada, since that could jeopardise their (re-exports) to the EC (Interview 20-2-2001-I, DFAIT; cf. GAO, 2001: 8). Moreover, the EC was seen as an important potential market for US and Canadian (GM) products, thus raising the significance of this trade issue beyond its direct effects on current exports to the EC.

Bilateral initiatives

The United States Trade Representative (USTR) first became active in this issue in the summer of 1995, when the approval of Roundup Ready soya beans encountered opposition in Austria and Denmark and officials went over to discuss the issue (Interview 19-1-2001, USTR). As the European approval system came to a halt and the labelling requirements were tightened, discussions between trade officials intensified.

The option of going to the WTO was discussed internally in both the US and Canadian governments, but they did not pursue this route. Although US officials have pointed out the possibility of the WTO incompatibility of the EC's regulatory system to European officials, neither country has used the threat of a WTO complaint, nor have US and Canadian business groups pushed for such action (Interviews 7-8-2000, US Mission; 7-8-2000, Canadian Mission; 31-8-2000, European Commission; 26-9-2000, European Commission; 11-1-2001, USDA; 18-1-2001, AFBF; 19-1-2001, USTR; 25-1-2001, NCGA; 15-2-2001, DFAIT; 20-2-2001-I, DFAIT).

This has probably had two reasons. First, the chances of winning the case would have been small, since the European measures seem to fall within the latitude allowed by the WTO Agreements. At the very least, the EC would have had to reject a GM product in order to create a clear case for a WTO dispute settlement panel. Second, even if a case before the WTO were to be won, this would not address the underlying problem of consumer confidence. Although some interviewees indicated that protectionism may have been part of the motives behind the EC's measures, these measures were generally considered as the result of political problems within the EC rather than protectionism. Therefore, going to the WTO could even exacerbate the problems, since it could be perceived as the US or Canada trying to force GM foods on the EC.

The US and Canadian experiences in the beef-hormone case may have reinforced their reluctance to resort to the WTO. Although the case was a clear win in legal terms, it has not led to any change in the EC's legislation. In the GMO case, where public concerns and public involvement were still greater than in the beef-hormone case, this scenario was likely to occur again, maybe even in a worse form. Thus, the WTO did not seem to offer a key to opening the European market for GM foods.

Still, the regulation of GM products was discussed within the WTO's SPS and TBT Committees, which meet regularly to discuss possible barriers to trade arising from national measures covered by these agreements. At various points, the US and Canada voiced their objections to European measures, such as its labelling requirements (Interviews 7-8-2000, US Mission; 31-8-2000, European Commission). Biotechnology was also an important issue in the talks leading up to the WTO's Ministerial Conference in Seattle in November 1999, where the US and Canada proposed the establishment of a working group on biotechnology (GAO, 2001: 24).

Nevertheless, since most officials and business groups in the US and Canada traced the European restrictions to political problems and misinformation, they sought to reduce opposition against GM products through discussions on the substantive aspects of the issue and 'public diplomacy.' Partly, the contacts between officials took place in multilateral forums, like the OECD, the Codex Alimentarius Commission, and the negotiations over the Cartagena Protocol, but there have been several bilateral initiatives, too.

The regulation of GM products had been an important issue in the regular talks between US and EC officials when, in October 1999 and May 2000, US President Clinton and the President of the European Commission Prodi decided to create two new bilateral forums for discussing the issue. On the one hand, they established special meetings of the US-EU Senior Level Group, consisting of high-ranking officials from both sides. On the other hand, they created a Consultative Forum of twenty experts from the US and the EC to present an independent report on the issue of agricultural biotechnology (State Department, 2000a; Interviews 26-9-2000, European Commission; 19-1-2001, USTR). These initiatives have not yielded any concrete results, however.

The Consultative Forum published its report in December 2000. The report included a number of recommendations that seemed to support the more restrictive European approach, such as the mandatory pre-market examination of all GM food products, a restricted use of the substantial equivalence approach, traceability and time-limited approvals of GM food products, and mandatory labelling for products containing GM ingredients. Moreover, the Forum endorsed the precautionary principle (Consultative Forum, 2000). Still, the report's formulation left enough room for both sides to claim that their regulatory systems largely conformed to them and the report became 'one element in our continuing discussions,' as the US Department of State called it (State Department, 2000b; see also CEC, 2000f).

Apart from these contacts on the level of politicians and senior officials, discussions also took place at the level of regulators. Officials from FDA and the USDA have had regular contacts with their counterparts in the European Commission and the EC member states over regulatory issues and the revision of Directive 90/220 (Interviews 11-1-2001, USDA; 16-1-2001, FDA).

Bilateral contacts between Canadian and European officials took place in similar ways, although they were less extensive. The European regulation of GM products was discussed during regular bilateral meetings and in meetings between officials from both sides (CEC, 2001a). Moreover, the CFIA and European Commission officials started to discuss the molecular characterisation involved in risk assessments in November 1999, a topic on which Canadian and US regulators had previously already reached an agreement (Interview 21-2-2001, CFIA). In addition, both US and Canadian officials and business groups have met with Members of the European Parliament, European interest groups, and European journalists to convince them of the safety of GM foods (Interviews 7-8-2000, US Mission; 15-2-2001, BioteCanada; 20-2-2001-I, DFAIT).

At the level of scientists and regulatory officials, the differences between Canada, the US and the EC appear to have been much smaller than at the political level (Interviews 9-11-2000, European Commission; 16-1-2001, FDA; 20-2-2001-I, DFAIT; 21-2-2001, CFIA). This probably reflects the similarity in underlying scientific and regulatory assumptions. The main divergence seems to occur in the positions taken by interest groups and politicians on both sides of the Atlantic.

Besides their attempts to influence the EC's thinking about GMOs, US and Canadian officials have also worked domestically with producers to help them export IP (or non-GM) varieties, although they did not set up IP systems themselves. Officials in both countries carried out market analyses for their producers. In addition, the USDA's Grain Inspection Packers and Stockyards Administration announced that it would start to accredit commercial laboratories and tests for discerning GM from non-GM grain varieties in May 2000 (USDA, 2000). It did so in co-operation with EC officials who dealt with testing issues (Interview 11-1-2001, USDA). The NCGA also worked with the US government to formulate a programme for non-GM maize exports to the EC (Interview 25-1-2001, NCGA). The Canadian and US governments have therefore not actively promoted exports of IP or non-GM crops among domestic producers, but they have on some occasions sought to facilitate those exports.

Despite the initiatives which US and Canadian officials, firms and business groups have taken, they have not been successful in relaxing the EC's regulatory standards. US soya bean producers have refrained from planting GM varieties that have not been approved in the EC, while US maize producers and Canadian canola producers have experienced a decrease in exports to the EC. In the next two subsections, I will discuss the developments in the domestic debates and regulatory standards in the US and Canada, and the extent to which they can be linked to the European regulatory trade measures.

5.5.2 Domestic developments in the US

The rise in public interest group activism

The first years after FDA had published its Statement of Policy, not much happened as regards the American approach to GM foods. The approval of the Flavr Savr tomato set the tone for a series of approvals by FDA (and the other regulatory agencies involved) that were fairly uncontroversial in American politics and among the public at large.

As the controversy was heating up in Europe, however, some of the heat also reached the US. The main instigators of the debate in the US were environmental groups, which became much more vocal during 1997 and afterwards. In September 1997, a number of environmental groups sued the EPA for gross negligence in its approval of GM crops (Levidow, 1999: 15). A similar lawsuit was filed in May 1998 by a group of public interest groups that argued that FDA should impose mandatory labelling on GM foods (CFS, 1998). Although the lawsuits were unsuccessful, they marked the beginning of the more active involvement of public interest groups in a policy area that had previously remained outside the public debate.

During 1998 and 1999, the public debate about GM foods started to become stronger in the US. Aided by the many transnational links between public interest groups in Europe and the US, US environmental groups started campaigns to warn the public of the dangers of GM crops and foods. American consumer groups like the Center for Food Safety and Consumers Union also argued for the mandatory labelling of GM foods.

Significant input for this demand came from the newly established Transatlantic Consumers Dialogue (TACD), which started its work in 1998. In a number of declarations, European and American consumer groups called for more stringent approval systems and mandatory labelling on both sides of the Atlantic (TACD, 1999b; 2000a). In its calls for labelling, the US consumer group Consumers Union pointed at polls among US consumers which indicated that a majority favoured the labelling of GM foods (Consumers Union, 1999a; 1999b).

Another source of transatlantic co-operation between consumer groups was formed by Consumers International. Although it was much more difficult to formulate a consensus position in an organisation that brought together consumer groups from all around the world, Consumers International called for a ban on the use of antibiotic marker genes in October 1996 (Consumers International, 1996) and it continued to be a forum for contacts between different consumer groups. Consumers International also hosted the TACD secretariat, which resulted in a close link between the two forums.

In contrast to the EC, however, US companies proved less susceptible to the public pressure, although some changes occurred. In 1999, a few companies announced that they would stop using GM ingredients in their food products (Food Online, 2000a). Later that year, Cargill announced that it would continue to buy GM soya and maize varieties that had been approved in both the US and the EC, but farmers had to contact their local buyer for varieties that had been approved in the US but not in the EC (ASA, 1999d). Thus, even though Cargill did not decide to discontinue the use of GM crops, it did limit itself mainly to those varieties that had been approved in the EC as well.

These initiatives did not lead to a change in farmers' attitudes toward GM food crops. Although the European regulations have prevented the planting of GM soya bean varieties that have not been approved in the EC (e.g. the LibertyLink soya bean), the position of US maize and soya bean farmers regarding the regulation of GM crops in their own country has not changed. The main reason for this is probably that in these agricultural systems, the economies of scale occur at the level of the system as a whole. As a consequence, it is all or nothing: either all farmers can use a GM variety, or no farmer can.

This differs from the role which export-oriented firms play in cases where the economies of scale occur at the firm level. Then, only the export-oriented firms have to adjust their whole production to the most stringent standard, which gives them a competitive disadvantage vis-à-vis their domestic competitors who do not have to do so. As a result, the export-oriented firms have an incentive to press for more stringent domestic regulations in order to dilute this disadvantage. A good example of this mechanism is Vogel's analysis of the effects of US automobile emission standards on European car manufacturers (see the description in section 1.3 of this study).

In the case of GM soya and maize, this mechanism did not occur since, effectively, there is no distinction between domestic and export-oriented producers: all farmers' produce is handled together, so that every farmer produces both for the domestic and export markets and does not even know for whom s/he is producing. Consequently, no farmer suffers a competitive disadvantage from having to apply more stringent standards than others.

The amount of identity-preserved crops sold to Europe has been too small to make much of a difference (ASA, 2000a: 63). In contrast to Japan, which annually imports considerable amounts of US IP soya for its tofu production, European industries have so far been reluctant to pay the premium for IP crops. Moreover, the producers of IP crops produce specifically for export and do not have to compete on domestic markets. Since IP crops sell at a premium (for soya typically some two to three times the price of ordinary soya beans (Interview 31-8-2000, ASA)) they also have no interest in imposing their standards on other exporters.

Formalising the FDA's approach

Despite the first signs of activism on the part of consumer and environmental groups, the FDA's policies remained firmly in place. The approval of new GM crops and foods did not slow down, nor did FDA consider mandatory labelling of GM foods. Industry groups, from all parts of the industry chain, continued to support FDA's policies. In November 1997, the FDA Modernization Act was signed into law. It sought to streamline the FDA's procedures and relieve unnecessary burdens on firms during FDA's procedures. It did not involve a change in FDA's policies regarding GM foods (FDA, 1997b).

As the public debate heated up, however, the federal government came under increasing pressure from both sides in the debate to do something. Public interest groups demanded a more stringent approval process, if not a moratorium, and mandatory labelling, while producer groups wanted the federal government to stand up for its policy, but also to allay concerns on the part of consumers.

During 1999, US Congress and FDA reacted to the debate through a number of hearings. On 18 October 1999, FDA announced a series of public meetings to take place later that year (FDA, 1999b). During those meetings, all interested groups could express their opinions about FDA's approach to GM foods. Consumers Union demanded to have GM foods go through a food additive review, and to impose mandatory labelling (Consumers Union, 1999a). Business groups, from all links in the production chain, broadly supported the FDA's current approval procedure process and rejected mandatory labelling (e.g. BIO, 1999d; 1999e). Still, some expressed support for a mandatory process if this would strengthen consumer confidence (ASA, 1999c; GMA & FMI, 1999).

In November 1999, 38 agri-food trade associations sent a letter to President Clinton urging him not to change the FDA's labelling policies. In the letter they also pointed at the negative consequences such a change would have for the US position in international debates, where it had consistently rejected labelling proposals (GMA, 1999).

US Congress also held hearings on the subject. Interest groups were allowed to express their opinion on the approval process and labelling before hearings by the US Senate Committee on Agriculture. In April 2000, the Subcommittee on Basic Research, belonging to the House of Representatives' Committee on Science, released a report after a series of hearings, which strongly supported the current policies and rejected the claims by environmental and consumer groups (House, 2000).

The growing interest of members of Congress in GM foods was not only witnessed by the hearings, but also by a number of bills introduced in both the Senate and the House. On 16 November 1999, Representative Kucinich and 50 co-sponsors introduced a bill that would require the mandatory labelling of GM foods (BIO, 1999c; AFBF, 2000c; FoE, 2000). Kucinich also introduced a bill that would require FDA to treat all GM foods as food additives. In early 2000, similar bills were introduced in the Senate by Senator Boxer, requiring mandatory labelling, and by Senator Moynihan, imposing a food additive review on GM foods (AFBF, 2000c; BIO, 2000b; FoE, 2000).

Although these bills were only supported by a minority of representatives and senators, they were strongly opposed by US business groups. In letters to members of Congress, 35 trade associations urged them to oppose the labelling bills introduced by Kucinich and Boxer (GMA, 2000a; 2000b). In the end, these bills did not reach the hearing stage, since not enough support for them could be mustered among Members of Congress (Interview 22-1-2001, Consumers Union).

Finally, on 3 May 2000, the Clinton White House and FDA announced a number of plans to strengthen federal oversight of GM foods (FDA, 2000b; White House, 2000). The main innovation concerned the substitution of a mandatory notification process for the voluntary process that had previously been in place. Producers of GM foods would be required to notify any new GM foods 120 days prior to their planned marketing. The subsequent process remained the same, however. The plans did not foresee the mandatory labelling of GM foods. In general, the plans expressed support for the existing oversight system and did not intend to change it fundamentally. Rather, they sought to formalise established practices in order to increase consumer confidence in their effectiveness.

In their first reactions, business groups reacted favourably. The mandatory process was supported by representatives of the biotechnology industry (BIO, 2000d), farmers (AFBF, 2000b), seed traders (ASTA, 2000), food processors (GMA, 2000c) and soya bean growers (ASA, 2000c) as a way to increase consumer confidence without modifying the substantive review process. Consumer groups, such as Consumers Union and the Center for Food Safety, either found the proposals disappointing or opposed them (CFS, 2000; Consumers Union, 2000c).

The StarLink incident and further developments

The stronger opposition against GM foods in the EC as compared to the US has often been linked to a lower confidence among European consumers in food safety and food safety regulators. The lower confidence has been partly explained by the recurring food scares in the EC during the second half of the 1990s, most notably the BSE crisis (see section 4.5.2 of this study). For a long time, no similar scares occurred in the US and there were no incidents to fuel opposition against GM foods.

Yet, this seemed to change in September 2000, when the US branch of Friends of the Earth discovered traces of StarLink maize in human food (GE Food Alert, 2000a). StarLink maize had only been approved for non-food purposes because of its possible allergenicity, although FDA considered these risks to be remote (FDA, 2000c). Later that year, traces of the protein that was produced by StarLink and allegedly caused allergic reactions, were found in other food products and even in maize that was not sold under the name StarLink (FDA, 2000c; GE Food Alert, 2000d).

In response to the discovery, the affected food products were recalled (Kraft Foods, 2000). At the same time, opponents of GM foods argued that the incident showed the weakness of the existing regulatory framework, a claim that gained additional significance since FDA was working on concrete proposals based on its announcement of 3 May. According to GE Food Alert, a coalition of groups that oppose GM foods, the recall 'underscore[d] the need for stronger government regulation over genetically engineered foods,' and it urged mandatory food additive reviews of all GM foods and mandatory labelling (GE Food Alert, 2000b; 2000c).

Despite the considerable stir which the StarLink incident had caused, it did not seem to affect the FDA's proposals. When, in January 2000, FDA published its concrete proposals for formalising the pre-market notification procedure, it maintained 'there [did] not appear to be any new scientific information that raise[d] questions about the safety of bioengineered foods currently being marketed' (FDA, 2001a: 4708). The proposal introduced mandatory notification 120 days prior to the marketing of a GM food, as had been announced in May 2000, but it did no go any further.

In a draft guidance on the voluntary labelling of GM foods, FDA also 'reaffirm[ed] its decision to not require special labelling of all bioengineered foods' (FDA, 2001b). In the guidance on voluntary labelling, FDA discussed a number of positive and negative claims that would (not) be allowable under its regulations. In doing so, it reinforced a number of differences with EC standards. Most importantly, it considered the use of a 'GM free' or 'GMO free' label to be misleading, since in FDA's terminology 'genetic modification' referred both to biotechnology and traditional breeding techniques.

In the meantime, the National Corn Growers Association (NCGA) had taken action in response to the StarLink incident. Some StarLink maize had also been exported to Japan, where it had not been approved. In contrast to the EC, Japan was an important export market for US maize producers and in its 2001 position on biotechnology, the NCGA only supported GM varieties that had been approved in both the US and Japan (NCGA, 2001). In that way, it took a similar step as the ASA had done with regard to GM soya bean varieties that had not been approved in the EC. The NCGA also called for closed marketing systems for GM varieties that had not been approved for all uses; these varieties should not be used in the bulk production of commodity maize. According to an NCGA official, this decision had already been taken before the StarLink incident (Interview 25-1-2001, NCGA). Finally, the NCGA 'encourage[d] biotech providers to avoid the use of antibiotic markers that unnecessarily raise[d] consumer concerns' (NCGA, 2001).

5.5.3 Domestic developments in Canada

The Novel Foods Regulations

Like in the US, the Canadian system for overseeing GM foods was rather uncontroversial in its first years of operation. Canadian environmental and consumer groups have not had the benefit of a TACD or TAED, like their American counterparts. The contacts between Canadian and European consumer groups have thus gone through Consumers International, the global consumer organisation, or on an ad hoc basis, although they have remained fairly limited (Interview 19-7-2001, Consumers Association of Canada). Nevertheless, Canadian public interest groups became more vocal during the last years of the 1990s, as well. In September 1999, Greenpeace and the Council of Canadians started a campaign against GM foods in the supermarkets in an effort to change public opinion on this issue (Western Producer, 1999a).

The campaigns succeeded in raising public concerns over GM foods. Consequently, in December 1999, distiller Seagram announced it would no longer buy GM maize (Food Online, 2000b; Western Producer, 2000a). Still, until now Canadian farmers have not changed their position on GM foods. They have suffered only minor losses as a result of the European standards, for which they have been able to compensate on other markets. Moreover, consumer concerns about GM foods always remained below traditional concerns, such as those relating to pesticides and food additives (Interview 19-7-2001, Consumers Association of Canada).

After the guidelines on novel foods had been published, consultations on the issue continued, with a view to developing formal regulations. The first draft of these Novel Foods Regulations was published in 1995. After a review of public comments, a second draft appeared in 1998. Two main changes had been made to the initial proposal. First, the definition of novel food had become narrower by excluding foods with a history of safe use. Second, the definition of 'major change,' was introduced to 'restrict novel food notifications due to introduction of new processes only to those that are truly new and cause substantial changes in the food.' A 'major change' was defined in terms of the adverse effects the change might have (Health Canada, 1999a).

In the public comments on this second draft, a consumer interest group feared that the new definition of 'novel food' would be too narrow, while industry groups expressed concern that it was still too broad. However, Health Canada did not adopt suggestions to limit the scope of the Regulations even further to novel foods produced by biotechnology. After this round of comments, only the definition of 'major change' was modified to focus on foods falling 'outside the accepted limits of natural variations for that food' rather than on 'adverse effects,' because the latter term was thought to be confusing (Health Canada, 1999a).

The final version of the Novel Foods Regulations did not foresee a change in the approval criteria themselves. Nor did it impose the mandatory labelling of GM foods, which some public interest groups had called for. As a result, the Regulations basically formalised the existing voluntary procedure under the Guidelines. A novel food had to be notified at least 45 days prior to its sale or advertising. Health Canada would review the notification and marketing could only take place after it had agreed to the food's acceptability (Health Canada, 1999b).

Formulating voluntary labelling standards

As to the issue of labelling, the Canadian government maintained its preference for voluntary solutions. In September 1999, the Canadian Council of Grocery Distributors, representing Canadian food retailers, entered into a project to formulate voluntary standards, together with the Canadian General Standards Board (CGSB). The project was intended to formulate standards for the voluntary labelling of GM and GM-free food products. It was supported by Agriculture and Agri-Food Canada, the Canadian federal department of agriculture (CFIA, 1999).

In response to this initiative, 27 public interest groups refused to participate in the committee that was going to prepare the standards, arguing that the development of voluntary labelling standards was only a way for the industry to prevent the enactment of mandatory labelling requirements. In addition, the groups presented a proposal for mandatory labelling based on the use of genetic modification techniques in and the segregation of GM and non-GM foods throughout the production process. The labelling requirement would also cover food additives produced by but not containing GMOs, and animals raised with GM feed (Council of Canadians, 1999).

The Consumers Association of Canada did join the process, however. In contrast to more radical groups like Greenpeace and the Council of Canadians, the Consumers Association opposed mandatory labelling and supported the development of guidelines on voluntary labelling (Interview 19-7-2001, Consumers Association of Canada). The most controversial issues in the process were the scope of a label (i.e. what would count as 'genetically modified'), and what the label would say; in addition, the verification of the label was also an issue for debate (Interviews 15-2-2001, BioteCanada; 21-2-2001, CFIA; 19-7-2001, Consumers Association of Canada). These controversies were reflected in the first draft standard, which was released in July 2001 (CGSB, 2001).

Further initiatives and developments

The adoption of the Novel Foods Regulations and the voluntary labelling initiative did not end the controversy surrounding GM foods. During 2000, the Bloc Québecois, one of Canada's opposition parties in parliament, started to press for more stringent regulations. In a number of initiatives, the Bloc requested hearings on the issue, and demanded the mandatory labelling of GM foods. In February and March 2001, two private members' bills were introduced in the House of Commons that would impose mandatory labelling on GM food products: one by Member of Parliament (MP) Caccia of the governing Liberal Party (Canadian Parliament, 2001a), and one by MP Wasylycia-Leis of the opposition National Democratic Party (Canadian Parliament, 2001b). Although these initiatives were supported by a number of public interest groups, which claimed that 93% of Canadians supported mandatory labelling (Council of Canadians, 2001b), the Canadian government did not respond to these demands for mandatory food labelling and preferred to wait for the outcome of the CGSB process (see e.g. Canadian Parliament, 2001c). The

Consumers Association of Canada did not support the bills either, although it did support a mandatory label that would mention the technique if a product had been changed through genetic modification (Interview 19-7-2001, Consumers Association of Canada), which came close to at least one element of the EC's labelling requirements.

Despite the government's refusal to alter its standards on GM foods, it had asked the Royal Society of Canada to form an expert panel on the future of food biotechnology in 2000. The panel was to study the issues surrounding these food products (Royal Society of Canada, 2000). In January 2001, the expert panel released a report in which it was highly critical of existing review procedures. It advocated a 'precautionary regulatory assumption' and recommended, among other things, that a 'rigorous scientific assessment (...) should replace the current regulatory reliance on "substantial equivalence" as a decision threshold' (Royal Society of Canada, 2001: x). Moreover, it questioned the independence of the regulatory agencies in the field of biotechnology and argued for external, independent reviews of approvals, and for a study of 'the problems related to the increasing domination of the public research agenda by private, commercial interests' (Royal Society of Canada, 2001: xi). The panel did not, however, recommend the mandatory labelling of all GM foods, although this recommendation was explicitly restricted to health and safety considerations and was made conditional upon the implementation of the panel's other recommendations (Royal Society of Canada, 2001: 225-226).

In a reaction to the report, the Council of Canadians, the Canadian Health Coalition and Greenpeace, three of the most vocal opponents of GM foods in Canada, called upon the government to strengthen the approval process, to install a moratorium on all GMOs, and to adopt mandatory labelling of GM products (Council of Canadians, 2001a). The Consumers Association of Canada, which had been largely supportive of the Canadian approval process, also found that the report included many of their specific concerns (Interview 19-7-2001, Consumers Association of Canada).

The Government of Canada, on the other hand, stressed that the report '[did] not raise concerns about the safety of GM foods currently in the marketplace' (Government of Canada, 2001a). Likewise, BioteCanada, the trade association for the biotechnology industry, described the report as 'a useful first step to a much larger public discussion that needs to take place,' but continued to emphasise the 'feasibility of implementation and economic impacts' as well as the importance of 'science-based' risk assessments (BioteCanada, 2001). In November 2001, the Government of Canada published an action plan to address the issues raised by the Royal Society, but it mainly called for clarification and further specification of current standards and practices (Government of Canada, 2001c).

5.6 Conclusions

The main events in the GM foods process are outlined in table 5.1. In this section, the analysis of the process in the previous sections will be used to arrive at answers to the two main questions: did a California effect occur, and what factors accounted for that outcome?

5.6.1 A California effect or not?

For a California effect to take place, two things have to occur. First, the exporting country has to strengthen its standards and, second, this strengthening has to be attributable to the regulatory trade measures of the importing ('initiator') country. In this subsection I will first examine whether the US and Canadian standards have been strengthened. Then I will discuss to what extent any strengthening can be attributed to the European measures taken in the second half of the 1990s.

As was explained above, the European standards gradually became more stringent during the 1990s. In terms of the general approach, the EC had already chosen a different trajectory with the horizontal approach of Directive 90/220. The US and Canada, on the other hand, chose to regulate groups of products, regardless of the way they were produced. Consequently, they could largely work within the existing framework for different product categories (e.g. foods). The EC, on the other hand, focused on genetic modification as a production technique and adopted directives specifically aimed at GMOs.

The EC approach at the same time implied a broader and a more limited scope for the regulations. It was broader, since it covered all GMOs, regardless of their use or purpose. It was more limited, because it excluded new products derived from techniques other than biotechnology, such as conventional breeding techniques in the case of GM plants.

Originally, the US and Canada adopted a voluntary notification procedure, in which companies were advised, but not formally required, to submit new GM food products to FDA and Health Canada, respectively. EC Directive 90/220, by contrast, contained a formal approval procedure for GM (food) products. This difference may have been smaller in practice than in theory, however, since producers in Canada and the US thought they had an interest in good and visible regulatory oversight of their products and treated the system as de facto mandatory.

Despite the difference between the product and process-based approaches, the US, Canadian and EC standards differed much less when it came to the concrete evaluation of GM food safety. Both the European and the US and Canadian approaches focused on differences between GM food products and existing food products. All three countries took similar aspects into consideration, like the possible presence of toxic substances and allergens, and the risks of antibiotic resistance marker genes. All three also relied on industry data rather than tests carried out by themselves in evaluating GM food products.

	In the EC	In the US	In Canada	At the international level
1986		Adoption of the Coordinated Framework		
1990	Adoption of Directive 90/220			
1992		Adoption of FDA's Statement of Policy		
1993				OECD report on substantial equivalence
May 1994		Approval of Flavr Savr tomato		
September 1994			Adoption of Health Canada's Guidelines	
23 January 1997	Approval of Bt-maize; Austria and Luxembourg adopt provisional bans			
27 January 1997	Adoption of the Novel Foods Regulation and strengthening of labelling requirements			
1998-1999		Rise in public interest group activism		
June 1999	Adoption of the 'de facto moratorium'			
1999		The ASA blocks the marketing of EC non-approved varieties		
September 1999			Start of CGSB process on voluntary labelling standards	
October 1999			Adoption of Novel Foods Regulations	
January 2000	Further strengthening of labelling requirements			
February 2000				Agreement is reached on the Cartagena Protocol
March 2000				First meeting of the Codex Task Force on GM foods
May 2000		President and FDA announce a mandatory notification process		
September 2000		StarLink incident		
March 2001	Adoption of Directive 2001/18			

Tabel 5.1: Main Events in the GM foods process

The main difference between the European and North American approaches therefore lay in the way in which products were triggered into the assessment procedure. In the EC, the technology of genetic modification provided such a trigger, while in Canada and the US it was the characteristics of the food product itself that did so. This difference did not apply to the EC's Novel Foods Regulation, however, which was adopted in 1997 and covered other types of novel foods besides GM foods. Moreover, once a product was in the assessment process, the safety evaluation criteria were largely similar between the three countries. In addition, neither country required the mandatory labelling of GM food products, unless they presented a food risk or were not equivalent to existing food products.

Since the mid-1990s, the differences between the EC and the US and Canada have gradually become greater. The EC's approval system broke down under the influence of sceptical member state governments and the ensuing de facto moratorium on the approval of new GM products. Directive 2001/18, which replaced Directive 90/220, introduced more stringent standards in a number of ways. Some of these changes will probably also affect the standards under the EC's Novel Foods Regulation. Moreover, the EC adopted mandatory labelling requirements for (food) products containing DNA or proteins resulting from genetic modification.

To what extent have the US and Canadian systems been strengthened in that same period? They can be said to have been strengthened in two ways. First, both the US and Canada formalised their voluntary procedures; Health Canada in the Novel Foods Regulations of October 1999, the US government in its announcements of 3 May 2000 and FDA's proposals of January 2001. In that regard, developments in the US and Canada indicate that standards have been strengthened to a certain degree.

At the same time, however, neither country adopted significantly more stringent approval criteria or decided to ban GM food crops or products that had not been approved in the EC. Nor did they adopt mandatory labelling of GM foods as a class. Both maintained their existing labelling requirements and supported voluntary GM and/or GM-free labelling.

Second, US soya bean growers have refrained from planting GM soya varieties that have not been approved in the EC. Since only Roundup Ready soya beans have been approved in the EC, US soya bean growers have effectively limited themselves to this GM variety. One's appreciation of this fact depends on one's point of view. On the one hand, it can be argued that it is the resulting effect that counts and then the American practice has become more stringent than its rule. On the other hand, the change in practice has not led to a change in regulations, which would imply that the change is incomplete.

Yet, the soya bean growers' move was meant as a marketing decision and has always been presented as such. The voluntary marketing ban on certain GM soya bean varieties will therefore most probably be revoked once the EC approves these varieties. This would have been less likely if the varieties had not been approved in the US either. Hence, the soya bean growers' decision is arguably a weaker California effect than a strengthening of standards would have been.

To what extent can these changes be attributed to the European measures and their trade effects? In general, the regulatory developments in both the US and Canada have probably been driven primarily by domestic political processes. There have not been any direct negotiations between the EC and Canada and the US on their respective regulatory frameworks, like in the leghold trap and data protection issues. Moreover, the reactions of regulatory agencies seem to have been a reaction to domestic political pressures from consumer groups and, sometimes, producers, rather than to the trade effects of the EC measures.

Still, the changes in the US and Canada can be linked to the EC measures in at least two ways. First, the EC measures may have had an effect on the public debate in the US and Canada, and on the position and strength of consumer and environmental groups within it. It can be argued that the public debate has been fuelled by the debates in the EC, in particular in the US. The links between US and EC groups have been facilitated by the existence of global groups, such as Greenpeace, and by the establishment of formal links in the TAED and TACD. Within the TACD, GM foods have become an important topic of debate and as a result US consumer groups have arguably taken a stronger position on the issue. These links have been much weaker between European and Canadian groups. Still, the European debate may have trickled into Canada through global public interest groups (such as Greenpeace), through the contacts between Canadian and US groups and because Canadian groups have monitored the European developments.

The fact that the EC adopted more stringent measures during the late 1990s, may have provided an extra impetus to these groups in both the US and Canada, in that it lent credibility to their position and proved that a powerful government could be persuaded to act upon their concerns. In this indirect sense, the EC measures and their trade effects can be said to have contributed to the changes in the US and possibly also to Canadian public debates and thus to the strengthening of FDA's and Health Canada's standards.

This effect seems to be stronger in the US, where FDA's May 2000 announcements were a direct response to the increased consumer concerns and interest group activism of the late 1990s. In Canada, the process of developing formal regulations had already started before this and the first drafts were published in 1995. The formalisation of Health Canada's guidelines is therefore probably not the result of changes in the public debate, although these changes may have contributed to a sense of urgency in the process.

The second way in which the EC measures may have influenced the US and Canadian regulatory frameworks is through debates and negotiations in multilateral forums. As was shown in subsection 5.4.1, this issue has been debated in a number of forums, including the OECD, the Codex Alimentarius Commission, the WTO and the negotiations on the Cartagena Protocol. In these forums, the EC has defended its own approach and regulatory framework and by its economic and political weight it has probably exerted a considerable influence on the outcomes.

These outcomes have not been the same in all forums: the OECD has built on its existing work, which is more in line with the Canadian and US approaches; work in the WTO and the Codex Alimentarius Commission has not proceeded very rapidly over the last few years; and the Cartagena Protocol seems to be closer to the European approach. When it comes to the safety assessment criteria, hardly any progress has been made in determining binding global standards, but the Cartagena Protocol includes the precautionary principle, which, although its precise meaning and applications are unclear, seems to support the European approach. The issue of labelling has not been resolved either, but it is interesting to note that a growing number of countries (including Japan, Australia and New Zealand) have adopted mandatory labelling requirements for GM foods, which has left Canada and the US relatively isolated in the international arena.

These developments may have weakened the position of US and Canadian regulatory agencies that want to maintain their existing policies. As a result, adjustments to those policies may have become more acceptable or may at least have been considered a more serious option than before. Nevertheless, these adjustments have not yet taken place, and many specific aspects of the international standards still have to be elaborated. Consequently, existing international standards allow considerable differences in approach, including the US and Canadian approaches.

The influence of the EC measures on the actual planting of certain GM soya bean varieties has been more direct. Because the EC has only approved Roundup Ready soya beans, US soya bean farmers have so far refrained from planting other varieties, since this would have ended their export opportunities to the EC. Hence, the trade effects of the EC measures have had a direct impact on US soya bean planting decisions.

All in all, the regulation of GM foods in the US and Canada has become somewhat more stringent in that the approval systems have been formalised in both countries and the actual use of certain GM crops has been limited in the US. The EC measures and their trade effects may have indirectly contributed to the formalisation of the approval systems, through their effects on the position and strength of US and Canadian consumer and environmental groups, and through the EC's impact on international negotiations and agreements. The limitations on the actual use of certain GM soya bean varieties is directly attributable to the fact that these varieties have not been approved in the EC.

5.6.2 Explaining the outcomes

As in the other case studies, I will now explain the outcomes of the GM foods issue using the hypotheses drawn up in chapter 2. These hypotheses fell under three general headings: those relating to constraints, to preferences and to participation expansion.

Changing constraints
Relating to constraints, four hypotheses were formulated. First, a *regulatory trade measure and a retaliatory measure were hypothesised to have a greater effect on another country's political balance, the greater that measure's effect on the other country's exports*. In the GM foods issue, neither the US nor Canada has adopted retaliatory measures, so the effect of retaliation cannot be discussed. The effect of the EC's regulatory trade measures can, however.

The (potential) direct loss of exports as a result of the European regulatory trade measures was limited for both the US and Canada. The US exported a relatively small amount of its maize production, only a few percent, to the EC. Although US maize exports to the EC were reduced significantly because some GM maize varieties in use in the US had not been approved in the EC, this did not affect US producers to a great extent. US soya bean producers depended much more on the European market for exports, as about 15% of US soya bean production is normally exported to the EC. These exports have hardly been affected by the European regulatory trade measures although partly, of course, this is the result of the US soya bean growers' decision not to use GM varieties that have not been approved in the EC.

Hence, the difference in the importance of the European market for US maize and soya bean producers may explain why US soya bean producers have chosen not to use EC non-approved varieties, while US maize producers have also grown EC non-approved varieties and thereby accepted a decline in exports. This conclusion is reinforced by the US maize growers' decision not to use GM varieties that have not been approved in Japan, which to them is a much more important export market than the EC.

Canadian canola producers hardly depended on the European market for their exports. Although exports of canola to the EC have been eliminated by the European regulatory trade measures, the producers have not been affected by these losses, in particular since other export markets have expanded at the same time. This may again explain why Canadian canola growers have not decided to block the use of EC non-approved varieties, like the US soya bean growers.

Exports of non-GM and IP varieties has not increased much as a result of the European regulatory trade measures, although Canadian producers of non-GM soya beans were reported to have experienced a small increase in exports to the EC. This effect has been limited, however, since a higher premium is paid for these varieties on other markets (mainly in Japan) than in the EC. As a result, the production of non-GM and IP varieties in the US and Canada has not increased as a result of the European regulatory trade measures.

Apart from these direct effects on US and Canadian exports, both countries have also experienced indirect effects, through third countries that (re-)export to the EC.

Some of these countries have become more reluctant to import GM products from the US and Canada, because they fear that this may jeopardise their exports to the EC. Thus, the trade effects of the European regulatory trade measures are wider than the direct exports to the EC themselves. It is difficult to estimate how large these indirect effects are, however. Still, they seem to have contributed to the US and Canadian desire to reach some degree of harmonisation at the international level in multilateral forums. This may partly explain why the two countries agreed to the Biosafety Protocol even if it encompassed a number of elements that conformed more closely to the European position.

The second hypothesis stated that *a regulatory trade measure or a retaliatory measure will have a greater effect on another country's political balance, the more that measure is targeted at pivotal actors in the other country*. The European regulatory trade measures affected actors that were pivotal, in that they had opposed more stringent regulatory standards and that they played a crucial role in the regulatory process. Given the limited trade effects of the European measures, they did not change their positions. Moreover, the degree of targeting did not differ between GM maize, soya beans and canola, so this cannot explain any of the differences between them. Consequently, targeting did not play an important role in this issue.

Third, it was hypothesised that *a regulatory trade measure will have a greater effect on regulatory standards in the target country, the lesser the costs of complying with that measure for actors in the target country*. In this issue, the costs of complying with the European regulatory standards were very high for both US and Canadian producers. These costs can be divided into direct and indirect costs.

Direct costs would have entailed the loss of productivity as a result of more stringent standards. In this issue, more stringent standards would have meant blocking or restricting the use of certain GM varieties and/or adopting the mandatory labelling of certain GM products. Although precise estimates of the benefits of GM crops currently in use vary, most US and Canadian producers consider them to be an important source of competitive advantage, as has been reflected in the high and rising adoption rates of GM crops by those producers.

These benefits are probably similar for maize, soya beans and canola. Together with the relatively small exports of GM products to the EC, they may explain why US maize and soya bean producers, as well as Canadian canola producers, have opposed the adoption of more stringent standards by regulatory authorities in the two countries.

US soya bean producers did block the marketing of GM varieties that had not been approved in the EC, thus losing potential benefits. Although this was mostly due to the US soya bean producers' greater dependence on exports to the EC when compared to US maize and Canadian canola producers, differences in costs may also explain part of the decision. US soya bean producers took this decision before the GM variety in question (LibertyLink soya beans) had actually been distributed, while US maize producers have used EC non-approved varieties for a longer period of time. As it becomes increasingly more expensive to reverse a decision to use certain varieties as they have been used for a longer period of time, this may also explain why it was less expensive for US soya bean producers to take this decision than for US maize producers. The US maize producers' decision not to use GM varieties that have not been approved in Japan mainly affected StarLink maize, which had already been removed from the market because of the StarLink incident in the autumn of 2000.

Apart from these high direct costs, both the US and Canadian producers and governments also had large indirect stakes in the issue. These indirect costs of complying with the European regulatory standards would have involved the effects that such a decision would have on related or future issues. The GM foods issue was related to the more general debate on the EC's agricultural policies. The US and Canadian governments (and producers) had sought to liberalise agricultural trade and European agricultural policies to reap the benefits of their (allegedly) more efficient way of producing agricultural products. Since agricultural biotechnology was another source of enhanced efficiency on the part of US and Canadian producers and was seen as an important strategic advantage in the future, complying with the European regulatory standards, which would have curbed the development and use of this technology, would have entailed large indirect costs to both countries. This probably reinforced their reluctance to adopt more stringent regulatory standards.

The fourth hypothesis relating to constraints stated that *a regulatory trade measure will have a greater effect on regulatory standards in the target country, if it is supported by both public interest groups and domestic producers in the initiator country*. This hypothesis refers to the Baptist-bootlegger coalitions that Vogel has argued play an important role in the adoption of regulatory trade measures. In my theoretical framework they were argued to be important in that they constrain the initiator country's win-set, thereby making the regulatory trade measure more credible.

In the beef-hormone issue it was concluded that this hypothesis needs to be modified by distinguishing between open and latent Baptist-bootlegger coalitions. Both types of Baptist-bootlegger coalitions indeed constrain the initiator country's win-set, but open coalitions also constrain the target country's win-set by reinforcing its suspicion of protectionism as a motive behind the regulatory trade measure.

In the GM foods issue, the European measures were strongly supported by European consumer and environmental groups. They were also actively supported by European retailers. European farmers and food processors were less active, although they did not openly oppose the measures either. Consequently, they did not undermine the credibility of the European measures. At the same time, they did not form an open Baptist-bootlegger coalition with public interest groups. This may have reinforced the perception by US and Canadian producers and officials that the 'real' issue was less a matter of protectionism than of political deadlock. This will be discussed more extensively below, but with regard to the hypothesis on Baptist-bootlegger coalitions the GM foods issue seems to support the conclusions drawn in the beef-hormone issue.

Changing preferences

The second group of hypotheses related to preferences. Three hypotheses were formulated. First, it was hypothesised that *a regulatory trade measure will have a greater effect on regulatory standards in the target country, the more it ties in with deeply-held values and perceived problems in the target country.* Together with the costs of complying with the European measures, this hypothesis explains much of the US and Canadian reactions. In both countries, agricultural biotechnology and GM foods have been much less controversial than in the EC. In terms of food safety, concerns among public interest groups and the public at large have been less than in the EC.

Still, GM foods led to more concerns than, for instance, the use of growth-hormones in meat, since it involved a much newer and potentially more far-reaching technology. As a result, GM foods have undergone more rigorous scrutiny than other foods, although this scrutiny has always focused on final products. Also, US and Canadian environmental and consumer groups have been more susceptible to arguments about the potential risks associated with GM crops and foods, which has led to a significant rise in concern during the late 1990s. It is this rise that has arguably led to the formalisation of risk assessment criteria by FDA; in Canada, the process of formalisation had been started earlier.

In comparison to the EC, however, these concerns remained confined to a number of environmental and consumer groups and did not translate to a wider range of business groups, like in the EC. US and Canadian business groups have consistently supported the prevailing regulatory approach in the two countries, which focused on characteristics of GM *products* both for safety assessments and labelling requirements. In both countries, this approach had been elaborated in the late 1980s and early 1990s and had already been used for some years when the concerns about GM food started to grow.

As a result, a broad consensus had arisen among officials and business groups that this was the right approach to regulating GM foods. Partly, this may be explained by constraints, as many producers had gained a vested interest in GM foods and the area planted with GM crops had become considerable. Apart from these interests, however, the US and Canadian regulatory approach also rested on a clear, and internally consistent regulatory philosophy based on a number of ideas: genetic modification as a technology does not pose fundamentally different or new risks than other or traditional means of altering foods; therefore, risk assessments and labelling requirements should focus on product characteristics; assessments of food safety risks should use the substantial equivalence approach to identify potential health risks; and any risk assessment should be based on scientifically ascertained risks rather than hypothetical risks.

Within this approach, both countries' regulatory agencies had arguably treated GM foods somewhat differently by giving more attention to GM foods than to foods developed through traditional techniques, but this could be justified as being necessary given the new character of GM foods and as a way to develop knowledge about the effects of GM foods. As subsequent tests and risk assessment did not yield any new or unforeseen risks, the underlying regulatory philosophy was reinforced rather than undermined.

Therefore, any change in regulatory standards that would have altered the fundamental tenets of this regulatory philosophy was likely to be illegitimate and to provoke much resistance among regulatory officials and business groups. In terms of approval procedures, the most US and Canadian regulatory officials could do was to formalise their existing consultation procedures. In terms of labelling, any changes aimed at imposing some sort of mandatory labelling based on genetic modification as a technique were also difficult to achieve. Together with the limited trade effects of the European regulatory trade measures, this explains much of the development in US and Canadian regulatory standards in the second half of the 1990s and the early 2000s.

According to the second hypothesis relating to preferences, *a regulatory trade measure will have a greater effect on regulatory standards in the target country, the more actors in the target country perceive it to be motivated by genuine concerns rather than protectionism.* Although the link to European agricultural policies and the debate over trade in agricultural products was important to US and Canadian officials and producers, there is less evidence that the European measures were seen as being outright protectionist. Most interviewees seem to acknowledge that other concerns played a more important role. At the same time, these concerns were not necessarily seen as 'genuine' or 'legitimate,' as many argued they were the result of misinformation or were politically motivated.

Still, the perceived absence of overtly protectionist motives may have strengthened the EC's case in a number of ways. First, it may have contributed to the appeal of the arguments behind the EC's regulatory trade measures among US and Canadian public interest groups. Second, it has probably led to a reduced willingness by the US and Canadian governments to use the WTO as a means of gaining market access. Since protectionism was not seen as the main motive behind the regulatory trade measures, going to the WTO could only have worsened the situation for US and Canadian producers, who would then be seen as trying to force potentially harmful products on European consumers.

Nevertheless, the perception of the European measures as the outcome of misinformation and political moves has also reduced the willingness of US and Canadian officials and producers to strengthen their own regulatory standards. Many observers in North America assume that the European measures will only be temporary and will be lifted once the political process starts moving again and European consumers learn more about GM food products. Consequently, strengthening US and Canadian regulatory standards is thought to be unnecessary in the long run, as well as ineffective given the perceived political motives behind the European measures.

The third hypothesis relating to preferences stated that *a regulatory trade measure will have a greater effect on regulatory standards in the target country if it conforms to international law and international standards*. Above it was argued that the European approval procedure probably conformed to WTO law, although the de facto moratorium could come close to a violation if it were to remain in place for a long time or become permanent. The EC's labelling requirements are probably more questionable under GATT/WTO law. However, as was argued above, the US and Canadian governments have been reluctant to use a WTO threat against the EC, since they felt that that might reinforce resistance against GM foods among European public interest groups and consumers. This has lent credibility to the European measures and, as will be discussed below, has led to a more passive role for European trade officials in the process.

In terms of the international harmonisation of regulatory standards, work has been carried out by several international organisations. Originally, the OECD's work, focusing on the concept of substantial equivalence, was important in defining a common approach to safety assessments of GM foods. This concept underlay both the US, Canadian and European food safety assessments of the early 1990s. In the late 1990s, some differences occurred as regards the interpretation of the substantial equivalence approach, with the US and Canadian governments taking a more narrow approach, and the EC broadening the concept.

Work in the Codex Alimentarius Commission has not yielded any standards relating to the most controversial issues between the US, Canada and the EC. The standards that have been formulated all relate to more or less generally accepted issues, such as the necessity to carry out a safety assessment and to label GM foods if they are potential allergens. The Biosafety Protocol could lead to a degree of harmonisation, but many issues still need to be elaborated. As was shown by the reservations made by the Canadian government when signing the Protocol, many provisions are still subject to debate and can be argued to support both the North American and the European approach.

All in all, international standards in this field have allowed enough room for interpretation to accommodate the regulatory standards adopted on either side of the Atlantic. While scientific consensus seems to exist over technical issues, such as molecular characterisation, such consensus is less likely for policy issues, like risk assessment criteria and labelling requirements. As the public and political debates took different courses in the EC and North America, the effectiveness of the existing international standards decreased.

Expanding participation

The final hypothesis related to participation expansion. It stated that *a regulatory trade measure will have a lesser effect on regulatory standards in the target country, if the target country succeeds in expanding participation in the initiator country to trade officials*. The trade aspects of this issue were raised by US and Canadian trade officials on several occasions, and the involvement of the USTR goes back to 1995. In addition, the US Department of State has been involved in the issue and has discussed it with European counterparts.

Although EC trade officials have thus been involved in the GM foods issue for a long time, their involvement does not seem to have changed the EC's position. Several factors may account for that. First, pressure from other groups and officials was probably much greater in this issue than in many others. In general, the range of groups and officials involved in the GM foods issue has been exceptionally wide, making it more difficult for any one group or official to dominate the debate.

Second, the GM foods issue has not risen to the level of a trade issue because the US and Canada have so far refrained from resorting to the WTO or threatening to do so. As was explained above, both countries had good reasons not to go to the WTO, but this also prevented European trade officials from assuming a more active role in the issue. Even then, it is doubtful whether these trade officials would have been able to make a decisive impact on European decision-making processes, given the strong support for current measures among interest groups, and a part of the member states and DGs, but at least it could have broadened support for a more liberal approach to GM food imports.

General conclusion

As in the beef-hormone issue, the GM foods issue hardly shows a change in the US and Canadian win-sets. On the one hand, this is the result of the relatively limited impact of the European measures. On the other hand, strengthening regulatory standards in the US and Canada would have entailed significant costs, both directly, as genetic modification arguably raises productivity, and indirectly, as the issue is linked to a wider debate on agricultural trade liberalisation and the extent to which the EC can ban agricultural imports that have been produced with new productivity-enhancing technologies. This is reinforced by a widely-shared perception among US and Canadian regulators and business groups that GM foods are safe to eat and, besides, do not require a fundamentally different approach than other (new) foods.

The EC win-set has contracted during the process, by a surge in public concerns over GM foods and public interest group activism, which was taken up by some of the EC member state governments and several business groups that avoided the use of GM foods and ingredients. Consequently, the positions of the EC, on the one hand, and the US and Canada, on the other, drifted apart during the second half of the 1990s. As in the beef-hormone issue, the EC position was reinforced by a number of food scares and the structure of the Common Agricultural Policy.

Some of the European concerns may have reached the other side of the Atlantic, leading to an increase in public interest group activism in the US and Canada. In general, however, public concerns about GM foods in the US and Canada have remained well below the levels found in the EC, and US business groups have continued to market GM foods. The only exception has been US soya bean growers, who have refrained from producing any GM soya bean varieties other than the one approved by the EC, even though they continued to support the technology and the US regulatory framework. Trade concerns have also given rise to attempts by the US and Canada to formulate common standards at the global level, but until now this has not led to changes in their domestic regulatory frameworks.

CHAPTER SIX

THE EUROPEAN DATA PROTECTION DIRECTIVE

6.1 INTRODUCTION AND BACKGROUND

6.1.1 Data protection and international trade

Information makes the world go around. The free flow of information is crucial to international trade in that the transfer of information is often necessary to conclude and execute contracts. In many instances, the information being transferred is of a personal nature: personal income, credit statuses, medical records or spending patterns can be important items of information for certain firms. In addition, the information itself can sometimes be used or sold as a product, for instance in direct marketing or credit reporting.

These uses have led to concerns on the part of those who fear that the use or abuse of information may lead to what they regard as unwarranted intrusions in individuals' lives. For example, through information on personal spending patterns, marketing efforts can be targeted more closely and directed to specific individuals. More specifically, by obtaining medical records, pharmaceutical firms can target their marketing efforts towards persons suffering from certain medical conditions.

Another example is the use of credit records to assess an individual's creditworthiness, which is highly valuable information for banks or firms engaged in distant sales. Yet another important category concerns employment data. Employers often have vast amounts of information on their employees' performance, absentee records and incomes, which they use for corporate planning but such information could also be useful for other firms and purposes (for instance, for marketing a pension plan).

Although personal information can be abused regardless of the way it is processed, the rise of data protection as a governmental policy is closely connected to the rise of information technology in the late 1960s and early 1970s. During that period, the dramatic increase in possibilities for processing and transferring (personal) information and linking information from different sources led to the first studies on the consequences for personal privacy. Western governments typically established a group of experts to study these consequences and during the 1970s various data protection laws were enacted in Western Europe and North America (Bennett, 1992: 45 ff.).

The debate over data protection gained a new impetus with the rise of the Internet in the second half of the 1990s, which offers even greater opportunities for the free exchange of (personal) information. On the one hand, that is seen as its foremost advantage but on the other, it may also lead to greater risks of abuse.

Concerns over data protection have not been confined to national borders. With the growing importance of international trade (both in goods and services), transborder data flows have also grown in significance, although most of these flows do not concern *personal* data (Raab & Bennett, 1994: 97-98). Still, as personal information can quite easily be transferred to another country and processed abroad, transborder data flows directly affect the level of domestic data protection.

The fear of 'data havens' (countries in which personal information can be processed under a less stringent system of data protection) led some European countries to allow restrictions on transborder data flows for the purpose of protecting privacy. At the same time, differences in data protection legislation, which could give rise to such restrictions, had the potential to disturb or restrict trade. Moreover, some were concerned that data protection laws were used for protectionist purposes, by impeding foreign firms' operations in a country (for a discussion of such concerns, see e.g. Cole, 1985; Ellger, 1987).

In debates over transborder data flows, the main controversy has therefore been between the protection of personal information as a human right and the free flow of information as an economic imperative. Proponents of more stringent data protection argue that the free flow of information has the potential to expose personal information to illegitimate uses, thereby intruding on a person's personal life. Although the concept of privacy includes much more than only the protection of personal information (Raab & Bennett, 1996: 537), the justification for the latter is often based on the broader principle of privacy as a human right (Bennett, 1992: 23 ff.; Flaherty, 1989: 7 ff.). Proponents of free data flows, on the other hand, argue that the free flow of information increases economic efficiency by reducing the costs of doing business and allowing a better informed use of resources (for instance, by directly targeting marketing efforts or combining credit information from different sources).

Although the tension between these two aspects of data flows features prominently in many debates, there are also tensions within the categories of human rights and economic interests themselves. Within the category of human rights, data protection may come into conflict with the freedom of expression, since data protection means that certain types of information cannot be freely disseminated. From an economic perspective, there is tension between the free flow of information as a way to increase efficiency and data protection as a means to build consumer confidence and thus markets. This tension is especially prevalent in debates concerning data protection in the context of electronic commerce. Hence, the (economic) desire to build a market for e-commerce is often translated into a call for better data protection policies.

Although most Western countries have adopted at least some data protection policies, they differ in the substantive principles underlying these policies, the types of information or sectors of society covered by them, the balance between legislation and self-regulation, and the way in which they are enforced. In this chapter I will examine the EC Data Protection Directive of 1995, which allowed restrictions on data flows to third countries, and its effects on the regulation of data protection in the US and Canada.

6.1.2 International work on data protection and transborder data flows

With the emergence of national data protection legislation in the late 1960s and early 1970s, a number of international organisations gained an interest in the international dimensions of the issue. The two most important ones were the Council of Europe (CoE) and the Organisation for Economic Co-operation and Development (OECD), which both became interested in the matter at around the same time, but for somewhat different reasons.

The Council of Europe approached data protection mainly as a human rights issue. Article 8 of the European Convention on Human Rights contained the right to privacy, which could come into conflict with Article 10, which lays down the freedom of expression, 'regardless of frontiers' (CoE, 1950). The balance between these two rights had been defined in the European Court of Human Rights' case law, but it was felt that a more specific instrument was needed to give effect to the right to privacy.

As a consequence, the Council of Europe had started to work on other legal instruments by the late 1960s. A Committee of Experts was set up to formulate guidelines for data protection laws in 1968. This resulted in two resolutions, adopted by the OECD Committee of Ministers in 1973 and 1974, which contained recommendations for data protection laws in the private and public sectors, respectively (CoE, 1981b: paragraph 4).

Already before the resolutions had been adopted, the Committee of Experts and the Conference of European Ministers of Justice had argued for a binding international agreement. Finally, in 1976, the Committee of Experts on Data Processing was given the task to prepare a data protection convention, which would be binding on all ratifying member states (CoE, 1981b: paragraphs 12 and 13).

During that same period, the OECD became involved in data protection issues due to its interest in the promotion of international trade. Consequently, its main focus was on the economic aspects of transborder data flows and the possible disruptions of those flows as a result of differences in national data protection laws. A group of experts' study of computer utilisation in the public sector marked the beginning of the OECD's involvement in the issue, which was followed by a symposium on data protection in 1977 (OECD, 1980b: paragraph 16).

Work on official guidelines started in 1978, carried out by a new Group of Experts. This work and the Council of Europe's work on a data protection convention were carried out in close co-operation. This co-operation also included the European Commission, which had developed an interest in transborder data flows between the EC member states (CoE, 1981b: paragraph 14-16; OECD, 1980b: paragraph 18).

As a result, the OECD Guidelines (OECD, 1980a; henceforth 'the Guidelines') and the Council of Europe Convention (CoE, 1981a; henceforth 'the Convention'), which were both adopted in 1980, are similar in their content and principles. Although the two organisations' points of reference differed, they both converged upon a largely similar set of principles. Moreover, both the OECD Guidelines and the Council of Europe Convention (or their explanatory memorandums) contain references to both the objectives of protecting privacy and preventing trade restrictions (cf. CoE, 1981a: preamble; 1981b: paragraph 25; OECD, 1980a: preamble; 1980b: paragraph 25).

The Convention and the Guidelines both recognise a number of key principles of data protection, which are grouped and formulated slightly differently. They both state that the purpose of data collection should be specified and that the use of those data should be limited to that purpose (Article 5b Convention; Paragraphs 9 & 10 Guidelines). Closely connected, they state that personal data should be relevant, accurate, complete and up to date (Article 5c & 5d Convention; Paragraph 8 Guidelines). Also, personal data should be obtained fairly and lawfully (Article 5a Convention; Paragraph 7 Guidelines).

Personal data should also be protected, physically and otherwise, against accidental and unauthorised loss, access, use or modification (Article 7 Convention; Paragraph 11 Guidelines).

Finally, the Convention and the Guidelines provide for a number of rights for data subjects (individuals whose data are being kept or used). Data subjects have the right to establish the existence of personal data relating to them, as well as who keeps and uses those data (Article 8a and 8b Convention; Paragraphs 12, 13a & 13b Guidelines). Furthermore, data subjects should have the right to correct data relating to them or have them erased if the data do not conform to the applicable legal requirements (Article 8c Convention; Paragraph 13d Guidelines). Countries should also establish adequate sanctions and remedies in case the law is not being complied with (Articles 8d & 10 Convention; Paragraph 19c & 19d Guidelines).

The Convention and the Guidelines also differ on a number of points (cf. OECD, 1980b: paragraph 20). First, they differ in the exact terminology they use to express the data protection principles. Sometimes one of the two instruments contains an explicit provision which the other lacks. For instance, the Convention foresees specific safeguards for special categories of data, such as data on race or political opinions (Article 6 Convention), which are thought to be inherently more sensitive to abuse. By contrast, the Guidelines contain a general provision against unfair discrimination (Paragraph 19e Guidelines), while the Committee preparing the Guidelines chose to leave the designation of categories of sensitive data for individual countries to decide (OECD, 1980b: paragraph 51).

Besides these terminological differences, there are also some differences in scope. Both instruments are limited to 'identified or identifiable' individuals (Article 2a Convention; Paragraph 1b Guidelines), but the Convention allows for an extension to legal persons (Article 3.2b Convention). The Convention is limited to automated data but allows for an extension to non-automated data (Article 3.1 and 3.2c Convention), while the Guidelines apply to all kinds of personal data, but allow a limitation to automated data (Paragraphs 2 & 3c Guidelines). Both the Convention and the Guidelines apply to both the public and the private sector (Article 3.1 Convention; Paragraph 2 Guidelines).

Furthermore, the two instruments differ because of the different status they have. Since the Convention is a legal instrument which is binding upon the countries that have ratified it, it has a more extensive and specific list of exceptions (Article 9 Convention) than the Guidelines, which are not binding and thus only touch upon the subject of exceptions in Paragraph 4 (cf. the discussion in OECD, 1980b: paragraph 46-47). In general, however, both formulate the exceptions in terms of vital state interests (like national security and public safety) and the interests of other individuals.

Finally, the Guidelines seem to give more room for self-regulation than the Convention. The provisions in the two instruments are equally brief, calling for 'necessary measures in (...) domestic law' (Article 4.1 Convention) and 'appropriate domestic legislation' (Paragraph 19a Guidelines), although in the Guidelines this is complemented by a call to 'encourage and support self-regulation' (Paragraph 19b Guidelines). In the Convention's explanatory report, it is explicitly stated that 'binding measures may usefully be reinforced by measures of voluntary regulation' but 'such voluntary measures are not by themselves sufficient to ensure full compliance with the convention' (CoE, 1981b: paragraph 39). The OECD's explanatory memorandum is more ambiguous at this point, although it seems to express a preference for legislative solutions. It states that the provision on self-regulation 'is addressed primarily to common law countries where non-legislative implementation of the Guidelines would complement legislative action' (OECD, 1980b: paragraph 70).

Apart from the protection to be offered to individuals, the Convention and the Guidelines also seek to reduce restrictions on transborder data flows for or under the guise of data protection motives. Article 12.2 of the Convention and Paragraph 17 of the Guidelines state the general rule that transborder data flows should not be restricted for data protection reasons between countries that adhere to the Convention or the Guidelines, respectively. Two exceptions are made: one if a country has adopted specific regulations for certain categories of personal data and the other country offers no equivalent protection for those categories (Article 12.3a Convention; Paragraph 17 Guidelines) and another if the data will be re-exported to a third country that does not adhere to the Convention or the Guidelines (Article 12.3b Convention; Paragraph 17 Guidelines).

The work by the Council of Europe and the OECD has had a great influence on the further (international) development of data protection law. Both the Convention and the Guidelines were meant to address a wider group of countries than only the Council of Europe or OECD member states. The Council of Europe's Convention was even opened for accession to non-member states (Article 23 Convention).

Given the broad convergence upon the same principles, they also became important reference points in international and national debates on data protection, both outside and within the Council of Europe and the OECD.

Outside these forums, the same substantive principles were reflected in the United Nations High Commissioner for Human Rights' data protection guidelines, which were adopted by the UN General Assembly in 1990 (UN, 1990). Although substantively similar, the UN Guidelines differ somewhat in their recommendation to establish a supervisory authority (UN, 1990: Paragraph 8).

Work on these issues also continued within the Council of Europe and the OECD. In 1985, the OECD member states adopted a declaration on transborder data flows, in which they reinforced the OECD Guidelines and pledged to avoid the creation of unjustified barriers to transborder data flows and to continue to work on common approaches and harmonised solutions (OECD, 1985). The Council of Europe adopted a number of recommendations on data protection in specific sectors in the early 1990s, which were meant to specify the Convention.

With the emergence of the Internet, both organisations also sought to apply their principles to this new medium. In doing so, however, they both recognised the continuing validity of their earlier work and did not change the Convention and the Guidelines themselves. At an OECD Ministerial Conference on e-commerce, the OECD members reaffirmed the 1980 Guidelines and stated that they 'continue to represent international consensus and guidance' (OECD, 1998b; see also OECD, 1998a). In the declaration, legislation and self-regulation were explicitly placed on a par as equally valid ways of implementing privacy policies. Almost six months later, the Council of Europe's Committee of Ministers also adopted guidelines for data protection on the Internet, which recognised that these new technologies 'are governed by the provisions of the Convention for the Protection of Individuals with regard to Automatic Processing of Personal Data' (CoE, 1999).

6.2 The EC data protection Directive

6.2.1 History and background

The EC gained an interest in data protection and the transborder flow of data in the late 1970s, as various member states had adopted national data protection laws that sometimes contained restrictions on transborder data flows. In the second half of the 1970s, the European Parliament (EP) adopted a number of resolutions calling for a European data protection Directive (EP, 1975; 1976; 1979). In that same period, the European Commission participated in the development of international data protection principles with the OECD and the Council of Europe. After the Council of Europe had adopted its Convention, the European Commission chose not to develop its own instrument. Instead, it recommended that the member states should ratify the Convention as a way to achieve harmonised levels of data protection across the EC (CEC, 1981).

In the course of the 1980s, however, this strategy proved to be rather unfruitful, due to both the particular characteristics of the Convention and to developments within the EC. The Council of Europe's Convention had a number of weaknesses for the purposes of the EC. The first set of weaknesses had to do with the ratification and implementation of the Convention. The Convention had only been ratified by some of the EC member states. By 1990, when the EC proposed its first draft data protection Directive, the Convention had been ratified by only seven out of the (then) twelve EC member states (Platten, 1996: 23; cf. CoE, 2000). Even if a member state had ratified the Convention, there was no mechanism to ensure (correct) implementation. Some member states simply retained their existing data protection laws, others did not adopt any domestic legislation after having ratified the Convention, and still others failed to implement certain specific provisions (Brühann, 1999: 12; Platten, 1996: 17-18). Moreover, the Convention left much room for interpretation, allowing differences in national implementation that only reinforced existing differences or created new ones (Mei, 1993: 308; Raab & Bennett, 1994: 101).

A second set of weaknesses related to the Convention's substantive provisions (cf. Brühann, 1999: 12; Platten, 1996: 18-19). The Convention's scope was limited to automated data processing. It did not make any provision for the determination of the applicable national law in case of transborder data flows, nor did it require restrictions on transborder data flows to third countries that did not have a sufficient level of data protection (it only allowed such restrictions). Finally, and closely related to the concerns about implementation, the Convention did not foresee the mandatory creation of national data protection authorities (or any specific domestic implementation mechanism, for that matter) (see also Raab & Bennett, 1994: 101-102).

As a consequence, the Convention did not bring about the degree and content of harmonisation that had been hoped for in the early 1980s. At the same time, as Brühann (1999: 13) has explained, the need for harmonisation became more pressing because of a number of developments within the EC.

First, differences in national data protection laws threatened to impede the free flow of information between the EC member states and the completion of the internal market (see also Platten, 1996: 23). Although the issue would have run into some legal complexities, member states would probably have been allowed to restrict transborder data flows between themselves on data protection grounds as long as no harmonisation had taken place on the European level (for a detailed legal analysis see Nugter, 1990: 264ff.).

Second, a number of EC member states decided to move ahead with the free movement of persons in the so-called Schengen Agreements. Part of those agreements was an international information system, which led to a call for data protection legislation by member states which already had data protection laws in place (see also Raab & Bennett, 1994: 104-105).

Thirdly, the differences in national data protection laws hindered the development of standardised technologies in the European market. The harmonisation of data protection legislation would also serve the development of this market.

By the mid-1980s the European Commission therefore again started to work on a European Directive. In 1989, a further impetus was provided by a declaration from the joint data protection commissioners and another declaration from the ministers working on the Schengen Agreements, which both requested European legislation (Brühann, 1999: 14; Platten, 1996: 23; Raab & Bennett, 1994: 104).

In 1990, the European Commission presented its first proposal (CEC, 1990). The proposal was based on Article 100A of the EC Treaty (now Article 95), the Treaty basis for harmonisation measures aimed at completing the internal market, which provided for co-operation between the Council of Ministers and the European Parliament in the decision-making process.

The reactions to this proposal were mixed. On the one hand, many member states and the EP were happy to see an EC-wide Directive in this field, but on the other they were also reluctant to accept the specifics of the text as it had been presented. The reactions by the member states were mainly conditioned by their existing data protection laws, each member state wanting the Directive to be as close as possible to its own system. France and the UK did not feel comfortable with many of the proposed Directive's features, which they felt were too close to the German system (Platten, 1996: 25). Many of these concerns were also reflected in the EP's opinion on the proposal (Brühann, 1999: 15).

The US government and US business groups also lobbied the EC. To that end, a delegation representing the Department of State and US business groups went to Brussels in 1991. Still, in the early 1990s, the issue of transborder data flows did not yet have the significance it would gain some years later and most US firms were more concerned about their operations in the EC itself than with possible barriers to Transatlantic data flows (Interview 24-1-2001, DMA).

In 1992, the European Commission presented a revised proposal, which had undergone a complete restructuring as compared to the first proposal, to include elements from French, Dutch and British data protection law as well (Brühann, 1999: 15; Platten, 1996: 25-26; Simitis, 1995: 449-450). Whereas the first proposal had made a distinction between the public and private sector, with somewhat different principles applying to each, the new proposal had abandoned that distinction (see CEC, 1992: 2). Also, the Council of Europe's data quality principles had obtained a more prominent position in the proposal.

Furthermore, the provisions on transfers of data to third countries had been modified. Initially, it had been proposed that such transfers would be prohibited if a third country did not provide 'adequate protection' for the personal data involved in the transfer. This assessment would be made for the third country as a whole, but the revised proposal specified the provision by establishing a case-by-case assessment of adequacy, rather than an overall approach (Murray, 1998: 996-997; cf. CEC, 1992: 35). The revised proposal also foresaw a number of exceptions to the general adequacy rule that were 'compatible with the protection of individuals' (CEC, 1992: 35). Finally, the term 'adequate' came under attack from groups that wanted to change it into 'equivalent,' as was the case in the Council of Europe's Convention. After lobbying by business groups, the word 'adequate' was retained, however (Interview 24-1-2001, DMA).

After the revised proposal had been presented, negotiations in the Council of Ministers started. The UK and Ireland opposed the harmonisation effort altogether, arguing instead for the ratification of the Council of Europe's Convention. They were supported by Denmark. The Mediterranean and Benelux countries broadly supported the objective of the proposed Directive, although some had specific concerns. A crucial role was played by Germany, which took a somewhat unclear position: on the one hand, it supported the objective of harmonisation at a high level of protection, but, on the other hand, it felt that the revised proposal was too different from the German system (Brühann, 1999: 16; Platten, 1996: 27).

The German position was especially important, since the three opposing countries needed Germany to form a blocking minority in the Council, which had to vote by qualified majority. After the negotiations in the Council had not witnessed much progress in the initial years after the revised proposal had been presented, the UK, Ireland, Denmark and Germany tabled a joint document by the end of 1993, demanding less stringent harmonisation and more room for manoeuvre for the member states under the Directive (Brühann, 1999: 16; Platten, 1996: 28-29). Since this was unacceptable to the other member states (as well as the European Commission), a stalemate resulted.

Business groups were also very active in the decision-making process (Brühann, 1999: 16-17; Platten, 1996: 27-28). Three sectors were particularly involved. The financial sector feared that the Directive would lead to extremely high costs, given the amount of (transborder) data flows that was involved in their daily business activities. In the Council, these concerns were voiced by the UK and the Netherlands. The direct marketing sector had already had some success in revising the first proposal. Originally, this proposal foresaw a system of 'opt-ins,' under which individuals would have to give their explicit consent for direct marketing purposes. In the revised proposal this had been changed into an 'opt-out' system, under which individuals could block the use of their personal data for these purposes (see also Raab & Bennett, 1994: 106). Still, the sector was worried about individuals' right of access to their own data. Finally, medical researchers feared that the Directive would make it impossible to use personal data for medical research if they had been collected for other purposes. Their concerns were expressed in the Council by Denmark.

A number of developments led to a solution to this stalemate in the following year. First, in December 1993 the European Commission presented its White Paper on Growth, Competitiveness and Employment, in which information technology was presented as one of the key areas in the development of the European economy (CEC, 1993b). In a follow-up document, the establishment of a framework for the protection of privacy was seen as essential for the development of an 'information society.' The document was endorsed by the European Council (consisting of the member states' heads of government) at their Corfu meeting in June 1994 and in the concluding statement, the Council of Ministers was called upon to make rapid progress on the data protection Directive (CEC, 1994b: 6; Brühann, 1999: 17; Platten, 1996: 30).

Second, Germany took over the presidency of the EC in June 1994. As with all EC presidencies, this led the German government to work more co-operatively toward the attainment of EC legislation and to become more flexible in its own demands. As a result, the Germans could be persuaded to support the existing proposal (Brühann, 1999: 17; Platten, 1996: 30). After some minor adjustments had been made to appease some specific concerns on the part of Ireland, Denmark and Greece (on the Greek position, see Simitis, 1995: 455-456), including an exemption for medical research, a political agreement was reached in December 1994, with only the UK opposing. Despite some last-minute lobbying by the UK delegation and further concessions by the other member states to address its concerns, the Council of Ministers adopted a common position on 20 February 1995 (Council, 1995). The UK abstained. In June of that year, the EP approved the common position subject to some minor amendments (EP, 1995a) and Directive 95/46/EC was finally adopted on 24 October 1995 (EC, 1995).

The thrust of the initial 1990 proposal had been retained throughout the decision-making process. Nevertheless, several more major as well as more minor changes had been made to the effect of allowing more flexibility in the application of the general principles. The same was true for the provisions on data flows to third countries, which had changed from a categorical to a case-by-case prohibition on data flows to countries without an adequate level of protection, and which had been refined to allow for some exemptions.

6.2.2 Directive 95/46 and data transfers to third countries

Directive 95/46

The Directive's substantive provisions are broadly similar to those in the Council of Europe Convention and the OECD Guidelines and each of the Convention's and Guidelines' principles outlined above can also be found in the Directive. Thus, the Directive contains the principle that 'personal data must be (...) collected for specified, explicit and legitimate purposes and not further processed in a way incompatible with those purposes' (Article 6.1(b) Directive). The data should also be 'adequate, relevant and not excessive in relation to the purposes for which they are collected and/or further processed' (Article 6.1(c)) as well as 'accurate and, where necessary, kept up to date' (Article 6.1(d)). Processing should be done fairly and lawfully (Article 6.1(a)).

Like the Convention and the Guidelines, the Directive also contains a provision on the security of processing. It states that data should be protected from 'accidental or unlawful destruction or accidental loss, alteration, unauthorized disclosure or access (…) and against all other unlawful forms of processing' (Article 17.1).

Again similar to the Convention and the Guidelines, the Directive provides for rights for data subjects. These rights include a right to know who keeps data on them and the purposes of the processing (Articles 10 & 12(a)). Data subjects should be able to correct data or have them erased if they do not conform to the Directive's provisions (Article 12(b)). Adequate remedies and sanctions and a liability regime should be in place to enforce the data subjects' rights (Article 22).

In addition, the Directive contains a detailed provision on sensitive data, whose processing shall be prohibited subject to a number of exceptions (Article 8). A completely new element can be found in Article 14, which establishes a number of grounds for data subjects to object to the processing of their data. According to article 14(b) data subjects have the right to block the processing of their data for direct marketing purposes (the 'opt-out' system). Article 15 introduces another new principle by stating that every person should have the right 'not to be subject to a decision which produces legal effects concerning him or significantly affects him and which is based solely on automated processing of data.'

The scope of the Directive is broad in that it covers both the public and private sectors, and both automated and manual data processing. Exceptions are made, however, for activities that fall outside the remit of the EC (for instance, public security and criminal law) and for data processing of a purely personal nature (for instance, a person's address book). Further exemptions to the data protection principles are provided in Article 13; they basically include the exceptions that had already been developed in the context of the Convention and the Guidelines. Article 9 seeks to balance data protection against the freedom of expression by allowing for exemptions for journalistic, artistic or literary purposes.

The main difference between the Directive and its international predecessors lies in the provisions on its implementation and enforcement. The Directive requires each member state to establish an independent supervisory authority to monitor the application of data protection legislation (Article 28.1 & 28.2). The supervisory authority should have a range of powers to monitor and enforce the law, including 'investigative powers,' 'effective powers of intervention,' and 'the power to engage in legal proceedings' (Article 28.3). In addition, the authority should hear claims from individuals and organisations regarding data protection (Article 28.4) and publish an annual report (Article 28.5).

Moreover, the processing of personal data for some purpose(s) should be notified to the supervisory authority before it takes place, subject to certain exceptions (Article 18). If the processing operation presents 'specific risks,' the authority has to check it before the processing takes place (Article 20).

All in all, the EC Directive is therefore characterised by at least two main features:

- It is comprehensive, covering both the private and public sectors and containing all substantive data protection principles that have been agreed upon in international forums;
- It establishes national supervisory authorities which have broad powers to handle data protection issues and act pro-actively to monitor the application of the data protection law. It is therefore aimed at preventing abuse of personal information.

Data transfers to third countries under Directive 95/46

Apart from providing for data protection legislation within the EC, the Directive also contains provisions on data flows to third countries, which are of particular relevance in the context of this study. Article 25.1 of the Directive states that such data flows may only take place if 'the third country in question ensures an adequate level of protection.' Article 25.2 continues by specifying that:

> 'the adequacy of the level of protection afforded by a third country shall be assessed in the light of all the circumstances surrounding a data transfer operation or set of data transfer operations; particular consideration shall be given to the nature of the data, the purpose and duration of the proposed processing operation or operations, the country of origin and country of final destination, the rules of law, both general and sectoral, in force in the third country in question and the professional rules and security measures which are complied with in that country.'

Article 26.1 provides for a number of exemptions to this general prohibition, including consent by the data subject, and data transfers that are necessary for the conclusion and/or performance of certain contracts, that are legally required on certain grounds, that are necessary to protect vital interests of the data subject, or that are made from a public register. Data transfers to countries without an adequate level of protection can also be covered by 'adequate safeguards,' for instance in the form of a special contract governing the transfer (Article 26.2).

The Directive foresees a special EC-wide procedure in case a third country does not offer an adequate level of protection. If the Commission finds that this is the case, all member states are required to prohibit data transfers to that country (Article 25.4). At the same time, the Commission may enter into negotiations with the third country in order to reverse that finding (Article 25.5), which is done if the third country can guarantee an adequate level of protection 'by reason of its domestic law or of the international commitments it has entered into' (Article 25.6).

The Commission's findings under both Article 25.4 and 25.6 have to go through a committee of member state representatives, which is established under Article 31 of the Directive. Besides this 'Article 31 Committee,' the Directive establishes a 'Working Party on the Protection of Individuals with Regard to the Processing of Personal Data' (Article 29), which consists of representatives of the national supervisory authorities and the supervisory authority established for the EC, as well as a Commission representative. The Working Party has no formal powers, but it is supposed to give advice and opinions on a number of data protection issues, including 'the level of protection in (...) third countries' (Article 30.1(b)).

Despite the guidance given in the text of the Directive, the adequacy standard laid down in Article 25 remains relatively vague and it was accompanied by substantial uncertainty about how it would be applied in practice. Still, at least three points become clear from the text of the provision. First, the Directive requires 'adequate' protection, which is not the same as 'equivalent' or 'the same level of' protection. In this regard, the Directive's formula is less stringent than that used in, for instance, the Council of Europe's Convention, which speaks of 'equivalent protection.' In practice, this means that the Directive does not require third countries to establish data protection legislation that is identical or even similar to the Directive.

Second, Article 25.2 speaks of 'the rules of law, *both general and sectoral*, in force in the third country' (emphasis added). This implies that a finding of adequacy need not relate to a country as a whole, but can be confined to certain sectors within that country. Thus, a country may have inadequate protection in one sector but an adequate level of protection in another. Then, data transfers to that country will be prohibited in one sector, but allowed in another.

Third, besides the laws in force in the third country, account should also be taken of 'professional rules and security measures which are complied with' (Article 25.2). This appears to pave the way for assuring an adequate level of protection by means of self-regulation as well as formal law, or at least partly so. However, as for the other points, the actual concrete and specific criteria that would be used in assessing a country's substantive and administrative measures for protecting personal data remained unclear from the text of the Directive.

The work by the Article 29 Working Party

In the years following the adoption of the Directive, the Article 29 Working Party did a great deal to clarify the meaning of Article 25. Although the Working Party did not have the power to decide which countries had or did not have adequate levels of protection, its opinion was very authoritative, if only because it was composed of the people who were supposed to apply the Directive, including the provisions on data flows to third countries.

After having published a number of discussion documents, the Working Party adopted a working document on the application of Articles 25 and 26 of the Directive in July 1998 (Working Party, 1998). In it, the Working Party outlined an approach for determining adequacy in third countries and for applying the exemptions of Article 26.

The Working Party's approach to assessing adequacy relied on two sets of principles which it regarded as the 'core' of the Directive: a set of core content principles, and a set of procedural or enforcement objectives. Together, these (sets of) principles 'could be seen as the minimum requirement for protection to be seen as adequate' (Working Party, 1998: 5). In specific cases, additional principles would have to be added or some of the core principles could be dropped, depending on the characteristics of the data transfer.

The Working Party discerned six core content principles (Working Party, 1998: 6):

- The purpose limitation principle: 'data should be processed for a specific purpose and subsequently used or further communicated only insofar as this is not incompatible with the purpose of the transfer;'
- The data quality and proportionality principle: 'data should be accurate and, where necessary, kept up to date' as well as 'adequate, relevant and not excessive in relation to the purposes for which they are transferred or further processed;'
- The transparency principle: 'individuals should be provided with information as to the purpose of the processing and the identity of the data controller in the third country, and other information insofar as this is necessary to ensure fairness;'
- The security principle: 'technical and organisational security measures should be taken (...) that are appropriate to the risks presented by the processing.' Moreover, if the data processing is contracted out to another person, that person 'must not process data except on instructions;'
- The rights of access, rectification and opposition: a 'data subject should have a right to obtain a copy of all data relating to him/her,' to have inaccurate data corrected, and, under certain circumstances, 'to be able to object to the processing of data relating to him/her;'
- Restrictions on onward transfers: onward transfers should only be allowed if the 'second recipient (...) is also subject to rules affording an adequate level of protection.'

All these principles would only be subject to the exceptions laid down in the EC Directive. In addition to these core principles, the Working Party identified a number of principles that could be applied in specific cases, such as additional safeguards for sensitive data, an opt-out of use for direct marketing purposes, and safeguards in case the data are used for automated individual decisions (Working Party, 1998: 6-7).

Apart from these content principles, the Working Party also took account of the way they were enforced. It claimed there was 'broad agreement that a system of "external supervision" in the form of an independent authority is a necessary feature of a data protection compliance system.' Since such authorities were mostly not to be found outside Europe, however, the Committee outlined three basic objectives which an enforcement system would have to conform to (Working Party, 1998: 7).

The system would have to:

- 'deliver a good level of compliance with the rules;'
- 'provide support and help to individual data subjects in the exercise of their rights' and;

– 'provide appropriate redress to the injured party where rules are not complied with;'

In the remainder of the Working Document, these principles are applied to a number of cases. Special attention is given to systems of self-regulation, which are defined as 'any set of data protection rules applying to a plurality of data controllers from the same profession or industry sector, the content of which has been determined primarily by members of the industry or profession concerned' (Working Party, 1998: 10). The Directive explicitly includes self-regulation as an element to be considered in the determination of 'adequacy' under Article 25.2.

As a rule, the Working Party stated that the same criteria should apply to self-regulatory and law-based systems. This involves an assessment of the substantive data protection principles incorporated in the self-regulatory code, and of its effectiveness, as measured by the three criteria outlined above: a good level of general compliance, support and help to individual data subjects, and appropriate redress (Working Party, 1998: 11). For each of these criteria, the Working Document specifies a number of questions to be asked in assessing the overall level of protection achieved by self-regulatory codes.

As to the practical implementation of Article 25, even though the Directive calls for a case-by-case assessment, the Working Party recognised that 'given the huge number of transfers of personal data leaving the Community on a daily basis and the multitude of actors involved in such transfers, no Member State (...) will be able to ensure that each and every case is examined in detail' (Working Party, 1998: 26). It therefore proposed to make adequacy findings pertaining to certain countries or sectors within countries, which would be for guidance in concrete decisions by data protection authorities. These findings should form a 'white list' of countries and sectors of countries that provide an adequate level of protection, rather than a 'black list' of countries and sectors with inadequate protection.

Taking into account these positive findings, the assessment of specific transfers should focus on transfers involving particularly great risks to data privacy. Priority should be given, for instance, to transfers involving sensitive data in the sense of Article 8 of the Directive, transfers carrying significant financial or personal safety risks, transfers for the sake of particularly significant decisions (like employment decisions), and transfers which may result in direct marketing approaches (Working Party, 1998: 27-28).

All in all, the Working Party adopted a rather stringent approach in applying the Directive's adequate protection test. As was said above, however, in the end it would not be the Working Party that was to make this assessment, but the European Commission, subject to the Article 31 Committee consisting of representatives from the member states. As the Directive entered into force in 1998, the Commission therefore started the first negotiations with third countries.

6.3 The European Directive and International Trade Law

The issues in the previous chapters related to trade in goods, and the European regulatory trade measures were covered by the GATT Agreement or, in two food safety issues, the SPS Agreement. Measures relating to transborder data flows, however, are not covered by these agreements, since they do not relate to (tangible) *goods*, but to (intangible) data processing *services*. With the growing importance of services and trade in services over the last decades, it was therefore decided to create a new agreement for trade in services during the Uruguay Round of negotiations. This General Agreement on Trade in Services (WTO, 1994e; henceforth 'GATS') became part of the final package of WTO Agreements, which was concluded in 1994.

Trade in services shows some specific characteristics when compared to trade in goods (Weiss, 1995: 1180). Most importantly for this study, many types of trade in services do not have a clear point of import, for instance when a consultant goes to another country to give advice. Consequently, barriers to trade that have traditionally been important in trade in goods, such as tariffs, are much less relevant in trade in services, while (domestic) regulatory standards are relatively more important.

Therefore, although the GATS was modelled after the GATT in many ways, including the GATT's key provisions, the specific set-up of the GATS and the formulation of many provisions differ in significant respects that probably also have consequences for the way the Agreement should be interpreted. Nevertheless, the body of GATT case law has relevance for the interpretation of the GATS and a comparison between provisions in the two agreements should yield valid conclusions about the GATS, even if some of the implications will only become clear at a later stage (cf. Jackson, 1998: 308; and Weiss, 1995: 1195, both with regard to the GATS Most Favoured Nation provision).

Article I GATS discerns four types of services that are covered by the Agreement, two of which may relate to transborder data flows:

- The supply of a service from the territory of one Member into the territory of any other Member;
- The supply of a service in the territory of one Member to the service consumer of any other Member.

Restrictions on transborder data flows may affect these types of trade in services, and may thus be subject to scrutiny under GATS. As under the GATT, an assessment of compatibility with the GATS should proceed in two steps. First, it has to be determined whether a measure (in this case the EC data protection Directive) violates one of the GATS' obligations. Second, if this is the case, it has to be assessed whether the measure can still be justified under an exception.

The GATS obligations

The first step (determining whether an obligation has been violated) is more difficult under GATS than under the GATT. While the GATT lays down a number of obligations that apply generally to almost all trade in goods, the GATS distinguishes between general obligations and specific commitments. The key general GATS obligation in this respect is the most-favoured nation principle of Article II GATS:

> 'With respect to any measure covered by this Agreement, each Member shall accord immediately and unconditionally to services and service suppliers of any other Member treatment no less favourable than that it accords to like services and service suppliers of any other country.'

Unlike its GATT counterpart, however, member states could make specific exemptions from this principle in an Annex to the Agreement.

In addition to this general obligation, member states can undertake specific commitments in a Schedule to the agreement. In the Schedule, each member indicates whether and under which conditions it will grant market access to foreign services. In total, a member can indicate the conditions for market access of 155 activities for each of the four modes of supply discerned in Article I GATS, which amounts to a maximum of 620 specific commitments. The EC, for instance, made 392 out of the possible 620 specific commitments (Trebilcock & Howse, 1999: 287).

Several GATS obligations cover only these specific commitments. For instance, the national treatment principle, another cornerstone of the GATT, only applies to 'the sectors inscribed in the Schedule (...) subject to any conditions and qualifications set out therein' (Article XVII GATS). When it comes to domestic regulations, Article VI provides that 'in sectors where specific commitments are undertaken, each Member shall ensure that all measures of general application affecting trade in services are administered in a reasonable, objective and impartial manner.'

The assessment of a violation of GATS is therefore more complicated than under GATT. Still, a case could be made under the most-favoured nation principle of Article II GATS, which applies generally subject to the specific exemptions made by the member states in an Annex. As was discussed in section 3.4.1, GATT case law has drawn a clear distinction between 'internal' regulations, which are covered by the Most Favoured Nation and National Treatment provisions of GATT Articles I and III, and 'external' regulations, which are covered by GATT Article XI. Import bans based on process standards fall under Article XI.

This distinction is not likely to apply to GATS, however, for two reasons. First, the GATS Most Favoured Nation provision is formulated differently than the equivalent GATT provision. GATS Article II relates to 'any measure covered by this Agreement,' while GATT Articles I and III relate to 'all laws, regulations and requirements affecting their internal sale, offering for sale, purchase, transportation, distribution or use.' Moreover, the two GATT provisions define their obligations with regard to 'the *products* of the territory of any contracting party' (emphasis added), which the Tuna-Dolphin panels took as the most important argument for excluding process standards from GATT Article III's scope (GATT, 1991: paragraphs 5.11-5.13; GATT, 1994: 5.8). GATS Article II, by contrast, offers a Most Favoured Nation treatment to 'services and *service suppliers* of any other Member' (emphasis added). As a result, its scope is probably not meant to be limited to services as such, but also to the way they are produced.

Second, and equally importantly, an EC ban would not relate to the import of services, but to the export of personal information. For example, the EC Directive does not foresee a ban on the import of a credit report drawn up by a US credit reporting agency, but on the export of personal information that is needed to draw up the report from the EC to the US. In that sense, the EC Directive is an internal regulation that applies to firms in the EC. Yet, by attaching certain conditions relating to adequate protection, it affects service suppliers in other countries.

Consequently, an EC ban on a data transfer would probably by covered by GATS Article II. According to this provision, a country is not allowed to discriminate between 'like services.' Since the EC data protection Directive distinguishes between services and service suppliers on the basis of the safeguards for data protection in place for those services in third countries, this would seem to be analogous to a distinction on the basis of production methods under the GATT, which would violate Article II GATS. Even if it were accepted that service suppliers that do not offer similar safeguards are 'unlike,' the Directive's focus on countries' safeguards could lead to distinctions between 'like' service suppliers from different countries, in that service suppliers that effectively offer a similar level of protection will be treated differently, either because suppliers from one country may be denied data transfers from the EC or because they become subject to closer scrutiny and more stringent requirements (for instance the use of model contracts) because their country has a different data protection regime.

The GATS exceptions

If the argument concerning GATS Article II is to be accepted, then the second step is to assess whether the European Directive can be justified under an exception. Article XIV GATS contains a number of general exceptions, which are modelled after the GATT's Article XX exceptions. Insofar as is relevant to this case, it reads as follows:

> 'Subject to the requirement that such measures are not applied in a manner which would constitute a means of arbitrary or unjustifiable discrimination between countries where like conditions prevail, or a disguised restriction on trade in services, nothing in this Agreement shall be construed to prevent the adoption or enforcement by any Member of measures:
> (...)
> (c) necessary to secure compliance with laws or regulations which are not inconsistent with the provisions of this Agreement including those relating to:

> (...)
> (ii) the protection of the privacy of individuals in relation to the processing and dissemination of personal data and the protection of confidentiality of individual records and accounts.'

Since the purpose of the Directive is to protect the privacy of European citizens, it seems to be covered by this provision. In addition, however, the Directive should also conform to the 'chapeau' of Article XIV GATS. Given the almost identical wording of this chapeau and that of Article XX GATT, it seems that the requirements are broadly the same under both chapeaux.

As was shown in section 3.4.2, the chapeau has played an increasingly important role in the interpretation of Article XX GATT. According to this case law, a measure fails to live up to the requirements of the chapeau if it is applied without regard to differences in the conditions in other countries. Thus, if the EC had simply required third countries to adopt legislation identical to its Directive, it would have violated the chapeau of Article XIV GATS.

The EC would also have violated the chapeau's requirements if it had not pursued international co-operation in order to remedy the perceived deficiencies in third countries' legislation. Moreover, under this case law, the application of a trade measure is subject to the requirements of reasonability and due process. For instance, the EC could not have used different time periods in allowing third countries to conform to the Directive's requirements.

It is unlikely, however, that the EC Directive would have violated any of these requirements. First, it was closely linked to the protection of the personal information of European citizens, thereby excluding the protection of personal information of the third countries' citizens. Second, Article 25 of the Directive allowed for considerable flexibility, both in its general exceptions to the requirement of 'adequate protection' and in the means it foresaw for obtaining an adequacy finding. Finally, the Directive foresaw talks between the European Commission and a third country's government in case the third country's level of protection was not deemed to be adequate.

As a result, the EC Directive seemed to be safely within the limits of what the GATS allows, at least in the way that its provisions were formulated. Still, potential conflicts between the Directive and GATS could have arisen if the EC had been too inflexible in its demands toward third countries (for instance, by requiring in practice that third countries should adopt all of the Directive's provisions) or if it allowed for unjustifiable differences in its treatment of third countries. As long as it avoided these pitfalls, however, the EC Directive would seem to be justified under the GATS.

6.4 The European Directive and the US

6.4.1 The initial situation in the US

Early developments in US data protection policies

The United States is the cradle of the legal concept of privacy. In a famous article published in 1890, the American lawyers Brandeis and Warren argued for a right to privacy under the common law, which included what is here referred to as 'data protection.' Subsequently, a body of case law was built up under the common law to protect various types of privacy invasion (Regan, 1995: 33-35).

In addition to these common law protections, the US Constitution has also provided some safeguards against intrusions of privacy. Although the US Constitution does not contain an explicit right to data protection or (informational) privacy, the US Supreme Court has inferred some limited data protection rights from existing constitutional provisions. In the 1977 case of Whalen v. Roe, the Supreme Court even identified a constitutional right to informational privacy, which was based on interests in 'avoiding disclosure of personal matters' and 'independence in making certain kinds of important decisions' (as cited in Schwartz & Reidenberg, 1996: 76).

Yet, the protection offered by these constitutional safeguards has been limited in a number of ways. First, the safeguards relate exclusively to activities by the government or by private actors that are closely related to the government. Relations between citizens and private organisations are excluded from their scope. Second, the constitutional data protection rights put limits on what the government can do, but they do not require the government to protect personal data in an active way (Schwartz & Reidenberg, 1996: 32-35).

Given these limitations, the US has also adopted data protection legislation, both at the federal and state levels. In contrast to the European states and the EC, however, neither the federal nor any state government has adopted comprehensive data protection legislation to cover all or most data processing activities. At the federal level, some sort of comprehensive legislation has only been enacted for the public sector; for the private sector, only a number of specific laws have been adopted that focus on certain sectors or types of information.

An additional difference with the European approach is that the US has never opted for a specialised governmental authority to oversee data protection law and practices. Rather, the system provides specific powers of oversight to several sectoral regulators and relies primarily on legal action in Court by private citizens who feel that their rights have been violated. As a result, the enforcement of the US system of data protection is reactive (after a violation of the law has taken place) rather than pro-active (before a data transfer takes place).

The early developments in US data protection legislation were heavily influenced by a 1973 report commissioned by the (then) Department of Health, Education and Welfare (HEW). In the report, a set of 'fundamental principles of fair information practice' was formulated (HEW, 1973: 41). These principles included the rights of data subjects to know of the existence of personal data relating to them and their content (what later became known as the principle of 'notice'), to block the use of these data for other purposes ('choice'), and to correct and amend data ('access'), as well as the obligations for data users to safeguard the data's reliability for their purposes and to prevent their abuse (which roughly corresponds to the principle of 'security' as it was later called). These principles had an important impact on the legislation of the day and, as we will see below, they would resurface in the US debate on data protection policies in the late 1990s.

Federal legislation in the public sector

At the federal level, the most important data protection law in the public sector is the Privacy Act of 1974 (5 USC 552a). The Privacy Act covers personal data held by federal agencies. It sets standards for data protection in these agencies that are broadly comparable to the substantive principles embodied in the EC Directive. In 1988, the Computer Matching and Privacy Protection Act amended the Privacy Act to set limits on some forms of computer matching by federal agencies (Flaherty, 1989: 357-358; Schwartz & Reidenberg, 1996: 100 ff.).

Despite the broad correspondence between the substantive principles embodied in the Privacy Act and the basic principles underlying the European Directive, the Act suffers from a number of weaknesses. From the perspective of the EC, one important deficiency of the Privacy Act is that it only covers US citizens and legal residents (5 USC 552a(a)(2)). European residents not legally resident in the US are therefore excluded from protection under the Act, even if their personal information is held by an American federal agency.

Moreover, although the Privacy Act provides that consent from the data subject is necessary for a federal agency to disclose personal information, this requirement is subject to twelve exemptions, some of which are quite broad (5 USC 552a(b)). The most widely debated exemption in the literature is the one relating to 'routine uses' (5 USC 552a(b)(3)). The Act defines a routine use as a use 'for a purpose which is compatible with the purpose for which it was collected' (5 USC 552a(a)(7)), but in practice this exemption has been used to justify almost any type of disclosure, which has severely restricted the scope of the Privacy Act's restriction on disclosures (Schwartz & Reidenberg, 1996: 95 ff.).

Apart from these limits on the substantive data protection principles, the Privacy Act does not establish an independent supervisory authority. The Office of Management and Budget (OMB), part of the Executive Office of the President, is responsible for the co-ordination of the Act's implementation by federal agencies. In that capacity, the OMB has issued a number of guidelines, but its role has been purely administrative (Flaherty, 1989: 325-327; Schwartz & Reidenberg, 1996: 125). As a result, it has not played the roles commonly played by data protection authorities, that is actively to monitor compliance with the Act, to hear and investigate complaints, and to give advice on data protection legislation.

Besides the Privacy Act, several laws on other issues in the public sector contain provisions on data protection. For instance, as Flaherty (1989: 306) claims, 'the provisions on confidentiality in the Tax Reform Act of 1976 (...) are much longer than comparable national data protection laws.' Similarly, the Freedom of Information Act (FOIA) limits the disclosure of personal data in a number of ways (Schwartz & Reidenberg, 1996: 108 ff.).

Although these laws complement and refine the assessment of US data protection legislation in the public sector, they do not detract from the general picture sketched above. Thus, data protection in the US federal public sector conforms to a large extent to the substantive principles underlying the EC data protection Directive (Murray, 1998: 1010), and is fairly comprehensive. Its enforcement, though, is less strict than in the European data protection authority approach.

Federal legislation in the private sector

In the private sector, the situation is far more fragmented and great differences exist in the level of data protection between sectors. Some sectors are subject to relatively stringent data protection laws, whereas others are almost unregulated. Many firms and sectors have established self-regulatory privacy codes, but these codes differ in their content and level of enforcement.

In contrast to the public sector, the US private sector is not subject to comprehensive (or 'horizontal') data protection legislation. Rather, the laws that have been adopted cover specific (sub-)sectors of the economy or specific issues. These laws have often been adopted in response to concrete examples of abuse. For instance, the Video Privacy Protection Act, which protects information relating to video sales and rentals, was adopted after a magazine had published the video titles which a candidate for the Supreme Court had rented (Schwartz & Reidenberg, 1996: 10). Other sectors are largely unregulated, which is reflected in the often-quoted statement that medical information receives less statutory protection than video rental records (e.g. Schwartz & Reidenberg, 1996: 11).

The financial sector is generally considered to have the most stringent data protection legislation in the private sector. Until the late 1990s, there was no general law protecting personal information by financial institutions (cf. Schwartz & Reidenberg, 1996: 262). However, some financial activities, such as credit reporting, were regulated fairly stringently. In fact, the Fair Credit Reporting Act (FCRA) of 1970 was the first piece of data protection legislation in the US. It contains many of the core content principles discerned by the EC's Article 29 Working Party, such as purpose limitation, individual rights of access and rectification, and protection of sensitive data (Schwartz & Reidenberg, 1996: 290 ff.). In the late 1990s, data protection in the financial sector was strengthened by the Gramm-Leach-Bliley Act, which will be discussed below in section 6.4.2.

The FCRA relies mainly on private litigation for its enforcement. However, the Federal Trade Commission (FTC) also has some authority to oversee compliance.

Until the early 1990s, the FTC was reluctant to use this authority, but it became gradually more active during the 1990s (Schwartz & Reidenberg, 1996: 304).

Other sectors are much less closely regulated. The most notable example is the direct marketing industry, which is not regulated by any federal sectoral law. Although laws that are aimed at other sectors sometimes also put limits on the use of personal information for direct marketing purposes (for instance the Video Privacy Protection Act mentioned above), this sector relies almost completely on self-regulation (Schwartz & Reidenberg, 1996: 308-310).

Self-regulatory codes have been developed by firms and industry associations in most sectors. As a result, they differ in their content. Enforcement of these codes typically takes place by the firms and industry associations themselves, through internal or external audits and the handling of complaints in so-called 'alternative dispute resolution' mechanisms. Industry associations often have the authority to impose penalties on member firms that have breached the code, ranging from warnings to suspension of membership, but privacy advocates argue that trade associations are usually reluctant to apply these sanctions and that the enforcement of self-regulatory codes is typically weak (Interview 9-1-2001, EPIC; see also Murray, 1998: 994 with regard to self-regulation in the direct marketing sector).

Apart from these internal enforcement mechanisms, self-regulatory codes also have legal effect under Section 5 of the Federal Trade Commission Act (FTCA, 15 USC 45(a)(1)). Under Section 5, 'unfair and deceptive acts or practices in or affecting commerce' are prohibited. If a firm violates a self-regulatory code it has publicly pledged to adhere to, this is actionable under the terms of this provision. The FTC has powers to enforce it in a number of ways. Like in the case of the FCRA, the FTC has been reported to have been rather passive in pursuing this aim, although (as we will see below) it stepped up its activities in the second half of the 1990s.

The scope of the FTC's powers is also limited in a number of ways. The FTC only has authority in the field of commerce, which excludes non-profit organisations. Furthermore, the FTC Act exempts several important sectors in the economy, most notably banks and airlines (15 USC 45(a)(2)). The FTC does not bring individual claims; rather, it collects individual complaints and takes action against a firm when it shows a pattern of violations of its code (Interview 10-1-2001, FTC).

Legislation at the federal level is complemented by state data protection laws, which differ widely. Most states have privacy acts for the public sector. For the private sector, some states have codified (parts of) the common law privacy safeguards, while others have adopted specific, sectoral legislation such as that which exists at the federal level (Heydrich, 1999: 416). This does not lead to a significant increase in overall data protection, however. All in all, data protection in the private sector is therefore characterised by specific and piecemeal legislation, complemented by various self-regulatory codes.

The adequacy of the US standards and the potential impact of the EC Directive

Because of the fragmented character of the US regime, it was impossible to determine the 'adequacy,' in the sense of the EC Directive, of US data protection law as a whole. In the public sector, constitutional and statutory protections combined to offer a relatively comprehensive set of data protection rights, although enforcement was generally weak because there was no data protection authority.

The private sector showed an uneven pattern, in which (parts of) the financial sector would seem to have come closest to the adequacy criteria, while others (such as the direct marketing and medical sectors) would have had greater difficulties in meeting the Directive's and Working Party's criteria (Murray, 1998: 1016-1017). Much would have depended on the specific laws and self-regulatory codes in place and being complied with. The task would have been complicated even further by the fact that many data flows are not confined to one sector or one purpose (Schwartz & Reidenberg, 1996: 379-380). For instance, medical data and credit reports can be used for direct marketing, and there is also a close link between financial services and telecommunications (Schwartz & Reidenberg, 1996: 265-266).

This would have meant either the constant threat of an interruption of data flows or the need to rely on the exceptions of Article 26.1 of the Directive. Flows of personal information, either about consumers or about employees in foreign subsidiaries, are essential for a significant part of trade. Therefore, the possibility of interruptions would have led to significant insecurity and unpredictability in US-EC trade flows, something that was unattractive for both US and EC firms. It is difficult to give a quantitative estimate of the costs this would have entailed, but it could potentially have affected data flows in almost all sectors of the economy (for an analysis of the potential consequences in a range of sectors, see Swire & Litan, 1998, in general and in particular the overview at pages 248-260).

Still, most of the potential trade effects would have occurred in service industries, since trade in services relied more on the kind of data flows that were covered by the Directive than trade in goods. Trade in services was relatively less important than trade in goods, making up less than 30% of US exports between 1995 and 2000 (calculated from DoC, 2001). Nevertheless, it was important in its own right as well as a 'new' area of trade that had great potential for the future. Moreover, both the US and the EC exported more than one third of their total services exports to the other, making their trade relation in services even closer than in goods (Krenzler & Wiegand, 1999: 155).

The second option, relying on the Directive's exceptions, was not very attractive as a permanent solution either. The potentially most important exceptions would be the consent of the individual and contractual clauses providing for additional data protection. Although consent could be obtained in many circumstances, problems would arise if individuals refused to give their consent and if a data transfer was not foreseen at the time when the data was collected.

The contractual solution had been used before, under German data protection law, in a planned data transfer between the German railway company and US Citibank in 1994. Although this contract could be seen as a possible model for future contracts, it was likely to be a viable solution only for large-scale data transfers between large firms, which had the means and experience to establish and monitor such contracts (Heydrich, 1999: 434-437). Moreover, US firms would possibly have had to incur significant costs to comply with additional data protection safeguards, while for European consumers it would have been unclear which protection their personal information would have received once transferred to the US.

A number of developments in the second half of the 1990s led to a considerable strengthening of US data protection standards in (parts of) the private sector. Despite these developments, the protection afforded in the US still fell short of the European Directive's adequacy criteria. Nevertheless, they formed an important background to the talks with the EC following the adoption of the Directive. I will therefore discuss these domestic US developments first.

6.4.2 Domestic developments after the adoption of the European Directive

In the mid-1990s, the issue of data protection gained a strong impetus because of the emergence of the Internet and e-commerce. Like in the EC (and Canada, as we will see below), the US government became interested in this issue in the first half of the 1990s and started a series of (regulatory) initiatives that were meant to support the growth of the Internet. Data protection was an important part of these initiatives, since it was seen as crucial to the further development of e-commerce and because the Internet seemed to increase the threats to personal privacy.

In 1993, the Vice-President of the United States created the Information Infrastructure Task Force (IITF). In 1995, the IITF's Privacy Working Group (PWG) published its 'Principles for Providing and Using Personal Information,' which were meant to serve as guidance for legislators and drafters of voluntary codes alike (IITF, 1995). The PWG discerned a number of principles for data users and data subjects. These principles included use and purpose limitation ('acquisition,' PWG, 1995: Principle II.A), notice (Principle II.B, see also Principle III.A on 'awareness'), security ('protection;' Principle II.C), choice (as part of 'fairness,' Principle II.D), access (as part of 'empowerment,' Principle III.B) and redress (Principle III.C). In the 'Framework for Global Electronic Commerce,' released by the White House in 1997, these principles were reduced to two basic principles of notice and choice (White House, 1997: under 'Issues' at point 5).

Six months earlier, the FTC had formulated four basic fair information practices, as the outcome of a workshop on consumer privacy and the Internet. These principles were based on the 1973 HEW report and the work done by the PWG and included notice, choice, access and security (FTC, 1997: 9-12). These principles were also highlighted in a January 1998 paper by the Department of Commerce on 'elements of effective self-regulation for protection of privacy' (DoC, 1998a). Among these principles, access was the most controversial. Many US business groups considered this to be an unreasonable and unduly burdensome requirement, at least in the forms suggested by the FTC (Interview 24-1-2001, DMA). As a result, the Model Privacy Code of the Direct Marketing Association, for instance, includes notice and choice (in the form of opt-out), but not access (DMA, 1998a; 2000).

All these government initiatives were still predicated on self-regulation by private firms. Still, Commerce's elements paper stressed the necessity of effective consequences in the enforcement of privacy codes (DoC, 1998a: point B.3) or 'self-regulation with teeth' as it had become known (Interview 23-1-2001, Commerce). The FTC also assumed a more active role in the enforcement of Section 5 FTCA in relation to privacy statements on web sites. In 1998, this resulted in the first enforcement action against a web site, Geocities, which, contrary to its privacy statement, had used its customers' personal information for direct marketing purposes (FTC, 1998b; 1999a).

The FTC used the four principles mainly for policy guidance, if only because the FTC had no legal basis to apply or enforce them as legal principles (Interview 10-1-2001, FTC). As of 1998, however, the FTC also used the principles in annual surveys of data protection policies on the Internet. These surveys and the FTC's recommendations for governmental action gradually became more critical. The first report noticed that data protection practices were insufficient, but argued that the industry should be given more time to develop self-regulatory codes. Legislation was only recommended for protecting children under twelve years of age, which was enacted later that year (FTC, 1998a). The 1999 report found some progress and continued to argue for self-regulatory approaches (FTC, 1999b: 12-14; 1999c).

In its May 2000 report, however, the FTC came to a different conclusion. Although a survey of Internet sites revealed some progress in the application of data protection principles, the FTC argued that not enough progress had been made and that the self-regulatory approach was no longer the best way to address the issue. Instead, it recommended the adoption of legislation by US Congress to establish mandatory data protection principles for Internet sites, as well as an implementing agency (FTC, 2000a: 34-38). Although the US administration did not endorse these recommendations (as it had done with the legislation for children), this represented an important shift in thinking by the main governmental privacy body in the US.

Apart from the FTC, US Congress also demonstrated a great deal of activity in the field of data protection in the second half of the 1990s. To an important extent these activities were related to the Internet and e-commerce, and by the year 2000 dozens of bills were pending before Congress. The principles used in these bills varied widely. Some used the four principles elaborated by the FTC, but others focused only on notice and choice. The role of the FTC as an enforcement agency also differed between bills. Still, the momentum had shifted considerably in the field of data protection policies since the early 1990s.

Important legislation was also adopted outside the area of electronic privacy. For instance, in the financial sector, the Gramm-Leach-Bliley Act was adopted in 1999 (US, 1999). Title V of the Act contained extensive provisions on data protection, providing for notice requirements (Section 502(a)), opt outs (Section 502(b)), and limits on the use of information, among other things for direct marketing purposes (Section 502(c) and (d)). The enforcement of the data protection provisions was placed under sectoral regulators, such as the Office of the Comptroller of the Currency for banks. In total, six sectoral regulators were made responsible for various financial subsectors, with the FTC having residual authority over any financial institution that did not fall under one of the sectoral regulators (Section 505(a)).

In the health care sector, which until then had largely been unregulated at the federal level, important advances were made with the Health Insurance Portability and Accountability Act of 1996 (HIPAA; US, 1996). Section 261 of the Act stated the necessity of establishing 'standards and requirements for the electronic transmission of certain health information.' In Section 264, US Congress was given three years to enact legislation protecting personal health information, or otherwise the Department of Health and Human Services (HHS) would gain the authority to promulgate regulations on this issue. As Congress was not able to reach agreement on legislation, HHS indeed issued regulations for 'Privacy and Individually Identifiable Health Information' in December 2000 (HHS, 2000b).

The HIPAA Regulations were significant for a number of reasons. First, they filled an important gap in federal data protection legislation. Second, they related both to electronic and manual health information. In an earlier proposal, HHS had limited the scope of the regulation to electronic data, but after receiving many comments on this feature, it broadened the scope (HHS, 2000a). This showed that the debate on electronic privacy had the potential to affect a much wider range of data protection issues that also included non-electronic data (Interview 9-1-2001, EPIC).

Despite these activities, the US approach of sectoral, targeted legislation and an important role for self-regulation remained intact. There was little support for comprehensive data protection legislation, and the range of accepted substantive principles was more narrow than in the EC. The FTC had become more active in enforcing privacy codes and as an advocate for (on-line) privacy legislation and the creation of a data protection authority, but enforcement was still mainly a private matter.

Hence, the US and the EC had to come up with something else if they wanted to avoid disruptions of trade flows or at least a perennial threat of disruptions. At the same time, the domestic developments in the US provided some basis for a solution and in the second half of the 1990s the EC and the US engaged in talks with a view to arriving at an agreement.

6.4.3 Setting the stage for an agreement

Initially, the awareness among US government and business of the Directive's implications for Transatlantic data flows seems to have been limited (Interviews 23-1-2001, Commerce; 24-1-2001, DMA). Within the US government, the Directive was mainly dismissed as a bureaucratic, top-down and inflexible (in short: a European!) instrument for dealing with data protection issues (also: Interview 9-1-2001, EPIC). According to Bennett and Raab (1997: 256), the US response at that time was a combination of distrust (as to the EC's possible protectionist motives), resentment about the EC's attitude toward US data protection policies, and scepticism about the EC's willingness and ability to block data transfers. In order to discuss these issues and to raise the US understanding of the European Directive, European officials (including data protection commissioners) embarked on several trips to the US to explain the Directive in the years after its adoption (Interview 28-11-2000, Article 29 Working Party).

In the years after 1995, it became increasingly clear to the US government and US firms that their system of data protection would not qualify as 'adequate' under the Directive. At the same time, Transatlantic data flows had gained increasing importance because of the development of the Internet. Up to mid-1997, some officials in the US administration wanted to take a hard line against the EC and to deal with the matter as a trade issue. Others, however, were wary of the trade dispute that would arise and wanted to engage in talks (Interview 23-1-2001, Commerce). Business groups did not support resorting to the WTO either (Interview 24-1-2001, DMA).

As a consequence, the US government and the European Commission started talks in late 1997. In these talks, the US and the EC explored the possibility of reaching an agreement on a set of principles. It would be up to US companies to decide whether or not to subscribe to these principles, but any US company subscribing to them would automatically be considered to offer an adequate level of protection for the purposes of the data protection Directive. During 1998, this approach was discussed and in the second half of 1998, it became crystallised under the name of the 'Safe Harbour' approach (Interview 23-1-2001, Commerce).

Initially, the European Commission was reluctant to accept a separate agreement based on a self-regulatory solution, whereas the Directive had foreseen adequacy findings on the basis of domestic standards. In the end, however, the European Commission agreed to the Safe Harbour approach, acknowledging that the US was unlikely to adopt comprehensive legislation in response to the Directive (Interview 17-10-2000, DG Internal Market). The Directive was to enter into effect on 25 October 1998, but the national data protection authorities agreed to treat data flows to the US favourably during the course of the negotiations.

In the US, the Department of Commerce (or: 'Commerce') was the lead agency, which negotiated with the European Commission and discussed the proposals with domestic actors. Within the US government, an interagency group was formed that was consulted during the negotiations. This group consisted of officials from a wide range of agencies, including an official from the United States Trade Representative (USTR) and several officials from the White House staff. At a later stage, someone from the FTC became a member of this group as well, although its role was mainly domestic and it was not engaged in the actual negotiations (Interviews 10-1-2001, FTC; 23-1-2001, Commerce).

To the US government, it was critical to reach an agreement on a self-regulatory approach, with as little government interference as possible. Moreover, it hoped to obtain adequacy findings for some sectors that had relatively stringent data protection laws, most notably the financial sector (Interview 23-1-2001, Commerce).

From the outset, US business groups were heavily involved in the Safe Harbour process, through formal consultations, workshops and discussion seminars. Initially, most US firms greeted the concept of a Safe Harbour agreement with some suspicion, since they were afraid that the self-regulatory element in the agreement would not be strong enough. Moreover, some feared that a Safe Harbour agreement might be the first step toward more comprehensive domestic legislation (Interviews 23-1-2001, Commerce; 24-1-2001, DMA).

US privacy advocacy groups were also involved in the process through formal consultations. They saw the European Directive as an opportunity to push for privacy legislation in the US and their aim was to turn the debate away from the trade implications of the European Directive to the deficiencies in US data protection law. Moreover, they hoped that the European Directive, as an example of comprehensive data protection legislation, could increase the credibility of such an approach in the US (Interview 9-1-2001, EPIC).

At an early stage, it became clear that the goal of comprehensive legislation was unrealistic. Still, several participants in the Safe Harbour process were well aware of the possible domestic ramifications of an agreement, as became apparent in several comments on the first draft of a Safe Harbour agreement (Consumers Union, EPIC et al., 1998; DMA, 1998b; ACB, 1999a).

Within the European Commission, DG XV (later DG Internal Market; I will refer to the later name throughout this study), which had been responsible for the data protection Directive, also took the lead in the negotiations. Other DGs did not play a formal role in the process; some (such as DG I/Trade) asked to be kept informed of the developments, but they were not actively involved in the process themselves. Only after a final draft had been published, in March 2000, did DG Internal Market commence formal interservice consultation with other DGs. During that consultation, some other DGs (most notably DG Sanco and DG Information Society) had some minor comments, but in the end they did not try to change the outcome of the negotiations (Interview 17-10-2000, DG Internal Market).

The issue of the WTO (in this case: GATS) compatibility of the European Directive was raised on several occasions during the regular meetings between DG Trade and US officials from the Department of State and the USTR. The USTR threatened to resort to the WTO at the beginning of the negotiations and again at a later stage, when the negotiations were moving slowly. Yet, DG Trade did not foresee any legal problems before a WTO panel and, consequently, did not itself become involved in the Safe Harbour negotiations (Interview 14-11-2000, DG Trade). As a result, the debate over the WTO/GATS compatibility of the Directive remained confined to the regular trade talks between European and US trade officials, without much impact on the Safe Harbour talks between DG Internal Market and the Department of Commerce.

European interest groups were not formally involved in the negotiations. Unlike the US Department of Commerce, the European Commission did not launch formal consultations. BEUC, the European consumers' organisation, asked to be informed about the proposals and to have the opportunity to comment on them. Initially, however, this request was not granted. Only after the Department of Commerce had published the first Safe Harbour draft on the Internet, was the European Commission more willing to give information and to discuss the Safe Harbour proposals with BEUC (Interview 5-9-2000, BEUC).

In 1998, almost at the same time as the Safe Harbour negotiations started, the Transatlantic Consumer Dialogue (TACD) was set up. The TACD consisted of US and EC consumer groups and the Safe Harbour issue was the first instance of co-operation between them (Interview 5-9-2000, BEUC). As a result, BEUC produced all its position papers together with US groups within the TACD.

European business groups did not have a formal input in the process either. Still, they were also interested in the Safe Harbour negotiations because they wanted to be able to transfer data to US firms. Their main interest was in creating a predictable framework for transferring data that would relieve European firms of liability for the way US firms would handle the information. In formulating their position, business groups worked closely together, and also with their US counterparts (Interview 23-11-2000, FEDMA). In informal debates with Commission officials they would normally support the US position and argue that the proposals were sufficient as they were (Interview 17-10-2000, DG Internal Market).

On the European side, the Article 29 Working Party played the most important role besides DG Internal Market, since it had to give an opinion on all proposals. These opinions were non-binding, which limited their impact, but the European Commission still found it important to obtain a positive opinion from the Working Party. The Working Party was consistently very critical about the proposals, but DG Internal Market viewed it as a welcome ally in the negotiations, giving more weight to demands for strengthening the proposals (Interview 17-10-2000, DG Internal Market).

The Article 31 Committee had to agree to any Safe Harbour agreement and therefore had an important role in the European decision-making process. The relationship between the member state representatives in the Article 29 Working Party and the Article 31 Committee varied between the member states, but the broad patterns of support were similar in both. To most Northern European member states, the idea of reaching an agreement based on a self-regulatory approach was quite acceptable, while most Southern European countries were more reluctant to endorse this approach. This was also reflected in the pattern of support for and opposition against the specific Safe Harbour drafts that were to follow (Interview 28-11-2000, Article 29 Working Party). It is difficult to say to what extent the member state positions in the Article 31 Committee were the direct result of the Article 29 Working Party's opinions, since the Article 31 Committee may also have used the Working Party's opinions to justify its own positions (Interview 17-10-2000, DG Internal Market).

6.4.4 The Safe Harbour negotiations

The first Safe Harbour draft

After a first round of discussions, the Department of Commerce presented its first official Safe Harbour proposal in November 1998 (DoC, 1998b). The proposal consisted of seven Safe Harbour principles, with which companies wanting to be in the Safe Harbour would have to comply. Six of these were substantive principles, which broadly reflected the principles covered by the OECD Guidelines and the EC Directive.

The principle of 'notice' stated that individuals should be informed about the information collected about them and the purposes for which it had been collected. The 'choice' principle provided for an opt-out for uses unrelated to the original use of the data and an opt-in for sensitive information. No further definition of 'sensitive data' was given, but medical information was mentioned as an example.

According to the 'onward transfer' principle, individuals should have a choice as to how third parties use information about them. In addition, the organisation transferring the data should require that the third party has at least the same level of data protection. Moreover, an opt-in for sensitive data was foreseen.

The 'security' principle contained the well-established rule that organisations should take 'reasonable precautions' to prevent loss, unauthorised use, and the like. In addition, it required reasonable measures to assure the reliability of the data. The 'data integrity' principle stated that personal information should be relevant to the purpose for which it was collected, as well as accurate, complete and current, 'to the extent necessary.'

Finally, the 'access' principle provided for 'reasonable' access for individuals to personal information about them with a view to correcting or amending it if it was inaccurate. 'Reasonableness' was defined in terms of the 'nature' and the 'sensitivity' of the data. For instance, access would have to be granted if the information was used in 'substantive decision-making' about the individual.

The scope of these six substantive principles was limited by a number of general exceptions. The principles would not apply to manual data. Nor would they cover 'proprietary' information, i.e. business information protected by law, such as information about the technologies used by a firm or relating to a firm's business operations or marketing strategies. Moreover, exceptions were made on the grounds of national security, risk management, information security, the public interest in general, regulatory compliance, law enforcement, and other legal obligations, but these terms were not defined any further.

In addition to these substantive provisions, the Safe Harbour proposal also contained a principle on enforcement. According to this enforcement principle, in order to qualify for the Safe Harbour, organisations should put in place mechanisms for assuring compliance, recourse for individuals, and consequences if an organisation did not comply with the substantive principles. In order to achieve that level of enforcement, organisations should at least have 'readily available, affordable and independent recourse mechanisms,' systems for verifying compliance, as well as remedies and sanctions in case of non-compliance.

In a note to the enforcement principle, it was explained that these requirements could be satisfied by taking part in a private sector self-regulatory programme with effective enforcement, compliance with US supervisory authorities, and co-operation with European data protection authorities. In the introduction to the principles, it was more generally stated that firms could qualify for the Safe Harbour if they complied with a self-regulatory code that satisfied the Safe Harbour principles, or if they fell under US laws and regulations that guaranteed the same level of protection.

In the debates that were to follow this first proposal, many interested groups and organisations referred to the OECD Guidelines as a point of reference. The Guidelines had been adopted by both the US and the EC and were widely recognised as an international standard in this field. However, the ambiguity of the Guidelines allowed considerable room for interpretation. As a result, they could be used to argue both that the Safe Harbour principles were too lax or that they were too stringent. Moreover, as we saw in section 6.1.2, the Guidelines did not elaborate on the implementation of the substantive principles and it was exactly this issue that would prove to be crucial during the negotiations.

In their reactions to the proposal, business groups supported the concept of the Safe Harbour proposal as a means of increasing predictability in transatlantic data flows. Still, some groups claimed that adherence to their self-regulatory codes should be sufficient to qualify for the Safe Harbour (e.g. DMA, 1998b), while others (notably in the financial sector) argued that privacy legislation in their sector was already adequate or would automatically qualify firms in their sector for the Safe Harbour (AIA, 1998; SIA, 1998).

At the same time, most business groups underlined their support for a self-regulatory and sectoral approach and were critical of specific principles in the proposal. Although all principles received critical comments by some groups, most attention focused on the access and onward transfer principles. The other principles were less controversial, with the security and data integrity principles being the least disputed.

The onward transfer principle was criticised for unduly restricting data flows between organisations. Some pointed out that the OECD Guidelines did not contain a similar provision (USCIB, 1998) and called for its deletion as an independent principle from the Safe Harbour proposal (DMA, 1998b; IIA, 1998). Others argued that the principle should be relaxed in order to accommodate data transfers between firms (e.g. ACB, 1998; CSI, 1998) and that the transferring firm should not be held liable for a violation of the data protection principles by the receiving firm (USCoC, 1998).

Another bone of contention was the access principle, which many business groups felt was too broad. Many groups requested that the principle be narrowed in order to limit the right of access, for several reasons. First, some firms were concerned that too broad an access principle would require the restructuring of information systems and invite wide-scale use by consumers, leading to high costs for the firms involved (e.g. DMA, 1998b; IIA, 1998; USCIB, 1998).

Second, many firms wanted to protect information that would reveal competitively valuable information, such as information about operating procedures, marketing strategies, information systems, and the like. They therefore argued for a specific exception for so-called 'proprietary information,' which would cover legally protected information (CSI, 1998; DMA, 1998b).

Finally, business groups composed of service and direct marketing firms wanted the Safe Harbour principles to stipulate that direct marketing activities (e.g. sending a catalogue) would not be considered a 'substantive decision' for the purpose of the access principle. This was important, since in the proposal the right of individual access was to be broadest for information used for substantive decision-making.

In these early stages, many points also required clarification, especially with regard to the implementation of the principles. Most business groups expressed support for the self-regulatory nature of the Safe Harbour principles, although some felt that the self-regulatory element was not strong enough (Interview 24-1-2001, DMA; see also e.g. IIA, 1998).

US public interest groups were less happy with the proposal. They argued that it fell short of both the EC Directive's adequacy requirement and the level of protection they envisaged for US legislation. In a letter sent on behalf of eleven consumer and privacy advocacy groups (Consumers Union, EPIC et al., 1998), the proposal was argued to be too weak to offer sufficient protection. In addition to numerous points of criticism aimed at the substantive principles, the groups deplored the absence of separate use limitation and purpose specification principles, which were contained in both the OECD Guidelines and the EC Directive (see also ACLU, 1998).

Moreover, the proposal was argued to offer insufficient means of enforcement. Both the eleven groups and the American Civil Liberties Union claimed that self-regulation had not proven to be a effective means of protecting data privacy. Consequently, both argued for the establishment of a privacy agency or at least some sort of governmental oversight.

On the European side, the most important consultations were with the Article 29 Working Party. In its opinion on the November 1998 proposal, it stated that 'the current patchwork of narrowly-focused sectoral laws and voluntary self-regulation [in the US, S.P.] cannot at present be relied upon to provide adequate protection in all cases' (Working Party, 1999a: 2). Agreeing in principle with the Safe Harbour approach, the Working Party also found the proposal to be inadequate.

As to the substantive principles, the Working Party criticised the absence of a purpose specification principle, the limitation of the access principle to 'reasonable access,' and the exclusion of proprietary and manually processed information. Furthermore, the general exceptions were deemed to be 'too vague and open-ended' (Working Party, 1999a: 3-4).

Notwithstanding these substantive points of criticism, the Working Party's main argument against the proposal related to its enforcement. It claimed that the protection offered was 'seriously weakened by the lack of a requirement for independent compliance monitoring.' Moreover, the Working Party argued that individuals would have to be able to rely on independent adjudication. Existing US agencies, such as the FTC, could play such a role (Working Party, 1999a: 3).

The second Safe Harbour draft

Since the Article 31 Committee did not approve the proposal either, DG Internal Market and the Department of Commerce continued their negotiations. In April 1999, a second version of the Safe Harbour principles was published (DoC, 1999a). In comparison to the first version, a number of important changes had been made, alongside a multitude of more minor adjustments.

The general exceptions for proprietary information, risk management, information security and regulatory compliance had been deleted. In addition, several changes had been made to the seven principles, reflecting concerns raised in the comments on the first draft. With regard to the comments discussed above, the April 1999 version contained a number of modifications. In the onward transfer principle, the opt-in for sensitive data had been deleted. The criteria for granting access to individuals were complemented by the expense and difficulty of access. The concept of 'sensitive data' was defined more thoroughly to include 'medical and health information, information revealing racial or ethnic origin, political opinions, religious or philosophical beliefs, trade union membership or information concerning the sex life of the individual' (DoC, 1999a: Choice Principle).

In order to clarify the meaning of the principles, the Department of Commerce had also added several 'Frequently Asked Questions' (FAQs), which explained how the principles would have to be applied. Initially, the precise status of the FAQs was not clear, but it was soon agreed that they would constitute an 'authoritative interpretation' of the principles and in that sense be a part of the agreement.

Although they were meant as interpretations of the principles, the FAQs sometimes went a bit further by introducing new elements. For instance, the FAQ on sensitive data introduced five (in later versions six) exceptions to the right of opt-in for sensitive data. The FAQ on access defined a number of exceptions to the access right. Instead of the general exception for proprietary information, the FAQ established an exception to the right of access for 'confidential commercial information,' which US law defined as 'information which an organization has taken steps to protect from disclosure, where disclosure would help a competitor in the market.' Furthermore, according to the FAQ, access could be denied if it was 'likely to' lead to any one of eight conditions, including 'breach of an express promise or an implied promise' and 'breach of a contractual obligation of confidentiality.'

In this draft of the principles and the FAQs, a number of points were highlighted that had not been resolved in the negotiations between Commerce and DG Internal Market. To start with, taking into account only the most important issues, the European Commission wanted to include manually processed data. It also required explicit choice and notice to be given if personal data were transferred to another organisation that did not adhere to the Safe Harbour principles. It objected to the limitation of individual access to 'reasonable access,' although it would consider other ways of providing that the access right was not absolute.

Moreover, it wanted to include a text in the FAQ on access that would indicate that marketing decisions could be substantive or involve sensitive information. Also, the exception for 'confidential commercial information' would have to be limited to 'trade secrets,' a narrower term in US law. Finally, it felt that the FAQ's denial of access if it was 'likely to' have certain consequences was too lax.

Most US business groups were generally happy with the changes made in the new proposals, although none approved of the proposal as it was and some were generally unhappy with it (e.g. ACB, 1999a). As to the access principles, it was generally felt that the changes made in the principle and the text of the FAQ addressed most of the US businesses' concerns. There was broad support for the inclusion of 'reasonable' in the access principle and the exclusion of confidential commercial information (see e.g. AIA, 1999a; CBA/US, ABA and FSR, 1999; CSI, 1999a; DMA, 1999a; NRF, 1999).

The onward transfer principle provoked more criticism. Some argued for a number of exemptions to be included in the documents (CBA/US, ABA and FSR, 1999; CSI, 1999a) or restated the wish to prevent the liability of the transferring organisation for the data protection practices of the receiving organisation (AIA, 1999a; CSI, 1999a).

The TACD continued to oppose the proposals, claiming in particular that the proposal did not provide effective enforcement, and that consumers would not be able to access the information held on them (TACD, 1999a). They were supported by the US trade union AFL-CIO, which strongly denounced the proposal (AFL-CIO, 1999).

The Article 29 Working Party was happy with some of the changes, such as the limitation to the exceptions and the definition of sensitive information. It restated some of its earlier criticism concerning the substantive principles and supported the European Commission's demands in the negotiations.

The Working Party's most serious concerns related to the enforcement, however, since 'data protection rules only contribute to the protection of individuals to the extent to which they are followed in practice' (Working Party, 1999b: 6). Consequently, it demanded the independent investigation of complaints, and a clarification of which body was going to determine the applicable sanctions and how. Moreover, it 'confirm[ed] its concern that self-certification may lead to abuses' (Working Party, 1999c: 6). As a result, the Article 29 Working Party did not consider the April 1999 proposal to be adequate, a position it restated in a message to the Article 31 Committee, which was to meet on 14 July 1999 (Working Party, 1999d).

The third Safe Harbour draft

Given the unresolved issues on both sides, it was not possible to finalise the Safe Harbour agreement before the US-EU summit in June 1999. In a declaration, the two sides stated that 'work on the substantive aspects of data protection [was] particularly well advanced' but 'on the procedural and enforcement aspects (...) further work [was] needed' (EU & US, 1999).

Over the summer of 1999, some important changes were made to the enforcement of the agreement. Before that time, US officials had assumed that enforcement would take place in Europe by European data protection authorities. These authorities themselves did not agree to this approach, however. They argued that the agreement would have to be enforced by US agencies, since the European agencies had no authority to enforce standards in the US and it would have been rather expensive for them to monitor the behaviour of firms in the US (Interview 28-11-2000, Article 29 Working Party). In the summer of 1999, the Article 31 Committee voiced its discontent concerning the current arrangement of the enforcement system and demanded a different approach (Interview 23-1-2001, Commerce).

As a result, the role of the FTC in the enforcement of the agreement was strengthened. In the third public draft Safe Harbour documents, published in November 1999 (DoC, 1999b), it was now explicitly stated that if an organisation relied on self-regulation, 'its failure to comply with such self-regulation must also be actionable under Section 5 of the Federal Trade Commission Act prohibiting unfair and deceptive acts or another law or regulation prohibiting such acts.'

Furthermore, the FTC's policy in dealing with complaints under the Safe Harbour agreement was addressed in a new FAQ, on dispute resolution and enforcement. This FAQ explained the various ways of complying with the Safe Harbour agreement. Individuals should have recourse to independent dispute resolution bodies after having raised the issue with the organisation itself. Moreover, it stated that 'the FTC has committed to reviewing on a priority basis referrals received from privacy self regulatory organizations, such as BBBOnline and TRUSTe, and EU member countries alleging non-compliance with the safe harbor principles to determine whether Section 5 of the FTC Act prohibiting unfair or deceptive acts or practices in commerce has been violated.'

In another new FAQ, on co-operation with European data protection authorities, US firms were given the option of enforcing their Safe Harbour commitments by undertaking to co-operate with European data protection authorities in the investigation and resolution of complaints, and to comply with any advice given by those authorities.

Several of the outstanding substantive issues had been resolved as well, some in favour of the Department of Commerce, others in favour of the European Commission. US firms could now choose whether or not to apply the principles to manually processed data, but they would have to do so in order to transfer them from the EC.

The onward transfer principle explicitly provided that if a US firm had made sure the level of protection in the third party firm was adequate, it would 'not be held responsible when a third party to which it transfers such information processes it in a way contrary to any restriction or representations.' Moreover, no explicit notice and choice were required for data transfers to organisations that did not adhere to the Safe Harbour principles.

The word 'reasonable' had been deleted in the access principle, but the right was limited insofar as 'the burden or expense of providing access would be disproportionate to the risks to the individual's privacy (...) or where the rights of persons other than the individual would be violated.' Marketing decisions had not been included as 'substantive decisions' in the FAQ on access, but the definition of exceptions in terms of access being 'likely to' cause certain effects had been abandoned. At the same time, two new employment-related exceptions had been inserted.

In their comments on the November 1999 draft, several business groups expressed their support for the changes made to the onward transfer and access principles (DMA, 1999b; ITI, 1999), although some insisted that the access principle would be too expensive for firms to implement or were not happy with the deletion of the word 'reasonable' (ACB, 1999b; AIA, 1999b). Nevertheless, several business groups maintained their earlier points of criticism as regards certain aspects of the principles and the FAQs. In general, however, the main issues for US industries seemed to have been addressed and attention shifted to relatively minor points and the transition period allowed for implementing the agreement.

Consumer and privacy advocacy groups continued to oppose the agreement in its entirety. The TACD pointed specifically to the limitations on individual access rights and the weakness of the enforcement mechanism (TACD, 1999d). Moreover, they deplored the fact that the agreement's safeguards would not extend to US citizens. One other group even claimed that US citizens would 'receive second class privacy treatment' (CDT, 1999).

The Article 29 Working Party also found that the November 1999 draft 'remain[ed] unsatisfactory' (Working Party, 1999e: 13). According to the Working Party, the exceptions allowed in general and in the FAQ on access were too broad. It was also concerned about the change in the onward transfer principle that would relieve transferring organisations from responsibility for the way receiving organisations used personal information. Moreover, it felt that the notice and choice principles were too ambiguous. In addition, the Working Party remained unsatisfied with the enforcement mechanism, which it argued was too weak and too much oriented towards e-commerce.

Finalising the agreement

In the months after the November 1999 draft, the Department of Commerce and DG Internal Market worked toward what was to become the final agreement. One of the most contentious remaining issues was the status of the US financial sector. The Department of Commerce had already requested that data protection in the financial sector be recognised as adequate by the European Commission. That request was strengthened by the enactment of the Gramm-Leach-Bliley Act in November 1999. Despite this new layer of data protection legislation, the European Commission and the Article 29 Working Party still considered the protection offered in the US financial sector to be inadequate and in the negotiations the Department of Commerce and DG Internal Market were not able to reach an agreement on this issue.

Moreover, the enforcement of the Safe Harbour agreement in the financial sector was deemed insufficient by DG Internal Market. It had already been agreed that the FTC would constitute an acceptable enforcement agency for the purposes of the Safe Harbour agreement, but the financial sector was largely excluded from its remit. Other, sectoral agencies could be recognised as being acceptable as well, but according to the European Commission, the role of the sectoral financial regulators in the field of data protection was too unclear to extend the Safe Harbour to the financial sector.

In the end, it was decided to exclude the financial sector from the scope of the Safe Harbour altogether and to review its status with a view to its inclusion in the agreement by the end of 2001. Until then, the sector would have to rely on the Directive's exceptions, in particular consent by the individual. Apart from the FTC, only the Department of Transport was recognised as an enforcement agency under the Safe Harbour agreement, which opened the opportunity for airlines and other transportation firms to subscribe to the Safe Harbour.

Together with some changes in the principles and the FAQs themselves, this paved the way for a new proposal in March 2000 (DoC, 2000a). The texts of most principles and FAQs had been settled by this time. Apart from a number of minor and textual changes, some important changes were made, mainly to address the Working Party's concerns.

Thus, in the onward transfer principle, the clause waiving the responsibility of US firms for the handling of personal information by third party firms was complemented by two exceptions: the transferring organisation could be held responsible if it had so agreed, or if it 'knew or should have known the third party would process it in such a contrary way and the organization has not taken reasonable steps to prevent or stop such processing.' The access principle remained unchanged, but the exceptions in the FAQ were rewritten. Furthermore, the exceptions for promises and contracts were deleted.

The reactions of US business groups to the March 2000 draft did not reveal any new positions. In general, the groups repeated some of the comments they had given earlier. Groups from the financial sector insisted that the Gramm-Leach-Bliley Act, together with older legislation in this sector, should lead to a finding of adequacy, but they also seemed to accept that the financial sector had been placed outside the agreement for the time being (explicitly so: CSI, 2000).

The TACD saw 'some movement forward' and in respect to access, notice and consent even 'substantial improvement' (TACD, 2000b). Nevertheless, it argued for 'a stronger framework with a clear enforcement mechanism.' The TACD's gravest concerns related to the handling of individual complaints under the agreement, which it felt did not offer enough safeguards to aggrieved individuals.

Work on the details of the agreement continued in the following months. In May 2000, the Article 29 Working Party gave its opinion on the proposals as they then were. It noted that 'the latest amendments to the principles and the related documents incorporate several suggestions made by the Working Party in its previous Opinions' (Working Party, 2000: 2). Despite these amendments, the Working Party did not accept the proposal as it was. It still had problems with the access, choice and onward transfer principles, which it found to be too lax. The enforcement mechanisms were also subjected to criticism, in particular with regard to the jurisdiction of the FTC, and the relation between the FTC and the dispute resolution bodies foreseen in the FAQ on dispute resolution and enforcement.

Notwithstanding the critical notes from both the Article 29 Working Party and the FTC, the blocking minority in the Article 31 Committee started to break down. Until then, a group of countries had consistently refused to accept the Safe Harbour proposals, but it was now felt that the EC had obtained just about the most that it could from the US (Interview 17-10-2000, DG Internal Market). After the blocking minority had been dissolved, all member states fell into line and the Safe Harbour proposal, as it then was, was adopted unanimously.

The European Parliament adopted a critical report and did not yet endorse the proposal (EP, 2000), but it could not block the agreement's adoption. The Department of Commerce published the final version of the Safe Harbour agreement and the FAQs on 21 July 2000 (DoC, 2000b). Only some minor changes had been made to the March 2000 text. The European Commission adopted the adequacy decision on this final package a few days later (EC, 2000e).

6.5 The European Directive and Canada

6.5.1 The initial situation in Canada

Until the mid-1990s, the legal framework for data protection in Canada was largely similar to that in the United States, in that there was comprehensive legislation in the public sector and only specific legislation in the private sector, complemented by self-regulation. At the same time, however, the Canadian situation differed from the American in a number of important ways.

As for the similarities, the legal safeguards for data protection in Canada's public sector largely paralleled those in the US. Thus, the Canadian Supreme Court had established a number of data protection rights based on provisions of the Canadian Charter of Human Rights and Freedoms. Although the Charter did not contain an explicit right to privacy, a number of other rights had been relied upon to provide protection against intrusions of privacy. This protection suffered from the same limitations as that in the US, however, being limited to state actions, and only setting negative limits on what governments could do (Harris, 1997).

In addition, in 1982, Canada had enacted the Privacy Act, which supplanted provisions that had been in place since 1977 (Flaherty, 1989: 243). The Privacy Act covered only the federal public sector, but it contained a broad range of substantive data protection principles, such as limitations on the collection and retention of personal information, data quality requirements, individual rights of access, and limitations on the use and disclosure of data (Flaherty, 1989: 253-256).

In the private sector, no comprehensive legislation was in place. Besides some common law protection of privacy, only a few industries (such as the credit and telecommunications industries) were subject to data protection laws. As a general policy, the Canadian government had primarily stimulated the adoption of self-regulatory codes, after the model of the OECD Guidelines, which Canada had ratified in 1984. Several such codes had been developed during the 1980s and early 1990s, but the effective protection they offered differed (Bennett, 1996: 480-481).

This situation was paralleled in the provinces, most of which had adopted data protection laws in the public sector, but not in the private sector. As a result, the Canadian data protection policies of the 1980s and early 1990s were to a great extent comparable to the US approach of comprehensive legislation in the public sector and a sectoral, largely self-regulatory approach in the private sector.

Yet, as was noted above, the Canadian situation of the mid-1990s also differed from that in the US in a number of ways, three of which are important to this study. To begin with, Canada had established the office of the Privacy Commissioner of Canada, who was charged with the responsibility of overseeing the Privacy Act. The Privacy Commissioner's tasks and powers were similar to those of European data protection authorities: it heard and investigated complaints under the Privacy Act, and closely monitored the state of and developments in Canadian data protection practices (Flaherty, 1989: 247).

This difference with the US was important for two reasons. First, it led to a higher level of data protection, since the Canadian Privacy Act was enforced more pro-actively. As was described above, the US had chosen to allocate the overseeing of its Privacy Act to the Office of Management and Budget, which acted in an almost purely administrative capacity. In Canada, these administrative tasks had been given to the Treasury Board (Flaherty, 1989: 248-249). In addition, the Privacy Commissioner had been established to deal exclusively with the protection of individual privacy. As a consequence, it was actively involved in investigating claims, supporting the claims of aggrieved individuals and trying to mediate between them and government organisations.

Second, it made a significant political difference, since the Privacy Commissioner amounted to an institutionalised advocate of data protection policies within the Canadian federal government. In its annual reports, the Commissioner not only described its own activities, but also gave its opinion on legislative and other actions to be taken. In so doing, the Commissioner consistently pushed for more stringent legislation, also in the private sector.

A further important difference with the US occurred in 1993, when the province of Quebec adopted a comprehensive data protection law, covering both the public and private sectors. Even though this law did not cover federally regulated industries, such as banks, telecommunications and transportation (Bennett, 1996: 483), its scope was broader than that of any other law in Canada (or North America, for that matter). Moreover, a number of firms in federally regulated industries that were working in Quebec promised to comply voluntarily with the law (Interview 13-2-2001, Industry Canada). Quebec's privacy commissioner (the 'Commission d'Accès à l'Information;' see Comeau & Ouimet, 1995: 665-667) was given the authority to oversee data protection in all sectors under the scope of the law.

Quebec's privacy law created a divergence among the Canadian provinces that in itself gave rise to calls for harmonisation. This was reinforced by a provision in the law that opened the possibility of restricting data transfers to other jurisdictions (Bennett, 1996: 482). The law also helped privacy advocates, in that it increased the acceptability of a legislative approach among Canadian policy-makers (Interview 12-2-2001, PIAC).

The final important difference with the US was formed by the Canadian Standards Association's (CSA) Model Code for the Protection of Privacy. In 1990, CSA had brought together a number of groups to discuss the desirability and feasibility of a model privacy code that could serve as a standard for firms. In the first half of the 1990s, CSA developed such a model code, in co-operation with government and business and consumer groups. Consensus on a model code was finally reached in September 1995, and the code was adopted as a national standard in March 1996 (CSA, 1996; henceforth 'the model code;' see also Bennett, 1996: 486).

One of the most difficult issues in the process had been the consent principle: the familiar controversy over opt-ins and opt-outs, as well as the forms in which consent could be given. However, and in contrast to the debate in the US, access was much less of an issue in the CSA process (Interviews 12-2-2001, PIAC; 7-3-2001, CMA).

The model code had been closely modelled on the OECD Guidelines and contained ten principles with which a firm would have to comply. These principles included the familiar internationally agreed-upon data protection principles. Thus, they provided for purpose specification (Principle 2 CSA Model Code) and the limitation of data collection (Principle 4), and use, disclosure and retention (Principle 5) in the light of that purpose. Also, personal information had to be as accurate, complete and up-to-date as necessary (Principle 6) and security safeguards had to be in place (Principle 7).

The organisation holding personal information was held accountable for that information and had to designate privacy officers to oversee the implementation of the model code (Principle 1). Individuals had to be able to file complaints with the privacy officers (Principle 10). As part of the accountability principle, firms were also held responsible for the handling of information they had transferred to third parties and they were encouraged to 'use contractual or other means to provide a comparable level of protection while the information is being processed by a third party' (Point 4.1.3 CSA Model Code).

Furthermore, the model code contained a right of individual access (Principle 9), including the right to have data amended if they are inaccurate or incomplete (Point 4.9.5 CSA Model Code). Consent was required for the use or disclosure of information, with some exceptions (Principle 3). As part of the consent principle, consumers were given a right to an opt-out for the transfer of information to other organisations (for instance for direct marketing purposes; Point 4.3.7(b) CSA Model Code). The concept of 'sensitive data' was also defined in the context of the consent principle. It was decided not to establish fixed categories of sensitive data, although it was stated that 'some information (for example, medical records and income records) is almost always considered to be sensitive' (Point 4.3.4 CSA Model Code).

CSA's model code was important in that it established a standards approach to data protection, which was later endorsed by the International Organization for Standardization (ISO) and applauded by the EC's Article 29 Working Party (Working Party, 1997). Even more significantly, in the context of Canada's domestic politics, the principles enshrined in the model code represented a consensus among business and consumer groups, which could (and would) form the basis for future legislation in this area. The model code was less important as a standard, however. Although it was used as the basis for voluntary codes by trade associations, only one firm registered with the CSA for compliance with the CSA model code itself (Interview 12-2-2001, PIAC).

Therefore, the Canadian political context of the mid-1990s was relatively favourable for the adoption of more stringent data protection legislation. The Privacy Commissioner of Canada was an institutionalised privacy advocate that consistently pushed for more stringent legislation and this had led to the acceptance of an independent data protection authority. Quebec's legislation had set a precedent for other provinces and the federation, and formed a potential barrier to interprovincial data flows as well as a cause of competitiveness concerns among more stringently regulated firms. Finally, CSA's model code for privacy protection could serve as a model for legislation which was supported by business and consumer groups alike.

6.5.2 Reactions to the European Directive and further developments

The move toward comprehensive data protection legislation

The development of Canadian data protection legislation after 1995 is closely linked to the rise of the Internet and e-commerce. In 1994, Industry Canada had established the Information Highway Advisory Council (IHAC), which mainly consisted of representatives from industry. The IHAC was set up in order to study fifteen issues that had been identified in an Industry Canada discussion paper. One of these issues was the protection of personal information, which was further elaborated upon in a joint Industry Canada/IHAC discussion paper published in October 1994 (Industry Canada & IHAC, 1994). This paper outlined a number of issues and options with regard to privacy protection.

About a year later, in September 1995, the IHAC published its report on the development of the information highway. In it, the Council recommended that the federal government adopt legislation to protect personal information, both on-line and off-line (IHAC, 1995: Rec. 10.1 and 10.2). It argued that this was necessary to create sufficient consumer confidence in the new commercial opportunities offered by the Internet.

Around that same time the European Directive gained the attention of Canadian privacy specialists. In the mid-1990s, officials from Industry Canada started to warn about the possible trade effects of the Directive and to urge for domestic legislation to remedy the situation. As a result, the European Directive became an important element in the Canadian government's thinking about data protection legislation (Interviews 12-2-2001, PIAC; 13-2-2001, Industry Canada).

This was also acknowledged by contemporary observers of the process. In a 1996 article, Bennett (1996: 484) claimed that Quebec's legislation 'was drafted with the EU language in mind' and that 'the impact of the EU Data Protection Directive on Canada has been a constant underlying theme within the recent debates'. In an article published in 1997, Bennett and Raab (1997: 259) stated that 'concern about the EU Data Protection Directive [was] manifested in the Canadian policy debate from the moment it arrived on the agenda in 1990.'

Until IHAC's September 1995 recommendation, Canadian business groups had all favoured self-regulatory solutions rather than legislation. Only one month later, however, the Canadian Direct Marketing Association (CDMA) was the first business group openly to declare its support for a legislative approach to data protection, based on the model code that had just been agreed upon within the CSA (Privacy Commissioner of Canada, 1995b; CDMA, 1998). The CDMA (later the Canadian Marketing Association, CMA) had several reasons for supporting legislation (Interview 7-3-2001, CMA). First, it sensed the Canadian government was working toward legislation and wanted to make sure it would be based on the CSA model code, since there was broad consensus surrounding the code and it provided considerable flexibility to firms. Second, the CDMA was afraid that future legislative initiatives would be driven by incidents or privacy scares and thought that the relatively quiet environment of the mid-1990s was a good one for developing legislation.

In May 1996, Industry Canada published an action plan for developing the information highway, in which it endorsed the adoption of a legal framework for privacy protection in order to create consumer confidence in electronic commerce. It stated that 'the ministers of Industry and Justice (...) will bring forward proposals for a legislative framework governing the protection of personal data in the private sector' (Industry Canada, 1996: 25). In September of that year, the Minister of Justice announced that Canada would have federal privacy legislation in the private sector by the year 2000 (Bennett & Raab, 1997: 258).

The Privacy Commissioner had been calling for comprehensive legislation before this (e.g. in its 1993-1994 and 1994-1995 annual reports; see Privacy Commissioner of Canada, 1994; 1995a). The EC data protection Directive provided an additional argument for this call. Hence, before an October 1996 Parliament committee hearing on pending privacy legislation in the financial sector, the Commissioner now also referred to the EC data protection Directive and the consequences it could have for Canadian firms (Privacy Commissioner of Canada, 1996).

The same argument also surfaced in an Industry Canada and Justice Canada discussion paper, published in 1998. After having restated older arguments for legislation, it stated that 'the ability to provide effective protection for personal information (...) may affect the exchange of data with European Union member states' since 'the Directive has the potential to make the protection of personal information a major non-tariff trade barrier with Canada.' Without legislation, so the paper continued, Canadian firms would have to rely on contractual solutions, which 'will be fraught with uncertainty and could become lengthy and expensive.' In conclusion, it was proposed to adopt 'light, flexible and effective legislation' to address this and other deficiencies of the existing legal framework (Industry Canada & Justice Canada, 1998a: 7-8).

In their comments on the paper, business and public interest groups expressed support for legislation on the basis of the CSA model code. In addition, there was broad support for the Privacy Commissioner of Canada as the overseeing agency. At the same time, the groups differed considerably on the specifics of the legislation, for instance relating to exemptions, disclosure without consent, the enforcement powers of the Commissioner, and, more generally, the need to specify the CSA standards (Industry Canada & Justice Canada, 1998b).

The Personal Information Protection and Electronic Documents Act

In September 1998, Industry Canada, supported by the Department of Justice Canada, launched the Canadian Electronic Commerce Strategy, which was meant to develop the use of the Internet in Canada (Industry Canada, 1998). Part of this Initiative was Bill C-54 (Government of Canada, 1998; henceforth 'Bill C-54'). Bill C-54 foresaw comprehensive data protection legislation on the basis of the CSA's model code. In fact, the model code had been integrated into the law as Schedule 1, and Section 5(1) of the proposed law required compliance with this schedule.

The law itself provided for some specifications concerning the model code's principles and laid down a number of specific exceptions. For instance, Sections 8 and 9 of Bill C-54 formulated precise rules for access and the refusal of access. The allowable reasons for refusal would include 'confidential commercial information' and 'prohibitive costs' (Section 9(3) Bill C-54).

Although the proposed law was developed in the context of Canada's Internet strategy, it applied to on-line, off-line and manual data processing alike. Initially, the law would cover only federally regulated industries, such as banks, telecommunications and interprovincial transportation (for the precise limits, see Section 2(1) Bill C-54), but three years after it had entered into force, the law would also cover provincially regulated industries (Section 30(2) Bill C-54). The main limitation on the law's scope concerned the exclusion of non-profit organisations, as it was limited to 'commercial activities' (Section 4(1) Bill C-54).

The Privacy Commissioner's authority would be extended to the new law and would thus cover the private sector as well. The law would give the Commissioner the right to initiate complaints (Section 11(2) Bill C-54). The Commissioner would have wide powers to investigate complaints (Section 12(1)) and would have the express authority to attempt to resolve such complaints (Section 12(2)). If the resolution attempt failed, the Commissioner would have the authority to file a complaint with the Federal Court on the aggrieved individual's behalf (Section 15). The Court could order an organisation 'to correct its practices' and award damages, which would be limited to CAN$ 20,000 (Section 16). In addition, the Privacy Commissioner would have the right to initiate audits of an organisation's data protection practices if it had reason to believe that the organisation had violated the law and it would have wide powers of investigation for that purpose (Section 18).

The most controversial issue in the subsequent debate over Bill C-54 related to the constitutional question of federal and provincial authority over data protection policies. Eventually, the proposed federal law would cover all sectors of the economy, including provincially regulated industries, although provincially regulated industries could be exempted if a province had adopted 'substantially similar' legislation (Section 27(2)(d) Bill C-54).

The federal government based its proposal on Section 91(2) of the Canadian Constitution, which gave the federal parliament authority over 'the regulation of trade and commerce,' arguing that data flows were almost always inter-provincial, in particular after the emergence of the Internet. The provinces, however, could point to Section 92(13), which gave them the authority over 'property and civil rights in the province,' which would arguably also cover data protection. In an October 1998 Federal-Provincial-Territorial meeting, the provincial justice ministers therefore 'expressed their strong concerns (...) about a significant intrusion into provincial and territorial jurisdiction' by the proposed law and 'requested the Federal government withdraw the Bill' (CICS, 1998)

The constitutional issue gained a specific edge because the province of Quebec was the only one to have adopted data protection legislation. The constitutional position of the province of Quebec had for a long time been a highly contentious and divisive issue in Canadian politics, and Quebec's government saw the proposed federal law as another incursion into its authority, even though the federal Minister of Industry had indicated that Quebec's law would qualify for the exemption foreseen by Section 27(2)(d) of the Bill (Government of Quebec, 1999b).

Furthermore, although the two were broadly similar in terms of underlying principles, Quebec's law differed from the federal proposal on a number of specific points (MRCI, 1999: 3-4). Therefore, the Quebec government argued that the federal law would subject some firms to a double and sometimes contradictory legal regime. This would be so even if Quebec's own data protection law was deemed to be essentially similar, since such an exemption would only apply to intra-provincial data flows (see also Government of Quebec, 1999a: 4).

Consequently, Quebec vehemently opposed the proposed law. In the federal parliament this position was reflected by the Bloc Québecois, a party that supported greater autonomy for Quebec within Canada. The proposal enjoyed broad support among the other parties, including the governing Liberal Party.

The idea of a legislative approach had been accepted by most business groups by now. The only exception was formed by some groups in the medical sector. Canadian pharmacists argued that medical information used for therapeutic purposes should fall outside the scope of the law. It feared the data protection provisions in Bill C-54 would stifle the development of on-line information systems and the delivery of health care (CPhA, 1999). This position was also taken by the Ontario Ministry of Health in a submission to the federal parliament (cf. Doray, 1999). At the same time, the Canadian Medical Association (CMA, which I will refer to as CMA/Medical to distinguish it from the Canadian Marketing Association, or CMA/Marketing), argued for more stringent protection for health information, in order to ensure the trust of patients in their physicians (CMA/Medical, 1999a; 1999b).

Other business groups had more specific concerns. The Canadian Bankers Association (CBA; I will refer to it as 'CBA/Canada' to distinguish it from the (US) Consumer Bankers Association) prepared a detailed critique of the bill's provisions. Besides a number of substantive issues (like a call for broader exceptions to the right of individual access and the consent principle), the CBA/Canada's main points of criticism related to the possibilities for banks to combat fraud and the enforcement powers given to the Privacy Commissioner, which CBA/Canada claimed to be 'excessive and unnecessary' (CBA/Canada, 1999a; 1999b). As a result, so it argued, 'the Bill [was] far from the "light and flexible" regulation espoused by Industry Canada in its earlier discussions about the direction of the framework privacy legislation.'

Public interest groups argued for more stringent data protection provisions on a number of points (see e.g. PIAC, 1998). On a number of occasions, they joined forces to oppose calls for a relaxation of the legislation by the insurance industry (PIAC et al., 1999a) and calls for an exemption of personal health information (PIAC et al., 1999b). In October 1999, PIAC, one of the leading public interest groups in the process, and the Canadian Marketing Association issued a joint declaration in which they called for the adoption of Bill C-54 (CMA/Marketing, 1999; PIAC, 1999).

That same month, the bill was reintroduced as Bill C-6, but under the same name (Industry Canada, 1999). Things proceeded quickly from here. The bill was adopted as the 'Personal Information Protection and Electronic Documents Act' (henceforth 'PIPEDA') and received royal assent on 13 April 2000 (Canada, 2000). Medical information had not been exempted from its scope, but the application of its privacy provisions to personal medical information was postponed until one year after the date at which the law was to come into effect (1 January 2001). The provisions dealing with provincially regulated industries and the exemptions for substantially similar provincial legislation (now Section 26(2)(b) PIPEDA) remained unchanged, and the same was true for the Privacy Commissioner's enforcement powers.

Compared to the original Bill C-54, the law had been strengthened on a number of points, most of which had been urged by privacy advocacy groups during the process. For instance, the law was given primacy over other federal laws (Section 4(3) PIPEDA). It now contained a principle that limited the allowable purposes of data collection, use and disclosure to 'purposes a reasonable person would consider are appropriate in the circumstances' (Section 5(3) PIPEDA). The exception to the access principle because of 'prohibitive costs' had been deleted, and the limit had been removed from the amount of punitive damages to be awarded by the courts. In addition, the law contained protection for whistle-blowers (Sections 27 and 27.1 PIPEDA).

Other amendments had somewhat broadened the exceptions to the law's data protection principles. Most notably, the PIPEDA opened the possibility of collecting, using and disclosing 'publicly available' information without the data subject's consent (Sections 7(1)(d), 7(2)(c.1) and 7(3)(h.1) PIPEDA).

The talks on an adequacy finding

With the adoption of the PIPEDA, Canada had established 'European-style' data protection legislation. Above, it was noted that the European data protection Directive (and indeed the European approach in this field from the 1970s) is characterised by two features: its comprehensiveness in terms of scope and substantive principles, and the enforcement by an independent overseeing agency.

The Canadian legislation exemplifies both features. Both the private and public sectors are now covered by similar data protection laws, the PIPEDA covering private firms as well as governmental organisations that fall outside the scope of the Privacy Act (cf. Section 4(2) PIPEDA). The PIPEDA relies heavily on the CSA's model code. As was noted above, the CSA's model code contains all internationally agreed upon data protection principles, and the PIPEDA itself adds some guarantees to these.

Apart from the comprehensive scope of its legislation, Canada has also established an independent overseeing agency for both the public and private sectors. The Privacy Commissioner of Canada's authority under the Privacy Act has been extended to the PIPEDA. As a result, the private sector is also subject to independent oversight.

Already in the December 1996 Joint Canada-EU Action Plan, the EC and Canada had agreed to 'address data protection and privacy issues with a view to facilitating data flows between Canada and the EU, while guaranteeing the rights of individuals' (Canada & EU, 1996: Section I, point 2(n), last indent). All along the legislative process, officials from Industry Canada remained in contact with officials from DG Internal Market to discuss the adequacy of the proposed Canadian laws under the European Directive. These discussions became gradually more specific as the Canadian process proceeded (Interview 13-2-2001, Industry Canada). In May 2000, after the PIPEDA had been adopted, the talks became more formal. In general, the Canadian law was considered to be adequate, but some specific issues remained (Interviews 17-10-2000, DG Internal Market; 28-11-2000, Article 29 Working Party; 13-2-2001, Industry Canada).

These issues were reflected in the opinion adopted by the Article 29 Working Party in January 2001 (Working Party, 2001). In general, the Working Party was positive concerning the Canadian legislation, but it raised a number of specific points. First, the PIPEDA would only apply to provincially regulated industries in 2004, and the criteria and procedure for determining substantial similarity between provincial laws and the PIPEDA were still unclear (Working Party, 2001: 5-6). Second, the Working Party stressed the importance of 'contractual and binding provisions able to provide a comparable level of protection' for onward transfers to third parties (Working Party, 2001: 6). Under the PIPEDA, such model contracts would be drawn up by the Privacy Commissioner of Canada (Section 23(2)(c) PIPEDA). Third, the Working Party found the definition of sensitive data, which had been adopted straight from the CSA Code, to be unclear (Working Party, 2001: 3-4). These were all issues that could be dealt with within the framework of the PIPEDA, however, and the European Commission adopted its adequacy finding in December 2001 (EC, 2001b).

6.6 Conclusions

Table 6.1 provides an overview of the main events in the data protection process. The analysis of these events in the previous sections provides the basis for answering two questions: did a California effect occur, and what factors contributed to that outcome?

	In the EC	In the US	In Canada	At the international level
1974		Adoption of the Privacy Act		
1980				Adoption of the OECD Guidelines
1982			Adoption of the Privacy Act and creation of the Privacy Commissioner	
1990	First proposal for a data protection Directive			
1990			Start of the CSA process	
1993			Quebec adopts comprehensive data protection legislation	
First half and mid-1990s	Emergence of the Internet and e-commerce; Regulatory initiatives in the EC, the US, and Canada; Rise in interest in data protection issues			
September 1995			Agreement is reached on the CSA standard; IHAC calls for data protection legislation and is followed by the CDMA	
October 1995	Adoption of Directive 95/46			
September 1996			Announcement of comprehensive federal legislation	
Autumn 1997	Start of talks on an agreement			
November 1998	First Safe Harbour draft			
September 1998			Introduction of Bill C-54	
April 2000			Adoption of the PIPEDA	
May 2000		The FTC calls for an online data protection law with an independent enforcement agency		
July 2000	Adoption of the Safe Harbour Agreement			

Table 6.1: Main events in the data protection process

6.6.1 A California effect or not?

As in the other case study chapters, I will now discuss whether a California effect has taken place, that is to what extent data protection standards in the US and Canada have been strengthened, and to what extent this can be attributed to the European data protection Directive. In the next subsection, I will then turn to the explanation of these outcomes.

To summarise the developments outlined above, the situation in the US and Canada before the European Directive was highly similar in terms of the legal protection in place for personal data, but differed with regard to its implementation. Both countries had limited constitutional and common law protection for personal information. When it came to legislative protection, both had fairly comprehensive data protection legislation in the public sector, whereas personal data in the private sector were protected by a variety of specific, sectoral laws and self-regulation.

The enforcement mechanisms differed, however, as Canada had established a federal Privacy Commissioner to oversee its public sector data protection legislation, while the US did not have such an institution and relied primarily on private litigation in court. In the private sector, the US Federal Trade Commission had some powers to enforce self-regulatory codes, but neither country had a specialised data protection agency.

This situation contrasted with the European approach, reflected in the EC Directive, which emphasised comprehensive legislation (for both the public and private sectors) and oversight by an independent, specialised data protection agency. The US therefore fell short of the EC Directive's criteria in two ways (scope of legislation and enforcement), while Canada fell short in terms of the scope of its legislation and enforcement in the private sector.

In the US, this situation did not change much, although some new sectoral data protection legislation was adopted in the second half of the 1990s. In addition, the FTC adopted a more active stance on the enforcement of self-regulatory codes, in particular on the Internet.

To avoid a disruption of trade flows under the EC Directive, the US engaged in negotiations in order to arrive at a so-called Safe Harbour agreement of voluntary standards which US firms could adhere to. In the course of the negotiations, the proposals were gradually strengthened and clarified on the issue of enforcement, while the substantive principles were sometimes strengthened and sometimes weakened.

Can the Safe Harbour agreement be said to constitute a strengthening of US data protection? To start with, any assessment of the agreement's immediate effects is made more difficult by its voluntary character. No firm is automatically bound by the agreement and its immediate effects will therefore very much depend on the number of firms that choose to comply with the Safe Harbour principles. Given the remaining uncertainties, some firms (both in the US and Europe) may still choose to use contract clauses rather than to work under the Safe Harbour agreement (Interview 23-11-2000, FEDMA).

Having said this, the Safe Harbour agreement may constitute a strengthening in a number of ways. First, the agreement is not limited to specific sectors. The financial sector has been excluded from the agreement's scope, but its position will be re-evaluated within a few years. As a result, the Safe Harbour agreement forms a broad, cross-sectoral set of data protection principles, whereas the US has until now only known sectoral codes. This in itself can be regarded as a strengthening.

Second, the principles themselves may at some points be more stringent than existing legislation and self-regulatory codes in the US. For instance, the debate over the exceptions to the right of individual access has led to a text that may well exceed existing data protection standards in some sectors.

Third, the FTC will play an active role in monitoring the Safe Harbour principles. It has promised to give priority to complaints under the Safe Harbour agreement, which may lead to a stricter enforcement of the agreement than of domestic self-regulatory codes. In addition, the European Commission and European data protection authorities are likely to evaluate the agreement's effectiveness and to act upon complaints as they arise, which may also contribute to the stricter enforcement of the principles. The same is true for US privacy advocates that can use the principles as a new legalthere is some indication that the FAQ on access has been cited as a model in US legislative debates (Interview 23-1-2001, Commerce).

Third, the FTC's role as a governmental advocate of data protection legislation may be strengthened by its new role in the enforcement of the Safe Harbour principles. In conjunction with the more active role it has assumed in the protection of personal information on the Internet, this may lead to a consistent voice for more stringent legislation within the US government.

The Safe Harbour agreement may therefore have a number of direct and indirect effects on the protection of personal information in the US, although most are still hypothetical at the moment. Insofar as US data protection standards are going to be strengthened by the Safe Harbour agreements, the strengthening is a direct effect of the EC data protection Directive, since the Safe Harbour negotiations were a direct response to the Directive and the threat it posed to EC-US data flows.

In Canada, data protection legislation has changed more radically since the mid-1990s. In April 2000, a comprehensive data protection law was adopted that will apply to the private sector. In combination with the existing data protection law in the public sector, Canada now has comprehensive data protection legislation. Moreover, the new law will be enforced by the Privacy Commissioner of Canada, which was already responsible for overseeing the public sector Privacy Act.

Canada's data protection standards have therefore evolved toward the 'European' model in that they involve comprehensive legislation and active enforcement by a specialised data protection authority. In comparison to the situation in the mid-1990s, this is a clear strengthening.

It is more difficult, however, to relate these developments to the European Directive. As was explained above, a number of developments that led to the formulation of the new legislation took place in the first half of the 1990s and around 1995. Quebec's comprehensive data protection legislation, which was adopted in 1993, may have provided an impetus for legislative efforts at the federal level. The Canadian Standards Association started to work on a data protection standard in the early 1990s and it finalised it in 1995. The development of a Canadian Internet policy, of which the data protection legislation formed a part, was initiated during the mid-1990s.

In terms of timing, many of the developments that led to the new law preceded the adoption of the EC Directive. Still, the European Directive seems to have played an important role in Industry Canada's thinking on the issue and its decision to move ahead with legislation. It therefore formed a significant part of the driving forces behind Bill C-54. During the legislative process, officials from Industry Canada also remained in contact with their counterparts in the European Commission to discuss how the Canadian law would fit into the Directive's adequacy criteria, so the Canadian legislation may also have been influenced by the European Directive in some of its specific provisions.

Given the other forces at play in the 1990s, Canada might well have adopted data protection legislation in the absence of the EC Directive. However, it is likely that the Directive, and more specifically the Directive's potential trade effects, influenced the choice for a legislative solution, the timing of the legislative initiatives, and some of the law's provisions. In that sense, the Canadian data protection law for the private sector may be considered to be an example of the California effect.

6.6.2 Explaining the outcomes

Given these assessments of the European Directive's influence on US and Canadian data protection standards, how can these outcomes be explained? What explains the outcomes of the Safe Harbour negotiations and the Canadian move toward comprehensive data protection legislation? In this subsection I will answer these questions in relation to the hypotheses drawn up in chapter 2. According to the theoretical framework developed in that chapter the political balance, and thereby the outcomes of decision-making processes in another country can be affected through actors' constraints and preferences, and by expanding participation. I will discuss the hypotheses linked to each of these three ways.

Changing constraints

Four hypotheses were formulated in relation to actors' constraints. First, it was hypothesised that *a regulatory trade measure or a retaliatory measure will have a greater effect on another country's political balance, the greater that measure's effect on the other country's exports*. In this case, the European Directive threatened to affect almost all trade flows between the EC and the US and Canada that involved transfers of personal information from firms in the EC to firms in those two countries. In practice, many transfers could have been made under one of the Directive's exceptions, most notably consent by the data subject and the use of model contract clauses. These solutions were not viable for all transfers, however, and model contracts were mainly an option for large firms that had sufficient resources to deal with the legal and technical aspects involved in them. Moreover, the absence of an adequacy finding would have increased the uncertainty for all parties involved. All in all, the Directive therefore affected a wide range of Transatlantic trade flows and it had a significant potential impact on US and Canadian exports to the EC.

In the previous chapters it was concluded that the size of the (potential) trade effects is important for determining the necessity to act on the part of the US and Canadian governments and their willingness to reach an agreement. This conclusion seems to be borne out by this case study as well. Because the European data protection Directive had such a great potential impact on their countries' exports, the US and Canadian governments could not afford to ignore the issue, but had to do something in order to prevent Transatlantic data flows from being interrupted.

At the same time, the EC also had an interest in keeping data flows to the US (and, to a lesser extent, to Canada) going. A disruption of data flows would have affected not only firms in those countries, but also European firms that wanted to transfer these data. This may explain why the EC was willing to accept a separate agreement for EC-US data flows, although this was not foreseen by the Directive. The part of the hypothesis relating to retaliatory measures is not relevant here, since retaliation was never an issue in the process.

The second hypothesis stated that *a regulatory trade measure or a retaliatory measure will have a greater effect on another country's political balance, the more that measure's effects are targeted at pivotal actors in the other country.* In this case, the European Directive was not particularly targeted towards firms or sectors of the economy that had a special position in the policy process. It was a broad-ranging measure that could have affected a wide range of firms and industries in the US and Canada, insofar as they received personal data from firms in the EC. The Directive had the most impact on industries that relied heavily on the exchange of personal information, such as the financial, direct marketing and information technology industries. Indeed, it was mainly business groups from these industries that were involved in the Safe Harbour talks and the legislative process in Canada. Still, compared to the issues studied in the previous three chapters, the data protection Directive was not particularly targeted, but that does not seem to have had an important impact on the outcome of the processes.

According to the third hypothesis, *a regulatory trade measure will have a greater effect on regulatory standards in the target country, the lesser the costs of complying with that measure for actors in the target country.* The costs of complying with data protection requirements are difficult to quantify. Still, it seems fair to say that compliance with the European Directive would have entailed high costs for US and Canadian firms, although these costs may have differed between sectors, according to the sectoral laws already in place, the content of self-regulatory codes in their sector, and the degree to which they complied with those codes.

The costs may also have been smaller for Canadian firms that already complied with Quebec's 1993 data protection law. The CSA model code probably did not make a great difference since only one Canadian firm registered with the CSA under the model code, but it may have had an important indirect effect through trade associations' voluntary codes that were based on the CSA model code. In that sense, the costs of complying with the European standards may have been smaller for Canadian than for US firms, but it is difficult to give precise estimates of this difference and it was probably mainly true for Canadian firms covered by Quebec's data protection law. Even then, it is difficult to substantiate whether complying with a multitude of sectoral laws and codes, as exist in the US, is less expensive than complying with one comprehensive piece of legislation.

The potential compliance costs thus seem to have been significant in both countries. Given the difficulties in quantifying these costs, however, support for, or opposition against, imposing legislation and more stringent standards seems to have been mainly based on a strategic assessment of the costs and benefits of data protection policies. This ties in better with the hypothesis on deeply held values and perceived problems that will be discussed below.

Fourth, it was hypothesised that *a regulatory trade measure will have a greater effect on regulatory standards in the target country, if it is supported by both public interest groups and domestic producers in the initiator country*. This hypothesis related to so-called 'Baptist-bootlegger coalitions.' In this issue, the European Directive and the possibility to block data flows to other countries were supported by European consumer groups and data protection officials in the member states. There is no indication that European government officials used data protection policies as a protectionist device.

European firms did not specifically support the data protection Directive, at least not for protectionist motives. European firms even shared many of the concerns of their North American counterparts. The importance of most substantive issues were also the same on both sides of the Atlantic, for instance the opt-in/opt-out controversy for direct marketing firms. Thus, firms on both sides faced similar problems, divisions among firms ran more between sectors of the economy than between firms in different countries, and a Baptist-bootlegger coalition was not a driving force behind the Directive and its provisions on data transfers to third countries.

Initially, US (and possibly also Canadian) officials were sceptical about the EC's willingness and ability to block data transfers. The Directive may have gained credibility, however, by the Article 29 Working Party's critical assessment of the Safe Harbour proposals and the Article 31 Committee's continuous rejections of those proposals. This was mainly the result of the important role played in the EC's data protection policies by the national data protection commissioners, who were staunch defenders of a strict interpretation of the Directive.

Changing preferences

The second way in which another country's political balance can be changed is through actors' preferences. The first hypothesis in this category was that *a regulatory trade measure will have a greater effect on regulatory standards in the target country, the more it ties in with deeply-held values and perceived problems in the target country*. This seems to have played a very important role in this case. To start with, the issue of privacy and data protection gained a new impetus in both the US and Canada with the emergence of the Internet and e-commerce. As a consequence, both countries experienced an increase in interest and concrete initiatives in this issue around the mid-1990s. The European Directive tied in well with these concerns.

At the same time, Canada and the US differed (between themselves and with the EC) when it came to the preferred way of dealing with this issue. These differences related both to the form, the content, and the implementation of data protection policies. As to the form, a legislative approach in the private sector, in particular one comprehensive law, was strongly opposed by US firms and business groups. US privacy advocacy groups had always supported comprehensive legislation, but they had not been able to muster enough support among legislators or business groups. The opponents of comprehensive legislation argued for targeted, sectoral legislation, combined with self-regulation in other sectors. Comprehensive legislation, so they argued, would be too inflexible and would impede economic development. The approach taken in the European Directive therefore differed substantially from mainstream thinking in the US.

This was also true for the content of data protection policies. The US debate has evolved around the four principles that were first formulated in the 1973 HEW report and that were restated by the FTC and the Department of Commerce in 1997 and 1998. These principles include notice, choice, access and security, but the access principle is still very controversial among US business groups. As a result, many legislative initiatives taken in the second half of the 1990s were limited to these four principles or only some of them. The set of data protection principles in the European Directive was much wider and less controversial within the EC.

Finally, the ideas concerning implementation also differed between the US and the EC. In the US, no independent overseeing agency had been established in the public or private sector and the concept of a government agency overseeing data flows was looked upon very unfavourably. Again, privacy advocacy groups had argued for the creation of such an agency, but this had not been supported by the US administration or business groups. In the second half of the 1990s, the FTC took on some of the roles normally played by a data protection commissioner, and in 2000 it spoke out in favour of an independent overseeing agency. Nevertheless, its 2000 recommendation was not supported by the US administration and the FTC's role remained limited compared to European (or the Canadian) data protection commissioners.

In terms of concrete perceived problems, the European Directive therefore did not tie in with the state of the US debate and a solution in line with the Directive would have required an enormous change in thinking. This is reflected in the solution which the US government eventually found. First, it negotiated a separate agreement for US firms wanting to receive personal information from firms in the EC, and did not try to change its domestic standards (at least, not in response to the European Directive). Second, the agreement was based on a voluntary, self-regulatory approach, and the enforcement would be carried out by the FTC through its authority under Section 5 FTCA.

The substantive standards in the Safe Harbour agreement are much wider than those found in US laws or self-regulatory codes. That is probably why it has not yet had much impact on concrete initiatives for domestic standards in the US, except for the FAQ on access, the principle that is currently at the 'frontier' of the US data protection debate.

In Canada, the situation was different to that in the US. In terms of the form of data protection policies, the situation was similar to that in the US until the mid-1990s, when all Canadian business groups and the Canadian government supported a self-regulatory approach in the private sector.

When it came to the content, however, Canada came closer to the EC. In the CSA standard-setting process, Canadian business groups, privacy advocates and government officials had agreed upon a wide set of data protection principles. The access principle, which was most controversial in the US, provoked much less debate in Canada, and apart from that the CSA model code contained almost all the substantive principles also embodied in the EC Directive.

The implementation of the public sector Privacy Act had already been entrusted to the independent Privacy Commissioner of Canada. As a result, the idea of having an independent overseeing agency was probably more accepted, and there was a logical, existing candidate for oversight in the private sector. This consensus on the content and implementation of data protection policies probably also increased the acceptability of a legislative solution.

The EC Directive thus tied in much more closely with the Canadian debate than with that in the US. This may explain why the Canadian government chose to pursue a legislative solution based on a wide set of data protection principles, while the US government opted for a separate agreement based on a self-regulatory approach. Like in the leghold trap issue, it was easier to form a coalition around policies that had strong roots in domestic political developments than to find support for a different type of approach, and this explains most of the differences between Canada and the US in their reactions to the European Directive.

Although perceived problems may thus explain much of the two countries' responses to the Directive, it is more difficult to assess whether the Directive has changed the preferences of US or Canadian actors. In the US, the preferences of privacy advocacy groups, business groups and governmental agencies do not seem to have changed much because of the Directive or the Safe Harbour talks. The FTC did change its position in 2000, which hardly seems to have been the result of a change in constraints. The Directive and the Safe Harbour talks may have contributed to this change, but that point is difficult to substantiate. Moreover, it has not yet led to a change in regulatory standards in the US.

In Canada, the main change in position took place when Industry Canada moved toward support for a legislative solution, followed by the C(D)MA. Insofar as this was the result of the European Directive, this was mostly so because of its trade effects. The Privacy Commissioner of Canada also used the European Directive to support his call for legislation, but it is not likely that the European Directive actually induced him to take this position. At the same time, the European Directive seems to have reinforced the credibility and legitimacy of domestic arguments for data protection legislation. In that sense, it may also have affected domestic actors' preferences.

All in all, perceived problems in the domestic debates determined much of the two countries' responses to the European Directive. In addition, the Directive may have affected the domestic debates on data protection policies and thus also have had an influence through domestic actors' preferences.

The second hypothesis relating to preferences stated that *a regulatory trade measure will have a greater effect on regulatory standards in the target country, the more actors in the target country perceive it to be motivated by genuine concerns rather than protectionism.* As was noted in section 6.4.3 above, some US officials initially suspected some protectionism on the part of the EC, a concern that had already been raised concerning national data protection laws in the 1970s and 1980s. However, most US officials and business groups do not seem to have regarded the European Directive as a protectionist measure.

During the Safe Harbour process, suspicions of protectionism were probably reduced even further by the EC's willingness to find a solution and by the European data commissioners' promise to treat data flows to the US favourably during the talks. As a result, protectionism does not seem to have been much of an issue during most of the process.

The same is true in Canada. Although there were some concerns about the possible trade effects of the European Directive, there is no indication that it was seen as a protectionist measure by either Canadian officials or Canadian business groups. Because Canada decided to pursue a legislative approach fairly soon after the adoption of the Directive, trade aspects only played a small role in the EC-Canadian debate anyway.

This has probably facilitated a regulatory solution to the Directive's potential effects on data flows to the two countries. To the US government and firms, it may have increased their trust in the feasibility of an agreement with the EC, even if the negotiations proved more difficult and took longer than originally foreseen. In Canada, it may have strengthened the legitimacy of the argument that new legislation was necessary to avoid a disruption of trade with the EC. If other Canadian actors had perceived the Directive as a protectionist measure, such an argument would probably have encountered more negative reactions.

The final hypothesis related to international law and stated that *a regulatory trade measure will have a greater effect on regulatory standards in the target country if it conforms to international law and international standards*. In this issue, two sets of international law were relevant: the WTO Agreements (in particular the GATS), and the OECD Guidelines. The Council of Europe Convention hardly played a role in the Canadian and US debates, but most of its provisions are also embodied in the OECD Guidelines.

Starting with WTO law, in section 6.3 it was concluded that the European Directive and the threat to block data flows to the US and Canada were probably consistent with the GATS and thereby WTO law. Above it was argued that this was an important reason for the US not to resort to the WTO over this issue. It also explains why trade officials were hardly involved in this matter.

At first sight, this may lead to the conclusion that WTO law did not play a role in this issue and was 'neutral' in the talks between the US and the EC. Shaffer (1999: 425-426) has argued, however, that the WTO compatibility of the European Directive supported the EC since the WTO rules protected it against retaliation by the US. Since the EC Directive would probably have survived scrutiny under GATS, the US did not have a legitimate, or at least legal, means of retaliating by imposing trade measures or threatening to do so. As a result, the US government had an additional reason to negotiate with the European Commission rather than to call the EC's bluff. It is doubtful whether the US would have retaliated in the absence of these WTO rules anyway, but the rules may have reduced the credibility of US threats even further. Thus, Shaffer's observation points to an interesting effect of WTO law and suggests that it is not neutral, even if (or here: exactly because) a regulatory trade measures is WTO compatible.

The OECD Guidelines were another set of international standards that were relevant in this case. The Guidelines had been ratified by the EC, the US and Canada, and they acted as a point of reference, both in internal debates and in talks between them. Above, in section 6.4.4, it was pointed out that the OECD Guidelines left considerable room for interpretation and could be used by all actors involved to support at least part of their argument. Still, they provided a generally accepted baseline for debates over data protection standards; subsequent debates then focused on the precise content of the standards and issues that were left open in the Guidelines (such as the preferred means of enforcement), but the more fundamental issues could quite easily be resolved. The Guidelines were therefore rather effective as a framework to set the stage or to define the terms in which the debate was to be held; they did not provide a ready code of applicable data protection standards, so the debate centred around the way they should be specified.

Expanding participation

Expanding participating was mentioned as a third way in which another country's political balance can be changed by regulatory trade measures. The hypothesis relating to participation expansion stated that *a regulatory trade measure will have a lesser effect on regulatory standards in the target country, if the target country succeeds in expanding participation in the initiator country to trade officials*. In this issue, participation expansion seems to have played hardly any role in the process. In the US-EC process, some US officials tried to shift the issue to the trade arena, and they raised the WTO compatibility of the European Directive in talks with EC trade officials. This did not lead to an increased involvement of trade officials on either side, however, and the talks remained largely limited to the Department of Commerce in the US and DG Internal Market in the EC.

This may have been so for several reasons. First, as was discussed above, the European Directive was probably compatible with WTO law. Second, European data protection commissioners did not block any data transfers to the US during the talks on the Safe Harbour agreement, so there were no concrete disruptions of trade either. Third, the call for WTO action remained confined to a small part of the US administration and was not broadly supported by US firms, which would probably have lent little credibility to a threat to resort to the WTO. Finally, data protection policies had become a largely de-politicised issue in the EC and it aroused little attention from politicians or interest groups apart from those that had a direct stake in it.

This stands in marked contrast to the GM foods issue, which was much more controversial. As a result, the weight attached to the issue, by both proponents and opponents, was much greater in the GM foods issue than in the data protection issue. The issue of data protection and the talks between the US and the EC were thus allowed to become technical by other participants. The main players in the EC, apart from DG Internal Market, were the Article 29 Working Party and the Article 31 Committee, both consisting of data protection specialists.

The (mainly informal) EC-Canadian talks were held between Industry Canada and DG Internal Market. Since Canada had decided to move toward its own data protection law, the trade aspects did not really come up in these talks, and they were confined to discussions of substantive issues. Hence, participation was not broadened in the EC-Canadian relationship either.

General conclusion

The EC data protection Directive led to an expansion of the US and Canadian win-sets and thereby a California effect because of its strong potential trade effects on Transatlantic trade. The effects of disruptions of data flows on European firms also increased the EC's willingness to reach an agreement (i.e. its win-set), in particular with the US. The credibility of the EC measures was increased by the fact that the process remained confined to a relatively small group of data protection specialists.

At the same time, the apparent absence of protectionism reduced opposition against an agreement in the US and legislation in Canada.

Both the US and Canadian reactions to the European Directive were conditioned by the existing political debates in the two countries. As a result, the US sought to conclude a separate agreement based on voluntary standards and enforced by the FTC. In Canada, a number of domestic political developments had led to a greater acceptance of legislation and provided an independent impetus for legislative action.

Although they formed the reason why the US and Canada reacted to the European Directive in the first place, trade concerns hardly played a role in the subsequent processes themselves. Resorting to the WTO was not an option because of the European Directive's apparent WTO compatibility. The OECD data protection guidelines offered a shared framework for thinking about data protection standards that facilitated agreement, even if they provided less guidance in the way of specific data protection standards.

CHAPTER SEVEN

SUMMARY AND CONCLUSIONS

In the previous four chapters I examined four issues in which differences in regulatory standards between the EC, and the US and Canada affected or threatened to affect US and Canadian exports to the EC. For all these four 'regulatory trade measures' I examined to what extent they have led to a strengthening of domestic regulatory standards in the US and Canada, and what factors contributed to those outcomes, making for a total of eight cases.

In this concluding chapter I will bring together the conclusions from the eight case studies to arrive at an answer to the research problem of this study and a more general answer to its central theme: under what conditions will regulatory trade measures lead to a strengthening of regulatory standards in other countries?

To that end, I will first briefly summarise the four issues and their outcomes in the US and Canada. Then, I will test the hypotheses drawn up in chapter two against the case studies' conclusions to arrive at a set of general conclusions relating to the California effect in the Transatlantic relationship. Finally, I will discuss the applicability of these conclusions to a wider range of cases, issue areas and trade relations.

7.1 THE EIGHT CASES AND THEIR OUTCOMES

The eight cases that were analysed in this study differ markedly in their outcomes. Some cases are (clear) examples of the California effect, while in others no appreciable strengthening of regulatory standards has taken place, or at least not as a result of a European regulatory trade measure. In order to set the stage for the general conclusions to be drawn in the next section, I will therefore first summarise the main developments and outcomes in each of the cases.

It is tempting to try to devise a ranking of the eight cases based on the size of the California effect that can be found in them. Such a ranking would be misleading, however, since it would imply a comparison between the effects in terms of their magnitude, which is only partly possible.

In general, the size of a California effect has two dimensions: the extent to which regulatory standards have been strengthened, and the extent to which this strengthening is the result of another country's regulatory trade measure. A California effect is absent if there is no strengthening of regulatory standards whatsoever, or if the strengthening is completely unrelated to another country's regulatory trade measure; it is very strong if there is a considerable strengthening of standards that can be attributed primarily to another country's regulatory trade measure.

Problems arise in two instances, however. First, although in principle it may be possible to formulate a measure for the stringency of standards *within* an issue area, this is nearly impossible *between* issue areas. For example, what is to count as a greater increase in stringency: the strengthening of Canadian trapping standards or the adoption of the Canadian data protection legislation? And if one or the other is deemed to be a greater increase, then what is the criterion for this judgement? Several aspects of stringency suggest themselves, such as the relative increase in substantive standards, the mode of implementation, or the number of people (and/or animals) affected by the standards. Something can be said for each of these approaches, but this choice will always be arbitrary and even then it may be impossible to compare, say, changes in substantive standards in two different issue areas.

Second, the relative weight to be attached to the two dimensions of a California effect is unclear. If in one case there has been a considerable strengthening of standards, which is partly linked to a regulatory trade measure, while in another the strengthening has been limited but directly linked to a regulatory trade measure, then which is to count as a stronger California effect? A good example is formed by the European data protection Directive, which led directly to the Safe Harbour agreement and partly to the Canadian data protection law. Since both the strengthening of standards and the extent to which such a strengthening is the result of a regulatory trade measure are matters of degree, some sort of criterion would be needed to arrive at a comparison between these cases.

Therefore, a clear ranking order of the eight cases under study here is not possible. Still, a more general ranking can be made avoiding the problems discussed above. Table 7.1 provides an overview of the four issues and eight cases in terms of the occurrence of a California effect.

The beef-hormone issue stands out as the one in which no strengthening of standards has occurred in either the US or Canada. The EC banned the imports of meat produced with growth-hormones in 1989. Since the US and Canada allowed the use of six different hormones as growth-promoters, this led to a prolonged dispute with the EC. Despite the European ban, the US and Canada have so far been unwilling to reverse the approval of the six hormones, to change their approval processes or to restrict the use of these hormones and the meat produced with them. As a result, no California effect has occurred in these cases.

In each of the other issues, at least some strengthening of regulatory standards has taken place that was at least to some extent the result of a European regulatory trade measure. In the case of genetically modified (GM) foods and food products, the EC has gradually adopted more stringent standards, both by blocking the approval of new GM varieties since 1998, and by imposing more stringent labelling requirements. Moreover, the 2001 EC Directive on GMOs contained a set of more stringent approval criteria. This has led to an increasing divergence with US and Canadian standards, which have allowed a wide variety of GM foods onto the market and have refused to install mandatory labelling related to the production process.

		Strengthening of standards?	Link to EC measures?	California effect?
Leghold trap issue	US	Yes (potentially)	Yes (directly through the Understanding and indirectly through the BMP process)	Yes
	Canada	Yes	Yes (directly through the Agreement)	Yes
Data protection issue	US	Yes (potentially)	Yes (directly through Safe Harbour agreement)	Yes
	Canada	Yes	Yes (partly)	Yes
GM foods issue	US	Limited (formalisation of existing approach) In practice (for the soya bean growers)	Indirectly (through increasing activism in the US) Directly (for the soya bean growers)	Limited
	Canada	Limited (formalisation of existing approach)	Possibly indirectly (through increasing activism in Canada)	Possibly and limited
Beef-hormone issue	US	No	Irrelevant	No
	Canada	No	Irrelevant	No

Table 7.1: The outcomes in the eight cases

In this issue, it can be argued that two types of strengthening have occurred that are more or less closely related to the European measures. First, both the US and Canada have formalised their assessment procedures for GM foods and food products. In the US, this formalisation was mainly a response to increased activism on the part of public interest groups and the desire to retain consumer confidence in GM foods and food products. The rise in activism and consumer concerns can be attributed partly to the European regulatory trade measures, in that these measures may have lent credibility to the arguments of the critics of these products in the US. This is a somewhat stretched use of the concept of a California effect, however. Moreover, the substantive risk assessment standards were not strengthened.

In Canada, the process of formalising the assessment procedure for GM foods and food products was started earlier than in the US, before the strengthening of the European regulatory regime, and before the rise in activism in Canada. This suggests that the Canadian decision to formalise its assessment procedure was taken before and in isolation of the rise in public interest group activism or the European regulatory trade measures. The European measures may have expedited the process, but this claim is difficult to substantiate.

Second, US soya bean producers have decided not to market GM soya bean varieties that are not approved in the EC. This is a direct result of the interest which US soya bean producers have in exporting to the EC. Since it is very difficult and expensive to separate different soya bean varieties throughout the production chain, producing EC non-approved varieties would effectively cut off any export opportunities to the EC. This decision has always been presented as a purely commercial move, however; it has not been accompanied by a call for more stringent standards in the US itself, and it will be reversed once the EC has approved the other varieties that have now already been approved in the US. In that sense, it is a weak effect in terms of regulatory change. Moreover, the decision not to produce EC non-approved varieties has been limited to the US soya bean industry. US maize producers have taken a similar decision with regard to Japan, but not to the EC, resulting in a strong decline in US exports of GM maize for human consumption to the EC.

In addition to the effects of the EC measures on domestic activism in the US and Canada, some degree of strengthening of regulatory standards may have resulted from the Cartagena Protocol on trade in GM organisms (GMOs) and products. The Cartagena Protocol reflects many of the European concerns over the possible risks of GMOs and GM products. Since both the US and Canada have agreed to the text of the Protocol (even if the US is not able to become a party to it and Canada has not yet ratified it), this seems to imply a move toward more stringent regulatory standards in this field. It remains to be seen, however, how the provisions of the Protocol will be interpreted in practice and what effect they will eventually have on domestic standards in the two countries.

The GM foods and food products issue therefore shows some strengthening of regulatory standards in the US and Canada, but this strengthening is fairly limited and only partly the result of EC regulatory trade measures.

The data protection and leghold trap issues demonstrate much clearer examples of the California effect. The EC data protection Directive opened the possibility of blocking data flows to countries without an 'adequate' level of protection. In the mid-1990s, when the Directive was adopted, this applied to the US and Canada, since both countries had no general data protection laws covering the private sector. Rather, they relied on sectoral legislation and self-regulation that was mainly enforced in the courts. Moreover, the data protection principles used in these laws and self-regulatory codes were more limited than the ones used in the European Directive.

This led to the conclusion of a Safe Harbour agreement between the US and the EC, which contains a set of voluntary data protection standards for US firms wanting to receive personal data from the EC. The substantive standards in this agreement are more stringent than those found in most US laws, regulations or voluntary codes, and unlike the prevalent sectoral approach in US legislation, the Safe Harbour agreement cuts across sectors of the economy. Moreover, enforcement of the Safe Harbour agreement will be subject to priority treatment by the Federal Trade Commission (FTC) and will probably come under close scrutiny by the EC and privacy advocacy groups.

Indirectly, a strengthening of domestic US standards could result from the Safe Harbour principles serving as a model or benchmark in the domestic debate over data protection policies, and from US firms becoming used to working with these principles. The FTC's role as an advocate for more stringent data protection legislation may also be strengthened by its special role under the Safe Harbour agreement.

Nevertheless, both the direct and indirect effects of the Safe Harbour agreement on US data protection standards are at the moment hypothetical and will depend to a great extent on the scale on which US firms will actually choose to work under the agreement. For now, these effects have therefore been limited.

In Canada, a general data protection law for the private sector was adopted in 2000, leading to a remarkable divergence from US data protection policies. The Canadian law was partly a response to the potential trade effects of the European data protection Directive, although domestic considerations also played an important role. This case therefore presents an example of a significant strengthening of standards, but one that was only partly the result of an EC regulatory trade measure.

Finally, the EC leghold trap Regulation threatened to ban the import of furs from countries that allowed the use of leghold traps or did not adhere to internationally agreed 'humane trapping standards.' The US and Canada did not qualify for either exemption, since the use of leghold traps was allowed in the vast majority of US states and Canadian provinces and territories. The Canadian government had been working on national trapping standards, but these were voluntary. In the US, no such standards existed in the early 1990s. Both countries participated in attempts to formulate humane trapping standards in the International Organization for Standardization, but this process did not yield any standards.

In the end, the dispute over the European leghold trap Regulation led to two agreements: one between the EC and the US, and one between the EC and Canada (and the Russian Federation). The substantive standards in the two agreements are identical and more stringent than existing domestic trapping standards in either country. The main difference is that the EC-Canadian agreement is formally binding, whereas the EC-US agreement is a voluntary 'Understanding.' As a result, the EC-Canadian agreement is more stringent than the EC-US agreement. On the other hand, the EC-Canadian agreement built upon existing voluntary national Canadian trapping standards, while the concept of nationwide trapping standards was new to the US. In the US, the move toward formulating such national standards, known as Best Management Practices, was largely motivated by increasing domestic activism against trapping and leghold traps, although the European import ban functioned as an important trigger for this move.

An interesting feature of the leghold trap issue is that the EC agreed to more stringent standards as well. The standards in the agreements with the US and Canada applied to all types of traps, not just leghold traps, and when implemented they would probably mean a considerable strengthening of standards in most EC member states. So far, they have not been implemented, however.

Thus, the outcomes of these cases differ significantly. Although it is impossible to establish a precise ranking based on the size of the California effect, it seems fair to say that the beef-hormone issue shows no California effect and the GM foods issue a very limited California effect in either country, although a little more so in the US than in Canada. The data protection and leghold trap issues form better examples of a California effect, although in the leghold trap issue arguably more so in Canada than in the US.

Apart from this general assessment of the cases in terms of a strengthening of standards, the cases also show more specific outcomes in terms of changes in substantive standards and of the form these standards took in Canada and the US. In the next section I will turn to the factors that account for these differences in outcomes, using the hypotheses formulated in chapter 2.

7.2 Explaining the outcomes

In chapter 2, a number of hypotheses were formulated about the factors that will increase or decrease the likelihood of a California effect. In general, three ways were discerned in which regulatory trade measures can affect the political balance in another country and thereby the stringency of regulatory standards in that country: by changing the constraints facing interest groups and government officials in the other country, by changing their preferences, and by expanding participation in the domestic regulatory policy-process. Conversely, countries affected by a regulatory trade measure can also use these mechanisms to undercut support for the measure in the country imposing it.

Table 7.2 gives an overview of the values of the hypothesised explanatory variables in each of the cases. In this section I will systematically compare the four issues and eight cases to find out to what extent the hypotheses are confirmed or contradicted by the results of the case studies.

7.2.1 Changing constraints

The first way in which regulatory trade measures and retaliatory measures can affect the political balance in another country is by changing constraints in that other country. Four hypotheses were drawn up with regard to constraints:

- A regulatory trade measure or a retaliatory measure will have a greater effect on another country's political balance, the greater that measure's effect on the other country's exports;
- A regulatory trade measure or a retaliatory measure will have a greater effect on another country's political balance, the more that measure's effects are targeted at pivotal actors in the other country;
- A regulatory trade measure will have a greater effect on regulatory standards in the target country, the lesser the costs of complying with that measure for actors in the target country;
- A regulatory trade measure will have a greater effect on regulatory standards in the target country, if it is supported by both public interest groups and domestic producers in the initiator country.

The size and targeting of trade effects

I will take the first and second hypotheses together, since both relate to the impact of the regulatory trade measure or the retaliatory measure on producers in the other country. To begin with, however, two observations should be made about the determination of the size of the trade effects of regulatory trade measures. First, the extent of these trade effects cannot normally be taken as given, but is itself the outcome of a political process in which different groups try to present their estimate of the trade effects as the 'true' estimate. This makes it difficult to pin down a precise value for these trade effects.

Second, the extent of the trade effects of a regulatory trade measure does not depend exclusively on the exports from the US and Canada to the EC, but may be much wider. For example, in the leghold trap issue, the EC was not only important as an importer of US and Canadian fur, but also as a centre for fur fashion. As a consequence, the importance of the EC market for furs exceeded the EC's importance as a mere importer of furs, since an EC import ban could have affected exports to other markets as well. The same was true in the GM foods issue, where US and Canadian exports to countries outside the EC have also been affected by the European restrictions, if those other countries themselves had close trading ties with the EC. Thus, some countries that exported food products to the EC refused to import GM products from Canada and the US because they feared that that in turn would jeopardise their (re-)exports to the EC.

Hence, the extent of trade effects is hardly an objective fact that can be taken as given in a political process, but is partly the outcome of the political process itself and partly the result of strategic choices by the actors concerned. Having said this, the cases seem to confirm the importance of the size and targeting of trade effects for the occurrence of a California effect, in that these costs seemed to determine the necessity on the part of the US and Canadian governments to do something in order to avoid the import ban from coming into force, and their willingness to reach an agreement.

Not only is this true for the country affected by the regulatory trade measure, but also for the country imposing it. For the target country, the (potential) trade effects of a regulatory trade measure largely determine the necessity to avoid an import ban. For the initiator country, the effects of its regulatory trade measure on its own importing firms and the effects of possible retaliation do the same. To a great extent, these two effects go hand in hand: the greater the potential trade effects of a regulatory trade measure on a target country, the greater the effects will be on importing firms in the initiator country and the greater the potential retaliatory measures will also be. Thus, the greater the trade effects of a regulatory trade measure, the more willing both sides will be to reach an agreement.

There seem to be two exceptions to this general conclusion. First, two countries will not be equally willing to reach an agreement if the effects are more targeted in one country than in the other. Then, the country in which the effects are relatively more targeted will have a greater interest in reaching an agreement.

		Size of trade effects			Targeting		Costs of compliance	
		Of EC measure on US and Canada	Of EC measure on EC itself	Of retaliatory measures on EC	Of EC measure on US and Canada	Of retaliatory measures on EC	Direct costs	Indirect costs
Leghold trap issue	**US**	Large	Large	Irrelevant	No	Irrelevant	Of a ban on traps high; of trapping standards low	Low
	Canada	Large	Large	Irrelevant	Yes	Irrelevant	Of a ban on traps high; of trapping standards low	Low
Data protection issue	**US**	Large	Large	Irrelevant	No	Irrelevant	High	Low
	Canada	Large	Moderate	Irrelevant	No	Irrelevant	High	Low
GM foods issue	**US**	Maize: small; Soy: moderate	Small	Irrelevant	No	Irrelevant	High	High
	Canada	Small	Small	Irrelevant	No	Irrelevant	High	High
Beef-hormone issue	**US**	Small	Small	Small	No	No	High	High
	Canada	Small	Small	Small	No	No	High	High

Table 7.2: The explanatory variables in the eight cases

Baptist-bootlegger coalition	Deeply held values and perceived problems	Perception of protectionism	Conformity with international law		Participation expansion
			With GATT/ WTO law	With international standards	
No or latent	Ban on leghold traps not legitimate; Trapping standards legitimate (after BMP process)	No	No	Irrelevant	Yes and successful
	Ban on leghold traps not legitimate; Trapping standards legitimate	No			
No	Purpose legitimate; EC approach not legitimate	No	Yes	Yes	No
	Purpose and EC approach legitimate	No			
Latent	EC approach not legitimate	No or somewhat	Probably yes; labelling more dubious	Probably yes	Yes, but not successful
	EC approach not legitimate	No or somewhat			
Open	EC ban not legitimate	Yes	No	No	Yes, but not successful
	EC ban not legitimate	Yes			

This may partly explain why Canada was more willing to reach an agreement in the leghold trap issue than the US. Targeting was largely absent in the other cases, but this does not seem to have had an appreciable effect on the outcomes of these cases. Strong conclusions about this hypothesis are therefore not warranted.

Second, the initiator and the target country will not be equally willing to reach an agreement if the trade effects are greater for one country than for another, relative to its total trade or total economy. This may explain why the EC was more willing to give in to US rather than to Canadian demands in the leghold trap issue and why the EC was willing to consider a separate agreement with the US in the data protection issue.

These two hypotheses therefore relate to three (potential) interruptions of trade flows: the trade effects of a regulatory trade measure on a target country, the effects of a retaliatory measure by a target country, and the effects of a regulatory trade measure on importing firms in the initiator country. I will discuss the consequences of each of these three (potential) interruptions in the four issues, starting with the trade effects of the regulatory trade measure on the target country.

In the beef-hormone issue, the trade effects for both the US and Canada were very limited: US and Canadian exports before the European ban were small (less than 1% of each country's total beef production) because of the EC's restrictive import regime, and there were enough alternatives for the European market. As a result, there was little need for the US and Canadian governments to avoid the European import ban and they could afford to engage in a prolonged trade dispute.

In the leghold trap issue, by contrast, the trade effects of a European import ban would have been enormous. US and Canadian trappers were highly dependent on exports and most exports went to the EC, either for final consumption or at some stage of the production process. Moreover, in Canada, the effects of the import ban would have fallen most heavily on a small group of aboriginal trappers, something the Canadian government wanted to avoid for political reasons. As a result, both the US and Canadian governments had a high stake in trying to avoid a European trade ban, especially since most harm could already be done by a temporary ban. This may explain their attempts to reach a solution that would avoid the implementation of the import ban. It may also partly explain why Canada was in a worse bargaining position than the US and had to accept a stronger agreement.

In the GM foods issue, the trade effects differed between sectors. For US maize and Canadian canola producers, the European market was not very important and they decided to forego exports to the EC. US soya bean producers, on the other hand, relied more heavily on exports to the EC. This may explain why the soya bean producers decided to block the marketing of GM varieties that had not been approved in the EC, while the other two groups of producers did not. This conclusion is supported by the fact that US maize producers did take the decision to block the marketing of GM varieties that had not been approved in Japan, a much more important market to them than the EC. All in all, however, the direct trade effects of the European restrictions on GM foods and food products have been too small for the US and Canada to require something to be done by their governments.

In the data protection issue, the trade effects of the European measure are the most difficult to estimate. The possibility to block data flows applied to all transactions, which potentially involved all Transatlantic trade that relied on transfers of personal information. However, most trade does not rely on such transfers and even if it does many data flows could in actual practice be covered by one of the exceptions in the European Directive. Still, this was an issue that touched upon a wide variety of trade flows, and it could therefore hardly be ignored by the US and Canadian governments. Again, this may account for the initiatives they took to address it.

The hypotheses about the size and targeting of trade effects also apply to retaliatory measures. In the issues studied here, only the beef-hormone issue led to retaliation. The US retaliated between 1989 and 1995, and again as of July 1999; Canada retaliated as of August 1999. The size of the retaliation was relatively limited, compared to total EC (agricultural) exports to the US and Canada. The 1999 US retaliation amounted to US$ 116.8 million, while the Canadian retaliation was limited to CAN$ 11.3 million.

The retaliatory measures were not very targeted either. They excluded the United Kingdom, since it had always opposed the hormones ban. In practice, the 1999 US retaliation affected mainly Danish pork exporters, which indeed became active in an attempt to avoid retaliation. Their political clout was too small to affect European decision-making on this issue, however. The US plans to rotate the retaliation every six months (the 'caroussel' approach) had the potential to affect a wider range of exporters from more EC member states. Even then, however, the extent of the retaliatory measures would probably be too small to affect EC decision-making processes.

These conclusions tie in well with the two hypotheses, in that they show that limited retaliatory measures did not affect the EC's decision-making processes and hardly induced the EC to make concessions in order to avoid them. Targeting led to a greater involvement by the affected producers, but in this case these producers were not able decisively to influence the EC's decisions. The difference in the amount of retaliation between the US and Canadian measures may explain why the European Commission has focused its efforts on the US and has sought to reach an agreement with the US before Canada, although this is probably more the result of the greater importance of US-EC (agricultural) trade in general.

Nevertheless, it is impossible to draw strong conclusions about these hypotheses in relation to retaliatory measures, since retaliation did not play a role in the other cases. In the leghold trap issue, a GATT/WTO case could have ended in retaliation, but this was hardly an issue in the process. In the other two issues, retaliation was not considered a viable option by most groups and officials in the US and Canada. As a result, there is little evidence on the effects of retaliation in issues other than the beef-hormone issue, and the conclusions should be treated as being preliminary.

Finally, regulatory trade measures may affect importers of the products that are banned. As a result, these importing firms may oppose an import ban. This was shown most clearly in the data protection issue, where European firms had a clear interest in continued flows of personal data to the US (and, to a lesser extent, Canada). As a result, they were involved in the Safe Harbour talks (at least in an informal way) and urged for an agreement. The potential effects of a disruption of data flows to the US was probably an important reason for the EC to engage in talks and to accept an agreement based on a voluntary scheme rather than binding standards.

In the beef-hormone issue, some importers were affected by the import ban in 1989. It was in particular British tongue canners who opposed the import ban. They were not able to reverse the import ban, however, which seems to be logical given their small size. In general, US and Canadian beef imports had been relatively limited before 1989, so only a small number of producers were affected by the ban. The same was true in the GM foods issue, where also only a small part of imports was affected. Still, the relatively greater importance of EC-US trade in agricultural products may explain why the EC focused its attention in both food issues mainly on the US and to a lesser extent on Canada.

In the leghold trap issue, however, there is no indication that European importers of North American wild fur were active in the process, although they provided some information to the Canadian and US governments. Given the importance of wild fur from these two countries, this would seem to contradict this part of the conclusion.

All in all, the hypothesis on the extent of trade effects seems to be confirmed, insofar as the extent of the trade effects affects the necessity to avoid an import ban on the part of a target country and its willingness to reach an agreement. At the same time, the extent of the trade effects also affects the initiator country's willingness to reach an agreement, which can be interpreted as a decrease in the commitment to implement the import ban. Yet, this part of the conclusion rests mainly on the events in the EC-US data protection case; it appears to be contradicted by the fact that fur importers were relatively uninvolved in the leghold trap issue, whereas an import ban would have affected them, too. No strong conclusions can be drawn about the effect of retaliation, although the (absence of an) effect in the one issue in which the US and Canada retaliated (the beef-hormone issue) confirms the hypothesis. Furthermore, the hypothesis should be refined by taking into account that the extent of trade effects cannot be taken as given, but is itself the outcome of a political process.

The hypothesis on targeting seems to account well for some differences in response between the US and Canada in the leghold trap issue, and is supported somewhat by the (absence of any) effects of the US and Canadian retaliation in the beef-hormone issue. Apart from this, targeting does not seem to have played an important role in most cases, however. Generally, targeting hardly seems to have played a role apart from the extent of the trade effects; when a regulatory trade measure has sizeable trade effects, targeting may increase the political costs of the measure, but when these effects are small anyway, targeting does not make much of a difference. The hypothesis is therefore only confirmed in a limited way.

This is probably due to the nature of regulatory trade measures as opposed to human rights related economic sanctions, from which the concept of targeting was borrowed in the theoretical framework. The groups that are affected by human rights related economic sanctions need not be the same as the groups that violate human rights, since the products covered by these sanctions are not related to human rights as such. Regulatory trade measures, by contrast, affect the same groups that are affected by the (process) standards that are the subject of the measure. Thus, they are more likely to play a role in the political standard-setting process, at least in liberal democracies. As a result, regulatory trade measures are almost always targeted at important actors in the political process. Then, only the extent of the trade effects is relevant. Only in special cases, such as the leghold trap case in Canada, in which some groups have a special position in the political process for other than economic reasons will targeting play a role.

The costs of compliance

The third hypothesis related to the costs of complying with a regulatory trade measure. It was hypothesised that a California effect is more likely if these costs are lower. This hypothesis seems to be borne out by the case studies. It needs to be refined, however, in that the costs of complying have to be divided into direct and indirect costs. The direct costs relate to the changes that have to be made to the production of a product by complying with the standards which the regulatory trade measure imposes on that product. The indirect costs comprise of the (potential) costs in related areas that may be affected by the outcome in the dispute over the regulatory trade measure.

For example, in the beef-hormone issue, the direct costs of complying with the European hormone ban would have entailed the loss of productivity in meat production resulting from such a ban in the US and Canada. The indirect costs were formed by the wider trade in agricultural products, for which the outcome of the beef-hormone dispute could set an important precedent. The US and Canadian governments and producers feared that if the EC could get away with the hormone ban, it would use similar regulatory measures to protect other parts of its market for agricultural products in the future.

The distinction between direct and indirect costs is important for several reasons. Most conspicuously, the indirect costs are typically much higher than the direct costs. At the same time, they are more diffuse, more difficult to estimate, and therefore based mainly on a strategic assessment by the actors involved. As a result, disputes over indirect costs tend to be disputes over principles rather than over concrete measures. They are meant to establish the principles on which similar future issues will be decided, rather than to facilitate concrete trade flows at the present.

Therefore, higher indirect costs are likely to impede a strengthening of standards. This can be seen most clearly in the two food issues, the beef-hormone and GM food issues. Both issues were closely related to other agricultural trade issues and the long-standing dispute between the EC and the US and Canada over agricultural trade liberalisation in consecutive negotiating rounds under the GATT/WTO. As a result, the costs for the US and Canada of giving in to the European regulatory trade measures by strengthening domestic regulatory standards, or even standards for export products, were very high. This resulted in a contraction of the two countries' win-sets in these two issues.

By contrast, the leghold trap Regulation had less wide implications. It related to a more general debate about the use of unilateral trade measures to protect animal welfare in other countries, but the amount of trade potentially affected by similar EC measures was not so large. Similarly, the data protection Directive was a fairly isolated issue, which was important to future measures in the field of data protection, but much less so in other issue areas.

The level of both the direct and the indirect costs depends on the form that a change in domestic standards takes. A change that requires a different type of standard will entail higher costs than a strengthening of a given type of standard. This is probably so for two reasons. First, if government officials, firms and consumers in a country are used to working with certain standards, it will be more expensive for them to adjust to a different set of standards than to an incremental change of existing standards. This is an economic factor that relates directly to the constraints facing actors. Second, an existing set of standards is normally supported by a coalition of groups and officials. Changes within that set of standards may require an adjustment of that coalition, but usually the adjustment will be much greater if support has to be mustered for an entirely new approach. This factor relates partly to the adjustment costs and thus the constraints which actors face, and partly to their preferred policies. Hence, it also relates to the hypothesis on deeply-held values and perceived problems, which will be discussed below. Here, I will discuss the general point that a change within an existing approach is easier to achieve than a change of approach, as well as how differences in adjustment costs have affected the outcomes in the cases. Below, at the hypothesis on deeply-held values and perceived problems, I will discuss the role of these values and perceived problems in the eight cases.

The eight cases show that a change within an existing approach is easier to achieve than a change between approaches. In the leghold trap issue, Canada had been working on formulating national trapping standards for some time when the European Regulation was adopted. As a result, some standards already existed and the approach was supported by a coalition of trappers and government officials that had become used to working with these standards. However, a ban on one type of traps, in this case leghold traps, would have met with much more resistance by trappers, who would then have lost a valued tool. Similarly, in the US, banning leghold traps was not an option to most trappers and wildlife regulators, but once they had started to formulate voluntary trapping standards (the 'Best Management Practices'), it was much more acceptable to agree to a set of international voluntary trapping standards. As a consequence, an agreement on trapping standards with the EC was much more acceptable than an outright ban on leghold traps, even if the actual standards in that agreement may have exceeded existing trapping standards.

In the data protection issue, a similar mechanism was at work. In the US, a legislative approach to data protection, backed up by an independent data protection authority, would have implied a fundamental change of standards, away from the prevailing approach (at least in the private sector) that relied on sectoral laws, self-regulation, and enforcement through the courts and by the Federal Trade Commission (FTC). Such a change would have entailed high costs both in terms of adjustments which firms would have had to make to their business practices and of political resistance to such a change. The Safe Harbour Agreement, however, relied on self-regulation and enforcement by the FTC, which was much more in line with existing policies.

The Canadian government did decide to adopt data protection legislation in the private sector, partly in response to domestic developments and partly in response to the European Directive. Even then, the approach taken in the law built on existing work and was therefore markedly Canadian. In the first half of the 1990s, Canadian firms, public interest groups and governments had worked on voluntary data protection standards in the Canadian Standards Association (CSA). In 1995, this work resulted in a model code that was supported by all participants in the process. These standards in turn formed the basis for the data protection law, even to the extent that they became an integral part of the law in the form of a schedule. The adoption of legislation for data protection in the private sector was a novelty to Canada. Yet, because such a broad coalition had supported the CSA model code, the political costs of adopting the legislation were much smaller than they would have been in the absence of the model code; they were also much smaller by basing the legislation on the code than they would have been if it had been based, for instance, directly on the European Directive.

The beef-hormone issue shows that the costs of changing domestic standards may also prevent any strengthening from taking place. The US and Canadian governments had approved the use of six hormones (or rather, of implants or feed additives containing one or more of these hormones) and set limits on the hormone residues in meat. These Maximum Residue Limits (MRLs) had been calculated on the basis of the Acceptable Daily Intake (ADI) of these hormones. The ADIs had been estimated on the basis of the results of animal tests with these hormones, using a safety factor.

The European measures required a complete ban on the use of all growth-hormones, including the six allowed in the US and Canada. Banning these substances would have been very expensive to US and Canadian farmers, and would have invited a great deal of political resistance. A solution based on MRLs would probably have been much more acceptable, even if they had been more stringent (for instance, by using a higher safety factor). Even then, it is not certain whether these more stringent MRLs would have been acceptable to the US and Canada, but at least it would have offered some room for compromise. Yet, since this approach was unacceptable to the EC, any solution along these lines was ruled out. In the end, this led to a complete stalemate and no California effect occurred.

In the GM foods and food products issue, the US and Canada had adopted a set of approval criteria for GM foods that was based on a comparison of product characteristics. Likewise, mandatory labelling was based on product characteristics, not on the process by which they were produced as such. In chapter 5, it was shown that this approach did not differ fundamentally from the approach in the original European Directives, and that the technique of genetic modification did play a role in triggering certain review procedures in the US and Canada. Moreover, a voluntary approval process had already been in place for GM foods in both countries since the early 1990s.

Although this offered some room for adjustment, a complete ban on GM foods, like the 'de facto moratorium' established by the EC in 1998, was completely at odds with the US and Canadian approaches. The same was true for European labelling requirements, which gradually incorporated elements of process labelling. Thus, the most the US and Canadian regulatory authorities could do without fundamentally changing their approach was to formalise their existing approaches.

The decision by US soya bean producers only to use GM varieties that had been approved in the EC was the result of the economies of scale involved in bulk products like soya. Because it is very expensive to separate different types of soya beans in the production process, using varieties not approved in the EC would have meant the loss of most of the European market (as had happened to US maize producers). This was purely a marketing decision that involved a trade-off between commercial benefits and costs. Nevertheless, in terms of costs, this decision was probably easier to take since it had been taken before these varieties were actually marketed. This is in line with the developments in the beef-hormone issue, in that the political costs of a change in standards seem to become higher if a particular practice has been used for a longer period of time.

The US and Canada also agreed to the Biosafety Protocol, which incorporates a number of principles that seem to tie in more closely with the development of EC policies on GM foods. For instance, it stresses the precautionary principle at a number of points. In that sense, the acceptance of the Protocol by the two countries is remarkable. At the same time, however, the provisions of the Protocol leave considerable room for interpretation and do not unambiguously support a 'European' approach. Moreover, they relate only to international trade in certain GM products and do not directly affect Canadian or US domestic standards.

All in all, the costs of complying with the standards in a regulatory trade measure seem to play an important role in explaining the form which compliance will take. Adjustments tend to take place in the form of incremental changes within existing approaches rather than shifts to a new approach. Moreover, if the only way of complying with the standards in the regulatory trade measure is to take a new approach, this may prevent a change from taking place at all.

Two remarks should be made, however. First, the costs are only one element among others. If it is true, as was argued above, that the size and targeting of trade effects largely determine the necessity to avoid an import ban and the willingness to reach an agreement, then it is unlikely that the US and Canada would have adjusted their domestic standards in the hormones and GM foods issues, even if more changes within the existing approach had been available. Second, as was noted above, the costs of complying are probably not the only reason why existing approaches are preferred over new approaches. This may also partly be the result of actors' preferences and their susceptibility to certain (types of) arguments. I will therefore come back to this point below, under the hypothesis on deeply-held values and perceived problems.

Thus, the hypothesis on adjustment costs is confirmed by the case studies. Compliance costs can be divided into direct and indirect compliance costs, whereby the latter are determined by links to other issues in the trade relations between the target and initiator countries. Indirect compliance costs mainly played a role in the two food issues, which were closely linked to the debate over agricultural trade. Both types of costs have an important impact on the likelihood that a target country will strengthen its standards in response to a regulatory trade measure, and the way in which it will do so. As was shown above, the US and Canada normally sought to respond in ways that were compatible with existing policies and standards.

Baptist-bootlegger coalitions

The final hypothesis relating to constraints dealt with the credibility of regulatory trade measures. It stated that regulatory trade measures will have a greater effect on regulatory standards in the target country if they are supported by 'Baptist-bootlegger' coalitions of domestic producers and public interest groups, since that will increase the credibility of the threat to impose or maintain an import ban. The domestic producers may have an interest in the regulatory trade measure as a protectionist device (to keep out products from foreign competitors), while the public interest groups may support the measure out of principle.

The clearest example of a Baptist-bootlegger coalition among the regulatory trade measures studied here, and indeed a very good example of such a coalition in general, is the coalition of European agricultural and consumer groups that has supported the European ban on the use of growth-hormones in meat production. Consumer groups supported the ban because of the possible health risks associated with these hormones, while farmers wanted protection against cheaper US and Canadian beef. The farmers' demand for protection was part of the wider protectionist tendencies in the EC's Common Agricultural Policy (CAP). It was also fuelled by the European farmers' demand to be compensated for the increasing regulatory burdens placed on them, or otherwise to be protected against foreign imports that are produced according to less stringent standards.

This is such a clear example of a Baptist-bootlegger coalition because it was a very open one, in which the two groups jointly issued a statement in support of the ban. In the other issues, no such open statements were issued and it is more difficult to conclude that there have been Baptist-bootlegger coalitions. In the leghold trap issue, the import ban was mainly supported by animal protection groups. In the late 1980s, European fur farmers may have lent silent support to the ban, but this position was probably not mainly motivated by protectionism. Therefore, this potential coalition was latent at best and in the later stages of the process, fur farmers even actively opposed the European measures.

In the GM foods issue, European farmers, food processors and retailers have supported more restrictive European measures with regard to GM foods. Among European business groups, this support has been strongest and most open among retailers, which have come close to the positions taken by consumer groups in many respects. Farmers and food processors seem to have acquiesced in the measures rather than having actively supported them. The positions taken by European business groups in this case seem to have been determined mostly by concerns about the confidence of European consumers and the stability of European markets. The structure of the CAP may have reinforced the farmers' position, or at least prevented them from opposing the European restrictions, but this seems to have been less of an issue for food processors and retailers, who might gain from more liberal trade in agricultural products. Even if protectionism has played a role in this issue, the resulting agreement between consumer groups and some business groups can at most be labelled a latent Baptist-bootlegger coalition, like in the leghold trap issue, and not an open one.

In the data protection issue, European business groups do not seem to have supported the EC measures in an active way. The problems confronting firms in relation to data protection issues were largely similar on both sides of the Atlantic and related more to specific sectors. For instance, direct marketing firms in the US and Europe worked together on many issues relating to data protection policies. Although the favoured approaches may have differed between European, US and Canadian business groups, there is no indication that European firms supported the data protection Directive for protectionist motives.

Now, what effect did the existence or absence of Baptist-bootlegger coalitions have in the four issues? In terms of my theoretical framework, the existence of a coalition should reduce the EC's win-set and thereby strengthen its bargaining position vis-à-vis the US and Canada. The developments in the hormone issue seem to confirm this: the strong support by the two main interest groups seems to have led to a very narrow EC win-set. This may also help to explain why no agreement could be reached, as the reduction of the EC's win-set may have prevented it from overlapping with the US and Canadian win-sets.

It is likely, however, that the existence of an open Baptist-bootlegger coalition in the EC also had an impact on the US and Canadian win-sets, something that was not predicted by the hypotheses. The open support from European farmers for the import ban may have reinforced the US and Canadian suspicion that the hormone ban in fact had protectionist rather than health protection objectives. This may then have reduced their win-sets, too. I will come back to the effect of these perceptions below, when the hypothesis on protectionism and genuine concerns is discussed, but suffice it to say here that the existence of a Baptist-bootlegger coalition may have an effect through that mechanism as well, and may therefore reduce the effects of a regulatory trade measure on other countries' domestic standards.

Consequently, latent Baptist-bootlegger coalitions seem to be more effective than open coalitions in strengthening the credibility of a regulatory trade measure without adversely affecting other countries' willingness to change their domestic standards. The leghold trap and GM foods issues are cases in point. In these issues, the protectionist effects of the European measures may have been welcome to some business groups, even though they did not specifically seek those effects. This probably reduced potential resistance to the measures within the EC, thus making them more credible, while at the same time it did not affect the US and Canadian willingness to consider regulatory change.

The case studies also show that the credibility of a regulatory trade measure is affected by the range of government officials involved. In the data protection issue, decisions to block data flows and decisions on the adequacy of third countries' data protection policies were left entirely to data protection specialists. The officials involved were DG Internal Market, which had developed the EC Directive, national data protection commissioners in the Article 29 Working Party, and national data protection specialists in the Article 31 Committee. This significantly increased the threat to block data transfers to third countries without an adequate level of protection. In the leghold trap issue, the credibility of the European Regulation was substantially reduced after DG I/Trade became involved and gained the initiative. In the two food issues, participation by European DGs was more balanced. The credibility of a regulatory trade measure is therefore also affected by the officials that participate in the process and the position they take within it. This points to a link between credibility and participation expansion, and I will discuss this issue further under that hypothesis.

Hence, the hypothesis on Baptist-bootlegger coalitions is supported in some ways, but has to be refined in others. Baptist-bootlegger coalitions seem to improve the credibility of a regulatory trade measure. Yet, if these coalitions are open, like in the beef-hormone issue, they may also reduce the target country's win-set by confirming suspicions of protectionism. This is an additional effect over and above the effect found by David Vogel. Partly, this may be explained by the fact that David Vogel formulated his Baptist-bootlegger hypothesis in the context of the *adoption* of regulatory trade measures, whereas I have used it as a factor affecting the *credibility* of those measures once they exist.

7.2.2 *Changing preferences*

The second way in which countries can try to affect other countries' win-sets is by changing preferences. The distinction between preferences and constraints is a matter of definition. In chapter 2, preferences were defined at the level of policies; if an actor succeeds in changing another actor's ranking of policy alternatives given their consequences (i.e. by using arguments), that is considered to be a change in preferences. Since regulatory trade measures (and retaliation) are normally supported by arguments, these mechanisms are also important in an analysis of the California effect. In chapter 2, three hypotheses were formulated concerning the conditions under which regulatory trade measures and retaliatory measures will affect the political balance in another country through the use of arguments:

- A regulatory trade measure will have a greater effect on regulatory standards in the target country, the more it ties in with deeply-held values and perceived problems in the target country;
- A regulatory trade measure will have a greater effect on regulatory standards in the target country, the more actors in the target country perceive it to be motivated by genuine concerns rather than protectionism;
- A regulatory trade measure will have a greater effect on regulatory standards in the target country if it conforms to international law and international standards.

Deeply-held values and perceived problems

The first hypothesis related to deeply-held values and perceived problems in the country affected by the regulatory trade measure. On the basis of this hypothesis, a regulatory trade measure is expected to have a stronger effect on regulatory standards in the target country if the standards embodied in that measure 'touch base' with values that are widely held in the country affected by it or with problems that have already been discussed and recognised as important in that country. By contrast, if the standards in the regulatory trade measure 'come out of the blue,' the measure will have less effect.

As was indicated above, this hypothesis is closely linked to the one concerning the costs of compliance. There it was concluded that the costs of compliance are lower if the required change of standards can be achieved within an existing approach, since such a change will require a smaller adjustment of practices, and it will require a more minor realignment in the coalition supporting the standards. The first factor relates to the (economic) adjustment costs of changing standards, the second both to those costs and to the perceived appropriateness of such a change. Thus, this second factor also relates to domestic actors' preferences in that a change within an existing approach will normally tie in more closely with the preferences of the actors supporting that approach than a change in approach.

Above, under the hypothesis concerning the costs of compliance, it was shown that the US and Canada tended to respond to the European measures in ways that were compatible with domestic developments. In most cases, this can be explained with reference to both adjustment costs and preferences, since both factors point to the same outcome. It is therefore difficult to isolate the effects of these two explanatory variables and thereby to assess the relative weight of the two hypotheses, since they predict similar outcomes. As a result, it is also difficult to isolate the effects through constraints (costs) from the effects through preferences (appropriateness).

In the data protection issue, however, the two hypotheses may lead to different predictions. In both countries, the adjustment costs of adopting data protection legislation were probably high, although they may have been somewhat lower in Canada than in the US. This may explain why Canada adopted legislation and the US did not, but such an explanation is not entirely satisfactory. The adjustment costs of complying with data protection legislation are difficult to estimate and depend largely on the law to be adopted and on the standards that were previously in place. Moreover, it is not clear whether compliance with one comprehensive data protection law would actually be more expensive to US firms than compliance with the plethora of data protection laws and codes that are currently in place. This is also reflected in the decision by the Canadian (Direct) Marketing Association to support legislation even though the outcome of the legislative process was unclear at that point. Thus, the choice to pursue legislation seems to be based more on the perceived appropriateness of a comprehensive legislative approach than on a purely material cost-benefit calculation. In terms of my theoretical framework, this would be considered a matter of preferences rather than constraints. The outcomes in the data protection issue therefore seem to conform more to the hypothesis on deeply-held values and perceived problems than the hypothesis on the costs of adjustment. In any case, they suggest that values and perceived problems may play an independent role in shaping the outcomes.

In the other cases, the hypothesis on deeply-held values and perceived problems by and large predicts the same outcomes as the hypothesis on the costs of adjustment. In the leghold trap issue, North American animal protection groups had campaigned against leghold traps for a long time when the import ban was adopted, in particular in the US. They used the European ban as a way to strengthen their arguments in the domestic debate, and they also played an important role in the process leading to its adoption in the first place.

Because of the long-standing controversy over leghold traps in the two countries, the purpose of the import ban was a very illegitimate one as far as North American trappers and wildlife regulators were concerned. The import ban thus became part of the ongoing domestic controversies over the issue of leghold traps, and became associated with an animal protection (or even animal rights) position. Arguably, this made it more difficult for the US and Canadian governments to accept a ban on leghold traps.

Conversely, deeply-held values and perceived problems played a role in changing the EC's position, because the US and Canadian governments could use the animal protection argument against the European Community. Purportedly, the Regulation sought to improve animal welfare, not to ban trapping as such. Given that position, however, it was difficult to defend a ban on one specific type of trap while excluding other, possibly equally cruel traps from that ban. It was this argument, together with the GATT/WTO incompatibility of the import ban that led to the European Commission's acceptance of an agreement on humane trapping standards rather than requiring an outright ban on leghold traps.

In the beef-hormone and GM foods issues, the two hypotheses lead to the same predictions, since the adjustment costs were high and the European concerns were seen as illegitimate by all except a minority of groups (even apart from the allegedly protectionist intent of the European measures, which I will discuss below). In the beef-hormone issue, the EC's arguments were not even supported by most US and Canadian consumer groups. In the GM foods issue, the European arguments were picked up by a wide range of consumer and environmental groups in both countries, but this was probably more the result of the activities of transnational public interest groups than of the EC's restrictive measures. Still, the concerns among US and Canadian public interest groups did lead to some strengthening of domestic standards.

Thus, deeply-held values and perceived problems may account, at least to some extent, for the way the US and Canada reacted to the European regulatory trade measures. Such an effect of regulatory trade measures through preferences may occur by lending credibility to arguments in the domestic debate. Thus, the arguments by proponents of more stringent data protection policies in the US and Canada have probably been strengthened by the European Directive as an example of comprehensive data protection legislation enforced by independent supervisory authorities. US privacy advocates, for instance, actively sought to use the European Directive to intensify the domestic US debate about the level of data protection offered by existing legislation. In the other cases, public interest groups did the same, but in those cases the EC's arguments were less legitimate and therefore had less impact.

To wrap up the argument, the hypothesis on deeply-held values and perceived problems seems to account for much of the difference in the way the US and Canada responded to the European data protection Directive. This factor therefore seems to play an independent role as well, by increasing the legitimacy of some specific response among domestic actors, thereby reducing the political costs of strengthening regulatory standards in the target country.

Protectionism and genuine concerns

The second hypothesis related to the perceived motive behind a regulatory trade measure: if actors in a target country perceive a measure as being based on 'genuine' concerns (like the protection of consumers or the environment), then that measure will have stronger effects than if it is perceived as a protectionist device. It is difficult to assess what actors in another country see as the main motive behind a regulatory trade measure. Allegations of protectionism are a recurring theme throughout these cases and seem to be part of the regular debates over regulatory trade measures. Moreover, the perception of a regulatory trade measure may differ between actors within the same country that support or oppose the standards contained in the regulatory trade measure.

Still, some general conclusions about the way the four European measures were perceived in the US and Canada do seem possible, by combinations of public statements and the interviews. Then, the two food issues stand out as the most controversial among US and Canadian officials and business groups. They were both seen as part of a wider set of European agricultural policies, which have always been denounced as protectionist by the two countries. The EC ban on growth-hormones was generally considered to be the most blatantly protectionist measure among these four. As was argued above, this was partly the result of the open Baptist-bootlegger coalition that supported the import ban in the EC. The leghold trap Regulation and the data protection Directive have also sometimes been branded as protectionist, but this aspect seems to have played a much less important role.

This is not to say that the European concerns in the leghold trap and data protection issues have always been considered 'genuine.' The leghold trap Regulation, in particular, has often been forcefully denounced as being motivated by prejudice and bad information, as well as a hidden agenda to eliminate trapping altogether. As a result, the purpose of the leghold trap Regulation was considered to be highly illegitimate among US and Canadian officials and trappers (but of course not among animal protection groups). The same is true for some North American observers of the beef-hormone and GM foods issues, who saw the European measures as neither protectionist nor legitimate, but simply as political moves fuelled by ignorance on the part of European voters and/or consumers. This reflects differences in values and perceived problems and ties in with the hypothesis discussed above.

Still, a regulatory trade measure seems to be more effective if it is not perceived as being motivated by protectionism. If a regulatory measure is perceived to be protectionist in its intent, changes in target countries' regulatory standards are probably less likely for two reasons. First, changing regulatory standards in response to a regulatory trade measure is even more illegitimate if that measure is widely considered to be motivated by protectionism. Then, changing those standards will more readily be interpreted as yielding to foreign pressure.

Second, if a regulatory trade measure is perceived as a protectionist measure, firms and officials in the target country will be uncertain whether giving in to those measures will actually lead to sustained access to the initiator country's market. In the beef-hormone issue, this played an important role in US beef producers' reluctance to agree to a compensation package with the EC: they feared that the EC would soon find other ways of blocking beef imports after an agreement had been reached. In the data protection issue, on the other hand, it was easier for the US and the EC to reach the Safe Harbour agreement once US firms and officials became convinced that protectionism was not a motive behind the European Directive, since this increased the confidence on their part that the EC would negotiate in good faith.

All in all, the hypothesis on genuine concerns and protectionism has to be refined on the basis of these case studies. If actors in a target country perceive a regulatory trade measure to be fuelled by protectionist motives, it will be much less legitimate to strengthen domestic standards in response to that measure. A perception of genuine concerns helps to defray accusations of protectionism, but it does not seem to make a difference in itself when the concerns are seen as illegitimate by actors in the target country. This ties is with the hypothesis on deeply-held values and perceived problems, though; a perception of genuine concerns therefore does not seem to play an independent role.

Compatibility with international (trade) law

The final hypothesis that related to preferences was the one on international law and international standards. It was hypothesised that regulatory trade measures will have a greater effect if they are compatible with international (trade) law. For regulatory trade measures, two types of international law are important: GATT/WTO law and (voluntary or binding) international standards.

WTO (and previously GATT) law sets limits on the regulatory trade measures which countries are allowed to take. Among the four regulatory trade measures studied here, the leghold trap Regulation and the beef-hormone ban violated WTO law (or, to be more precise, the import bans contained in these measures violated WTO law). In the beef-hormone issue, this was determined in two panel cases and a case before the WTO's Appellate Body. In the leghold trap issue, the import ban was not implemented and there was no case before the GATT or WTO, but a European import ban would quite clearly have violated GATT/WTO law.

The European data protection Directive seemed to conform to WTO (in this case: GATS) law, at least as long as the EC required third countries to have a similar level of protection and not identical standards. The EC's restrictions on GM foods and food products have been somewhat more ambiguous, but it can be argued (as was done in chapter 5) that until now the approval procedure has stayed within the latitude which WTO law allows; the labelling requirements are more problematic, but this case is not clear-cut either.

At first sight, the GATT/WTO compatibility does not seem to have any relation to the outcomes in the cases. The leghold trap Regulation, which was probably the clearest violation of GATT/WTO law, led to a California effect; so did the data protection Directive, which was WTO compatible. The restrictions on GM foods, which were probably partly WTO compatible and partly dubious, led to a minor California effect. Finally, the import ban on hormone-treated beef, which was officially deemed to be WTO inconsistent by subsequent panels and the Appellate Body, led to a stalemate, with neither a California effect nor a withdrawal of the European import ban.

Yet, as was argued in the conclusions to the case studies, GATT/WTO law did affect the processes and outcomes in the cases. These effects can be summarised in three conclusions. The first conclusion is that GATT/WTO law seems to be more effective as a threat when a regulatory trade measure has not been implemented than to reverse existing measures, since the reversal of an existing measure requires an active decision, the political costs of which will increase once a measure has been implemented. These costs depend on three factors. First, regulatory trade measures tend to reinforce their support base because firms that have opposed them will either go out of business or adjust to the new market conditions. Thus, firms that imported US and Canadian prime beef and offal had to adjust after the import ban, which also eliminated their incentives to oppose the import ban. Second, it is more difficult for a regulatory body to reverse a decision if this will affect its credibility. This is particularly important in the approval of products (such as growth-hormones or food products, but this would probably also be true of, for instance, chemicals or pharmaceuticals). Reversing such an approval will undercut the regulator's credibility in other cases. Third, withdrawing a measure that is intended to protect a non-economic value for trade reasons will encounter strong resistance, both from public interest groups and from policy officials.

As long as a regulatory trade measure has not been implemented, GATT/WTO law may be useful as a means of preventing it from coming into force. This was shown most clearly in the leghold trap issue, where the US and Canada did not want to resort to the GATT or WTO, but used the threat of a GATT/WTO complaint to put pressure on the EC. In the end, this threat was arguably the most important factor leading to the two main changes in the EC's position: first, the European Commission's acceptance of negotiations on an agreement on trapping standards, and second, the Council's acceptance of the two agreements. Even though this did not prevent the US and Canada from having to change their domestic standards because of the European Regulation, at least they could do so in their preferred way (through trapping standards) and they could force the EC to accept those standards, too.

The second conclusion about the role of GATT/WTO law is that its influence seems to have increased with the transition from GATT to WTO. In the leghold trap issue, DG I (later DG Trade) became active in late 1994, just before the WTO Agreements would come into force. Around that same time, trade law considerations seem to have gained more prominence within the European Commission more generally. This is most clearly seen by two potential regulatory trade measures that have not been studied in this volume because they did not materialise. In 1993, the EC adopted an amendment to its cosmetics Directive, which would ban the marketing of cosmetics tested on animals. As was noted in chapter 3 on the leghold trap issue, this ban has not yet been implemented, and the European Commission has tabled a proposal to exclude the trade aspects from the Directive. Concerns over WTO compatibility raised by DG I/Trade seem to have played the most important role in this decision. Apparently, these considerations were less important in 1993 than they later became. Another potential regulatory trade measure that did not come into existence was the EC's ban on the use of BST, a hormone used to promote milk production in cows. As was discussed in chapter 4, the BST issue was very similar to the beef-hormone issue. Still, the EC decided to ban the use of BST in the EC, but not to block imports of milk produced with BST, despite calls for import restrictions from European farmers.

These examples point to a stronger role of WTO law than had previously been the case with GATT law, at least in the EC's use of regulatory trade measures. Partly, this may also be the result of the EC's experiences with earlier regulatory trade measures (i.e. the leghold trap Regulation and the ban on growth-hormones), which may have made the European Commission more aware of the negative consequences of using WTO incompatible measures. Nevertheless, the change from GATT to WTO seems to have contributed to this rise in awareness since the new WTO rules made it impossible for the EC (or any other WTO member) to block dispute settlement proceedings, something that could be (and was) done before if a measure was likely to be deemed GATT incompatible. Thus, even though GATT/WTO incompatibility has not led to the withdrawal of regulatory trade measures in the issues studied here, it does seem to have had an important effect on related issues.

The third and final conclusion is that even though GATT/WTO law limits the use of regulatory trade measures, it may also protect the country imposing these measures. This is most clearly the case if a regulatory trade measure complies with GATT/WTO law. Then, the GATT/WTO rules prevent target countries from resorting to retaliation. This may have been a factor in the data protection issue and maybe also in the GM foods issue, although in both cases it is doubtful whether the US (and, for that matter, Canadian) governments would have retaliated anyway, since they were well aware of the negative ramifications which retaliation would have had. Yet, even if a regulatory trade measure does not comply with GATT/WTO law, the country imposing it may be protected by the fact that GATT/WTO proceedings typically take many years to complete. In some cases, such as the leghold trap issue, this may prevent a country from resorting to the WTO at all, since most damage will have been done before the proceedings are completed. In other cases, it will at least be a disincentive for countries to go to the WTO and gain some additional time for the initiator country. Here, again, this effect has probably been heightened by the strengthening of dispute settlement rules in the WTO as compared to the GATT.

Apart from the GATT/WTO regime, international standards that seek to harmonise domestic standards also played a role in most of the issues. In the leghold trap issue, their role was small, since the standardisation process in the International Organization for Standardization (ISO) did not yield any standards. Still, much of the work done in ISO was used in the agreements on humane trapping standards. In the beef-hormone issue, the Codex Alimentarius Commission had set standards for the use of growth-hormones in beef production. In the GM foods issue, several forums were important: the OECD had carried out a great deal of work on risk assessment, the Codex Alimentarius Commission became more involved in the late 1990s, and in 2000 the Cartagena Protocol on trade in genetically modified organisms was concluded. In the data protection issue, the most important international standards were the OECD Guidelines on data protection, which the EC, the US and Canada had endorsed.

Most of these standards (except for the Cartagena Protocol, once it is ratified) are non-binding. They seek to offer guidance and to create a common understanding between countries about certain issues, but they are not (legally) binding on those countries. The standards of the Codex Alimentarius Commission have an indirect legal effect, because they serve as benchmarks in WTO proceedings under the Agreement on Sanitary and Phytosanitary Standards (SPS). According to the SPS Agreement, domestic standards are presumed to be compatible with WTO law if they are based on Codex standards. As can be seen from the legal analysis of the beef-hormone reports in chapter 3, the meaning of this provision was relaxed in the Appellate Body report in order to avoid a de facto harmonisation on the basis of Codex standards. Therefore, they still serve as guidelines rather than international food standards.

Two conclusions can be drawn concerning the role of these international standards. First, they serve as benchmarks in debates between actors but, at least in these four issues, they do not offer much guidance in the way of specific standards. Rather, they set a framework within which subsequent debates could evolve. The Codex Alimentarius MRLs were specific, but they were not followed by the EC.

Second, and most importantly, the international standards only affected outcomes to the extent that they enjoyed broad support in domestic political processes. Thus, the OECD Guidelines on data protection were widely accepted in the EC, the US and Canada, making them an effective framework for discussion. By contrast, the MRLs for hormones in beef that were adopted by the Codex Alimentarius Commission were highly controversial from the outset and were only adopted after a vote that pitted the EC against the US and Canada. As a result, these MRLs were not acceptable to most domestic actors in the EC and did not affect the EC's position.

In the GM foods issue, the OECD's work on substantial equivalence served as an important framework in the first half of the 1990s, probably similar to the role played by the OECD Guidelines on data protection. In the second half of the 1990s, however, some of the OECD's underlying premises became less accepted by interest groups and some officials in the EC, and the concept of substantial equivalence was interpreted differently in the EC than in the US and Canada. As a result, the concept became less useful as the basis for an international agreement.

It is striking that at the level of scientists and officials with a scientific background, the original formulation by the OECD is still widely accepted and there seems to be relatively little disagreement between Europeans and North Americans. It is at the level of public interest groups that the differences have occurred and it is the increased participation of public interest groups and the increased concerns among the public at large that have caused a shift in the acceptability of this approach. To explain the outcomes of a case, it is therefore important to examine which groups and officials actually participate in the process, and what is their position on the international standards.

Therefore, the hypothesis on conformity with international law has to be refined, as well. Conformity with international standards helps to increase the legitimacy of a regulatory trade measure, while non-conformity may undermine it, but only insofar as these standards are accepted by actors in the target country. This is demonstrated by the role of the OECD Guidelines in the data protection issue, and of the OECD's work on biotechnology in the GM foods issue. In the beef-hormone issue, the unacceptability of the Codex standards among most European actors reduced their role. The incompatibility of a regulatory trade measure with international trade law (GATT/WTO law) will confirm a perception of protectionism among actors in the target country, thereby decreasing the regulatory trade measure's legitimacy. Although there is no direct link between GATT/WTO incompatibility and the outcomes of the cases, international trade law seems to have played important roles in the background. This role seems to have grown with the move from GATT to WTO.

7.2.3 Expanding participation

The final hypothesis stated that a regulatory trade measure will have a lesser effect on regulatory standards in the target country, if the target country succeeds in expanding participation in the initiator country to trade officials. This is called participation expansion and it played a role in several issues. The clearest example of successful participation expansion is the leghold trap issue, where the US and Canadian governments succeeded in involving DG I/Trade in the process, which led to the most important shifts in the EC's position.

In the beef-hormone issue, trade officials also became involved in the process, but this did not lead to an appreciable change in the EC's position. As was argued above, this issue and the leghold trap issue did probably lead to changes in related issues, where DG I/Trade also became involved (i.e. the ban on BST and the ban on cosmetics tested on animals), but in the beef-hormone issue the EC's position remained stable. Several factors may account for that. First, DG I/Trade became involved in the late 1980s, when the WTO had not yet been created. If it is true that the change from GATT to WTO led to an important increase in the salience of trade law issues in the EC, this explains why DG I/Trade did not then push as hard as it might have done later. Second, legally speaking, the beef-hormone issue was less clear than the leghold trap issue, especially in the period before the SPS Agreement. Third, in the late 1980s the European Commission was initially relatively flexible and willing to reach an agreement during the talks with the US, only to be constrained by other actors within the EC (such as the European Parliament, consumer groups and some member states) and the discovery of a large black market for hormones within the EC. Hence, participation expansion might have been a successful strategy around 1987, but its effect was reversed by other factors in the EC's political process that left DG I/Trade with little room for manoeuvre.

In the data protection issue, the USTR sought to raise the WTO (GATS) compatibility of the European Directive in talks with DG I/Trade, but that did not lead to participation expansion. As was explained in the case study, this was probably due to the apparent WTO compatibility of the Directive, the fact that no concrete data flows were blocked, and because the call for a WTO case remained confined to only a few US officials.

In the GM foods issue, the trade aspects of the issue have been raised, and special working groups have been set up under the EC-US agreements about Transatlantic trade. It is likely that European trade officials have supported a more liberal regime for GM food products, together with DG Enterprise, but this call has not led to changes in the EC's position. Again, this is probably due to the massive resistance from other officials, interest groups and member states. Moreover, the WTO incompatibility of the European regulatory standards is unclear and it is generally unlikely that the US or Canada will actually resort to the WTO over this issue.

Thus, two steps can be discerned in the process of participation expansion. First, trade officials become involved when either a regulatory trade measure violates WTO law and officials from the target country threaten to go to the WTO, or concrete trade flows are blocked. They do not become involved when trade continues, or when the threat to go to the WTO is not credible. Second, trade officials are able to change the political balance if they succeed in excluding other participants who are less concerned with the trade aspects of an issue.

As was already mentioned above, participation expansion operates mainly through the credibility of a regulatory trade measure. If trade officials become involved in an issue and raise trade (law) concerns over a regulatory trade measure, it is less likely that the regulatory trade measure will actually be implemented. However, if trade officials and trade concerns do not play a role and the issue is left largely to policy officials, as was the case in the data protection issue, the regulatory trade measure becomes much more credible.

Hence, the hypothesis on participation expansion is supported by the leghold trap issue, whereas it did not work in the other issues. Participation expansion seems to work mainly by undermining the credibility of a regulatory trade measure, but it only seems to work under the conditions outlined above. This hypothesis is therefore partly confirmed by the case studies.

7.2.4 Providing an answer to the research problem

All in all, no hypothesis has been contradicted by the case studies. Still, some were supported by only a few observations, which makes it more difficult to reach any strong conclusions; others had to be refined. Nevertheless, the theoretical framework formulated in chapter 2 worked well in accounting for most outcomes in the cases and it is in that sense confirmed by the case studies.

In this subsection, I will present an integrated account of the California effect. This account will be used to arrive at a more general explanation of the outcomes in the eight cases, which forms the answer to my research problem. In chapter 1, the research problem was formulated as follows:

> *Under what conditions will EC process standards in the fields of environmental and consumer protection that affect or have the potential to affect US and Canadian exports lead to a strengthening of standards in the US and Canada?*

Above, the various hypotheses concerning these conditions were discussed. Here, they will be integrated into a general conclusion. This general conclusion and the relations between explanatory variables are summarised schematically in figure 7.1. In this figure, the explanatory variables that were found to have been important in the case studies have been related to other variables and each other. If an increase in one variable leads to an increase in another variable, this is indicated by a '+.' If the relation is an inverse one, this is indicated by a '-'. At the right-hand side, the figure leads to the adoption of more stringent regulatory standards in the target country, that is, a California effect.

Although this scheme suggests a set of deterministic relationships, all relations are more likely to be probabilistic, although it is not possible to determine the probabilities with the type of research design used here. Moreover, some of the relations depicted in figure 7.1 are supported more strongly by the case studies than others. Hence, the caveats formulated above at each of the hypotheses should be taken into account when interpreting the scheme.

Following the scheme from right to left, the decision to adopt more stringent regulatory standards involves a trade-off between the political costs of the regulatory trade measure (which equal the political benefits of strengthening domestic regulatory standards, keeping all domestic political factors constant) and the political costs of strengthening domestic regulatory standards in order to comply with the regulatory trade measure. Both types of costs are determined by a number of other factors.

The political costs of the regulatory trade measure are determined by the (potential) economic impact of the measure. The relation between the (potential) economic impact and the political costs of the measure is qualified by the degree of targeting of these measures on pivotal actors in the target country. The (potential) economic impact depends on the size of the trade effects, and is qualified by the credibility of the regulatory trade measure, that is, the likelihood that it will actually be implemented. The credibility is increased by a Baptist-bootlegger coalition, but decreased by participation expansion to trade officials.

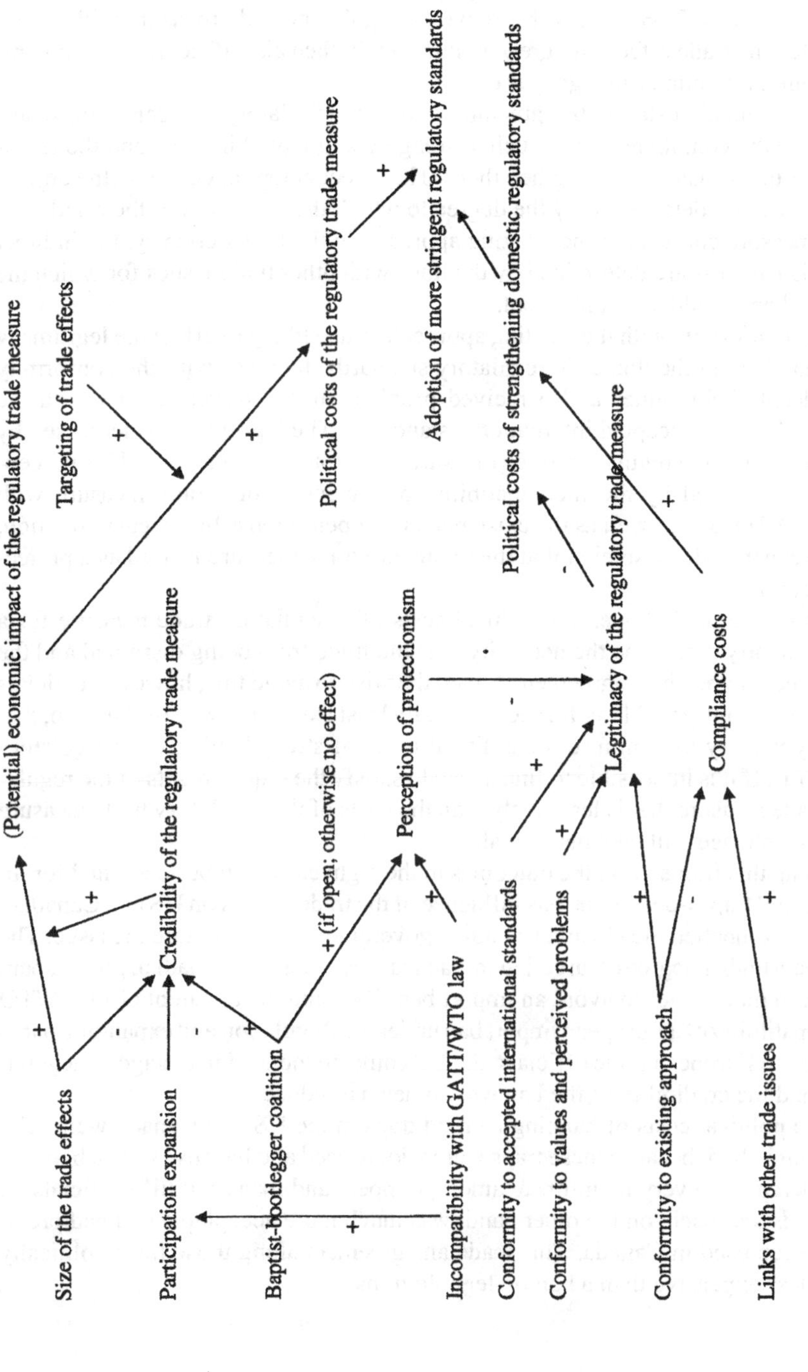

Figure 7.1: Explaining a California effect

Participation expansion is more likely if the regulatory trade measure is incompatible with GATT/WTO law. Moreover, a regulatory trade measure will be less credible if its trade effects are greater, since it will then also affect importing firms in the initiator country to a greater extent.

The political costs of strengthening domestic regulatory standards are determined by the compliance costs such a strengthening would involve and the legitimacy of the decision to strengthen them. The direct compliance costs (the adjustment costs) are determined by the degree to which the standards in the regulatory trade measure conform to the existing approach in the target country; the indirect compliance costs are determined by the links with other trade issues for which the issue at hand could set a precedent.

The conformity with the existing approach is also likely to affect the legitimacy of strengthening the domestic regulatory standards, together with the conformity with deeply-held values and perceived problems in the target country, and the conformity with accepted international standards. The legitimacy is decreased by a perception of the regulatory trade measure as a protectionist device. This perception is confirmed by the incompatibility of the regulatory trade measure with GATT/WTO law, as well as the existence of an open Baptist-bootlegger coalition, which enhance the suspicion that the regulatory trade measure is used as a protectionist tool.

As was argued above, the political costs of a regulatory trade measure for a target country determine the necessity to avoid trade from being disrupted and the willingness to reach an agreement. Given the wish to avoid this, however, officials in a target country will look for the politically least expensive way of doing so, that is, they will try to minimise the political costs of strengthening their regulatory standards. If it is impossible to find a way to satisfy the requirements of the regulatory trade measure that is less costly than the costs of the regulatory trade measure itself, no change will take place at all.

Using this framework, the outcomes in the eight cases can be accounted for. In the leghold trap issue, the serious influence of the trade effects on US and Canadian trappers compelled the US and Canadian governments not to ignore the issue. The relatively higher degree of targeting in Canada meant that the Canadian government was even more eager to avoid an import ban. By using the apparent GATT/WTO incompatibility of a European import ban under the Regulation and expanding participation to European trade officials, the EC could be induced to engage in negotiations and the credibility of the ban was somewhat reduced.

The political costs of banning leghold traps in the US and Canada were relatively high, both because these traps were widely used and because such a ban was considered to be very illegitimate among trappers and many wildlife officials. A standards approach, on the other hand, was much more acceptable and had previously been used in Canada. This made an agreement along those lines politically much less expensive than a ban on leghold traps.

The leghold trap issue shows an interesting additional phenomenon in that the EC itself also agreed to more stringent trapping standards in the agreements with the US and Canada. This is unique among these four issues, and strictly speaking it is beyond the scope of my research problem, which is concerned with the effects of regulatory trade measures on the US and Canada. Still, this outcome is interesting in itself and was the result of a successful attempt by the US and Canada to take over the initiative in this issue. This was again made possible by the fact that European trade officials had a high stake in avoiding the implementation of the import ban, which would probably have led to a GATT/WTO dispute, while at the same time they had to cope with high domestic political costs of refusing to implement the ban because of the strong support for the ban in the European Parliament, among animal welfare groups, and by some member states. As a result, the US and Canada were able to use the EC's regulatory trade measure against the EC itself, a situation that did not occur in any of the other issues.

In the data protection issue, it was again the extent of the potential trade effects that compelled the US and Canada to act. Targeting did not play a role here. The potential effects of a disruption of data flows also reduced the credibility of the European measures, since European officials and firms had an interest in avoiding disruptions, as well. This led to a lower credibility of the EC's threat to block data flows, as was reflected in the initial scepticism among many US officials and firms concerning the EC's willingness to block data transfers. In the end, however, the fact that the European data protection community was relatively closed and the US did not succeed in expanding participation to other types of officials assured more credibility.

In terms of the political costs of strengthening data protection standards, the legitimacy of the issue was fairly high in both the US and Canada. The European approach, however, was much less legitimate in the US, and the agreement with the EC was based on the prevailing US approach of self-regulation without an independent overseeing agency. In Canada, domestic developments (the CSA standard, Quebec's law, and the existence of the Privacy Commissioner of Canada) had increased the legitimacy of comprehensive legislation and independent oversight. The apparent absence of protectionism on the part of the EC, witnessed among others in the absence of a Baptist-bootlegger coalition, probably increased the legitimacy of adopting more stringent standards in both countries. In the whole process, the OECD Guidelines served as a background to talks and as a common set of principles, although these Guidelines offered room for the EC, Canadian and Safe Harbour approaches at the same time so that the specific responses were not determined by them.

In the GM foods issue, the political costs of the EC's regulatory trade measures were limited, in particular since the size of the trade effects was relatively small. The only producers for which these costs were non-trivial were US soya bean growers, who decided to suspend the marketing of GM soya bean varieties that had not been approved in the EC, although they explicitly did not support a strengthening of domestic US regulatory standards.

The costs of strengthening domestic standards were enormous, both in terms of direct and indirect compliance costs and because many of the European measures were illegitimate as far as US and Canadian officials and business groups were concerned. Concerns raised by US and Canadian consumer and environmental groups lent some legitimacy to the European measures, however, and if these measures had an effect on US and Canadian regulatory standards, it was mainly through this channel. The perception of protectionism played a small direct role, although US and Canadian officials and business groups were wary of the effects on other agricultural trade issues (which led to increased indirect compliance costs).

In the beef-hormone issue, the situation was similar, but more extreme. Here, the regulatory trade measure was credible, mainly since it enjoyed the broad support of European consumer groups and farmers, but its political costs in the US and Canada were insignificant given the low beef exports from the US and Canada to the EC. The political costs of strengthening domestic regulatory standards were even higher than in the GM foods issue. First, the use of growth-hormones was economically very important to US and Canadian beef producers. Second, the issue was perceived to have close links to other agricultural trade issues. Third, and closely related to the second point, the European hormones ban was seen as a protectionist instrument, because of the close link to surpluses in the European market, the open support of European farmers for the ban, and the GATT/WTO incompatibility of the ban as was determined in a series of WTO cases. Finally, the ban on growth-hormones was considered to be very illegitimate in the US and Canada since these hormones were deemed to be safe, even by most consumer groups in those countries.

The conclusions as depicted in figure 7.1 therefore seem to account well for the outcomes in these four issues and eight cases. In the remainder of this chapter, I will discuss to what extent these conclusions are likely to be applicable to other cases.

7.3 Generalising the conclusions to other cases

Strictly speaking, the conclusions drawn in the previous section only relate to the four issues and eight cases examined in this study. However, these cases were studied in order to gain an insight into the general phenomenon of the California effect. Therefore, it is important to assess to what extent the conclusions of this study can be generalised to other cases. In this final section, I will answer that question for three types of generalisations: to other (future) environmental and consumer protection issues; to other issue areas (including labour standards, and human rights); and to other countries or trade relations.

Generalisation will take place by critically examining some of the assumptions underlying the conclusions of this study in order to arrive at well-reasoned hypotheses concerning the factors that are likely to be important in other cases to which these assumptions do not apply. The outcomes of other cases may differ from those examined in this study for one or more of the following four reasons:

- The initial values of some of the explanatory variables may be different. For instance, trade dependence on the EC may be greater for some neighbouring countries than it is for the US or Canada;
- The relative weight of the various factors discussed above may differ. Thus, even if the extent of trade effects and the role of deeply-held values and perceived problems may play a role in another case, it may well be that one factor or another is relatively more important than in the cases studied here;
- Additional explanatory variables may be important in other cases, requiring an extension of the theoretical framework;
- The causal relations inferred in this study may be contradicted or reversed in other cases.

These four situations pose different types of challenges to my theoretical framework. The first situation would fit well into the framework, as long as the outcome conforms to what the hypothesis predicts. Then, the initial values may differ, but the hypotheses do not, and in the end a theory is all about the hypotheses. The second and third situation would require modifications of the theoretical framework. They do not squarely contradict the framework, but some elements would have to be changed, added or removed in order to apply it to other cases. Whether this constitutes an important modification to the framework depends on the type of modification that would have to be made. The fourth situation would contradict my theoretical framework. Then, the framework would have to be partly or completely replaced by another framework in order to account for the different causal relations in another case.

In addition, the level of abstraction has to be taken into account. It may well be that the conclusions of this study apply to another case when factors are formulated at a relatively high level of abstraction, but not in the way they have been specified in this study. Of course, the higher the level of abstraction, the less informative the theory will be. For instance, arguing that a decision to strengthen standards involves a trade-off between the political costs and benefits of doing so is a truism that is void of any meaning apart from the specification given to the factors that determine those costs and benefits. Still, those factors, too, can be formulated at a more or less abstract level. Keeping this in mind and using the basic fourfold scheme presented above, I will now discuss to what extent the theoretical framework derived from my conclusions is likely to hold true in other cases.

7.3.1 Generalising the conclusions to other issues

To begin with, I will look at the possibility of generalising the outcomes of this study to other issues in the fields of environmental and consumer protection in the Transatlantic relation. In section 1.5, a number of assumptions were discussed that have to be accepted if generalisations are to be made. Some of these assumptions were shown to be less relevant if use is made of systematic theory and process-tracing. Nevertheless, other assumptions remain crucial, and they are important in generalising the conclusions to other issues and cases.

Most crucially, it has to be assumed that other cases reflect similar patterns of causal relations, which largely depends on the conditions under or the limits within which the conclusions are supposed to apply. In this study's research problem, these limits were fairly narrowly drawn to include only cases involving process standards in the fields of environmental and consumer protection in the EC-US and EC-Canadian relations after the Cold War.

The conclusions of this study should also hold true for these cases, which include mainly the cases examined in this study, but also the cases not studied and cases in the (near) future under similar conditions. These cases may exhibit different initial values of the explanatory variables, but the hypotheses should still apply.

Furthermore, the conclusions may also largely hold true when some restrictions on the research problem are relaxed. First, EC regulatory trade measures were defined in terms of the existence of a legal basis for restricting trade. In some cases, there may be no such legal basis, but the EC (or another country) may threaten to interrupt trade anyway. The credibility of such a threat would depend on the likelihood of a legal basis being adopted. Given the complexity and length of EC procedures, an EC threat to interrupt trade in the absence of an existing legal basis would not seem to be very credible. Still, this likelihood can be expressed within the theoretical framework, which includes the credibility of a regulatory trade measure. All other hypotheses are likely to be applicable as well. As a consequence, the theoretical framework should equally apply to threats without a legal basis and threats with such a legal basis.

Second, when product and not process standards are concerned, many of the hypotheses should remain the same. Even though product standards are always imposed on products and not on countries, like the EC measures on leghold traps and data protection, governments may become involved in disputes over product standards when exports from firms in their country are threatened. Thus, many of the same dynamics may be at play in those processes and in the processes examined here. Even if they do not become involved in a trade dispute, they may play a role in domestic processes involving the strengthening of the product standards. Thus, there is little reason to expect fundamentally different or additional factors to be important in those cases, although the initial values of the explanatory variables may differ, and possibly the relative weight of the factors amongst themselves.

Third, all cases studied here took place mainly in the 1990s, that is, after the Cold War. As was explained in subsection 1.4.4, this delimitation served to exclude the influence, if any, of the larger political and military context of the Transatlantic relation. The impact of that context on California-effect types of processes is unclear. The military or security context does not seem to have played a role in the cases studied here. The larger political context was probably important in some cases, particularly the GM foods issue, where, for instance, the US Department of State was also involved. Similarly, within the European Commission, DG External Affairs deals with Transatlantic trade relations within a broader political framework. Still, from the case studies, it is not apparent that (or indeed how) this affected the outcomes.

At the very least, the theoretical framework is likely to hold true in future cases that evolve within a political context similar to that in the cases studied here. If larger political considerations play a more important role, some additional factors may have to be included and some causal relations may be different. However, even then, much of the impact of the larger political considerations may be explained within my theoretical framework, similar to the way trade considerations are incorporated within it. Within a government, broader political considerations (including security considerations) will probably be advanced by a specific agency or type of official. Within the European Commission, that would be DG External Affairs, in the US the Department of State, and in Canada the foreign affairs section of the Department of Foreign Affairs and International Trade. These broader political considerations could be hypothesised to become important if participation is expanded to these officials and if they are able to gain an edge over other officials and groups participating in the process. The conditions under which this is likely to occur would have to be the subject of further study.

Still, both when there are cases that conform to all the restrictions in my research problem and when some of these restrictions are relaxed, two other assumptions underlying generalisations from multiple case studies are important. First, studies using a small number of cases (like this study) are less well suited to cope with probabilistic causal relations. It is likely that the conclusions reached in this study are in fact probabilistic relations, in that the precise strength of the relations may vary somewhat across cases, even in the same issue area and trade relation. Consequently, predictions made for other cases on the basis of this study's conclusions should always be made cautiously, acknowledging the potential for 'random' variation between cases. At the same time, when the probabilistic nature of the causal relations is accepted, small differences in outcomes between cases would not automatically invalidate the conclusions of this study.

Second, measurement errors or problems of interpretation can render generalisations invalid. Even though great care was taken to establish measurements or interpretations on the basis of various sources, many of the variables in this study are vulnerable to differences in interpretation.

To complicate things even further, differences in interpretation are often crucial components of the political processes underlying the California effect. For instance, in measuring the variable 'size of trade effects,' which on the face of it would seem to be the most objective explanatory variable, differences in measurement turned out to play quite an important role in some cases, in particular when indirect or future trade effects were at stake. In the end, interpretations by participants in the political process are the most important, not some objective measure subsequently determined by a researcher.

This is even more true for variables such as 'perception of protectionism' or 'legitimacy of regulatory change.' Although I believe that a strong case can be made for the interpretations given in this study, some room for interpretation always remains. This is likely to be particularly problematic when these variables are used in other case studies by other researchers.

7.3.2 Generalising the conclusions to other issue areas

The research problem and the cases in this study involved consumer and environmental protection standards. Yet, the effects of (regulatory) trade measures have been discussed in a much wider range of issues, including at least human rights and labour standards. In this subsection I will discuss the possibility of generalising (some of) the conclusions of this study to these two issue areas.

In subsection 1.4.1, it was argued that human rights-related economic sanctions differ from environmental and consumer protection standards in at least two important respects. First, human rights often involve important issues of power and authority in the target country. Therefore, they touch upon the very power base of that country's government. Second, human rights violations are usually not linked to competitiveness concerns. Likewise, human rights-related economic sanctions are not imposed on specific products that do not conform to or have not been produced according to certain standards. Rather, they are an instrument to hit (certain groups in) the target country.

Despite these differences, my theoretical framework was based partly on the literature on human rights-related economic sanctions, and both the hypotheses proposed in the literature and the outcomes of this study suggest at least an analogy between the two areas in terms of which factors are likely to effect regulatory change (quite apart from the question whether economic sanctions are intended to produce change or are used as a form of punishment; for a discussion of this issue, see Nossal, 1989).

This analogy or similarity is borne out by the conclusions of some studies in the field of human rights-related economic sanctions. For instance, Glasius (1999: 311-340) found a set of explanatory variables for the effects of international sanctions against human rights violations in Indonesia that is strikingly similar to many of the conclusions reached in this study. Similar results have also been reported as regards particular hypotheses or factors, for instance the economic impact of economic sanctions (Hufbauer, Schott & Elliott, 1990: 101-102) and the role of deeply-held values (Klotz, 1996). Many of these conclusions are certainly hotly contested by other authors in the field, and it would be far beyond the scope of this study to review this literature, much less to take a position on these complicated issues. Nevertheless, the available literature seems to warrant a prima facie conclusion that there are important similarities between the factors determining the effects of human rights-related sanctions, and those determining the effects of regulatory trade measures.

At the same time, these similarities probably relate more to the theoretical approach and some more abstract variables than to the specific hypotheses drawn up in this study. Differences between cases involving human rights and the cases studied here are likely to result from four sources. First, the initial values for some explanatory variables are probably different. The 'compliance costs' or the 'political costs of strengthening standards' are usually much higher when human rights are involved, since they often affect the government's power base. Therefore, the resistance against regulatory change is probably much stronger when it comes to human rights. Consequently, the political benefits of strengthening standards (or: the political costs of the economic sanctions) probably have to be much higher, too.

Second, the relative weight of the factors may be different. As was indicated above when discussing the conclusions about the hypothesis on targeting, targeting is likely to play a more important role when economic sanctions are concerned, because the products to be hit are less closely related to the standards that are not observed. Hence, targeting may be a deliberate strategy to increase the political costs of the sanctions, whereas in the case of regulatory trade measures it is usually much more difficult selectively to target some groups but not others.

Third, some additional factors may have to be included in a theoretical framework to explain the effects of human rights-related economic sanctions. For instance, the benefits of violating human rights may depend on their necessity for the governing regime to remain in power. Thus, Glasius (1999: 323) found that the 'desirability' of the human rights violations for the Indonesian government was one of the most important factors in explaining the effects of sanctions, and Hawkins (1997: 408) identified low 'domestic costs of easing repression' as an important prerequisite for economic sanctions to produce change.

Fourth, some causal relations may not hold true in the case of human rights-related economic sanctions. For instance, the role of deeply-held values and perceived problems will often be smaller or absent, given the overriding concerns with power and authority that lie at the root of many human rights violations. This will depend, however, on the particular country and the issue at stake. For instance, Hawkins (1997: 408) argued that even in authoritarian regimes 'some domestic actors are able to use international pressure as a tool to advance their own agendas within the regime.' These domestic actors may include both business groups and 'soft-line factions' within the ruling elite. Other studies have shown that close cultural links between the country imposing sanctions and the country affected by them may also have a 'socialising' effect (in the terminology of Klotz, 1996, who studied the effects of sanctions against South Africa). In other countries, in which the ruling elite are less divided and do not have close cultural ties with the countries imposing the sanctions, this mechanism will probably play a much smaller role, however, and the differences with the cases studied here will be greater. Moreover, values may play a more important role if the direct domestic political challenge to a regime is smaller, as was argued above.

Another issue area for which the results of this study may be relevant is the field of labour standards. Although some labour standards have important human-rights aspects, they are also related to competitiveness concerns and have been part of the same discussion as trade and environmental standards (see section 1.4.1). As they are more or less 'in between' environmental and consumer protection standards on the one hand, and human rights on the other, the possibilities for generalisation are also likely to be somewhere in between. Thus, in principle, the theoretical framework in this study could also be used to study regulatory trade measures related to labour standards.

Differences are likely to flow from two of the same sources as discussed above in the context of human rights. The economic costs of strengthening labour standards may be much higher than in the cases studied here, in particular when it comes to standards relating to child labour or wages. The political costs may be much higher when the standards relate to the rights of trade unions and collective bargaining. The importance of targeting depends on the character of the regulatory trade measure: if it is not directly related to products produced according to less stringent standards, these measures have the character of an economic sanction and targeting would be a more important factor.

The role of values and perceived problems may be the same as in the cases studied here, in that regulatory change will be more difficult if the standards to be imposed do not conform to deeply-held values and perceived problems. These values and perceived problems may differ more radically from those in the countries imposing the regulatory trade measures than in the cases studied here, but this would not invalidate the hypothesis itself.

7.3.3 Generalising the conclusions to other countries

In terms of countries, this study was limited to cases in EC-US and EC-Canadian relations (in short: the Transatlantic relation). An important question is therefore to what extent the outcomes of this study can be generalised to other countries and relations. This relates both to the initiator (in this study the EC) and the target (here the US and Canada).

Until now, the US and the EC have been the main potential sources of a California effect at the global level. In section 1.4.3, it was argued that both have unique characteristics that cannot be found in any other country. Many of the EC's specific characteristics, in particular the relation between the EC and the member state levels, played an important role in some cases. Still, it was possible to explain most of the outcomes in the processes by using hypotheses that were developed in the context of national states, in particular the US. Thus, the Baptist-bootlegger coalition hypothesis was not developed with particular reference to the EC, but it still proved fruitful in explaining the EC's behaviour in some cases, although it was irrelevant in others. Similarly, the distinction made between types of officials worked just as well for the EC as for the US and Canada, and many of the same political processes between officials and government agencies seemed to play a role.

Therefore, there is no reason to expect that the hypotheses relating to the EC as an initiator are fundamentally any different from those relating to the US. When other, smaller countries act as initiators, the hypotheses are also likely to hold true. The main difference will then probably be the size of the trade effects, in that the target country will probably be much less dependent on the small country than on the US or the EC, but of course this may be different if the initiator and the target have some special trading relationship. In any case, the theoretical framework is still likely to apply at the level of abstraction at which the hypotheses have been formulated. The specification of the hypotheses in concrete cases will probably differ when another initiator is studied.

As to the target country, many of the same conclusions are likely to hold true for other target countries as well. In fact, the hypotheses on participation expansion and deeply-held values and perceived problems were advanced by Schoppa (1993) in relation to Japan. Still, the theoretical framework may have to be modified as regards a number of other points, depending on the type of target country involved.

First, the theoretical framework used in this study assumes an important role for organised interests in the target country, and relies on a distinction between different types of business groups and public interest groups. In non-Western, non-liberal and/or non-democratic countries, these interests may be absent, organised differently, or have different links to the government. Consequently, Trumbull (2000: 93) argued that a California effect is only likely to take place in democratic countries, where 'the interests of business [are] checked by government officials who rely on popular elections for their offices.'

This remark should be qualified in that the absence of popular or public interest group involvement need not preclude a California effect altogether, but such an effect would rely entirely on export considerations by government officials. Yet, as Trumbull (2000: 93) stressed, the process leading to a California effect 'is not automatic, nor purely economic [but] instead fundamentally political.' In general, political pressure for the strengthening of regulatory standards depends to a great extent on pressure by interest groups and the public at large. This is also borne out by the cases examined in this study, not only with regard to elected officials but also to public interest groups. Given the important role of public interest groups and public concerns in these cases, a California effect is less likely in non-democratic than in democratic regimes, and in countries that lack public interest groups than in countries that have well-organised public interest groups.

Second, some new factors may play a role when other target countries are involved. For instance, in section 2.4.2, it was argued that regulatory trade measures are more likely to be successful if the relation between initiator and target is generally friendly and co-operative (cf. Li, 1993; Schoppa, 1999). Apart from the apparent difficulties involved in measuring this factor, the hypothesis could not be tested in this study, since there was no appreciable variation on this variable between EC-US and EC-Canadian relations. However, when other countries are involved this may well be possible and this hypothesis would have to be added to the theoretical framework, possibly as a variable that determines the legitimacy of the regulatory trade measure in the target country or that qualifies the relation between deeply-held values or perceived problems and the legitimacy.

A whole set of new factors may enter the equation when the regulatory trade measure is part of a broader package of regulatory reform in exchange for increased market access, as is the case for instance for the candidates for European Union membership in Central and Eastern Europe, the countries that have an association agreement with the EC, or Mexico when it wanted to become part of the North American Free Trade Agreement with the US and Canada. As was argued in section 1.4.3, these processes are likely to involve a much broader range of considerations that may override any considerations related to the specific regulatory standard at issue, rendering most of the hypotheses in the framework irrelevant.

At the same time, a California effect could be expected to be more likely in this situation, partly for political and strategic reasons that are not part of the theoretical framework, and partly because the potential economic impact of complying with the more stringent standards is much greater. Even then, the form which a strengthening will take in the target country will probably be highly dependent on existing approaches in that country, as well as deeply-held values and perceived problems, at least in practice if not formally. This, however, is a fairly general prediction, and a separate study would be required to pinpoint more specifically how these processes work.

Thus, the theoretical framework will have to be modified if other target countries are involved. Depending on the specific target country, most explanatory variables may be retained, or important elements in the framework may have to be restructured, rewritten or deleted. In general, the occurrence of a California effect appears to become increasingly less likely the more target countries differ from the US and Canada in terms of being a liberal democracy with strong public interest groups and having close co-operative relations with the initiator. At the same time, the initial values of some other explanatory variables may lead to a greater likelihood of a California effect. Trade dependence on the initiator, in particular, will often be higher than the US and Canadian dependence on the EC in the cases examined here while, conversely, the dependence of the initiator on the target may be smaller.

List of Interviews

7-8-2000 US Mission (Beef-Hormone and GM Foods)
Interview with two officials of the US Mission in Brussels (also GM foods)

7-8-2000 Canadian Mission (Beef-Hormone and GM Foods)
Interview with an official of the Canadian Mission in Brussels

14-8-2000 BEUC (Beef-Hormone and GM Foods)
Interview with a representative of the European Consumers Association

29-8-2000 EuropaBio (GM Foods)
Interview with a representative of the European Association of Biotechnology Firms

31-8-2000 ASA (GM Foods)
Interview with two representatives of the American Soybean Association's
West European Office

31-8-2000 European Commission (GM Foods)
Interview with an official of the European Commission

5-9-2000 BEUC (Data Protection)
Interview with a representative of the European Consumers Association

26-9-2000 European Commission (Beef-Hormone and GM Foods)
Interview with an official of the European Commission

26-9-2000 COPA/COGECA (Beef-Hormone and GM foods)
Interview with a representative of the European Farmers Association

29-9-2000 EuroCommerce (Beef-Hormone and GM foods)
Interview with a representative of the European Retailers Association

29-9-2000 Canadian Mission (Leghold Traps)
Interview with an official of the Canadian Mission in Brussels

17-10-2000 DG Internal Market (Data Protection)
Interview with an official of DG Internal Market

24-10-2000 Canadian Mission (Data Protection)
Interview with two officials of the Canadian Mission in Brussels

9-11-2000 DG Enterprise (Leghold Traps: Cosmetics Directive)
Interview with an official of DG Enterprise

9-11-2000 European Commission (GM Foods)
Interview with an official of the European Commission

14-11-2000 DG Trade (Data Protection)
Interview with an official of DG Trade

23-11-2000	FEDMA (Data Protection) Interview with a representative of the Federation of European Direct Marketing Associations
28-11-2000	Article 29 Working Party (Data Protection) Interview with a member of the Article 29 Working Party
30-11-2000	UECBV (Beef-Hormone) Interview with a representative of the European Meat Traders Association
8-12-2000	DG Trade (Leghold Traps) Interview with an official of DG Trade
9-1-2001	EPIC (Data Protection) Interview with a representative of the Electronic Privacy Information Center (Interview continued on 26-1-2001)
10-1-2001	FTC (Data Protection) Interview with two officials of the Federal Trade Commission
11-1-2001	AMI (Beef-Hormone) Interview with a representative of the American Meat Institute
11-1-2001	USDA (Beef-Hormone and GM Foods) Interview with two officials of the United States Department of Agriculture
15-1-2001	NTA (Leghold Traps) Interview with two representatives of the National Trappers Association
16-1-2001	FDA (Beef-Hormone and GM Foods) Interview with an official of the Food and Drug Administration
17-1-2001	HSUS/AWI (Leghold Traps) Interview with two representatives of the Humane Society of the United States and one representative of the Animal Welfare Institute
18-1-2001	AFBF (Beef-Hormone and GM Foods) Interview with a representative of the American Farm Bureau Federation
19-1-2001	IAFWA (Leghold Traps) Interview with two officials of the International Association of Fish and Wildlife Agencies
19-1-2001	USTR (Beef-Hormone, GM Foods and Leghold Traps) Interview with four officials of the United States Trade Representative
22-1-2001	Consumers Union (Beef-Hormone and GM Foods) Interview with a representative of Consumers Union
23-1-2001	Commerce (Data Protection) Interview with a former official of the Department of Commerce
24-1-2001	DMA (Data Protection)

	Interview with two representatives of the Direct Marketing Association
25-1-2001	NCGA (GM Foods) Interview with a representative of the National Corn Growers Association
29-1-2001	DB (Leghold Traps) Interview with a representative of the Dutch Society for the Protection of Animals ('DierenBescherming')
9-2-2001	AAFC (Beef-Hormone) Interview with an official of Agriculture and Agri-Food Canada
9-2-2001	Canadian Mission/INAC (Leghold Traps) Interview with a former official of the Canadian Mission in Brussels and an official of Indian and Northern Affairs Canada
12-2-2001	PIAC (Data Protection) Interview with a representative of the Public Interest Advocacy Centre
13-2-2001	Industry Canada (Data Protection) Interview with two officials of Industry Canada
15-2-2001	BioteCanada (GM Foods) Interview with a representative of BioteCanada
15-2-2001	FIC (Leghold Traps) Interview with an official of the Fur Institute of Canada
15-2-2001	DFAIT (Beef-Hormone and GM Foods) Interview with an official of the Department of Foreign Affairs and International Trade
20-2-2001-I	DFAIT (Beef-Hormone, GM Foods and Leghold Traps) Interview with three officials of the Department of Foreign Affairs and International Trade
20-2-2001-II	DFAIT (Beef-Hormone) Interview with an official of the Department of Foreign Affairs and International Trade
21-2-2001	CFIA (GM Foods) Interview with three officials of the Canadian Food Inspection Agency
22-2-2001	Animal Alliance (Leghold Traps) Interview with a representative of the Animal Alliance of Canada/ Canadian Alliance for Furbearing Animals
7-3-2001	CMA (Data Protection) Interview with a representative of the Canadian Marketing Association (By phone)

19-7-2001 Consumers Association of Canada (Beef-Hormone and GM Foods) Interview with a representative of the Consumers Association of Canada (By phone)

REFERENCES

AAFC (1995) *Labelling of Novel Foods Derived through Genetic Engineering*, Communiqué, 1 December 1995

ACB (1998) *Draft International Safe Harbor Principles*, Letter to the Department of Commerce, 14 October 1998, available at www.ita.doc.gov/td/ecom/menu.html

ACB (1999a) Letter to the Department of Commerce, 11 May 1999, available at www.ita.doc.gov/td/ecom/menu.html

ACB (1999b) *Draft International Safe Harbor Principles – November 15, 1999*, Letter to the Department of Commerce, 3 December 1999, available at www.ita.doc.gov/td/ecom/menu.html

ACLU (1998) *Draft International Safe Harbor Privacy Principles*, Letter to the Department of Commerce, 18 November 1998, available at www.ita.doc.gov/td/ecom/menu.html

AFBF (2000a) *Biotechnology – The Farm Perspective*, Retrieved on 5 July 2000, available at www.fb.com/issues/biotech/biotech_farmers.html

AFBF (2000b) *Statement by Bob Stallman, President American Farm Bureau Federation, Regarding Federal Proposal on Biotech Oversight*, News Release, 12 May 2000, available at www.fb.org/news

AFBF (2000c) *The Issue: Labeling Bioengineered Foods*, Retrieved on 5 July 2000, available at www.fb.org/issues/backgrd

AFL-CIO (1999) *Proposed International "Safe Harbor" Privacy Principles*, Letter to the Department of Commerce, 14 May 1999, available at www.ita.doc.gov/td/ecom/menu.html

Ahn, D. (1999) 'Environmental Disputes in the GATT/WTO: Before and after US-Shrimp Case,' *Michigan Journal of International Law*, Vol. 20, pp. 819-870

AIA (1998) *International "Safe Harbor" Principles*, Letter to the Department of Commerce, 19 November 1998, available at www.ita.doc.gov/td/ecom/menu.html

AIA (1999a) *International "Safe Harbor" Privacy Principles*, Letter to the Department of Commerce, 11 May 1999, available at www.ita.doc.gov/td/ecom/menu.html

AIA (1999b) *International "Safe Harbor" Privacy Principles – November 15, 1999 Revisions*, Letter to the Department of Commerce, 3 December 1999, available at www.ita.doc.gov/td/ecom/menu.html

Anderson, S.B. (1987) 'Wild Furbearer Management in Eastern Canada,' in: M. Novak et al. (eds) *Wild Furbearer Management and Conservation in North America*, Toronto: Ontario Trappers Association/Ontario Ministry of Natural Resources, pp. 1039-1048

Animal Alliance, CAHT & HSUS (1999a) *Urban Trapping Action Kit*, also available at www.animalalliance.ca/projects/index.html

Animal Alliance, CAHT & HSUS (1999b) *Humane and Effective Solutions to Urban Wildlife Concerns: Alternatives to Painful Trapping Methods*, August 1999, unpublished

Arts, B. (1998) *The Political Influence of Global NGOs*, Utrecht: International Books

ASA (1999a) *Key Message Points Regarding Soybean Seedstock Derived through Biotechnology*, 6 October 1999, available at www.amsoy.org/documents/biotechsum.htm

ASA (1999b) *ASA Urges Government to Defend the Value of Biotechnology*, News Release, 7 October 1999, available at www.amsoy.org/documents/biotech99.htm

ASA (1999c) *ASA Supports Biotechnology at Food and Drug Administration Public Hearing*, News Release, 18 November 1999, available at www.amsoy.org/documents/fdabiotech.htm

ASA (1999d) *Cargill's Position on Biotechnology*, letter received by ASA on 7 December 1999, available at www.amsoy.org/documents/cargill-1299.htm

ASA (2000a) 'Factors Affecting the Demand for Biotech and Conventional Soybeans in 2000. A Decision Guide for Soybean Farmers from the American Soybean Association,' *Soybean Digest*, January 2000, pp. 62-69, available at www.amsoy.org

ASA (2000b) *The Impact of the Biosafety Protocol and the So-Called "Precautionary Principle" on Trade, plus Experience with Safeguards long Utilized to Protect Biodiversity in Nations that Import Agricultural Commodities*, by Kimball Nill, Technical Issues Director ASA, Retrieved on 17 August 2000, available at www.amsoy.org/biotech/cbd.htm

ASA (2000c) *ASA Welcomes White House Biotechnology Initiatives*, Press Release, 3 May 2000, available at www.asa-europe.org/releases/releaseAW.htm

ASTA (2000) *ASTA Supports U.S. Government's Efforts to Increase Consumer Confidence in Bioengineered Foods*, Press Release, 5 May 2000, available at www.amseed.com/documents

AWI (1990a) 'Environmental Committee Approves Ban on Furs Caught in Leghold Traps,' *AWI Quuarterly*, Vol. 39, No. 2, p. 3

AWI (1990b) *Letter and leaflet on leghold traps*, sent to MEPs in September 1990

AWI (1990c) 'European Parliament Votes to Ban Import of Furs Beginning 1995,' *AWI Quarterly*, Vol. 39, No. 3, pp. 3 & 6

AWI (1990d) *Animals and their Legal Rights*, 4th edition, Washington, DC: AWI, 1990

AWI (1992a) 'North American Fur Industry Fights to Undercut EC Regulation,' *AWI Quarterly*, Vol. 41, No. 3, p. 4

AWI (1992b) 'Humane Trap Standards Groups Gets New Chair,' *AWI Quarterly*, Vol. 41, No. 4, p. 18

AWI (1993) 'Pro-Steel Jaw Leghold Trap "Experts" Meet behind Closed Doors to Produce a Final Draft of "Humane" Trap Standards,' *AWI Quarterly*, Vol. 42, No. 2, p. 12-13

AWI (1994a) 'Footsnares Can Reduce Injuries to Trapped Coyotes,' *AWI Quarterly*, Vol. 43, No. 1, p. 10

AWI (1994b) 'Friends of Furbearers: Delegations that Voted for Removal of the Word "Humane" from the Title of the Trap Standards,' *AWI Quarterly*, Vol. 43, No. 1, p. 11

AWI (1995) *Economic Status of the United States Fur Trade*, July 1995, unpublished

AWI (1996) 'More Strides in the Campaign against the Leghold Trap,' *AWI Quarterly*, Vol. 45, No. 4, pp. 8-9

Baldwin, D.A. (1985) *Economic Statecraft*, Princeton NJ: Princeton University Press

Becker, G.S. (1983) 'A Theory of Competition among Pressure Groups for Political Influence,' *Quarterly Journal of Economics*, Vol. 98, No. 3, pp. 371-400

Becker, G.S. (1985) 'Public Policies, Pressure Groups, and Dead Weight Costs,' *Journal of Public Economics*, Vol. 28, pp. 329-347

Beermann, D.H. (1995) 'Existing and Emerging Strategies for Enhancing Efficiency and Composition of Meat Animal Growth,' in: CEC (ed.), *Scientific Conference on Growth Promotion in Meat Production. Proceedings*, Brussels, 29 November to 1 December 1995, pp. 43-61

Bennett, C.J. (1992) *Regulating Privacy. Data Protection and Public Policy in Europe and the United States*, Ithaca and London: Cornell University Press.

Bennett, C.J. (1996) 'Rules of the Road and Level Playing-Fields: The Politics of Data Protection in Canada's Private Sector,' *International Review of Administrative Sciences*, Vol. 62, No. 4, pp. 479-491

Bennett, C.J. & C.D. Raab (1997) 'The Adequacy of Privacy: The European Union Data Protection Directive and the North American Response,' *The Information Society*, Vol. 13, No. 3, pp. 245-263

BEUC (1998) *Comments on the Proposal for Amending Directive 90/220/EEC on the Deliberate Release of GMOs into the Environment*, BEUC/267/98, 25 August 1998, available at www.beuc.org/public/papers/pa1998/content98.htm

BEUC (1999a) *Consumers Attitude to Biotechnology in Europe*, Address by Jim Murray, Director of BEUC, to the Biovision Forum, Lyon, 26-29 March 1999, BEUC/058/99

BEUC (1999b) *Position du BEUC au Sujet de l'Interdiction de la Viande Traitee aux Hormones dans l'UE [Position of BEUC in regard to the prohibition of meat treated with hormones in the EU]*, BEUC/083/1999, 21 April 1999

BIO (1999a) *BIO Responds to Nature Report on Bt Threat to Monarch Butterflies*, News Release, 19 May 1999, available at www.bio.org/newsroom/news.asp

BIO (1999b) *Academic Researchers and Industry Associations Agree Report on Bt Crop Impact on Monarch Butterflies Overblown*, News Release, 21 June 1999, available at www.bio.org/newsroom/news.asp

BIO (1999c) *BIO Responds to Labeling Bill*, News Release, 10 November 1999, available ate www.bio.org/newsroom/news.asp

BIO (1999d) *Scientific and Food Safety Issues Statement (The Food and Drug Administration Public Meeting)*, News Release, 18 November 1999, available at www.bio.org/newsroom/news.asp

BIO (1999e) *Public Information Issues Statement (The Food and Drug Administration Public Meeting)*, News Release, 18 November 1999, available at www.bio.org/newsroom/news.asp

BIO (2000a) *BIO Opposes Mandatory Labelling Bill Introduced by Sen. Boxer*, News Release, 23 February 2000, available at www.bio.org/newsroom/news.asp

BIO (2000b) *BIO Opposes Bill Introduced by Senator Moynihan*, News Release, 30 March 2000, available at www.bio.org/newsroom/news.asp

BIO (2000c) *BIO Statement Regarding USDA Planting Estimates of Genetically Modified Seeds*, News Release, 30 June 2000, available at www.bio.org/newsroom/news.asp

BIO (2000d) *BIO Supportive of FDA Announcement on Biotech Policies*, News Release, 3 May 2000, available at www.bio.org/newsroom/news.asp

BIO (2000e) *BIO Statement Regarding Purported New Findings on Bt Corn and Monarch Butterflies*, News Release, 21 August 2000, available at www.bio.org/newsroom/news.asp

BioteCanada (2001) *Royal Society Report a first Step in Needed Broader Consultation*, News Release, 5 February 2001, available at www.biotech.ca/EN/nr.Feb.05.2001.RoyalSociety.html

Breaux, J.B. et al. (1995a) *Letter by 14 Members of Congress to European Commissioner Leon Brittan*, dated 2 May 1995, reprinted in NTA 1996

Breaux, J.B. et al. (1995b) *Letter by 20 Members of Congress to USTR Mickey Kantor*, dated 29 September 1995, reprinted in NTA 1996

Brewster, B.K. et al. (1994) *Letter by 31 Members of Congress to USTR Mickey Kantor*, dated 8 June 1994, reprinted in NTA 1996

Brittan, L. (1995) *Letter from European Commissioner Leon Brittan to Members of US Congress*, dated 4-7-1995

Brock, K. (2000) 'Finding Answers in Difference: Canadian and American Aboriginal Policy Compared,' in: D.M. Thomas (ed.), *Canada and the United States: Differences that Count*, 2nd ed., Peterborough ON: Broadview Press, pp. 338-358

Brühann, U. (1999) 'La Directive Européenne Relative à la Protection des Données: Fondements, Histoire, Points Forts [The European Data Protection Directive: Foundations, History, Strong Points],' *Revue Française d'Administration Publique*, Vol. 89, pp. 9-19

BSE Inquiry (2000) *BSE Inquiry Report. Volume 1: Findings and Conclusions*, Report on the BSE crisis commissioned by five UK government departments, available at www.bseinquiry.gov.uk/pdf/index.htm

Busch, M.L. & H.V. Milner (1994) 'The Future of the International Trading System: International Firms, Regionalism, and Domestic Politics,' in: R. Stubbs & G.R.D. Underhill (eds.), *Political Economy and the Changing Global Order*, New York: Macmillan, pp. 259-276

CAC (2000a) *Matters Referred to the Task Force by the Codex Alimentarius Commission and Other Codex Committees*, Document CX/FBT/00/2, prepared for first session of the Codex Ad Hoc Intergovernmental Task Force on Foods Derived from Biotechnology, at Chiba, Japan, 14-17 March 2000, available at www.codexalimentarius.net/ccfbt1/bt00_01e.htm

CAC (2000b) *Review of the Work by International Organizations on the Evaluation of the Safety and Nutrition Aspects of Foods Derived from Biotechnology*, Document CX/FBT/00/3, prepared for first session of the Codex Ad Hoc Intergovernmental Task Force on Foods Derived from Biotechnology, at Chiba, Japan, 14-17 March 2000, available at www.codexalimentarius.net/ccfbt1/bt00_01e.htm

CAC (2000c) *Consideration of the Elaboration of Standards, Guidelines or Other Principles for Foods Derived from Biotechnology*, Document CX/FBT/00/4, prepared for first session of the Codex Ad Hoc Intergovernmental Task Force on Foods Derived from Biotechnology, at Chiba, Japan, 14-17 March 2000, available at www.codexalimentarius.net/ccfbt1/bt00_01e.htm

CAC (2000d) *Report of the First Session of the Codex Ad Hoc Intergovernmental Task Force on Foods Derived from Biotechnology*, 14-17 March 2000, Document ALINORM 01/34, available at www.codexalimentarius.net/Rep9901e.htm

CAC (2000e) *Report of the Twenty-Eighth Session of the Codex Committee on Food Labelling*, 5-9 May 2000, Document ALINORM 01/22, available at www.codex alimentarius.net/Rep9901e.htm

CAC (2001a) *Proposed Draft Recommendations for the Labelling of Food and Food Ingredients Obtained through certain Techniques of Genetic Modification/Genetic Engineering (Proposed Draft Amendment to the General Standard for the Labelling of Prepackaged Foods)*, February 2001, Document CX/FL 01/7

CAC (2001b) *Report of the Second Session of the Codex Ad Hoc Intergovernmental Task Force on Foods Derived from Biotechnology*, 25-29 March 2001, Document ALINORM 01/34A, available at www.codexalimentarius.net/Rep9901e.htm

CAC (2001c) *Report of the Twenty-Ninth Session of the Codex Committee on Food Labelling*, 1-4 May 2001, Document ALINORM 01/22A, available at www.codexalimentarius.net/Rep9901e.htm

Canada (2000) *Personal Information Protection and Electronic Documents Act*, Assented to on 13 April 2000, available at www.parl.gc.ca/36/2/parlbus/chambus/house/bills/government/C-6/C-6_4/C-6TOCE.html

Canada & EU (1996) *Joint Political Declaration on Canada-EU Relations and Joint Canada-EU Action Plan*, Signed on 17 December 1996, available at www.dfait-maeci.gc.ca/english/geo/europe/EU/ACTION-E.htm

Canadian Parliament (2001a) *Bill C-287. An Act to Amend the Food and Drugs Act (Genetically Modified Food)*, 1st Session, 37th Parliament, 49-50 Elizabeth II, 2001, available at www.parl.gc.ca/37/1/parlbus/chambus/house/bills/private/C-287/C-287_1/C-287TOCE.html

Canadian Parliament (2001b) *Bill C-310. An Act to Amend the Food and Drugs Act (Mandatory Labelling for Genetically Modified Foods)*, 1st Session, 37th Parliament, 49-50 Elizabeth II, 2001, available at www.parl.gc.ca/37/1/parlbus/chambus/house/bills/private/C-310/C-310_1/C-310TOCE.html

Canadian Parliament (2001c) *Answers by Lyle Vanclief, Minister of Agriculture and Agri-Food, to Oral Questions by MP Suzanne Tremblay*, 1st Session, 37th Parliament, Edited Hansard, Number 054, 3 May 2001: 1445-1450, available at www.parl.gc.ca/37/1/parlbus/chambus/house/debates/054_2001-05-03/han054_1445-e.htm and /han054_1450-e.htm

Canadian Press (1999) *Beef Hormones Linked to Premature Onset of Puberty and Breast Cancer*, by Dennis Bueckert, 31 July 1999, available at www.purefood.org/Toxic/hormoncancer.cfm

Canola Council (1999) *Markets and Statistics: History of Seed Exports*, updated on 13 December 1999, available at www.canola-council.org

Canola Council (2000) *Markets and Statistics: History of Oil & Meal Exports*, updated on 20 April 1999 and 12 October 1999, respectively, available at www.canola-council.org

CBA/Canada (1999a) *The Personal Information Protection and Electronic Documents Act*, 2 February 1999, available at www.cba.ca/eng/cba_on_the_issues/reports/personal.htm

CBA/Canada (1999b) *Bill C-6, Personal Information Protection and Electronic Documents Act*, Submission by the Canadian Bankers Association to the Standing Senate Committee on Social Affairs, Science and Technology on Bill C-6, 29 November 1999, available at www.cba.ca/eng/cba_on_the_issues/reports/billc6.htm

CBA/US, ABA and FSR (1999) *International Safe Harbor Privacy Principles and Related Documents*, Letter to the Department of Commerce, 17 May 1999, available at www.ita.doc.gov/td/ecom/menu.html

CDMA (1998) *Direct Marketing Industry Welcomes Federal Privacy Bill*, News Release, 1 October 1998, available at www.the-cma.org/media/nr_privacybill.html

CDT (1999) *Letter to the Department of Commerce*, 3 December 1999, available at www.ita.doc.gov/td/ecom/menu.html

CEC (1980) *Proposal for a Council Regulation Concerning the Use of Substances with a Hormonal Action and Those Having a Thyrostatic Action in Domestic Animals*, Submitted on 3 November 1980, OJ C 305, 22-11-1980, pp. 2-4

CEC (1981) *Commission Recommendation Relating to the Council of Europe Convention for the Protection of Individuals with Regard to Automatic Processing of Personal Data*, adopted on 29 July 1981, OJ L 246, 29-8-1981, p. 31

CEC (1984) *Proposal for a Council Directive Amending Directive 81/602/EEC Concerning the Prohibition of certain Substances Having a Hormonal Action and of any Substances Having a Thyrostatic Action*, COM (84) 295 final, Submitted on 13 June 1984, OJ C 170, 29-6-1984, pp. 4-8

CEC (1985a) *Use of Hormones in Stockfarming*, Press Release, DN: P/85/28, 1 April 1985, available at europa.eu.int/rapid/start/cgi/guesten.ksh

CEC (1985b) *Amendment of the Proposal for a Council Directive Amending Directive 81/602/EEC Concerning the Prohibition of certain Substances Having a Hormonal Action and of any Substances Having a Thyrostatic Action*, COM (85) 607 final, Submitted on 8 November 1985, OJ C 313, 4-12-1985, pp. 4-5

CEC (1985c) *Amended Proposal for a Council Directive Prohibiting the Use in Livestock Farming of certain Substances Having a Hormonal Action*, COM (85) 832 final, Submitted on 18 December 1985, OJ C 351, 31-12-1985, pp. 13-15

CEC (1987) *Hormones: American Measures against Community Imports: Commission Reaction*, Press Release, DN: IP/87/509, 24 November 1987, available at europa.eu.int/rapid/start/cgi/guesten.ksh

CEC (1988) *Proposal for a Council Directive on the Protection of Natural and Semi-Natural Habitats and of Wild Fauna and Flora*, COM (88) 381 final, submitted by the Commission on 16 August 1988, OJ C 247, 21-9-1988, pp. 3-13

CEC (1989) *Proposal for a Council Regulation (EEC) on the Importation of Certain Furs*, COM (89) 198 final, submitted by the Commission to the Council on 28 April 1989, OJ C 134, 31-5-1989, pp. 5-7

CEC (1990) *Proposal for a Council Directive Concerning the Protection of Individuals in Relation to the Processing of Personal Data*, COM (90) 314 final, Submitted on 27 July 1990, OJ C 277, 5-11-1990, pp. 3-12

CEC (1991) *Amendment to the Proposal for a Council Regulation (EEC) on the Importation of Certain Furs*, COM (91) 86 final, submitted by the Commission on 25 March 1991, OJ C 97, 13-4-1991, pp. 10-11

CEC (1992) *Amended Proposal for a Council Directive on the Protection of Individuals with Regard to the Processing of Personal Data and on the Free Movement of Such Data*, COM (92)422, 15 October 1992

CEC (1993a) *Commission Proposal for a Council Regulation (EEC) Concerning the Prohibition on the Use in Stockfarming of certain Substances Having a Hormonal or Thyrostatic Action and of Beta-Agonists*, COM (93) 441 final, Submitted on 14 October 1993, OJ C 302, 9-11-1993, pp. 8-11

CEC (1993b) *Growth, Competitiveness, Employment. The Challenges and Ways forward into the 21st Century*, White Paper, COM (93) 700, 5 December 1993

CEC (1994a) *Biotechnology and the White Paper on Growth, Competitiveness and Employment. Preparing for the next Stage*, Communication from the Commission to the Council, the European Parliament and the Economic and Social Committee, COM (94) 219, 1 June 1994

CEC (1994b) *Europe's Way to the Information Society. An Action Plan*, Communication from the Commission to the Council and the European Parliament and to the Economic and Social Committee and the Committee of the Regions, COM (94) 347, 19 July 1994

CEC (1995a) *Answer by the European Commission to EP Written Question P-1212/95*, given on 24 May 1995, OJ C 209, 14-8-1995, p. 51

CEC (1995b) *Answer by the European Commission to EP Written Question E-1296/95*, given on 12 June 1995, OJ C 213, 17-8-1995, p. 46

CEC (1995c) *Mr Fischler Denounces Codex Alimentarius Decision on Hormones*, Press Release DN: IP/95/704, 7 July 1995, available at europa.eu.int/rapid/start/cgi/guesten.ksh

CEC (1995d) *Answer by the European Commission to EP Written Questions E-1677/95 through E-1683/95*, given on 20 July 1995, OJ C 273, 18-10-1995

CEC (1995e) *Answer by the European Commission to EP Written Question E-2223/95*, given on 4 October 1995, OJ C 311, 22-11-1995, p. 42

CEC (ed.) (1995f) *Scientific Conference on Growth Promotion in Meat Production. Proceedings*, Brussels, 29 November to 1 December 1995

CEC (1995g) *Letter from Horst Krenzler, Director General DG I, and P. Wilmott, Director General DG XXI, to the permanent representatives of the member states*, dated 8 December 1995

CEC (1995h) *Proposal for a Council Regulation (EC) Amending Council Regulation (EEC) No 3254/91 Prohibiting the Use of Leghold Traps in the Community and the Introduction into the Community of Pelts and Manufactured Goods of Certain Wild Animal Species Originating in Countries which Catch them by Means of Leghold Traps or Trapping Methods which Do not Meet International Humane Trapping Standards*, COM (95) 737 final, 15 December 1995

CEC (1996a) *Letter from DG I to the Dutch Permanent Representative to the EU*, dated 26 January 1996 (letter in Dutch)

CEC (1996b) *Communication from the Commission to the Council and the European Parliament on Trade and Environment*, COM (96) 54 final, 28 February 1996

CEC (1996c) *Report on the Review of Directive 90/220/EEC in the Context of the Commission's Communication on Biotechnology and the White Paper*, COM (96) 630, 10 December 1996

CEC (1997a) *Proposal for a Council Decision Concerning the Signing and Conclusion of an International Agreement between the European Community, Canada and the Russian Federation on Humane Trapping Standards*, COM (97) 17 final, 24 January 1997

CEC (1997b) *Situation and Outlook. Beef Sector*, CAP 2000 Working Document, April 1997, available at europa.eu.int/comm/agriculture/publi/index_en.htm

CEC (1997c) *The European Commission has Decided to Propose further Labelling of Genetically Modified Organisms*, Press Release IP/97/259 of 2 April 1997, available at europa.eu.int/rapid/start/cgi/guesten.ksh

CEC (1997d) *The General Principles of Food Law in the European Union*, Commission Green Paper, COM (97) 176 final, 30 April 1997

CEC (1997e) *Consumer Health and Food Safety. Communication of the European Commission*, COM (97) 183 final, 30 April 1997, available at europa.eu.int/comm/food/fs/sc/index_en.html

CEC (1997f) *Amended Proposal for a Council Decision Concerning the Signing and Conclusion of an Agreement on International Humane Trapping Standards between the European Community, Canada, and the Russian Federation*, COM (97) 251 final, 29 May 1997

CEC (1997g) *Proposal for a Council Decision on the List Referred to in the Second Paragraph of Article 3(1) of Council Regulation (EEC) No 3254/91 Prohibiting the Use of Leghold Traps in the Community and the Introduction into the Community of Pelts and Manufactured Goods of certain Wild Animals Species [sic] Originating in Countries which Catch them by Means of Leghold Traps or Trapping Methods which Do not Meet International Humane Trapping Standards and in Article 1(1)(a) of Commission Regulation (EC) No 35/97 Laying Down Provisions on the Certification of Pelts and Goods Covered by Council Regulation (EEC) No 3254/91*, COM (97) 52 final, 5 June 1997

CEC (1997h) *Animal Trapping Standards*, Press Release, 19 June 1997, DN: IP/97/543, available at europa.eu.int/rapid/start/cgi/guesten.ksh

CEC (1997i) *Agenda 2000. For a Stronger and Wider Union*, Communication of the Commission, Volume I, DOC 97/6, 15 July 1997, available at europa.eu.int/comm/enlargement/agenda2000/strong/index.htm

CEC (1997j) *Final Consolidated Report to the Temporary Committee of the European Parliament on the Follow-up of Recommendations on BSE*, COM (97) 509 final, 20 October 1997

CEC (1997k) *Proposal for a Council Decision Concerning the Signing an Conclusion of an International Agreement in the Form of Agreed Minute between the European Community and the United States of America on Humane Trapping Standards*, COM (97) 726 final, 11 December 1997

CEC (1997l) *Signature of the Agreement on International Humane Trapping Standards by the European Community and Canada*, Press Release, 17 December 1997, DN: PRES/97/397, available at europa.eu.int/rapid/start/cgi/guesten.ksh

CEC (1997m) *Signature of the Agreement on International Humane Trapping Standards by the European Community and the United States of America*, Press Release, 18 December 1997, DN: PRES/97/403, available at europa.eu.int/rapid/start/cgi/guesten.ksh

CEC (1998a) *WTO Ruling on EU Hormone Ban is a Victory for European Consumers*, Press Release DN: IP/98/45, 16 January 1998, available at europa.eu.int/rapid/start/cgi/guesten.ksh

CEC (1998b) *Proposal for a European Parliament and Council Directive Amending Directive 90/220/EEC on the Deliberate Release into the Environment of Genetically Modified Organisms*, COM (1998) 85, 23 February 1998

CEC (1998c) *Proposal for a Council Decision Concerning the Provisional Prohibition of the sale in Austria of Genetically Modified Maize* (Zea mays L.) *with the combined Modifications for Insecticidal Properties Conferred by the Bt-endotoxin Gene and Increased Tolerance to the Herbicide Glufosinate Ammonium*, COM (1998) 339, 2 June 1998

CEC (1998d) *Proposal for a Council Decision Concerning the Provisional Prohibition of the sale in Luxembourg of Genetically Modified Maize* (Zea mays L.) *with the combined Modifications for Insecticidal Properties Conferred by the Bt-endotoxin Gene and Increased Tolerance to the Herbicide Glufosinate Ammonium*, COM (1998) 340, 2 June 1998

CEC (1999a) *WTO Decisions Regarding the EC Hormones Ban*, Communication of the Commission to the Council and the Parliament, 16 February 1999, available at mkaccdb.eu.int/miti/dsu

CEC (1999b) *Letter from Sir Leon Brittan, Vice-President of the European Commission, and Franz Fischler, European Commissioner for Agriculture, to Charlene Barshefsky, USTR, and Dan Glickman, Secretary of Agriculture*, dated 23 February 1999, available at mkaccdb.eu.int/miti/dsu

CEC (1999c) *Amended Proposal for a European Parliament and Council Directive Amending Directive 90/220/EEC on the Deliberate Release into the Environment of Genetically Modified Organisms*, COM (1999) 139, 26 March 1999

CEC (1999d) *Hormones – First Commission Debate*, Press Release, 17 May 1999, available at europa.eu.int/comm/food/fs/him/him_index_en.html

CEC (1999e) *Growth Hormones in Meat Pose Risk to Consumers – Different Levels of Evidence*, Press Release, 17 May 1999, available at europa.eu.int/comm/food/fs/him/him_index_en.html

CEC (1999f) *Abusive Use and Difficulties of Controls of Growth Hormones Increase Risks*, Press Release, 17 May 1999, available at europa.eu.int/comm/food/fs/him/him_index_en.html

CEC (2000a) *White Paper on Food Safety*, COM (1999) 719 final, 12 January 2000, available at europa.eu.int

CEC (2000b) *Economic Impacts of Genetically Modified Crops on the Agri-Food Sector. A Synthesis*, Working Document DG Agriculture, April 2000, available at europa.eu.int/comm/agriculture/publi/index_en.htm

CEC (2000c) *Proposal for a Directive of the European Parliament and of the Council Amending for the seventh Time Council Directive 76/768/EEC on the Approximation of the Laws of the Member States Relating to Cosmetics Products*, COM (2000) 189 final, 5 April 2000

CEC (2000d) *Proposal for a Directive of the European Parliament and of the Council Amending Council Directive 96/22/EC Concerning the Prohibition on the Use in Stockfarming of certain Substances Having a Hormonal or Thyrostatic Action and of Beta-Agonists*, COM (2000) 320 final, 24 May 2000, available at europa.eu.int/comm/food/fs/him/him_index_en.html

CEC (2000e) *Facts on GMOs in the EU*, MEMO/00/43, 13 July 2000, available at europa.eu.int/comm/food/fs/biotech/biotech_index_en.html

CEC (2000f) *The EU-US Consultative Forum on Biotechnology. Commentary on the Report from the Commission Services*, available at europa.eu.int/comm/external_relations/us/biotech/ec_commentary.htm

CEC (2001a) *EU-Canada Trade Initiative Progress Report*, 21 June 2001, available at europa.eu.int/comm/external_relations/canada/sum06_01/ecti.htm

CEC (2001b) *Proposal for a Regulation of the European Parliament and of the Council Concerning Traceability and Labelling of Genetically Modified Organisms and Traceability of Food and Feed Products Produced from Genetically Modified Organisms and Amending Directive 2001/18/EC*, COM (2001) 182 final, 25 July 2001

CEC (2001c) *Proposal for a Regulation of the European Parliament and of the Council on Genetically Modified Food and Feed*, COM (2001) 425 final, 25 July 2001

CFIA (1997) *Summary of Comments on the Communiqué "Labelling of Novel Foods Derived through Genetic Engineering (December 1, 1995)*, Information Letter, April 1997

CFIA (1998a) *Labelling of Genetically Engineered Foods in Canada*, May 1998, available at www.inspection.gc.ca/english/ppc/biotech/labeti/response.shtml

CFIA (1998b) *Summary Report. Canada – U.S. Bilateral Discussions on Agricultural Biotechnology*, July 15-16, 1998, Ottawa, Canada, available at www.inspection.gc.ca/english/plaveg/pbo/usda02e.shtml

CFIA (1999) *Voluntary Labelling Project Announced for Foods Derived from Biotechnology*, News Release, 17 September 1999, available at www.inspection.gc.ca/english/corpaffr/newcom/19990917e.shtml

CFIA (2000) *Response of the Federal Departments and Agencies to the Petition Filed May 9, 2000 by the Sierra Legal Defence Fund under the Auditor General Act: Review of Federal Laws, Regulations and Policies on Genetically Modified Organisms*, 7 September 2000, available at www.inspection.gc.ca/english/ppc/biotech/enviro/sierrae.shtml

CFS (1998) *Landmark Lawsuit Challenges Food and Drug Administration (FDA) Policy on Genetically Engineered Foods*, Press Release, 27 May 1998, available at www.centerforfoodsafety.org/li/GEpress1.html

CFS (2000*) New FDA Policy Fails to Require Testing or Labeling of Genetically Engineered Foods*, Press Release, 3 May 2000, available at www.centerforfoodsafety.org/inthenews/CFSresponsetoWH.html

CGSB (1996) *Animal (Mammal) Traps - Mechanically Powered, Trigger-Activated Killing Traps for Use on Land*, CAN/CGSB-144.1-96, Ottawa: CGSB, November 1996

CGSB (2001) *Draft Standard for Voluntary Claims about Foods that are and are Not [Products of Gene Technology]*, C**/CGSB-32.315, First Draft, July 2001

Chambers, G.R. (1999) 'The BSE Crisis and the European Parliament,' in C. Joerges & E. Vos (eds) *EU Committees: Social Regulations, Law and Politics*, Oxford and Portland: Hart Publishing, pp. 95-106

Charnovitz, S. (1992) 'Environmental and Labour Standards in Trade,' *The World Economy*, Vol. 15, pp. 335-356

Charny, D. (1991) 'Competition among Jurisdictions in Formulating Corporate Law Rules: An American Perspective on the "Race to the Bottom" in the European Communities,' *Harvard International Law Journal*, Vol. 32, pp. 423-456

CHC (2000a) *Beef Hormones Food Safety Fact Sheet*, available at www.healthcoalition.ca

CHC (2000b) *Letter to Jean Chrétien and other Party Leaders*, 20 November 2000, available at www.healthcoalition.ca/chretienletter11202000.html

Checkel, J.T. (1997) 'International Norms and Domestic Politics: Bridging the Rationalist-Constructivist Divide,' *European Journal of International Relations*, Vol. 3, No. 4, pp. 473-495

CIAA (1997) *The Labelling of Products Derived from Herbicide-Resistant Soya and Insect-Resistant Maize: Toward a Balanced Approach*, Position MIN/393/97E Final, 13 October 1997, available at www.ciaa.be/en/Documents/positions/scientreg/MIN393.html

CIAA (1999) *EU Food Labelling and Consumer Information. Preparing for the 21st Century*, Position MIN/140/99E-Final, 23 July 1999, available at www.ciaa.be/en/Documents/positions/scientreg/MIN14099E.html

CICS (1998) *Federal-Provincial-Territorial Meeting of Ministers Responsible for Justice. Regina, Saskatchewan – October 29-30, 1998*, Press Release, Ref. 830-632/28, available at www.scics.gc.ca/cinfo98/83063228_e.html

CMA/Marketing (1999) *Consumers and Business Call for early Passage of Federal Privacy Legislation*, News Release, 7 October 1999, available at www.the-cma.org

CMA/Medical (1999a) *"Listening to our Patient's Concerns": Comments on Bill C-54, Submitted to the House of Commons Standing Committee on Industry*, 18 March 1999, available at www.cma.ca/advocacy/political/1999/03-18/index.htm

CMA/Medical (1999b) *"Putting Patients first": Comments on Bill C-6, Submitted to the Senate Standing Committee on Social Affairs, Science and Technology*, 29 November 1999, available at www.cma.ca/advocacy/political/1999/11-29/index.htm

CoE (1950) *Convention for the Protection of Human Rights and Fundamental Freedoms*, ETS No. 005, Rome, opened for signature on 4 November 1950, available at conventions.coe.int/Treaty/EN/CadreListeTraites.htm

CoE (1981a) *Convention for the Protection of Individuals with Regard to Automatic Processing of Personal Data*, ETS No. 108, opened for signature on 28 January 1981, available at conventions.coe.int/Treaty/EN/CadreListeTraites.htm

CoE (1981b) *Explanatory Report to the Convention for the Protection of Individuals with Regard to Automatic Processing of Personal Data*, available at conventions.coe.int/Treaty/EN/CadreListeTraites.htm

CoE (1999) *Guidelines for the Protection of Individuals with Regard to the Collection and Processing of Personal Data on Information Highways*, Recommendation No. R(99)5, adopted by the Committee of Ministers on 23 February 1999, available at cm.coe.int/ta/-rec/1999/99r5.htm

CoE (2000) *Convention for the Protection of Individuals with Regard to Automatic Processing of Personal Data: Status as of 21/09/00*, Retrieved on 21 September 2000, available at conventions.coe.int/Treaty/EN/CadreListeTraites.htm

Cole, P. E. (1985) 'New Challenges to the US Multinational Corporation in the European Economic Community: Data Protection Laws,' *International Law and Politics*, Vol. 17, pp. 893-947

Collinson, S. (1999) '"Issue-Systems", "Multi-Level Games" and the Analysis of the EU's External Commercial and Associated Policies: A Research Agenda,' *Journal of European Public Policy*, Vol. 6, No. 2, pp. 206-224

Comeau, P.A., & A. Ouimet (1995) 'Freedom of Information and Privacy: Québec's Innovative Role in North America,' *Iowa Law Review*, Vol. 80, No. 3, pp. 651-668

Consultative Forum (2000) *The EU-U.S. Biotechnology Consultative Forum. Final Report*, December 2000, available at europa.eu.int/comm/external_relations/us/biotech/biotech.htm and at www.useu.be/ISSUES/biotreport2000.htm

Consumers International (1996) *International Consumers Organisation Warns that Genetically Altered Food Poses Health Concern*, Press Release, 29 October 1996, available at www.consumersinternational.org/news/press_archive/genetic.html

Consumers International (1999) *OECD Consultation of NGOs on Genetically Engineered Food*, Remarks by Michael Hansen, 20 November 1999, available at www.consumers international.org/campaigns/biotech/hansen.html

Consumers Union (1999a) *Consumers Union's Comments on Docket No. 99N-4282, Biotechnology in the Year 2000 and beyond Public Meetings*, Retrieved on 5 July 2000, available at www.consumersunion.org/food/fdacpi100.htm

Consumers Union (1999b) *Testimony of Mark Silbergeld, Co-Director, Washington Office, Consumers Union of U.S., before the Committee on Agriculture, United States Senate Hearings on Biotechnology*, 7 October 1999, available at www.consumersunion.org/food/senag1099dc.htm

Consumers Union (2000a) *Genetic Engineering is not an Extension of Conventional Plant Breeding*, by Michael K. Hansen, Retrieved on 5 July 2000, available at www.consumers union.org/food/widecpi200.htm

Consumers Union (2000b) *Consumers Union Supports Genetically Engineered Food Labeling Bill Sponsored by U.S. Senator Barbara Boxer*, Press Release, 22 February, available at www.consumersunion.org/food/boxerwc200.htm

Consumers Union (2000c) *Consumers Union Labels FDA's New Policy for Genetically Engineered Foods "Disappointing"*, Press Release, 3 May 2000, available at www.consumersunion.org/food/genfooddc400.htm

Consumers Union, EPIC et al. (1998) *Additional Preliminary Comments of Consumer and Privacy Groups on the Department of Commerce "Safe Harbor" Proposal*, Letter to the Department of Commerce, 19 November 1998, available at www.ita.doc.gov/td/ecom/menu.html

Cook, T.D. & D.T. Campbell (1979) *Quasi-Experimentation. Design & Analysis Issues for Field Settings*, Boston etc.: Houghton Mifflin Company

COPA/COGECA (1999a) *Remarks of COPA and COGECA on the Communication of the Commission on WTO Decisions Regarding the EU Hormones Ban*, Pr (99)25F1/P(99)27F1, 11 March 1999

COPA/COGECA (1999b) *Position of COPA and COGECA on a Commission Proposal to Prohibit the Use of BST (COM (1999)544 final)*, Pr(99)94F1/P(99)98F1, 10 December 1999

COPA/COGECA (2000) *Position of COPA and COGECA on the Use of Gene Technology in Agriculture*, Pr(00)06F1/P(00)06F1, 21 January 2000

COPA/COGECA & BEUC (1999) *European Consumers and Farmers Unanimous on the EU Ban of Hormone Treated Beef*, Joint Statement of BEUC, EUROCOOP, COPA and COGECA, CdP(99)19-1, Press Release, 29 April 1999

Cortell, A.P. & J.W. Davis, Jr. (1996) 'How Do International Institutions Matter? The Domestic Impact of International Rules and Norms,' *International Studies Quarterly*, Vol. 40, pp. 451-478

Cosbey, A. & S. Burgiel (2000) *The Cartagena Protocol on Biosafety: An Analysis of Results*, International Institute for Sustainable Development Briefing Note, available at www.iisd.ca

Council (1987) *Council Resolution of 19 October 1987 on the Continuation and Implementation of a European Community Policy and Action Programme on the Environment (1987-1992)*, OJ C 328, 7 December 1987, pp. 1-43

Council (1995) *Common Position (EC) No 1/95 with a View to Adopting Directive 95/.../EC of the European Parliament and of the Council of ... on the Protection of Individuals with Regard to the Processing of Personal Data and on the Free Movement of such Data*, adopted on 20 February 1995, OJ C 93, 13 April 1995, pp. 1

Council (1996) *1978th Council - Environment*, Press Release, 9 December 1996, PRES/96/360

Council (1997a) *1989th Council - General Affairs*, Press Release, 24 February 1997, PRES/97/48, available at europa.eu.int/rapid/start/cgi/guesten.ksh

Council (1997b) *2011th Council - General Affairs*, Press Release, 2 June 1997, PRES/97/177, available at europa.eu.int/rapid/start/cgi/guesten.ksh

Council (1997c) *2017th Council - Environment*, Press Release, 19 June 1997, PRES/97/204, available at europa.eu.int/rapid/start/cgi/guesten.ksh

Council (1997d) *2024th Council - General Affairs*, Press Release, 22 July 1997, PRES/97/246, available at europa.eu.int/rapid/start/cgi/guesten.ksh

Council (1997e) *2047th Council - General Affairs*, Press Release, 24 November 1997, PRES/97/356, available at europa.eu.int/rapid/start/cgi/guesten.ksh

Council (1997f) *Special Council Meeting - General Affairs*, Press Release, 12 December 1997, PRES/97/393, available at europa.eu.int/rapid/start/cgi/guesten.ksh

Council (1999) *2194th Council Meeting – Environment, Luxembourg, 24/25 June 1999*, Press Release, PRES/99/203, available at europa.eu.int/rapid/start/cgi/guesten.ksh

Council (2001) *Decisions Adopted by Written Procedure. Environment. Deliberate Release of Genetically Modified Organisms (GMOs)*, Press Release, PRES/01/50, 15 February 2001, available at europa.eu.int/rapid/start/cgi/guesten.ksh

Council of Canadians (1999) *Joint letter to federal Health, Agriculture and Industry ministers on labelling genetically engineered foods*, 16 November 1999, available at www.canadians.org/left.html

Council of Canadians (2001a) *Expert Panel on GMOs Confirms Need for Immediate Moratorium, Say GMO Critics*, Media Release, 5 February 2001, available at www.canadians.org/campaigns/campaigns-genfoodmedia010205.html

Council of Canadians (2001b) *GE Labelling Bill Gets Country-Wide Support. More than 80 Groups, 93% of Canadians Say Label Now*, Media Release, 6 June 2001, available at www.canadians.org/campaigns/campaigns-genfoodmedia010606.html

CPhA (1999) *Bill C-54: Personal Information Protection and Electronic Documents Act*, Submitted to the Parliamentary Committee of Industry, 18 March 1999, available at www.cdnpharm.ca/cphanew/nv/C54-English.htm

Crasson, D. (1996) *Study into Trapping in five European Union Countries*, Study commissioned by the IFTF, July 1996

Crombez, C. (1996) 'Legislative Procedures in the European Community,' *British Journal of Political Science*, Vol. 26, pp. 199-228

CSA (1996) *Model Code for the Protection of Personal Information. A National Standard of Canada*, CAN/CSA-Q830-96, March 1996

CSI (1998) *CSI Comments on Safe Harbor Principles Draft*, Letter to the Department of Commerce, 11 November 1998, available at www.ita.doc.gov/td/ecom/menu.html

CSI (1999a) Letter to the Department of Commerce, 14 May 1999, available at www.ita.doc.gov/td/ecom/menu.html

CSI (2000) *Provisional "Safe Harbor" Agreement*, Letter to the Department of Commerce, 6 April 2000, available at www.ita.doc.gov/td/ecom/menu.html

Czaplinski, W. & G. Danilenko (1990) 'Conflicts of Norms in International Law,' *Netherlands Yearbook of International Law*, Vol. 21, pp. 3-42

Dale, G. (1996) 'The European Union's Steel Leghold Trap Ban: Animal Cruelty Legislation in Conflict with International Trade,' *Colorado Journal of International Environmental Law and Policy*, Vol. 7, No. 2, pp. 441-461

Danish EPA (1998) *New GMO Agreement with Industry and Agriculture*, News Release, 26 November 1998, available at mstex03.mst.dk/news/02060000.htm

Deliens, L., & Van Goor, H. (1984) 'Retrospectieve Vertekening in Interviews - Een Empirisch Onderzoek naar het Gebruik van Interviews bij het Opsporen van Beleidsprocessen uit het Recente Verleden' [Retrospective Bias in Interviews - An Empirical Study of the Use of Interviews in Tracing Policy Processes in the Recent Past], *Sociologische Gids*, Vol. 31, No. 5, pp. 390-411

Demaret, P. (1993) 'Environmental Policy and Commercial Policy: The Emergence of Trade-Related Environmental Measures (TREMs) in the External Relations of the European Community,' in: M. Maresceau (ed.), *The European Community's Commercial Policy after 1992: The Legal Dimension*), Dordrecht: Martinus Nijhoff, pp. 305-386

DFAIT (1999) *Canada Retaliates against the EU*, Press Release No. 174, 29 July 1999, available at 198.103.104.118/minpub/Publication.asp?FileSpec=/Min_Pub_Docs/102518.htm

DFAIT (2000) *Comments from the Government of Canada on the European Community Proposal for European Parliament and Council Directive Concerning: A Permanent Ban for Use on Farm Animals of 17ß Oestradiol and a Provisional Ban, Pending further Scientific Evaluation, of Testosterone, Progesterone, Trembolone Acetate, Zeranol and Melengestrol Acetate*, Submitted to the WTO's SPS Committee, 15 December 2000

Dietrich, W.F. (1996) 'Harmonization of Automobile Emission Standards under International Trade Agreements: Lessons from the European Union Applied to the WTO and the NAFTA,' *William and Mary Environmental Law and Policy Review*, Vol. 20, pp. 175-221

DiStefano, J.J. (1987) 'Wild Furbearer Management in the Northeastern United States,' in: M. Novak et al. (eds.) *Wild Furbearer Management and Conservation in North America*, Toronto: Ontario Trappers Association/Ontario Ministry of Natural Resources, pp. 1077-1090

DMA (1998a) *Privacy Promise. Member Compliance Guide*, Effective 1 July 1999, published in September 1998

DMA (1998b) *Draft International Safe Harbor Privacy Principles*, Letter to the Department of Commerce, 19 November 1998, available at www.ita.doc.gov/td/ecom/menu.html

DMA (1999a) *Letter to the Department of Commerce*, 14 May 1999, available at www.ita.doc.gov/td/ecom/menu.html

DMA (1999b) *Letter to the Department of Commerce*, 3 December 1999, available at www.ita.doc.gov/td/ecom/menu.html

DMA (2000) *Direct Marketing Association Guidelines for Ethical Business Practice*, Revised version, September 2000

DoC (1998a) *Elements of Effective Self-Regulation for Protection of Privacy*, Discussion Draft, January 1998, available at www.ntia.doc.gov/reports/privacydraft/198dftprin.htm

DoC (1998b) *International Safe Harbor Privacy Principles*, 4 November 1998, available at www.ita.doc.gov/td/ecom/menu.html

DoC (1999a) *International Safe Harbor Privacy Principles*, 19 April 1999, available at www.ita.doc.gov/td/ecom/menu.html

DoC (1999b) *Draft International Safe Harbor Privacy Principles Issued by the U.S. Department of Commerce*, 15 November 1999, available at www.ita.doc.gov/td/ecom/menu.html

DoC (2000a) *Draft International Safe Harbor Privacy Principles Issued by the U.S. Department of Commerce*, 17 March 2000, available at www.ita.doc.gov/td/ecom/menu.html

DoC (2000b) *Final Safe Harbor Documents*, 21 July 2000, available at www.ita.doc.gov/td/ecom/menu.html

DoC (2001) *Table 1.1. Gross Domestic Product*, Bureau of Economic Analysis, Last Revised on 27 July 2001, available at www.bea.doc.gov/bea/dn/nipaweb

Doray, R. (1999) *The Implications of Bill C-54 on Medical Information: An Analysis of the Submission to the House of Commons Standing Committee on Industry by the Ontario Ministry of Health Concerning Bill C-54 (Personal Information Protection and Electronic Documents Act)*, Study Commissioned by Industry Canada, Submitted on 14 June 1999, available at www.e-com.ic.gc.ca/english/privacy/632d296.html

Doyle, E. (1999) *Environmental Benefits and Sustainable Agriculture through Biotechnology*, Executive Summary of the Ceres Forum at Georgetown University, November 10-11, 1999, unpublished paper

Doyle, M.E. (2000) *Scientific Literature Review: Human Safety of Hormone Implants Used to Promote Growth in Cattle*, Food Research Institute, University of Wisconsin, July 2000, unpublished report

Dutch Government (2001) 'Knelgevallen Nertsenhouderij' [Difficult Cases Mink Farming], *Staatscourant*, No. 33, 15 February 2001, p. 7

Earnshaw, D. & D. Judge (1996) 'From Co-operation to Co-decision: The European Parliament's Path to Legislative Power,' in: J. J. Richardson (ed.), *European Union. Power and Policy-Making*, London and New York: Routledge, pp. 96-126

EC (1981) *Council Directive 81/602/EEC Concerning the Prohibition of certain Substances Having a Hormonal Action and of any Substances Having a Thyrostatic Action*, Adopted on 31 July 1981, OJ L 222, 7-8-1981, pp. 32-33

EC (1983) *Council Directive 83/129/EEC Concerning the Importation into Member States of Skins of certain Seal Pups and Products Derived therefrom*, Adopted on 28 March 1983, OJ L 91, 9-4-1983, pp. 30-31

EC (1985) *Council Directive 85/649/EEC Prohibiting the Use in Livestock Farming of certain Substances Having a Hormonal Action*, Adopted on 31 December 1985, OJ L 382, 31-12-1985, pp. 228-231

EC (1987) *Council Decision 87/561/EEC on Transitional Measures Concerning the Prohibition on Administration to Farm Animals of certain Substances Having a Hormonal Action*, Adopted on 18 November 1987, OJ L 339, 1-12-1987, pp. 70-71

EC (1988a) *Council Directive 88/146/EEC Prohibiting the Use in Livestock Farming of certain Substances Having a Hormonal Action*, Adopted on 7 March 1988, OJ L 70, 16-3-1988, pp. 16-18

EC (1988b) *Council Directive 88/299/EEC on Trade in Animals Treated with certain Substances Having a Hormonal Action and their Meat, as Referred to in Article 7 of Directive 88/146/EEC*, Adopted on 17 May 1988, OJ L 128, 21-5-1988, pp. 36-38

EC (1990a) *Council Directive 90/219/EEC on the Contained Use of Genetically Modified Micro-Organisms*, Adopted on 23 April 1990, OJ L 117, 8-5-1990, pp. 1-14

EC (1990b) *Council Directive 90/220/EEC on the Deliberate Release into the Environment of Genetically Modified Organisms*, Adopted on 23 April 1990, OJ L 117, 8-5-1990, pp. 15-27

EC (1991) *Council Regulation (EEC) No. 3254/91 Prohibiting the Use of Leghold Traps in the Community and the Introduction into the Community of Pelts and Manufactured Goods of Certain Wild Animal Species Originating in Countries Which Catch Them by Means of Leghold Traps or Trapping Methods Which Do Not Meet International Humane Trapping Standards*, Adopted on 4 November 1991, OJ L 308, 9-11-1991, pp. 1-3

EC (1992a) *Council Regulation (EEC) No. 880/92 on a Community Eco-Label Award Scheme*, Adopted on 23 March 1992, OJ L 99, 11-4-1992, p. 1-7

EC (1992b) *Council Regulation 2068/92 Fixing, for the Period 1 July 1993 to 30 June 1996, the Intervention Prices for Adult Bovine Animals*, Adopted on 30 June 1992, OJ L 215, 30-7-1992, p. 58

EC (1993) *Council Directive 93/35 Amending for the sixth Time Directive 76/768/EEC on the Approximation of the Laws of the Member States Relating to Cosmetic Products*, Adopted on 14 June 1993, OJ L 151, 23-6-1993, pp. 32-37

EC (1994a) *Commission Regulation (EC) No 1771/91 Laying down Provisions on the Introduction into the Community of Pelts and Manufactured Goods of Certain Wild Animal Species*, Adopted on 19 July 1994, OJ L 184, 20-7-1994, pp. 3-4

EC (1994b) *Council Regulation (EC) No. 3281/94 Applying a Four-Year Scheme of Generalized Tariff Preferences (1995 to 1998) in Respect of certain Industrial Products Originating in Developing Countries*, Adopted on 19 December 1994, OJ L 348, 31-12-1994, pp. 1-8

EC (1995) *Directive 95/46/EC of the European Parliament and of the Council on the Protection of Individuals with Regard to the Processing of Personal Data and on the Free Movement of such Data*, Adopted on 24 October 1995, OJ L 281, 23-11-1995, pp. 31-50

EC (1996a) *Commission Decision 96/281/EC Concerning the Placing on the Market of Genetically Modified Soya Beans (Glycine max L.) with Increased Tolerance to the Herbicide Glyphosate, Pursuant to Council Directive 90/220/EEC*, Adopted on 3 April 1996, OJ L 107, 30-4-1996, pp. 10-11

EC (1996b) *Council Directive 96/22/EC Concerning the Prohibition on the Use in Stockfarming of certain Substances Having a Hormonal or Thyrostatic Action and of Beta-Agonists, and Repealing Directives 81/602/EEC, 88/146/EEC and 88/299/EEC*, Adopted on 29 April 1996, OJ L 125, 23-5-1996, pp. 3-32

EC (1997a) *Commission Regulation (EC) No 35/97 Laying down Provisions on the Certification of Pelts and Goods Covered by Council Regulation (EEC) No 3254/91*, Adopted on 10 January 1997, OJ L 8, 11-1-1997, pp. 2-4

EC (1997b) *Commission Decision 97/98/EC Concerning the Placing on the Market of Genetically Modified Maize (Zea mays L.) with the Combined Modification for Insecti-*

cidal Properties Conferred by the Bt-Endotoxin Gene and Increased Tolerance to the Herbicide Glufosinate Ammonium Pursuant to Council Directive 90/220/EEC, Adopted on 23 January 1997, OJ L 031, 1-2-1997, pp. 69-70

EC (1997c) *Regulation (EC) No 258/97 of the European Parliament and of the Council Concerning Novel Foods and Novel Food Ingredients*, Adopted on 27 January 1997, OJ L 43, 14-2-1997, pp. 1-7

EC (1997d) *Council Regulation (EC) No. 552/97 Temporarily Withdrawing Access to Generalized Tariff Preferences from the Union of Myanmar*, Adopted on 24 March 1997, OJ L 85, 27-3-1997, pp. 8-9

EC (1997e) *Commission Decision 97/404/EC Setting up a Scientific Steering Committee*, Adopted on 10 June 1997, OJ L 169, 27-6-1997, pp. 85-87

EC (1997f) *Commission Directive 97/35/EC Adapting to Progress for the Second Time Council Directive 90/220/EEC on the Deliberate Release into the Environment of Genetically Modified Organisms*, Adopted on 18 June 1997, OJ L 169, 27-6-1997, pp. 72-73

EC (1997g) *Council Decision 97/602/EC Concerning the List Referred to in the second Subparagraph of Article 3(1) of Regulation (EEC) No 3254/91 and in Article 1(1)(a) of Commission Regulation (EC) No 35/97*, Adopted on 22 July 1997, OJ L 242, 4-9-1997, pp. 64-66

EC (1997h) *Commission Decision 97/579/EC Setting up Scientific Committees in the Field of Consumer Health and Food Safety*, Adopted on 23 July 1997, OJ L 237, 28-8-1997, pp. 18-23

EC (1997i) *Commission Recommendation 97/618/EC Concerning the Scientific Aspects and the Presentation of Information Necessary to Support Applications for the Placing on the Market of Novel Foods and Novel Food Ingredients and the Preparation of Initial Assessment Reports under Regulation (EC) No 258/97 of the European Parliament and of the Council*, Adopted on 29 July 1997, OJ L 253, 16-9-1997, pp. 1-36

EC (1997j) *Consolidated Version of the Treaty Establishing the European Community*, 97/C 340/03, Approved on 2 October 1997, OJ C 340, 10-11-1997, pp. 173-308

EC (1998a) *Council Decision 98/142/EC Concerning the Conclusion of an Agreement on International Humane Trapping Standards between the European Community, Canada and the Russian Federation and of an Agreed Minute between Canada and the European Community Concerning the Signing of the Said Agreement*, Adopted on 26 January 1998, OJ L 42, 14-2-1998, pp. 40-57

EC (1998b) *Commission Decision 98/188/EC Amending Council Decision 97/602/EC Concerning the List Referred to in the second Subparagraph of Article 3(1) of Regulation (EEC) No 3254/91 and in Article 1(1)(a) of Commission Regulation (EC) No 35/97*, Adopted on 2 March 1998, OJ L 70, 10-3-1998, pp. 28-30

EC (1998c) *Council Regulation 1139/98 Concerning the Compulsory Indication of the Labelling of certain Foodstuffs Produced from Genetically Modified Organisms of Particulars other than those Provided for in Directive 79/112/EEC*, Adopted on 26 May 1998, OJ L 159, 3-6-1998, pp. 4-7

EC (1998d) *Council Decision 98/487/EC Concerning the Conclusion of an International Agreement in the Form of an Agreed Minute between the European Community and the United States of America on Humane Trapping Standards*, Adopted on 13 July 1998, OJ L 219, 7-8-1998, pp. 24-37

EC (1998e) *Council Regulation (EC) No. 2820/98 Applying a Multiannual Scheme of Generalised Tariff Preferences for the Period 1 July 1999 to 31 December 2001*, Adopted on 21 December 1998, OJ L 357, 30-12-1998, pp. 1-112

EC (1999a) *Commission Decision 1999/301/EC Amending Decision 87/257/EEC on the List of Establishments in the United States of America Approved for the Purpose of Importing Fresh Meat into the Community and Amending Council Decision 79/542/EEC Drawing up a List of third Countries from which the Member States Authorise Imports of Bovine Animals, Swine, Fresh Meat and Meat Products*, Adopted on 30 April 1999, OJ L 117, 5-5-1999, pp. 52-57

EC (1999b) *Commission Decision 1999/302/EC Amending Decision 94/360/EC on the Reduced Frequency of Physical Checks of Consignments of certain Products to be Imported from third Countries, Pursuant to Council Directive 90/675/EEC*, Adopted on 30 April 1999, OJ L 117, 5-5-1999, pp. 58-59

EC (1999c) *Commission Decision 1999/417/EC Amending Decision 1999/301/EC Amending Decision 87/257/EEC on the List of Establishments in the United States of America Approved for the Purpose of Importing Fresh Meat into the Community and Amending Council Decision 79/542/EEC Drawing up a List of third Countries from which the Member States Authorise Imports of Bovine Animals, Swine, Fresh Meat and Meat Products*, Adopted on 16 June 1999, OJ L 159, 25-6-1999, pp. 56-57

EC (1999d) *Council Decision 1999/468/EC Laying down the Procedures for the Exercise of Implementing Powers Conferred on the Commission*, Adopted on 28 June, OJ L 184, 17-7-1999, pp. 23-26

EC (1999e) *Council Decision 1999/879/EC Concerning the Placing on the Market and Administration of Bovine Somatotropin (BST) and Repealing Decision 90/218/EEC*, Adopted on 17 December 1999, OJ L 331, 23-12-1999, pp. 71-72

EC (1999f) *Commission Decision 2000/2/EC Amending Council Decision 79/542/EEC Drawing up a List of third Countries from which the Member States Authorise Imports of Bovine Animals, Swine, Equidae, Sheep and Goats, Fresh Meat and Meat Products and Repealing Decision 1999/301/EC*, Adopted on 17 December 1999, OJ L 1, 4-1-2000, pp. 17-19

EC (2000a) *Commission Regulation (EC) No 49/2000 Amending Council Regulation (EC) No 1139/98 Concerning the Compulsory Indication on the Labelling of certain Foodstuffs Produced from Genetically Modified Organisms of Particulars other than those Provided for in Directive 79/112/EEC*, Adopted on 10 January 2000, OJ L 6, 11-1-2000, pp. 13-14

EC (2000b) *Commission Regulation (EC) 50/2000 on the Labelling of Foodstuffs and Food Ingredients Containing Additives and Flavourings that Have Been Genetically Modified of Have Been Produced from Genetically Modified Organisms*, Adopted on 10 January 2000, OJ L 6, 11-1-2000, pp. 15-17

EC (2000c) *Commission Decision 2000/136/EC Amending Commission Decision 2000/2/EC Amending Council Decision 79/542/EEC Drawing up a List of third Countries from which the Member States Authorise Imports of Bovine Animals, Swine, Equidae, Sheep and Goats, Fresh Meat and Meat Products and Repealing Decision 1999/301/EC*, Adopted on 16 February 2000, OJ L 45, 17-2-2000, pp. 41-42

EC (2000d) *Commission Decision 2000/236/EC Amending Council Decision 79/542/EEC Drawing up a List of third Countries from which the Member States Authorise Imports of Bovine Animals, Swine, Equidae, Sheep and Goats, Fresh Meat and Meat Products*, Adopted on 22 March 2000, OJ L 74, 23-3-2000, pp. 19-20

EC (2000e) *Commission Decision 2000/520/EC Pursuant to Directive 95/46/EC of the European Parliament and of the Council on the Adequacy of the Protection Provided by the Safe Harbour Privacy Principles and Related Frequently Asked Questions Issued by the US Department of Commerce*, Adopted on 26 July 2000, OJ L 215, 25-8-2000, pp. 7-47

EC (2001a) *Directive 2001/18/EC of the European Parliament and of the Council on the Deliberate Release into the Environment of Genetically Modified Organisms and Repealing Council Directive 90/220/EC*, Adopted on 12 March 2001, OJ L 106, 17 April 2001, pp. 1-39

EC (2001b) *Commission Decision 2002/2/EC Pursuant to Directive 95/46/EC of the European Parliament and of the Council on the Adequate Protection of Personal Data Provided by the Canadian Personal Information Protection and Electronic Documents Act*, Adopted on 20 December 2001, OJ L 2, 4-1-2002, pp. 13-16

ECJ (1988) *United Kingdom of Great Britain and Northern Ireland v Council of the European Communities*, Case 68/86, 23 February 1988, [1988] ECR, pp. 855-903

Eichener, V. (1993) *Social Dumping or Innovative Regulation? Processes and Outcomes of European Decision-Making in the Sector of Health and Safety at Work Harmonization*, EUI Working Paper SPS No. 92/98

Eichener, V. (1997) 'Effective European Problem-Solving: Lessons from the Regulation of Occupational Safety and Environmental Protection,' *Journal of European Public Policy*, Vol. 4, No. 4, pp. 591-608

Ellger, R. (1987) 'Data Protection Laws as Non-Tariff Barriers to the Transborder Flow of Information,' in: E. Mestmäcker (ed.), *The Law and Economics of Transborder Telecommunications*, Baden-Baden: Nomos, pp. 122-143

Emerson, R. M. (1962) 'Power-Dependence Relations,' *American Sociological Review*, Vol. 27, No. 1, pp. 31-41

Environment Voters (2001) *2000 Federal Election Campaign Briefing Paper*, unpublished

EP (1975) *Resolution on the Protection of the Rights of the Individual in the Face of Developing Technical Progress in the Field of Automatic Data Processing*, adopted on 21 February 1975, OJ C 60, 13-3-1975, p. 48

EP (1976) *Resolution on the Protection of the Rights of the Individual in the Face of Developing Technical Progress in the Field of Automatic Data Processing*, adopted on 8 April 1976, OJ C 100, 3-5-1976, p. 27

EP (1979) *Resolution on the Protection of Rights of the Individual in the Face of Technical Developments in Data Processing*, adopted on 8 May 1979, OJ C 140, 5-6-1979, pp. 34-38

EP (1985) *Resolution Closing the Procedure for Consultation of the European Parliament on the Proposal from the Commission of the European Communities to the Council for a Directive Amending Directive 81/602/EEC Concerning the Prohibition of certain Substances Having a Hormonal Action and of any Substances Having a Thyrostatic Action*, Document A2-100/85, Adopted on 11 October 1985, OJ C 288, 11-11-1985, pp. 158-160

EP (1988a) *Resolution on the Effects and Risks of Using the Growth Hormones and the BST Hormone in the Dairy and Meat Industries*, Document A2-30/88, Adopted on 5 July 1988, OJ C 235, 12 September 1988, pp. 41-44

EP (1988b) *Resolution on the Use of Hormones in Meat Production*, Joint Resolution Replacing Documents B2-713, 753 and 754/88, Adopted on 16 September 1988, OJ C 262, 10 October 1988, pp. 167-170

EP (1988c) *Written Declaration on the Steel-Jawed Leghold Trap*, Document 9/88, Adopted on 16 September 1988, OJ C 262, 10-10-1988, pp. 221-222

EP (1989) *Resolution on the Harmonization of Legislation within the European Community on the Manufacture, Sale and Use of the Leghold Trap*, Document A2-303/88, Adopted on 17 February 1989, OJ C 69, 20-3-1989, pp. 198-201

EP (1990a) *Report on the Proposal from the Commission to the Council for a Regulation on the Importation of Certain Furs*, Document A3-138/90, 7 June 1990

EP (1990b) *Proposal for a Council Regulation on the Importation of Certain Furs*, Texts Adopted by the European Parliament on 10 September 1990, OJ C 260, 15-10-1990, pp. 18-25

EP (1995a) *Decision on the Common Position Established by the Council with a View to the Adoption of a European Parliament and Council Directive on the Protection of Individuals with Regard to the Processing of Personal Data and on the Free Movement of such Data*, Adopted on 15 June 1995, OJ C 166, 3-7-1995, pp. 105-107

EP (1995b) *Resolution on Leghold Traps*, Documents B4-1465, 1466, 1467, 1482, 1487 and 1490/95, Adopted on 14 December 1995, OJ C 17, 22-1-1996, pp. 167-168

EP (1996a) *Report on the Proposal for a Council Regulation (EC) Amending Council Regulation (EEC) No 3254/91 Prohibiting the Use of Leghold Traps in the Community and the Introduction into the Community of Pelts and Manufactured Goods of certain Wild Animal Species Originating in Countries which Catch them by Means of Leghold Traps or Trapping Methods which Do not Meet International Humane Trapping Standards*, Document A4-151/96, 2 May 1996

EP (1996b) *Proposal for a Council Regulation Amending Council Regulation (EEC) No 3254/91 Prohibiting the Use of Leghold Traps in the Community and the Introduction into the Community of Pelts and Manufactured Goods of certain Wild Animal Species Originating in Countries which Catch them by Means of Leghold Traps or Trapping Methods which Do not Meet International Humane Trapping Standards*, Texts Adopted by the European Parliament on 19 June 1996, OJ C 198, 8-7-1996, pp. 101-110

EP (1996c) *Decision Setting up a Temporary Committee of Inquiry*, Document B4-0964/96, Adopted on 18 July 1996, OJ C 261, 9 September 1996, pp. 132-135

EP (1997a) *Resolution on the Results of the Temporary Committee of Inquiry into BSE*, Documents B4-0078, 0079, 0080, 0083 and 0096/97, Adopted on 19 February 1997, OJ C 85, 17 March 1997, pp. 61-62

EP (1997b) *Resolution on Leghold Traps*, Document B4-154/97, 21 February 1997, OJ C 85, 17 March 1997, p. 173

EP (1997c) *Report on the Signing and Conclusion of an International Agreement between the European Community, Canada and the Russian Federation on Humane Trapping Standards*, Document A4-187/97, 23 May 1997

EP (1997d) *Report on the Report from the Commission on the Review of Directive 90/220/EEC in the Context of the Commission's Communication on Biotechnology and the White Paper*, Document A4-0239/97, 3 July 1997

EP (1997e) *Report on the Proposal for a Council Decision Concerning the Signing and Conclusion of an Agreement on International Humane Trapping Standards between the Euopean Community, Canada and the Russian Federation*, Document A4-325/97, 22 October 1997

EP (1997f) *Legislative Resolution Embodying Parliament's Opinion on the Amended Proposal for a Council Decision Concerning the Signing and Conclusion of an Agreement on International Humane Trapping Standards between the European Community, Canada and the Russian Federation*, Document A4-325/97, Adopted on 18 December 1997, OJ C 14, 19-1-1998, p. 177

EP (1998) *Legislative Resolution Embodying Parliament's Opinion on the Proposal for a Council Decision Concerning the Signing and Conclusion of an International Agreement in the Form of an Agreed Minute between the European Community and the United States of America on Humane Trapping Standards*, Document A4-197/98, Adopted on 16 June 1998, OJ C 210, 6-7-1998, p. 31

EP (1999) *Report on the Proposal for a European Parliament and Council Directive Amending Directive 90/220/EEC on the Deliberate Release into the Environment of Genetically Modified Organisms*, Document A4-0024/99, 28 January 1999

EP (2000) *Report of the Draft Commission Decision on the Adequacy of the Protection Provided by the Safe Harbour Privacy Principles*, Document A5-177/2000, 22 June 2000

Esty, D. C. & D. Geradin (1998) 'Environmental Protection and International Competitiveness. A Conceptual Framework,' *Journal of World Trade*, Vol. 32, No. 3, pp. 5-46

EU & US (1999) *Joint Report on Data Protection Dialogue to the EU/US Summit, 21 June 1999*, available at www.ita.doc.gov/td/ecom/menu.html

EU Food Law (1995a) 'Presidency Writes to Codex,' *EU Food Law*, March 1995, pp. 5-6

EU Food Law (1995b) 'Codex to Discuss Scientific Standards,' *EU Food Law*, April 1995, pp. 12-14

EU Food Law (1995c) 'Codex Votes in Favour of Hormones in Meat,' *EU Food Law*, July 1995, pp. 7-8

EuroCommerce (1998) *EuroCommerce Welcomes the Adoption of the Regulation on Detailed Labelling Rules for Foodstuffs Produced from Genetically Modified Soya and Maize*, Press Release, 28 May 1998, available at www.eurocommerce.be/main.html

EuroCommerce (1999) *Position Paper on the Labelling of Foods Containing Genetically Modified Soya and Maize*, 15 November 1999, available at www.eurocommerce.be/main.html

EuropaBio (1999a) *European Parliament: Need for a Strong, Science-Based Regulatory Framework for GMOs*, Position Paper, 15 February 1999, available at www.europabio.be/code/en/m_press.cfm?id_news=37

EuropaBio (1999b) *Biotechnology Industry Channeling Program Helps US Farmers to Sell Novel Trait Corn Crops which Have not yet Obtained EU Import Clearance*, Position Paper, 15 April 1999, available at www.europabio.org/code/en/m_press.cfm?id_news=32

EuropaBio (1999c) *Biotechnology Industry Regrets Greek Ban on GM Crops*, Position Statement, 21 April 1999, available at www.europa-bio.be/code/en/m_press.cfm?id_news=31

EuropaBio (2000a) *European Bio-Industries Welcome Biosafety Protocol Agreement*, Press Release, 31 January 2000, available at www.europa-bio.be/code/en/m_press.cfm?id_news=18

EuropaBio (2000b) *For the Moment, the Gene Genie is Staying in its Bottle*, Press Release, 25 March 2000, available at www.europa-bio.be/code/en/m_press.cfm?id_news=28

EuropaBio (2000c) *European Bioindustries fully Accept Liability under Existing National and EU Laws*, Press Release, 13 April 2000, available at www.europa-bio.be/code/en/m_press.cfm?id_news=11

Evans, P.B. (1993) 'Building an Integrative Approach to International and Domestic Politics: Reflections and Projections,' in P.B. Evans, H.K. Jacobson, & R.D. Putnam (eds.), *Double-Edged Diplomacy. International Bargaining and Domestic Politics*, Berkeley: University of California Press, pp. 397-430

Evans, P.B., H.K. Jacobson & R.D. Putnam (eds.). (1993) *Double-Edged Diplomacy. International Bargaining and Domestic Politics*, Berkeley: University of California Press

FACE (1999) *Technical Support for the Preparation of the Implementation of the Agreement on International Humane Trapping Standards between the European Community, Canada and the Russian Federation - Evaluation of the Situation in the Member States*. Final Report to the European Commission, Environment, Nuclear Safety and Civil Protection, unpublished

Falkner, R. (2000) 'Regulating Biotech Trade: The Cartagena Protocol on Biosafety,' *International Affairs*, Vol. 76, No. 2, pp. 299-313

FAO & WHO (1991) *Strategies for Assessing the Safety of Foods Produced by Biotechnology. Report of Joint FAO/WHO Consultation*, available at www.who.int/fsf/GMfood/index.htm (conclusions and recommendations also reprinted in CAC 2000a, appendix 1 to annex 1)

FAO & WHO (1996) *Biotechnology and Food Safety. Report of a Joint FAO/WHO Consultation*, available at www.fao.org/WAICENT/faoinfo/economic/esn/biotech/tabconts.htm (conclusions and recommendations also reprinted in CAC 2000a, appendix 2 to annex 1)

FAO & WHO (2001) *Codex Alimentarius Commission Discussed Safety of Genetically Modified Foods, Approves Toxin Limits and Guidelines for Organic Livestock Farming*, Press Release 01/44 Joint WHO/FAO, 6 July 2001, available at www.fao.org/WAICENT/OIS/PRESS_NE/PRESSENG/2001/pren0144.htm

Fara, G.M. et al. (1979) 'Epidemic of Breast Enlargement in an Italian School,' *The Lancet*, 11 August 1979, pp. 295-297

Farber, D.A. & P.P. Frickey (1991). *Law and Public Choice. A Critical Introduction*, Chicago and London: University of Chicago Press

FDA (1992) 'Statement of Policy: Foods Derived from New Plant Varieties,' *Federal Register*, Vol. 57, No. 104, 29 May 1992, pp. 22984-23005

FDA (1994a) *Conference on Scientific Issues Related to Potential Allergenicity in Transgenic Food Crops*, April 18-19, 1994, Handout, available at www.cfsan.fda.gov/~lrd/bioallrg.html

FDA (1994b) 'Secondary Direct Food Additives Permitted in Food for Human Consumption; Food Additives Permitted in Feed and Drinking Water of Animals; Aminoglycoside 3'-Phosphotransferase II; Final Rule,' *Federal Register*, Vol. 59, 23 May 1994, pp. 26700-26711

FDA (1995) *FDA's Policy for Foods Developed by Biotechnology*, by James Maryanski, available at vm.cfsan.fda.gov/~lrd/biopolcy.html

FDA (1997a) *Guidance on Consultation Procedures. Foods Derived from New Plant Varieties*, October 1997, available at vm.cfsan.fda.gov/~lrd/consulpr.html

FDA (1997b) *The FDA Modernization Act of 1997*, 21 November 1997, available at www.fda.gov/opacom/backgrounders/modact.htm

FDA (1998) *Guidance for Industry: Use of Antibiotic Resistance Marker Genes in Transgenic Plants*, 4 September 1998, available at vm.cfsan.fda.gov/~dms/opa-armg.html

FDA (1999a) *Statement on Biotechnology Issues*, by James H. Maryanski, FDA Biotechnology Coordinator, before the Senate Committee on Agriculture, Nutrition and Forestry, 7 October 1999, available at www.hhs.gov/progorg/asl/testify/t991007a.html

FDA (1999b) *FDA Announces Public Meetings on Bioengineered Foods*, News Release, 18 October 1999, available at www.fda.gov/bbs/topics/NEWS/NEW00695.html

FDA (2000a) *Foods Derived from New Plant Varieties Derived through Recombinant DNA Technology. Final Consultations under FDA's 1992 Policy*, May 2000, available at vm.cfsan.fda.gov/~lrd/biocon.html

FDA (2000b) *FDA to Strengthen Pre-Market Review of Bioengineered Foods*, News Release, 3 May 2000, available at www.fda.gov/bbs/topics/NEWS/NEW00726.html

FDA (2000c) *Aventis CropScience Finds Bioengineered Protein in Non-StarLink Corn Seed*, News Release, 21 November 2000, available at www.fda.gov/oc/po/firmrecalls/aventis11_00.html

FDA (2001a) 'Premarket Notice Concerning Bioengineered Foods. Proposed Rule,' *Federal Register*, Vol. 66, No. 12, 18 January 2001, pp. 4706-4738

FDA (2001b) *Guidance for Industry: Voluntary Labeling Indicating whether Foods Have or Have not Been Developed Using Bioengineering*, Draft Guidance, January 2001, available at www.cfsan.fda.gov/~dms/biolabgu.html

Fearon, J. D. (1994) 'Domestic Political Audiences and the Escalation of International Disputes,' *American Political Science Review*, Vol. 88, No. 3, pp. 577-592

FIC (undated) *Answers*, booklet published in co-operation with the IFTF

Flaherty, D. H. (1989) *Protecting Privacy in Surveillance Societies*, Chapel Hill and London: University of North Carolina Press

Fleishman-Hillard Research (1999) *Human Dimensions of Trapping and Furbearer Management. A Report to IAFWA*, May 1999, unpublished

FMI (1999) *EC – Hormone Ban, Implementation of WTO Recommendations*, Letter to the Office of the USTR, 22 April 1999, available at www.fmi.org/gr/comments/more/422-99.html

FoE (2000) *The Genetically Engineered Food Right-to-Know Act, S. 2080*, available at www.foe.org/safefood/boxer-s2080.htm

Food Online (2000a) 'Frito-Lay Angers Farm Groups with GM Policy,' *Food Online*, 2 February 2000, available at www.foodonline.com/content/news/search/adv_search.asp

Food Online (2000b) 'Seagram Says No to GM Corn,' *Food Online*, 10 February 2000, available at www.foodonline.com/content/news/search/adv_search.asp

Fredriksson, P. G. & D.L. Millimet (2000) *Strategic Interaction and the Determination of Environmental Policy and Quality across US States*, unpublished paper

Friman, H. R. (1993) 'Side-Payments Versus Security Cards: Domestic Bargaining Tactics In International Economic Negotiations,' *International Organization*, Vol. 47, No. 3, pp. 387-410

FTC (1997) *Public Workshop on Consumer Privacy on the Global Information Infrastructure*, 6 January 1997, available at www.ftc.gov

FTC (1998a) *Privacy Online: A Report to Congress*, June 1998, available at www.ftc.gov

FTC (1998b) *Internet Site Agrees to Settle FTC Charges of Deceptively Collecting Personal Information in Agency's first Internet Privacy Case*, News Release, 13 August 1998, available at www.ftc.gov/opa/1998/9808/geocitie.htm

FTC (1999a) *Decision and Order in the Matter of Geocities, a Corporation*, Docket No. C-3850, 5 February 1999, available at www.ftc.gov/os/1999/9902/9823015.do.htm

FTC (1999b) *Self-Regulation and Privacy Online. A Report to Congress*, July 1999, available at www.ftc.gov

FTC (1999c) *Self-Regulation and Privacy Online*, Prepared Statement before the Subcommittee on Telecommunications, Trade, and Consumer Protection of the Committee on Commerce, United States House of Representatives, 13 July 1999, available at www.ftc.gov/os/1999/9907/pt071399.htm

FTC (2000a) *Privacy Online: Fair Information Practices in the Electronic Marketplace. A Report to Congress*, May 2000, available at www.ftc.gov

FTC (2000b) *Privacy Online: Fair Information Practices in the Electronic Marketplace*, Prepared Statement before the Committee on Commerce, Science, and Transportation,

United States Senate, 25 May 2000, available at www.ftc.gov/os/2000/05/testimony privacy.htm

FVO (1998a) *Final Mission Report. Canada. Residues. 5 to 14 May 1998*, available at europa.eu.int/comm/food/fs/inspections/vi/reports/canada/index_en.html

FVO (1998b) *Final Report on a Mission to the USA, 20-31 July 1998. Evaluation on Residue Control in Meat, Milk and Dairy Products, Aquaculture Fish and Game Meat*, available at europa.eu.int/comm/food/fs/inspections/vi/reports/usa/index_en.html

FVO (1999a) *Final Report of a Mission Carried out in the USA from the 28th June to the 2nd July 1999 to Assess the Implementation of a New Testing Regime in the Framework of the US/EU Interim Agreement of April 1989 Concerning Trade in Non-Hormone Treated Bovine Meat*, Document XXIV/1186/99 – MR – final, available at europa.eu.int/comm/food/fs/inspections/vi/reports/usa/index_en.html

FVO (1999b) *Final Report of a Mission Carried out in the United States of America from 4 November to 12 November 1999 in Order to Evaluate the Implementation and the Enforcement of the Non-Hormone Treated Cattle (NHTC) Programme*, Document DG(SANCO)/1076/1999 – MR final, available at europa.eu.int/comm/food/fs/ inspections/vi/reports/usa/index_en.html

FVO (2000a) *Report of a Mission Carried out in the United States of America from 24 January to 4 February 2000 in Order to Evaluate the Implementation and the Enforcement of the Non-Hormone Treated Cattle and the EU Additional Residue Testing Programmes*, Document DG(SANCO)/1030/2000 – MR final, available at europa.eu.int/ comm/food/fs/inspections/vi/reports/usa/index_en.html

FVO (2000b) *Final Report of a Mission Carried out in Canada from 19 September to 29 September 2000 in Order to Evaluate the Control of Residues in Live Animals and Animal Products*, Document DG(SANCO)/1188/2000 – MR final, available at europa.eu.int/comm/food/fs/inspections/vi/reports/canada/index_en.html

G8 (1999) 'Communiqué of the G8 Heads of Government Meeting at Cologne, June 1999,' reprinted in Annex 1 to: *OECD's Work on Biotechnology*, OECD News Release of 16 September 1999, available at www.oecd.org/media/release/biotechnology.htm

Galtung, J. (1967) 'On the Effects of International Economic Sanctions. With Examples from the Case of Rhodesia,' *World Politics*, Vol. 19, No. 3, pp. 378-416

GAO (2001) *International Trade. Concerns of Biotechnology Challenge U.S. Agricultural Exports*, Report to the Ranking Minority Member, Committee on Finance, U.S. Senate, GAO-01-727, June 2001, available at www.gao.gov/nav.html

Gaskell, G., M.W. Bauer, J. Durant & N.C. Allum (1999) 'Worlds Apart? The Reception of Genetically Modified Foods in Europe and the U.S.' *Science*, Vol. 285, No. 5426, pp. 384-387

GATT (1952) *Belgian Family Allowances (Allocations Familiales)*, Report of the Panel, G/32 – 1S/59, Adopted on 7 November 1952, available at www.wto.org/english/tratop_e/ dispu_e/gt47ds_e.htm

GATT (1984) *Canada – Administration of the Foreign Investment Review Act*, Report of the Panel, L/5504 – 30S/140, Adopted on 7 February 1984, available at www.wto.org/ english/tratop_e/dispu_e/gt47ds_e.htm

GATT (1988) *Canada – Measures Affecting Exports of Unprocessed Herring and Salmon*, Report of the Panel, BISD 35S/98, Adopted on 22 March 1988, available at www.wto. org/english/tratop_e/dispu_e/gt47ds_e.htm

GATT (1991) 'United States – Restrictions on Imports of Tuna,' Report of the Panel, Not Adopted, Submitted to the parties on 16 August 1991, *International Legal Materials*, Vol. 30, pp. 1594-1623

GATT (1994) 'United States – Restrictions on Imports of Tuna,' Report of the Panel, Not Adopted, Released in June 1994, *International Legal Materials*, Vol. 33, pp. 839-903

GE Food Alert (2000a) *Contaminant Found in Taco Bell Tace Shells, Food Safety Coalition Demands Recall by Taco Bell, Philip Morris*, Press Release, 18 September 2000, available at www.gefoodalert.org/recall/Btnewsrelease6_0.htm

GE Food Alert (2000b) *Pending FDA Policy on Genetically Engineered Foods under Fire in Wake of Regulatory Breakdown over Kraft Taco Shells*, Press Release, 28 September 2000, available at www.gefoodalert.org /html/policyfire.htm

GE Food Alert (2000c) *Re: Imminent FDA Rulemaking on Genetically Engineered Foods*, Press Memo, 5 October 2000, available at www.gefoodalert.org/html/fdamemo.htm

GE Food Alert (2000d) *Contamination by Starlink Corn Found in Western Family® Taco Shells Purchased in Oregon. Company Sells to U.S., Japan, and other Pacific Rim Countries*, Press Release, 25 October 2000, available at www.gefoodalert.org/recall/westernrelease.htm

Genschel, P. & T. Plümper (1997) 'Regulatory Competition and International Cooperation,' *Journal of European Public Policy*, Vol. 4, No. 4, pp. 626-642

George, A.L. & T.J. McKeown (1985) 'Case Studies and Theories of Organizational Decision Making,' *Advances in Information Processes in Organizations*, Vol. 2, pp. 21-58

Geradin, D. (1997) 'Trade and Environmental Protection in the Context of World Trade Rules: A View from the European Union,' *European Foreign Affairs Review*, Vol. 2, pp. 33-61

Glasius, M.E. (1999) *Foreign Policy on Human Rights. Its Influence on Indonesia under Soeharto*, Antwerpen: Intersentia-Hart

Globe and Mail (2000) 'Europeans Seek to Ban Canadian Beef, Pork,' by André Picard, *Globe and Mail*, 20 November 2000

GMA (1998) *Biosafety Protocol Could Choke off Global Trade, GMA Coalition Tells President*, News Release, 17 December 1998, available at www.gmabrands.com/news/docs/NewsRelease.cfm?DocID=210

GMA (1999) *Letter on labelling of GM foods sent to President Clinton by 38 organisations*, 12 November 1999, available at www.gmabrands.com/news/docs/Correspondence.cfm?DocID=446

GMA (2000a) *Letter on Rep. Kucinich's mandatory labelling bill sent to members of the House of Representatives by 35 trade associations*, 27 January 2000, available at www.gmabrands.com/news/docs/Correspondence.cfm?DocID=491

GMA (2000b) *Letter on Sen. Boxer's mandatory labelling bill sent to members of the U.S. Senate by 35 trade associations*, 10 February 2000, available at www.gmabrands.com/news/docs/Correspondence.cfm?DocID=510GMA (2000c) *FDA's Reaffirmation of Biotech Safety Will Help Ensure "Continued Consumer Confidence" in Regulation*, News Release, 3 May 2000, available at www.gmabrands.com/news/docs/NewsRelease.cfm?DocID=567

GMA & FMI (1999) *Letter with recommendations on FDA's GM foods policies sent to FDA's Commissioner on 17 November 1999*, available at www.gmabrands.com/news/docs/Correspondence.cfm?DocID=485

Golub, J. (1996) 'State Power and Institutional Influence in European Integration: Lessons from the Packaging Waste Directive,' *Journal of Common Market Studies*, Vol. 34, No. 3, pp. 313-339

Government of Canada (1998) *Bill C-54. Personal Information Protection and Electronic Documents Act*, 1st Session, 36th Parliament, 46-47 Elizabeth II, 1997-1998, available at www.parl.gc.ca/36/1/parlbus/chambus/house/bills/government/C-54/C-54_1/C-54TOCE.html

Government of Canada (2001a) *Government of Canada Welcomes Royal Society Expert Scientific Panel Report on the Future of Food Biotechnology*, News Release, 5 February 2001, available at www.hc-sc.gc.ca/english/archives/releases/2001/2001_13e.htm

Government of Canada (2001b) *Cartagena Protocol on Biosafety. Notice of Canada's Signature and Government Position Regarding Implementation of the Cartagena Protocol on Biosafety*, Statement, 5 April 2001, available at www.ec.gc.ca/press/2001/010405-2_n_e.htm

Government of Canada (2001c) *Action Plan of the Government of Canada in Response to the Royal Society of Canada Expert Panel Report*, 23 November 2001

Government of Quebec (1999a) *Letter by Minsters David Cliche and Robert Perreault to John Manley, Minister of Industry Canada*, dated 25 January 1999, available at www.autoroute.gouv.qc.ca/une/extraits.htm

Government of Quebec (1999b) *Le Gouvernement du Québec Demande le Retrait du Projet C-54* [The Government of Quebec Demands the Withdrawal of Bill C-54], Press Release, 18 March 1999, available at www.autoroute.gouv.qc.ca/une/extraits.htm

Grant, W. (1997) *The Common Agricultural Policy*, New York: St. Martin's Press

Greenpeace (undated) *Gokken met Genen* [Gambling with Genes], available at www.greenpeace.nl/gmoinfo/rapport.shtml

Hamilton, D.A. & L.B. Fox (1987) 'Wild Furbearer Management in the Midwestern United States,' in: M. Novak et al. (eds) *Wild Furbearer Management and Conservation in North America*, Toronto: Ontario Trappers Association/Ontario Ministry of Natural Resources, pp. 1100-1116

Hamilton, D.A., B. Roberts, G. Linscombe, N.R. Jotham, H. Noseworthy & J.L. Stone (1998) 'The European Union's Wild Fur Regulation: A Battle of Politics, Cultures, Animal Rights, International Trade and North America's Wildlife Policy,' *Transactions of the 63rd North American Wildlife and Natural Resources Conference*, Washington DC: Wildlife Management Institute, pp. 572-588

Hammonds, H. (1990), 'A U.S. Perspective on the EC Hormones Directive,' *Michigan Journal of International Law*, Vol. 11, pp. 840-844

Hancock, D.L., J.F. Wagner & D.B. Anderson (1991) 'Effects of Estrogens and Androgens on Animal Growth,' in: A.M. Pearson & T.R. Dutson (eds), *Growth Regulation in Farm Animals*, London and New York: Elsevier Applied Science, pp. 255-297

Harris, H.A. (1997) *Privacy Rights According to the Supreme Court of Canada*, Presented at the 1997 CAPA Conference, 30 October 1997, Ottawa, Ontario, available at www.privcom.gc.ca/speech/archive/02_05_a_971030_e.htm

Harrop, S. (1997) 'Reconciling Animal Welfare and Trade Law,' in: A. Nollkaemper (ed.) *Trapped by Furs? The Legality of the European Community's Fur Import Ban in EC and International Law*, Rotterdam: Center for International Natural Resources Law, pp. 77-87

Hathaway, O.A. (1998) 'Positive Feedback: the Impact of Trade Liberalization on Industry Demands for Protection,' *International Organization*, Vol. 52, No. 3, pp. 575-612

Haverland, M. (1998) *National Autonomy, European Integration and the Politics of Packaging Waste*, Amsterdam: Thela Thesis

Haverland, M. & S.B.M. Princen (1998) 'Causaliteit in Meervoudige Case-Studies' [Causality in Multiple Case Studies], *Sociale Wetenschappen*, Vol. 41, No. 4, pp. 24-41

Hawkins, D.G. (1997) 'Domestic Response To International Pressure: Human Rights In Authoritarian Chile,' *European Journal of International Relations*, Vol. 3, No. 4, pp. 403-434

Health Canada (1994) *Guidelines for the Safety Assessment of Novel Foods*, published in September 1994, available at www.hc-sc.gc.ca

Health Canada (1999a) *Novel Foods and Ingredients – Regulatory Impact Analysis Statement*, 30 September 1999, available at www.hc-sc.gc.ca/foodaliment/english/subjects/novel_foods_and_ingredient/novel_foods_and_ingredient.html

Health Canada (1999b) 'Food and Drugs Regulations – Amendments; Schedule No. 948 (Novel Foods Regulations),' *Canada Gazette*, Part II, 27 October 1999

Health Canada (2000) *Novel Food – Decisions*, available at www.hc-sc.gc.ca/foodaliment/english/subjects/novel_foods_and_ingredient/novel_foods_and_ingredient.html

Health Canada & CFIA (2000) *Canada's Response to European Commission Mission Carried out to Evaluate the Control of Residues in Live Animals and Animal Products*, 15 December 2000, available at europa.eu.int/comm/food/fs/inspections/vi/reports/canada/index_en.html

HEW (1973) *Records, Computers and the Rights of Citizens*, Report of the Secretary's Advisory Committee on Automated Personal Data Systems, July 1973, DHEW Publication No. (OS) 73-94

Heydrich, M.W. (1999) 'A Brave New World: Complying with the European Union Directive on Personal Privacy through the Power of Contract,' *Brooklyn Journal of International Law*, Vol. 25, No. 2, pp. 407-443

HHS (2000a) *HHS Announces Final Regulation Establishing first-ever National Standards to Protect Patients' Personal Medical Records*, Press Release, 20 December 2000, available at www.hhs.gov/news/press/2000pres/20001220.html

HHS (2000b) 'Standards for Privacy of Individually Identifiable Health Information; Final Rule,' *Federal Register*, Vol. 65, No. 250, 28 December 2000, pp. 82462-82829

Hirschman, A.O. (1980 (1945)) *National Power and the Structure of Foreign Trade*, 2nd ed., Berkeley: University of California Press

HNN (1995) 'WWF Denmark Supports Indigenous Trappers,' *High North News*, No. 10, 15 May 1995, available at www.highnorth.no

Hoekman, B.M. & M.M. Kostecki (1995) *The Political Economy of the World Trading System. From GATT to WTO*, Oxford: Oxford University Press

Hogenboom, B. (1998) *Mexico and the NAFTA Environment Debate. The Transnational Politics of Economic Integration*, Utrecht: International Books

Horn, F. (1988) *Reservations and Interpretative Declarations to Multilateral Treaties*, Amsterdam etc.: North-Holland

House (2000) *Seeds of Opportunity: An Assessment of the Benefits, Safety, and Oversight of Plant Genomics and Agricultural Biotechnology*, Report prepared by the Subcommittee on Basic Research of the Committee on Science, 13 April 2000, available at www.house.gov/science

Howells, G.G. & T. Wilhelmsson (1997) *EC Consumer Law*, Aldershot: Ashgate

Howse, R. (1998) 'The Turtles Panel. Another Environmental Disaster in Geneva,' *Journal of World Trade*, Vol. 32, No. 5, pp. 73-100

HSUS (1997) '74% of Americans Want Steel Jaw Leghold Traps Outlawed,' *Washington Times*, Advertisement, 20 January 1997, p. F5

Hufbauer, G.C., J.J. Schott & K.A. Elliott (1990) *Economic Sanctions Reconsidered. History and Current Policy*, 2nd ed., Washington DC: Institute for International Economics

Hurd, I. (1999) 'Legitimacy and Authority in International Politics,' *International Organization*, Vol. 53, No. 2, pp. 379-408

IAFWA (1997) *Improving Animal Welfare in U.S. Trapping Programs: Process Recommendations and Summaries of Existing Data*, unpublished report

IAFWA (2000) *Performance of Restraining Traps to Capture Furbearers in the United States*. Progress Report, May 2000, unpublished

IFT (1999) 'Regulatory Scene has Active Month,' *Food Science Communicators' Alert*, Vol. 6, No. 4, available at www.ift.org

IFT (2000) 'Genetically Modified Organisms (GMOs). A Backgrounder by the Institute of Food Technologists,' *Food Technology*, Vol. 54, No. 1, pp. 42-45, available at www.ift.org

IHAC (1995) *Connection, Community, Content: The Challenge of the Information Highway*, September 1995, available at www.strategis.ic.gc.ca/SSG/ih01070e.html

IIA (1998) *Comments of the Information Industry Association (IIA) on the International Safe Harbor Privacy Principles*, Letter to the Department of Commerce, 19 November 1998, available at www.ita.doc.gov/td/ecom/menu.html

IITF (1995) *Privacy and the National Information Infrastructure: Principles for Providing and Using Personal Information*, Report by the Privacy Working Group of the Information Policy Committee of the Information Infrastructure Task Force, 6 June 1995, available at www.iitf.nist.gov/ipc/ipc/ipc-pubs/niiprivprin_final.html

Industry Canada (1996) *Building the Information Society: Moving Canada into the 21st Century*, available at strategis.ic.gc.ca/SSG/ih01103e.html

Industry Canada (1998) *Canada Moves to Promote E-Commerce: Personal Privacy Protection and Electronic Signatures Recognized in Law*, News Release, 1 October 1998, available at www.ic.gc.ca/cmb/Welcomeic.nsf/englisharchives

Industry Canada (1999) *Privacy Legislation Reintroduced in House of Commons*, News Release, 15 October 1999, available at www.ic.gc.ca/cmb/Welcomeic.nsf/englisharchives

Industry Canada & IHAC (1994) *Privacy and the Canadian Information Highway. Building Canada's Information and Communications Infrastructure*, October 1994, available at www.strategis.ic.gc.ca/SSG/ih01094e.html

Industry Canada & Justice Canada (1998a) *The Protection of Personal Information. Building Canada's Information Economy and Society*, Discussion Paper, 24 January 1998, available at e-com.ic.gc.ca/english/privacy/632d9.html

Industry Canada & Justice Canada (1998b) *The Protection of Personal Information. Summary Report of the Responses to the Discussion Paper*, available at e-com.ic.gc.ca/english/privacy/632d19.html

ISB (1994a) 'Flavr Savr Tomatoes Approved for Sale,' *ISB News Report*, June 1994, available at gophisb.biochem.vt.edu/articles/JUN9401.htm

ISB (1994b) 'The New Tomato: An Inside View,' *ISB News Report*, July 1994, available at gophisb.biochem.vt.edu/articles/JUL9416.htm

ISB (1998a) 'GMOs under Attack in the UK,' *ISB News Report*, August 1998, pp. 2-4, available at gophisb.biochem.vt.edu/articles/AUG9802.htm

ISB (1998b) 'Poisonous Potatoes: A Case Study in Miscommunicating Science,' *ISB News Report*, September 1998, pp. 1-3, available at gophisb.biochem.vt.edu/articles/SEP9801.htm

ISB (2000) 'Commercialization of Path-Breaking Transgenic Salmon Faces Stumbling Blocks, *ISB News Report*, April 2000, available at gophisb.biochem.vt.edu/articles/apr0004.htm

ISO (1999a) *Animal (Mammal) Traps - Part 4: Methods for Testing Killing-Trap Systems Used on Land or Underwater*, ISO 10990-4, 1st edition, 1 November 1999

ISO (1999b) *Animal (Mammal) Traps - Part 5: Methods for Testing Restraining Traps*, ISO 10990-5, 1st edition, 1 November 1999

ITI (1999) Letter to the Department of Commerce, 3 December 1999, available at www.ita.doc.gov/td/ecom/menu.html

Jackson, J.H. (1998) *The World Trading System. Law and Policy of International Economic Relations*, 2nd ed., Cambridge MA and London: The MIT Press

Jackson, R.J. & D. Jackson (2001) *Politics in Canada. Culture, Institutions, Behaviour and Public Policy*, 5th ed., Toronto ON: Prentice Hall

James, C. (1998) *Global Review of Commercialized Transgenic Crops: 1998*, ISAAA Briefs No. 8, Ithaca NY: ISAAA, available at www.isaaa.org/publications/briefs/Brief_8.htm

James, C. (2000a) *Global Status of Commercialized Transgenic Crops: 1999*, ISAAA Briefs No. 17, Ithaca NY: ISAAA, available at www.isaaa.org/publications/briefs/Brief_17.htm

James (2000b) *Global Status of Commercialized Transgenic Crops: 2000*, ISAAA Briefs No. 21: Preview, Ithaca NY: ISAAA, available at www.isaaa.org/publications/briefs/Brief_21.htm

Jans, J.H. (2000) *European Environmental Law*, 2nd ed., Groningen: Europa Law Publishing

JECFA (1999) *Fifty-Second Meeting. Summary and Conclusions*, 2-11 February 1999, available at www.fao.org/es/ESN/jecfa/#meetings

JMC (2000) *Report*, Joint Management Committee Meeting, Edmonton, Alberta, June 15-16, 2000, Agreement on International Humane Trapping Standards, unpublished

Joseph, J. (1994) 'The Tuna-Dolphin Controversy in the Eastern Pacific Ocean: Biological, Economic, and Political Impacts,' *Ocean Development and International Law*, Vol. 25, pp. 1-30

Kaempfer, W.H. & A.D. Lowenberg (1999) 'Unilateral Versus Multilateral International Sanctions: A Public Choice Perspective,' *International Studies Quarterly*, No. 43, pp. 37-58

Kapteyn, P.J.G. & P. VerLoren van Themaat (1998) *Introduction to the Law of the European Communities*, 3rd ed., London: Kluwer Law International

Keohane, R. O. & J.S. Nye (1977) *Power and Interdependence. World Politics In Transition*, Boston and Toronto: Little, Brown and Company

Keohane, R.O. & J.S. Nye (1987) 'Power and Interdependence Revisited,' *International Organization*, Vol. 41, No. 4, pp. 725-753

Kerry, J.F. et al. (1994) *Letter from 11 Members of Congress to USTR Mickey Kantor*, dated 16 August 1994

King, G., R.O. Keohane & S. Verba (1994) *Designing Social Inquiry. Scientific Inference in Qualitative Research*, Princeton NJ: Princeton University Press

Klotz, A. (1996) 'Norms and Sanctions: Lessons From the Socialization Of South Africa,' *Review of International Studies*, Vol. 22, pp. 173-190

Knopf, J W. (1993) 'Beyond Two-Level Games: Domestic-International Interaction in the Intermediate-Range Nuclear Force Negotiations,' *International Organization*, Vol. 47, No. 4, pp. 599-628

Kraft Foods (2000) *Kraft Foods Announces Voluntary Recall of all Taco Bell Taco Shell Products from Grocery Stores. Tests Indicate Presence of Unapproved Variety of Corn*, News Release, 22 September 2000, available at www.kraftfoods.com/corporate/news/tln_09222000.html

Krasner, S.D. (1983) 'Structural Causes and Regime Consequences: Regimes as Intervening Variables,' in: S. D. Krasner (ed.), *International Regimes*, Ithaca and London: Cornell University Press, pp. 1-21

Krenzler, H.G. & G. Wiegand (1999) 'EU-US Relations: More than Trade Disputes?' *European Foreign Affairs Review*, Vol. 4, pp. 153-180

Krueger, A.B. (2000) 'From Bismarck to Maastricht: The March to European Union and the Labor Compact,' *Labour Economics*, Vol. 7, pp. 117-134

Kuyper, P.J. (1994) 'The Law of GATT as a Special Field of International Law. Ignorance, further Refinement or Self-Contained System of International Law?' *Netherlands Yearbook of International Law*, Vol. 25, pp. 227-257

Lamming, G.E. et al. (1987) 'Scientific Report on Anabolic Agents in Animal Production,' *The Veterinary Record*, Vol. 121, pp. 389-392

Lancet (1999a) 'Data on Toxicity of GM Potatoes Slated,' *Lancet*, Vol. 353, No. 9166, p. 1769

Lancet (1999b) 'Health Risks of Genetically Modified Foods,' *Lancet*, Vol. 353, No. 9167, p. 1811

Langille, B.A. (1997) 'Eight Ways to Think about International Labour Standards,' *Journal of World Trade*, Vol. 31, No. 4, pp. 27-53

LA Times (1999) 'U.S., European Lock Horns in Beef Hormone Debate,' by Paul Jacobs, *LA Times*, 9 April 1999, available at www.purefood.org/Toxic/beefhormone.cfm

Lee, E. (1997) 'Globalization and Labour Standards: A Review of Issues,' *International Labour Review*, Vol. 136, No. 2, pp. 173-189

Levidow, L. (1999) 'Regulating Bt Maize in the United States and Europe. A Scientific-Cultural Comparison,' *Environment*, Vol. 41, No. 10, pp. 10-22

Levinson, A. (1996) 'Environmental Regulations and Industry Location: International and Domestic Evidence,' in: J. N. Bhagwati & R. E. Hudec (eds.), *Fair Trade and Harmonization. Prerequisites for Free Trade? Vol. 1: Economic Analysis*, Cambridge MA and London: MIT Press, pp. 429-457

Li, C.P. (1993) 'The Effectiveness of Sanction Linkages: Issues and Actors,' *International Studies Quarterly*, Vol. 37, pp. 349-370

Lieberson, S. (1992) 'Small N's and Big Conclusions: An Examination of the Reasoning in Comparative Studies Based on a Small Number of Cases,' in: C. C. Ragin & H. S. Becker (eds.), *What is a Case? Exploring the Foundations of Social Inquiry*, Cambridge: Cambridge University Press, pp. 105-118

Linscombe, G. (1987) 'Wild Furbearer Management in the Southeastern United States,' in: M. Novak et al. (eds) *Wild Furbearer Management and Conservation in North America*, Toronto: Ontario Trappers Association/Ontario Ministry of Natural Resources, pp. 1091-1099

Liss, C. (1990) 'Trapping and Poisoning,' in: *Animals and their Legal Rights*, 4th edition, Washington, DC: AWI, pp. 157-189

Lowey, R.M. et al. (1994) *Letter by 27 Members of the House of Representatives to USTR Mickey Kantor*, dated 25 August 1994

Lynge, F. (1997) 'Conflicting Interests of Animal Welfare and Indigenous People,' in: A. Nollkaemper (ed.) *Trapped by Furs? The Legality of the European Community's Fur Import Ban in EC and International Law*, Rotterdam: Center for International Natural Resources Law, pp. 39-46

MacNeil, J.D. (1995) 'Agriculture and Agri-Food Canada's National Monitoring Program for Residues of Growth Promoting Substances in Meat,' in: CEC (ed.) *Scientific Confer-*

ence on Growth Promotion in Meat Production. Proceedings, Brussels, 29 November to 1 December 1995, p. 596

MAFF (1998) *Government Announces Fuller Evaluations of Growing Genetically Modified Crops*, News Release, No. 414/98, 21 October 1998, available at www.defra.gov.uk/news/newsrel/1998/981022b.htm

MAFF (1999a) *Enforcement Powers for GM Food Labelling now in Place*, News Release, No. 99/99, 19 March 1999, available at www.defra.gov.uk/news/newsrel/1999/990319d.htm

MAFF (1999b) *Canada Excludes UK Food Exports from Trade Sanctions*, News Release No. 267/99, 29 July 1999, available at www.defra.gov.uk/news/newsrel/1999/990729b.htm

MAFF (1999c) *EU Beef Hormones Ban: New Independent UK Scientific Assessment*, News Release No. 355/99, 19 October 1999, available at www.defra.gov.uk/news/newsrel/1999/991019b.htm

MAFF (2000) *Fur Farming (Prohibition) Act 2000 Receives Royal Assent*, News Release No. 423/00, 1 December 2000, available at www.defra.gov.uk/news/newsrel/2000/001201c.htm

Mahler, V.A. (1991) 'Domestic & International Sources of Trade Policy: The Case of Agriculture in the European Community & the United States,' *Polity*, Vol. 24, No. 1, pp. 27-47

Majone, G. (1996) *Regulating Europe*, London and New York: Routledge

Margaronis, M. (1999) 'The Politics of Food,' *Nation*, Vol. 269, No. 22, pp. 11-14

Martin, L.L. & K. Sikkink (1993) 'U.S. Policy and Human Rights in Argentina and Guatemala, 1973-1980,' in: P.B. Evans, H.K. Jacobson, & R.D. Putnam (eds.), *Double-Edged Diplomacy. International Bargaining and Domestic Politics*, Berkeley: University of California Press, pp. 330-362

Mayer, F.W. (1992) 'Managing Domestic Differences in International Negotiations: The Strategic Use of Internal Side-Payments,' *International Organization*, Vol. 46, No. 4, pp. 793-818

Mayer, D. & D. Hoch (1993) 'International Environmental Protection and the GATT: The Tuna/Dolphin Controversy,' *American Business Law Journal*, Vol. 31, No. 2, pp. 187-244

McMahon, J.A. (2000) *Law of the Common Agricultural Policy*, Harlow: Longman

McNiel, D.E. (1998) 'The first Case under the WTO's Sanitary and Phytosanitary Agreement: The European Union's Hormone Ban,' *Virginia Journal of International Law*, Vol. 39, pp. 89-134

Mei, P. (1993) 'The EC Proposed Data Protection Law,' *Law & Policy in International Business*, Vol. 25, pp. 305-334

Melchior, H.R., N.F. Johnson & J.S. Phelps (1987) 'Wild Furbearer Management in the Western United States and Alaska,' in: M. Novak et al. (eds) *Wild Furbearer Management and Conservation in North America*, Toronto: Ontario Trappers Association/Ontario Ministry of Natural Resources, pp. 1117-1128

Meng, W.P. (1990) 'The Hormone Conflict between the EEC and the United States within the Context of GATT,' *Michigan Journal of International Law*, Vol. 11, pp. 819-839

Meyer, H.H.D. (1991) 'The Illegal Practice and Resulting Risks versus the Controlled Use of Licensed Drugs: Views on the Present Situation in Germany,' *Annales de Recherche Vétérinaire*, Vol. 22, pp. 299-304

Milner, H. V. (1988) *Resisting Protectionism. Global Industries and the Politics of International Trade*, Princeton NJ: Princeton University Press

Milner, H.V. (1991) 'The Assumption of Anarchy in International Relations Theory: a Critique,' *Review of International Studies*, Vol. 17, pp. 67-85

Milner, H.V. (1998) 'Rationalizing Politics: The Emerging Synthesis of International, American, and Comparative Politics,' *International Organization*, Vol. 52, No. 4, pp. 759-786

Moravcsik, A. (1993) 'Introduction: Integrating International and Domestic Theories of International Bargaining,' in: P. B. Evans, H. K. Jacobson & R. D. Putnam (eds.), *Double-Edged Diplomacy. International Bargaining and Domestic Politics*, Berkeley: University of California Press, pp. 3-42

Moravcsik, A. (1997) 'Taking Preferences Seriously: A Liberal Theory of International Politics,' *International Organization*, Vol. 51, No. 4, pp. 513-553

Moravcsik, A. (1998) *The Choice For Europe. Social Purpose & State Power From Messina To Maastricht*, London: UCL Press

MRCI (1999) *L'Impact the l'Adoption du Projet the Loi Fédérale C-54 sur la Protection des Renseignements Personnels au Québec* [The Impact of the Adoption of Federal Bill C-54 on the Protection of Personal Information in Quebec], March 1999, available at www.autoroute.gouv.qc.ca/une/extraits.htm

Murray, P.J. (1998) 'The Adequace Standard under Directive 96/46/EC: Does U.S. Data Protection Meet this Standard?' *Fordham International Law Journal*, Vol. 21, pp. 932-1018

Muth, R.M., D.A. Hamilton, J.F. Organ, D.J. Witter, M.E. Mather & J.J. Daigle (1998) 'The Future of Wildlife and Fisheries Policy and Management: Assessing the Attitudes and Values of Wildlife and Fisheries Professionals,' *Transactions of the 63rd North American Wildlife and Natural Resources Conference*, Washington DC: Wildlife Management Institute, pp. 604-627

NCGA (2001) *NCGA Position. Biotechnology*, Position No. I-A-1, February 2001, available at www.ncga.com/biotechnology/main/position.htm

Netherlands (1995) 'Wijziging Regeling Aanwijzing Bedreigde Uitheemse Dier- en Plantesoorten en Wijziging Vrijstellingsregeling Bedreigde Uitheemse Dier- en Plantesoorten,' *Staatscourant*, No. 251, 28 December 1995, p. 16-17

Netherlands (1996a) 'Rectificatie Wijziging Regeling Aanwijzing Bedreigde Uitheemse Dier- en Plantesoorten en Wijziging Vrijstellingsregeling Bedreigde Uitheemse Dier- en Plantesoorten,' *Staatscourant*, No. 2, 3 January 1996

Netherlands (1996b) *Letter to DG I from the Dutch Permanent Representative to the EU*, dated 16 February 1996 (letter in Dutch)

Netherlands (1996c) *Métis Nation Northwest Territories versus Dutch State*, Case 96/289 before The Hague District Court, Decision of 28 March 1996 (decision in Dutch)

Nollkaemper, A. (1996) 'The Legality of Moral Crusades Disguised in Trade Laws: An Analysis of the EC "Ban" on Furs from Animals Taken by Leghold Traps,' *Journal of Environmental Law*, Vol. 8, No. 2, pp. 237-256

Nollkaemper, A. (ed.) (1997) *Trapped by Furs? The Legality of the European Community's Fur Import Ban in EC and International Law*, Rotterdam: Center of International Natural Resources Law

Nollkaemper, A. (1998) 'Rethinking States' Rights to Promote Extra-Territorial Environmental Values,' in: F. Weiss, E. Denters & P. De Waart (eds.), *International Economic Law with a Human Face*, The Hague: Kluwer, pp. 175-201

Noseworthy, H. (1997) 'European Community/Canada/Russian Federation Agreement on International Humane Trapping Standards and European Community/United States of

America Agreed Minute on Humane Trapping Standards. Is there a Difference? Is one Agreement "Better" than the Other?' in: NTA, *US/EU Understanding*, unpublished

Nossal, K.R. (1989) 'International Sanctions as International Punishment,' *International Organization*, Vol. 43, No. 2, pp. 301-322

Novak, M. (1987a) 'The Future of Trapping,' in: M. Novak et al. (eds) *Wild Furbearer Management and Conservation in North America*, Toronto: Ontario Trappers Association/Ontario Ministry of Natural Resources, pp. 89-97

Novak, M. (1987b) 'Traps and Trap Research,' in: M. Novak et al. (eds) *Wild Furbearer Management and Conservation in North America*, Toronto: Ontario Trappers Association/Ontario Ministry of Natural Resources, pp. 941-969

Novak, M. (1987c) 'Wild Furbearer Management in Ontario,' in: M. Novak et al. (eds) *Wild Furbearer Management and Conservation in North America*, Toronto: Ontario Trappers Association/Ontario Ministry of Natural Resources, pp. 1049-1061

NRF (1999) Letter to the Department of Commerce, 14 May 1999, available at www.ita.doc.gov/td/ecom/menu.html

NTA (1994) *Wildlife Management in Jeopardy*, Prepared for presentation to the Congressional Sportsmen's Caucus, 18 May 1994

NTA (1996) *Wildlife Management in Jeopardy, Part 2. An Update on the Illegal EU Fur Embargo*, Prepared for presentation to the Congressional Sportsmen's Caucus, 24 July 1996

NTA (2000) *Annual Report*, York PA, 15-16 August 2000

NTA & Trappers' Alliance (1995) *The Banning of Traps and Furs. Science - Wildlife - People in Jeopardy*, January 1995

Nugter, A.C.M. (1990) *The Transborder Flow of Personal Data within the EC*, Deventer: Kluwer

Odell, J.S. (1985) 'The Outcomes of International Trade Conflicts: The US and South Korea, 1960-1981,' *International Studies Quarterly*, Vol. 29, pp. 263-286

Odell, J.S. (1993) 'International Threats and Internal Politics. Brazil, the European Community, and the United States, 1985-1987,' in: P.B. Evans, H.K. Jacobson & R.D. Putnam (eds.), *Double-Edged Diplomacy. International Bargaining and Domestic Politics*, Berkeley: University of California Press, pp. 233-264

OECD (1980a) *Guidelines Governing the Protection of Privacy and Transborder Flows of Personal Data*, adopted on 23 September 1980, available at www.oecd.org/dsti/sti/it/secur/prod

OECD (1980b) *Explanatory Memorandum to the Guidelines Governing the Protection of Privacy and Transborder Flows of Personal Data*, available at www.oecd.org/dsti/sti/it/secur/prod

OECD (1982) *Biotechnology. International Trends and Perspectives*, by A.T. Bull, G. Holt & M.D. Lilly, available at www.oecd.org/dsti/sti/s_t/biotech/index.htm

OECD (1985) *Declaration on Transborder Data Flows*, Adopted on 11 April 1985, available at www.oecd.org/dsti/sti/it/secur/prod/e_dflow.htm

OECD (1986) *Recombinant DNA Safety Considerations*, available at www.oecd.org/dsti/sti/s_t/biotech/index.htm

OECD (1992) *Safety Considerations for Biotechnology*, available at www.oecd.org/dsti/sti/s_t/biotech/index.htm

OECD (1993) *Safety Evaluation of Foods Derived by Modern Biotechnology. Concepts and Principles*, available at www.oecd.org/dsti/sti/s_t/biotech/index.htm

OECD (1998a) *Implementing the OECD "Privacy Guidelines" in the Electronic Environment: Focus on the Internet*, DSTI/ICCP/REG(97)6/FINAL, published on 7 September 1998, available at www.oecd.org/dsti/sti/it/secur/index.htm

OECD (1998b) *Declaration on the Protection of Privacy on Global Networks*, Made by OECD Ministers at the Conference "A Borderless World: Realising the Potential of Global Electronic Commerce," 7-9 October 1998, Ottawa, Canada, available at www.olis.oecd.org/olis/1998doc.nsf/linkto/sg-ec(98)14-final

OECD (1999) *Foreign Trade by Commodities 1993-1998*, OECD Statistics, Paris: Organization for Economic Cooperation and Development

Ogus, A. (1996) *Regulation. Legal Form and Economic Theory*, Oxford: Clarendon Press

Ogus, A. (1999) 'Competition between National Legal Systems: A Contribution of Economic Analysis to Comparative Law,' *International and Comparative Law Quarterly*, Vol. 48, No. 2, pp. 405-418

OSTP (1984) 'Proposal for a Coordinated Framework for Regulation of Biotechnology,' *Federal Register*, Vol. 49, No. 252, 31 December 1984, pp. 50856-50907

OSTP (1985) 'Coordinated Framework for Regulation of Biotechnology; Establishment of the Biotechnology Science Coordinating Committee,' *Federal Register*, Vol. 50, No. 220, 14 November 1985, pp. 47174-47195

OSTP (1986) 'Coordinated Framework for Regulation of Biotechnology; Announcement of Policy and Notice for Public Comment,' *Federal Register*, Vol. 51, No. 123, 26 June 1986, pp. 23302-23350

Paarlberg, R. (1997) 'Agricultural Policy Reform and the Uruguay Round: Synergistic Linkage in a Two-Level Game?' *International Organization*, Vol. 51, No. 3, pp. 413-444

Palmeter, D. & P.C. Mavroidis (1998) 'The WTO Legal System: Sources of Law,' *American Journal of International Law*, Vol. 92, No. 3, pp. 398-413

Pardo Quintillán (1999) 'Free Trade, Public Health Protection and Consumer Information in the European and WTO Context. Hormone Treated Beef and Genetically Modified Organisms,' *Journal of World Trade*, Vol. 33, No. 6, pp. 147-197

Patterson, L.A. (1997) 'Agricultural Policy Reform in the European Community: A Three-Level Game Analysis,' *International Organization*, Vol. 51, No. 1, pp. 135-165

Patterson, L.A. (1999) *A Comparison of Biotechnology Regulatory Policy in the United States and the European Union*, Paper prepared for the biennial conference of the European Community Studies Association, Pittsburgh PA, 2-6 June 1999

Patterson, L.A. (2000) 'Biotechnology Policy. Regulating Risks and Risking Regulation,' in: H. Wallace and W. Wallace (eds) *Policy-Making in the European Union*, 4th ed., Oxford: Oxford University Press, pp. 317-343

Peltzman, S. (1976) 'Toward a More General Theory of Regulation,' *Journal of Law and Economics*, Vol. 19, pp. 211-240

Petersmann, E.-U. (1995) *International and European Trade and Environmental Law after the Uruguay Round*, London: Kluwer Law International

Peterson, J. (1989) 'Hormones, Heifers and High Politics – Biotechnology and the Common Agricultural Policy,' *Public Administration*, Vol. 67, pp. 455-471

Peterson, J. & E. Bomberg (1999) *Decision-Making in the European Union*, New York: St. Martin's Press

Pfeffer, J. (1981) *Power in Organizations*, Boston: Pitman

Phillips, P.W.B. & W.A. Kerr (2000) 'Alternative Paradigms. The WTO versus the Biosafety Protocol for Trade in Genetically Modified Organisms,' *Journal of World Trade*, Vol. 34, No. 4, pp. 63-75

PIAC (1998) *Comments of the Public Interest Advocacy Centre (PIAC) on Part I of Bill C-54: Protection of Personal Information in the Private Sector*, 2 December 1998, available at www.piac.ca/c54comde.htm

PIAC (1999) *Consumers and Business Call for early Passage of Federal Privacy Legislation*, News Release, 7 October 1999, available at www.piac.ca/newpage5.htm

PIAC et al. (1999a) *National Coalition Forms for Protection of Personal Information through Federal Bill C-54*, News Release by eight consumer and privacy advocacy groups, 14 April 1999, available at www.piac.ca/april99.htm

PIAC et al. (1999b) *Canadians in Support of Bill C-6*, Letter by 28 consumer and privacy advocacy groups to Canadian Senators, 15 November 1999, available at www.piac.ca/letterto.htm

Pierson, P. (1996) *Dismantling the Welfare State? Reagan, Thatcher, and the Politics of Retrenchment*, Cambridge: Cambridge University Press

Platten, N. (1996) 'Background to and History of the Directive,' in: D. Bainbridge (ed.), *EC Data Protection Directive*, London: Butterworths, pp. 13-32

Preston, R.L. (1999) 'Hormone Containing Growth Promoting Implants in Farmed Livestock,' *Advanced Drug Delivery Reviews*, Vol. 38, pp. 123-138

Privacy Commissioner of Canada (1994) *Information Highway Needs National Privacy Code*, News Release, 9 August 1994, available at www.privcom.gc.ca/media/nr-c/archive/02_05_b_940809_e.asp

Privacy Commissioner of Canada (1995a) *Time for Privacy Rules for Federal Private Sector*, News Release, 17 August 1995, available at www.privcom.gc.ca/media/nr-c/archive/02_05_b_950817_e.asp

Privacy Commissioner of Canada (1995b) *Commissioner Applauds CDMA Call for National Privacy Laws*, News Release, 3 October 1995, available at www.privcom.gc.ca/media/nr-c/archive/02_05_b_951003_e.asp

Privacy Commissioner of Canada (1996) *Privacy and Financial Sector Legislation: Proposals for Change*, Statement before the Standing Committee of Banking, Trade and Commerce, 3 October 1996, available at www.privcom.gc.ca/speech/archive/02_05_a_961003_e.asp

Putnam, R.D. (1988) 'Diplomacy and Domestic Politics: the Logic of Two-Level Games,' *International Organization*, Vol. 42, No. 3, pp. 427-460

Raab, C.D. & C.J. Bennett, C. J. (1994) 'Protecting Privacy across Borders: European Policies and Prospects,' *Public Administration*, Vol. 72, pp. 95-112

Raab, C.D. & C.J. Bennett (1996) 'Taking the Measure of Privacy: Can Data Protection Be Evaluated?' *International Review of Administrative Sciences*, Vol. 62, No. 4, pp. 535-556

Raiffa, H. (1982) *The Art and Science of Negotiation*, Cambridge MA: Harvard University Press

Regan, P.M. (1995) *Legislating Privacy. Technology, Social Values, and Public Policy.* Chapel Hill and London: University of North Carolina Press

Rehbinder, E. & R. Stewart (1985) *Environmental Protection Policy*, Berlin and New York: Walter de Gruyter

Renaville, R. et al. (1995) 'Aspects of the Use of Anabolic Steroids in Animal Production,' in: CEC (ed.) *Scientific Conference on Growth Promotion in Meat Production. Proceedings*, Brussels, 29 November to 1 December 1995, pp. 63-86

Revell, B.J. (1988) 'Linkages in the EC Beef Sector,' in: CEC (ed.) *Disharmonies in EC and US Agricultural Policy Measures*, Luxembourg: Office for Official Publications of the European Communities, chapter 10

Revesz, R.L. (1992) 'Rehabilitating Interstate Competition: Rethinking the "Race-to-the-Bottom" Rationale for Federal Environmental Regulation,' *New York University Law Review*, Vol. 67, pp. 1210-1254

Revesz, R.L. (1997) 'The Race to the Bottom and Federal Environmental Regulation: A Response to Critics,' *Minnesota Law Review*, Vol. 82, No. 2, pp. 535-564

Risse, T. (1998) *Progress in the Study of Transnational Relations and World Politics: Theoretical Propositions and Empirical Evidence*, Personal working paper, available at www.iue.it/Personal/Risse/Rissedoc/Welcome.html

Rood, J. (2000) 'Transatlantic Economic Relations in a New Era,' in: P. van Dijck & G. Faber (eds.) *The External Economic Dimension of the European Union*, The Hague: Kluwer Law International, pp. 177-193

Royal Society of Canada (2000) *The Royal Society of Canada Announces the Expert Panel on the Future of Food Biotechnology*, Press Release, 17 February 2000, available at www.rsc.ca/foodbiotechnology/indexEN.html

Royal Society of Canada (2001) *Elements of Precaution: Recommendations for the Regulation of Food Biotechnology in Canada*, January 2001, available at www.rsc.ca/foodbio technology/indexEN.html

SCF (2000) *Opinion Concerning a Submission from the Italian Authorities Raising Concerns for the Safety of certain Products Approved under the Notification Procedure of Regulation (EC) 258/97*, Expressed on 7 September 2000, Document CS/NF/DOS/11 ADD 4 REV 2 Final, available at europa.eu.int/comm/food/fs/sc/scf/outcome_en. html#opinions

Scharpf, F.W. (1997) 'Introduction: The Problem-Solving Capacity of Multi-Level Governance,' *Journal of European Public Policy*, Vol. 4, No. 4, pp. 520-538

Schelling, T.C. (1980 (1960)) *The Strategy of Conflict*, 2nd ed., Cambridge MA: Harvard University Press

Schenkelaars, P. (1996) 'Outlooks on the Public Information and Participation in the Context of the European Biotechnology Directives 90/219/EEC and 90/220/EEC,' in: A. van Dommelen (ed.) *Coping with Deliberate Release. The Limits of Risk Assessment*, Tilburg: International Centre for Human and Public Affairs, pp. 159-176

Schlagenhof, M. (1995) 'Trade Measures Based on Environmental Processes and Production Methods,' *Journal of World Trade*, Vol. 29, No. 6, pp. 123-155

Schoenbaum, T.J. (1997) 'International Trade and Protection of the Environment: The Continuing Search for Reconciliation,' *American Journal of International Law*, Vol. 91, No. 2, pp. 268-313

Schoppa, L.J. (1993) 'Two-Level Games and Bargaining Outcomes: Why Gaiatsu Succeeds in Japan in Some Cases but not Others,' *International Organization*, Vol. 47, No. 3, pp. 353-386

Schoppa, L. J. (1999) 'The Social Context in Coercive International Bargaining,' *International Organization*, Vol. 53, No. 2, pp. 307-342

Schwartz, P. M. & J.R. Reidenberg (1996) *Data Privacy Law. A Study of United States Data Protection*, Charlottesville, VI: Michie Law Publishers

SCVPH (1999) *Assessment of Potential Risks to Human Health from Hormone Residues in Bovine Meat and Meat Products*, Opinion of 30 April 1999, available at europa.eu.int/ comm/food/fs/him/him_index_en.html

SCVPH (2000) *Review of Specific Documents Relating to the SCVPH Opinion of 30 April 99 on the Potential Risks to Human Health from Hormone Residues in Bovine Meat and Meat Products*, Opinion of 3 May 2000, available at europa.eu.int/comm/food/fs/him/ him_index_en.html

Sebenius, J.K. (1983) 'Negotiation Arithmetic: Adding and Subtracting Issues and Parties,' *International Organization*, Vol. 37, No. 2, pp. 281-316

Sebenius, J.K. (1991) 'Negotiation Analysis,' in: V.A. Kremenyuk (ed.), *International Negotiation*, San Francisco and Oxford: Jossey-Bass, pp. 203-215

Sejrsen, K., N. Oksbjerg, M. Vestergaard & M.T. Sorensen (1995) 'Growth Hormone and Related Peptides as Growth Promoters,' in: CEC (ed.) *Scientific Conference on Growth Promotion in Meat Production. Proceedings*, Brussels, 29 November to 1 December 1995, pp. 87-119

Sevenster, H.G. (1998) *Eco-imperialisme binnen de Europese Unie: Een Juridisch Probleem? [Eco-imperialism in the European Union: A Legal Problem?]*, Deventer: W.E.J. Tjeenk Willink

Shaffer, G. (1999) 'The Power of EU Collective Action: The Impact of EU Data Privacy Regulation on US Business Practice,' *European Law Journal*, Vol. 5, No. 4, pp. 419-437

Shieff, A. & J.A. Baker (1987) 'Marketing and International Fur Markets,' in: M. Novak et al. (eds.) *Wild Furbearer Management and Conservation in North America*, Toronto: Ontario Trappers Association/Ontario Ministry of Natural Resources, pp. 862-877

SIA (1998) *Comments on Draft International Safe Harbor Privacy Principles*, Letter to the Department of Commerce, 19 November 1998, available at www.ita.doc.gov/td/ecom/menu.html

Siegers, J.J. (1992) 'Interdisciplinary Economics,' *De Economist*, Vol. 140, No. 4, pp. 531-547

Silverglade, B. (2000) 'The WTO Agreement on Sanitary and Phytosanitary Measures: Weakening Food Safety Regulation to Facilitate Trade?' *Swiss Political Science Review*, Vol. 6, No. 2, pp. 83-89

Simitis, S. (1995) 'From the Market to the Polis: The EU Directive on the Protection of Personal Data,' *Iowa Law Review*, Vol. 80, No. 3, pp. 445-469

Sinclair, I. (1984) *The Vienna Convention on the Law of Treaties*, 2nd ed., Manchester: Manchester University Press

Skocpol, T. & M. Somers (1980) 'The Uses of Comparative History in Macrosocial Inquiry,' *Comparative Studies in Society and History*, Vol. 22, pp. 174-197

Skogstad, G. (1998) 'Ideas, Paradigms and Institutions: Agricultural Exceptionalism in the European Union and the United States,' *Governance*, Vol. 11, No. 4, pp. 463-490

Slough, B.G., R.H. Jessup, D.I. McKay & A.B. Stephenson (1987) 'Wild Furbearer Management in Western and Northern Canada,' in: M. Novak et al. (eds.) *Wild Furbearer Management and Conservation in North America*, Toronto: Ontario Trappers Association/Ontario Ministry of Natural Resources, pp. 1062-1076

SSC (1999) *Opinion on Antimicrobial Resistance*, 28 May 1999, available at europa.eu.int/comm/food/fs/sc/ssc/out50_en.html

Staatscourant (2001) 'Nederlands Verbod op Nertsfokkerij Kan Einde Inluiden van Fok in Europese Unie' [Dutch Prohibition on Mink Farming May Mean End of Farming in European Union], *Staatscourant*, Nr. 129, 9 July 2001, p. 5

State Department (2000a) *Fact Sheet: U.S.-EU Biotechnology Cooperation Agreement*, Concluded at U.S.-EU Summit in Lisbon May 31, available at usinfo.state.gov/topical/global/biotech/00053102.htm

State Department (2000b) *Report of the U.S.-EU Biotechnology Consultative Forum*, Fact Sheet, 19 December 2000, available at www.useu.be/ISSUES/fact1200.html

Statistics Canada (2001a) *Number and Value of Pelts Produced, by Kind for Canada, by Season*, retrieved from CANSIM, available at www.statcan.ca/english/CANSIM

Statistics Canada (2001b) *Gross Domestic Product (Expenditure-Based)*, Last Modified on 31 July 2001, available at www.statcan.ca/english/Pgdb/Economy/Economic/econ04.htm

Stevens, T. et al. (1994) *Letter by 14 Members of Congress to USTR Mickey Kantor*, dated 1 July 1994, reprinted in NTA 1996

Stigler, G.J. & G.S. Becker (1977) 'De Gustibus Non Est Disputandum,' *American Economic Review*, Vol. 67, No. 2, pp. 76-90

Stone, J. (1997) 'Resolving the Animal Welfare and Legal Issues of the EU Fur Import Prohibition; View of Canada,' in: A. Nollkaemper (ed.) *Trapped by Furs? The Legality of the European Community's Fur Import Ban in EC and International Law*, Rotterdam: Center for International Natural Resources Law, pp. 23-30

Swanborn, P.G. (1996) *Case-Study's. Wat, wanneer en hoe? [Case Studies. What, when, and how?]*, Amsterdam and Meppel: Boom

Swinbank, A. (1993) 'CAP Reform, 1992,' *Journal of Common Market Studies*, Vol. 31, No. 3, pp. 359-372

Swire, P.P. & R.E. Litan (1998). *None of your Business. World Data Flows, Electronic Commerce, and the European Privacy Directive*, Washington, D.C.: Brookings Institute

TACD (1999a) *Safe Harbor Proposal and International Convention on Privacy Protection*, Doc No. Ecom-8-99, April 1999, available at www.tacd.org/cgi-bin/db.cgi?page=view&config=admin/docs.cfg&id=57

TACD (1999b) *TACD Brussels Meeting, 23-24 April 1999: TACD Recommendations on Food, Electronic Commerce and Trade and European Commission Services' Responses*, available at www.tacd.org/cgi-bin/db.cgi?page=view&config=admin/docs.cfg&id=59

TACD (1999c) *Hormone Treated Beef*, Doc No. Food-10-99, September 1999, available at www.tacd.org/cgi-bin/db.cgi?page=view&config=admin/docs.cfg&id=10

TACD (1999d) *Comments of Consumer and Privacy Groups on the Department of Commerce "Safe Harbor" Proposal (15 Nov 1999)*, Letter to the Department of Commerce, 3 December 1999, available at www.ita.doc.gov/td/ecom/menu.html

TACD (2000a) *Consumers' Concerns about Biotechnology and Genetically Modified Organisms*, Doc Food-5pp-00, February 2000, available at www.tacd.org/cgi-bin/db.cgi?page=view&config=admin/docs.cfg&id=73

TACD (2000b) *Submission of the Trans Atlantic Consumer Dialogue (TACD) Concerning the U.S. Department of Commerce Draft International Safe Harbor Privacy Principles and FAQs, Published on March 15, 2000*, Letter to the Department of Commerce, 31 March 2000, available at www.ita.doc.gov/td/ecom/menu.html

Todd, A.W. & E.K. Boggess (1987) 'Characteristics, Activities, Lifestyles, and Attitudes of Trappers in North America,' in: M. Novak et al. (eds) *Wild Furbearer Management and Conservation in North America*, Toronto: Ontario Trappers Association/Ontario Ministry of Natural Resources, pp. 59-76

Tomlinson, J. (1999) *Globalization and Culture*, Cambridge: Polity Press

Trachtman, J.P. (1992) 'GATT Dispute Settlement Panel. United States – Restrictions on Imports of Tuna,' *American Journal of International Law*, Vol. 86, No. 1, pp. 142-151

Trebilcock, M.J. & R. Howse (1999) *The Regulation of International Trade*, 2nd edition, London and New York: Routledge

Trumbore, P.F. (1998) 'Public Opinion as a Domestic Constraint in International Negotiations: Two-Level Games in the Anglo-Irish Peace Process,' *International Studies Quarterly*, Vol. 42, pp. 545-565

Trumbull, G. (2000) 'More Trade, Safer Products,' *Swiss Political Science Review*, Vol. 6, No. 2, pp. 89-93

Tsebelis, G. (1995) 'Decision Making in Political Systems: Veto Players in Presidentialism, Parliamentarism, Multicameralism and Multipartyism,' *British Journal of Political Science*, Vol. 25, pp. 289-325

UK (2000) *Fur Farming (Prohibition) Act*, 200 Chapter 33, 23 November 2000, available at www.legislation.hmso.gov.uk/acts/acts2000/20000033.htm

UN (1969) 'Vienna Convention on the Law of Treaties,' Adopted on 22 May 1969, Opened for Signature on 23 May 1969, *International Legal Materials*, Vol. 8, pp. 679-713

UN (1990) *Guidelines for the Regulation of Computerized Personal Data Files*, General Assembly Resolution 45/95, Adopted on 14 December 1990, available at www.unhchr.ch/html/menu3/b/71.htm

UN (1992) *Rio Declaration on Environment and Development*, Adopted on 14 June 1992, available at www.unep.org/Documents/Default.asp?DocumentID=78&ArticleID=1163

UN (2000) *Cartagena Protocol on Biosafety to the Convention on Biological Diversity*, Adopted by the Conference of the Parties to the Convention on Biological Diversity on 29 January 2000, available at www.biodiv.org/biosafety/protocol.asp

US (1996) *Health Insurance Portability and Accountability Act*, H.R. 3103, Signed into law on 21 August 1996 as Public Law 104-191, available at thomas.loc.gov/cgi-bin/query/z?c104:H.R.3103.ENR:

US (1999) *An Act to Enhance Competition in the Financial Services Industry by Providing a Prudential Framework for the Affiliation of Banks, Securities Firms, and other Financial Service Providers, and for other Purposes (Gramm-Leach-Bliley Act)*, S.900, Signed into law on 12 November 1999 as Public Law 106-102, available at thomas.loc.gov/cgi-bin/query/z?c106:S.900.ENR:

US (2000) *Trade and Development Act*, Signed into law on 18 May 2000, Public Law No. 106-200, available at thomas.loc.gov/cgi-bin/query/z?c106:H.R.434.ENR:

USCIB (1998) *USCIB Comments on the DoC Draft International Safe Harbor Privacy Principles*, Letter to the Department of Commerce, 19 November 1998, available at www.ita.doc.gov/td/ecom/menu.html

USCoC (1998) *Letter to the Department of Commerce*, 20 November 1998, available at www.ita.doc.gov/td/ecom/menu.html

USDA (undated*) ERS Fact Sheet: The Adoption of Genetically Engineered Crops for Pest Management*

USDA (1998) 'Biotechnology in Agriculture Confronts Agreements in the WTO,' *Agriculture in the WTO*, WRS-98-4, December 1998, pp. 34-35, available at www.ers.usda.gov/publications/so/view.asp?f=international/wrs-bb/1998/wto/

USDA (1999) 'Consumer Concerns Elicit Policy Changes,' *The European Union's Common Agricultural Policy: Pressures for Change*, WRS-99-2, October 1999, pp. 45-52, available at www.ers.usda.gov/publications/wrs992

USDA (2000) *USDA to Standardize Biotech Grain Testing System*, Press Release, 4 May 2000, available at www.useu.be/ISSUES/grain0504.html

US Mission (2000) *"Carousel" Revised Retaliation List in EU Disputes Delayed*, Press Release, 20 June 2000, available at www.useu.be/issues/retal0620.html

USTR (1997) *Letter from USTR Charlene Barshefsky to the German Minister of Foreign Affairs Klaus Kinkel*, dated 10 December 1997

USTR (1998) *Appellate Body Finds EC Hormone Ban Inconsistent with WTO Obligations under SPS Agreement*, Press Release 98-02, 15 January 1998, available at www.ustr.gov/releases/1998/01/index.shtml

USTR (1999a) *U.S. Expresses Concern Following Discussion Regarding EU Beef Ban*, Press Release 99-18, 5 March 1999, available at www.ustr.gov/releases/1999/03/index.shtml

USTR (1999b) *USTR Announces Final Product List in Beef Hormones Dispute*, Press Release 99-60, 19 July 1999, available at www.ustr.gov/releases/1999/07/index.shtml

USTR (2000) *USTR Announces Procedures for Modifying Measures in EC Beef and Bananas Cases*, Press Release 00-41, 26 May 2000, available at www.ustr.gov/releases/2000/05/index.shtml

Van Calster, G. (2000) 'The EU, Trade, Environment and Unilateralism: Passing the Buck,' *European Foreign Affairs Review*, Vol. 5, pp. 9-34

Vernon, R. (1995) 'The World Trade Organization: A New Stage in International Trade and Development,' *Harvard International Law Journal*, Vol. 36, No. 2, pp. 329-340

Vingerling, P. (1997) 'Leghold Traps: The Animal's Point of View,' in: A. Nollkaemper (ed.) *Trapped by Furs? The Legality of the European Community's Fur Import Ban in EC and International Law*, Rotterdam: Center for International Natural Resources Law, pp. 7-12

Vogel, D. (1995) *Trading up. Consumer and Environmental Regulation in a Global Economy*, Cambridge MA and London: Harvard University Press

Vogel, D. (1997a) *Consumer and Environmental Regulation and Transatlantic Trade*, Paper presented at the Conference on Institutions, Markets and (Economic) Performance, Utrecht, 11-12 December 1997

Vogel, D. (1997b) 'Trading Up and Governing Across: Transnational Governance and Environmental Protection,' *Journal of European Public Policy*, Vol. 4, No. 4, pp. 556-571

Wagner, R.H. (1988) 'Economic Interdependence, Bargaining Power, and Political Influence,' *International Organization*, Vol. 42, No. 3, pp. 461-483

Wallace, H. & W. Wallace (eds.) (1996) *Policy-Making in the European Union*, 3rd ed., Oxford: Oxford University Press

Wallace, H. & W. Wallace (eds.) (2000) *Policy-Making in the European Union*, 4th ed., Oxford: Oxford University Press

Waters, M. (1995) *Globalization*, London and New York: Routledge

Weiss, F. (1995) 'The General Agreement on Trade in Services 1994,' *Common Market Law Review*, Vol. 32, pp. 1177-1225

Western Producer (1999a) 'Senate Considers Hearings on GMO Issue,' *The Western Producer*, 7 October 1999, available at www.producer.com/articles/19991007/news/19991007news04.html

Western Producer (1999b) 'GM Canola Exports May Be at Risk,' *The Western Producer*, 7 October 1999, available at www.producer.com/articles/19991007/news/19991007news05c.html

Western Producer (1999c) 'Chrétien Fights GMO Battle on Diplomatic Front,' *The Western Producer*, 16 September 1999, available at www.producer.com/articles/19990916/market_quotas/19990916mkt06.html

Western Producer (2000a) 'Seagram Fuzzy on Accepting GM Corn,' *The Western Producer*, 6 January 2000, available at www.producer.com/articles/20000113/market_quotas/20000113mkt02.html

Western Producer (2000b) 'GM Canola Situation Unpredictable,' *The Western Producer*, 20 January 2000, available at www.producer.com/articles/20000120/market_quotas/20000120mkt01.html

WFRR (1999) 'Beef Hormones: Dispute Splits U.S., EU Scientists; Research Continues on Risk to Humans,' Special Report, *World Food Regulation Review*, Vol. 9, No. 5

White House (1997) *A Framework for Global Electronic Commerce*, 1 July 1997, available at www.ecommerce.gov/framewrk.htm

White House (2000) *Clinton Administration Agencies Announce Food and Agricultural Biotechnology Initiatives: Strengthening Science-Based Regulation and Consumer Access to Information*, News Release, 3 May 2000, available at vm.cfsan.fda.gov/~lrd/whbio53.html

Winham, G.R. (1998) 'The World Trade Organization: Institution-Building in the Multilateral Trading System,' *The World Economy*, Vol. 21, No. 3, pp. 349-368

Working Party (1997) *Opinion 1/97 on Canadian Initiatives Relating to Standardisation in the Field of Protection of Privacy*, Adopted on 29 May 1997, Document XV/5023/97-Final, WP 2, available at europa.eu.int/comm/internal_market/en/dataprot/wpdocs/wpdocs_97.htm

Working Party (1998) *Transfers of Personal Data to Third Countries: Applying Articles 25 and 26 of the EU Data Protection Directive*, Adopted on 24 July 1998, Document DG XV D/5025/98, available at europa.eu.int/comm/internal_market/en/dataprot/wpdocs/wpdocs_98.htm

Working Party (1999a) *Opinion 1/99 Concerning the Level of Data Protection in the United States and the Ongoing Discussion between the European Commission and the United States Government*, Adopted on 26 January 1999, Document 5092/98/EN/final, WP 15, available at europa.eu.int/comm/internal_market/en/dataprot/wpdocs/wpdocs_99.htm

Working Party (1999b) *Opinion 2/99 on the Adequacy of the "International Safe Harbor Principles" Issued by the US Department of Commerce on 19th April 1999*, Adopted on 3 May 1999, Document 5047/99/EN/final, WP 19, available at europa.eu.int/comm/internal_market/en/dataprot/wpdocs/wpdocs_99.htm

Working Party (1999c) *Opinion 4/99 on the Frequently Asked Questions to be Issued by the US Department of Commerce in Relation to the Proposed "Safe Harbor Principles,"* Adopted on 7 June 1999, Document 5066/99/EN/final, WP 21, available at europa.eu.int/comm/internal_market/en/dataprot/wpdocs/wpdocs_99.htm

Working Party (1999d) *Working Document on the Current State of Play of the Ongoing Discussions between the European Commission and the United States Government Concerning the "International Safe Harbor Principles,"* Adopted on 7 July 1999, Document 5075/99/EN/final, WP 23, available at europa.eu.int/comm/internal_market/en/dataprot/wpdocs/wpdocs_99.htm

Working Party (1999e) *Opinion 7/99 on the Level of Data Protection Provided by the "Safe Harbor" Principles as Published together with the Frequently Asked Questions (FAQs) and other Related Documents on 15 and 16 November 1999 by the US Department of Commerce*, Adopted on 3 December 1999, Document 5146/99/EN/final, WP 27, available at europa.eu.int/comm/internal_market/en/dataprot/wpdocs/wpdocs_99.htm

Working Party (2000) *Opinion 4/2000 on the Level of Protection Provided by the "Safe Harbor Principles,"* Adopted on 16 May 2000, Document CA07/434/00/EN, WP 32, available at europa.eu.int/comm/internal_market/en/dataprot/wpdocs/wpdocs_2k.htm

Working Party (2001) *Opinion 2/2001 on the Adequacy of the Canadian Personal Information and Electronic Documents Act*, Adopted on 26 January 2001, Document 5109/00/EN, WP 39, available at europa.eu.int/comm/internal_market/en/dataprot/wpdocs/index.htm

Wright, S. (1994) *Molecular Politics. Developing American and British Regulatory Policy for Genetic Engineering, 1972-1982*, Chicago and London: University of Chicago Press

WTO (1994a) *General Agreement on Tariffs and Trade 1947*, Text as of July 1986, Part of Annex 1A to the Agreement Establishing the World Trade Organization, Adopted on 15 April 1994, available at www.wto.org/english/docs_e/legal_e/final_e.htm

WTO (1994b) *General Agreement on Tariffs and Trade 1994*, Part of Annex 1A to the Agreement Establishing the World Trade Organization, Adopted on 15 April 1994, available at www.wto.org/english/docs_e/legal_e/final_e.htm

WTO (1994c) *Agreement on the Application of Sanitary and Phytosanitary Measures*, Part of Annex 1A to the Agreement Establishing the World Trade Organization, Adopted on 15 April 1994, available at www.wto.org/english/docs_e/legal_e/final_e.htm

WTO (1994d) *Agreement on Technical Barriers to Trade*, Part of Annex 1A to the Agreement Establishing the World Trade Organization, Adopted on 15 April 1994, available at www.wto.org/english/docs_e/legal_e/final_e.htm

WTO (1994e) *General Agreement on Trade in Services*, Annex 1B to the Agreement Establishing the World Trade Organization, Adopted on 15 April 1994, available at www.wto.org/english/docs_e/legal_e/final_e.htm

WTO (1996a) *United States – Standards for Reformulated and Conventional Gasoline*, Report of the Panel, WT/DS2/R, 29 January 1996, available at www.wto.org/english/tratop_e/dispu_e/distab_e.htm

WTO (1996b) *United States – Standards for Reformulated and Conventional Gasoline*, Report of the Appellate Body, AB-1996-1, WT/DS2/AB/R, 29 April 1996, available at www.wto.org/english/tratop_e/dispu_e/distab_e.htm

WTO (1997a) *EC Measures Concering Meat and Meat Products (Hormones). Complaint by the United States*, Report of the Panel, WT/DS26/R/USA, 18 August 1997, available at www.wto.org/english/tratop_e/dispu_e/distab_e.htm

WTO (1997b) *EC Measures Concering Meat and Meat Products (Hormones). Complaint by Canada*, Report of the Panel, WT/DS48/R/CAN, 18 August 1997, available at www.wto.org/english/tratop_e/dispu_e/distab_e.htm

WTO (1998a) *EC Measures Concerning Meat and Meat Products (Hormones)*, Report of the Appellate Body, AB-1997-4, WT/DS26/AB/R and WT/DS48/AB/R, 16 January 1998, available at www.wto.org/english/tratop_e/dispu_e/distab_e.htm

WTO (1998b) *United States – Import Prohibitions of certain Shrimp and Shrimp Products*, Report of the Panel, WT/DS58/R, 15 May 1998, available at www.wto.org/english/tratop_e/dispu_e/distab_e.htm

WTO (1998c) *EC Measures Concerning Meat and Meat Products (Hormones)*, Arbitration under Article 21.3c of the Understanding on Rules and Procedures Governing the Settlement of Disputes, Award of the Arbitrator, WT/DS26/15 and WT/DS48/13, 29 May 1998, available at www.wto.org/english/tratop_e/dispu_e/distab_e.htm

WTO (1998d) *United States – Import Prohibitions of certain Shrimp and Shrimp Products*, Report of the Appellate Body, AB-1998-4, WT/DS58/AB/R, 12 October 1998, available at www.wto.org/english/tratop_e/dispu_e/distab_e.htm

WTO (1999a) *Japan – Measures Affecting Agricultural Products*, Report of the Appellate Body, AB-1998-8, WT/DS76/AB/R, 22 February 1999, available at www.wto.org/english/tratop_e/dispu_e/distab_e.htm

WTO (1999b) *European Communities – Measures Concerning Meat and Meat Products (Hormones)*, Original Complaint by the United States. Recourse to Arbitration by the European Communities under Article 22.6 of the DSU, Decision by the Arbitrators, WT/DS26/ARB, 12 July 1999, available at www.wto.org/english/tratop_e/dispu_e/distab_e.htm

WTO (1999c) *European Communities – Measures Concerning Meat and Meat Products (Hormones)*, Original Complaint by Canada. Recourse to Arbitration by the European Communities under Article 22.6 of the DSU, Decision by the Arbitrators, WT/DS48/ARB, 12 July 1999, available at www.wto.org/english/tratop_e/dispu_e/distab_e.htm

Yin, R.K. (1994) *Case Study Research. Design and Methods*, 2nd ed., Thousand Oaks CA: Sage

Ziegler, A.R. (1996) *Trade and Environmental Law in the European Community*, Oxford: Clarendon Press

INDEX

Aboriginal trappers 89, 93-94, 110-111, 114, 115, 116, 117, 121, 138, 141-142

Agreement on Sanitary and Phytosanitary Standards (SPS)
- *See also* precautionary principle, and World Trade Organization General 52
- In the beef-hormone issue 158, 159-166
- In the GM foods issue 233-237, 238
- Labelling requirements 236-237
- Relation to Cartagena Protocol 238-242
- Risk assessments 161-162, 164-165
- Role of international standards 158, 160-161, 163-164, 355
- Unjustifiable distinctions in levels of protection 162-163, 165-166

Agreement on Technical Barriers to Trade (TBT)
- *See also* World Trade Organization General 51
- In the beef-hormone issue 155
- In the GM foods issue 236, 237

Agricultural biotechnology
- *See* genetic modification

Agricultural Marketing Service (AMS) 180
- *See also* United States Department of Agriculture (in the beef-hormone issue)

Agriculture and Agri-Food Canada (AAFC)
- In the beef-hormone issue 152
- In the GM foods issue 208, 209, 254

Allowable Daily Intake (ADI) 157-158, 178

Alternative specification 69

American Civil Liberties Union (ACLU) 301

American Soybean Association (ASA) 244, 257

Animal and Plant Health Inspection Service (APHIS) 202, 210
- *See also* United States Department of Agriculture (in the GM foods issue)

Animal tests
- *See* cosmetics Directive

Animal Welfare Institute (AWI) 92

Antibiotic resistance marker genes
- *See also* genetic modification
- Groups supporting or opposing a ban 226, 227, 248, 252
- Regulation in the EC 221
- Regulation in the US 206-207
- Risks of 197
- Use in genetic modification 195-196

Article 29 Working Party
- Opinion on Canadian initiatives and legislation 310, 316
- Role in the Safe Harbour talks 298, 301-302, 303-304, 305-306, 307
- Role under the EC data protection Directive 280-281
- Work on international data transfers 281-283

Article 31 Committee
- Role in the Safe Harbour talks 298-299, 302, 304, 307
- Role under the EC data protection Directive 280

Austria
In the GM foods issue 217, 218, 225, 245, 257
In the leghold trap issue 120-121, 122, 142

Automobile emission standards 3, 6-7

Ballot Issues Coalition (BIC) 128

Baptist-bootlegger coalitions
Conclusions 345-347
Definition and background 6, 63
Hypothesis 72, 73, 77
In the beef-hormone issue 187-188
In the data protection issue 322-323
In the GM foods issue 263-264
In the leghold trap issue 138-139

Belgian family allowances (GATT case) 98

Belgium
In the beef-hormone issue 149
In the GM foods issue 218
In the leghold trap issue 82, 121, 122, 142

Best Management Practices (BMP) 128-129, 133, 134-135

BEUC
See also Transatlantic Consumer Dialogue
In the beef-hormone issue 171-172, 177, 187
In the data protection issue 298
In the GM foods issue 224

Bill C-6
See Personal Information Protection and Electronic Documents Act

Bill C-54
See Personal Information Protection and Electronic Documents Act

BioteCanada 255

Biotechnology
See genetic modification

BSE
General 169-170
Role in the beef-hormone issue 170-172
Role in the GM foods issue 224, 251

BST 154, 175, 182, 190, 354, 356

Bt-maize
See also genetic modification (types of)
Approval and unilateral bans in the EC 217, 257

California effect
Definition 35
Occurrence in the beef-hormone issue 183, 185, 330
Occurrence in the data protection issue 318-320, 332-333
Occurrence in the GM foods issue 256, 258-260, 330-332
Occurrence in the leghold trap issue 132, 134-136, 333

Canadian Bankers Association (CBA) 314

Canadian Direct Marketing Association (CDMA)
See Canadian Marketing Association

Canadian Food Inspection Agency (CFIA)
In the beef-hormone issue 152, 181
In the GM foods issue 208, 209, 210, 247

Canadian General Standards Board (CGSB)
In the GM foods issue 254, 257
In the leghold trap issue 85, 130

Canadian Health Coalition (CHC)
In the beef-hormone issue 182
In the GM foods issue 255

Canadian Marketing Association (CMA) 311-312, 314, 317

Canadian Medical Association (CMA) 314

Canadian Mission to the European Union 117

Canadian Pharmacists Association (CPhA) 314

Canadian Standards Association (CSA) 309-310, 311, 312, 316, 317, 322, 324, 343

Carousel approach 176-177, 186

Cartagena Protocol
  See also Global Industry Coalition, and labelling
  Background and content 230-233
  Relation to GATT/WTO law 237-242
  Role in producing a California effect 259-260, 332

Center for Democracy and Technology (CDT) 305

Center for Food Safety (CFS) 248, 251

Chief of Government
  See two-level game approach

Codex Alimentarius Commission
  See also labelling
  General 52, 157
  In the beef-hormone issue 157-159, 184, 185, 355
    See also Joint FAO/WHO Expert Committee on Food Additives
  In the GM foods issue 228-230, 257, 266
  Role under SPS Agreement 158, 160-161, 163-164, 355

Comitology system 60

Commission of the European Communities (CEC)
  See European Commission

Common Agricultural Policy (CAP)
  General 153-154
  Multifunctionality, concept of 174
  Reforms in the 1990s 173-174
  Role in the beef-hormone issue 153-154, 176, 345
  Role in the GM foods issue 226, 267, 346
  Role in international trade negotiations 172-173

Compliance costs
  See costs of compliance

Confederation of Agri-Food Industries (CIAA) 226

Congress
  See United States Congress

Congressional Sportsmen's Caucus 113

Constraints
  Definition of 38-39
  Role in producing a California effect 39, 40-45, 48-49, 66-69, 72

Consultative Forum 246-247

Consumers Association of Canada
  In the beef-hormone issue 182
  In the GM foods issue 254, 255

Consumers Union
  In the beef-hormone issue 182
  In the data protection issue 301
  In the GM foods issue 248, 250, 251

Convention on Biological Diversity (CBD) 230, 231, 238

Convention on International Trade in Endangered Species (CITES) 111, 124-125, 241-242

Coordinated framework
See Office of Science and Technology Policy

COPA/COGECA
In the beef-hormone issue 174-175, 176, 177, 187
In the GM foods issue 226

Cosmetics Directive 143-144, 353-354, 356

Costs of compliance
Conclusions 341-345
Hypothesis 68, 69
In the beef-hormone issue 187
In the data protection issue 321-322
In the GM foods issue 262-263
In the leghold trap issue 138

Council of Canadians 253, 254, 255

Council of Europe (CoE) 271-274, 274-275, 276, 277, 278-279, 281

Council of Ministers (of the EC) 59-60, 61

Court of Justice of the European Communities
See European Court of Justice

CSA Model Code
See Canadian Standards Association

Data protection Directive
See Directive 95/46

Deeply-held values and perceived problems
Background and hypothesis 70-71, 77
Conclusions 348-350
In the beef-hormone issue 188-189
In the data protection issue 323-325
In the GM foods issue 264-265
In the leghold trap issue 139-142

De facto moratorium 217-218, 235-236, 257

Delaware effect
See race to the bottom

Deliberate release of GMOs
See Directive 90/220

Denmark
In the beef-hormone issue 150-151, 168, 175, 176, 177, 186
In the data protection issue 277, 278
In the GM foods issue 217, 218, 223-224, 225, 245
In the leghold trap issue 82, 115, 120, 121, 142

Department of Commerce (DoC) 293-294, 296, 298, 299, 302, 306, 307, 323, 327

Department of Foreign Affairs and International Trade (DFAIT) 117, 365

Department of Health and Human Services (HHS) 203, 295

Department of Health, Education and Welfare (HEW) 288-289, 293, 323

Department of Indian and Northern Affairs Canada (INAC) 117

Dependence 40-45

Directive (in EC law) 60

Directive 81/602 (ban on growth-hormones) 150

Directive 85/649 (ban on growth-hormones) 150-151

Directive 88/146 (ban on growth-hormones) 150-151

Directive 90/219 (contained use of GMOs) 211

Directive 90/220 (deliberate release of GMOs)
See also de facto moratorium, and labelling (of GM foods in the EC)
Content 211-212
Revision (Directive 2001/18) 219-221

Directive 95/46 (data protection)
Background and history 274-278
Content 278-281

Directive 96/22 (ban on growth-hormones) 157, 184

Directive 2001/18
See Directive 90/220 (revision)

Direct Marketing Association (DMA) 294

Directorate General (DG)
See European Commission

Directorate General I/Trade
See also European Commission
In the beef-hormone issue 191
In the data protection issue 297-298
In the leghold trap issue 114, 115, 117, 118, 119, 120, 131, 142, 143, 144, 145

Directorate General III/Enterprise
See also European Commission
In the GM foods issue 223, 227
In the leghold trap issue 131

Directorate General VI/Agriculture
See also European Commission
In the beef-hormone issue 159, 191
In the leghold trap issue 131

Directorate General XI/Environment
See also European Commission
In the GM foods issue 211, 223, 227
In the leghold trap issue 83, 115, 117, 118, 120, 131, 141, 142

Directorate General XII/Research
See also European Commission
In the GM foods issue 223

Directorate General XV/Internal Market
See also European Commission
In the data protection issue 297, 298, 302, 306, 316, 327

Directorate General XXI/Customs
See also European Commission
In the leghold trap issue 115

Directorate General XXIV/Sanco
See also European Commission, and Food and Veterinary Office
In the beef-hormone issue 171, 191
In the data protection issue 297
In the GM foods issue 227

Domestic audience costs 46-47

Domestic firms 62, 63, 68-69

Drowning traps
See traps, types of

Eco-labelling 21

Economic sanctions 11-12, 37, 40, 47, 48, 70, 341, 366-368

Economic theory of regulation 62

Electronic Privacy Information Center (EPIC) 297, 301
See also Transatlantic Consumer Dialogue (in the data protection issue)

Environmental Protection Agency (EPA) 106, 202, 248

EuroCommerce 176, 225-226

EuropaBio 226-227

European Commission
General: role in EC decision-making 58, 60

In the beef-hormone issue 149, 150, 155, 156-157, 167, 171, 173-174, 177-178
See also Directorates General I/ Trade, VI/Agriculture, and XXIV/Sanco, Food and Veterinary Office, Scientific Committee on Veterinary Measures Relating to Public Health, and Scientific Steering Committee
In the data protection issue 271, 274-275, 276, 277-278, 280, 283, 296, 297, 298, 307, 316
See also Directorates General I/Trade, XV/Internal Market, and XXIV/Sanco
In the GM foods issues 211, 212, 213, 214, 215, 216-217, 218, 219, 220, 221, 223, 227, 246
See also Directorates General III/Enterprise, XI/Environment, XII/ Research, and XXIV/Sanco, and Scientific Steering Committee
In the leghold trap issue 83, 110, 112, 115, 116, 117, 118-121, 122, 131, 144
See also Directorates General I/Trade, III/Enterprise, VI/Agriculture, XI/Environment, and XXI/Customs

European Council 59, 278

European Court of Justice 60, 151

European Parliament (EP)
General 59-61
In the beef-hormone issue 150, 154, 170-171, 185
In the data protection issue 274, 276, 278, 307
In the GM foods issue 215, 220, 221, 226-227, 247
In the leghold trap issue 83-84, 110-111, 116, 119-120, 122, 123, 133, 141

Export-oriented firms 62-63, 68-69

Fair Credit Reporting Act 290-291

Federal Food, Drugs and Cosmetics Act (US) 203-204, 205-206

Federal Provincial Committee for Humane Trapping (FPCHT) 85

Federal Trade Commission (FTC) 290-291, 294-295, 297, 304, 317, 318, 319, 323-324

Finland
In the GM foods issue 218

Fish and Wildlife Service 129
See also United States Department of Agriculture (in the leghold trap issue)

Flavr Savr tomato 204

Food additives
Regulation in Canada 208
Regulation in the US 203-204
See also Generally Recognized as Safe

Food and Agriculture Organization (FAO) 228
See also Codex Alimentarius Commission, and Joint FAO/WHO Expert Committee on Food Additives

Food and Drug Administration (FDA)
In the beef-hormone issue 151, 189
In the GM food issue 202-208, 210, 247, 248, 250-252, 257

Food and Drugs Act (Canada) 208

Food and Veterinary Office (FVO) 179-181, 182

Food Marketing Institute (FMI) 168

Food Safety Inspection Service 152, 180
See also United States Department of Agriculture (in the beef-hormone issue)

Foreign Investment Review Act (GATT case) 97

France
In the beef-hormone issue 150, 170
In the data protection issue 276
In the GM foods issue 217, 218, 220, 222, 223-224, 225
In the leghold trap issue 121

Freedom of Information Act (FOIA) 290

Friends of the Earth (FoE) 224, 251

Fur farming
Prohibitions in Europe 132
Significance in Europe and North America 82, 90, 120

Fur Information Council of America 113

Fur Institute of Canada (FIC) 85, 117, 130, 133

General Agreement on Tariffs and Trade (GATT)
See also World Trade Organization
For case law, see also Belgian family allowances, Foreign Investment Review Act, Tuna-Dolphin case, and Unprocessed herring and salmon
Background 50-51
Domestic regulation under GATT 96-97
General exceptions 98-104
Most Favoured Nation principle 96
National Treatment principle 96
Regulatory trade measures based on process standards 98, 104-107

General Agreement on Trade in Services (GATS) 284-287
See also World Trade Organization

Generalised System of Preferences (GSP) 15

Generally Recognized As Safe (GRAS) 203-204

Genetic modification
See also antibiotic resistance marker genes, and substantial equivalence
Estimated use in agriculture 194
History 193-194
Promises and risks 196-199
Types of 194-195

Genuine concerns
See protectionism

Germany
In the beef-hormone issue 156
In the data protection issue 277, 278, 293
In the GM foods issue 218, 223-224, 225
In the leghold trap issue 82, 121, 122, 123, 137, 142

Global Industry Coalition 232

Grain Inspection Packers and Stockyards Administration 247
See also United States Department of Agriculture (in the GM foods issue)

Gramm-Leach-Bliley Act 295

Greece
In the data protection issue 278
In the GM foods issue 217, 218
In the leghold trap issue 82, 121

Greenpeace 224, 253, 254, 255, 259

Growth-hormones
See also Allowable Daily Intake, Codex Alimentarius Commission, Directives 81/602, 85/649, 88/146, and 96/22, and Maximum Residue Level
Functions and effects 147-148
Risks of 148-149
Types of 147

Health Canada
In the beef-hormone issue 152, 181
In the GM foods issue 208-210, 253, 257

See also Novel Foods Regulations (Canada)

Health Insurance Portability and Accountability Act (HIPAA) 295

HEW
See Department of Health, Education and Welfare

HHS
See Department of Health and Human Services

Hormone Free Cattle Programme (HFC) 156, 179-180
See also Non-Hormone Treated Cattle Programme

Hormones
See Growth-hormones

House of Commons
See Parliament of Canada

House of Representatives
See United States Congress

Humane trapping standards
Issues in formulating 81-82
In the EC-US and EC-Canadian agreements 124-126
In ISO 111-113, 127, 133

Human rights
See economic sanctions

Importing firms 62, 68

INAC
See Department of Indian and Northern Affairs Canada

Industry Canada 311, 312, 316, 320

Influence effect
See trade effects

Information Highway Advisory Council (IHAC) 311, 317

Information Infrastructure Task Force (IITF) 293
See also White House (in the data protection issue)

Interdependence 41-42, 43-45

Interest groups, types of 62

Interim Agreement on exports of non-hormone treated beef
See Hormone Free Cattle Programme

International Association of Fish and Wildlife Agencies (IAFWA) 113, 117, 128-129, 135

International Fur Trade Federation (IFTF) 139

Internationalisation 1, 2, 3, 10, 11

International Organization for Standardization (ISO)
See also humane trapping standards
General 51
In the data protection issue 310

International standards
Background and hypothesis 52, 53-54, 72-73, 77
Conclusions 354-356
In the beef-hormone issue 190
In the data protection issue 326
In the GM foods issue 266

International Trade Organization (ITO) 50

Ireland
In the beef-hormone issue 149, 150-151
In the data protection issue 277, 278
In the leghold trap issue 82

Issue linkage 43-47, 66-67

Issue redefinition 74

Italy
In the beef-hormone issue 149, 184
In the GM foods issue 217, 218, 220
In the leghold trap issue 82, 121

Joint FAO/WHO Expert Committee on Food Additives (JECFA) 158, 178, 184, 185

Joint Management Committee (JMC) 125, 126-127, 131

Killing traps
See traps, types of

Labelling
See also Agreement on Sanitary and Phytosanitary Standards
Of GM foods in Canada 209-210, 254
Of GM foods in the Codex Alimentarius Commission 229-230
Of GM foods in the EC 213, 215-216, 218-219, 221, 222
Of GM foods in the US 205-206, 251, 252
Of GM foods under the Cartagena Protocol 232
Of hormone-treated beef 167, 172, 175, 176, 177, 179, 182, 185

Labour standards 12, 368

Lamming report 150, 184

Leghold traps
See Regulation 3254/91, and traps, types of

Luxembourg (in the GM foods issue) 217, 218, 257

Mad cow disease
See BSE

Maximum Residue Level (MRL) 158, 178

Measures affecting agricultural products (WTO case) 165

Ministry of Agriculture, Fisheries and Food (MAFF) 225

Most Favoured Nation principle
See General Agreement on Tariffs and Trade

Multifunctionality
See Common Agricultural Policy

Multinational corporations 75-76

National Corn Growers Association (NCGA) 247, 252

National Institutes of Health (NIH) 202

National Trappers Association (NTA) 87, 92, 110, 113, 117, 123, 127, 128, 129
See also Ballot Issues Coalition

Negotiation analysis 41, 43-44

Netherlands
In the beef-hormone issue 170
In the data protection issue 276, 277
In the GM foods issue 218
In the leghold trap issue 82, 111, 116-117, 120-121, 122, 132, 133, 137, 138, 142

Non-Hormone Treated Cattle Programme (NHTC) 180
See also Hormone Free Cattle Programme

No Observable Effect Level (NOEL) 157-158

North American Free Trade Agreement (NAFTA) 2, 3, 8

Novel Foods Regulation (EC)
See Regulation 258/97

Novel Foods Regulations (Canada) 252-253, 257
  See also Health Canada (in the GM foods issue)

Occupational health and safety standards 9

Office of Management and Budget (OMB) 289

Office of Science and Technology Policy (OSTP) 202

Organisation for Economic Co-operation and Development (OECD)
  General 52
  In the data protection issue 271-274, 278, 299, 300, 308, 309, 317, 326
  In the GM foods issue 199-201, 228, 229, 257, 259-260, 266

Parliament of Canada 59, 254-255

Participation expansion
  Background and hypothesis 71-72, 73, 78
  Conclusions 356-357
  In the beef-hormone issue 190-191
  In the data protection issue 327
  In the GM foods issue 266-267
  In the leghold trap issue 144

Personal Information Protection and Electronic Documents Act 312-315

Pivotal groups 67, 72

Policy officials 58, 71, 74

Precautionary principle
  General 165, 199
  In the Cartagena Protocol 231, 232
  In the EC's regulation of GM foods 211, 220, 229
  In the SPS Agreement 165, 234-236

Preferences
  Definition of 38-39
  Role in producing a California effect 39, 47-49, 66, 69-71, 72-73

Privacy Act (Canada) 308, 317

Privacy Act (US) 289, 317

Privacy Commissioner of Canada 308-309, 312, 313, 314, 316, 317, 324, 325

Privacy Working Group (PWG) 293

Process-tracing 27-29

Protectionism
  Background and hypothesis 70, 71, 77
  Conclusions 350-352
  In the beef-hormone issue 189
  In the data protection issue 325-326
  In the GM foods issue 265-266
  In the leghold trap issue 142-143

Public Interest Advocacy Centre (PIAC) 314-315

Public interest groups 62, 63, 63-64, 68, 71, 74, 75

Public opinion
  See two-level game approach

Quebec 309, 311, 314, 317

Race to the bottom 1-2, 10, 11

Ratification
  See two-level game approach

Regulation (in EC law) 60

Regulation 258/97 (Novel Foods Regulation) 213-215, 218, 221, 227, 257

Regulation 3254/91 (ban on leghold traps)
  Background and history 82-84
  Content 84
  Proposed amendments 115-116

Regulatory standards
See standards

Regulatory trade measures, definition of 19, 35

Reservation value 41, 43-44, 46

Restraining traps
See traps, types of

Retaliation
See also carousel approach
General 56, 63, 68-69, 70, 72, 77, 339, 354
In the beef-hormone issue 155, 156, 159, 168, 175-176, 184, 186-187
In the data protection issue 321, 326
In the GM foods issue 261
In the leghold trap issue 137, 143

Retaliatory measures
See retaliation

Reverberation
See two-level game approach

Royal Society of Canada 255

Safe Harbour agreement
Background 296-299
Final draft and adoption 306-307, 317
First draft 299-302
Second draft 302-304
Third draft 304-306

Scientific Committee on Veterinary Measures Relating to Public Health (SCVPH) 177-178, 184

Scientific Steering Committee (SSC) 171, 227

Seal skins, European ban on 90-91, 94-95, 133, 138

Senate
See United States Congress

Shrimp-Turtle case 102-104, 133

Single European Act (SEA) 9, 60

Spain (in the GM foods issue) 218

Sponsoring officials 58

SPS Agreement
See Agreement on Sanitary and Phytosanitary Standards

Standardisation bodies
See Canadian General Standards Board, Canadian Standards Association, and International Organization for Standardization

Standards
Process standards 12-13
Product standards 12-13
Product-related process standards 13
Stringency of standards 19-20

Standards for reformulated and conventional gasoline (WTO case) 106-107

StarLink incident 251-252

Submersion traps
See traps, types of

Substantial equivalence
See also genetic modification
Concept and definition 200

Sweden (in the GM foods issue) 218, 222, 225

Targeting
Background and hypothesis 67, 69, 77
Conclusion 335, 338, 340-341
In the beef-hormone issue 186-187
In the data protection issue 321
In the GM foods issue 262
In the leghold trap issue 137-138

TBT Agreement
See Agreement on Technical Barriers to Trade

Technical Committee on Humane Trapping Standards (TC 191)
See humane trapping standards (in ISO)

Terms of trade
See trade effects

Trade effects
Background and hypothesis 40-45, 66-69, 77
Conclusions 335, 338-340
Influence effect of trade 42
In the beef-hormone issue 186
In the data protection issue 320-321
In the GM foods issue 261-262
In the leghold trap issue 136-137

Trade officials 58, 67-68, 71-72, 73

Transatlantic Business Dialogue (TABD) 53

Transatlantic Consumer Dialogue (TACD)
General 53
In the beef-hormone issue 183
In the data protection issue 298, 303, 305, 307
In the GM foods issue 248-249, 259

Transatlantic Environmental Dialogue (TAED) 53

Transnational coalitions 74-75

Transnational interest groups 74-75

Trapping standards
See humane trapping standards

Traps, types of 80-81

Tuna-Dolphin case
Background and outcome 7-8
Cases before the GATT 97, 99-101, 133
Role in the leghold trap issue 95, 114

Two-level game approach
General 35-37
Application to the EC 61
Chief of Government 58
Public opinion, role of 35, 57
Ratification 35
Reverberation 69
Win-set 35-36

UECBV 175-176

Unitary states/countries, assumption of 54-55

United Kingdom (UK)
In the beef-hormone issue 149, 150-151, 156, 168, 169-170, 175, 177, 178, 186
In the data protection issue 276, 277, 278
In the GM foods issue 222, 224, 225, 227
In the leghold trap issue 82, 109, 120, 121, 122, 132, 133, 142

United States Congress
General 59
In the beef-hormone issue 176
In the data protection issue 294-295
In the GM foods issue 230, 250-251
In the leghold trap issue 87, 113-114, 117, 127

United States Department of Agriculture (USDA)
In the beef-hormone issue 180
See also Agricultural Marketing Service, and Food Safety Inspection Service
In the GM foods issue 196, 243, 244, 247
See also Animal and Plant Health Inspection Service
In the leghold trap issue 113, 117
See also Fish and Wildlife Service

United States Trade Representative (USTR)
In the data protection issue 297, 297-298
In the beef-hormone issue 155, 167-168, 176-177
In the GM foods issue 245
In the leghold trap issue 113-114, 117, 123, 133

Unprocessed Herring and Salmon (GATT case) 100-101

Vienna Convention on the Law of Treaties 100, 238-241

White House
In the data protection issue 293, 297
See also Information Infrastructure Task Force
In the GM foods issue 251

Win-set
See two-level game approach

World Health Organization (WHO) 228
See also Codex Alimentarius Commission, and Joint FAO/WHO Expert Committee on Food Additives

World Trade Organization (WTO)
See also Agreement on Sanitary and Phytosanitary Standards, Agreement on Technical Barriers to Trade, General Agreement on Tariffs and Trade, and General Agreement on Trade in Services
For case law, see also Measures affecting agricultural products, Shrimp-Turtle case, and Standards for reformulated and conventional gasoline
General 50-52
Effects of WTO law:
Background and hypothesis 53-54, 72-73, 77
Conclusions 352-354
In the beef-hormone issue 190
In the data protection issue 326
In the GM foods issue 266
In the leghold trap issue 143-144
Relation to other multilateral treaties 238-242

EUROPEAN MONOGRAPHS

1. Lammy Betten (ed.), *The Future of European Social Policy* (second and revised edition, 1991).
2. J.M.E. Loman, K.J.M. Mortelmans, H.H.G. Post, J.S. Watson, *Culture and Community Law: Before and after Maastricht* (1992).
3. Prof. Dr. J.A.E. Vervaele, *Fraud Against the Community: The Need for European Fraud Legislation* (1992).
4. P. Rawortli, *The Legislative Process in the European Community* (1993).
5. J. Stuyck, *Financial and Monetary Integration in the European Economic Community* (1993).
6. J.H.V. Stuyck, A.J. Vossestein (eds.), *State Entrepreneurship, National Monopolies and European Community Law* (1993).
7. J. Stuyck, A. Looijestijn-Clearie (eds.), *The European Economic Area EC-EFTA* (1994).
8. R.B. Bouterse, *Competition and Integration – What Goals Count?* (1994).
9. R. Barents, *The Agricultural Law of the EC* (1994).
10. Nicholas Emiliou, *The Principle of Proportionality in European Law: A Comparative Study* (1996).
11. Eivind Smith, *National Parliaments as Cornerstones of European Integration* (1996).
12. Jan H. Jans, *European Environmental Law* (1996).
13. Siofra O'Leary, *The Evolving Concept of Community Citizenship: From the Free Movement of Persons to Union Citizenship* (1996).
14. Laurence Gormley (ed.), *Current and Future Perspectives on EC Competition Law* (1997).
15. Simone White, *Protection of the Financial Interests of the European Communities: The Fight against Fraud and Corruption* (1998).
16. Morten P. Broberg, *The European Commission's Jurisdiction to Scrutinise Mergers* (1998).
17. Doris Hildebrand, *The Role of Economic Analysis in the EC Competition Rules* (1998).
18. Christof R.A. Swaak, *European Community Law and the Automobile Industry* (1999).
19. Dorthe Dahlgaard Dingel, *Public Procurement. A Harmonization of the National Judicial Review of the Application of European Community Law* (1999).
20. J.A.E. Vervaele (ed.) *Compliance and Enforcement of European Community Law* (1999).
21. Martin Trybus, *European Defence Procurement Law: International and National Procurement Systems as Models for a Liberalised Defence Procurement Market in Europe* (1999).
22. Helen Staples, *The Legal Status of Third Country Nationals Resident in the European Union* (1999).
23. Damien Geradin (ed.) *The Liberalization of State Monopolies in the European Union and Beyond* (2000).
24. Katja Heede, *European Ombudsman: Redress and Control at Union Level* (2000).
25. Ulf Bernitz, Joakim Nergelius (eds.) *General Principles of European Community Law* (2000).
26. Michaela Drahos, *Convergence of Competition Laws and Policies in the European Community* (2001).

27. Damien Geradin (ed.), *The Liberalization of Electricity and Natural Gas in the European Union* (2001)
28. Gisella Gori, *Towards an EU Right to Education* (2001)
29. Brendan P.G. Smith, *Constitution Building in the European Union* (2002)
30. Friedl Weiss, Frank Wooldridge, *Free Movement of Persons within the European Community* (2002)
31. Ingrid Boccardi, *Europe and Refugees: Towards an EU Asylum Policy* (2002)
32. John Vervaele, André Klip (eds.), *European Cooperation between Tax, Customs and Judicial Authorities* (2002)
33. Wouter P.J. Wils, *The Optimal Enforcement of EC Antitrust Law: Essays in Law and Economics* (2002)
34. Damien Geradin (ed.), *The Liberalization of Postal Services in the European Union* (2002)
35. Nick Bernard, *Multilevel Governance in the European Union* (2002)
36. Jill Wakefield, *Judicial Protection through the Use of Article 288(2)EC* (2002)
37. Sebastiaan Princen, *EU Regulation and Transatlantic Trade* (2002)
38. Amaryllis Verhoeven, *The European Union in Search of a Democratic and Constitutional Theory* (2002)
39. Paul Torremans, *Cross Border Insolvencies in EU, English and Belgian Law* (2002)